W9-CEG-326

God's Last Words

God's Last Words

*Reading the English Bible from the
Reformation to Fundamentalism*

David S. Katz

Yale University Press
New Haven and London

For information about this and other Yale University Press publications, please contact:
U.S. Office: sales.press@yale.edu   yalebooks.com
Europe Office: sales@yaleup.co.uk   www.yalebooks.co.uk

Set in Bembo by SNP Best-set Typesetter Ltd., Hong Kong
Printed in Great Britain by St. Edmundsbury Press Ltd.

ISBN 0–300–10115–5

Library of Congress Control Number 2003021344

A catalogue record for this book is available from the British Library.

10 9 8 7 6 5 4 3 2 1

In memory of

Hugh Trevor-Roper,
Lord Dacre of Glanton

(1914–2003)

Contents

Acknowledgments

Scholarship is often a very solitary calling. Ultimately, writing a book means getting down to it, even if distracted by a view of palm trees and – if there weren't so many palm trees – the blue of the Mediterranean. Before, during, and after the writing are the days at the coal face, and so my thanks go first to the librarians in the Upper Reading Room of the Bodleian Library, Oxford, especially Vera Ryhajlo. Some of them think that I own Seat U151, but I have been sitting there for only thirty years, and have remained loyal even when the desk was re-oriented from south-facing to the east. My fellow sitters in the URR have stayed the same: Kevin Sharpe, Alon Kadish, Glyn Redworth, and George Bernard. I thank them for their silent companionship.

Almost ritualistically, I always thank the two people who have most influenced my work. The dedication of this book to the late Hugh Trevor-Roper reflects the first debt. When we first met, Hugh was still in his fifties, and was the ruler of modern history at Oxford. At our last meeting he was no less a commanding presence, though blind and living alone. I hope that he would have liked this book, filled with the sort of historical characters that he found amusing and attractive.

My second debt is to Richard H. Popkin, even in Californian retirement still the leader of a motley crew of followers around the world who think that 'everything connects', in his famous phrase. Dick is able not only to find key documents in obscure archives, but also to understand the significance of a text which everyone else has failed to recognize as the crucial missing piece of the puzzle. I know that he will read this book and launch fearlessly into dark corners that I missed completely.

I should especially like to acknowledge the President and Fellows of Wolfson College, Oxford, for electing me to a Visiting Fellowship, during which much of the research for this book was completed.

Many thanks as usual to Peter Robinson, my agent at Curtis Brown, and

to the people at Yale University Press who worked so efficiently in producing the book: Robert Baldock, Diana Yeh, and Candida Brazil.

But I give my most heartfelt thanks, of course, to Professor Amy Singer,
en iyi arkadaşım ve aynı zamanda hayat arkadaşım. Who could ask for
anything more?

June 2003

Preface: The Biblical Reader and the Shifting Horizon of Expectations

Martin Luther built his Protestant faith on three pillars: faith, grace, and Scripture. The simplicity of his interpretation of Christianity guaranteed its success, for these three *solas* – *sola fide*, *sola gratia*, and *sola scriptura* – were axiomatic, requiring religious insight rather than external validating authority. The third *sola* predicated the only Protestant source of authority, the Bible itself, whose divine origins no more needed demonstrating than the place of the earth at the centre of the universe. The Bible contained God's Last Words, His message to mankind when His presence on earth was manifestly visible. The great intellectual movements which swooped over Europe passed over the biblical bedrock, at first apparently without making a dent. It was only when scholars began quite innocently to include Scripture in their more general textual work that cracks began to appear.

This book is the story of the vicissitudes of the English Bible between the European Renaissance and American Fundamentalism, as each era surveyed the Protestant pillar of *sola scriptura*, often thereby causing unintentional but severe structural damage. Yet the principle of the inerrant Bible has never been quite eradicated, but instead has remained enormously influential in England and the United States, where many millions of Christians still view the Bible as literally God's Last Words.

The question of biblical authority, however, is not of interest to theologians alone. For the English Bible is the text which forms the very foundation of the cultural base common to both Great Britain and America. Its words comprise a shared world of images and metaphors, a secret multi-layered language that could defy both censorship and central authority. This entire world is grounded on the simple fact that at least since the Reformation, the Bible in Britain has been available to anyone who could read, who could hear, who could see and follow the narratives of pictures.

The momentous effects of this cultural axiom have never been fully brought out by historians who have written about the English Bible, not even in the relatively rarefied realms of the history of ideas. This is more than a tale of texts and editions, however, or even of the growth of the popular press and the history of the book. The English Bible can only be understood against the wider canvas of numerous subjects such as prophecy, millenarianism, copyright, the occult, Darwin, the novel, and American Fundamentalism. Denying the English Bible the scope of its contemporary references is to truncate its influence and to distort its significance in manufacturing the common code of the English-speaking world.

But codes have to be read, deciphered, and understood, and this is reflected in the subtitle of this book. Reading has become a very hot topic in recent years, so much so that it is almost a cliché to speak of it as a cliché. There has been a proliferation of theoretical studies during the past three or four decades which have dealt extensively with the reader's response to the text he or she is reading. Even scholars who shrink from fashionable subjects will need to have a look at the work that has been done in the field of 'reception theory', if only because much of it is useful even to those historians who are really moved only by facts and figures. Oddly enough, although the Bible has been the subject of a mountain of literary criticism, not enough work has been done which emphasizes what Stanley Fish called 'the informed or at-home reader' of the English Bible, in the context of the intellectual world roughly in the period between the Reformation and the modern Fundamentalist movement.[1]

In the foreshortened and potted history of reception theory, or reader-response criticism, a key milestone is the inaugural lecture of Professor Hans Robert Jauss, given at the University of Constance in April 1967 and later published under the title, 'Literary History as a Challenge to Literary Theory'. Jauss proclaimed that his brief was no less than to bridge the gap between those two disciplines. 'Their methods conceive the *literary fact* within the closed circle of an aesthetics of production and of representation', he complained, and in 'doing so, they deprive literature of a dimension that inalienably belongs to its aesthetic character as well as to its social function: the dimension of its reception and influence.' Jauss pointed out that Marxist aesthetics, if it looked at the reader at all, treated him as it did the author of the text, examining his social position and place in a structured society. So too did the Formalists give the reader a purely passive role, mutely following the directions in the literary work.

Jauss rejected this entire approach. Instead, he emphasized what he called 'a dialogical and at once processlike relationship between work, audience, and new work'. Jauss called for 'an aesthetics of reception [*Rezeptionsästhetik*] and influence' which would also take on board 'the historical sequence of literary works as the coherence of literary history'. Importantly, he also explained what he meant by those terms. Aesthetics comes into it because 'the first reception of a work by the reader includes a test of its aesthetic value in comparison with works already read.' This is a historical process because 'the understanding of the first reader will be sustained and enriched in a chain of receptions from generation to generation; in this way the historical significance of a work will be decided and its aesthetic value made evident.' In brief, Jauss explains,

> A corresponding process of the continuous establishing and altering of horizons also determines the relationship of the individual text to the succession of texts that form the genre. The new text evokes for the reader (listener) the horizon of expectations and rules familiar from earlier texts, which are then varied, corrected, altered, or even just reproduced.

Jauss goes on to talk about texts that create an 'aesthetic distance' between the given horizon of expectations and the work which the reader has before him. If this distance is small, that is, if the work under discussion fulfils rather than challenges his expectations, then it might be described as 'culinary', or entertainment art. But if the gap is great, then a shifting of horizons can take place, creating a new and different set of expectations in later readers. At that point in time, they will find it difficult to recreate the sense of novelty and excitement which earlier readers felt when first confronted with the same text: 'the original negativity of the work has become self-evident and has itself entered into the horizon of future aesthetic experience, as a henceforth familiar expectation.' Sometimes, new works can create so radical a break 'that an audience can only gradually develop for them'.[2]

For English-speaking audiences, the approach of reader-response criticism and reception theory is widely associated with the work of Stanley E. Fish. Fish emphasized his opposition to 'the assumption that there *is* a sense, that it is embedded or encoded in the text'. Instead, Fish insisted, 'the reader's activities are at the center of attention', especially 'the making and revising of assumptions'. Therefore, in 'a word', Fish concludes, 'these activities are interpretive'. Fish also posited the concept of 'interpretive communities', which are 'made up of those who share interpretive strategies not for reading (in the conventional sense) but for writing texts, for constituting their properties and assigning their intentions.' Fish makes the same point as Jauss, that 'these strategies exist prior to the act of reading and therefore determine the shape of what is read rather than, as is usually assumed, the other way around.' These 'interpretive communities' are never stable because their strategies are learned and constantly changing.[3] Stanley Fish described his method as follows:

> The concept is simply the rigorous and disinterested asking of the question, what does this word, phrase, sentence, paragraph, chapter, novel, play,

poem, *do?*; and the execution involves *an analysis of the developing responses of the reader in relation to the words as they succeed one another in time.*

In brief, he writes, 'Literature is a kinetic art, but the physical form it assumes prevents us from seeing its essential nature, even though we so experience it.'[4]

Although the emphasis on the reader and the reception of the text were proclaimed by Jauss and, slightly later on, by Fish, neither man would claim absolute originality for this extraordinarily fruitful turn of mind. Jauss himself pays tribute to Karl Popper (1902–94), who had recently employed the very same term in relation to the history of science. Popper argued that in scientific research, each hypothesis or observation presupposes expectations, 'namely those that constitute the horizon of expectations which first makes those observations significant and thereby grants them the status of observations.' The most important moment for progress in science (and life?) is the 'disappointment of expectations':

> It resembles the experience of a blind person, who runs into an obstacle and thereby experiences its existence. Through the falsification of our assumptions we actually make contact with 'reality.' The refutation of our errors is the positive experience that we gain from reality.[5]

Perhaps more importantly, Jauss draws on his reading of another recent text, *Wahrheit und Methode* ('Truth and Method'), by Hans-Georg Gadamer (1900–2002). To understand why Gadamer is important for Jauss, and hopefully for us, we need to come to terms, however briefly, with the history of interpretation in general, known by the frightening name of hermeneutics.

The idea that interpretation is a theoretical science was a commonplace among early modern scholars of the Bible, who tried to make sense of the single most important text ever entrusted to mankind. The Greek neologism first appeared in print in the middle of the seventeenth century in Germany; twenty-five years later, 'Hermeneutick' was already an English word.[6] But it was the distinguished German theologian Friedrich Schleiermacher (1768–1834) who really first stressed the role of the reader in the process of interpretation, biblical and otherwise. He promoted the notion of 'congeniality', a state in which the reader recreates the original experience of the author. Schleiermacher employed the image of a 'hermeneutic circle' whereby a study of parts of a text leads naturally to a conjecture about the meaning of the whole, followed by an almost endless revision and correction of this general conception, based on a return to examining the parts and applying new insights to general understanding. The historical gap between the work and the reader is to be bridged by the back-and-forth movement of the hermeneutic circle, combined with moments of almost supernatural insight.

Our ultimate goal is to step into the author's shoes and to understand what he meant at the moment he wrote his text.

For our immediate purposes at least, the next two stages in the development of hermeneutics are less relevant. The lives of Schleiermacher and Wilhelm Dilthey (1833–1911) overlapped for less than a year, but give thereby a superficially striking image of a chain of tradition. Dilthey added both an historical and a psychological element to the task of hermeneutics, in an attempt to experience other minds and subjects. Edmund Husserl (1859–1938) was chief among those who focused on phenomenology in the science of interpretation. He argued that we can somehow 'bracket' out all transient and specific elements of thought, leaving only the structure of consciousness itself available for investigation, outside of real time. This marvellously theoretical aspiration was famously rejected by his pupil Martin Heidegger (1889–1976), who refused to see understanding as a human activity outside of history. Understanding, rather, is the process by which the world comes to humankind. As Heidegger put it, 'An interpretation is never a presuppositionless apprehending of something presented to us'; indeed, 'In every case interpretation is grounded in *something we see in advance* – in a *fore-sight.*' The implications of Heidegger's philosophy for literary criticism are clear, no matter in how condensed a form it comes down to English departments: to read drama we must know what a play is, and what a theatre is. Recognizing a genre and knowing what came before in that genre is taken for granted by the author of any literary work, even if he or she is intent on subverting the reader's expectations. Heidegger's emphasis on language also made him a kindred spirit and authority figure for scholars of literature.[7]

Which brings us to Hans-Georg Gadamer, whose book *Truth and Method* has been so influential in Germany since its appearance in 1960, but like much central European scholarship of that era, was not translated into English until much later, in 1975.[8] Gadamer was pleased that, thanks to Heidegger, history was once again the handmaiden of interpretation. But Gadamer rejected the assumption of Enlightenment philosophers since Descartes that the world was out there, waiting to be discovered, ready to come to us. He also argued that the temporal distance (*Zeitabstand*) between the interpreter and the work under scrutiny is not a tragic obstacle to be overcome (as Schleiermacher bewailed) but an historical fact to be celebrated. No doubt, we need to take on board all that the historical gap implies. The reader needs to understand that his own position in the relative future affects the way he reads the text. He himself may be favourable to modern notions of democracy and toleration, which may have been negative values to the author of a work in the past. Gadamer uses the term *Vorurteil* ('prejudice') here in a constructive sense, emphasizing the value of tradition and authority in preserving the judgements of brilliant people who over the years have read and commented on a particular text. As he put it, 'Understanding is not to be thought of so much as an action of one's subjectivity, but as the placing of oneself within a process of tradition, in which past and present are constantly fused.'[9] Furthermore, 'Every age has to understand a transmitted text in its own way, for the text is part of the whole of the tradition in which the age takes an objective interest and in which it seeks to understand itself.'[10]

Gadamer used the term *wirkungsgeschichtliches Bewusstsein* ('effective-historical consciousness') to describe the process by which we recognize that there can be no absolute starting point (as Descartes had claimed), since our own 'horizon of understanding' is constantly changing and being altered by texts that have come down to us by tradition, endorsed by authority. We 'fuse' our horizon with that of the past, what Gadamer calls *Horizontsverschmelzung*. In this way, Schleiermacher's 'hermeneutic circle' becomes an interpretative process whereby we employ our preconceptions, prejudgements, prejudices, and mere guesses as a way of using part of a text in order to imagine the whole, exploiting the 'horizons' of those who have interpreted the text before us. But we need always remember that we cannot help but be trapped within that circle, for there is no such thing as an unsituated interpreter who can look at a text from above and pronounce its true, universal, and eternal meaning. All understanding, Gadamer tells us, is hermeneutical: interpretative and situated in history.

For a literary critic, Gadamer's message is that the author's intention is only part of the story. We also need to look at the reception of a text, a work of art, or an historical event. Henry VIII's intentions alone during the English Reformation insufficiently reflect the importance of that great process. Far more significant are the results of Henry's choices and the effects they had in a wide variety of areas and over the centuries up to and including our own day.

Gadamer was enormously influential for people like Jauss and Fish in the lit. crit. world because he provided serious philosophical justification for the view that a text can never have a subjective interpreter or an objective meaning. Each interpreter carries traces of previous works that he or she has read, and this foreunderstanding or prejudice is the force that drives the hermeneutic circle round and enables understanding itself. Without literary history, there can be no understanding of a text.

Which brings us back to the English Bible. When we speak of the Bible as the cultural base of Anglo-American culture, we are really talking about the way a particular text was perceived by a wide variety of readers over a great expanse of time. Each era came with its own 'horizon of expectations', and without examining the lens through which the Bible was read, it is impossible to recreate the experience of the 'informed or at-home reader', which is an important part of what historians do. Everyone knows that a modern reader comes to the Scriptures with the achievements of science and archaeology ringing in the ears. Even the most ardent believer needs to face the challenge of geology and the dating of artefacts. We know that in the second half of the nineteenth century, Darwin's theories were a key issue. It should not come as a surprise that there were other key issues in earlier times. In the Renaissance, learned men rushed to apply the tools of textual analysis to the Testaments, fully confident that God's Word would open up and reveal shades of further truth. During the English Civil War, there was a symbiotic relationship between politics and religion, as the practical application of the biblical message was hammered out. Newtonian science, the rise of the novel, the development of a concept of authorial copyright, and the new discipline of anthropology all had an effect on forming the horizon of expectations for the informed reader of the Bible at different times in history.

The wonderful thing about the history of biblical reader response is that, just at the moment when it seemed that Holy Writ would henceforth be read just like any other book, the American Fundamentalist movement appeared and pummelled the debate back to the earliest and most straightforward Protestant approach of *sola scriptura*. This view very nearly denied that there could ever be textual problems in Scripture, and ensured that the belief that the Bible contained God's Last Words would gain new strength for the twenty-first century.

CHAPTER I

The Prehistoric English Bible

The Bible tells us that history has a beginning and an end, so it is only natural that the history of the Bible should be structured upon the same model. Every (English) schoolboy knows that the Creation of the English Bible occurred in AD 1525, when William Tyndale (1494?–1536) printed his translation of the New Testament. William Tyndale, the Creator of the English Bible, and much more: M.M. Knappen, in his influential history of Tudor Puritanism, made him the Creator of that too.[1] Historians shy away from admitting that they write according to models: indeed, the very word 'model' makes us cringe with loathing. Yet it is undeniable that for many centuries the history of the world, of Parliament, of religion, was written on the biblical model. It was a search for King Edward I, the Creator of the Model Parliament; Martin Luther, the first Protestant; or even the anonymous First Jew in Hampstead. Even after Butterfield warned us against ends-oriented Whig history, the biblical model remained most satisfying, especially for the generation that saw during the Second World War what one man could do to change the course of history.

During the past twenty years, historians have revised their ideas on how to understand history in general, and the history of the English Reformation in particular. We now see how little most people really wanted change, and were not very satisfied with the changes once they came. The biblical model has given way to a more evolutionary one. Luther becomes much more understandable as a passenger on a history train with express stops at Wyclif and Hus, on a line beginning with Augustine. The so-called 'precursors' of the biblical model – those lucky fellows who had the wit to proclaim the 'correct' concepts of the future, like religious toleration or heliocentrism – can now be seen in some cases to be genuine contributors to a view that becomes more developed down the evolutionary path. If we are interested in finding the actual sources of the English Bible, as opposed to its precursors, in looking behind Tyndale for the prehistoric English Bible, then we need to begin with the humanists who made his achievement possible.

Burckhardt writes not only about the rise of humanism, but also about its decline, and the fall of the humanists themselves: 'Though they still served as models to the poets, historians and orators, personally no one would consent to be reckoned of their number.' The chief charges against them were self-conceit, profligacy, and irreligion:

> Why, it may be asked, were not these reproaches, whether true or false, heard sooner? As a matter of fact, they were heard at a very early period, but the effect they produced was insignificant, for the plain reason that men were far too dependent on the scholars for their knowledge of antiquity – that the scholars were personally the possessors and diffusers of ancient culture. But the spread of printed editions of the classics, and of large and well-arranged handbooks and dictionaries, went far to free the people from the necessity of personal intercourse with the humanists, and, as soon as they could be but partly dispensed with, the change in popular feeling became manifest. It was a change under which the good and bad suffered indiscriminately.[2]

Compare Burckhardt's picture of the position of the Italian, Greek, and Latin humanists, with that of their Jewish contemporary counterparts. Rabbi Elijah Menahem Halfan described the new-found popularity of Jewish scholars as somewhat exasperating. 'In the last twenty years,' he wrote,

> knowledge has increased, and people have been seeking everywhere for instruction in Hebrew. Especially after the rise of the sect of Luther, many of the nobles and scholars of the land sought to have thorough knowledge of this glorious science (Kabbalah). They have exhausted themselves in this search, because among our people there are but a small number of men learned in this wisdom, for after the great number of troubles and expulsions, but a few remain. So seven learned men grasp a Jewish man by the hem of his garment and say: 'Be our master in this science!'[3]

In both cases, the scholar was tolerated as long as he was necessary. 'About the middle of the sixteenth century,' Burckhardt explains, 'these associations seem to have undergone a complete change. The humanists, driven in other spheres from their commanding position, and viewed askance by the men of the Counter-reformation, lost the control of the academies'.[4] History is written in the academies, the universities, and the story that is told does not always give credit to the Hebraic humanists who made the English Bible possible.[5] This is a shame, because Tyndale's Old Testament has an especially rich prehistory, in the Hebrew grammars and lexicons which have some claim to be seen as comprising the prehistoric English Bible.

I

Martin Luther, in one of his most famous complaints, protested that the 'Romanists profess to be the only interpreters of Scripture, even though they never learn anything contained in it their lives long.' This was one of the walls which the Roman Catholics had built to protect themselves. Luther's advice to the neophyte interpreter of the Bible was simple: 'Think it over for yourself.'[6] But what exactly was the Bible over which Luther and his Romanist opponents were quarrelling? At the very outset of the Reformation, there was a good deal of common ground in relying on the Vulgate, the translation of St Jerome (*c.* 342–420) which was meant to replace both the Septuagint and the various Latin manuscripts which were in use among the early Christians. Specifically, the recension of the Vulgate with most authority was the so-called Paris Version (1226), which was not in itself a better edition, but came into existence to service the practical need of producing a standard text for quotation. The division of the text into chapters of similar length by Stephen Langton (d. 1228) made the Vulgate even easier for reference. Vernacular translations, the most famous English ones being those associated with John Wyclif (*c.* 1320–84) and the Lollards, were not particularly accurate, but were startling for the very fact of being in a language other than Latin.

The Renaissance devotion to classical civilization, however, would inevitably spill over into other areas of textual analysis, including the Scriptures. The cry of '*ad fontes*' was one which had direct application to the book of books. Furthermore, the leading figures in the Renaissance invented the tools of modern historical writing, and showed what could be winkled out of a cold and lifeless text. The most famous case was that of Lorenzo Valla (*c.* 1406–57), who exposed the Donation of Constantine as a forgery. This document supposedly testified to the legal act by which the Emperor Constantine (*c.* 280–337), upon his conversion to Christianity in 312, recognized the superior dignity of the bishop of Rome and granted him vast parts of Italy. Valla noticed, among other things, that the word *feodum* appeared in the text, even though both the word and the institution of feudalism which it represented were unknown in fourth-century Rome.

This habit of close reading, of textual criticism, very soon came to biblical studies, not necessarily with immediately revolutionary results. After all, even Valla himself was a devoted Christian, and ended his life with a papal post. The goal was to be *trium linguarum gnarus*, knowledgeable about the three languages of Latin, Greek, and Hebrew. Much ground-clearing needed to be accomplished. The original texts needed to be provided and improved, grammars, lexicons, and manuals of the relevant languages produced, and commentaries written to synthesize this new knowledge. The development of printing helped standardize and disseminate this erudition, but it was a slow process. Most importantly, it was not immediately perceived as a threat to the established Christian order, even after the appearance of Protestantism, and certainly not before the Council of Trent thirty years later.

The essentially orthodox nature of early biblical scholarship can be seen quite clearly by looking in some detail at the first major project of post-Renaissance scriptural study, the Complutensian Polyglot (Alcalá, 1514–17).[7] This great *Biblia Sacra Polyglotta* was a Spanish initiative, undertaken immediately before the Reformation, in the generation that saw the conquest of Granada, the discovery of the New World, and the expulsion of the Jews and the Muslims from Iberia. Indeed, the driving figure behind the work was the famous Cardinal Francisco Ximenes de Cisneros (1437–1517): confessor to Queen Isabella, provincial of the Franciscan order in Castile, primate of Spain, and Inquisitor-General of Castile and Leon.[8] Ximenes studied at Salamanca and Rome until 1465, and established the University of Alcalá (*Complutum* in Latin) in 1500 as a tri-lingual college.[9] The cardinal was of impeccable orthodox credentials, despite having been imprisoned for six months in his youth by a previous archbishop of Toledo. William Prescott, the great nineteenth-century historian of Spain, gives a most unattractive physical description of Ximenes:

> His complexion was sallow; his countenance sharp and emaciated; his nose aquiline; his upper lip projected far over the lower. His eyes were small, deep-set in his head, dark, vivid, and penetrating. His forehead ample, and, what was remarkable, without a wrinkle, though the expression of his features was somewhat severe. His voice was clear, but not agreeable. His enunciation was measured and precise. His demeanour was grave, his carriage firm and erect; he was tall in stature, and his whole presence commanding.[10]

Ximenes was also a great crusader against *marranos*, burning over 2,500 backsliding Jews, in no way deterred by his love of the Hebrew language from persecuting its purveyors.

According to the story, Ximenes began to learn Hebrew when he was over sixty in order to work on this new type of Bible. The work itself was paid for by Ximenes: it cost over 50,000 ducats, including 4,000 ducats alone for the purchase of seven manuscripts of the Hebrew Bible.[11] Indeed, the point of this new edition was to lay the various versions of Scripture side by side and enable the Renaissance scholar to arrive at the divine truth which had been clouded by centuries of mis-copying and obscurantism, and which now could be revealed by the textual tools which had been developed in the past fifty years.

The Complutensian Polyglot was begun in about 1502 in the religious *fin-de-siècle* before Luther's rebellion, and finished just as the Protestant threat began for the Church. The Medici Pope Leo X (1513–21), the second son of Lorenzo the Magnificent, was always a soft touch for the humanists, and on 22 March 1520 he issued a bull giving permission for its printing, but the Bible was not circulated in its six volumes until 1522, perhaps only after the death of Leo X on 1 December 1521.[12] Six hundred copies of the Complutensian Polyglot were printed, including about three on vellum, one of which now is in the Vatican Library. Its price was set at 6.5 ducats by the pope himself: too dear for casual use. It may be that Leo X got very cold feet once the work was actually done: he it was who made the shady deal with Albrecht of Mainz (1490–1548) over the sale of indulgences for the rebuilding of St Peter's which sparked off Luther's crusade, and it was Leo who had to excommunicate Luther in January 1521.[13] Ximenes himself at least lived to see the volumes printed, and was very gratified, as is told in a contemporary anecdote:

> I have often heard John Brocarius, son of Arnoldus Brocarius, who printed the Polyglot, relate to his friends, that, when his father had put the finishing stroke to the last volume, he deputed him to carry it to the Cardinal. John Brocarius was then a lad; and having dressed himself in a very elegant suit of clothes, he approached Ximenes, and delivered the volume into his hands. 'I render thanks to thee, O God!' exclaimed Ximenes, 'that thou hast protracted my life to the completion of these biblical labours!' And afterwards conversing with his friends, the Cardinal would often observe, that the surmounting of the various difficulties of his political situation afforded him not half the solace of that which arose from the finishing of his Polyglot. Ximenes died the same year (1517), not many weeks afterwards.[14]

The structure of the Polyglot showed what could be done by applying the spirit of the Renaissance to biblical scholarship. The first four volumes included the Old Testament and Apocrypha. The Vulgate appears in the centre of the page; the Septuagint with interlinear Latin translation on the inside column; and the Hebrew text on the outside column. Below the text of the Pentateuch is the Aramaic targum of Onkelos, and a Latin translation. The margin notes Hebrew and Aramaic roots. The apocryphal books accepted by the Church appear in the Septuagint Greek version, with the Vulgate printed interlinearly, and in a separate column, although III Maccabees appears in the Greek only.[15]

The contribution of Ximenes and his Polyglot to Old Testament scholarship can hardly be overestimated. His edition was the first to divide the Hebrew text into chapters; it was also the first time that the Septuagint was printed, using manuscripts from the Vatican library, the library of St Mark at Venice, and from Ximenes's own private collection. In the dedication to Leo X, the editors boasted that they had used 'the oldest examples out of the apostolic library', although they missed Vatican B, one of the most ancient uncial manuscripts.[16] Sometimes they cheated a bit, in accordance with time-honoured practice: when passages were present in the Vulgate but absent in the Septuagint, they filled in the gaps by translating into Greek from the Latin. The first volume of the Old Testament part of the Polyglot is particularly interesting, containing a variety of introductory material, such as Jerome's own preface to the Pentateuch and the original bull of Leo X approving the publication of the Polyglot. More importantly, Ximenes also printed here the introductions to the Hebrew and Aramaic dictionary which appeared in the last volume, and two guides for studying the Bible. The last volume of the Old Testament, the fourth of the entire Polyglot, was the final one printed, and bears the date of 10 July 1517.

The New Testament was actually printed first, according to the colophon dated 10 January 1514, and forms the sixth volume of the Polyglot. The New Testament appears in Greek, and thus predates Erasmus's more famous edition by two years. A sort of primitive concordance appears in the margin, noting similar passages in other parts of the Bible.

In many ways, the fifth volume of the Polyglot was the most revolutionary, consisting as it did of innovative study aids. Among the highlights were the Hebrew and Aramaic pronouncing lexicons, far superior to that of Johann Reuchlin (1455–1522) and far more user-friendly. The Hebrew lexicon included Latin catchwords and Hebrew roots in the margins, and passages from the Latin Old Testament to provide examples of the use of Hebrew words. Ximenes also printed a short Hebrew grammar for general use. The primacy of the Hebrew and even Aramaic elements in scriptural study was thus stated unequivocally, and made even more explicit in the dedication to Pope Leo X:

> Certainly since there can be no word, no combination of letters, from which there does not arise, and as it were spring forth, the most concealed senses of the heavenly wisdom; and since the most learned interpreter cannot explain more than one of these, it is unavoidable that after translation the Scripture yet remains pregnant and filled with both various and sublime insights which cannot become known from any other sources than from the very fountain of the original language.[17]

This proclamation of reliance on the primary text of Scripture, and the need to look at the Bible as one would do any other ancient document, is probably more representative than the oft-quoted remark of the preface that

> We have placed the Latin translation of the blessed Jerome as though between the Synagogue and the Eastern Church, placing them like the two thieves one on each side, and Jesus, that is the Roman or Latin Church, between them.[18]

Such a prodigious work as the Complutensian Polyglot quite obviously could only be accomplished with a good deal of effort from a wide variety of sources. Certainly, at the end of the fifteenth century, a near monopoly of Hebrew scholarship was in the hands of Jews. Ximenes's chief Jewish adviser was the convert Alfonso de Zamora (*c.* 1474–1544), the son of an exile of 1492 who had returned to Spain and been baptized six years later. Zamora became professor of Hebrew at Salamanca, and even published a letter to the Jews of Rome calling on them to follow his lead and convert to Christianity. Zamora was aided in his Hebraic work by two other converts from Judaism, Pablo Coronel and Alfonso de Alcalá. A Christian named Nebrija worked with them as well. Benjamin Kennicott, the great eighteenth-century English biblical critic, would claim that one of the problems with the Complutensian Polyglot was that the Hebraists were former Jews and therefore used Masoretic manuscripts in which the variations between the texts had already been smoothed over. More recent criticism, however, suggests that Zamora and his colleagues seem to have been using a manuscript dating from no later than the ninth century, before the codification of the Masorites, which can be determined by certain idiosyncrasies in the vocalization. As this so-called Babylonian Codex no longer survives among Ximenes's manuscripts in Madrid, we will never have final proof, but the work of the Jewish converts seems to have been more flexible than Kennicott understood.[19]

This curious Jewish codex was not the only manuscript that went missing, to the intense frustration of modern scholars. Johann David Michaelis, the authoritative eighteenth-century German biblical critic, added the following paragraph to the fourth edition (1788) of his introduction to the New Testament:

In this situation it was natural for every friend to criticism, to wish that the manuscripts used in this edition, which might be supposed to have been preserved at Alcala, should be collated anew; and in the third edition of this Introduction I expressed the same in speaking of the Codex Rhodiensis. But the inconceivable ignorance and stupidity of a librarian at Alcala, about the year 1749, has rendered it impossible that these wishes should ever be gratified. Professor Moldenhawer, who was in Spain in 1784, went to Alcala, for the very purpose of discovering those manuscripts: and being able to find none, suspected that they were designedly kept secret from him, though contrary to the generous treatment which he had at other times experienced in that country. At last he discovered that a very illiterate librarian, about thirty-five years before, who wanted room for some new books, sold the ancient vellum manuscripts to one Toryo, who dealt in fire works, as materials for making rockets. Oh, that I had it in my power to immortalize both librarian and rocket-maker! This prodigy of barbarism I would not venture to relate, till Professor Tychsen, who accompanied Moldenhawer, had given me fresh assurances of its truth. I will not lay it to the charge of the Spanish nation in general, in which there are men of real learning; but the author of this inexcusable act was the greatest barbarian of the present century, and happy only in being unknown.

Michaelis follows this horrific account with a long quotation in footnote from Professor Tychsen himself, who adds that having been sold, these irreplacable manuscripts

> were put down in the librarian's account como membranas inutiles. Martinez, a man of learning, and particularly skilled in the Greek language, heard of it soon after they were sold, and hastened to save these treasures from destruction: but it was too late, for they were already destroyed, except a few scattered leaves, which are now preserved in the library. That the number of manuscripts was very considerable, appears from the following circumstance. One Rodan assured Bayer, that he had seen the receipt which was given to the purchaser, from which it appeared that the money was paid as two different payments.[20]

Not everyone believes this story. Charles Butler, the eighteenth-century Bible scholar, accepted Michaelis's second-hand testimony.[21] William H. Prescott, the indefatigable nineteenth-century American scholar of the Spanish-speaking world, also repeated it, although he described it somewhat ambiguously as 'one of the most whimsical anecdotes in literary history'. 'The name of the librarian, unfortunately, is not recorded', he laments. 'It would have been as imperishable as that of Omar.'[22] Prescott was taken to task for this insult to national pride by his Spanish counterpart, Modesto Lafuente y Zamalloa, who denounced him for believing that the manuscripts were sold 'como papel viejo á un polvorista'. This 'calumniosa fábula' was disproven, Lafuente claims, by Señor Sabau y Larroya, secretary of the Real Academia de la Historia and translator of Prescott, who found and identified all of the so-called missing manuscripts safe in the library of the University of Madrid, which absorbed that of Alcalá when the Complutensian University moved to the capital in 1836.[23] So too did Christian D. Ginsburg, the final word in his day about biblical manuscript collation, reject this 'whimsical story which was believed throughout Europe for about sixty years'. As Ginsburg explains, although this ' "prodigy of barbarism" has been exploded by the ascertained fact that all the MSS. which were known to belong to Cardinal Ximenes, and which were preserved in the library at Alcalá are now in the University Library at Madrid, still the Hebrew MSS. and the printed editions used for the Complutensian text have hitherto not been definitely identified', which he then proceeds to do.[24] It may be that Michaelis's two professorial colleagues

were the victims of a practical joke, but the story of Toryo the biblical rock-
eteer is justly part of the Polyglot's past.

II

A passing knowledge of Greek was the essential intellectual characteristic of
a Renaissance humanist, and one would have thought that a proper edition
of the New Testament would be the first item on any biblical agenda. Paradoxically, this was not the case, and both Greek biblical scholarship and printing in Greek lagged behind parallel efforts in the Hebrew. It may be that the
humanist ideal was so connected with the search for Greek manuscripts that
began in earnest with the fall of Constantinople in 1453, that the notion of
exploiting the new invention of printing in order to produce cheaper editions for actual use was slow to be grasped. The only parts of the Bible to
be printed in Greek before 1500 were two Latin/Greek psalters.[25]

Since the Complutensian Polyglot was not distributed until 1522, the real
watershed was the publication of Erasmus's Greek New Testament in 1516,
his *Novum instrumentum*. Erasmus himself was well aware that even in an age
of constant discoveries of ancient manuscripts it would not be wise to over-
estimate his achievement of producing the *editio princeps* of the most fundamental document of Christianity. Erasmus protested that his production was
'*praecipitatum fuit verius quam editum*', and we need not dismiss his words
entirely as false modesty.[26] Nevertheless, it should not be forgotten that
Erasmus's Greek New Testament was part of a triple project. The printing of
the Greek text was in many ways secondary to the *Annotations*, a work of
extended commentary, not on the Greek text, but on the very Vulgate which
Erasmus sought to correct.[27] The third part of the project was a completely
new Latin translation of the New Testament, not meant to replace the Vulgate
in either school or church, but intended as a more accurate translation of the
Greek original.

Erasmus was already fifty years old when the first edition of his New Testament was published, and perhaps it is far-fetched to seek at that stage the
youthful origins of his biblical enthusiasms, but the motivations behind his
achievement remain very significant, and may clear up some misunderstanding.[28] It seems clear now that until Erasmus was in his early thirties, the parts
of the Renaissance intellectual menu which were most attractive to him, as
to most other late fifteenth-century humanists, were precisely the sources most
far removed from religion. When Erasmus went to Oxford in the spring of
1499 accompanying Lord Mountjoy, he was known primarily as a poet. His
encounter with John Colet (1467?–1519), then lecturing in Oxford on the
Vulgate, may or may not have been the direct cause of his new-found dedi-

cation to the scholarly life, as some of his biographers have claimed, but certainly it is true that Erasmus began to devote himself to Greek only afterwards. Erasmus applied himself to the letters of St Jerome, and eventually began to explore the possibility of editing his entire works. The crown of these was of course the Vulgate, which Erasmus could safely say had become defective through careless copying, like any ancient manuscript.

Certainly from the turn of the new half-millennium we find Erasmus searching for Greek texts of the Gospels and the Psalms. Back again in Holland, he was encouraged by the Observant Franciscan mystic Jean Vitrier to study Origen, which he did while continuing with his Greek and working on a commentary on the Epistle to the Romans. He also tried to learn Hebrew 'but stopped because I was put off by the strangeness of the language, and at the same time the shortness of life.'[29]

In 1504 Erasmus's attention was focused immediately while he was looking for Greek texts in the abbey of Parc near Louvain. It was there that he stumbled upon a manuscript of Lorenzo Valla's notes on the text of the Vulgate. Erasmus published this important document the following year as *Adnotationes in novum testamentum*. Valla symbolizes for us, and perhaps for Erasmus as well, that part of the Renaissance turn of mind devoted to the close reading of texts. Valla's exposure of the Donation of Constantine demonstrated that the new scholarship could have wide-ranging effects. Valla's application of the methods he made famous to the most holy Greek text of them all was surprisingly tame. As expected, he compared a number of manuscripts of the Vulgate, including Greek, and argued for the greater authenticity of the earlier copies. While criticizing some of St Jerome's translations as inaccurate, there is no indication that Valla was considering rejecting the Vulgate for Christian use.

It seems likely that Erasmus, like Valla, did not see his study of the Greek text of the Vulgate as inherently revolutionary or fundamentally different from working on any first- or second-century Greek manuscript. Indeed, his celebrated *editio princeps* of the Greek New Testament seems to have been the outgrowth of other projects and interests: learning Greek, editing the works of St Jerome, and writing an extended commentary on the Vulgate, the *Annotations*, which would reflect what he had discovered from his work with the Greek originals. In August 1514, Erasmus wrote a letter to Reuchlin from Basle in which he reported that

> I have written annotations on the entire New Testament, and so have now in mind to print the New Testament in Greek with my comments added. They say that you have a very accurate copy, and if you will give Johann Froben access to it, you will do a service not only to me and to him but to all students of the subject. The volume shall be returned to you intact and spotless. Farewell, and pray let me hear from you.[30]

Apparently it was his publisher Johann Froben (1460?–1527) who grasped the significance of being the first house to print a Greek New Testament, an important achievement in itself, but also useful for demonstrating that the press could produce an extended Greek text in what was still a fairly esoteric type. Once it was agreed to print the entire Greek text, it seemed to make more sense to translate it directly into Latin, rather than reproduce the Vulgate which would not always adequately reflect the original. The *Annotations*, however, remained a commentary on the Vulgate, which was not printed here. Finally, if more proof were needed to show the haphazard qualities of Erasmus's great work, the first edition of 1516 actually makes no mention of the fact that this copy was the *editio princeps* of the Christian message.

What were the manuscript sources that Erasmus used? Certainly, it seems as if Erasmus was more interested in producing some sort of printed Greek text, without worrying overmuch about the quality of the recension. He used only four manuscripts for the first edition, none of which was earlier than the eleventh century: most were manuscripts left to the Dominicans in Basle by Cardinal Ivan Stojkovic of Ragusa, a delegate to the Council of Basle who died there in 1443. Reuchlin lent him a twelfth-century manuscript of the Book of Revelation, but it was missing the last folio and thus the last six verses of the text (xxii. 16–21). Erasmus's solution was simply to translate the missing verses back into Greek from the Vulgate Latin. More convincing proof is hardly needed to demonstrate that Erasmus never saw his Greek text as being definitive; merely handy. Having the New Testament in published form was very useful, since books could be circulated and corrected in the margins. The printed copies could be sent to the manuscripts and be collated in that fashion from a single printed text. Erasmus's text was the one which served as the basis for future collations and editions, from Luther's German translation to the so-called 'received text' published by the Elzevir family at Leiden in 1633. The fact of Erasmus's being the *editio princeps* was secondary, since Ximenes had done the work even without Erasmus. But Ximenes, unlike his Dutch contemporary, was not interested in raising fundamental questions about the biblical text itself.

Perhaps Erasmus was merely recording what he saw in the manuscripts, but he must certainly have realized that the variations between his Greek text and the Latin Vulgate would not go unnoticed. The most notorious difference between Erasmus's text and the others was that he left out the 'comma Johanneum' (I John v. 7), the essential proof text for the Trinity. He defended himself against all critics by promising to restore the verse if it could be found in a single manuscript. Eventually one was produced, the Codex Britannicus or Montfortianus (now in Trinity College, Dublin). Erasmus suspected that it was a contemporary forgery, which it was, but nevertheless he restored the verse in his third edition of 1522. Officially he could argue that since the verse was in the Vulgate it must have been in the Greek manuscript used by St Jerome.[31] In any case, he continued to express doubts about its authenticity both in his annotations and in private letters. His other eccentricities were also controversial. He omitted the words 'For thine is the kingdom, and the power, and the glory, for ever. Amen' from the Lord's Prayer, arguing (correctly) that this doxology slipped into the text of the New Testament via the liturgy. His Latin was also controversial, such as his translation of the Greek *logos* in St John's Gospel by the word *sermo* instead of the Vulgate's *verbum*.

The main point was that Erasmus sought and received the approbation of Pope Leo X, to whom his New Testament was dedicated. Three thousand copies were sold in the first two editions (1516 and 1519), while Erasmus widened his search for older and more reliable Greek manuscripts of the New Testament. A third edition appeared in 1522, and his fourth edition of 1527 utilized Ximenes's Polyglot, especially for the Book of Revelation. A fifth and final edition appeared in 1535.

All of these worthy contributions of Erasmus made no impression on the band of critics and detractors who attacked his New Testament the moment it appeared. One of these was Johann Eck (1486–1543), Luther's famous opponent. Others included his countryman Martin Dorp, and Jacob Zuñiga of Spain. Perhaps his most formidable adversary was Edward Lee (1482?–1544), later archbishop of York. Ironically, Lee was a humanist, a friend of More, who had gone as far as to answer Erasmus's call in the first edition of the Greek New Testament to send corrections and additions to the author. Lee may have felt that his contributions were slighted, or he may have had a change of heart, but when he rose to action, among his chief objections was the omission of the proof text from John. On this basis, Lee accused Erasmus of being a closet Arian determined from the outset to undermine the theological basis of the Trinity. The result of Erasmus's labours, he said, would be that 'the world would again be racked by heresy, schism, faction, tumults, brawls, and tempests'. Erasmus for his part was contemptuous of attributing such disastrous results to his humanistic endeavours. 'My New Testament has been out now for three years. Where are the heresies, schisms, tempests, tumults, brawls, hurricanes, devastations, shipwrecks, floods, general disasters, and anything worse you can think of?'[32] Indeed, Erasmus noted in the preface to the fourth edition of 1527, 'if the verse had been left in, it would not have refuted the Arians, because it does not say that the three heavenly witnesses are of one substance, but only that they are of one mind.'[33]

So too did Jacques Lefèvre d'Etaples (1450?–?1537), the great French humanist, object to Erasmus's rendering of Hebrews ii. 7 as 'a little lower than the angels', pointing out that the Hebrew has 'Elohim', God, instead of 'angels' in the eighth psalm, which is quoted. The author of Hebrews used the Septuagint, which has 'angels'. As a point of principle, Erasmus (like

Jerome) insisted that it was his duty to reproduce the original text, warts and all. This dispute with Lefèvre eventually occupied a considerable amount of space in the second edition, and touched on an important issue in biblical translation which is still not resolved.

Erasmus's New Testament was a great success, not least for the audacity of the attempt. His methodology was delineated in the three prefaces he included in the first edition: *Methodus* (enlarged in the second edition as *Ratio Theologica*), *Apologia*, and *Paraclesis*. In this last 'exhortation', Erasmus argues that the Bible should be made available in the vernacular, although he himself never produced one in Dutch. He did, however, write a paraphrase in Latin, which was soon translated into French, German, English, and (tellingly) Czech. Edward VI decreed that Erasmus's paraphrase of the Gospels be set up in all English churches. In a famous aside, Erasmus proclaimed that he would like to see the Bible in the hands of 'the farmer, the tailor, the mason, prostitutes, pimps, and Turks.'[34] Most humanist scholars probably found that their biblical needs were satisfied somewhere between Erasmus's paraphrase and his Greek New Testament. Pope Leo X, for his part, was so pleased at being associated with such a worthy and pioneering project that he sent a letter of thanks which was printed at the head of every subsequent edition. Erasmus had hoped to dedicate his paraphrases of each of the four Gospels to Henry VIII, Francis I, Charles I (V), and Ferdinand of Austria. Despite certain scholarly doubts and criticisms, it would be difficult to denigrate Erasmus's contribution to biblical scholarship in publishing the first edition of the Greek text of the New Testament, however faulty and based on late manuscripts.

That being said, sixteenth-century New Testament scholarship did not cease with Erasmus. Simon de Colines (1480–1546) the French printer combined Erasmus's Greek text with that of the Complutensian Polyglot plus some of his own additions to produce a new version in 1534, which lacked the proof text from John. His more famous son-in-law Robert Estienne (1503–59) combined art and scholarship in his celebrated folio Greek New Testament published at Paris in 1550. He had already come out with duodecimo versions in 1546 and again in 1549, but in none of these French editions did he dare mention the dreaded name of Erasmus, although clearly it was the same text in all essentials. The folio edition had not only beautiful type, but variant readings collated by his son Henri Estienne (1528?–98). The fourth edition was printed at Geneva once Estienne fled Paris in about 1552 and aligned himself with the Calvinist cause. The Greek text was divided up into verses for the first time by Estienne, which may show that it was meant to be used, not only admired.

Calvin's successor at Geneva, Theodore Beza (1519–1605), also tried to keep the Greek text in pace with the latest advances in New Testament scholarship. His Greek New Testament was published in 1565, and appeared in many

editions in both folio and quarto, sometimes including Beza's own Latin translation in addition to the Vulgate, with extensive annotations. Beza used Henri
Estienne's notes, and his own Codex Bezae, the sixth-century uncial manuscript he found in the monastery of St Irenaeus at Lyons in 1562, and which
he eventually gave to Cambridge University. Beza also utilized the Codex
Claromontanus, the Clermont uncial manuscript of the same period of Paul's
epistles.

The odd part about this post-Erasmian New Testament scholarship is the
degree of inaccuracy that was thought to be acceptable. Even Beza, for all his
possession of two sixth-century codices, declined when at all possible from
deviating too strongly from the accepted text. The point was to have a Greek
text which was reasonably accurate, if not perfect. In this, someone like Beza
is not so very different from Jewish scholars who used (and continue to use)
early sixteenth-century recensions of the Hebrew Old Testament without
querying those jots and tittles which do not materially affect the biblical
message. The terminal point of this trend of thinking came in 1633 when the
Elzevir Press in Leiden printed the second edition of their Greek New
Testament in their line of cheap editions of standard texts. They called their
version the *textus receptus*, and in creating this phrase crowned Robert Estienne's third edition of 1550 with Beza's corrections as the basis for further
discussion. As this was in essence Erasmus's work, in many ways it can be seen
as the Dutch humanist's final victory.

III

The provision of a much-corrected text of the Greek original had the secondary effect of highlighting the fact that in many respects the Latin Vulgate
was no longer an adequate reflection of what was now perceived as the Word
of God. It is enlightening that even Cardinal Cajetan (1469–1534), who would
be ranged in history as one of the 'losers' in having backed Luther's adversaries, did not see the Vulgate as the final word. In his view, the Vulgate was
merely a translation from the original Hebrew and Greek manuscripts, and
was never intended to be authoritative. Although this claim was decisively
rejected by the Council of Trent, it shows how humanism could still triumph
over sectarianism in the early days of the Reformation.[35]

There were those scholars, then, who were content to improve the existing text of the Vulgate simply by comparing the Latin with an available
Hebrew or Greek manuscript. While a significant advance over complacency,
it was not sufficient even for Latinists. Only new research, a determined effort
to discover older manuscripts of the Vulgate, would bring us closer to the
inspired text of St Jerome himself. In principle at least, such an attitude should

be sufficiently orthodox even for those who saw the Vulgate as the second edition of a very popular book. Robert Estienne was the first in the field in a Paris edition of 1528, crowned in 1546 with a grand folio reprint at Lyons of the third edition of the revised Vulgate.[36] As a humanist layman under the protective patronage of Francis I, Estienne's corrected Vulgates were highly suspicious. Eventually, Estienne fled to Calvinist Geneva, where he published further revisions of his Vulgate.[37]

Other scholars apart from Estienne tried to correct the existing text of the Vulgate by searching out ancient manuscripts and applying them. The Council of Trent tried to put a stop to excessive speculation by its decree of April 1546 that only the Vulgate might be used for quotations in sermons or public disputations. It was clear even to conservative Romanists that the immediate task was to produce an orthodox and standard revised version of the Vulgate. This would be the famous Sixtine edition, whose name testifies that it was due to the initiative of Pope Sixtus V (1585–90), who breathed life into a comatose biblical commission which had already been sitting for forty years without any tangible results to show for their deliberations. Sixtus himself was very much involved in preparing this official Vulgate, sifting through the variant readings and revising the proofs. Indeed, a press was established at the Vatican to print this edition, which finally appeared in three volumes in 1587.

In a sense, Sixtus V complicated matters almost as much as he tried to put an end to divisive disputes. For with the publication of his new Vulgate, he issued a bull which forbade any further editions. It was unrealistically utopian to expect that a work of this kind could be absolutely free from error, and the celebrated Cardinal Robert Bellarmine (1524–1621) was quick to point out that there were plenty of those. There was, however, a possible solution which might both save face and promote scholarship. While Sixtus did rule that no further full-blown editions of the Vulgate might be published, it was recognized that sixteenth-century Vatican printers, unlike St Jerome, did not enjoy the collaboration of the Holy Ghost, and errors might have inadvertently crept into the work. The new pope (after three rapidly deceased) Clement VIII (1592–1605) in 1592 therefore ordered the withdrawal of all copies of the Sixtine Vulgate, even if it meant buying them back. By the end of the year, a corrected edition was produced with the help of Bellarmine and others, but with Sixtus's name remaining on the title page to spare his posthumous blushes. This revised Sixtine Vulgate was the final version and did not include variant readings – they simply were no longer required. Pope Sixtus V therefore virtually caused the death of Roman Catholic scholarship on the Vulgate until the modern period, as any such activity would have been in direct violation of the papal bull which established his edition as authoritative for all time.

It was almost easier to retranslate the Hebrew and Greek into the elegant Renaissance Latin so much in contemporary favour. An early version was produced at Lyons in 1528 by Sanctes Pagninus, an Italian Dominican, but his attempt was so literal as to be an aid to translation rather than a rival to the Vulgate. Erasmus's Latin New Testament dominated the field, but Pagninus's 1528 Old Testament was published with approbations from the short-reigning Dutch pope Adrian VI (1522–3) and his troubled successor Clement VII (1523–34). Michael Servetus (1511–53) issued a revised edition at Lyons in 1542, but his heresy effectively killed it. Sebastian Münster (1489–1552) published a Hebrew/Latin Old Testament in Basle in 1535, two folio volumes from the Froschauer Press. As in Münster's other works, the influence of the rabbis was more apparent than the saints'.[38]

Perhaps more famous was the Zurich Latin Bible of 1543, dominated by the work of Leo Jud (*c.* 1482–1542), a scholar of Jewish background as his name indicates, but whose father was already a priest. Leo Jud was one of Zwingli's closest colleagues, and his Latin Bible included a preface by Heinrich Bullinger (1504–75), Zwingli's successor in 1531.[39] The first Bible to be read as literature also appeared from the Protestant camp with the publication of French humanist Sebastian Castellio's (1515–63) Bible at Basle in 1551, followed by other editions. His Bible was history and literature, appearing in elegant Renaissance Latin unimpeded by verse divisions. Anticipating later concerns, Castellio bridged the gap between the Testaments with Latin selections from Josephus set in italics in the 1554 edition, which was also printed at Basle.

IV

The Renaissance emphasis on textual analysis, on reintegrating the classical text with the original classical meaning, was bound to have religious implications. No longer was Greek and Roman literature to be used as a vehicle for demonstrating Christian values and ethics; now it came to be seen again as texts written within a specific temporal and cultural context. We have already seen how these methods were applied to Holy Scripture, although at first with the New Testament alone, which was always seen to be more the work of man than of God, and therefore a legitimate proving ground for philological tinkering.[40] Every jot and tittle of the Old Testament might still be seen as divinely inspired, written with the finger of God on Mount Sinai, but it was inevitable that one day the Renaissance would come to the Pentateuch as well.

That revolution in biblical studies was long delayed, for not until the seventeenth century, even in Roman Catholic circles, was the Old Testament considered fair game. Nevertheless, the initial interest of Renaissance scholars in the Old Testament was not narrowly textual, but included many occult applications of the biblical message. Pico della Mirandola (1463–94) was the first to introduce the Jewish mystical tradition, the kabbalah, as a Christian tool for biblical analysis. Frances Yates speaks of 'the occult philosophy' of the Renaissance: 'This philosophy, or outlook, was composed of Hermeticism as revived by Marsilio Ficino (1433–99), to which Pico della Mirandola added a Christianised version of Jewish Cabala. These two trends, associated together, form what I call "the occult philosophy".'[41] Pico began to study Hebrew, Aramaic, and Arabic in the early 1480s at Perugia, and developed an interest in the kabbalah before 1486, the year of his famous 900 theses, of which 47 came directly from kabbalistic sources and a further 72 were his own conclusions based on kabbalistic research. One of his theses proclaimed that 'no science can better convince us of the divinity of Jesus Christ than magic and the Kabbalah'.[42] Indeed, the kabbalistic techniques of gematria (whereby each letter stands for a significant numerical value) and notarikon (whereby words are seen as abbreviations) efficiently served Christian needs. The first three letters of the Hebrew Bible, beth–resh–aleph, for example, could easily be an abbreviation for ben–ruach–av, son–spirit–father. The placing of the Hebrew letter shin in the median position of the tetragrammaton produced an approximation of the name 'Jesus'. As the unspeakable word becomes pronounceable, so too is the ineffable made tangible, the spirit made flesh. Even the vertical arrangement of the four letters of the Hebrew tetragrammaton seemed to produce the stick figure of a man.[43]

Pico's determination to use the kabbalah in the context of Christian theological discussion promoted the first genuine scholarly interest in this important Jewish tradition, and at exactly the same time that the Jews were being expelled from Spain. Iberian Jews were instrumental in raising the study of the kabbalah to new heights in Italy, for one of the intellectual effects of the Expulsion from Spain was to turn the entire mystical tradition away from its focus on the origins of the world to its eventual apocalyptic destruction. The flight from Spain was the birth pangs of the Messiah, and the kabbalah was reinterpreted during the sixteenth century to reflect these new pessimistic orientations in an era of holocaust. Pico and his spiritual descendants, then, were latching on to a Jewish philosophy in the process of rapid development, as a contemporary Jewish intellectual movement came to influence Christian theology. Furthermore, since kabbalah was fundamentally biblical, it was not a prisca theologia, and thereby was spared the suspicious scepticism that might be connected with the parallel hermetic interest in the Egyptian tradition.

Pico's influence is justly celebrated. Burckhardt proclaimed that 'He was the only man who loudly and vigorously defended the truth and science of all ages against the one-sided worship of classical antiquity.' Indeed, 'Looking at Pico, we can guess at the lofty flight which Italian philosophy would have taken had not the counter-reformation annihilated the higher spiritual life of the people.'[44] So too did Frances Yates stress Pico's notion of the 'dignity of Man as Magus', noting that the idea of man 'having within him the divine creative power and the magical power of marrying earth to heaven, rests on the gnostic heresy that man was once, and can become again through his intellect, the reflection of the divine *mens*, a divine being.' Through Pico's influence, Johannes Reuchlin was led to kabbalistic and Hebraic wisdom, which he studied in Italy under Jacob ben Jehiel Loans, the Jewish court physician of Frederick III. Reuchlin produced in 1506 the first proper Hebrew grammar in Latin, published the first full treatises on kabbalah written by a gentile and, as we shall see, was not without his detractors.[45]

Certainly, to some extent, the fascination which Pico and Reuchlin had with Hebrew and kabbalah was part of Renaissance eclecticism, the notion that the truth could be found scattered in a wide variety of sources. Yet, more importantly, there was also the belief that the kabbalah was part of the original divine message given by God on Mount Sinai, and that it had remained pure, untainted by the intervention of the rabbis and their obfuscating Talmud. Those drawn to Jewish sources soon found themselves in dire need of guidance, such as could be had only from living Jews. Many rabbis and even medical doctors found themselves sought after by their intellectual Christian neighbours as purveyors of whatever Hebrew knowledge they may have had, no matter how haphazardly it had been acquired. Eventually, their monopoly would be weakened both by the printing of kabbalistic works, and the rise of Lurianic kabbalah, the new variety of the mystical tradition which was being developed at Safed in Palestine, but for nearly a century Jewish teachers were much in demand.

Pico had his Rabbi Yohanan Isaac Allemanno, whom he met in Florence in 1488 and engaged as his teacher. We know little about Allemanno, but it appears that he was acquainted with Lorenzo de Medici as well. Allemanno's son Isaac taught Pico's nephew Giovanni Francesco.[46] Flavius Mithridates, that mysterious Sicilian Jew who converted to Christianity, translated kabbalistic texts for Pico, and taught Hebrew, Aramaic, and Arabic not only in Italy, but in France and Germany as well. He also translated the Koran into Latin for the duke of Urbino, and preached a sermon before the pope on the suffering of Jesus.[47]

Indeed, the point has been made that the entire direction of translation was altered. Before the Renaissance, many philosophical treatises were translated into Hebrew by Jews for the use of other Jews. From the beginning of the fifteenth century, on the other hand, Jews and converts from Judaism were translating Hebrew works into Latin or Italian, and themselves writing in these languages.[48] It has recently been argued that (apart from a Judaized Plato), contemporary Jews were little interested in the Renaissance notion of two sources for ancient theology, pagan and Christian, preferring the single path that led from Mount Sinai.[49] Yet the example of Abraham Yagel (1553–1623), physician and tutor to moneyed Jewish families in northern Italy, shows that many Jews were drawn to classical authors, as he compared them with Jewish sources and concluded that his own tradition was superior to that of Greece and Rome.[50] A great scholar like Azariah de' Rossi (*c.* 1511–*c.* 1578), whose masterpiece *Me'or Einayim* [Enlightenment of the Eyes] was written in the mid-1570s, demonstrated that Jews might participate fully in the intellectual ferment of the Renaissance.

The Reformation strengthened this interest and respect for Jewish learning, not so much in the kabbalistic vein, but more directly as respect for the Jews as the guardians of the Old Testament, which came to be seen as their most important historical function.[51] The Word of God was His legacy to mankind, and His word was in Hebrew. The principle of *sola scriptura* demanded mastery of the Hebrew language. Yet even in rationalistic Protestantism, Hebrew soon acquired mystical signification and kabbalistic intonations. Hebrew was the vernacular of Adam and Eve in the Garden of Eden, when Adam gave names to the animals and there was no poetic ambiguity between words and the things to which they referred. The Bible tells us that God created the universe by speaking, and the language He spoke was almost certainly Hebrew. There was always the hope that one day mankind might recreate this entire technology by a study of the intricacies of the Hebrew language, and thereby take part in the divine process.[52]

During the first half of the sixteenth century, then, Protestants and Roman Catholics alike were united in the belief that in order to reach full Christian understanding it was necessary to study the Old Testament, the Hebrew language, and even the Jewish mystical tradition, the kabbalah. The Jews of Europe, and especially in Italy, were therefore given positive associations, and a number of Jewish intellectuals found themselves popular and in demand as representatives of an entire people.

Erasmus, we recall, was defeated by the prospect of learning Hebrew 'by the strangeness of the language, and at the same time the shortness of life'. A difficult language at the best of times, one can only gnash one's teeth at the challenge which faced the Christian humanists and the Renaissance Hebraists at the end of the fifteenth century. The very first Hebrew grammar written by a Christian was the work of Conrad Pellican (1478–1556), the Swiss Protestant scholar: twenty quarto leaves, it was printed from woodcut blocks at Strasburg. It was an extract from a larger work, and was mainly an account of how Pellican divined the rules of Hebrew grammar on his own. The grammar itself is a mere nineteen pages, followed by a sampler of texts from Isaiah and Psalms (five pages), and a short list of Hebrew words, with their Latin and Greek equivalents.[53]

Johannes Reuchlin, the German humanist politician, produced his more substantial *De rudimentis Hebraicis* published in 1506 and printed back-to-front like a Hebrew book. Reuchlin had to pay Jews to teach him the language, and this first proper grammar in Latin of the Old Testament language was pathbreaking, not the least because, as Reuchlin lamented, 'before me among the Latins no one appears to have done this.' Reuchlin's book was part grammar (very briefly done), part dictionary, and part primer: a mere description of the Hebrew alphabet for absolute beginners.[54] Reuchlin's lead was followed by Wolfgang Fabricius Capito (1478–1541) the German Reformer, who published a small Hebrew grammar at Basle in 1518. Other such works would follow throughout the sixteenth century,[55] but Hebrew studies after Reuchlin's death would not receive its next boost until the appearance of Sebastian Münster at Basle.

Sebastian Münster was a second-generation Christian Hebraist, a pupil of Pellican, and by 1524 (like him) a Protestant, having abandoned the Franciscans who had accepted him while still a very young man. Münster taught Hebrew at Heidelberg, and in 1528 was appointed professor of Hebrew at Basle, where he remained until his death. Münster was not only a Hebraist, of course, but also mathematician, cosmographer, and cartographer. But his Hebraic studies alone were prodigious and pioneering. His first Hebrew grammars were unexceptional, published in 1520 and 1524.[56] At about this time he discovered the work of Elijah ben Asher Levita, the great Jewish grammarian, who had already published both a Hebrew grammar at Rome (1508) and an Aramaic dictionary at Isny (1514). Münster immediately recognized the futility of trying to hack a pathway through the Hebrew woods on his own: 'In all the grammatical works written by Christians before Elias began his work,' he confessed, 'the true fundamental [grounding] was missing.' Indeed, he lamented, 'We have become teachers before being students'.[57]

Elijah Levita (1468?–1549), also known as Eliyahu Bachur, was not only a leading Hebrew philologist and lexicographer, but one of those Jews during the period of the Renaissance who actively promoted Christian Hebraism, as a point of principle. Although born near Nuremberg, Levita lived most of his life in Italy, and was in contact with most of the leading Christian Hebraists of his day.[58] Postel claimed Levita among his closest friends in Venice.[59] At Rome, Levita lived for thirteen years (1514–27) in the home of Cardinal Egidius da Viterbo, and taught him kabbalah while translating manuscripts for him. Acting on the recommendation of one of his pupils, King Francis I invited Levita to lecture at the Collège Royal in Paris. Levita refused, explaining that being the only Jew allowed to live in France would be detrimental to his religious observances.[60]

Levita's life changed in the sack of Rome (1527), which ruined him. He returned to Venice and from about 1529 for ten years worked as a proof-reader for the press owned by Daniel Bomberg (d. 1549), which was a Christian business publishing Hebrew books. Levita remained in Venice, except for the period 1539–44 when he took a job with Paul Fagius's press at Isny (Württemberg) and printed there some of his most important works.[61] Levita's Hebrew grammars and dictionaries, and his Aramaic dictionary and biblical concordance, brought him to the attention of the Christian scholarly world. His *Bove-Bukh*, a sort of Jewish *Decameron* written in Yiddish, brought him fame in the Jewish world, and gave him a lasting place in the history of Yiddish literature.[62] But for Sebastian Münster, what was important were the books that Levita wrote and published at Rome between 1518 and 1519, and which seemed even to gentile scholars to put the field on an entirely new footing.[63]

To his credit, Münster immediately gave up significant creative work and dedicated himself to bringing Levita before the gentile Latin-reading public. Münster's next work, the *Grammatica Hebraica absolutissima* (1525) was quite simply a translation of Levita's *Sefer ha-Bachur* (1518), and he made no attempt to hide this fact.[64] Indeed, in the catalogue of the British Library it is listed as Münster's translation of the work of 'Elijah, ben Asher, the Levite'. Münster also published at this time a translation of Levita's *Sefer ha-Harkavah*, and a Hebrew dictionary.[65] Münster tried to summarize this scholarship in his *Opus grammaticum consummatum*, published in Basle in 1542, which became the most complete grammar available to Christians, a fine piece of work.[66]

These ponderous products were inherently unobjectionable. So too was his translation of the Old Testament into Latin, the first such achievement by a Protestant, printed in parallel columns to the Hebrew.[67] Even Münster's Aramaic grammar of 1527, the first written by a Christian, was very nearly beyond reproach.[68] What annoyed his fellow humanists was Münster's attraction to aspects of the Jewish tradition which did not seem to have much bearing on biblical scholarship. How could one explain his work on the Jewish calendar,[69] or his edition of the Books of Joel and Malachi with the commentary of David Kimchi?[70] Münster also published a translation of Moses of Coucy's catalogue of the 613 commandments,[71] and Maimonides's 'Thirteen Articles of Faith'.[72] Worst of all, however, was his translation of the Gospel of Matthew into Hebrew, the first Hebrew translation of any portion of the New Testament, and dedicated to King Henry VIII of England, no less.[73] Even Postel, who was no saint, was outraged, and attacked Münster in print.[74]

V

Apart from the not inconsiderable difficulty of actually learning the language, there was the slow development of Hebrew printing. Despite the fact that the technology of printing was most advanced in Germany, it was in northern Italy that the Hebrew language was first set in movable type.[75] The first surviving example of Hebrew printing is a psalter with David Kimchi's commentary which appeared in Bologna in 1477, and is therefore the first part of the Hebrew Bible to be printed.[76] This was followed in 1482 at Bologna by a Pentateuch with vowels, cantillation marks, the Aramaic paraphrase of Onkelos, and Rashi's standard commentary.

But Hebrew printing really came of age near Mantua in the town of Soncino when a family of south German Jews inaugurated their press in 1484 by printing the Talmudic tractate *Berachot*. The way in which they arranged the commentaries around the Aramaic text would become standard practice. The following year (1485) they published a Hebrew edition of the Prophets, and in 1488 made history by printing the *editio princeps* of the complete Hebrew Bible. A second edition followed in 1491–3, printed without date or place of publication, but thought by scholars to be the work of the Soncino Press transmigrated to Naples. Except for a brief three-year hiatus, between 1494 and 1504, the Soncino Press was the only Hebrew publisher in the world. Their work was not only of intrinsically high quality, but like Erasmus's Greek New Testament had a great effect on subsequent scholarship since there was no effective competition. Luther used the Soncino third edition printed at Brescia as the basis of his translation of the Old Testament. This indeed was the last production of the Hebrew Bible or parts thereof until 1510–11, when Gershom ben Moses Soncino (d. 1533 or 1534) published a beautiful edition of the former Prophets with the commentary of Isaac Abravanel. This gap in Hebrew publishing may have some historical significance or it may reflect the vicissitudes of the Soncino family. Abravanel was himself a Spanish refugee who fled to Italy and there lived out the remainder of his life in contemplation of the disaster that had befallen the Jewish people in 1492. Jewish life was turned upside down in the *fin-de-siècle* Mediterranean world, and it may be that Hebrew publishing by Jews was one of the victims. The Soncinos for their part removed to the Ottoman Empire, printing their works in Salonica (1527) and from 1530 in Constantinople. By mid-century they were in Cairo, printing until 1557. The Soncinos published altogether about one hundred Hebrew and an equal number of Latin works.

By the time the Soncino family left Italy, Hebrew printing was no longer a Jewish monopoly. Daniel Bomberg of Antwerp settled in Venice as a young man and with a good deal of Jewish help published during his lifetime about two hundred Hebrew books. The most famous was his first rabbinic Bible, the Hebrew text with standard commentaries, which appeared at Venice in 1516–17.[77] Bomberg's Bible was meant primarily for a Jewish readership, it would appear, although he went to the trouble of turning to the Medici pope Leo X for a licence forbidding any other printer from producing a rabbinical Bible until 1525.[78]

Bomberg's chief Hebrew adviser was the apostate known as Felix Pratensis (d. 1539), and after his death, Bomberg returned to Antwerp.[79] Bomberg followed up the success of the rabbinical Bible with the first complete edition of both the Babylonian and Jerusalem Talmuds (1520–3), and his pagination in this work has remained standard among Jews until today. So too was Bomberg's second rabbinical Bible, published at Venice, 1524–5, an important model for all later editions. His Jewish assistant, later baptized, was Jacob ben Hayim, a refugee from Tunisia who set the text. This edition utilized full Masoretic equipment and was based on fourteenth-century manuscripts.[80]

Although somewhat of a calm followed Bomberg's storm, a number of other Hebrew Bibles did appear before the next great edition, the Royal Poly glot of Antwerp (1569–72). Sebastian Münster's *Hebraic Biblia* in two volumes at Basle (1534–5), used the Hebrew text of Bomberg's first edition as the basis for his own Latin translation. Robert Estienne, the great Protestant printer of Geneva, preferred to use the more accurate Jacob ben Hayim text as the basis for his quarto Old Testament published between 1539 and 1544. Bomberg's son worked for Christopher Plantin (c. 1520–89), the leading crypto-Protestant printer who fled France for the Low Countries and began publishing books at Antwerp from 1555. By the mid-1570s he had more than twenty-two presses, an empire which in one form or another survived until the mid-nineteenth century. Plantin's copy of Bomberg's rabbinical Bible in its second edition was very successful, not least among North African Jews.

In a sense, all of this activity was a prelude to the last great pioneering edition, the Royal Polyglot of Antwerp, the *Biblia regia*, printed at Antwerp by Christopher Plantin between 1569 and 1572.[81] The work was fitfully paid for in part by Philip II, who thereby earned a dozen sets on vellum, apart from the 1,200 copies printed. The first four volumes comprised the Hebrew Old Testament including Aramaic targums, relying in great measure on the Complutensian Polyglot with necessary corrections from Bomberg's second rabbinical Bible.[82] The man behind the Hebrew was Benedictus/Benito Arias Montanus/Montano (1527–98), the Spanish Benedictine who had studied at the University of Alcalá, and first director of the Escorial library. Unlike many of the Hebrew midwives of printed Bibles, Arias Montanus probably was not of significantly Jewish descent: he was a member of the Order of Santiago which carefully guarded *limpieza de sangre*.

The Hebrew text was divided for the first time into verses and is the basis of our present system. It formed the first column of four printed over two pages: Hebrew–Vulgate–Latin translation of the Greek Septuagint-Septuagint, with the Aramaic Targums and Latin translation at the bottom of the page. The entire Hebrew text was reprinted interlinearly with a revised version of Pagnini's Latin translation. The same volume also included the Greek New

Testament of the Complutensian Polyglot with an interlinear Latin translation. Another Greek New Testament was published in volume 5, including Syriac and Latin translations.

Even more interesting than the published texts were the aids to study included in the Royal Polyglot. The sixth volume contained lexicons, and grammars of Hebrew, Aramaic, and Greek, plus a grammar of Syriac. The eighth and last volume of the Polyglot printed not only indexes and a list of variant readings, but also helpful essays on biblical subjects and an explanation of the Jewish Masoretic principles.

Apart from Plantin and Arias Montanus, a number of other scholars were associated with the Antwerp Polyglot and give it an interesting pedigree. The first volume of the Antwerp Polyglot included Hebrew poems not only by Arias Montanus, but also by Guy Le Fèvre de la Boderie (1541–98), one of the trio of brothers who were known for their Hebrew and kabbalistic studies. Their entry into this story is intriguing not the least because of their possible motives for participation. In the decade after the publication of the Antwerp Polyglot they would be heavily involved with presenting an esoteric philosophy which used elements from Hermeticism, Pythagoreanism and kabbalah. Guy translated into French the *De harmonia mundi* of Francesco Giorgi of Venice, which was a striking example of how numerical calculations could be used to express what the kabbalists saw as the divine organization of the universe. The brothers Guy and Nicolas (1550–1613) in their laudatory prefaces stressed the way in which Solomon's Temple was the scale model of God's plan and the key to further understanding.[83] As if to make their devotion to Christian kabbalah even more manifest, the same volume included Nicolas's French translation of the *Heptaplus* by Pico della Mirandola (first published 1489), his commentary on the Creation story in Genesis.[84]

The La Boderie brothers would be involved with many of the main protagonists of esoteric lore in France during the period of the wars of religion. Guy published as early as 1570 a discourse of the eternal secrets,[85] and eight years later, at the same time as he worked on Giorgi's book, he published a poem on French cultural heroes, entitled *La Galliade*.[86] La Boderie used Giorgi's ideas on universal harmony in his contacts with the Pléiade poets. Even more telling, Guy Le Fèvre de la Boderie was part of the circle around François d'Alençon, the brother of the French king, the heir to the throne, and the leader of the *politique* faction. With such kabbalistic leanings, it is not surprising that the La Boderie brothers were involved with Guillaume Postel, as always the centre of anything esoteric in late sixteenth-century France.[87] In brief, Guy and Nicolas Le Fèvre de la Boderie were loudly trumpeting a kabbalistic philosophy at a time when the Church of the Counter-Reformation had already made it perfectly clear (at least from 1553) that this was not a proper path for Christian wisdom.

Another scholar with strong Hebraic interests who worked on the Antwerp Polyglot was Gilbert Génébrard (1537–97), professor of Bible at the Collège de France. Unlike the La Boderie brothers, Génébrard was rather conventional, and opposed kabbalah and its study. He was also an outspoken supporter of the Catholic League, and although in 1593 he became archbishop of Aix-en-Provence, he would be out of favour when Henry IV became king and would end his days in disgrace.[88] Among Hebraists he would remain known, not the least because of his Latin version of the travels of Eldad ha-Dani, the late ninth-century self-styled ambassador from the Lost Ten Tribes of Israel. Génébrard's panegyric to the Antwerp Polyglot thus gave a certain amount of balance to the La Boderie brothers.[89]

In any case, the Antwerp Polyglot was made eminently respectable by the somewhat ungracious patronage of Philip II. The money was given so fitfully that Christophe Plantin its printer went into deep debt, his title of Architypographer in some measure an empty honour. Plantin seems to have had rival offers from Protestant princes, but whether because of confessional loyalty or the perceived inability of remaining in Antwerp after crossing the Spanish ruler of the Low Countries, Plantin refused them all.[90]

Arias Montanus received papal approval for his Polyglot after paying a visit to Rome, possibly because of Catholic fears that a rival polyglot by the Jewish convert Immanuel Tremellius was in the works. Nevertheless, the Antwerp Polyglot was the object of exceedingly strenuous attacks from a variety of sources. Leon de Castro, the professor of Hebrew at the University of Salamanca, denounced Arias Montanus to the Inquisition, arguing that he was guilty of Judaizing tendencies in making use of the Hebrew Masoretic text when it conflicted with the Vulgate. The investigation dragged on for years, but in the end the Inquisitorial authorities were convinced by the expert testimony regarding the accused's orthodoxy given by Juan de Mariana (1536–1623), the great Jesuit historian of Spain. Arias Montanus later even represented Philip II at a Church council in Toledo (1582–3), declined the offer of a bishopric, and spent the last years of his life in isolation at a monastery near Seville.[91]

The papal fears about a rival version from Immanuel Tremellius (1510–80) were only partially justified. Tremellius was born a Jew in the ghetto at Ferrara, and was introduced to Christianity by the future Pope Paul III and converted to Catholicism by the English Cardinal Reginald Pole (1500–58), being baptized in 1540. Tremellius began teaching Hebrew at Lucca, and by 1542 had converted to Protestantism and was teaching at Strasburg. He made a friend of Thomas Cranmer (1489–1556) and was appointed Regius professor of Hebrew at Cambridge in 1548. When Mary came to the throne in 1553 he was forced to decamp with many other Protestant professors to the Continent, where he taught at Heidelberg and Sedan. With his son-in-law

Francis Junius (1545–1602) he produced in 1575–9 an Old Testament and Apocrypha in a literal Latin translation. While achieving a good deal of popularity among Protestants, it was not in the end a rival to the achievements of the Antwerp Polyglot.[92]

VI

One aspect of the Renaissance Hebraic tradition which has gone almost completely unnoticed by modern historians is the growing place of Syriac studies from the middle of the sixteenth century.[93] The Syriac language is in essence a form of Aramaic written in a script other than Hebrew. The existence of a Syriac New Testament (the Peshitta Version) used by Christians in the Near East aroused mixed emotions in Renaissance scholars. Many believed that Syriac rather than Aramaic was the mother tongue of Christ and that it might be possible to uncover the original text of the Gospel of Matthew and even the Epistle to the Hebrews in that language. The status of the Syriac New Testament was thus worryingly unclear from the very beginning: it might even have a claim to greater antiquity than the Vulgate.

The story of the beginning of Syriac studies in the West is recounted romantically in the preface to the first printed edition of the Syriac New Testament, published in 1555. It seems that three Maronite clergy turned up to the meetings of the Fifth Lateran Council (1512–17), and asked permission to be allowed to celebrate the mass in the Syriac language. The clergyman assigned to the case was Theseus Ambrosius (1469–1540), also known as Teseo Ambrogio degli Albonesi, who had a Syrian priest translate the material into Arabic, which was then translated by a Jew into Latin. The result of his labours was the first grammatical introduction to Syriac, which also called for the design of the first Syriac types. Ambrosius in this work discusses not only Syriac, but Armenian as well, and provides short accounts of other exotic languages such as Samaritan, Coptic, and Ethiopic. Since type for these languages was often lacking, blank spaces were left to be filled in by hand. At the end of the book, Ambrosius printed twenty-four exotic and fantastic alphabets and his correspondence with the great Postel.[94] One interesting technical feature of the book is that Ambrosius claims that it was dictated rather than written, and he gives a description of himself doing so and chatting with friends in the print shop.[95]

It may have been the tragic loss of the Syriac type and his papers in the siege of Pavia by Francis I, or the immensity of the pioneering task, but Ambrosius was unable to produce a printed Syriac New Testament before his death in 1540. He passed on his research and his Syriac manuscripts to the German Catholic humanist and diplomat Johann Albrecht von Widmanstadt

(d. 1557). He studied Syriac with a Maronite bishop, and received some help from Moses the Syrian Jacobite priest who represented himself as the agent of his patriarch. With financial backing from Charles V, Widmanstadt got his Syriac New Testament printed in 1555, casting his own types in tin, and conforming to the Syriac canon which not only left out a number of epistles, but also the Book of Revelation and the proof text of the Trinity from John.

One thousand copies of the Syriac New Testament were printed, half of these earmarked for use in the East. The Jacobite patriarch was supposed to get 300 copies and Moses 200 for delivery to his brethren back home, but without his patron's knowledge or consent, Moses simply flogged the copies anywhere he could. The remainder of the print run was redated 1562 and sold in Europe. Despite the chicanery of the actual sale, the achievement of Ambrosius and Widmanstadt was undeniable, for their edition is still respected by modern scholars. Widmanstadt's little Syriac grammar of 1556 was a sort of companion volume which set the seal on their work.

Syriac studies remained in vogue for a number of years. An even better grammar was produced in 1569 by Immanuel Tremellius, who published a folio edition as well to go with his own version of the Syriac New Testament printed the same year. Tremellius's New Testament had four columns: Greek, Syriac (also in Hebrew letters), the Vulgate, and Tremellius's own Latin, which was literal rather than literary.

VII

As is apparent, despite what is presented in many histories of Tudor Puritanism, one needs to do quite a bit of foregrounding before bringing on stage the subject of the English Bible, let alone Tyndale, as majestic and important as he undoubtedly was for the history of the Holy Book in England. William Tyndale was born in the Welsh border country and entered Magdalen Hall, Oxford in 1510, when he was probably about sixteen years old. He took his MA in 1515, and left shortly thereafter for Cambridge, where he stayed until the end of 1521. Tyndale thus managed to just miss both John Colet at Oxford and Erasmus at Cambridge, but something of their spirit must have remained at both institutions. He spent some time as a tutor in Gloucestershire, and at some point resolved to translate the New Testament into English.[96] Tyndale seems at that time to have conceived of that project less as a humanistic exercise than as a tool in local religious disputes:

> For when I was so turmoiled in the country where I was that I could no longer there dwell (the process whereof were too long here to rehearse) I this wise thought in myself, this I suffer because the priests of the country

be unlearned, as God it knoweth there are a full ignorant sort which have seen no more Latin than that they read in their portesses and missals which yet many of them can scarcely read.

'And so I gat me to London', Tyndale recalled. There he presented an oration of Isocrates which he had translated from the Greek to Sir Henry Guildford the master of the horse, 'the king's grace controller'. This gift opened the door to the famously taciturn Cuthbert Tunstall (1474–1559), who had recently been created bishop of London. Although in some ways the model of a Renaissance prelate, Tunstall was in no mood to make any changes that smacked of Protestantism. Tyndale presented his plan for an English Bible, 'Whereupon my lord answered me, his house was full, he had more than he could well find, and advised me to seek in London, where he said I could not lack a service.'[97]

Tyndale was forced to delay his project, and became preacher at St Dunstan's-in-the-West: 'And so in London I abode almost a year,' he recounted, 'and marked the course of the world'.[98] Among those who were impressed with Tyndale's vision was Humphrey Monmouth (d. 1537), a cloth merchant with Lollard connections. Monmouth took Tyndale into his own house under the guise of a chaplain. Tyndale was able to remain there for nearly half a year, where, according to Monmouth, 'he lived like a good priest', that is, 'He studied most of the day and night, ate only sodden meat, drank small single beer, and never wore linen.'[99] Despite these advantages, insufficient progress was being made on his translation, and he 'understood at the last not only that there was no room in my lord of London's palace to translate the new testament, but also that there was no place to do it in all England, as experience doth now openly declare.'[100]

Tyndale removed to the Continent in May 1524, first to Hamburg and then to Wittenberg, to consult with Luther in the place where the Protestant Revolution began. Monmouth continued to support Tyndale, sending him £10 to pray for his parents' souls, and then a year later, £10 more.[101] Tyndale returned to Hamburg the following April, working all the while on his English New Testament, assisted by William Roy (*fl.* 1527).[102] They soon moved on to Cologne, where they contracted with Peter Quentell to print the work. The printers got as far as the signature K (ten sheets) when another patron of the same publishing house got wind of what was coming off the presses, and denounced Tyndale to the town senate, which issued an injunction stopping all further printing.[103]

Tyndale and Roy took the printed pages and fled to Worms, arriving in October 1525. There, in more sympathetic surroundings, they agreed with a printing house, probably that of Peter Schöffer (1425?–1502), to produce the entire work again. The English New Testament was soon completed, for in

December of that year Henry VIII was informed by Edward Lee from Bordeaux that an Englishman had produced a vernacular version of Scripture at Luther's request, and was intending to send copies to England.[104] Even if Lee's reference was only to the Cologne fragments rather than to the finished Worms edition, it was clear that progress was being made at a rapid rate. Henry was sufficiently alarmed to include an explicit declaration in his *Answer to Luther* (1526) that all 'untrue translations' of the Bible would be burnt and even their readers punished, although he did hold out the hope that one day an English Bible might appear.[105]

Unauthorized versions of Scripture had been banned in England in 1410 at the beginning of the Lollard movement, so sufficient legal menace existed to render Tyndale's project precarious. Bishop Tunstall of London no doubt had cause to remember the man who had asked for a humanist's help a few years back, but now was determined to crush the work that he might equally have approved. In October 1526, he denounced it from St Paul's Cross, and gave orders to his archdeacons to pass on the word that all copies of Tyndale's translation which had been spirited into England were to be turned in within thirty days on pain of excommunication. Tunstall then summoned the booksellers of London and ordered them not to sell Tyndale's New Testament.[106] On 3 November 1526, Archbishop William Warham gave the bishop of Exeter a list of books 'containing heretical pravity', including 'The New Testament of Tindall', and ordered him to have them hunted down.[107]

Most of the copies were brought over from Antwerp to supply a constant demand.[108] Robert Barnes (1495–1540) and Simon Fish (d. 1531) were among those who sought to increase the flow. Some of these 'New Testamenters' when caught provide us with useful information about how this was done. John Pykas, a Colchester baker, confessed in March 1528 that 'about a Two yeres last past, he bowght in Colchestre, of a Lumbard of London, a New Testament in English, and payd for it Foure Shillinges.' A certain Robert Nectone testified that he 'sold fyve of the said New Testaments to Sir William Furboshore Synging man, in Stowmarket in Suffolk, for vii or viii Grotes a pece.' He also 'sold Sir Richard Bayfell two New Testaments unbound, about Cristmas last; for the which he payd iijs. iiijd.' According to Nectone, 'About Cristmas last, there came a Duche man, beyng now in the Flete [Prison], which wold have sold this Respondent ij or iij Hundreth of the said N. Testaments in English.' These were going at 'ixd. a pece'. Some of these were 'New Testaments of the biggest', while others were copies 'of the smal Volume'.[109] On 19 November 1530, four men (one of them called John Tyndale and possibly a brother) were paraded through the City to Cheapside Cross, their clothes decorated with copies of Tyndale's New Testament. At their destination they were made to throw the heretical translation on to a fire specially prepared, before being displayed in the pillory.[110]

Even Humphrey Monmouth, Tyndale's first patron, was arrested in May 1528, but he had already burnt all of Tyndale's letters, treatises, sermons, and 'copies of books written by his servant'. Monmouth claimed that he had destroyed them more 'for fear of the translator' than for their content, and that the first he had heard of Tyndale's heterodoxy was when Tunstall 'preached at St. Paul's Cross, and said that he had translated the New Testament naughtily.' Monmouth testily pointed out that he had supported other clergymen: was he to be blamed if one of them turned out badly?[111]

We can gain some idea of the impact of Tyndale's New Testament in English from a story told about Robert Barnes, the Protestant pioneer who in late 1526 was under house arrest at the Augustinian friary in London. A pair of Essex Lollards came to visit him and brought along their manuscript Gospels in English. Barnes was unimpressed, noting that it was 'A point for them, for that they be not to be regarded toward the new printed Testament in English, for it is of more cleaner English.' Barnes sold them a better copy of Tyndale's New Testament for 'iijs. ijd.' 'and desyred them, that they wold kepe yt close'.[112]

Tyndale must surely have been gratified that his New Testament was so much in demand, and sought after by people who thereby put themselves at personal risk, like the Lollards in the century before the Reformation. The Protestant martyrologist John Foxe (1516–87) claimed that Tyndale turned some of this opposition to his advantage. Tyndale, according to Foxe, knew that there was a good deal of truth in the criticism of the first edition of his New Testament, which 'was much complained of by the clergy as full of errors.' As Foxe recounts,

> Tonstall, then bishop of London, returning from Cambray, to which place More and he had been sent by the king, as he came through Antwerp, bargained with an English merchant who was secretly a friend of Tindal, to procure him as many of his New Testaments as could be had for money. Tindal gladly received this; for being about a more correct edition, he found he would be better enabled to proceed if the copies of the old were sold off; he therefore gave the merchant all he had, and Tonstall, paying for them, brought them over to England, and burnt them publicly in Cheapside.

Foxe testifies that

> This was called a burning of the word of God; and it was said the clergy had reason to revenge themselves on it, for it had done them more mischief than all other books whatsoever. But a year after this, the second edition being finished, great numbers were sent over to England, when [George] Constantine, one of Tindal's partners, happened to be taken: believing that some of the London merchants furnished them with money,

he was promised his liberty if he would discover who they were: upon this he said the bishop of London did more than all the world besides, for he bought up the greatest part of a faulty impression.

The end result was that

> The clergy, on their condemning Tindal's translation, promised a new one: but a year after, they said, that it was not necessary to publish the scripture in English, and that the king did well not to set about it.[113]

Faulty though it was, Tyndale's octavo English New Testament of 1526 was the first completed volume. Of the original 3,000 copies, only two seem to have survived. The first is illuminated, with the title page missing, and was bought not so long ago by the British Library for £1 million from the Bristol Baptist College.[114] The second surviving copy, in St Paul's Cathedral Library, has 71 leaves missing. The book is graced with a number of small woodcuts of various evangelists and apostles. The textual differences between the complete New Testament and the quarto fragment are insignificant, and are most likely due to the fact that Tyndale had switched printers. The most important change is that Tyndale dropped the marginal notes in the smaller final printed copy, some of which returned to anger his opponents in later editions as his 'pestilent glosses'. Scholars are in agreement that Tyndale actually did translate directly from the Greek, using as aids other translations, especially the Vulgate, Erasmus's Latin (which was printed with the original Greek text), and Luther's German New Testament of 1522. As for Lollard manuscript New Testaments, it would seem that the echoes of Wycliffite versions that appear in Tyndale are more likely due to currents of speech than to actual textual consultation.[115] Tyndale revised the manuscript himself once again, and published his definitive translation in octavo at Antwerp in 1535.[116]

From our point of view, and certainly in terms of humanistic achievement, however, it is Tyndale's translation of parts of the Old Testament which attracts attention. Greek and Latin were part of the intellectual baggage of any Renaissance intellectual, and it is no surprise that Tyndale should have been able to utilize existing linguistic tools in the service of biblical scholarship. Hebrew was another matter entirely.

As was usually the case, the first portion of the Old Testament to be translated into the vernacular was the Book of Psalms, which according to the title page appeared on 16 January 1530. The publisher was given as 'Francis foxe'; the place of publication as 'Argentine', that is, Strasburg. In fact, as everyone knew, the 16° book of 240 leaves was printed by Martinus de Keyser at Antwerp.[117] The translator, however, was not Tyndale, but almost certainly his associate George Joye (d. 1553). Like Tyndale, Joye used many aliases, including Clarke, Geach, Gee, and Jaye, but he was the Bedfordshire fellow of

Peterhouse, Cambridge who became a well-known Protestant controversialist and Bible translator. Thomas More (1478–1535) at least thought that Joye was the one who had translated the Psalms, and John Stokesley (1475–1539), the bishop of London, included 'the psalter in English by Joye' as one of the forbidden books in his list of Advent Sunday, 1531.[118]

But the book of interest is Tyndale's Pentateuch, the *editio princeps* in English, printed by Johannes Hoochstraten at Antwerp, although the title page claims that it came from the press of Hans Luft at Marburg.[119] This information comes from the colophon at the end of Genesis, which also supplies the date: 17 January 1530. It is a handy book, an octavo in 378 leaves, and not entirely in black letter, unlike the previous English Bibles. The book includes a certain number of woodcuts, and in addition to the prologues, many marginal notes for which Tyndale would become notorious.[120] Tyndale followed the Pentateuch with the Book of Jonah, apparently printed by Martinus de Keyser of Antwerp in 1531.[121] In addition, Tyndale left in manuscript the entire Old Testament from Joshua to Chronicles, which was printed in the 'Matthew' Bible of 1537. The English Bible was born, if not quite created.

VIII

One of the most interesting shifts of policy during the Tudor period was the government's toing and froing over the question of the vernacular Bible. In May 1530, Tyndale was denounced as a heretic and a perverter of God's word. Within less than a year, however, King Henry VIII was ordering Thomas Cromwell (1485?–1540), his henchman and architect of Tudor authority, to scour the European countryside for Tyndale and to offer him the job of producing an authorized version of the English Bible. Cromwell wrote to Stephen Vaughan (d. 1549), an English merchant at Antwerp, giving him the job of convincing Tyndale to come home at once and set to work. Vaughan replied in January 1531, in separate letters to Henry VIII and Cromwell, that Tyndale was afraid that he would be arrested the moment he set foot in England. To Cromwell he added that he himself was deeply impressed with Tyndale: 'Would God he were in England!' Vaughan exclaimed. Two months later, Vaughan wrote again in the same spirit, but with nothing more definite to report.

What had happened to cause such a dramatic turn-about in English religious policy? Thomas Cromwell has been left with the image of a cruel and devious politician, but he was also an intellectual, almost a humanist. Foxe claimed he had memorized Erasmus's New Testament during a journey to and from Rome.[122] Presumably it was the Latin that he studied, perhaps to compensate for a patchy education, but there may be some truth to the matter. Cromwell was therefore probably pushing an English Bible even at this early stage, and would be consistent in this in his later career. A.G. Dickens, whose devotion to Thomas Cromwell sometimes exceeds even that of G.R. Elton, the Tudor statesman's greatest admirer, objects that

> I find the merely secular and destructive Cromwell, the Biblical *saboteur*, a little too simple for the known facts. Must the unfortunate man never be allowed a motive outside the straight role assigned him by Gardiner's Tudor saga? One whose Biblical interests long antedated his power to turn them to political ends need not be denied a belief in the educative power of the Scriptures for a new type of Christian society. And if he really believed that the English Bible would finally destroy the influence of the priesthood, this must have been the greatest of all his miscalculations![123]

Anne Boleyn may have had some influence: the British Library has her copy, printed on vellum, of Tyndale's New Testament of 1534.[124] She made Henry read Tyndale's polemical work on *The Obedience of a Christian Man* (1528), a very Erastian document which promoted the notion of the king who would arise to deliver the people from the powerful and corrupt Catholic Church.[125] Tyndale argued that kings were God's anointed servants, and thus had a religious function to perform for the reformation of the faith. It may simply be that Henry was warming to the idea of being Supreme Head of the Church, and conceived of this as an active job involving policy-making.

In any case, the romance between Tyndale and King Henry VIII was short-lived. In April 1531, Vaughan reported to Henry that he had had a meeting with Tyndale in a field outside Antwerp, and enclosed with his letter a manuscript copy of Tyndale's reply to the attacks of Thomas More.[126] This latest document disabused Henry of any hope of cooperating with the cantankerous cleric, made manifest in Tyndale's book about the *Practice of Prelates* (1530) in which he positively denounced Henry's divorce. Thomas Cromwell wrote another letter to Vaughan, the draft copy of which shows so many corrections that we might conclude that it was written in nervous haste after a tongue-lashing from the king, since the changes do not significantly alter the tone of the letter.[127] Cromwell reported that

> The king's highness therefor has commanded me to advertise you that his pleasure is that you should desert and leave any further to persuade or attempt the said Tyndale to come into this realm, alleging that he, perceiving the malicious, perverse, uncharitable and indurate mind of the said Tyndale, is in manner without hope of reconciliation in him and is very joyous to have his realm destitute of such a person . . . that should Tyndale return unto the same there to manifest his errors and seditious opinions which (being out of the realm by his most uncharitable, venemous and

pestilent books, crafty and false persuasions) he has partly done already, his
highness right prudently considers if he were present by all likelihood he
would shortly (which God defend) do as much as in him were to infect
and corrupt the whole realm, to the great inquietation and hurt of the
commonwealth of the same.

Cromwell closes by explicitly warning him that even though he had been so
favourably impressed by Tyndale during their meetings in Antwerp, should
Vaughan continue to show favour to the man it would most certainly incur
the wrath of the king and personal ruin.[128]

Nevertheless, ever devious, Vaughan's reply demonstrates that when
Cromwell finally sent the letter, he included a secret postscript instructing
Vaughan to give it one more go with Tyndale. He held two additional inter-
views with Tyndale, and reported to both Cromwell and the king (apparently
now calmer) during May and June 1531. During their first meeting, Tyndale
offered to return to England and accept any punishment, on condition that
Henry would agree to publish a translation of the English Bible, and not necessarily the one that Tyndale had done.[129] But Henry was fed up: he tried in
vain to get Emperor Charles V to arrest Tyndale,[130] and when Vaughan wrote
to Cromwell again in November 1531, Tyndale was already old news.[131]

In 1534, Convocation under Cranmer wrote formally to Henry asking for
an English translation of Scripture, and a new project was under way. With
the aim of improving Christian understanding of the original Hebrew text,
Thomas Cromwell in 1535 decreed a series of injunctions at the two English
universities, which were augmented at Cambridge by his commissioner
Thomas Legh (d. 1545), soon to be the villain of the Pilgrimage of Grace.
One of Legh's additions ordered the university to provide at its own expense
a public lecture in either Hebrew or Greek, in return for relieving it of a tax
which had been levied the previous year. This agreement was ratified in an
act of Parliament passed at the beginning of 1536 and pertaining now to both
Oxford and Cambridge. The new lectureship was to be named after the king,
and might now in addition to Greek and Hebrew be devoted to any of the
seven liberal arts or Latin. In other words, a new teaching post was created
by the king, but the Hebrew language was no longer on any (probably short)
list of subjects. This was changed four years later when the number of lec-
tureships at each university was increased to five, now to be paid for by the
cathedral church of Westminster. According to the new regulations, the
approved subjects were deemed specifically to be divinity, civil law, medicine,
Greek, and Hebrew. These were the Regius professorships. In 1546, the financial responsibility for the Hebrew, Greek, and divinity chairs was shifted to
the new foundations, Christ Church at Oxford and Trinity College, Cambridge. The Regius professor of Hebrew was initially required to lecture for

five hours per week, but this crushing burden was reduced to the more man-
ageable proportions of one weekly hour from 1564.[132]

The English Bible carried on even without Tyndale, or so it would seem.
In 1535, an English Catholic tricked Tyndale into leaving the safety of the
English House in Antwerp, whereupon he was arrested. Despite appearances,
this was apparently done without English collusion. Stephen Vaughan, who
had worked so hard to bring Tyndale home, wrote to Cromwell on 13 April
1536, pleading that 'If now you sende but your lettre to the Pryvey Coun-
sail, I could delyver Tyndall from the fyre, so it came by tyme, for elles it
wilbe to late.'[133] But this was too much to ask: Tyndale was condemned as a
heretic, and given the mercy of being strangled before his body was burnt.
His last words at his martyrdom at Antwerp in October 1536, according to
Foxe, were 'Lord, open the King of England's eyes!'[134]

The work of producing the first full edition of the Bible in England was
given to Miles Coverdale (1488–1568), a Yorkshireman educated at Cambridge,
a former Augustinian friar who had worked with Tyndale at Hamburg on the
first Pentateuch. He would become bishop of Exeter in 1551 under Edward
VI, and after return from his Marian exile, would be given a quiet rectory in
London under Elizabeth.[135] Why a man with a biography so similar to the
rejected Tyndale was chosen for this work is not clear, but it may be a combination of a more pliant nature and the promise of a grovelling dedication
to the king which made him more attractive. Coverdale's Bible, published at
either Cologne or Marburg in 1535, made no pretence of being an original
work, but was 'faithfully and truly translated out of Douche [German] and
Latin'.[136]

Coverdale's Bible was just a stopgap, however, made more unsatisfactory in
August 1536 when Cromwell, as deputy to the Supreme Head of the English
Church, issued injunctions to the clergy to provide both Latin and English
Bibles for parishioners to read in the church.[137] These injunctions were largely
ignored, not only because it was not clear exactly which English Bible was
meant, but because the Pilgrimage of Grace, the mass uprising of the north,
delayed the implementation of any reforming legislation.[138] Cromwell was
enough of a humanist to realize that Tyndale's translation was too good to
lose, even if it was impossible to work with the man. In any case, Tyndale was
now dead, having been executed by the Imperial authorities.

In August 1537, Thomas Cromwell licensed a folio edition of the Old and
New Testaments which was said on the title page to have been 'truly and
purely translated into Englysh by Thomas Matthew'. Cromwell knew that
'Thomas Matthew' did not exist, and that the man behind the edition was
John Rogers (c. 1500–55), later to be the first martyr in Mary's persecutions,
but meanwhile chiefly known as the late William Tyndale's close associate.
Essentially, this version of the Bible is a melding of the best of Coverdale and

Tyndale. From Ezra to the end of the Apocrypha, including Jonah, is Coverdale's version, but the entire stretch from Joshua to Chronicles is almost certainly Tyndale's, drawn from a manuscript given to Rogers for safe keeping. The Pentateuch and the New Testament are basically Tyndale's as well. Even the place of publication and the name of the printer are mysterious, although the work was probably done in Antwerp. It is more than likely that not even King Henry VIII knew that he was endorsing the work of the awful William Tyndale when he allowed the book to appear 'with the Kinges most gracyous lycêce'.[139]

Thomas Cromwell was therefore able to issue a second set of royal injunctions in September 1538, ordering each parish to obtain 'one book of the whole Bible of the largest volume in English' by the following Easter, set up in church for people to read. At the same time, he commissioned a revision by Coverdale of Matthew's Bible, corrected with further application to Sebastian Münster's Latin translation of the Hebrew Old Testament (1534–5), with due attention to Erasmus's Latin New Testament and the Complutensian Polyglot. The work was begun in Paris, but when many of the finished sheets were confiscated at the end of 1538, they shifted the entire lot – presses, type, and printers – to London, where the so-called 'Great Bible' was finished in folio by April 1539.[140] Cromwell spent a good deal of his own money in this project, and by the time of his execution the following year, had managed to get printed enough copies for all of the 8,500 English parishes, although few of those outside London were willing to lay out the subsidized cost of purchase. 'Cromwell's Bible' almost fell with him, but assiduous work by Cranmer out-manoeuvred the opposition. In the end, a royal proclamation of 1541 ruled that parishes had six months to purchase a Bible or to pay a £2 fine. It was finally cheaper just to buy the Holy Book. By the end of 1545 most churches had them, and the royal commissioners two years later made sure that the last recalcitrant parishes obeyed. Tyndale, in one form or another, was finally set up throughout England.[141]

IX

Modern historiography has returned in recent years to the notion of 'great men' in history. Twenty years ago, the accepted wisdom in English publishing houses was that 'biographies won't sell'; now they are all the rage. Although individuals (like Churchill) can be debunked, it is no longer quite so fashionable to deny the role of great men in the historical process. William Tyndale was a great man, and not merely because he was the first to translate and publish (most of) the English Bible. Tyndale was the beneficiary of a good deal of pioneering scholarship in the Greek and Hebrew text, right in the middle of the period when there was still a modicum of cooperation between Jewish and gentile scholars, before the Counter-Reformation put an end to all that. In his appreciation and utilization of these advances, Tyndale put himself squarely in the Renaissance tradition. But he was also a champion and publicist for the Protestant Reformation, as his 'pestilent glosses' and various polemical writings abundantly show. We have become accustomed to thinking of the Renaissance and the Reformation as two separate historical tunnels, especially after Luther made it quite clear to Erasmus and the human ist world in 1525 that he would have nothing to do with newfangled notions of human free will.

Tyndale the Protestant, however, demonstrates a good deal of Renaissance spirit, especially if we take note of P.O. Kristeller's controversial claim that the humanists were more interested in how ideas were obtained and expressed than in the content of those ideas themselves. Rhetoric, eloquence, and style were their primary concerns. As long as the views expressed were derived from antiquity and presented in an elegant and learned format, then it really did not matter if you were Platonist or Aristotelian. The cover was almost as important as the book.[142]

A good deal of printers' ink has been spilled over such questions as 'Did Tyndale really know Hebrew?' or, 'How much did he rely on previous translations?' and the central question, 'How accurate a translation from the Hebrew is Tyndale's Old Testament?'[143] We could do worse than to listen to Tyndale himself, keeping Kristeller in mind. Concluding the preface to his Pentateuch, Tyndale asked his readers to remember that

> Notwithstanding yet I submit this book and all other that I have either made or translated, or shall in time to come, (if it be God's will that I shall further labour in his harvest) unto all of them that submit themselves unto the word of God, to be corrected of them, yea and moreover to be disallowed and also burnt, if it seem worthy when they have examined it with the Hebrew, so that they first put forth of their own translating another that is more correct.[144]

Tyndale was far less concerned than his modern critics with providing the ultimate translation into English of the Old Testament. The important thing was to publish a basic text of Holy Writ over which scholars could argue, a standard basis for discussion, a printed English translation which came to the scholar's library, instead of him having to seek it out under the beds and behind the wardrobes of Lollards up and down the country. In this, Tyndale was just like his hero Erasmus, who was quite happy to publish the Greek text of the New Testament out of defective late medieval manuscripts. When he found the last folio of the Book of Revelation lacking, he just made it up for himself, translating the Vulgate back into Greek. This was not forgery; he made no attempt to hide this literary sleight of hand, for it was perfectly in keeping with the main purpose behind the entire enterprise – to provide a basic text on which all further discussion could centre.[145]

Tyndale thus combines both Renaissance and Reformation trends, and stands at the beginning of a new enterprise – the printed English Bible. But he also marks the end of another line of medieval biblical scholarship represented by the Lollard followers of John Wyclif. The Lollards thought it enough to produce a vernacular text, any English Bible, even if it was merely a translation of the increasingly inaccurate Vulgate. They would no more have thought of going *ad fontes*, turning to the Hebrew and Greek, searching out and collating early biblical manuscripts, than an Italian humanist would think of praising Scholasticism. Like in everything else, the Lollard underground had to give way to the heavy artillery of the Reformation.[146]

We all know that there is nothing so permanent as temporary, and Tyndale's achievement turned out to be well nigh eternal. About 90 per cent of the King James Authorized Version (1611) is verbatim Tyndale, and even the Revised Version of 1881–5 retains Tyndale to the degree of 80 per cent.[147] It was John Reynolds (1549–1607), the president of Corpus Christi College, Oxford, who first suggested producing a new translation of the Bible to replace Tyndale's. Indeed, it was one of the few points of agreement at the Hampton Court Conference in January 1604, where the idea was first given a public airing before King James I (1603–25), who accepted it enthusiastically. The responsibility for the work was divided among six 'companies', each of which took on a particular part of the Bible. The directors were Lancelot Andrewes (1555–1626) at Westminster; Edward Lively (1545?–1605) at Cambridge; and John Harding at Oxford, each of whom was in charge of two companies. The fifty or so men who did the actual work of translating were told to use the Bishops' Bible as the base, and to compare it not only with the originals, but with Tyndale and all other English versions.[148]

The first few years were occupied with initial ground-clearing, but by 1607 actual text was being produced. The translations were passed around for amendment and changes, and by 1610 were delivered to a committee of a dozen representatives sitting at Stationers' Hall. The two men responsible for supervising the printing were Miles Smith (d. 1624), later bishop of Gloucester; and Thomas Bilson (1547–1616), bishop of Winchester. Smith probably wrote the chapter headings, and Bilson the preface of 'The Translators to the Reader'.

According to this famous preface, the translators worked on their sacred text 'twise seuen times seuentie two dayes and more', which works out to about two years and nine months. The finished product was published by Robert Barker (d. 1645), the king's printer. Despite being often referred to as the Authorized Version, there is no evidence that it was authorized by anyone political or ecclesiastical.[149] Perhaps 'King James Version' is a better name to refer to that extraordinary work which has influenced the English language more than any other single book, even if it is the voice of Tyndale that shouts through the text. Not only did Tyndale introduce the word 'Jehovah' into English,[150] but numerous phrases such as 'powers that be', 'die the death', 'eat, drink and be merry' and many others as well. Tyndale proclaimed that 'the properties of the Hebrew tongue agreeth a thousand times more with the English than with the Latin.'[151] That this could become a permanent part of the English legacy was due to the Hebraic pioneers, both Jew and gentile, of the prehistoric English Bible.

CHAPTER 2

In Pursuit of a Useful Bible: Scriptural Politics and the English Civil War

Thomas Hobbes (1588–1679), when contemplating the vicissitudes of the scriptural text, was not unduly worried by the fact that the Bible had been in the hands of those with authority until it was revealed to all with the vernacular translations of more recent times. Despite this dubious custodianship, Hobbes wrote,

> yet I am perswaded they did not therefore falsifie the Scriptures, though the copies of the Books of the New Testament, were in the hands only of the Ecclesiasticks; because if they had had an intention so to doe, they would surely have made them more favorable to their power over Christian Princes, and Civill Soveraignty, than they are. I see not therefore any reason to doubt, but that the Old, and New Testament, as we have them now, are the true Registers of those things, which were done and said by the Prophets, and Apostles.[1]

As Hobbes correctly observed, there was a certain element in the biblical narrative which worked against political authority, and any unsupervised reading of Scripture could very easily bring that aspect to the fore. Hobbes was well aware of the danger here, and after the Restoration complained that 'Every man, nay, every boy and wench, that could read English thought they spoke with God Almighty, and understood what he said, when by a certain number of chapters a day they had read the Scriptures once or twice over . . . this licence of interpreting the Scripture was the cause of so many several sects, as having lain hid till the beginning of the late King's reign, did then appear to the disturbance of the commonwealth.'[2]

The era of the English Civil War in the middle years of the seventeenth century was the high-water mark in bibliolatry in the Protestant world before the emergence of Fundamentalism in our own time. The underlying social fact which enabled the Bible to play such a central role was that despite differences in class and education, England to a very large extent enjoyed in those years a common cultural base, a complex of images and metaphors which were understood and recognized by nearly everyone. This cultural common denominator was the English Bible, which since the Reformation was the text that was read the most, heard the most, and discussed the most at all levels of society. The Bible provided the vocabulary of a secret language which only needed to be invoked in order to be understood. A partial biblical phrase, a sanctified word or two, served the dual purpose of conveying a synecdochic message without fear of the censor, and ratifying it with the stamp of divine authority. There was a kind of scriptural politics at work during the period of the English Civil War – politics in the sense of the active application of theoretical intellectual views. Scriptural politics was the practical application of the English Bible in an era of common cultural assumptions.

I

What factors promoted the crystallization of such a common biblical culture in England during the sixteenth and the first half of the seventeenth centuries? Obviously, the most important prerequisite was the timely invention of printing, which enabled the Bible to be distributed cheaply and efficiently. Francis Bacon (1561–1626) believed that the three great inventions which had created his world were gunpowder, the mariner's compass, and printing.[3] John Foxe, the esteemed martyrologist, believed that the invention of movable type was the result of divine intervention:

> Notwithstanding, what man soever was the instrument, without all doubt God himself was the ordainer and disposer thereof; no otherwise than he was of the gift of tongues, and that for a singular purpose . . . the Lord hath given this gift of printing to the earth.[4]

Yet equally if not more important was the fact that a printed Bible was a standard and uniform text, and discussion about Scripture achieved a new kind of focus without having to worry about the vagaries of manuscript transmission.

One of the main reasons for the spread of the English Bible was not only the fact that it was printed, but that it was relatively cheap, and became more so with the breakdown of authority in the Civil War. The printing of bibles and liturgies was the monopoly of Robert Barker, the king's printer, who was much more interested in restricting the trade in Scripture to his own advantage than in spreading the divine Word. It was Robert Barker who printed the first edition of the Authorized or King James Version in 1611. Barker's most famous opponent was Michael Sparke (c.1588–1653), originally from the

Oxfordshire village of Eynsham, but now a bookseller in London. Sparke was a sort of publishing terrorist, a notorious infringer of copyrights, and the courageous publisher of no fewer than forty-two of the books and pamphlets written by professional radical William Prynne (1600–69). Indeed, Sparke's printing of Prynne's *Histriomastix* in 1633 earned him a £500 fine and a spell in the pillory. Attacking Barker's Bible monopoly was thus more than a religious issue with Sparke: it was a crusade.[5]

Sparke's system was to import English bibles published in Holland, which could be sold at a much cheaper rate than Barker's since the margin of profit was considerably smaller. Barker managed to take out a warrant to search for and seize all bibles printed abroad that could be found being unloaded in the ports. Sparke knew like everyone else that monopolies were already an anachronism, and that a monopoly on printing the Bible was more than anyone could reasonably enforce. He brought an action for trespass against Barker's agents and continued importing bibles from Holland without further molestation. Parliament in August 1645 prohibited the importing of foreign bibles, but only until they were examined by the Assembly of Divines and certified theologically correct, not on commercial grounds.

Sparke published an enormously useful pamphlet in 1641 on the entire vexed question of Bible monopolies, under the title of *Scintilla, or a Light broken into darke Warehouses*. This short work is essentially a price catalogue of English and Scottish bibles, drawing the conclusion that despite larger print runs, they cost substantially more than they did 'in times past'. A quarto English bible in the Geneva translation printed at London, for example, used to fetch seven shillings unbound, with notes and concordance. Now in 1641, Sparke records, the same bible, with a concordance but no notes and crammed on to fewer pages, sold at 9s. 4d. Furthermore, Sparke observed,

> There hath been at least 12,000. of these Bibles Quarto with Notes Printed in *Holland*, and sold very reasonable: and many brought from thence hither, and they have been seized by the Kings Printers, and the parties that Imported them, not only lost them, but were put in *Purgatory*, and there glad to lose their Bibles and all cost to get off; and then the Monopolists sold them again, and so kept al others in awe.

A helpful side note explained that by 'Purgatory', he meant the High Commission. Sparke argued that the current situation was all too sad. It was a 'Great pitty our Printing should be forced to be carryed to Strangers', Sparke wrote, 'better to have our own Nation set at work.' Apart from anything else, Sparke thought it was absurd that it was common to receive 'More punishment for selling a 4to Bible with Notes, then a 100. Masse Books in the High Commission.' Indeed, he claimed, 'I have known divers punished for selling Bibles, but none for Masse Books.' As for Sparke's tract itself, the author proclaimed on the title page, it was 'Printed, not for *profit*, but for the Common Weles good: and no where to be *sold*, but some where to be *given*.'[6]

Yet despite the rise in Bible prices that Sparke so angrily records, the Scriptures in English were readily available and were being read and assimilated. Apart from the obvious point that one did not necessarily have to purchase a bible to read it or have portions read aloud, the Scriptures also served as the most common subject of the hangings which adorned the walls of houses, not only to provide decoration, but also to keep out draughts. So-called 'godly tables' were specially produced as decorative posters, illustrating biblical stories and themes. Some people covered their walls with almanacs, ballads, and broadsides which very often referred to stories from the Scripture. Other houses had quotations from the Bible written on the walls or posts. The net effect was to underline the common and universal nature of the Bible as the ubiquitous standard of culture and morality.[7]

Historians since the time of Clarendon have mulled over the entire issue of the effects of printing the English Bible and making it generally available in a variety of forms ranging from the daunting folio volume chained up in the church, to the sprinkling of verses on the wall of a public house. Some general speculations seem to be in order. Firstly, a printed Bible, as opposed to a selection of biblical verses transmitted orally, allows the Protestant to conduct independent research, to read and re-read those parts of the text which have immediate relevance and use. This leads to a second surmise, that the printed vernacular Bible fostered intellectual independence. Many self-taught Puritans must have found themselves fully able to challenge divines on a wide variety of issues, so long as the mutually agreed weapon was the Book of Scripture. In some cases, poorly educated Puritans may actually have had an advantage over prelates, having only one book to read and study. This notion of intellectual independence shades into a third likely effect of the printed Bible, namely, that the incentive for reading having been created, it was natural that many newly literate Puritans went on to read other things, not necessarily with an eye to study, but in order to acquire useful information towards improving their lives. This predilection led one contemporary to refer to Protestants derisively as '*Hereticques* and two penye booke men'.[8] The increased demand for knowledge was an important factor in what has been called the 'educational revolution' of the seventeenth century, which made England a country of scholarly opportunity not matched again until our own time.

II

Although there can be no doubt that the English Bible was the most influential single text in the decades before and during the English Civil War, we need to be clear about *which* English Bible is under discussion. It is often forgotten that the famous Authorized Version of 1611 was never actually authorized, nor were parish churches ordered to obtain it. Its success in great part was due to the fact that no other folio Bible suitable for general parish use was printed after 1611. The English family Bible, all things being equal, was much more likely to be the Geneva version of 1560, produced by English exiles in the centre of international Calvinism. The Geneva Bible was from the start intended to be a best-seller. It was the earliest English Bible printed in roman type, and the first to divide the text into verses as well as chapters. It was published as a handy, compact quarto with maps and concordances, and its Calvinistic running commentary made it exceedingly popular for generations. Between 1560 and 1644 over 140 editions of the Geneva Bible or New Testament were published. The cost of the first printing was met by the exiles themselves, including John Bodley (the father of Thomas, the founder of the Library), who received a monopoly for printing the book for seven years from 1561.[9] In 1566, Archbishop Matthew Parker (1504–75) and the then bishop of London Edmund Grindal (1519?–83) asked Sir William Cecil for an extension of twelve years for the printers of the Geneva Bible, so pleased were they with the text and its popular success. 'For though one other special Bible for the churches be meant by us to be set forth, as convenient time and leisure hereafter will permit', they confessed, 'yet shall it nothing hinder, but rather do much good, to have diversity of translations and readings.'[10] The Geneva Bible remained popular when Grindal became archbishop of Canterbury (1576), and its translation was the one frequently quoted by Shakespeare, Raleigh, and others. By 1616, however, the Geneva Bible with its Calvinist commentary was no longer thought acceptable by church authorities, and demand for it had to be supplied by printing it abroad. In 1632, a man was even imprisoned for 'having taken in his house many new Bibles of the Geneva print with the notes', with the intention of selling them.[11]

The reasons for the fall of the Geneva Bible were not only religious. Archbishop William Laud (1573–1645) claimed at his trial that although it was true that he did try to suppress the Geneva version, his motive was not theological but commercial. Laud claimed that he saw it as his duty to protect the interests of English printers. Another problem was the fact that too many alternative versions of Scripture were on the market and had at one stage or another received official sanction. This instability of the English Bible was a powerful argument in the Roman Catholic polemical arsenal, since it implied a pervasive lack of authority.

Nevertheless, despite the ambiguous position of the Geneva Bible in the general theological scheme of things, that version continued to be printed during the first half of the seventeenth century, and met a very real demand. Indeed, in 1611, the very year of the Authorized Version, Robert Barker also brought out a duodecimo New Testament in the Geneva translation.[12] Barker's first quarto roman type Authorized Version, that is, the first edition which could compete with Geneva for general use, appeared in 1612, including a map and genealogies.[13] The Princess Elizabeth took a copy with her to Bohemia, stamped in gold with the Stuart arms.[14] Throughout the first half of the seventeenth century, a number of different and varied editions of the Authorized Version appeared, in an ultimately successful attempt to drive the Geneva Bible off the market. In 1612, alongside the quarto, Robert Barker produced a separate New Testament, printed in black letter, but using roman type for the headings, marginal references, and the contents of chapters. A telling feature of this New Testament was that it was deliberately printed with a woodcut title border reminiscent of the Geneva Bible in some of its incarnations, with emblems of Matthew, Mark, Luke, and John, and figures of *Fides* and *Hvmilitas*.[15]

Barker kept trying to supply all corners of the market, and to improve his stock. In 1613 he put out another folio Authorized Version, sadly marred by an amusing misprint at Ruth iii. 15 where Boaz is referred to as 'she', earning this edition the sobriquet, 'Great She Bible'.[16] Barker rectified this deficiency in another folio Authorized Version printed the same year, which also had many mistakes, some serious.[17] He published at the same time a black-letter quarto King James Version, the first of its kind, and including genealogies, map, and concordances, in direct imitation of the popular black-letter quarto Geneva Bibles.[18] The first duodecimo Authorized Version appeared in 1617.[19]

The competition between the Geneva Bible and the Authorized Version was a losing battle for the testimonial document of the English Calvinist pioneers. A number of further milestones were soon passed by the King James Bible. In 1629, the first Authorized Version was printed at Cambridge, in itself a slight liberalization of Robert Barker's monopoly. Henry VIII had allowed Cambridge University to print the Bible in a royal charter of 1534, but it produced its first Bible, in the Geneva version, only in 1591. Henry's royal charter was ratified by Charles I in 1628, and his first Authorized Version is the fruit of this agreement. Although the king's printers tried all they could to prevent its widespread dissemination, the accuracy of the Cambridge text as opposed to some of Barker's slipshod productions ensured its popular appeal.[20]

Barker's most notorious blunder was the so-called 'Wicked Bible' of 1631 which misprinted the Seventh Commandment and enjoined Christians that 'Thou shalt commit adultery'.[21] Peter Heylyn the Royalist historian records that

His Majesties Printers, at or about this time, had committed a scandalous mistake in our *English* Bibles, by leaving out the word *Not* in the Seventh

Commandment. His Majesty being made acquainted with it by the Bishop of *London*, Order was given for calling the Printers into the *High-Commission*, where upon Evidence of the Fact, the whole Impression was called in, and the Printers deeply fined, as they justly merited. With some part of this Fine *Laud* causeth a fair Greek Character to be provided, for publishing such Manuscripts as Time and Industry should make ready for the Publick view.[22]

The entire edition of 1,000 copies was ordered to be destroyed, and the printers were said to have been fined £300.[23] Whether this shameful misprint was the result of negligence, industrial sabotage, or even wishful thinking, it was immediately corrected and Barker produced six further editions of this quarto Bible, including genealogies and map.[24] Barker spent the last years of his life in King's Bench prison, dying there in January 1645.[25]

With the accession of William Laud to the throne of the archbishop of Canterbury, the need for greater precision and conformity came to dominate all levels of organization in the Anglican Church. The Authorized Version was one of the beneficiaries of this change in policy, having become virtually the sole biblical vehicle on the road to salvation. The coronation of Charles I at Edinburgh in June 1633 was the occasion for the introduction of the King James Version into Scotland.[26] An Authorized Version New Testament had already been printed at Edinburgh in 1628 in octavo.[27] The entire Bible, however, appeared only five years later, in an edition which became extremely controversial, not so much because of the text, but by virtue of the lurid way in which it was presented. Both the New Testament in the complete Bible and the separately issued New Testament printed the same year included a large number of plates which were thought by iconoclastic Protestants to be highly inappropriate.[28] These 76 plates were purloined from a small devotional book put out by the Jesuits at Antwerp in 1622. The last numbered plate, *De assumptione Deiparae*, was used as a frontispiece, and was thought by Protestants to be particularly offensive.[29]

Protestant objections to such Bible illustrations were quite predictable. One Englishman made his views known to two colleagues in Scotland in a rather blunt letter in 1638. 'That you may taste a little of our condition,' he complained,

> I have sent you two of your own Scots Bibles, your New Testament only, wherein they have placed such abominable pictures, that horrible impiety stares through them; these come forth by public authority; do you show them to such as you think meet; I send to each of you one of them.[30]

Michael Sparke, Prynne's publisher, was so incensed that he ventured once again into print to denounce the Roman Catholics and 'their wicked

Designes to set up, advance, and cunningly to usher in *Popery*; By introducing *Pictures* to the *Holy Bible*'. Sparke claimed that the man behind the trav-
esty was 'a strong and secret Papist' called Francis Ash, a bookbinder from
Worcester, who clandestinely imported Catholic literature for clients in the
West Country. As Sparke testified, Ash

> found an extraordinary *Trade*, especially to joyn *pictures* to the English Bible
> in 8$^{vo.}$ which *pictures* he had from Mr. *Robert Peake*, (who after went to
> *Basing-house*) so that Mr. *Ash* after took a voyage to *France* for *Popish Books*,
> and *pictures* for the *Bible*, which the *Papists* so much extolled, so that now
> the *Papists* of late will have *Bibles* in English, and the *Pope* cannot avoid it,
> but so that all their sorts must have *pictures*, and I fear Popish notes: and
> by this means *Ash* grew into an extraordinary way to get *Trade*; I am cred-
> ibly informed there, that in *France* he dealt for the *pictures* of all the *Popish*
> sorts, and the most excellent, as of *Vandikes Draft*, and there bargained with
> an excellent workman Mr. *Hollard* to ingrave and cut them, and gave a
> piece of money in hand to begin withall, and they there were begun, and
> divers proffers made of them since.[31]

The conjuncture of Charles I's Scottish coronation, the elevation of Laud
to the archbishopric of Canterbury, and these picture-Bibles was too much
for the Puritan interests to bear. Laud's connection with these idolatrous editions was made manifest by his insistence that they be called 'the Archbishop
of Canterbury's Bibles'. Laud's scourge William Prynne recorded his version
of what led the English Church to adopt such repulsive practices:

> the Archbishop had in his own private Study a Book of Popish pictures of
> the Life, Passion, and Death of our Lord Jesus Christ, and of the Virgin
> *Mary*, printed by *Boetius à Bolswert* in forein parts, *Anno* 1623. These very
> Pictures were all licensed by the Archbishops own Chaplain Doctor *Bray*;
> printed by his own printer and Kinsman *Badger*, in the year 1638. for one
> *Peake* a Stationer (now in armes against the Parliament) and publickly sold
> and bound up in Bibles; as was testified by Mr. *Walley* Clerk of Stationers
> Hall, and *Michael Sparke Senior*. Master *Willingham* likewise attested upon
> oath concerning these Pictures and Crucifixes put into the Bibles: that
> Captain *Peak* at Holborne Cundit, Bookseller, who printed these pictures
> for Bibles, did affirme, that he printed them *with the good liking, and by the*
> *speciall direction of the Archbishop, and his Chaplaine Dr. Bray: which Dr. Bray,*
> as he said, *carried him divers times to the Archbishop, to shew him the prints*
> *thereof, as they were cut and finished, who liked them all well, and gave his consent*
> *for the binding them up in Bibles*; saying, *That the Bibles wherein these pictures*
> *were bound up, they should be called* THE BISHOP OF *CANTERBURIES*
> BIBLES

As always with Prynne, it was the sheer volume of supporting detail which made his version of events so compelling. Prynne continued his denunciation of Laud with a more general indictment:

> he would corrupt, pollute all our Bibles and New Testaments with these Romish Images bound up in them, to which they are most repugnant. He would suffer no English Bibles to be printed or sold with marginall Notes to instruct the people, all such must be seized and burnt, as we shall prove anone: but himself gives speciall approbation for the venting of Bibles with Popish pictures taken out of the very Masse book, to seduce the people to popery and idolatry.

Laud's involvement with this first Scottish King James Bible would prove to be another nail in his coffin on the day of revolutionary reckoning.[32]

The wave of the immediate future, in any case, was not to be with the quasi-papistical illustrated bibles so repugnant to Puritans and serious Bible scholars, who were unhappy at seeing universal and abstract scriptural stories given unpleasantly concrete form. The important work which had been begun at Cambridge in 1629 in producing a more accurate text was continued at that university in a new version described by William Kilburne the biblical critic as

> the Authentique corrected *Cambridge Bible*, revised *Mandato Regio*, by the learned Doctor *Ward*, Doctor *Goad* of *Hadley*, Mr. *Boyse*, Mr. *Mead*, &c, and printed by the elaborate industry of *Thomas Buck* Esquire, and Mr. *Roger Daniel*, in *folio* in 1638.[33]

The editors of this new text made a number of useful changes, such as the standardization of the use of italics. One alteration which they made in the text would be ascribed to the Puritans, sometimes with the claim that Cromwell had paid £1,000 to obtain it. The verse in question was Acts vi. 3:

> Wherefore, brethren, look ye out among you seven men of honest report, full of the Holy Ghost and wisdom, whom we may appoint over this business.

This Cambridge Bible amended the text as '... whom ye may appoint', implying that the Apostles had turned over this power to the multitudes. This, at least, was a libel against Cromwell, since the change appeared years before he was in a position to demand anything from the University of Cambridge, and in an edition published by royal command. This particular Cambridge Bible remained the standard edition of the King James Bible until 1762, when further corrections were made by Dr F.S. Paris and H. Therold.[34]

A fully corrected edition of the King James Version was already esssential by 1638, not only on general scholarly grounds, but also because of the large number of spurious counterfeit bibles which were being produced abroad, especially in Holland. According to Kilburne again, writing at the very end of the interregnum,

> Moreover during the time of the late Parliament, great numbers of Bibles in a large 12° volume, were imported from *Holland* in 1656. with this false Title, (*Imprinted at* London *by Rob. Barker, &c. Anno* 1638.) wherein Mr. *Kiffin* and Mr. *Hills* cannot be excused, (if reports be true,) being contrary to the several Acts of Parliament of 20°, *Sep.* 1649, and 7. *Janu*, 1652. for regulating of Printing. Wherein are so many notorious *Erratas*, false English, Nonsense, and Corruptions, that in reading part of *Genesis*, I found 30. grand faults

Apart from the damage caused to both theology and aesthetics, Kilburne reasoned, the entire issue was objectionable, 'The very Importation of the Books being an offence contrary to the said Statutes, and ought deservedly to be suppressed; which notwithstanding are dispersed in the Countrey as aforesaid'.[35] A number of slightly different variations and editions of the spurious Bible of 1638 have survived.[36]

Once the Civil War had begun in earnest, of course, it was necessary to find a more organized solution to the problem of mass-producing cheap and accurate bibles for both general reference and short-term spiritual planning. It had always been believed that Cromwell's soldiers had been issued small bibles along with other essential military equipment. Only in the middle of the nineteenth century, however, did the actual bible turn up, in a copy owned by a private collector in Massachusetts, although other copies were later found in England. It was published at London in 1643 in octavo, bearing the imprimatur of Edmund Calamy (1600–66). The title page advertises this edition as

> The Souldiers Pocket Bible: Containing the most (if not all) those places contained in holy Scripture, which doe shew the qualifications of his inner man, that is a fit Souldier to fight the Lords Battels, both before the fight, in the fight, and after the fight; Which Scriptures are reduced to severall heads, and fitly applyed to the Souldiers severall occasions, and so may supply the want of the whole Bible, which a Souldier cannot conveniently carry about him: And may bee also usefull for any Christian to meditate upon, now in this miserable time of Warre.

The promised inspirational passages are mostly from the Geneva version of the Old Testament, collected under appropriate headings. This particular edition had a second childhood in the nineteenth century, and circulated in five different printings among the Union soldiers during the American Civil War, and at the end of the century in the Spanish-American War.[37]

This military Bible was among the most compact copies of Scripture produced during the period of the English Civil War. Quite in the other direction was the edition with marginal notes produced by John Canne (d. 1667), a leader of the English separatists living in Amsterdam, where he published his Bible in 1647. Canne's was the first English Bible to be printed with a proper apparatus of marginal references. In June 1653, six years after its first appearance, Canne's achievement was recognized when he received a licence for seven years 'to print a Bible with annotations, being his own work, and that no man, unless appointed by him, may print the said notes, either already printed or to be printed.'[38] This was in some sense an official publication, and was dedicated in its first edition to the English Parliament.[39] A very similar edition with full marginal references was produced by Cromwell's official printer Giles Calvert in the same year. It is sometimes called the 'Quaker Bible' because of Calvert's printing connections with the Society of Friends.[40]

Oddly enough, in light of Oxford University Press's identification with Bible publishing, the first English Bible they printed did not appear until 1675, fifteen years after the Restoration of Charles II. Two slightly different printings of this edition exist.[41] A second edition was published at Oxford in 1679, the first time that an English Bible risked being committed to precise chronology by printing in the margins the exact date when biblical events were said to have occurred. By this means, the birth of Christ, for example, was set at 4,000 years after Creation, about 240 years after the conventional Jewish reckoning.[42] The names of four London printers are given on the title page: Moses Pitt (d. 1696), Peter Parker, Thomas Guy (1645?–1724), and William Leak. William Maitland (1693?–1757), in his eighteenth-century history of London, describes Guy's career after he finished his training in 1668:

Mr. *Guy* was no sooner out of his Apprenticeship, than he set up his Trade, in the little Corner-house betwixt *Cornhill* and *Lombard-street*, with a Stock of about two hundred Pounds. At which Time, the *English* Bibles printed in this Kingdom being very bad, both in the Letter and Paper, occasion'd divers of the Booksellers of this City to encourage the Printing thereof in *Holland*, with curious Types, and fine Paper; and imported vast Numbers of the same, to their no small Advantage. Mr. *Guy*, soon coming acquainted with this profitable Commerce, became a large Dealer therein. But this Trade proving not only very detrimental to the Publick Revenue, but likewise to the King's Printer, all Ways and Means were devis'd to quash the same; which being vigorously put in Execution, the Booksellers, by frequent Seizures and Prosecutions, became so great Sufferers, that they judg'd a farther Pursuit thereof inconsistent with their Interest. Wherefore our Founder contracted with the University of *Oxford*, for their Privilege to print Bibles; and having furnish'd himself with Types from *Holland*, carried on a very great Trade in Bibles for divers Years, to his very great Advantage.

At least from a purely commercial point of view, Thomas Guy's venture was a great success. He invested much of the capital he earned from bibles in South Sea stock, got out in time, and before he died in 1724 endowed the London hospital which still bears his name.[43]

The birth of the Oxford English Bible has a rather prophetic ring to it. More importantly, by the Restoration, the disagreement over which version was to be the basis for quotation and interpretation had been settled in favour of the King James Bible, which had become the *de facto* Authorized Version. An abortive attempt was made to organize a new and perhaps more accurate translation of Scripture in 1652–3, but nothing came of this proposal: the Jacobean Bible remained.[44] The Geneva Bible dropped out of the race in 1644, when the last seventeenth-century version was published.[45] Despite the fact that this text of the Marian exiles would remain quoted throughout the interregnum, for all intents and purposes the remainder of our story until more modern times belongs to King James and the committee of scholars he appointed to produce a version of the Bible capable of withstanding the vicissitudes of a more religious age.

III

Having established the text of the divine Word, the use to which it might be put remained to be seen, and this led the English to a consideration of the separate functions of divine providence and chance. This was the first and most common manifestation of scriptural politics: the Bible as a providential prism. The precise role that *fortuna* played in human affairs was a question which troubled early modern thinkers and famously concerned Machiavelli:

> It is not unknown to me how many have been and are of opinion that worldly events are so governed by fortune and by God, that men cannot by their prudence change them, and that on the contrary there is no remedy whatever, and for this they may judge it to be useless to toil much about them, but let things be ruled by chance.

Machiavelli made his own views quite clear: 'I think', he wrote, 'that fortune is the ruler of half our actions, but that she allows the other half or thereabouts to be governed by us.'[46] Even before Calvin turned predestination into the central issue of Protestant theology, the question was much debated as to the precision of God's divine plan, and how we as human players might learn something about it.

During the middle years of the seventeenth century, it was taken for granted, and not only in Puritan circles, that the divine plan was extremely detailed if not complete, and that God was continuously intervening in worldly affairs, sowing small clues directing mankind's attention to His plea-sure.[47] Apart from conspicuous and meaningful signs and 'providences', the largest single collection of clues was to be found in God's last words, His legacy to mankind – the Bible.

The era of Puritanism and the English Civil War was one of heightened religious sensibilities, and one in which many commonly held views of earlier times freely made their appearance with continuously diminishing royal restraints until they were allowed to flourish relatively unfettered during the interregnum. The so-called 'godly' were convinced that the Bible provided an infallible guide in a wide variety of areas, and were prepared to seek guid-ance in Holy Writ. The end result was to create a climate of Bible worship unknown before the emergence of Fundamentalism nearly three hundred years later.

The underlying assumption of Puritan veneration for the Bible and its message, then, is that God has a divine plan, and that mankind can go a good deal along the way towards discovering it. The usual explanation was that God demonstrates His concern for His human creations by means of His 'general' and 'particular' providence. His 'general' providence consists in having created the world in the first place, in having ordained the courses of the planets, and the laws of physics. His 'particular' providence was His suspension of the laws that He Himself had ordained, in order to achieve a specific goal. The extreme cases of particular providence are what we would call 'miracles' and fulfilled prophecies. The Bible recounted numerous instances of God's particular prov-idence and demonstrated His extraordinary intervention on behalf of mankind in that crucial historical moment, so there was no reason to rule out the pos-sibility that He was still active in human affairs.

The biblical axiom of divine intervention as a regulatory mechanism worked in a wide variety of applications. Thieves might see capture and pun-ishment as their just reward. A righteous man unjustly suffering could compare himself with Job, enduring trial after trial towards eternal compen-sation. When punishments fit the crime, such as the contraction of syphilis after a lifetime of philandering, God's will seemed a full and justified explanation.

The necessity of distinguishing between an act of providence and pure chance hardly concerned those who were already convinced that they had succeeded in deciphering the meaning of a particular temporal event. Thomas Gataker studied the problem from the Puritan point of view in the early years of Charles I's reign and came to the conclusion that the essential ingredient for distinguishing between providence and the mere course of events was a clear connection between the sign and the resulting outcome.[48] A storm before a dangerous journey was likely to be a message from above. It was a good bet at all times that lightning had a hidden meaning, especially when it struck down someone or something. Even those who did not think that any notion of chance was an insult to God's Dominion were impressed by the context of a divine message.

In the very long run, it seemed likely that there was a connection between success in one's worldly calling and one's final and eternal destination. As Tyndale nicely put it in his translation of Genesis xxxix. 2, 'And the Lord was with Joseph, and he was a lucky fellow'.[49] Max Weber's Protestant ethic, however, was only one part of a complex equation. It was equally apparent that temporal failure might be a divine portent. It now seems clear that one of the reasons for the development of *laissez-faire* economics in the nineteenth century was the desire to allow God to manifest his providences unimpeded by human safeguards or cushions. If a man was doomed to become bank-rupt, he should be allowed to free-fall to the very bottom.[50]

Portents, prodigies, and providences might be useful aids in deciphering divine intention in regard to particular temporal happenings, but when it came to rather more long-term cosmic future events, such as the coming of the Messiah, it was clear that only one method would suffice: a systematic study of God's written code-book – the Bible.

Certainly Christians everywhere agreed that the Bible was a useful guide to general moral conduct. The Ten Commandments were enjoying a Euro-pean revival during the early modern period, and even in Roman Catholic countries were coming to replace the Seven Deadly Sins as the yardstick of human misconduct.[51] When it came to more specific advice on which course to choose out of several alternatives, one could always open the Bible at random and pull out a verse. Theologians might argue that this procedure implied that God could be compelled to intervene, and was in itself an infringement of the notion of God's absolute sovereignty, but biblical fishing remained popular. Conscious verse-mining was also unavoidable: 'Curse ye Meroz' was a popular tag for condemning neutrality in the English Civil War, for example, made famous by a contemporary sermon which exploited the verse for that purpose.[52] Creative exegesis of the Bible, combined with a careful study of providences and portents, might thus illuminate the path for mankind.

Undoubtedly, one of the chief pioneers of the prophetic field during the period of the English Civil War and after was the Baptist clergyman Henry Jessey (1601–63), and it is worth looking at him in some detail to see how from biblical soil might spring up an entire science of prophecy and predic-tion. At the age of thirty-four, Jessey assumed the leadership of Henry Jacob's church in London, which was the parent non-parochial congregation. Apart from his courageous support for the theological position which would become known as semi-separatism, Jessey was also prominent for his philo-semitism and his active support for Menasseh ben Israel and the readmission of the Jews to England. He was also a great believer in God's constant intervention in human affairs. Henry Jessey published an annual 'Scripture-Kalendar' between 1645 and his death in 1663.[53] In addition to the usual material found in almanacs during this period, Jessey would include a good deal of biblical and kabbalistic lore, lists of Jewish fasts, and assurances that 'the *fifth* is at hand', with supporting scriptural references. In his Scripture-Kalendars Jessey replaced the traditional anatomical figure common on almanacs with Daniel's image of the Fifth Monarchy. In the edition of 1661, he computed that since the beginning of the Civil War in 1640 there had been forty-seven changes of government in England, a clear fulfilment of the biblical promise to 'overturn, overturn, overturn'.[54] Towards this end, Jessey joined with Joseph Caryll, Jeremiah Whitaker, and William Strong in recommending and prefacing another prophetic chronology which appeared during this period, and which predicted that the fifth vial of the Book of Revelation would commence in 1666 and end in 1702 as the first horn of the ten-horned beast was symbolized in 1642; the Church's full glory would begin in 1777.[55]

In August 1660, Jessey published another work of this nature, 'a True *Relation* of some Late, Various, and Wonderful *Judgments*, or Handy-works of God, by Earthquake, Lightening, Whirlewind, great multitudes of Toads and Flyes; and also the striking with Sudden Deaths, of divers persons in several places'. Although no direct reference to the Restoration of Charles II was made, the implication was that the political changes of the past year would have some awe-inspiring divine effect.[56] This work seems to have been a trial run for his three-volume edition of 'prodigies', which appeared in 1661 and 1662.[57] Jessey's work was an account of 'many remarkable *Accidents*, and signal *Judgments* which have befel divers Persons who have Apostatized from the Truth, and have been Persecutors of the Lord's faithful Servants'.[58] More exactly, it was a list of strange occurrences between the summer of 1660 and the autumn of 1662; 146 prodigies seen in the skies, 75 observed on the earth, 26 in the rivers and seas, and 91 examples of divine judgment.[59] Jessey explained that 'let every one rather from these things be convinced, that upon us the ends of the world are come, and that God is now making hast to consummate his whole work in the earth, and to prepare the way for his Son to take unto himself his great power and reign.'[60] These were 'certain Harbengers and immediate fore-runners'.[61]

Not everyone, of course, was as credulous as Jessey regarding the divine significance of these apparitions. One of his eulogists suggested that the 'Scripture Calendar, then so despiz'd/ Deserves to be reviv'd, and better priz'd'.[62] Jessey himself, in the preface to the second of his three volumes, admitted

that some of the accounts might be exaggerated and in any case were sometimes unauthenticated.[63] Professor William Lamont, in his biography of the
famous Puritan divine Richard Baxter (1615–91), claims that Henry Jessey set
the serious study of prodigies back several decades.[64] Baxter himself, writing
of Jessey's works, pleaded in 1660 that the search for prodigies be continued,
but carried out with greater scientific thoroughness.[65] Baxter, caught up in
the exciting atmosphere of the 1650s, nevertheless still believed that much
could be accomplished by projects, programmes, and plans.[66] Thus, even for
a man like Richard Baxter, imbued with esoteric lore, Jessey's understanding
of divine intervention might seem over-credulous.

Henry Jessey may have sincerely believed that the biblical-style signs and
portents he had collected pointed the way to certain divine action. During
the interregnum, Jessey was widely respected and found signs of God's pleasure all around him. From the point of view of the newly restored Royalist
government, however, Jessey's latest researches seemed to imply divine dissat-
isfaction with the recent changes. Certainly Jessey included numerous examples of Nonconformists who went over to the Established Church and
subsequently met bad and often violent ends. Anthony Wood thought that
these 'pdigies were published by certaine fanaticall people at ye restoration of
K. Ch. 2. purposely to amuse ye Vulgar.' But Wood also took the trouble to
copy out part of a pamphlet in which it was argued that to 'overthrow the
government by King & Bps is y^t they aime at: and this, by the influence of
the pretended signes from heaven, upon ye peoples minds'. The author of the
pamphlet called for the government to take immediate steps, for 'ye wretch
gives them to rebell, & cast off ye yoke.'[67] Certainly, Jessey's selection of divine
portents had this effect on Philip Henry, a Nonconformist preacher who had
himself lost his living at the Restoration and was now deprived of his curacy
as well. Henry noted in his diary that 'I read a book cald *Annus mirabilis* con-
tayning a narrative . . . withnessing agt. Prophanes & persecution'. Henry
thought Jessey's books proved how just and righteous were the Lord's
judgments.[68]

The publication of such a work on such a grand scale, calling to witness
alleged signs of God's displeasure, was an incitement to disorder that the government could not ignore. Indeed, the Parliamentarians had years before
sought to regulate official fasts and days of humiliation for exactly the same
reasons. But when most of the copies of *Mirabilis annus* were seized, Jessey's
response was to issue a defiant second impression.[69] Worst of all, there was
some evidence that Jessey himself was involved with certain seditious parties,
or that at least they saw him as a potential ally.[70] Jessey was arrested three
days after Christmas 1660: he later complained that the soldiers who came to
apprehend him and to search his house took away and never restored some
of his papers, including 'another Collection of some other remarkables'.[71]

Henry Jessey spent the next two years in and out of prison, until he was finally released on 20 February 1663 by an order in Council. By August he fell ill with his last sickness, and died on 4 September 1663 at Woodmongers Hall in Dukes Place.[72] He was buried three days later in a mass funeral that was itself seen as a danger by the government informer, who reported that four to five thousand people were present, and 'there had been as many more but that it was thought not convenient'. Hanserd Knollys, the man who had baptized Jessey years before, preached the final eulogy, and told the crowd that he himself and several others had stood at Jessey's bedside to hear the great man's final words. Jessey was said to have prophesied 'that the Lord would destroy the power that now is in being, & did much encourage all the people to put their helping hand to that great worke, & that the Lord would make the tyme knowne vnto the saints here when this great worke should be brought to an end'.[73] Henry Jessey always believed that the biblical model provided humankind with the key to interpreting seemingly innocuous occurrences around us, seeing them as partially disguised divine messages. God's method of communication had not changed very much between the time of Moses and the era of Cromwell.

IV

The Bible, then, was more than the historical and literary production of the ancient Jews and early Christians: it was a living example of God's actions in this world and a guide to the behaviour which will bring us to external life in the next. Proper analysis of the Bible with reference to exceptional contemporary events might uncover entirely new levels of meaning. This was a view shared not only by simple country folk and their clergymen, but by those much higher up the ladder, beginning with Oliver Cromwell himself.

To say that Cromwell was a religious man would probably be the most banal statement we could make about seventeenth-century England. What Cromwell knew about God and His divine ways came directly from reading the Bible: there was no other authoritative source regarding the divine plans of the Maker of the universe. Based on his study of the Holy Book, Cromwell saw the workings of God all around him, especially as the Civil War began. After the battle of Marston Moor, for example, he wrote a letter of condolence to his brother-in-law, Colonel Valentine Walton, who had lost a son in the fight. In Cromwell's view, Marston Moor 'had all the evidences of an absolute victory obtained by the Lord's blessing upon the godly party principally.'[74] This was substantially the same assessment he made after the battle of Long Sutton the following year, when he was one of the leaders who fought and defeated a Royalist force three times the size of his own army.

Cromwell described the unlikely victory to a member of the House of Commons: 'And to see this, is it not to see the face of God!' He was reminded of what happened at his great rout at Naseby:

> when I saw the enemy draw up and march in gallant order towards us, and we a company of poor ignorant men, to seek how to order our battle – the General having commanded me to order all the horse – I could not (riding alone about my business) but smile out to God in praises, in assurance of victory, because God would, by things that are not, bring to naught things that are. Of which I had great assurance; and God did it. O that men would therefore praise the Lord, and declare the wonders that He doth for the children of men![75]

The image of Cromwell smiling with assurance before the battle of Naseby, infuriatingly confident, while not an attractive picture, is supremely indicative of a man who knew from his Bible that the Lord goes out with the troops of the righteous.

Cromwell was sure that God had a good deal to reveal to us, if only we would listen. 'I pray God teach this nation,' he wrote to Fairfax his commander during the Second Civil War, 'what the mind of God may be in all this, and what our duty is.' His entire world of metaphor was biblical:

> Surely it is not that the poor godly people of this Kingdom should still be made the object of wrath and anger, nor that our God would have our necks under a yoke of bondage; for these things that have lately come to pass have been the wonderful works of God; breaking the rod of the oppressor, as in the day of Midian, not with garments much rolled in blood, but by the terror of the Lord; who will yet save His people and confound His enemies, as in that day.[76]

Cromwell expressed himself in much the same way to William Lenthall, the speaker of the House of Commons, describing his victory over the Scots as 'nothing but the hand of God, and wherever anything in this world is exalted, or exalts itself, God will pull it down, for this is the day wherein He alone will be exalted.'[77]

Cromwell's letters to his friends and relations were no less full of references to God's divine plans and the clues scattered in Scripture. He wrote to Oliver St John in September 1648 after yet another victory, in completely religious terms, praising God and His glory. Cromwell was full of confidence about the outcome of the Civil War, and based his assurance on what he read in his Bible: 'This Scripture has been of great stay to me,' he informed St John, 'read it: *Isaiah* eighth, 10, 11, 14; – read all the chapter.' The reference was to a biblical warning to the wicked, prophesying that all their councils and efforts will ultimately come to naught, 'For God is with us.'[78] Cromwell wrote in a similar vein the following day to his good friend Philip, Lord Wharton, describing what he felt when 'we think of our God, what we are. Oh, His mercy to the whole society of saints, despised, jeered saints! Let them mock on. Would we were all saints. The best of us are (God knows) poor weak saints, yet saints'.[79]

Cromwell's scriptural frame of mind and his devotion to the idea that the Bible was not only a general code of ethical conduct but also a precise guide to action at any particular point in human history, comes out very clearly in his famous letter of 25 November 1648 to Colonel Robert Hammond. In two months, King Charles I would be on trial for his life and, having been found guilty, would be beheaded in Westminster. To Hammond, meanwhile, fell the unfortunate task of being the king's jailer, and he had written to Cromwell for his advice on what to do in this unprecedented constitutional and ethical situation. Cromwell's reply was that the victories of the Parliamentary army and the faith of the godly made it clear that it was God's will that Charles be brought to justice in this world as well as in the next:

> My dear friend, let us look into providences; surely they mean somewhat. They hang so together; have been so constant, so clear and unclouded. Malice, swoln malice against God's people, now called Saints, to root out their name; and yet they, by providence, having arms, and therein blessed with defence

The signs were all there to see if only we opened our eyes. 'Dear Robin,' warned Cromwell, 'tempting of God ordinarily is either by acting presumptuously in carnal confidence, or in unbelief through diffidence: both these ways Israel tempted God in the wilderness, and He was grieved by them.' By observing God's reaction to the behaviour of the people of Israel, Englishmen could learn what actions were expected of them, especially now that they had in some sense become a new Israel, God's chosen nation.[80]

If Cromwell ever needed the Lord's guidance, it was when he was sent to Ireland. In August 1649, already on board ship, he wrote a letter to his daughter Dorothy assuring her that the 'Lord is very near, which we see by His wonderful works, and therefore He looks that we of this generation draw near Him.' Even the current political crisis was proof of divine intervention, Cromwell asserted, for this 'late great mercy of Ireland is a great manifestation thereof.' So exalted was Cromwell by the visible manifestations of God's blessings that he relegated to a postscript his fatherly condolences to his daughter for having miscarried, probably the reason he wrote to her in the first place.[81] Writing to William Lenthall again, after the fighting was well under way, Cromwell had much the same story to tell, and explained what was happening in purely biblical terms:

Sir, what can be said to these things? Is it an arm of flesh that doth these things? Is it the wisdom, and counsel, or strength of men? It is the Lord only. God will curse that man and his house that dares to think otherwise. Sir, you see the work is done by divine leading. God gets into the hearts of men, and persuades them to come under you. I tell you, a considerable part of your army is fitter for an hospital than the field; if the enemy did not know it, I should have held it impolitic to have writ it. They know it, yet they know not what to do.[82]

Cromwell could cite numerous examples from his Bible proving that unexpected victory in battle was one of the benefits of being among the godly.

At Dunbar, indeed, Cromwell won a victory which seemed to be explicable only by divine intervention, any other interpretation requiring an even more intense degree of credulity. This is why Cromwell, in hot pursuit of the Royalist Scottish forces, brought his troops to a halt and had them sing the (very short) 117th Psalm before they continued on their destructive mission.[83] In his report to Lenthall, Cromwell continued this theme: 'It is easy to say, the Lord hath done this. It would do you good to see, and hear our poor foot go up and down making their boast of God.' Cromwell thought this was not enough: 'we pray you own His people more and more, for they are the chariots and horsemen of Israel.'[84]

Everywhere Cromwell looked, especially during the testing period of the English Civil War, he saw the hand of God in human affairs. The divine signs were not always easy to interpret. At the end of 1651, Cromwell wrote to the Reverend John Cotton in Boston, asking for a bit of spiritual advice. 'We need your prayers in this as much as ever', Cromwell pleaded,

How shall we behave ourselves after such mercies? What is the Lord a-doing? What prophecies are now fulfilling? Who is a God like ours? To know His will, to do His will, are both of Him.[85]

Cromwell's world view was hewn from the common bedrock of biblical culture. He knew from his study of Scripture what the Lord had done in the past for his chosen people Israel, and was thus able to predict what God would do in the future for his new Israel, the godly of England. The only difficulty was that the Bible was a source book to which all literate persons had equal access. No matter how many editorial improvements were made to the text itself, its interpretation would remain infinite. Cromwell put the Bible to political and military use. Others, more radical, saw the English Civil War as one vast millenarian providential sign, and themselves as the prophets who could help put into practice the divine programme outlined in the Book of Revelation.

V

A good deal of historiographical debate has ensued in the past forty years over the question of how to evaluate the influence of radical religion during the early modern period.[86] Much has also been written about the most prominent radical group in revolutionary England, the Fifth Monarchy Men.[87] But it is a serious distortion of events to see such millenarian groups as fundamentally different in their philosophical outlook from someone like Cromwell. The appeal of the notion of four world empires followed by a messianic age was practically irresistible to anyone who looked carefully at the seventh chapter of Daniel. It is in that most difficult book of the Old Testament that the image of four beasts is presented, symbolizing perhaps the rise and fall of four successive empires, followed by an everlasting kingdom. By Cromwell's time, it was generally thought that these empires were Babylon, the Medes/Persians/Assyrians, Greece, and Rome (including the Roman Catholic Church). The last beast had ten horns, or kings, and a little horn which destroyed the other ten. After this violent moment, the kingdom of the saints would arise and would be given to them for ever, the Fifth Monarchy.

The bare bones of this theory were hammered out over the centuries, certainly from the time of Joachim of Fiore (*c.* 1132–1202), who gave the chaotic succession of world events an internal structure and a predictable purpose.[88] For sixteenth- and seventeenth-century England, the main prophets of doom were Thomas Brightman (1562–1607) and Joseph Mede (1586–1668), who was in turn greatly influenced by the German professor Johannes Alsted (1588–1638). Brightman and Mede worked out the details of millenarianism in a series of books which were published during the revolutionary period once press censorship was no longer effective or applied. Professor B.S. Capp, in a much-quoted statistic, reckoned on the basis of a study of the books published by prolific ministers during the middle years of the seventeenth century that about 70 per cent expressed millenarian views.[89]

Like Cromwell, but in more radical fashion, the Fifth Monarchy Men saw the world around them through a biblical prism, and expressed themselves in the language of Holy Writ. This comes out quite clearly, for example, in the manifesto of the millenarian Venner Plot of 1657. Thomas Venner (d. 1661), a master cooper, was head of the church at Swan Alley, Coleman Street during the last years of the interregnum. He led a rising of Fifth Monarchy Men in April 1657 which got no further than a gathering of less than two dozen saints at Mile End plotting to attack a troop of horse and advance towards presumed followers in East Anglia. Government troops arrived in short order and arrested them. Venner was confined to the Tower for two years. After the Restoration, he led a more violent rising with about fifty followers and managed to kill about twenty soldiers before being captured. Venner and a dozen others were executed, and many others were tried.[90]

The manifesto from their first abortive revolt is indicative of the revolutionary uses to which the Bible might be put. The very first article demanded

> That all earthly governments, and worldly constitutions may be broken and removed by the first administration of the Kingdom of Christ, appointed unto him by the decree of the Father, and is the inheritance of the Saints, as joint heirs with him.

The sixth article affirmed Jesus Christ as 'the supreme absolute legislative power and authority'. This was immediately followed by a declaration of their faith in the Bible, which stated

> That the scriptures, being given by inspiration of God with his holy spirit, are the revealed will and rule of this legislator, to be constantly owned and submitted unto in times of war and peace, as a constant standing rule, for the inward and outward man . . . For so they were to the commonwealth of Israel, the only type of the Lamb's government.

Venner and his rebels hoped that the legislature of the new government might be known as the Sanhedrin, which 'shall be the Representative, for our Lord and King, of the whole body of the Saints, whose day this is, and people in the nations.' This Representative would have control over the army, the 'forces of Zion at sea and land'. Much of the latter part of the document is concerned with more mundane matters such as customs, excise, impressing, assessments, copyhold, and tithes, but the biblical inspiration of the new world order is paramount.[91]

Certainly no one could deny that these Fifth Monarchy Men ought to be classified among the *devotés* of radical religion. Yet it is also true that in their fundamental conception of God's divine plan, they were not so very different from more mainstream Puritans, including Cromwell himself. Their deviation was not that they took the books of Daniel and Revelation seriously, but that they saw it incumbent upon themselves to serve Jesus Christ by putting the cosmic scheme into operation. Their occasional tendency towards armed rebellion of the most impossible kind may have had the historiographical effect of sanitizing other groups which venerated the Bible no less but shrank from breaking man's law to put God's word into operation. Chief among these more cautious biblical radicals were the Saturday-Sabbatarians.

VI

A Frenchman, writing home in 1659, confessed that he had failed to understand why the English Calvinists believed themselves to be following a form of that religious doctrine laid down in Geneva. 'The religion of England,' he remarked, 'is preaching and sitting still on Sundays.'[92] This observation points to one of the most distinctive features of English religious life, the English Sunday, devoted to religious edification and complete abstinence from ordinary weekday activity. The strict English attitude towards the Sabbath was and always has been radically different from that which prevailed even in Protestant areas on the Continent. Indeed, it has been argued that Sabbatarianism is perhaps the only important English contribution to the development of Protestant theology.[93] Strict Sabbatarianism was also one of the permanent effects of the Puritan rule in seventeenth-century England. Even after the Restoration of the king in 1660, when the two decades of the Cromwellian period were regarded as a time of temporary national insanity, the almost Judaic observance of the Sunday rest continued to be a deeply rooted part of English life and culture. Most importantly, the general question of Sabbath observance itself reflects the way in which the biblical text was understood in post-Reformation England, and illustrates a fourth biblical use: as the foundation of law.

The explanation for the phenomenon of English Sabbatarianism must in the first instance be sought in the light of the Puritan emphasis on a direct understanding of the Word of God as it appears in the Bible, without priestly intermediaries. But although it was during the sixteenth and seventeenth centuries that the Old Testament regained a place of honour beside the newer partner that was thought to have superseded it, the extent to which the Mosaic law might be binding on Christians was still a thorny question. The Elizabethan religious settlement included among its Thirty-Nine Articles the affirmation that 'the Law given from God by Moses, as touching Ceremonies and Rites do not bind Christian men, nor the Civil precepts thereof ought of necessity to be received in any Commonwealth.'[94] Yet it was extremely difficult to find convincing theological justification for the partial exclusion of Old Testament injunctions, especially for Puritans who located the ultimate authority for their actions in both biblical books. Even for moderate Puritans, the Old Testament was still seen as a useful model, perhaps somewhat inexact, for the ordering of temporal affairs. This turn of mind was given fullest rein at the high-water mark of the English Revolution, in 1653, when Cromwell forcibly dissolved Parliament and prepared to put to the test godly notions about the best way to reorder government and society. But the ideas expressed then were hardly new: when the radicals sought guidance from the past, they turned to Jewish sacred history and the books of Moses.

Among the most interesting ideas which emerged in the early 1650s was a plan to model the new Parliament on the Jewish Sanhedrin of seventy members. The main obstacle seems to have been that seventy members alone would comprise an assembly which would be much too small to represent adequately all of the English counties, Scotland, Ireland, and Wales. Cromwell later claimed that he had therefore fixed 140 members on this Judaical basis, but until the last stage it had been intended to summon only 130 men to the nominated parliament.[95] A very strong biblical element appears at the very outset of the short life of Barebones Parliament, then, and illustrates, like Sabbatarianism itself, the penetration of the Old Testament ideas and values into the realm of political action.

This Jewish orientation is also apparent in the debates over legal reform which threatened to divide Barebones Parliament. The ultimate hope was that 'the great volumes of law would come to be reduced into the bigness of a pocket book, as it is proportionable in New-England and elsewhere'.[96] The reference was to the radical code of laws which had been enacted in Massachusetts in 1643 and revised the following year as 'The Laws and Liberties'.[97] One of the comprehensive plans which was not finally accepted in Massachusetts was John Cotton's 'Moses his Judicials', so called because it aimed at being a synthesis of the biblical commandments and common law practice. Although other plans were thought to be more workable, Cotton's code was printed in England and appealed to radical instincts everywhere.[98] As it was, the final code had numerous biblical overtones: the list of capital offences included idolatry, blasphemy, witchcraft, adultery, rape, sodomy, kidnapping, and cursing or smiting a parent. As Professor Woolrych puts it, 'the Bible and the Statutes at Large were almost equally consulted in the framing of it', this 'first modern code of the Western world'.[99]

Certainly, then, the Old Testament was widely regarded as a legal authority with a divine claim on the obedience of Christians. Yet even the faithful of New England argued that not all the injunctions of the Jews applied to them. These were the 'ceremonial' laws whose authority had ended with the coming of Christ. Jewish dietary regulations and the prohibition on mixing linen and wool fell into this superseded category, which included many of the 613 commandments in the Old Testament.

But what was one to do about the Sabbath? Its authority derived from the most central text of the Old Testament, the Ten Commandments, to which was accorded special respect even by those who argued that Christ had fulfilled and abrogated the Mosaic law. Nine of the commandments could easily be incorporated into existing codes of behaviour: murder, theft, and adultery were sins in any law. But the fourth commandment proved more difficult to assimilate by New England style Puritans and more moderate churchmen alike. The first problem was that God had ruled that on the Sabbath 'thou shalt not do any work, thou, nor thy son, nor thy stranger that *is* within thy gates'. Before the Civil War, both Church and State positively encouraged recreation and sports after the Sabbath prayer; this sacrilegious state of affairs was somewhat ameliorated afterwards. The second and insurmountable difficulty was the divine definition that 'the seventh day *is* the sabbath of the LORD'.[100] The Commandment stated very clearly that Saturday was the Sabbath, not Sunday, and the intention of this Mosaic rule was hardly disputed at any time. The Sabbath question in early modern England was twofold, therefore, in regard both to the manner and to the day of observance.

Let us look first at the more widespread problem of the proper way in which the Sabbath day should be honoured, whenever it occurred. Strict Sabbatarianism in its earliest English form was a doctrine associated with the unreformed Catholic Church. Even in medieval England the assumption remained that there was a moral core to the fourth commandment apart from its ceremonial husk.[101] The notion that Sunday should be spent in good works was eventually codified in legislation prohibiting Sunday markets. This Roman Catholic Sabbatarianism aroused the hostility of the Lollards because no justification could be found in the New Testament for the practice.[102]

So too did the continental Reformers reject Sabbatarianism as another evil papistical invention, along with pilgrimages and prayers to saints. The Church's habit of linking the Sabbath with saints' days in ecclesiastical legislation only reinforced this view.[103] 'If anywhere the day is made holy for the mere day's sake,' Luther advised, 'then I order you to work on it, to ride on it, to feast on it, to do anything to remove this reproach from Christian liberty.'[104] Calvin made a point of playing at bowls on Sunday to demonstrate his attitude to the question.[105] Tyndale protested that 'we be lords over the Saboth and may yet change it into the Monday, or any other day, as we see need . . . Neither needed we any holy day at all, if the people might be taught without it.'[106]

Until the later sixteenth century, the English Protestant position regarding the Sabbath was similar to that which prevailed in Reformed circles on the Continent. During the reigns of Henry VIII and Edward VI the Church in England took a middle ground: with the Lutherans they denounced the superstitious observance of the Lord's Day, but with the Catholics they promoted Sunday as a day given over in normal circumstances to worship, good works, and religious education.[107] By 1573, however, Richard Fletcher, a future bishop of London, could complain that it 'is said crediblelly in the countrie that . . . it is no greater a sinne to steal a horse on Munday then to sell him in fayre on the Sunday; that it is as ill to play at games as shoutinge, bowlinge on Sundaye as to lye with your neyghbors wiffe on Munday'.[108] Learned theological treatises provided the academic justification for this increasingly popular view. Richard Greenham led the way in 1592 with his *Treatise of the Sabbath*, followed three years later by his son-in-law Nicholas Bownde's study of *The Doctrine of the Sabbath*. By the Civil War fifty years later, it could even be claimed that 'England was at rest . . . till they troubled Gods Sabbath'.[109]

It is clear that this change in attitude was not officially inspired. Elizabeth vetoed a bill for 'the better and more reverent observing of the Sabbath day' in 1585 and ensured that a similar or identical measure would not escape the Lords' committee when the issue came up again in 1601. J.E. Neale points out that these were not Puritan measures: the first attempt at passing the bill was probably the legislative result of the collapse of the old scaffolding about the bear pit in the Paris Garden during a crowded Sunday performance, killing eight people and injuring many more. This tragedy seemed to confirm a growing popular feeling that Sabbath abuse might have unforeseen and unpleasant consequences. 'Her action may have been determined mainly by a resolve not to let Parliament interfere with any religious questions,' Neale suggests, 'but there can also be little doubt that she preferred a Merry to a Puritan England. What she had done was to veto a measure on which both Houses had set their hearts; and her chief statesman, Burghley, had been on the committee that steered it through the Lords.'[110]

When James I passed through Lancashire in 1617 on his way back from Scotland, he had occasion to 'rebuke some Puritans and precise people' for the 'prohibiting and unlawful punishing of our good people for using their lawful recreations and honest exercises upon Sundays, and other Holy-days, after the afternoon sermon or service'. James took advice from the local bishop and decided that every man was free to amuse himself on Sunday afternoon unless the Puritans could convince him otherwise.[111] The follow-ing year, in 1618, James extended this proclamation for Lancashire to the entire kingdom as the Declaration of Sports, which positively encouraged traditional recreations on Sunday, excepting 'bear and bull-baiting, interludes and at all times in the meaner sort of people by law prohibited, bowling.' The hope was that all able-bodied men would engage in sports that had some military value, especially archery. His son Charles I reissued the Declaration in 1633, noting that if Sunday sports were banned, 'the meaner sort who labour hard all the week should have no recreation at all to refresh their spirits'. Charles ordered that the Declaration be read from the pulpits of all parish churches, a step which his father had abandoned in the face of stiff opposition, even from the archbishop of Canterbury.[112] The popular sort of Sabbatarianism, on the other hand, is best illustrated by the possibly apocryphal story of the London clergy-man who first read the Declaration of Sports and then the Ten Com-mandments: 'Dearly beloved,' he told his congregation, 'ye have heard the commandments of God and man, obey which you please.' Measures for enforcing Sabbath observance appeared in the parliaments of 1621, 1624, and 1625 as well, and some of them became law.[113]

The explanation for this popular support of Judaical Sabbath observance on Sunday has long puzzled historians. 'The good and evil effects of this self-imposed discipline of a whole nation, in abstaining from organized amusement as well as from work on every seventh day,' wrote Trevelyan, 'still awaits the dispassionate study of the social historian.'[114] The Victorian historian S.R. Gardiner thought that one of the features of the Jewish Sabbath which was attractive to religious radicals was that it was incumbent upon them as individuals, not as members of any congregation. They could therefore observe the strict Sabbath quietly at home, and avoid any legal or social reprisals.[115] M.M. Knappen, the religious historian, saw the rise of Sabbatarianism as the natural result of a social need for orderly religion. In his view, the notion of a strict Sabbath worked its way up from the bottom and was in origin the medieval Catholic doctrine which had survived in Anglican teaching and religious legislation. Only in the seventeenth century, especially after the tragedy at the Paris Garden, did Sabbatarianism become a characteristically Puritan issue.[116]

A more dramatic explanation of popular support for the Jewish Sabbath concentrates on the economic utility of a regular day of rest. Margaret James was the pioneer of this approach more than seventy years ago, and no doubt drew some measure of inspiration from Weber's remarks on the Protestant ethic. Margaret James noted that although Puritans were anxious to observe the day of rest with great severity, and though 'religious exercises might be reserved for Sundays, the week was fully occupied in the work of economic salvation.' The Puritan obsession with work was one of the reasons that they campaigned for the suppression of saints' days, which were economically unproductive. Parliament could therefore be assured of support from business interests when it passed an ordinance in 1647 abolishing festivals and declaring the second Tuesday in every month an arbitrary secular holiday. The religious enthusiasm which had been distributed over a large number of festivals was now concentrated on the strict observance of the Sabbath.[117]

This economic approach to the Sabbath question was utilized by Christopher Hill in his study of pre-revolutionary English society. Hill argues that the Puritans promoted the Jewish Sabbath as a *regular* day of rest, in contrast to the haphazard hundred or so saints' days which were compatible with the agricultural society of medieval England. The newly emerging industrial society, on the other hand, required a more regular framework in order to develop further. The Puritans' objection to saints' days, then, was part of their general assault on the existing social and economic order. Following Margaret James, Hill notes that the fourth commandment also enjoins us to *work* on the remaining six days; the Sabbath day was meant to be a day of recovery from a hard working week. Sunday sports would continue to be popular in the countryside, where the medieval agricultural life was still dominant. In the modern industrializing cities, however, the emphasis would be on Sunday rest. Soon, the Puritans came to see this Sabbath day of rest as a time for religious edification, and began to argue that *rest* days should be deducted from ordinary work days, as would be done in the legislation of 1647 which created the Tuesday secular holidays. Generally, then, Hill claims, we should see the Puritan attack on Sunday sports as an attempt to impose the ethos of an urban civilization, particularly the new concern for labour discipline, on the whole realm, especially its dark corners. The Crown here again supported the economically backward areas of the country, which would be Royalist in the Civil War, against the values of the 'industrious sort of people'.[118]

On this basis, Hill is able to explain why nothing like the English Sunday developed in other Calvinist countries. Hill argues that the answer is to be sought in the peculiar features of economic and social development in England, where an industrial and urban way of life was established on a national scale earlier than elsewhere. The 'industrious sort of people', the early capitalists, required a new ethos and protection from overwork, which they could obtain by championing the Sabbath as a day of rest. The monarchy and the medieval landed class, however, encouraged traditional sports as a harmless occupation for idle agricultural workers. In Hill's view, the Bible had little influence on the creation of strict Sabbatarianism, which derived from the pressures and demands of society, only afterwards justified by an apposite biblical text. 'There were plenty of Bibliolators among the Puritan Sabbatarians', Hill explains, 'but there was also a rational case for the Sunday rest. It was the habit of the age to find Biblical texts to justify men in doing what they would have done even if no texts could be found.'[119]

Yet certainly not all biblical interpretation was utilitarian. As is often the case, one finds the most sensible approach in the writings of unfashionable classic authors. J.R. Tanner, writing in 1930 about James I's *Book of Sports*, insisted that the Sabbatarian controversy is 'vastly more important than it appears at first sight. The fundamental conflict was after all between those who contended for the exclusive authority of the Bible and those who contended for the co-ordinate authority of the Church.' This debate, Tanner continues, was part of the controversy which included the question of whether the Church might institute ceremonies not mentioned in the Bible, provided they were not contrary to the spirit of the law. It was only another application of their principle when the Puritans claimed for Sunday the characteristics of the Jewish Sabbath.[120] So too in the nineteenth century, Gardiner emphasized the biblical origins of the Puritan's strict Sabbath observance: 'The precepts of the Fourth Commandment were, according to his interpretation, of perpetual obligation. The Christian Lord's Day was but the Jewish Sabbath, and it was the duty of Christian magistrates to enforce its strict observance.' The opponents of the strict Sabbath, on the other hand, argued that the Christian Sunday was a human rather than a divine institution, handed down by oldest church tradition, and that therefore the Church was free to determine the exact form of its observance.[121]

Tanner and Gardiner bring us back again to the Old Testament and the second part of the fourth commandment. If, as they argue, the Sabbath question was primarily religious in nature, why have historians consistently revealed a blind spot towards the most radical of Sabbatarians, those who followed the commandment to the letter of the law and observed God's holy Sabbath on the seventh day, on Saturday? James I noted with distaste that 'all such kind of people . . . encline to a kind of Judaism'.[122] Indeed, the determination of the time of Sabbath observance was not a dilemma that began with the Puritans in seventeenth-century England. Only about a hundred years after Jesus made his dramatic declaration that the 'Sabbath was made for man, and not man for the Sabbath', Christians began using the expression 'Lord's Day' as their exclusive designation for Sunday.[123] Certainly by the fourth century the Sabbath was no longer observed on Saturday in accordance with Jewish law, but had been transferred to Sunday, perhaps in commemoration of the Resurrection, but more likely as a means of distinguishing Christians from Jews.[124]

We need to pay careful attention to the important distinction between the acceptance of the Church's insistence of Sunday as the Sabbath day and the belief in the continuing existence of a morally binding Sabbath. As we shall see, many churchmen and indeed less educated practitioners of the Christian faith were quite willing to accept the second principle, while finding no conclusive scriptural authority for the first.

The promulgation of the *Book of Sports* in 1618 only intensified the general Sabbatarian debate and with it the problem of justifying Sunday as the day to observe the Word of God in all its Mosaic rigour, for one could hardly obey one part of the commandment with uncompromising strictness while altering the other part completely. The first attempt to eliminate this ambiguity in a dramatic and highly public way was that of John Traske (1585–1636), the famous Jacobean Judaizer, who kept a whole range of Jewish laws, from the Sabbath to Passover. By the beginning of 1618, Traske and his sect of Judaizing Saturday-observers could no longer be ignored, even though the king seemed to be rather more amused than incensed by Traske's well-known practices. He was sentenced in Star Chamber on 19 June 1618 to be kept close prisoner in the Fleet for the rest of his life, given a monetary fine of unpayable proportions, and was finally whipped across London, branded in the forehead with the letter J, and nailed to the pillory by his ears. Traske recovered, renounced the open observance of the Saturday-Sabbath, and eventually joined the Baptist Church led by Henry Jessey. One of Traske's followers seems to have converted to Judaism in Amsterdam.[125]

But the silencing of Traske and his little band by no means put an end to those who were willing to cut the Gordian knot of biblical fidelity, or who were brave enough to air their doubts in public. It was Theophilus Brabourne

(1590–1661) who, after Traske, did the most for propagating the belief in the Saturday-Sabbath in England before the outbreak of the Civil War. Brabourne, a native of Norwich and the son of a Puritan hosier, began to write on the Saturday-Sabbath in 1628, but was not committed to prison until six years later. Brabourne appeared before Laud and the High Commission, and was pronounced 'a Jew, a heretic and schismatic, and adjudged . . . worthy to be severely punished.' During the interregnum he was free to promote these doctrines once again, although he seems to have steered clear of the organized churches which observed the Saturday-Sabbath. After the Restoration he wrote several pamphlets concerning liberty of conscience, while upholding the royal supremacy in religious affairs. Some of Traske's followers may have migrated to Brabourne's circle of acquaintance after 1636, but in any case in contemporary minds the two men were inextricably linked. As Peter Heylyn the Royalist historian of the Sabbath wrote, 'their Opinions, so farre as it concerned the *Sabbath*, were the very same; they onely making the conclusions, which of necessitie must follow from the former premisses'.[126]

By the time Peter Heylyn wrote his comprehensive 500-page history of the Sabbath in 1636, the validity of the seventh-day Sabbath was already an idea that had taken root in the fertile soil of the English religious landscape. For in that year Henry Jessey, the pioneer of the Baptist movement in England, was appointed pastor of the Jacob Church, the mother church of the English Baptists and of the English semi-separatist tradition. And Henry Jessey observed the Sabbath on Saturday. His adoption of that straightforward understanding of the fourth commandment would be crucial for the later development of Saturday-Sabbatarianism into an organized religious sect during the period of the Civil War.

Indeed, in a sense this is the story of the remarkable persistence of a revolutionary religious belief in seventeenth-century England, powerful and convincing enough to survive the watershed of the king's return in 1660 and to continue into modern times. The Saturday-Sabbath gradually became institutionalized in a Nonconformist sect in which the ideological foundation was sufficient to unite men who on political grounds should have been the most bitter of enemies, including millenarians, Fifth Monarchists, neutrals, and Royalists alike. That these men and their followers could amicably join forces after the Restoration is testimony to the power of religious ideas which might overshadow the political affiliations of the Civil War. Most importantly in the long term, in the latter part of the seventeenth century Saturday-Sabbatarianism was transplanted into English America, to Rhode Island, where thanks to a motley coalition of Quakers, Freemasons, and Jews the sect would flourish as the Seventh-Day Baptists. This group would be instrumental in the foundation of the Seventh-day Adventists after the 'Great Disappointment' of 22 October 1844 when Jesus declined to arrive manifestly as scheduled, and in the theological development of Fundamentalism at the beginning of the twentieth century.

But far more crucial than the institutional survival of the Seventh-Day men are the ideas which had been highlighted by their struggle against disintegration, and which continued to run through English and American Protestantism in the following centuries. It is well known that one of the most important theological results of the Protestant Reformation was that the Old Testament regained a place of honour next to the New, but the precise application of this distinction was never satisfactorily resolved, and at different points in religious history the problem of the Old Testament and of the Jewish antecedents of Christianity erupts with disturbing clarity. In the seventeenth century, in a culture which prized linguistic precision and confessional allegiance, this issue became centred around the observance of the Seventh-Day Sabbath, the day of rest that had been ordained in the Ten Commandments, the central text of the Old Testament which was revered by Christians of all persuasions. Those worried by the need to observe literally all of the Ten Commandments found the problem of the Old Testament brought home with terrifying power, for they were forced to make a public demonstration of their faith by putting aside Saturday, a working day, as the day of rest.

VII

The all-pervasive nature of biblical culture in seventeenth-century England might easily have the effect of blinding us to the seeds of change which were beginning to germinate at the end of the Civil War period. The authority of Scripture was based on the concept that it was the sole record of God's activity in this world and that without it mankind was completely lost. Even from the very earliest days of Protestantism, Luther himself was plagued by those, like the Anabaptists, who believed that they were in direct contact with God. Luther fought vigorously against 'Enthusiasm', and tried to keep his Reformation within the written tradition of Scripture. Towards the end of the English interregnum, the champions of Enthusiasm were the Quakers, who were developing a unique theology which would have repercussions in a wide variety of areas.

Certainly the most influential Quaker in the field of biblical criticism was Samuel Fisher (1605–65), the son of a Northamptonshire hatter who went up to Trinity College, Oxford and passed through Presbyterianism and Baptism before discovering the Quaker message when he was nearly fifty years old. Fisher was therefore a Quaker theologian for only about eleven years before his death in the Great Plague. Nevertheless, during this time he published a remarkable book, *The Rustick's Alarm to the Rabbies*, well over 900 pages of biblical criticism and reflections on the divine plan. Fisher had a selective approach to Jewish learning, trying to isolate the true and useful elements of biblical exegesis without entertaining wild Talmudic notions. He was disappointed by the fact that the English clergy had not been more forthcoming in supporting the recent debate over the readmission of the Jews. He was disgusted

> to hear their *Clergy* calling and sounding out to God . . . *Gather in thy ancient people the Jews,* and yet neither going out to gather the *Jews,* nor giving way to the *Jews,* when they would, to gather so much as into *England,* that they might be gathered to the Lord

In any case, Fisher argued, although the Jews did possess an enormous amount of scriptural knowledge, the original text of the Bible had become so corrupted over the years that it would be a vain hope to imagine that we could restore it to its pristine purity. Fisher thought it absurd to

> expect such eminent guidance as ye here seem to do from these *pidling Pricks and Points* into the *Kingdom of God,* and *Salvation,* so that the Terrours of *Hell* take hold on you at the very time and thought of the losse of no more, then that meer imagined *Antiquity* and pretended *divine original* of them from *mount Sinai,* that some sillily ascribe unto them.

Fisher ridiculed the slavish Hebraism of biblical textual critics like John Owen (1616–83) and others who

> Like Boyes, that ly brawling about *Bawbles,* which they prize above, and will not part with for far more serious & precious matters; blessing themselves more in a Bag of *Cherry-stones,* and fearing more to lose, & caring to keep them, then wise men do theirs, whose Riches lyes in that which can't be lost: So doth *J.O.* busie himself with fear and much trembling about these perishing *Points, Vowels, Accents,* about his *Cametz's* and *Patack's, Tsere's* and *Segols, Chiricks* and *Cholems, Sheva's* and *Sciurech's, Athnach's, Kibbutz's* and *Chametz Catuph's,* hoping he is rich and encreased with Goods, and hath need of nothing while he enjoyes them . . . Not knowing, that for all this, being out of, and against the true Light, he is poor, and wretched, and miserable, and blind, and naked

If this were not bad enough, Fisher railed, we are deluged with over-priced editions of the Bibles by self-appointed interpreters, who 'sell one *verse* of it, a little set out and flourisht, and amplified with no other *Trimming,* but their own *fallible vain thoughts* upon it, for Twenty shillings, which *Bible* might serve a whole Town to read in'. The fact of the matter, Fisher concludes, is that

> all the *Copies of the Original* that are in the World, and *Translations* too, come utterly to *moulder, perish,* and *passe away,* as the *Originals* themselves have

long since done; yet *Truth* is the same that it was before any *Letter* or *outward Text* of it was.

Since the original text of the Bible has been hopelessly corrupted, the only true source of divine wisdom must be the inner light.[127]

In *The Rustick's Alarm*, Fisher makes reference to the fact that

> Among many hundreds of *Jews*, the Truth hath been Testified to openly in their *Synagoguges* and *streets* of their Cities, in *Rome*, and elsewhere, and yet being in safety from them hath been witnessed; the Truth hath been Testified in *Turkie*, yea by the *Power of God* to some great *Bashaws*, and to the very *Grand Segnior* himself, and his *Councell*.[128]

We know that in 1656 Fisher did indeed go abroad on a quixotic mission to convert the pope and the sultan to Quakerism. His first stop was Holland, where he was very active in the Quaker mission there to convert the Jews, acting in concert with his colleagues John Stubbs and William Caton, both of whom had converted Fisher to the faith two years before. Caton recorded that

> Sam. Fisher was in their Synagogue at Amsterdam and among them at Rotterdam; they were pretty moderate towards him: (I meane they did not abuse him) but assented to much of that which he spoke: he had some discourse with two or three of their Doctors in private at Amsterdam, and they seemed to owne in words the substance of that which he declared: but they were in bondage as people of other formes are.[129]

Before he had left England, Fisher was asked by Quaker leader Margaret Fell to translate two of her pamphlets into Hebrew.[130] Fisher was unable to accomplish this, and gave the job to a Dutch Jew, who met Quaker leader William Ames in 1657.[131] There are a number of weighty reasons for believing that this Jew was Benedict/Baruch Spinoza (1632–77), who had been excommunicated from the synagogue on 27 July 1656, but who continued to live in Amsterdam for the next four years, during which time he was in close contact with the Quakers.[132] Margaret Fell's pamphlet, an open letter to Menasseh ben Israel, was duly translated into Hebrew, and Fisher took it with him on his journey to Rome and Constantinople.[133] Fisher's work of biblical criticism, *The Rustick's Alarm to the Rabbies*, was published at London in 1660, written chiefly against John Owen and Thomas Danson, the Nonconforming Hebraist. Spinoza began writing his *Tractatus theologico-politicus* in about 1665, when he was already living at Voorburg, and had it published anonymously in Amsterdam in 1670. The similarity between some of the major points brought forward by Samuel Fisher and the arguments of Spinoza may indicate a certain amount of cross-fertilization and give the English

Quaker some claim to being among the founding fathers of modern biblical criticism.

VIII

Samuel Fisher and the Quakers, with their disparagement of textual idolatry and their reliance on the inner light of inspiration, look to the modern historian like a futuristic Fifth Column among the Fifth Monarchists and the other proto-Fundamentalists of English Puritanism. At the beginning of the seventeenth century, the major issue was the establishment of a reliable biblical text, and the King James Version seemed to provide this. But even then it was realized that the problem was not the text itself but the commentary, and the concerted efforts to drive the Geneva Bible with its pestilent glosses off the market reflects this understanding. For while the biblical book itself could be controlled to a very great extent, there was no way in which divergent interpretations could be suppressed. After the fall of the godly English Republic and the Restoration of King Charles II, even die-hard Puritans realized that an error of interpretation may have been made. So too had Thomas Munzer and his rebellious German peasants in the 1520s raised the cry of 'God's word, God's word'. 'But my dear fellow', Luther objected, 'the question is whether it was said to you'.[134] For a very long period of time, Cromwell and the scriptural politicians of seventeenth-century England thought they knew the answer.

CHAPTER 3

Cracking the Foundations: Biblical Criticism and the Newtonian Synthesis

If it is true that the first half of the seventeenth century was the high-water mark of bibliolatry in England, it follows that from that point on the waters had to recede. The years after the appearance of the Authorized Version in 1611 were a time when Englishmen and women came to know their Bible as a natural resource. They became acquainted with the English Bible as the chief instrument of *sola scriptura*, a principle of faith which was accepted axiomatically since the beginning of the Protestant Revolution. The Bible throughout the early seventeenth century up to and including the period of the English Civil War was thought to be a stable foundation that could support a structure of any size. The most ardent supporters of *sola scriptura* were so convinced of the impregnability of biblical authority that they fearlessly investigated every conceivable aspect of Scripture, and were amazed to discover that their examinations themselves caused irreparable cracks in the entire edifice.

The key terminal points for our discussion at this stage will be two nearly simultaneous texts: Thomas Hobbes's *Leviathan* (1651) and Brian Walton's *Polyglot Bible* (1657). Hobbes and Walton were not such different characters as their work would have us believe, and each in his own way, through biblical criticism, had the effect of reducing the power of *sola scriptura* until it was hardly functional as a concept. It remained for Isaac Newton to devise a synthesis of science and religion that in many quarters has endured until the present day.

I

Certainly it is true that the first half of the seventeenth century did not lack for pious efforts to unravel the mysteries of the biblical text *as it stood*. This genre is very visible right at the beginning of the century, for example in the

study by Nicholas Gibbens of the questions and disputations regarding
the Holy Scriptures, published during the last year of Elizabeth's reign. In
this large quarto volume, Gibbens goes through fourteen chapters of Genesis
verse by verse, using many Jewish sources and showing a broad knowledge
of the Hebrew language. At some stage, Gibbens is compelled to deal with
the problem of the Hebrew text itself, since there is no point in bringing to
bear the full weight of *sola scriptura* if the object of scrutiny itself is suspect.
Gibbens addresses the question of where we are to put our faith in the case
of a discrepancy between the Hebrew text of the Jews and the Latin Vulgate
of St Jerome. Should we not think that perhaps Jerome had access to a better
copy of the Hebrew Old Testament than the one we have at present from
the Jews?

> For by these authorities it may seeme apparant, that the Hebrue text hath
> bin corrupted by the Iewes: which if it be; where is the truth of Scripture
> to be found, but either perished, or onelie remaining in that translation,
> which the Papists so greatlie magnifie? For answere whereunto, we
> affirrme and testifie by the authoritie of the Scriptures themselues, (which
> is the voice of God) of the Fathers, and of the aduersaries themsclues;
> that the Scriptures in the Hebrue tongue are pure, and vnspotted of all
> corruption.

Indeed, the entire notion of a Jewish conspiracy to pervert the word of God
which had been entrusted to Jews exceeds even the most bare standards of
possibility, for

> in regard that the Iewes haue euer bin dispersed, as it were throughout the
> world, it was not possible that they would, or could consent vniuersallie in
> all their copies to corrupt the Scripture, but the same must haue beene
> knowne vnto the world

Not only that, but 'the Iewes haue euer shewed such zeale and diligence, for
the preserving of the Scriptures vncorrupted in the Hebrue tongue; as that
the same without extreame and vniuersal negligence cannot decay for euer.'[1]
Having established the integrity of the text itself as a worthy object to
which to apply the axiom of *sola scriptura*, however, Gibbens goes on to enun-
ciate a rather more astonishing principle, which although well in line with
the thinking of his judicious rabbis, somewhat undermines the concept of the
biblical text as literally true. 'It is manifest hereby', Gibbens explains,

> that the Scripture applieth it selfe in a sort vnto the rudenesse of the Iewes,
> to whom it was first directed: deliuering onelie the truth of the Historie,
> in manner as was meetest for their capacitie: and although pretermitting
> nothing that was necessarie, yet leaueth the Doctrine to be afterward

expounded by the Prophets, and to be reuealed by the Sonne of righteousness.[2]

One could hardly find a clearer expression of the fundamental Jewish principle of accommodation, *dibra Torah k'lashon b'nei adam*, which would seem so radical when proposed in an entirely different context by Hobbes and Spinoza later in the century. As we shall see time and time again, many of the most far-reaching principles of biblical criticism emerge in quite orthdox garb on their earliest appearance, promoted by the very people who would have been genuinely horrified to see the later uses to which their ideas were put.

According to one of the common arguments which sought to keep speculation under control, the root of the problem was in the very existence of scholarly debate over the biblical text. Henry Walker, a.k.a. 'the Ironmonger', who also published works under his anagram 'Levek Hunarry', thought that all of these trivial scriptural disputes only served the real enemies of *sola scriptura*: 'Whilst we about nice poynts of Scripture strive, The Pope would us quite of the Scripture shrive.' Walker even argued that the disputes over the Bible created textual problems where none existed before:

> whosoever pleaseth to cast their eyes on the Bible, as it there stands opened
> . . . to be veiled with so blacke a mist, that there is now great difficultie
> found in the true reading thereof; even as there was many difficulties under
> the Law, till the veile was taken away, so is there now so great a veile, or
> rather vanity, of humerous Inventions under the Gospell at this day in the
> Church of *England*.

Walker's point is that 'the Pope is glad of these distractions amongst us, and would now take the opportunity to snatch away the Bible from us; he would faine take our Religion away; but we hope to send him backe againe to *Rome* with a powder'.[3] Henry Walker had a clear sense that what was at stake was the basic Protestant principle of *sola scriptura*, without which the achievements of the Reformation itself would be lost.

So too did Arthur Jackson (1593?–1666), another popular interpreter of the Bible, try to back off from over-ingenious interpretations of Scripture which only had the effect of reducing people's faith in the text itself:

> I have not at all meddled with the many doubts that have been raised by
> Interpreters concerning the different wayes of translating some passages in
> the Originall Text, but have onely endeavoured to unfold the meaning of
> the Text according to our last Translation; only I have for the most part
> taken in that reading also which is added in the margin of our Bibles.

Jackson knew that *sola scriptura* was not really about the close reading of the King James Version, but of the original text of God's divine Word in Hebrew, and he admitted that he would not be surprised to find many a reader who 'stumbles at this'. Nevertheless, Jackson was sceptical of the value of such intense linguistic discussion for most people, 'and such knotty disputes concerning the Originall must needs have mightily puzzled such readers, but could never have been any way profitable for them.' There was a time for 'the Hebrew pricked Bibles', but it was not always necessary to consult them when doing the scriptural ground-clearing that every Protestant need do while becoming acquainted with the text that formed the basis of this faith.[4]

John Downame made himself a place in the history of the English Bible largely by having produced a succession of concordances. Downame thought that the very success of the English Reformation was well nigh a miracle, as 'weake instruments, (a childe and a woman)' succeeded in defeating the 'mightie Engines' of the papacy. There were plenty of causes for optimism, and one of these

> may be set on the *Translation of the Scripture* into a Language understood by unlearned people, that they might *search the Scriptures*, and by searching of them might *finde in them*, what is most desired, *eternall life*; for they are Bookes not for the *Clergie* onely, (though for them especially) for which cause some Councels have decreed.

Downame produced what by the second edition were two massive folio volumes 'wherein The *Text* is Explained, *Doubts* Resolved, *Scriptures* Paralleled, and *Various Readings* observed.'[5]

So keen was the revolutionary Parliament to inspire guided reading of the Holy Text that on 30 March 1648 it approved the translation into English of the Dutch annotations on the whole Bible by Theodore Haak (1605–90). Haak's work was part of the spill-over from the Synod of Dort in 1618, which called for a new translation of the Bible into Dutch, perhaps influenced by James I's similar call after the Hampton Court Conference much earlier. Various translators, understudies, and revisers were subsequently chosen, and the six starters were given full employment with their families by the University of Leiden, which took care that the different provinces were represented. According to the book's approbation, when the Civil War Parliament considered the question of providing new biblical commentaries in conjunction with the project for a new translation of the Bible, Archbishop Ussher of Ireland 'was often heard to wish very heartily, both before and after that time, that the whole work might be *Englished*, as finding it the *plainest* and *impartialest*, and *freest* of *Excursions* and *Impertinencies*, of any he knew, that knew so many.' The approbations were followed by a list of distinguished divines including William Twisse, Samuel Clark, Anthony Tuckney, John Dury, Thomas Godwin, and Samuel Rutherford. The work itself consists of two large folios, 'at this time most seasonable, when so many are dangerously seduced by the mis-representation of the Will of God, through the wresting of Scripture.'[6]

The book met with general acclaim, even from competitors like Arthur Jackson, whose annotations on the Old Testament were published the following year. 'Reader, when I first undertook this Work of writing these Annotations upon the Scripture,' he reminds us, 'there was not, as I remember, any piece of this kind extant in English, save only the Geneva marginall Notes. But since that time (blessed be God, *the father of lights*) abundance of help hath come flowing in by more able Hands', chief among these works being the Dutch annotations.[7]

Annotations and quick commentaries such as these works, however, often created as many problems as they solved, since total immersion in the biblical text revealed an ever-increasing quantity of additional quandaries and contradictions. The various Scripture chronologies which appeared during the era of the Civil War were similarly meant to iron out apparent inconsistencies, but ended up only by exacerbating the situation. William Nisbet, a Scottish minister, for example, tried his hand at elucidating 'A Golden Chaine of Time leading unto Christ', a Scripture chronology which he published at Edinburgh in 1650 and at London with a different title page five years later. Nisbet begins his preface to the reader by admitting that the 'Studie of Chronologie, till of late, hath been either much contemned by some, or then but meanly regarded by others'. Indeed, he writes,

> *Erasmus* of Rotterdam affirmeth, that Chronologie is the same to the writers of Histories and other books, that lights are to houses in the which we dwell, and the Polstar to the Mariners in the vast sea, and that same that *Ariadneis* threed was to *Theseus* in the labyrinth. And if it be such to the writers of Histories, and other books, what must it be to the readers of them?

Nisbet's book itself was not particularly memorable. His numbering of the biblical years is perfectly standard. But even William Nisbet, for all his chronological orthodoxy, needed to make certain adjustments and to devise for himself certain general rules. For example, Nisbet argued that the Bible often rounds out numbers, a perceived fact which in itself solves a number of knotty problems. What such a reading of the Bible does to the iron-clad notion of *sola scriptura* is anyone's guess. But certainly works like Nisbet's must have had the effect of eroding the conviction that the Bible was a completely transparent text which did not require any further elucidation by experts in the field.[8]

A very similar work came from Thomas Allen (1608–73), the rector of Norwich who spent over a dozen years in New England after refusing to read Charles I's *Book of Sports* in 1636. According to popular legend, Allen used to say that he was happy to leave others to 'dispute' while he himself preferred to 'compute'. It is undeniable that his 'Chain of Scripture Chronology' is an impressive work, including a number of major, fold-out chronological tables. Allen was not one to give away his sources, nor to share too much of the credit: 'Chronology being *delightful* and *useful*,' he explained, 'hath many *friends*, and them *men* of *name*, who have labored therein, and written thereof, which this *Author* taking notice of, was unwilling to cumber the World with his *Labors* that way.'[9]

Yet sometimes the chronologers raised such important points that they could not be fully incorporated into the existing framework without making a number of crucial adjustments. Edward Fisher (d. 1656), the Royalist theologian, is known, if at all, as a defender of the strict Sabbath. But his first publication was a very interesting work on the harmony of Scripture. Fisher admitted that a saying had grown up among scholars, to the effect that '*Chronologers agree like Clocks. Scarce two of one mind throughout*'. The reasons for this were quite clear, he thought:

> The chiefe and maine ground of these differences is, because most, neglecting the Word of God, are drawne away with Fables, humane traditions, and uncertaine authorities, whereby they exceed the just and true number, some forty yeeres, some one hundred, some one thousand, nay some two thousand yeeres, and upwards.

If we are to rely on the principle of *sola scriptura*, then we should not abandon it at the slightest provocation:

> Others, who seeme much to follow the Scriptures, and Hebrew expositions, (unto whom without all peradventure we ought in this point to subscribe) doe indeed renounce them, when there is small cause to suspect them of falshood; and embrace them, when we know they seeke by all meanes to obscure the truth.

Fisher claimed that in his book, without abandoning the principle of *sola scriptura*, 'All Scriptures seemingly jarring in point of time are here reconciled' and 'Prophecies are shewed in their due time to be accomplished: Christ Jesus is proved [to] be the true Messiah'.

These promises were impossible to fulfil. Fisher knew that the span between Creation and the Flood was 1,656 years, and that it was sensible to demonstrate this axiomatic dating in his Scripture chronology. But to do so required a certain amount of dextrous ingenuity. Thomas Hobbes (1588–1679) showed the way.[10]

II

When Luther developed the concept of *sola scriptura* during the first three years of the Reformation, he was convinced that the text of the Bible was so clear that comprehension was simultaneous with reading. Although we could see in the Bible examples of how one ought to believe, indeed structures verging on allegory, basically it was God's intention that we should be attentive to the literal text of Scripture. The disadvantages of this method became immediately apparent, for the Bible is not meant to be an ordinary book of historical narrative and poetry. The entire text is held together by a complex series of references which shatter the narrative line. The first system is that based on types or figures, whereby certain patterns are repeated. The exile to Egypt is paralleled by the exile to Babylon centuries later. Adam prefigures Moses who is later reflected by Ezra the lawgiver, and who is fulfilled by Jesus. Little circles appear on the time-line of divine history. The second system is based on chains of prophecy and fulfilment. Not only are biblical figures themselves aware of being caught up in the web of prophecy, as when Daniel (ix. 2) consults Jeremiah (xxv. 12), but in a sense the entire Old Testament is one huge prophecy which is fulfilled by the New. Denying either or both of these two substructural systems brings with it a number of seismic after-shocks. Without a concept of types or figures, the history described in the Bible loses its unique qualities. It becomes, as Isaac La Peyrère argued, merely the history of the Jewish people, and one could never be sure that God did not enact other creations over the horizon. While it is true that figural history was in some ways ahistorical, awash with subplots and divine metaphors, at least it was the history of everyone, not merely that of the Jews. So too was it dangerous to tinker with prophecy. Denying the chain of prophecy and fulfilment cuts the link between the Old Testament and the New, and here too reduces the books of Moses and the prophets to the local history of a rather stiff-necked Middle Eastern tribe.

A purely literal reading of the biblical text such as somewhat naïvely envisioned by Luther at the outset of the Reformation was thus liable to bring a number of potentially disruptive effects in its train. Another threat to *sola scriptura* was the deconstructive tendencies of the humanist tradition. The close reading of historical texts associated with men like Lorenzo Valla seemed to place the Bible itself in some danger, and despite contemporary devotion to the method, there was a tacit understanding that the scriptural word was off limits. This in itself could be perceived as odd even in Luther's time, since it was clear from the Bible that its establishment was promulgated at a sort of ancient book launch held at the watergate of Jerusalem by the prophet Ezra in the fifth century BC.

Hobbes believed that his method of biblical interpretation would clear up most of the scriptural problems still remaining, and produce a biblical text free of the ambiguities that had obscured its understanding for centuries. Right at the beginning of the third part of *Leviathan*, turning to the question of a 'Christian Commonwealth', Hobbes proclaims that unlike his previous two sections regarding man, and the ordinary civil commonwealth, when dealing with God's plan one needs to take into account that 'there dependeth much upon supernatural revelations of the will of God'. As a result, the bounds of discussion must comprehend 'not only the natural word of God, but also the prophetical.' That being said, however, Hobbes explains,

> Nevertheless, we are not to renounce our senses, and experience; nor, that which is the undoubted word of God, our natural reason. For they are the talents which he hath put into our hands to negotiate, till the coming again of our blessed Saviour; and therefore not to be folded up in the napkin of an implicit faith, but employed in the purchase of justice, peace, and true religion. For though there be many things in God's word above reason; that is to say, which cannot by natural reason be either demonstrated, or confuted; yet there is nothing contrary to it, but when it seemeth so, the fault is either in our unskilful interpretations, or erroneous ratiocination.

'Therefore,' Hobbes concludes, 'when any thing therein written is too hard for our examination, we are bidden to captivate our understanding to the words; and not to labour in sifting out a philosophical truth by logic, of such mysteries as are not comprehensible, nor fall under any rule of natural science.' By 'captivate our understanding', Hobbes elucidates, he does not mean 'a submission of the intellectual faculty to the opinion of any other man; but of the will to obedience, where obedience is due.'[11]

There were, however, some general restrictions which applied even with regard to the divine world. Most importantly, the teachings of the Bible could not be contrary to simple logic:

> That which taketh away the reputation of wisdom, in him that formeth a religion, or addeth to it when it is already formed, is the enjoining of a belief of contradictories: for both parts of a contradiction cannot possibly be true: and therefore to enjoin the belief of them, is an argument of ignorance; which detects the author in that; and discredits him in all things else he shall propound as from revelation supernatural: which revelation a man may indeed have of many things above, but of nothing against natural reason.[12]

The very attempt to produce an illogical construction of the divine word is sufficient proof that the prophet is false and the commentary worthless.

Another caveat in biblical interpretation, Hobbes insists, is that the reader must pay equal attention to both the text and the context. As Hobbes explains with characteristic directness,

And in the allegation of Scripture, I have endeavoured to avoid such texts as are obscure or controverted interpretation; and to allege none, but in such sense as is most plain, and agreeable to the harmony and scope of the whole Bible; which was written for the re-establishment of the kingdom of God in Christ. For it is not the bare words, but the scope of the writer, that giveth the true light, by which any writing is to be interpreted; and they that insist upon single texts, without considering the main design, can derive nothing from them clearly; but rather by casting atoms of Scripture, as dust before men's eyes, make everything more obscure than it is; an ordinary artifice of those that seek not the truth, but their own advantage.[13]

These were rules for interpreting any text, but it was the Bible which concerned Hobbes, as the document which helped us to establish civil authority on a sound footing.

But it was not enough to interpret rightly the text as we have it: one must also understand something about the author's intentions and the target readership. In Hobbes's view, the Bible had two main functions. 'The Scripture was written to shew unto men the kingdom of God, and to prepare their minds to become his obedient subjects; leaving the world, and the philosophy thereof, to the disputation of men, for the exercising of their natural reason.' The Bible was never intended to teach us science, or 'Whether the earth's, or the sun's motion make the day and night' – that we need to discover for ourselves through the use of reason.[14] The function of Scripture itself is to make us obedient subjects and to prepare us for eternal salvation: in any apparent conflict between the observable natural world and the Scriptures, it is the Holy Writ which must give way.

Despite the fact that *Leviathan* is absolutely riddled with biblical references and quotations, which give the impression that Hobbes recognizes the Bible as the ultimate source of authority, in effect his general rules of interpretation and his remarks regarding the purpose and readership of the text have the effect of fatally undermining biblical authority. By subjecting the Bible to human logic and reason, he efficiently restricted the scope for miracles and other supernatural interventions, especially when we consider his mechanistic understanding of how events occur in the temporal world. Hobbes's insistence on seeing all scriptural references in their complete context also had a great effect, for he eliminated at a stroke the sort of text-mining which so characterized Puritan biblical interpretation.

Having established the rules of interpretation and expounded both the intention of the author and the limits of the text, Hobbes goes on to apply them to certain key terms and concepts in the Bible, again on a logical basis, namely the axiomatic faith that the words in Scripture have a consistent meaning and usage:

Seeing the foundation of all true ratiocination, is the constant signification of words; which in the doctrine following, dependeth not, as in natural science, on the will of the writer, nor, as in common conversation, on vulgar use, but on the sense they carry in the Scripture; it is necessary, before I proceed any further, to determine, out of the Bible, the meaning of such words, as by their ambiguity, may render what I am to infer upon them, obscure, or disputable.[15]

Otherwise, it would not be possible to claim that the Bible had any inner logic at all.

In Hobbes's view, there are three key concepts which appear in the Bible whose misinterpretation has been the cause of untold trouble ever since. The first of these is the nature of the human soul. Hobbes takes us through the biblical understanding of the concepts of 'spirit', 'body', 'substances', 'corporeal', and 'incorporeal'. His conclusion is startling, but essential to the whole structure of his argument – that since there can be no such thing as an incorporeal substance, both the soul and the heavenly angels must be corporeal.[16] 'The *soul* in Scripture, signifieth always, either the life, or the living creature; and the body and soul jointly, the *body alive.*' The soul itself is not eternal, and 'if by *soul* were meant a *substance incorporeal*, with an existence separated from the body, it might as well be inferred of any other living creature as of man.'[17] The historical source of this misinterpretation of the nature of the soul, Hobbes claims, can ultimately be traced back to the fact that the 'Grecians, by their colonies and conquests, communicated their language and writings into Asia, Egypt, and Italy; and therein, by necessary consequence their *demonology*'.[18]

The political results of this failure in biblical interpretation have been critical:

The maintenance of civil society depending on justice, and justice on the power of life and death, and other less rewards and punishments, residing in them that have the sovereignty of the commonwealth; it is impossible a commonwealth should stand, where any other than the sovereign hath a power of giving greater rewards than life, and of inflicting greater punishments than death.

The role of the Bible in creating this undesirable situation should be obvious:

Now seeing *eternal life* is a greater reward than the *life present*; and *eternal torment* a greater punishment than the *death of nature*; it is a thing worthy to be well considered of all men that desire, by obeying authority, to avoid the calamities of confusion and civil war, what is meant in Holy Scripture, by *life eternal*, and *torment eternal.*[19]

In other words, biblical interpretation was a matter of utmost importance, not only for divines, but also for the planners of civil society. Even more generally, Hobbes is also suggesting that one of the enemies of political authority is sloppy and irrational thinking.

In the same painstaking manner, Hobbes disposes of his next concept from the Bible, miracles, a category including prophecy and magic as well. 'By *miracles* are signified the admirable works of God: and therefore they are also called *wonders*.' Furthermore, since the purpose of miracles is often to eliminate doubt with regard to God's commandment, Hobbes notes that the common scriptural term for a miracle is 'a sign'.[20] Hobbes does not deny that miracles could occur, in theory at least. In actual fact, he sets so many limitations to what could properly be considered a miracle – especially the criteria of strangeness and inexplicability – that for all practical purposes we can regard miracles as a dead letter:

> From that which I have here set down, of the nature and use of a miracle, we may define it thus: A MIRACLE *is a work of God, (besides his operation by way of nature, ordained in the creation) done, for the making manifest to his elect, the mission of an extraordinary minister for their salvation.*

While Hobbes has nothing against miracles or prophecy in the comfortable distance of biblical times, he assures us that to accept these concepts as continually valid on the basis of scriptural evidence is to put the entire civil order in jeopardy. Every citizen must do as the Jews did when Moses was the civil sovereign and men were found prophesying in the Israelite camp. They went to Moses and complained, and left it to their political leaders to decide whether to accept or reject these so-called prophets:

> For when Christian men, take not their Christian sovereign, for God's prophet; they must either take their own dreams, for the prophecy they mean to be governed by, and the tumour of their own hearts for the Spirit of God; or they must suffer themselves to be led by some strange prince; or by some of their fellow-subjects, that can bewitch them, by slander of the government, into rebellion, without other miracle to confirm their calling, than sometimes an extraordinary success and impunity; and by this means destroying all laws, both divine and human, reduce all order, government, and society, to the first chaos of violence and civil war.[21]

Any contemporary reader would know that Hobbes was referring to his own time, when Cromwell and many others found in the Bible ample evidence of their own election and confirmation of the divinely ordained role they thought themselves privileged to play.

Indeed, Hobbes looked almost with disgust at people who claimed to be divinely inspired, in direct contact with God:

For if every man should be obliged, to take for God's law, what particular men, on pretence of private inspiration, or revelation, should obtrude upon him, in such a number of men, that out of pride and ignorance, take their own dreams, and extravagant fancies, and madness, for testimonies of God's spirit; or out of ambition, pretend to such divine testimonies, falsely, and contrary to their own consciences, it were impossible that any divine law should be acknowledged.[22]

Since we are no longer troubled by miracles and prophecies for all practical purposes in our own day, it is possible to discuss the very existence of a civil commonwealth without worrying about divine contradiction.

The third term which Hobbes discusses at length by means of scriptural analysis is that of the 'kingdom of God'. Indeed, Hobbes claims,

The greatest and main abuse of Scripture, and to which almost all the rest are either consequent or subservient, is the wresting of it, to prove that the kingdom of God, mentioned so often in the Scripture, is the present Church, or multitude of Christian men now living, or that being dead, are to rise again at the last day: whereas the kingdom of God was first instituted by the ministry of Moses, over the Jews only; who were therefore called his peculiar people; and ceased afterward, in the election of Saul, when they refused to be governed by God any more, and demanded a king after the manner of the nations.

Under the Jews, there was no division between political and religious authority. God's kingdom was the one under which they lived, and the misuse of the Bible to suggest that this entity is comprised of those who enjoy eternal bliss in heaven is a cause of inestimable political troubles on earth. Eventually, Christ will return to earth to take up his messianic mantle:

Which second coming not yet being, the kingdom of God is not yet come, and we are not now under any other kings by pact, but our civil sovereigns.[23]

This misunderstanding of a crucial biblical term has justified the pope's power, and the establishment of the political influence of the Roman Catholic Church, and the subsequent weakening of secular political authority. The Calvinists are hardly better, and certainly more actively destabilizing, with their claim that religious authority may override political rule. The only kingdom to which we can appeal is the one governed by our civil sovereign.

The Bible, then, is a very dangerous book when its interpretation is allowed to run unleashed, not only with disregard for reason and logical textual analysis, but also free from proper deference to established political authority. At the same time, we have no alternative than to devote ourselves to biblical interpretation if we are to understand our role in the divine plan:

Seeing therefore miracles now cease, we have no sign left, whereby to acknowledge the pretended revelations or inspirations of any private man; nor obligation to give ear to any doctrine, farther than it is conformable to the Holy Scriptures, which since the time of our Saviour, supply the place, and sufficiently recompense the want of all other prophecy; and from which, by wise and learned interpretation, and careful ratiocination, all rules and precepts necessary to the knowledge of our duty both to God and man, without enthusiasm or supernatural inspiration, may easily be deduced.[24]

The Bible is the very basis of a Christian commonwealth, and Hobbes addresses the question of biblical authority most directly. Interestingly, he deals with the thorny question of the authorship of the Pentateuch almost with a flourish:

We read in the last chapter of *Deuteronomy*, verse 6, concerning the sepulchre of Moses, *that no man knoweth of his sepulchre to this day*, that is, to the day wherein those words were written. It is therefore manifest, that those words were written after his interment. For it were a strange interpretation, to say Moses spake of his own sepulchre, though by prophecy, that it was not found to that day, wherein he was yet living.[25]

Hobbes goes on to prove, from the internal evidence of the scriptural text itself, that many parts of the Bible were written long after the events described therein took place.

Having amply demonstrated the vagaries of scriptural transmission, and thereby effectively having demolished any common-sense understanding of *sola scriptura*, Hobbes then asks, '*from whence the Scriptures derive their authority*'? Even more basically, he notes, we might equally frame the question, 'in other terms, as, *how we know them to be the word of God*, or, *why we believe them to be so*'. Hobbes argues that this key question of scriptural authority has been badly posed, which is the chief reason for so much dispute regarding its resolution: 'the difficulty of resolving it, ariseth chiefly from the improperness of the words wherein the question itself is couched.' The problem, as Hobbes sees it, is that we all believe that the Scriptures are the Word of God, Who is the author of the biblical text. This statement cannot be rationally demonstrated according to any standard of proof, and therefore belongs in the realm of belief rather than actual knowledge. When we ask what is the basis for this belief, we find such a myriad possible responses that the 'question truly stated is, *by what authority they are made law*.' Here too, the answer for Hobbes is quite clear: the authority of the Bible and the laws of God are ultimately political in nature:

He therefore to whom God hath not supernaturally revealed that they are his, nor that those that published them, were sent by him, is not obliged to obey them, by any authority, but his, whose commands have already the force of laws; that is to say, by any other authority, than that of the commonwealth, residing in the sovereign, who only has the legislative power.[26]

There is really no alternative: if the power of biblical interpretation resides elsewhere than in the sovereign, then there are only a few unattractive alternatives left. If we are to apply the principle of *sola scriptura* to its fullest individualistic extent, so that everyone will interpret the Bible for himself, then a particular interpretation 'obliges only him, to whom in particular God hath been pleased to reveal it.' Otherwise, the multiplicity of revelations, expressed for both genuine and dishonest reasons, would swiftly lead to a situation whereby 'it were impossible that any divine law should be acknowledged'. This could hardly be countenanced. If we base scriptural authority on public authority, then we are soon thrown upon the same dilemma. In a commonwealth, the power is in the hands of the civil sovereign, and we are back where we started. If we are speaking of a Church, then power is concentrated in the hands of a single Christian sovereign. But since 'the whole number of Christians be not contained in one commonwealth', then each individual Christian in each individual country is dependent for the interpretation of God's Word on his or her own individual Christian sovereign. Roman Catholics are thus grossly mistaken in supposing that all Christians are '*subject to one Vicar of Christ, constituted of the universal church*'.[27]

Indeed, Hobbes explains, 'it is manifest that the Scriptures were never made laws, but by the sovereign civil power.'[28] Historically, that

> part of the Scripture, which was first law, was the Ten Commandments, written in two tables of stone, and delivered by God himself to Moses; and by Moses made known to the people. Before that time there was no written law of God, who as yet having not chosen any people to be his peculiar kingdom, had given no law to men, but the law of nature, that is to say, the precepts of natural reason, written in every man's own heart.[29]

The inescapable conclusion of what Hobbes is saying, is that the biblical text is a human artefact and that its authority rests completely on human foundations as determined by the sovereign.

The implications of Hobbes's system of biblical interpretation can hardly be overestimated. Not only did Hobbes establish the absolute right of the sovereign to interpret the Scriptures, but he effectively undermined the importance of the Bible as an exact indicator of the divine plan. Since the Bible was a human production, then slavish devotion to the principle of *sola scriptura* must be a misguided impulse.

III

Brian Walton (1600–61) was born in the same year as Charles I, and died immediately after being elevated to the see of Chester after the Restoration. In temperament and political outlook he was not so different from Thomas Hobbes, who was twelve years older.[30] Walton was born in Yorkshire, and took his MA at Peterhouse, Cambridge in 1623. He was soon appointed to prestigious church posts, and eventually was made chaplain to King Charles I. By 1639 he was already a doctor of divinity. Walton became very well known in London, especially after publishing a book which defended the tithes of rent owed to the clergy, always a controversial subject. He managed to collect a prodigious body of precedents that proved the clergy's case beyond all doubt, which made him extremely unpopular with every group except the clergy.[31] As might be expected, when the Civil War broke out, Walton was among the first to suffer. His church preferments were revoked, his house was looted, he was imprisoned for a time, then forced to flee for his life. Walton was almost killed by Parliamentary soldiers, but managed to escape.[32] He made his way to Oxford, where the Royalist spirit was not extinguished, and from about 1645 was collecting materials for a new polyglot Bible, at which time he was incorporated in Oxford University. The actual project was under way by October 1653. Although most of the work on the Bible was done in London at the house of his (second) father-in-law, Dr William Fuller, Walton's first steps on this massive and innovative project were taken in Oxford.[33]

The idea of producing a new text of the Bible, with or without a new translation, had long been in the air, and it is not entirely clear what Walton's role was in the various machinations which preceded Cromwell's patronage of the project. Walton's Royalist record seems to have been forgiven if not forgotten at some stage, although his name does not appear in the earliest agitations for a new biblical text.

The first serious proposal was presented to Parliament some time in 1652. The text begins by citing a recent sermon to Parliament, in which it was pointed out that the Authorized Version New Testament was deliberately made 'to bringe it toe speake Prelaticall Languadge'. This alone would call for a new and revised version, but there were other weighty arguments as well, especially the fact that

in ye Originall Text of ye Holy Scriptures, ther is so great a Depth, that only by Degrees ther is a progresse of Light – towards the Attayning of perfection of the knowledge in the bettering of the Translation thereof: & Hence, the Most Learned Translators have found Cause, agayne & agyne of Revisinge & still Rectifyinge & Amendinge within a ffew years, of w^t they themselves had translated And published.

Thére was nothing wrong with admitting that mistakes and infelicities remained in even the most worthy translations. Indeed, 'this hath beene ye C[o]mendable practice Even of some Papists and of Sundry of the Reformed Religion'. In any case, the proposal continued,

> And it being now above 40 years since our new translation was finished, Divers of ye Heads of The Colledges, & many other Learned persons (y^t Comeing later, have the Advantage to stand as on the heads of The former) in y^r Publicke sermons, (& in print also) have often held out to y^{eir} hearers & readers, that ye Hebrew or Greeke may better be rendred, as they mention, then as it is in o^r Newest & Best Translation: Some of the places seeming to be very materiall, & Crying aloud for the Rectifiinge of them, if ye trueth be as it is so Affirmed & published by them.

What was required now was some official action, since 'wee heare that some have translated the New testament if not ye Old also: and would have them printed & Published in our Nation.' Such a step, without official supervision, could be catastrophic,

> Which if it should be Done on their owne heads, without Due Care for ye su[per]vising therof by Learned Persons; Sound in ye Fundamentals of the Christian Religion might be a President of Dangerous Consequence: Emboldening others to doe the Like. And might tend at Last to bringe in Other Scriptures or or [sic] an other Gospell instead of ye Oracles of God, & the Gospel of o^r Lord Jesus Christ.

The authors of this proposal did not stop at complaining: they had a plan, the first provision of which was

> That no Person or persons whatsoever within the Dominion of England, Scotland, or Ireland, without the Aprobation of persons heareafter named, or to be named by Authority, Shall presume to print or Publish any such Translation of ye Bible, or of ye New Testament.

This special committee was to be composed of John Owen, Ralph Cudworth (1617–88), William Jenkins (1613–85), William Greenhill (1591–1671), Samuel Slater (d. 1704), William Cowper, Henry Jessey, Ralph Venning (1612?–74), and John Row (1568–1646), Hebrew professor in Aberdeen. Two names are crossed off the original list: Thomas Goodwin (1600–80) and Joseph Caryll (1602–73). As if to add insult to injury, the parsimonious scribe has changed the last five letters of Goodwin's name to 'Owen'. But this is only to reserve them for more weighty business: the proposal suggested that Goodwin, Caryll and Anthony Tuckney (1599–1670) be the supervisors of the entire project, that is, to revise the entire Bible before any further printings be made. They were advised to pay careful attention to the translation done by Henry Ainsworth

(1571–1622), for 'its said, that there are M.S. of his Translations of some other Scriptures, both of the Old & New Testam[en]t'. In any case, they were to make use of whatever sources they wished in order to bring the English version closer to the original Hebrew and Greek. At the end of their work, a new revised translation of the Scriptures was to be produced, which 'shall accordingly be printed and published for the Generall Edification, and benefit, of the Whole Nation, to be Read both privately, And in the publicke Congregations.'[34] On the basis of this learned and judicious petition, a bill was brought to the House of Commons on 11 January 1652–3, 'for a New Translation of the Bible out of the original Languages' which was to include the names of those who would be authorized to do the actual work.[35]

The petition to Parliament was most likely connected in some fashion with the anonymous prospectus put out by Brian Walton at about the same time, in which he promoted the need for a new polyglot Bible. His prospectus opens with a firm commitment to the concept of *sola scriptura*:

> Whereas the ground of Faith is the Word of God, contained in the Scriptures, it must needs be a work of highest consequence to preserve those *Sacred Oracles* in their original purity, freed (as much as may be) from all possibility of Error, that may arise either by the negligence of Scribes, and injury of Times, or by the wilful corruption of Sectaries and Hereticks, which (as was foretold) abound in these latter times, and so to transmit them to Posterity.

Walton makes clear, however, that the question of obtaining the best texts of the divine Word is not merely a matter of improving existing translations. What was needed was more diligent application to

> the *Eastern Languages*: which in regard of their affinity and neernesse to the Original are fittest to expresse, and in regard of their Antiquity and general use in the first and purest Ages are the truest Glasses, to represent that sence and reading which was then generally received in the Church of Christ, to whose Care the custody of the Scriptures is committed: The comparing of which together hath always been accounted one of the best means to attain the true sence in places doubtful, and to finde out and restore the true reading of the Text where any variety appears.

Prefiguring the line of argument which would be used three centuries later after the discovery of the Dead Sea Scrolls, Walton points out (quite rightly) that it was extraordinary to perceive 'the *Harmonie* and *Consent* of so many ancient Copies and Translations made in several Ages, and Parts of the World, so far remote from one another, and continued to this day, agreeing in all matters of moment'. Walton understood this to be an example of the voice of God testifying from Heaven that those Books proceeded from a divine Author, who hath so marvellously owned and preserved them in all parts of the World among so many changes and revolutions that have happened, maugre the malice and power of Sathan, labouring by Hereticks, and Sectaries to corrupt, and by Persecutors to extirpate the Scriptures, and therewith Christian Religion.

Walton went on to describe the key editions of his day, and explained that it was not for him to denigrate the achievements of his predecessors:

> Though these Editions be justly had in high esteem . . . yet it must be confest that divers *Ancient* and *Vseful Translations* may be added, that there are *better Copies* now, then those followed in the former Editions, that many things useful then, yet needlesse now may be taken away, that a new *Apparatus* far more useful may be framed, and the several Languages digested in better Method, besides the greatnesse of the price, and vastnesse of the Volumes, which makes them scarce useful for private Libraries, being printed in such *Paper* and *Characters*, as served rather for *Pomp* then *Vse*, (that of *Paris* being sold at 45. or 50 li. the price of an ordinary *Librarie*) so that without detracting from the just praises of the publishers (whose Labours must be made use of, as they did of other mens that were before them) it may be said that a *more perfect* and *useful Edition* then any yet extant may be made in 5 or 6 *ordinary Volumes*, which may be had at a fourth or fift *part of the price*.

Walton promised that the finished Polyglot would be given to those who subscribed £10; £50 would fetch six copies. The work, however, would be not be commenced until enough money had been raised to produce the first volume, the Pentateuch, which Walton reckoned at £1,500. The same would hold true for the succeeding volumes, which should run at about £1,200 each. Walton asked for the first payment on or before 1 May 1653, and promised to deliver the entire Polyglot Bible within a little over three years. It is usually forgotten how radical Walton's proposal actually was: his Polyglot Bible was one of the first books published in England by subscription.[36]

The work began on schedule, in October 1653, and was finished four years later.[37] A distinguished group of scholars aided Walton in his project.[38] The Pentateuch was completed in September 1654. The second volume was finished in July 1655, the third exactly a year later, and the last three volumes were completed as planned in 1657. Walton used two presses simultaneously, and tried continuously to get government support for his project, without conspicuous success. On 11 July 1652, the Council of State decided to 'inform Dr Brian Walton that, on considering his petition offering an edition of the Bible in several tongues, Council are of opinion that the work propounded by him is very honourable and deserving encouragement, but find that the matter of his desires is more proper for the consideration of Parliament than Council.'[39] While not as encouraging a response as might have been expected, Walton was given the paper for his Polyglot duty free, and better quality at that, at 15 shillings per ream. He was also allowed to borrow books from state libraries.[40]

Walton's Polyglot was in many ways the most useful one ever printed. The Gospels appear in six languages, and the other New Testament books in five. Walton used the Septuagint quite fully, producing the Roman edition of 1587. The Latin Vulgate included is that of Clement VIII. His Aramaic Targum is more complete than previous editions. The fifth volume of his Bible includes the Greek, with a Latin translation, and also the Vulgate, and the versions written in Syriac, Arabic, Ethiopic, and the Persian copy of the Gospels. The sixth volume contains the first substantial collection of variant readings that had ever been printed.[41]

The entire conception of Walton's work was one tied umbilically to the Protectorate, with the emphasis on *sola scriptura* and looking to the Bible for providences. Towards that end, Walton dedicated his Polyglot to Cromwell, and was somewhat at a loss when Cromwell died just as the book was printed. At the Restoration, Walton excised his dedication to the Protector, and rechristened the work in the name of Charles II, a necessary alteration in the text, since the Polyglot immediately received the praise that was and would remain its due. Despite not a small number of errors and typographical blunders, the work continued to be an essential reference source. Walton's prolegomena regarding the sources of his Polyglot and the original languages remained an important summary, and was reprinted both in England and in Germany.[42]

That Walton's Polyglot should have earned a place on the 'Index Librorum Prohibitorum' at Rome was not surprising. His work was attacked even at home, especially by Dr John Owen. His objections were not to the scholarship of the Polyglot, but to the wisdom of the entire enterprise itself, the very act of comparing the differing versions of the Bible, which was bound to weaken blind faith in *sola scriptura*. Walton replied, and seems to have set the matter to rest.[43] Walton also produced a summary of the Oriental languages while working on the Polyglot, which appeared in several versions.[44]

Walton's massive contribution to biblical studies was well timed, but did not win him the complete protectoral pardon that he might have hoped for. His opinion was consulted by Parliament when it looked into the question of revising the Authorized Version in 1657, under the auspices of a 'Grand Committee of Religion'. Still, the Restoration was not far off, and when he petitioned to be reinstated in his benefices and reappointed chaplain in ordinary to the king, his wishes were granted.[45] Other awards followed swiftly. On 14

August 1660 he was made a prebendary of St Paul's Cathedral, and later the same year bishop of Chester, consecrated in Westminster Abbey on 2 December. When the Savoy Conference was called several months later, Brian Walton was a member. He was also given some additional livings to top up his bishopric.[46] His enjoyment of these rewards for near fidelity was not long lived, however. Walton died in his house in Aldersgate Street, London, on 29 November 1661, and was buried at St Paul's on 5 December. His monument there was destroyed in the Great Fire, and his library was sold in 1683.[47]

IV

Brian Walton was only one of a somewhat select group of learned Hebraists during the middle of the seventeenth century, and not even the best of them. He worked, for example, with Edmund Castell (1606–85), who was his Cambridge contemporary, and a most noteworthy expert on Oriental languages. Castell played a great role in the Polyglot Bible: he was responsible for the Samaritan, Syriac, Arabic, and Ethiopic texts, and later said that not only was his contribution unduly minimized, but that the research for the work came out of his own pocket, instead of being subsidized by Walton and his subscribers. But his efforts were well channelled into his own *Lexicon Heptaglotton*, which appeared at London in 1669 and became one of the most celebrated books in the field of English Oriental studies.

Castell, unlike Walton, was not attuned to the financial aspects of Hebraic scholarship, and lost a good deal of money. He was said to have employed at his own expense seven Englishmen and seven foreigners in his own house as research assistants, all of whom mysteriously died before the lexicon was completed. Castell claimed to have spent £12,000 on his work, an immense sum.[48] His financial distress put him in fear of debtors' prison, and he wrote to King Charles II, who declined to help him directly but recommended his work to others. Still, Castell dedicated his lexicon to the king, lamenting the loss of his library in the Great Fire, and the other misfortunes which befell him in the composition of his great book. 'I had once', he writes, 'companions in my undertaking, partners in my toil; but some of them are now no more, and others have abandoned me, alarmed at the immensity of the undertaking. I am now, therefore, left alone, without amanuensis or corrector, far advanced in years, with my patrimony exhausted, my bodily and mental strength impaired, and my eye-sight almost gone!' Indeed, Castell claimed, 'I considered that day as idle and dissatisfactory in which I did not toil sixteen or eighteen hours either at the Polyglot or Lexicon'.[49]

Charles did respond to some degree. In 1666, Castell was made chaplain in ordinary to the king, and the following year was appointed to the eighth prebendal stall in Canterbury Cathedral, although he was excused attendance. In these posts, he paralleled the good fortune of his mentor Brian Walton. He was also appointed to the professorship of Arabic at Cambridge in 1664, which was in the gift of the king. The chair itself was hardly a going concern, and cost him more to maintain than it brought in. He was elected to the Royal Society in 1674.

Bad luck continued to dog Castell, however, and the sales of his learned work went very poorly. There were still 500 copies unsold at his death, and his niece, who inherited the lot, kept them at a tenant's house in Surrey, where they became fodder for the rats. In the end, the paper was sold as scrap for £7. Castell himself took a number of country livings, and finally died in Bedfordshire in 1685. He left his Oriental manuscripts to the University Library at Cambridge, and his best books to Emmanuel College.[50]

Castell always stayed at Lightfoot's rooms when at Cambridge, which is not surprising, given their mutual interest in Eastern languages. John Lightfoot (1602–75) was certainly one of the foremost Hebraists who ever came out of England. He studied at Christ's College, Cambridge, and later on, as a young curate in Shropshire, attracted the patronage of Sir Rowland Cotton, who made him his domestic chaplain and encouraged him to pursue his Hebrew studies. Lightfoot followed Cotton to London, received a series of church livings, and continued his work on Eastern languages in a study that he had built in his garden.

When the time came to take sides, he supported Parliament against the king, but Lightfoot was no Roundhead. First of all, he was a Presbyterian, and as such sat in the Westminster Assembly of divines, arguing for an erastian position of strong government involvement in church affairs. Even worse, he believed that King Charles had been murdered by Cromwell and company, rather than judicially and legally executed. Nevertheless, these unpopular views did not prevent him from accepting a Hertfordshire rectory which he held until his death, nor the mastership of St Catharine Hall, Cambridge, followed in 1654 by the vice-chancellorship of the university. Lightfoot managed to weather the Restoration with his emoluments intact. Still siding with the Presbyterians, he took part in the Savoy Conference of 1661, constant in his beliefs even after Charles II had moved the goalposts well to the other side of the field.

John Lightfoot was one of the great Hebrew scholars of his generation. Gibbon, in a famous remark, noted that Lightfoot, 'by constant reading of the rabbis, became almost a rabbi himself'. Lightfoot's output was impressive, especially his series entitled *Horae Hebraicae et Talmudicae* (Cambridge, 1658–74). He was also a key figure in the production of Walton's Polyglot, revising the Samaritan Pentateuch and writing a geographical commentary on the maps of the Holy Land. Indeed, his son John became Walton's chaplain.[51]

Edward Pococke (1604–91) was Lightfoot's opposite number at Oxford. He was actually born there,[52] and finished his BA at Corpus Christi College, where in due course he became a fellow and devoted himself to Oriental studies. He excelled not only in Hebrew, but also in Arabic and Syriac. But it was the time he spent in Aleppo (1630–6) as chaplain to the English merchants there that gave him the breadth of scholarship for which he was celebrated, adding Samaritan and Ethiopic to his repertoire. Archbishop William Laud, who was a true scholar as well as a villain, had been chancellor of Oxford University since 1629, founded a lectureship in Arabic and appointed Pococke to the post. When he returned to England in early 1636, Pococke brought with him a large number of Oriental manuscripts, which would eventually form the basis of the Bodleian's collection.[53]

Within a year, however, Laud sent his protégé back to the East, this time to Constantinople, with the task of procuring even more manuscripts for Oxford, and simultaneously improving his Oriental tongues. Pococke remained there for three years, and when he returned to England in spring 1641, Laud was already in the Tower. Pococke spent the interregnum constantly under threat because of his close association with Laud, and required the intervention of great scholars close to Cromwell such as John Selden (1584–1654) to keep him out of trouble. Pococke was appointed Regius professor of Hebrew in 1648, but was constantly harassed at Oxford and periodically deprived of various rights and privileges. These annoyances ended with the Restoration, and Pococke lived out the remaining thirty years of his life in Christ Church, in view of the ancient fig tree which he had brought with him from Aleppo.[54]

Pococke is important for biblical studies not only for his analytical and textual work but also for his role in the history of printing. In 1650 he published his *Specimen historiae Arabum*, dedicated to Selden, in which he took an excerpt from the Universal History of Bar-Hebraeus (Abulfaragius) (1226–86), archbishop of the Eastern Jacobites and the last classical Syriac author, and used it as a basis for erudite articles on Arabic history, literature, and culture.[55] Pococke's book and one by his colleague John Greaves were the first two examples printed in Arabic type by Oxford University Press. Pococke's edition (1655) of Maimonides on the Mishna was the first Hebrew text from the Press.[56] Like Lightfoot, Pococke was an active participant in Walton's Polyglot project. Apart from lending manuscripts and giving constant advice, Pococke collated the Arabic version of the Pentateuch and contributed a critical appendix on the subject. John Locke (1632–1704), Pococke's colleague at Christ Church, described his character in a private letter years after his death:

The Christian World is a Witness of his great Learning; that, the Works he publish'd would not suffer to be conceal'd: nor could his Devotion and

Piety lie hid, and be unobserv'd in a College where his constant and regular assisting at the Cathedral Service, never interrupted by sharpness of Weather, and scarce restrain'd by down-right want of Health, shew'd the Temper and Disposition of his Mind. But his other Virtues and excellent Qualities, had so strong and close a covering of Modesty and unaffected Humility . . . they were the less taken notice and talk'd of by the Generality of those to whom he was not wholly unknown . . . He had often the Silence of a Learner, where he had the Knowledg of a Master: . . . He was a Man of no irregular Appetites; if he indulg'd any one too much, it was that of Study, which his Wife would often complain of (and, I think, not without Reason) . . . His Name, which was in great Esteem beyond sea, and that deservedly, drew on him Visits from all Foreigners of Learning, who came to Oxford to see that University . . . he was always unaffectedly chearful . . . His Life appear'd to me, one constant Calm.[57]

Lightfoot and Pococke represent the best of seventeenth-century Hebrew and Oriental scholarship. Their work was not so very different from that practised in the Renaissance since the days of Lorenzo Valla. Despite its extraordinary professionalism, it was nonetheless characterized by an underlying confidence in the deepest veracity of God's last words as they appear in Scripture. Once the human encrustations of centuries had been stripped away through the application of philological remedies, then the pure divine gold would be revealed. But the textual world of men like Lightfoot and Pococke was changing as the concept of God's testimony was broadened by natural science beyond the printed word.

V

One of the most persuasive myths used to justify the pursuit of natural philosophy (science) in the seventeenth century was that of the 'two books'. According to this analogy, God in His goodness has provided mankind with two alternative sources of essential information: the written Book of Scripture and the visible Book of Nature. Thus, even someone who is unable to hear or read the Word of God, even a non-Christian, can deduce the basic metaphysical truths by observing the surrounding world. Such a person should be able to invent for himself or herself at least the 'argument from design', the realization that the universe is of such complexity that it could only have been created by a superhuman intelligence – the story of the '*watch* upon the ground' found in 'crossing a heath', used with such effectiveness in the nineteenth century.[58] The observation of the stars and planets alone should produce the desired realization that everything has a place and an order in the divine chain of being.

The Newtonian synthesis was predicated on the idea that God had created the universe to operate in accordance with specific *laws*. These were laws which He Himself had promulgated in His role as absolute ruler of the universe. In normal circumstances these laws might be presumed to operate: there was an implicit divine promise involved here. We may never understand the ultimate causes of the laws of nature, as the Aristotelians hoped to do, but at least the 'efficient causes' might be divined, which would give us power over nature. Yet at the same time, just as the notion of a 'Book of Nature' derived from the palpable reality of a 'Book of Scripture', so too was the scientific method applicable in reverse to the Bible. Were not both books bodies of divine knowledge to be understood by the same laws of interpretation, just as the same scientific principles were held to apply anywhere in the universe, both in our world and in superlunary realms? Newton saw the Bible, especially the books of prophecy, as a sort of divine puzzle, set for instruction by God Himself, no less a puzzle than inscrutable nature around us. Like nature, the Bible was to be interpreted according to a fixed set of scientific rules, which would prise open the secrets of the Book of Scripture and reveal to us the past, the present, and even the future.

Newton's theological views are so crucial in the understanding of his particular mode of biblical interpretation that it is worth having a closer look at their antecedents and subsequent developments.[59] Side by side with the evolution of the tools of modern textual and philological scholarship was the flourishing of various occult approaches to the world. Hermeticism grew in the West at the same time as the definition of witchcraft as heresy and the persecution of its alleged practitioners. Paracelsus (1493?–1541) peddled his combination of supernatural philosophy and medical advances across Europe. Thinkers like Marsilio Ficino and Pico della Mirandola sought to unite diverse strands of Neoplatonism, Gnosticism, and kabbalah into a coherent whole.

What united these philosophies was the general conception of the universe, of nature, as an intelligent and living organism. As in the individual human being, there was an organic connection between the different parts of the whole. R.G. Collingwood, in his classic book on the idea of nature, called this the 'Greek view'.[60] Everything then was seen as interdependent. If you could fathom the ultimate nature of things, you could figure out their mutual attraction. By this reasoning, what we naïvely call the 'laws of nature' are really our expressions of the mutual relations of things that we observe around us. The natural world is alive with intelligence, if only we have ears to hear.

This animistic view of the universe is usually thought to have come to an end with René Descartes (1596–1650), who likened the universe to an efficient machine, instituted and planned by God. He explained that the entire Creation was made up of two components: (1) matter in extension, i.e. in three dimensions; and (2) matter *not* in extension, i.e. God and the human

mind, or soul. This distinction was the famous 'Cartesian dualism'. The entire
system, Descartes posited, was set in motion by God at Creation and has continued mechanistically ever since, one particle of matter pushing and displac-
ing another. There was literally no place that did not contain matter: the
universe is a *plenum*. What looks to us like a *vacuum* is actually filled to the
brim by a 'matière subtile' which allows motion to be conducted from A to
B and on for ever. There can never be action at a distance, since any motion
must be caused by a mechanistic push. In a very real sense, every breath we
take is the latest result of a colossal chain reaction that began with God's
divine nudge. Perhaps most important for the future development of physics,
Descartes also showed that Aristotle was wrong in having posited two sets of
laws, one for earth (sublunary physics) and a rather different one for the
heavens (celestial physics). All physical laws, Descartes argued, are universal in
God's creation.

Descartes's mechanistic system of physics had the advantage of emphasizing God's role as Creator of the universe, and of countering those near-
atheists, ancient and modern, who preferred to think that the world and the
matter contained therein had existed since time immemorial. The difficulty
of Cartesian physics is that a perfect Creator was more than likely to have
constructed a perfect temporal machine which would not require His intervention thereafter. This was the point that Leibniz (1646–1716) liked to stress.
In a sense, Descartes threatened the entire idea of providence, and even the
Calvinistic idea of predestination, which obviously was of vastly greater significance in England and in other Protestant countries than it was in France.

By the Restoration, English natural philosophers were already working on
a scheme which could save what was good in Cartesian theological physics
without abandoning the world to an eternal doomsday machine. Their brief
was to insist that matter was created *ex nihilo* as a result of God's will. Space
and time, however, were not created: they were inherent features of God's
existence: He is omnipresent (space) and eternal (time). Space and time are
the scene of God's creation, which is an act of His will, beginning with the
creation of matter. Having created matter as a result of His own volition, it
would be inconsistent with His divine character to have simply designed a
machine and then let it run eternally on its own steam, as it were. The reason
for this is that God is Ruler of the universe, and without having anything to
do, He would be a ruler in name only, a sort of figurehead. A ruler without
a dominion to rule is no ruler at all. God is therefore responsible not only
for creating matter and putting it into motion, the two components of all
natural phenomena according to mechanical philosophy, but also for preserving the motion in bodies, by constantly intervening in subtle ways to jog
things along. Sometimes we call this intervention 'providence'. For Restoration natural philosophers, this was the way the world goes round.

There is a very nice statement of this issue in the Leibniz–Clarke correspondence, where Samuel Clarke (1675–1729) served as the mouthpiece for the publicity-shy Isaac Newton (1642–1727):

The notion of the world's being a great machine, going on without the interposition of God, as a clock continues to go without the assistance of a clockmaker; is the notion of materialism and fate, and tends, (under pretence of making God a *supra-mundane intelligence,*) to exclude providence and God's government in reality out of the world. And by the same reason that a philosopher can represent all things going on from the beginning of the creation, without any government or interposition of providence; a sceptic will easily argue still farther backwards, and suppose that things have from eternity gone on (as they now do) without any true creation or original author at all, but only what such arguers call all-wise and eternal nature. If a king had a kingdom, wherein all things would continually go on without his government or interposition, or without his attending to and ordering what is done therein; it would be to him, merely a nominal kingdom; nor would he in reality deserve at all the title of king or governor. And as those men, who pretend that in an earthly government things may go on perfectly well without the king himself ordering or disposing of any thing, may reasonably be suspected that they would like very well to set the king aside: so whosoever contends, that the course of the world can go on without the continual direction of God, the Supreme Governor; his doctrine does in effect tend to exclude God out of the world.[61]

This emphasis on God's divine will as ruler of the universe was not a concept which developed out of a need to Protestantize Descartes. Historians of philosophy recognize this so-called 'voluntarist' position in the writings of Duns Scotus (1265?–1308) and William of Ockham (*c.* 1287–1347). They too had argued that of God's three fundamental attributes – wisdom, goodness, and power – it was the last which was essential for understanding the world that He had created. The English scientists of the Restoration saw that God's will was a force that surpassed the existence of nature as a mere machine. Without wishing to retreat to the 'intellectualist' position of Aquinas and theologians in the medieval West who spoke of the semi-immanence of natural law, they recognized that there was a greater intelligence at work around us all the time.

This stress on the power of God as an absolute ruler had immediate implications for anyone engaged in the study of the world as we find it. On the one hand, it was true that just because certain phenomena have been observed to occur in the past – such as things tending to fall down rather than up – there is no guarantee that they will continue to do so in the future. God could simply alter the rules of the natural game. On the other hand, God had never intended chaos to be a guiding principle of mundane life. God has established a world of physics within which one may speak of the 'laws of nature', which will continue to apply until the entire framework is altered in a significant way. The stable existence of the natural world is a kind of continuing promise that it will not be destroyed until the end of days, as God promised Noah after the Flood:

> And the bow shall be in the cloud; and I will look upon it, that I may remember the everlasting covenant between God and every living creature of all flesh that *is* upon the earth. (Gen. ix. 16)

Indeed, God's covenant with Noah, and His other promises throughout the Bible, gave Restoration scientists the assurance that it was worth studying the laws of nature, since there was nothing so permanent as temporary, especially when dealing with divine time. While God has it in His omnipotence to turn our physical world upside down without a moment's notice, His promises in the Book of Scripture put the stamp on what we may observe in the Book of Nature.

The influence of the Bible in Restoration science was therefore paramount: the promises God made in the Book of Scripture reaffirmed the existence of semi-permanent natural laws. On the other hand, what we know of God the absolute ruler of the universe comes from the picture of God we obtain from the Bible. The God of the Old Testament, from Creation, to the Flood, through to Mount Sinai, is a lawgiver. Some of His commandments are not only reasonable but well nigh universal. But a good number of the 613 biblical injunctions seem to our imperfect human reasoning to be arbitrary and unreasonable, or at least beyond our current capacity to comprehend. Like the laws of nature, we can only hope that one day, God's divine plan as revealed in the Bible will be somewhat clearer. From our point of view here, what is important is that the Cartesian physics which Newton and his contemporaries like Henry More (1614–87) and Robert Boyle (1627–91) received was crucially modified, not only by means of ideas inherited from the late medieval Nominalists, but more significantly by applying the wisdom of the Bible in the realm of natural philosophy. And just as Newton would argue (with Descartes) that there was only one set of rules which applied throughout the universe, both here on earth and beyond the moon, so too should the Book of Scripture be opened through the use of a consistent body of rules of interpretation, fixing biblical images with the exactitude of a precision scientific instrument. Both the Book of Nature and the Book of Scripture were worthy subjects for scholarly research, since both hid secrets that God had left for mankind to reveal in its growing wisdom.

VI

An examination of Newton's biblical criticism should probably begin with a consideration of his revision of conventional chronology. Newton's work on chronology first came to light through a combination of gossip and royal pressure. He had discussed his work with Signor Abate Conte Antonio Conti, the Abbé Conti, a Venetian nobleman and hanger-on, who in turn communicated this bit of news to Caroline of Anspach, the princess of Wales and wife of the future George II. She was Newton's greatest admirer. Newton was summoned to court and was requested to provide a copy, or at least a summary, of his work in this fascinating field. He worked up an 'Abstract', what would become his 'Short Chronology', and gave one to the princess, although he refused to pass it on to Conti as well. Not to be denied a look at this compelling document, Conti simply asked Caroline to order Newton to hand it over, and he could do nothing but comply.

As Newton suspected and feared, Conti immediately showed the manuscript around. This 20-page chronology of ancient history was a minor bombshell, since apart from anything else, Newton had cut off about four centuries from Greek history, basing his calculations on astronomy and the points of the equinox and refusing to accept any written Greek authority before Herodotus. Newton's summary was published without his permission as the *Abregé de la chronologie*, an appendix to the French translation of the history of the Jews by Humphrey Prideaux (1648–1724). Newton denounced the pirated edition, but refused to recant on the ideas expressed therein.[62] Conti, for his part, thought that he had found the Italian counterpart to the chronological research of the great man, and promoted the system of Giambattista Vico (1668–1744), who sent a copy of the first edition of *The New Science* to Newton via a rabbi of Livorno, but the book seems not to have been delivered.[63]

The importance of Newton's work can hardly be overestimated. For the first time, a scholar conversant in both the written sources and the Book of Nature had managed to combine the two approaches towards understanding the divine message. Once the biblical and gentile written record was linked to the unimpeachable astronomical time-line, it should have been easy to verify or correct the accepted chronological schema. Although Newton refused to allow anything further to be published under his name, after his death in 1727 it was inevitable that every word would appear in print. We know that Newton was working on the manuscript only a few days before his death. The following year, *The Chronology of Ancient Kingdoms Amended* was published, including the troubled 'Abstract' produced by John Conduitt (1688–1737), who had married Newton's niece.[64]

The reputation of Newton's work on chronology has not always been high. His most important biographer, Robert Westfall, described it as

A work of colossal tedium, it excited for a brief time the interest and opposition of the handful able to get excited over the date of the Argonauts
before it sank into oblivion. It is read today only by the tiniest remnant
who for their sins must pass through its purgatory.[65]

In many ways, this is an unfair assessment of a book whose importance out-
weighs its uselessness as a scientific decipherment of a significant problem.
The study of biblical chronology has always required a good deal of ingenuity and a substantial amount of patience and mathematical skill. Different
methods need to be applied in order to find the exact date of a biblical event.
The first is based on simple addition and subtraction. The Flood, for example,
can be calculated quite easily at 1656 *anno mundi* by adding up the ages of
the patriarchs. Adam, for example, was 130 years old when Seth was born,
and Seth was 105 when his son Enosh was born, and so on.[66] This method
is useful for generating a biblical chronology from the Creation of the world
until the Temple of Solomon. Unfortunately, some problems do exist.
Arphaxad's birth 'two years after the flood' (Gen. xi.10) does not square with
the dates given for his father Shem (Gen. v. 32). Even more worrying, one
obtains radically different figures depending on which text of the Bible is
used. Lower figures can be generated by using the Samaritan Pentateuch,
which will set the Flood at 1307 AM, while the Septuagint gives numbers
which lead the reader to determine it at 2242 AM. As we shall see, the introduction of these non-Hebrew biblical texts into the debate over chronology
in the seventeenth century was a minefield for biblical criticism.

As every careful Bible reader knew, this basic arithmetic could be supplemented by studying specific time lengths given in the text of Scripture itself.
Adding up the ages of the patriarchs from Abraham's entry into Canaan until
the going down of Jacob into Egypt gives the figure of 215 years. The Bible
in Exodus xii. 40 categorically states that the Israelites spent 430 years in
Egypt, which would place the Exodus at 2666 AM. Again, using the Samaritan and the Septuagint places the matter in further doubt, since both texts
say that the 430 years *includes* the earlier period from Abraham to Jacob,
making Israel's sojourn in Egypt only 215 years long, the same length as the
first Canaanite era. To make matters worse, Paul in Galatians iii. 17 affirmed
the latter interpretation, stating that the entire period from Abraham to Moses
was only 430 years in length.

The time between the Exodus and the beginning of Solomon's Temple is
given in 1 Kings vi. 1 as 480 years, which would set this date as 3146 AM.
This figure is particularly useful, as the time scale of the prophets is very
unclear. Carrying this reckoning further, we find that by simply adding up
the regnal lengths of the kings of Judaea from Solomon's fourth year, when
construction of the Temple began, to the destruction of the said Temple and

the kingdom itself, we arrive once again at the mystical figure of 430 years. This is odd, since if we use historical facts, this figure should not be more than about 372 years, on the assumption that Solomon began to reign in 962 BC, and in 958 began building the Temple, which was destroyed in 587–6 BC. Clearly, a good deal of calendrical corner rounding had taken place.

There was thus a good deal of ground-clearing to be done before trying to create the perfect synthesis of information. Others had dealt with the issue of chronology before Newton; its true study began with Archbishop James Ussher of Armagh (1581–1656). Ussher's greatest achievement was to have improved the system of chronology devised by J.J. Scaliger (1540–1609), the inventor of the 'Julian Period', a cycle of 7,980 years within which no day was in exactly the same position according to three parallel systems of measurement: the solar cycle of 19 years, the lunar cycle of 28 years, and the Roman civil cycle (Indiction) of 15 years. Scaliger had managed to bridge the gap between recorded history and the Old Testament, and thereby to calculate the day of Creation as Sunday, 25 October 3950 BC. Ussher, however, pointed out that Scaliger had missed the crucial fact that Terah was twice married and that Abraham's mother was his *second* wife. Furthermore, even assuming that the sun readjusted itself after standing still for Joshua and moving backwards for Hezekiah, recalculating the entire calendar pushed the date of Creation back to 4004 BC: Sunday, 23 October, to be precise. Scaliger, Ussher complained to his friend John Selden, 'intending higher matters, did not heed so much his ordinary arithmetic.'[67]

The systems of Ussher and Scaliger were marvels of exactitude which enabled the Christian world to assimilate the histories of the gentile nations to the biblical plan, and to provide a comforting framework within which to accommodate all known historical facts. Ussher pinpointed not only the Creation, but all other key dates, such as the Flood (2349 BC) and the Exodus (1492 BC). Edward Gibbon (1737–94) described the effect that the study of chronology had on his schoolboy mind:

> from Strauchius I imbibed the elements of chronology: the tables of Helvicus and Anderson, the annals of Usher and Prideaux distinguished the connection of events, and I engraved the multitude of names and dates in a clear and indelible series. But in the discussion of the first ages I overleaped the bounds of modesty and use. In my childish balance I presumed to weigh the systems of Scaliger and Petavius, of Marsham and Newton, which I could seldom study in the originals; the dynasties of Assyria and Egypt were my top and cricket-ball; and my sleep has been disturbed by the difficulty of reconciling the Septuagint with the Hebrew computation.[68]

Even more recently, Professor Hugh Trevor-Roper described the pleasure that as a boy he had derived from the labours of Archbishop Ussher:

When I was a child I was taken regularly, on Sundays, to our local parish church, from whose formal proceedings I fear my attention was inclined to wander. Happily, it found a rival attraction still within the holy circle of orthodoxy. The prayer books supplied in the pews contained a series of tables which, I now realize, came ultimately from the Archbishop: tables of fascinating complexity which enabled the reader to work out, via the Epact and the Golden Year, the date of Easter in any year, past or future. I never discovered what the Epact and the Golden Year were, but many a mechanical litany, many a dull sermon, formed a comfortable continuo while I conjured with these fascinating tables, checking that they worked and applying them to random years in the past and the future.[69]

Both Gibbon in the eighteenth century and Dacre two hundred years later give us a sense of the comforting quality of chronology whose claims brought strength to the faith of the devout Christian and fascinated even the doubting near-non-believer. The problem, however, with an exact science is that one needs to be exact: even the differences between Scaliger and Ussher, so much in agreement about the generalities, would in the long run undermine the whole. As Paul Hazard pointed out long ago, when the chronologists finished their task, and concluded their hair-splitting arguments, 'they will have sown more seeds of unrest in quiet minds, and done more to undermine faith in history, than all your open scoffers and anti-religious fanatics ever succeeded in doing.'[70] Paradoxically, the reason for this was the very fact that they were believers rather than sceptics.

Newton agreed with his predecessors that the main challenge of chronology was to find a way of organizing world events using Hebrew history as the base. Yet to this difficult task he added the ambitious project of incorporating the events recorded by the Egyptians, Assyrians, Babylonians, Persians, Greeks, and Romans, and possibly the Chinese, whose detailed chronology posed an especially difficult quandary. The problem, he lamented, was that 'All Nations, before they began to keep exact accounts of Time, have been prone to raise their Antiquities; and this humour has been promoted, by the Contentions between Nations about their Originals.'[71] His innovation was to use astronomical proofs in order to set a number of key dates as axes around which the entire chronology could revolve. As long as he could find a reliable ancient record of the position of the sun at the time of the equinox relative to the fixed stars, such as in his favourite Pliny, Newton knew that he could extrapolate backwards from their present astronomical position to arrive at the desired date, since the 'Equinox goes back fifty seconds in one year, and one degree in seventy and two years'. Others had tried to find the position of heavenly bodies at certain key points in history. The Polish astronomer Hevelius set the exact location of the sun over Eden at Creation, and

Newton's sometime protégé William Whiston (1667–1752) did his best to date the comet that in his view had caused the Flood. Following this astronomical method, Newton was able to calculate the date of the Argonautic expedition as 43 or 44 years after the death of Solomon, i.e. *c.* 936 BC. As for the period when Hesiod lived, Newton noted that

> Hesiod tells us that sixty days after the winter Solstice the Star *Arcturus* rose just at Sunset: and thence it follows that *Hesiod* flourished about an hundred years after the death of *Solomon*, or in the Generation or Age next after the *Trojan* war, as *Hesiod* himself declares.

The variation of the equinox, quite simply, was the key to chronology.[72]

Another of Newton's innovations was to calculate the average length of a king's reign in ancient times. 'The *Egyptians* reckoned the Reigns of Kings equipollent to Generations of men,' Newton noted, 'and three Generations to an hundred years'. As a result, 'so did the *Greeks* and *Latines*: and accordingly they have made their Kings Reign one with another thirty and three years a-piece'. Newton studied the records of the Jews, the Persians, the Hellenistic kings, and those of England and France and came up with a more representative figure of 18–20 years per monarch. Indeed, Newton concluded, in 'the later Ages, since Chronology hath been exact, there is scarce an instance to be found of ten Kings Reigning any where in continual Succession above 260 years'. In brief, 'Let the reckoning be reduced to the course of nature, by putting the Reigns of Kings one with another, at about eighteen or twenty years a-piece'. The net result was that the existing chronologies needed to be shortened by almost half. Using this method, and counting the reigns of mythological figures as real historical men who had been raised to divine status, Newton arrived at the same date for the Argonauts that he had calculated astronomically. What further proof could be desired? Biblical history could now be comfortably assimilated into the shortened ancient record.[73]

Newton's insistence on seeing the mythical gods as kings who had become divine in popular history was based on a method which had already acquired a kind of acceptance. It is usually called 'euhemerism', in memory of the philosopher Euhemerus who lived in the fourth century BC, and derives from the idea of explaining myth historically and, by extension, understanding religious beliefs or phenomena in non-supernatural terms. Since classical and biblical archaeology were not yet born, there was little material evidence for Newton to work with apart from literary sources. Mythology became history, and could be dealt with in this fashion. Not only that, but virtually every symbolic element in ancient culture could be euhemeristically explained. Newton even argued that hieroglyphs were originally an ordinary alphabet. Whereas others looked for complicated spiritual meaning in the cultural artefacts of ancient cultures, Newton tried to reduce everything to political history, with the aim of comparing these civilizations with that of the Israelites as recorded in the Bible.

The point of all this frenetic chronological activity was to prove the supreme antiquity of the Hebrews and their civilization. In this, of course, Newton had numerous allies. Most prominent among them was Theophilus Gale (1628–78), whose massive work on *The Court of the Gentiles* proved with multi-volume erudition that all of philosophy began with the Jews, whose religion is the only authentic one in the ancient world.[74] One problem was that even the Bible seems to suggest that the Egyptian and Assyrian royal houses predated the establishment of an Israelite kingship. Newton's response was to argue that there was a significant difference in kind: the Israelites had the first properly developed monarchy, while their neighbours ruled over petty little tribal groups which did not deserve the appellation of kingdom. In any case, the battle between the Israelites and the Egyptians for antiquity was for Newton merely the preliminary skirmish before the great fight between the Jews and the Greeks, between Moses and Homer. The commonly accepted view since the Renaissance was that it was to the Greeks that Western civilization owed its origins, and Newton took pains to restore the Hebrews to their rightful place.

We can get a clearer idea of Newton's views on this subject by looking for a moment at his manuscript, 'Theologiae gentilis origines philosophicae' (The Philosophical Origins of Gentile Theology).[75] Apart from his supreme confidence in pronouncing on prehistoric events for which there is hardly any record, this document provides an insight into Newton's genuine views on the earliest history and influence of the biblical text. It is perhaps for this reason that it remained hidden for nearly three centuries after he wrote it, until it turned up in his unpublished papers.

Newton argued that ancient peoples worshipped the same twelve gods under different names, with the gods being originally Noah and his sons and grandchildren. Why twelve gods exactly? Because the number twelve reflected the seven planets, the four elements, and the single quintessence, that is, the most prominent objects that nature presents to the primitive mind. In earliest times, people identified their most eminent ancestors with these supremely important icons. As this religion of Noah was transmitted to other nations farther away from the original time and place of the Flood, this mode of metaphysical thought was adapted to local conditions. Each nation would identify its own kings and heroes according to the same pattern. This is why one finds similarities among the mythologies of different peoples. Noah evolved into Saturn or Janus, but all of these characters are united in having three sons. Ham represented the original model of the supreme God, the divine who is depicted as a mature man in all civilizations. He might be called Zeus or Jupiter or Hammon, but the connection is the same. Interestingly,

Ham, who was so reviled by both Jewish and Christian theology, becomes a central figure for Newton's scheme. All peoples have a goddess who is a beautiful woman, Newton notes. This was originally Ham's daughter, and later became Aphrodite, Venus, or Astarte, among others. When one nation colonized another, as when Egypt or Phoenicia colonized Greece, the theology of the mother state was simply imported and adapted to local conditions.

The general point Newton was making here was that while at first glance the myths and religions of the world seem to present a chaos of conflicting views, in fact they have an underlying unity based on true biblical history as recounted in Genesis. Furthermore, as the beginnings of mythology were to be found in a primitive interpretation of the physical world, it might be said that gentile theology began with the study of natural philosophy.

Just as the mythological conceptions began with Noah and his family, so did the earliest religion. In his *Irenicum*, Newton proclaimed that 'All nations were originally of one religion & this religion consisted in the Precepts of the sons of Noah', that is, love of God and love of neighbour, 'the Moral law of all nations'. Noah was the key figure of Jewish history no less than of the world: Abraham's role was correspondingly reduced, as the man who simply revitalized an old principle, further strengthened by Isaac and Jacob. Moses taught the same thing to the Israelites, after they had forgotten Noah's precepts.

Basing himself on Genesis and supplementing the biblical text with other ancient sources, Newton described how Noachide religion spread. The Egyptians were the descendants of Ham. Noah's son Cush received the East, and two centuries after the Flood went beyond Arabia and conquered the family of Shem, establishing an empire in Babylon. It was Cush's son Nimrod who led an expedition from Babylon, establishing Nineveh and Assyria. No wonder, then, that the same themes should appear.

Despite these promising beginnings, Newton explains, Noachide religion was not destined to prevail outside the Jewish world. The Egyptians began the decline by creating false gods from their ancestors, and by developing sidereal theology. This was gentile theology, the corruption of true religion. A staunch anti-Trinitarian, Newton in this way was also able to explain the growth of that particular aberration. The promotion of Jesus Christ as a god was no different to what the Egyptians had done in worshipping dead men as divinities. Jesus was merely the latest prophet who, like Abraham and Moses, sought to recall the Jews to the original worship of Noah, not to form a totally new religion. Newton blamed the Egyptian Athanasius (293?–373) for corrupting Christianity by introducing the concept of Jesus's divinity. The coming of Jesus was therefore no longer the fulcrum of Christian history but merely the latest manifestation of a pattern in Jewish history which had begun with Abraham. Christianity, therefore, was hardly different from Judaism, in that it was simply the religion of Noah, which gave praise to God and His Creation. The main distinction between Judaism and Christianity was that to the first two precepts of Noah, Christianity adds a third one: that we should believe that Jesus is the Christ foretold in prophecy. Nothing is to be found here about the redemption of mankind by a man who was also a god. That was too similar to corrupt gentile and Egyptian theology to be true.

Ever on the lookout for divine teaching, Newton also developed a keen interest in the exact form of the Temple of Solomon. 'The Temple of *Solomon* being destroyed by the *Babylonians*, it may not be amiss here to give a description of that edifice', he explained in his *Chronology*.[76] Newton was taken with the idea that the Temple was a building that had God as its architect, and that there were no doubt divine secrets contained in its very proportions and structure. He spent a good deal of time trying to determine the exact length of a cubit.[77] Newton knew that Moses had restored the original Noachide religion, and had also given to the Israelites the basic form of the tabernacle which would later be recreated by Solomon. Moses installed a perpetual flame in the tabernacle, which itself served as a model of nature, with the fire representing the sun in a heliocentric universe:

> Now the rationale of this institution was that the God of Nature should be worshipped in a temple which imitates nature, in a temple which is, as it were, a reflection of God. Everyone agrees that a Sanctum with a fire in the middle was an emblem of the system of the world.[78]

When Solomon built his Temple according to the instructions given by God and recorded in the Book of Ezekiel, he also placed a fire in the centre, surrounded by seven lamps representing the seven planets. We were to understand by this that the heavens themselves were God's temple, no less than the building erected by Solomon. When false religion came to dominate the Egyptians, it was similarly reflected in their misunderstanding of nature. The fire in the centre was conceived, not as the sun, but as some fire in the centre of the earth. The earth was placed in the centre of the planets. It was not by accident that Ptolemy was an Egyptian.

VII

Newton's religion, as we have seen, was fundamentally biblical in nature and inspiration. It is not surprising, then, that he should have strong opinions about the text of the Bible itself. These views were most strikingly expressed in two 'letters' to John Locke, one discussing 1 John v. 7 (the Trinitarian proof text), and the other 1 Timothy iii. 16. In his covering letter, dated 14 November 1690, Newton instructed Locke that it at present you get only what concerns the first done into French, that of the other may stay till we see what successe the first will have. I have no entire copy besides that I send you, and therefore would not have it lost, because I may perhaps after it has gone abroad long enough in French put it forth in English.[79]

Locke had a copy made of these letters, and sent the manuscript to Jean Le Clerc (1657–1736), the reformed theologian who became professor of Philosophy at the Arminian Remonstrants' Seminary at Amsterdam. Le Clerc read the text and agreed to translate it into either Latin or French. 'Je croi pourtant', Le Clerc noted, 'qu'il pourroit être meilleur, si l'Auteur avoit lu avec soin ce que M. Simon a dit du sujet, dont il parle, dans la Critique du N.T.'[80] Newton had not known that Locke sent his 'letters' to Le Clerc, but did not seem to mind, and followed the theologian's advice to read Richard Simon's *Histoire critique du texte du Nouveau Testament*, published at Rotterdam only in 1689. Newton did make some changes in his text, which Locke passed on to Le Clerc, who intended to incorporate them in the Latin translation.[81]

Newton, however, got cold feet, and declined on this occasion, as on so many others, to expose his heterodoxy to public display. On 26 January 1692, he wrote to Locke asking for his manuscript back.[82] A few weeks later, Newton rather worriedly wrote again, noting that

I was of opinion my papers had lain still and am sorry to heare there is news about them. Let me entreat you to stop their translation and impression as soon as you can for I designe to suppress them. If your friend hath been at any pains and charge I will repay it and gratify him.[83]

Le Clerc complied with Newton's wish, and deposited the manuscript in the Remonstrants' Library, where it lay undisturbed until long after Newton's death.[84]

Inevitably, the manuscript was eventually published. The first edition appeared under the misleading title, *Two Letters of Sir Isaac Newton to Mr. Le Clerc*, at London in 1754.[85] A better copy was published from the original manuscript in 1785.[86] The original letter is the one which bears study, being among the New College manuscripts deposited at the Bodleian Library.[87]

Newton begins his discussion of the controversial Trinitarian proof text in I John v. 7 by noting:

But whilst we exclaim against the pious frauds of ye Roman Church, & make it a part of our religion to detect & renounce all things of that kind: we must acknowledge it a greater crime in us to favour such practises, then in the Papists we so much blame on that account. For they act according to their religion but we contrary to our's. In the eastern nations, & for a long time in the western the faith subsisted without this text & it is rather a danger to religion then an advantage to make it now lean upon a bruised reed. There cannot be better service done to the truth then to purge it of things spurious: & therefore knowing your prudence & calmnesse of temper, I am confident I shal not offend you by telling you my mind plainly: especially since 'tis no article of faith, no point of discipline, nothing but a criticism concerning a text of scripture wch I am going to write about.

Newton then begins a long discussion of the history of the text itself, the 'ancient Interpreters wch I cite as witnesses' being 'chiefly the Authors of the ancient Vulgar Latin of the Syriac & of the Ethiopic versions', based on information from Brian Walton's Polyglot Bible and other sources, not neglecting the Egyptian Arabic, the Armenian, and the Slavonic Bible.

The upshot of this discussion was to prove that 'So then the testimony of the three in heaven, wch in the times of those controversies would have been in every bodies mouth had it been in their books, was wholy unknown to the Churches of those ages.' Newton is particularly sarcastic about the claim that the early records had been censored of the Trinitarian text during the Arian controversy:

> Yes truly those Arians were crafty Knaves that could conspire so cunningly & slyly all the world over at once (as at the word of Mithridates) in the latter end of the reign of the Emperor Constantius to get all men's books into their hands & correct them without being perceived: Ay & Conjurers too, to do it without leaving any blot or chasm in the books, whereby the knavery might be suspected & discovered; & to wipe even the memory of it out of all men's brains, so that neither Athanasius nor any body else could afterwards remember that they had even seen it in their books before, & out of their own too so y^t when they turned to the consubstantial faith, as they generally did in the West soon after the death of Constantius, they could remember no more of it then any body else.

Newton's main grievance was against 'they that wthout proof accuse hereticks of corrupting books, & upon that pretense correct them at their pleasure without the authority of ancient manuscripts'.

Newton spent a great deal of time discussing the contribution of Erasmus to the misunderstanding of the proof text for the Trinity, without neglecting the role of Ximenes's Polyglot Bible in ratifying the mistake. Erasmus, it will be recalled, 'omitted it in his two first editions & inserted it unwillingly against the authority of his manuscripts in his three last', having promised to include the text if it could be found in a single manuscript.

> Hence notice was sent to Erasmus out of England that it was in a manuscript there; & thereupon to avoyd their calumnies (as he saith) he printed

it in his following editions notwithstanding that he suspected that manuscript to be a new one corrected by the latine. But since upon enquiry I cannot learn that they in England ever heard of any such manuscript but from Erasmus, & since he was only told of such a manuscript in the time of the controversy between him & Lee & never saw it himself: I cannot forbear to suspect that it was nothing but a trick put upon him by some of the Popish Clergy.

In brief, Newton challenged, 'Let those who have such a manuscript at length tell us where it is.' Actually, the manuscript turned up in Dublin in the mid-eighteenth century, but Newton was correct that the Codex Britannicus or Montfortianus was 'new', a sixteenth-century forgery without any authority.[88]

Newton's letter exhibits an extraordinary amount of thought and research into one of the most central problems of biblical research and Christian theology. Apart from his history and religious understanding, what is remarkable is the forthright manner of his expression, which seems so out of character with his politically cautious nature. Newton himself felt the change in tone, and concluded his letter to Locke by noting that

> You see what freedome I have used in this discourse & I hope you will interpret it candidly. For if ye ancient Churches in debating & deciding the great mysteries of religion, knew nothing of these two texts: I understand not why we should be so fond of them now the debates are over. And whilst it's ye character of an honest man to be pleased, & of a man of interest to be troubled at the detection of frauds, & both to run into those passions when the detection is made plainest: I hope this letter will to one of your integrity prove so much the more acceptable, as it makes a further discovery then you have hitherto met wth in Commentators.

In this, at least, Newton thought that he had gone beyond the work of Richard Simon, whose writings he had been advised to study.

Although he established that the text of Scripture is defective, not only because of the passage of time, but because various special interest groups over the centuries had deliberately falsified the original meaning, Newton still had no doubt that the prophetic portions of the Bible completely reflected the divine intention, and that it was here that the student of God's will should direct his gaze. Generally speaking, Newton's attitude to the prophecies was the exact opposite of the esoteric approach to texts which had been so popular during the Renaissance and which would remain an essential tool in biblical interpretation. Whereas the esoteric tradition saw mystical truths in even the most commonplace statements in the Bible, Newton's aim was to produce realistic interpretations of every supernatural scriptural passage.

Newton accepted that the Bible was written in a secret language, so that the text could be seen to be composed of 'hieroglyphs'. But these 'hieroglyphs' could be understood, the code could be cracked, by anyone who took the trouble to learn the key. As Newton himself put it,

> He that would understand a book written in a strange language must first learn ye language & if he would understand it well must learn the language perfectly. Such a language was that wherein the Prophets wrote, & the want of sufficient skill in that language is the main reason why they are so little understood . . . they all wrote in one & the same mystical language, as well known without doubt to ye sons of ye Prophets as ye Hieroglypic language of ye Egyptians to their Priests, and this language, as far as I can find, was as certain & definite in its signification as is the vulgar language of any nation whatsoever.[89]

Newton spelled out the rules for the interpretation of prophecy. 'I have thought my self bound to communicate it for the benefit of others,' he explained, 'remembring the judgment of him who hid his talent in a napkin.' This was a matter of great moment, since 'if God was so angry with the Jews for not searching more diligently into the Prophecies which he had given them to know Christ by: why should we think he will excuse us for not searching into the Prophecies which he hath given to know Antichrist by?' Newton set himself three tasks. The first was to 'lay down certain general Rules in Interpretation' so as to identify the 'genuine' one. His second task was to 'prepare the Reader also for understanding the Prophetique language'. The point of this was to make certain that 'the Language of the Prophets will become certain and the liberty of wresting it to private imaginations be cut of.' His final goal was to compare the different parts of the Apocalypse and reduce its message into 'Propositions'.

Newton follows these general remarks with fifteen 'Rules for interpreting the words and language in Scripture', set out in almost mathematical form. A number of general points emerge from his analysis. The first almost axiomatic principle is that the reader must 'assigne but one meaning to one place of scripture, unles it be by way of conjecture.' In other words, the images of the Bible are so consistent that it is impossible for them to have more than one meaning. In this they are perhaps even less flexible than words in a language. 'Thus', Newton explains,

> if any man interpret a Beast to signify some great vice, this is to be rejected as his private imagination becaus acording to the stile and tenour of the Apocalyps and of all other Prophetique scriptures a Beast signifies a body politique and sometimes a single person which heads that body, and there is no ground in scripture for any other interpretation.

The important thing is to 'keep as close as may be to the same sense of words, especially in the same vision'. That being said, one should 'chose those interpretations which are most according to the litterall meaning of the scriptures unles where the tenour and circumstances of the place plainly require an Allegory.' There is no necessity to see figurative language in each and every place in the Bible. So, for example,

> if they describe the overthrow of nations by a tempest of Hail, thunder, lightning and shaking of the world, the usuall signification of this figure is to be esteemed the proper and direct sense of the place as much as if it had been the litterall meaning, this being a language as common amongst them as any national language is amongst the people of that nation.

This last point is crucial: while Newton firmly believed that the Bible was built on allegory, with each figure having one set meaning which rendered its interpretation similar to learning the vocabulary of a new language, he also warned against the over-utilization of his method:

> He that without better grounds then his private opinion or the opinion of any human authority whatsoever shall turn scripture from the plain meaning to an Allegory or to any other less naturall sense declares thereby that he reposes more trust in his own imaginations or in that human authority then in the Scripture. And therefore the opinion of such men how numerous soever they be, is not to be regarded. Hence is it and not from any reall uncertainty in the Scripture that Commentators have so distorted it; And this hath been the door through which all Heresies have crept in and turned out the ancient faith.

Newton followed these general guidelines with more specific 'Rules for methodising the Apocalyps'. He insisted that one ought to 'prefer those interpretations which, caeteris paribus, are of the most considerable things. For it was Gods designe in these prophesies to typefy and describe not trifles but the most considerable things in the world during the time, time of the Prophecies.' For this reason, Newton thought that when we see references to the whore of Babylon or the woman clothed with the sun, we should prefer an interpretation which relates these figures not to individuals but to 'Kingdoms Churches and other great bodies of men', except when 'perhaps in any case the single person propounded might be of more note and moment then the whole body of men he stands in competition with, or some other material circumstance might make more for a single person then a multitude.' One should also take into account that the Apocalypse was meant to be a continuous narrative 'without any breach or interfering'.

Newton was very concerned that the interpretation of the Apocalypse should not become overly clever: 'Truth is ever to be found in simplicity, and not in the multiplicity and confusion of things.' This, of course, was Newton's belief not only in biblical interpretation, but in his search for general laws of physics which would be applicable not only in the mundane world, but throughout the known universe:

> It is the perfection of God's works that they are all done with the greatest simplicity. He is the God of order and not of confusion. And therefore as they that would understand the frame of the world must indeavour to reduce their knowledg to all possible simplicity, so it must be in seeking to understand these visions. And they that shall do otherwise do not onely make sure never to understand them, but derogate from the perfection of the prophecy; and make it suspicious also that their designe is not to understand it but to shuffle it of and confound the understandings of men by making it intricate and confused.

The interpretation of the Apocalypse was in a sense similar to the construction of a mechanical device. One should 'chose those constructions which without straining reduce contemporary visions to the greatest harmony of their parts.' The key is to avoid 'straining':

> For as of an Engin made by an excellent Artificer a man readily beleives that the parts are right set together when he sees them joyn truly with one another notwithstanding that they may be strained into another posture; and as a man acquiesces in the meaning of an Author how intricate so ever when he sees the words construed or set in order according to the laws of Grammar, notwithstanding that there may be a possibility of foreceing the words to some other harsher construction: so a man ought with equal reason to acquiesce in that construction of these Prophecies when he sees their parts set in order according to their suitableness and the characters imprinted in them for that purpose.

But the analogy with machinery should not be carried too far:

> Tis true that an Artificer may make an Engin capable of being with equal congruity set together more ways then one, and that a sentence may be ambiguous: but this Objection can have no place in the Apocalyps, becaus God who knew how to frame it without ambiguity intended it for a rule of faith.

VIII

A good deal of what Newton was saying about the Bible and its role as a model for scientific research was said by others, most notably Henry More and Robert Boyle. Newton's contribution was to submit biblical information to an uncompromising and rigid sense of law and order, with concomitant notions of consistency and uniformity. This principle of order was in itself based on the Bible, for was not God's very first recorded act the imposition of order upon chaos in accordance with His divine will?

Michel Foucault, in his search for the origins of the modern conception of the prison, argues that Descartes's analogy of the universe, and man within it, functioning like a vast machine, had the effect of producing what he calls 'disciplines'. These were general formulas which allowed for uninterrupted and constant coercion of individuals, such as one finds in the monastery, the workshop, and the army. He sees this as the moment when the art of the human body was born, producing 'docile bodies', and a new micro-physics of power based on 'small acts of cunning'. Indeed, Foucault tells us, 'Discipline is a political anatomy of detail', and notes that detail, which had long been a category of theology and asceticism, took on a wider role since every detail was important to God, Who had everything in His purview:

> A meticulous observation of detail, and at the same time a political aware-
> ness of these small things, for the control and use of men, emerge through
> the classical age bearing with them a whole set of techniques, a whole
> corpus of methods and knowledge, descriptions, plans and data. And from
> such trifles, no doubt, the man of modern humanism was born.[90]

Nowhere is this attention to detail more apparent than in the works of Isaac Newton. Both in his scientific and his biblical research, it was the combination of meticulous observation and the search for general laws which helped him bring order to what appeared to be a chaos of facts and data. Newton's comparison between the method of biblical prophecy and machinery also brings us back rather nicely to the world-image of Descartes and his followers. It also helps us understand why Newton was such an admirer of Joseph Mede (1586–1668) and his highly developed exegetical system of biblical 'synchronisms' which was so popular during the period of the English Civil War. Mede gave Newton a scientific method which generated intense study of the biblical text designed to winkle out God's hidden message. Mede was Newton's Newton in biblical scholarship: the man who had discovered the hidden laws of the Book of Scripture, just as Newton sought to perform the same service for the other Book.

CHAPTER 4

Streamlined Scriptures: The Demystification of the Bible

'If we were to look for a general characterization of the age of the Enlightenment,' wrote Ernst Cassirer in his classic study of that period, 'the traditional answer would be that its fundamental feature is obviously a critical and skeptical attitude toward religion.'[1] Voltaire (1694–1778) claimed that religion began when the first rogue met the first fool, and in a letter to Frederick William, prince of Prussia, coined his famous maxim that 'Si Dieu n'existait pas, il faudrait l'inventer.'[2] Diderot (1713–84) the Encyclopaedist dreamed of the day when religion and tyranny would perish together as 'the last king is strangled with the entrails of the last priest'. This intellectual movement symbolized by Voltaire and Diderot is described in European languages through the use of a metaphor of light: siècle des lumières . . . die Aufklärung . . . illuminismo . . . la Ilustración . . . Enlightenment. Only at the beginning of the eighteenth century were the centuries of darkness finally dispelled and the blinding power of priestcraft broken.

Certainly this view of the Enlightenment period has a strong basis in fact, and like most stereotypes it contains a very hard kernel of truth. The catchword of the period was 'Reason', by which was meant many different things. Some used the term to signify the demonstration of the existence and attributes of God by the use of mathematically inclined proofs. Others saw the function of reason in studying the miracles of the New Testament. Reason might also imply the formulation of Christian doctrine on the basis of eternal moral principles. But whichever understanding of reason was emphasized, all of its protagonists were united in the belief that the human intellect was charged with studying and examining the rational elements of Christian belief in an effort to determine which parts of that faith could be shown to be true. In any such discussion, the Bible would inevitably play a central part.

Yet not all students of religion during this period were as unshakeably hostile to organized religion as Voltaire and Diderot. Reason might also be a tool towards a deepened and more accurate religious faith, despite its attendant dangers. Philosophical perceptions had moved much farther ahead since the days of Descartes (1596–1650), who was able to construct the entire universe on the confident basis of his own reasonings. Descartes refused to make any initial metaphysical assumptions and began with his own self-consciousness: 'Cogito, ergo sum', I think, therefore I am. Having posited himself as an existing, thinking entity, Descartes then turned to those thoughts which must be seen as ideas innate in the mind. In experience, just as in mathematics, he reasoned, whatever is clearly and distinctly conceived must be true. The triangle, for example, has an independently real nature which is grasped the moment the concept of the triangle is understood: its reality needs no further demonstration than its very definition. On this basis, Descartes asserted that the first clear and distinct idea which a thinking entity finds outside itself is the idea of God, which like the triangle is inexplicable unless we concede that He exists. 'Clearly, the idea of God, that is, the idea of a supremely perfect being, is one I discover to be no less within me than the idea of any figure or number', he explained. Once we accept the idea of God as a perfect being, all-powerful, all-knowing, and eternal, then our other ideas fall into place under His goodness.[3]

Descartes's entire outlook was based on the optimistic premiss that a thinking individual can recreate the entire philosophical universe from his armchair. All of the relevant facts lie there before us, if only we have eyes to see. This confident assessment of the transparent and fully revealed physical universe gradually became eroded in the later seventeenth century as the scientific revolution opened up worlds within worlds unknown and unsuspected by medieval man. New discoveries were being made all of the time with the use of the microscope and the telescope alone, and it was becoming clear that experimentation would be an essential complement to the independent cogitation of a thinking entity.

There is no doubt that the decline of Cartesianism led to a loss of certainty, as philosophers began to doubt that they would ever reach an understanding of the final causes of the universe. Knowledge was reduced to the delineation of nature's laws, which were no more than an assertion of what had happened in the past and was likely to occur in the future. The supernatural and the metaphysical were barely subjects for contemplation in such a restricted philosophical world, since so little could unerringly be said about the subjects that really mattered. Yet despite these frequently expressed views in the generations after Descartes, all was not lost, and secularization was still very far away.

I

The first important group of scholars who tried to incorporate Reason into religious understanding in the post-Cartesian world was the Latitudinarians.

The term itself is often the subject of some confusion, but within this group one would have to include such figures as Edward Stillingfleet (1635–99), bishop of Worcester; John Tillotson (1630–94), archbishop of Canterbury; Thomas Tenison (1636–1715), Tillotson's successor; Simon Patrick (1626–1707), bishop of Ely; and William Lloyd (1627–1717), bishop of Worcester and elsewhere. The Latitudinarians were accused of many things: of being too reasonable, too permissive, and too Pelagian in their doctrine of grace and salvation. But the most important theological fact about them is that they were strictly orthodox, and conformed to the Thirty-Nine Articles of the Anglican Church. They were also great supporters of the Glorious Revolution, and were rewarded handsomely for their trouble by William III, who by 1702 had managed to appoint 21 of the 26 bishops: almost all were Latitudinarian in outlook and Whig in politics, unlike the majority of the clergy, which was predominantly High Church Tory.[4]

The main theological thrust of the Latitudinarian argument was that reason is an essential component of religious thought, not as a primary tool of research, but rather as a means for confirming the truth of revelation. The Latitudinarians were especially concerned by Roman Catholic apologetics, especially the system invented by the Jesuit François Veron (1575–1625), elegantly entitled the 'machine de guerre de nouvelle intention'. This scheme, derived from the works of Montaigne, consisted of a two-pronged attack: a sceptical 'Pyrrhonist' demolition of the Bible as a sufficient and adequate basis for Christian belief; and the assertion of Roman Catholicism on the principle of fideism, that is, the notion that since human intellect is inherently limited, only blind faith will suffice. Montaigne himself had been famous for his Pyrrhonism in philosophy as opposed to his fideism in religion. In the *machine de guerre*, this fideism was expressed as a reliance on the infallible authority and tradition enshrined in the Roman Catholic Church. The Latitudinarians rightly saw this system as a direct attack on the foundations of Protestantism, especially the claim that the Bible could not be used as a rule of faith, not only because it was a defective document as shown by modern biblical critics, but also because logically it required something outside itself to certify its truth. This outside verification, of course, could only be the Roman Catholic Church.[5]

A good example of this *machine de guerre* at work in England is provided in the work of John Sergeant (1622–1707). His argument was that even if the Latitudinarians were correct in their assumption that reason and the Bible could be joint rules of faith, the sheer number of biblical manuscripts which has survived, not to mention the problems of translation and interpretation, render this excessive devotion to human powers of comprehension unreasonable.[6]

In many ways, Sergeant was ahead of his time, but even when the work of Richard Simon appeared, and was translated into English four years later in 1682, the Latitudinarians ignored this challenge to their theology, which ultimately was biblically based, and heavily dependent on the reality of miracles. The Latitudinarians defined 'faith' much as they understood 'reason', with the sole difference being that the object of faith was divine rather than natural truth. Faith, according to Tillotson, was composed of three parts. The first was what he called 'persuasion of natural religion', which in turn had three components: (1) the existence of God with the providential attributes of wisdom, goodness, and power; (2) the immortality of the soul; and (3) the future state of rewards and punishments. Natural religion was demonstrated by a combination of the cosmological proof – that only God could have created such an orderly universe – and the notion of the *consensus omnium*, the claim that belief in God is a universal fact throughout the world at all times. This second point would remain part of the Latitudinarian arsenal even after men like Locke used travel accounts to erode belief in the universality of religion.

The second aspect of faith, according to Tillotson, is the 'persuasion of things supernatural, and revealed'. Since inspiration has now ceased, Tillotson was in large measure referring to the evidence of Scripture, God's last words revealed to man. This aspect was related to the third, 'persuasion of the supernatural revelation contained in the Scriptures', that is, belief not in the things revealed, but in the very fact that God was behind it all. This came down to an acceptance of miracles, which made Christian doctrine as certain as anything could be in this world. As Tillotson explained,

> But yet miracles are the principal external proof and confirmation of the divinity of a doctrine. I told you before, that some doctrines are so absurd, that a miracle is not a sufficient proof of them: but if a doctrine be such as is nowise unworthy of God, nor contrary to those notions which we have of him, miracles are the highest testimony that can be given to it, and have always been owned by mankind for an evidence of inspiration.

These scriptural miracles were witnessed by very many and could not be denied, unlike modern frauds which by definition could not be true once revelation was transmitted to mankind through the text of the Bible.[7]

The entire Latitudinarian construct, then, was based on divine revelation, which was demonstrated by the miracles of the New Testament. In their view, a reasonable man would recognize that the probability of the truth of Christianity was at least as great as any other proposition in the natural world, including historical events. These were true beyond any reasonable doubt and could be accepted as such. At no time, however, could revelation contradict reason, which is why the Latitudinarians rejected transubstantiation, for example. Since the Bible was the ultimate source of authority in religion, the Latitudinarians also argued that the Scriptures were completely plain and without the need for complex interpretation. God would not hide His revelation beneath layers of deception; if He exists, then what is written in the Bible must be true.

Far from reason and faith being contradictory or even completely distinct concepts, the Latitudinarians insisted that they were almost the same, differing only in the objects of inquiry. Reason involved coming to accept various types of evidence and the conclusions which can be drawn from it regarding the things of this world, including the principles of natural religion. Faith uses exactly the same process, but its object is the content and meaning of the divine revelation contained in the Bible. Faith, Tillotson wrote,

> is an act of the understanding, and does necessarily suppose some knowledge and apprehension of what we believe. To all acts of religion there is necessarily required some act of the understanding; so that, without knowledge, there can be no devotion in the service of God, no obedience to his laws. Religion begins in the understanding, and from thence descends upon the heart and life.

The source of this understanding, Tillotson continues, is the Bible:

> And as knowledge in general is necessary to religion, so more particularly the knowledge of the holy scriptures is necessary to our eternal salvation: because these are the great and standing revelation of God to mankind; wherein the nature of God, and his will concerning our duty, and the terms and conditions of our eternal happiness in another world, are fully and plainly declared to us.

The attainment of faith is therefore a completely rational process, as the believer is persuaded of the truth of biblical divine revelation. This did not require any divine intervention, for which the Latitudinarians were often accused of Pelagianism. They were certainly Arminians and rejected any sort of Calvinist predestination. The certainty which was achieved through faith was something less than mathematical certainty, without question, but was at least as firm as any aspect of certainty concerning the things of this world. Only an unreasonable man would demand more.[8]

Even in the seventeenth century it was recognized that not all of the elements in the Latitudinarian creed were original. There were many echoes of the Great Tew circle, especially the works of William Chillingworth (1602–44), who himself had written against the *machine de guerre*. Chillingworth had also argued that faith provided a weaker kind of certainty than mathematics, based as it was on the Bible and its miracles. This was, he wrote, 'Not so certain, I grant, as that which wee can demonstrate: But certain enough, morally certain, as certain as the nature of the thing will beare. So certain we may be, and God requires no more.' Faith in the Bible was a bit like Pascal's wager.

Indeed, it has been argued that the legal doctrine of 'truth beyond a reason-able doubt' owes its origins in the common law directly to the writings of the Latitudinarians. The end result, Chillingworth claimed, was that

> if men did really and sincerely submit their judgements to Scripture, and that only, and would require no more of any man but to doe so, it were impossible but that all controversies, touching things necessary and very profitable should be ended: and if others were continued or increased, it were no matter.

When choosing his religion, all that was needed was to follow a simple method: 'the Rule whereby he is to guide his choyce, if he be a naturall man, is Reason, if he be already a Christian, Scripture, which we say is the Rule to judge controversies by.' The first principle of Protestantism, Chillingworth affirmed, was that 'the Scripture is the word of God'. Accept that, and every-thing else falls into place.[9]

The problem, of course, with such a minimalist doctrine based on princi-ples confirmed by reason is that what seems reasonable to one person may seem unjustified to another, once the method is applied to specific cases. By the end of the seventeenth century, the Latitudinarians were embroiled in the question of the Trinity, which not only was difficult to square with reason, but was based on very weak scriptural foundations. Some Latitudinarians, such as Samuel Clarke and William Whiston, became deeply enmeshed in the Trinitarian controversy, having found the entire concept offensive to rational thought. So too did the Eucharist remain unclear for them. The Latitudinar-ians seem to be arguing that if any points of Christian doctrine are contro-versial then this in itself is a demonstration that they have not been revealed clearly in the Scripture and are by definition unnecessary for salvation. Unfor-tunately, such a sweeping view would demolish so many foundations of Christianity that little would be left. Indeed, by this token, Christianity would become merely a vague system of morality no different from any other equally accessible to pagans and Jews. It was at this point that the Latitudinarians dropped the ball, which was retrieved by Locke and passed to the Deists. Throughout, however, the playing field remained the text of the Bible itself.

II

The role of John Locke in the history of the English Bible remains some-what mysterious, not least because his writings do not always square with the public persona of the great rational thinker as proclaimed by numerous general histories of philosophy. Locke is most famous for having attacked the Platonist concept of 'innate ideas' used most recently by Descartes and others.

The human mind was seen instead as a *tabula rasa*, all our ideas deriving instead from experience, that is, either from sensation or reflection on what we experience. Locke is often portrayed as a scientist of the mind, using experiments as a starting-point and by means of inductive reasoning moving from the specific to the general, delaying the positing of truth until all the information is in. Certainly from the point of view of English-speaking audiences, this seemed like a method far superior to Descartes's deductive strategy, which began with the known truth and used experiments and experience in order to confirm the principles which were already innately grasped.

Locke's attitude to religion remains difficult to accommodate in this schematic view. It certainly is true that Locke believed that the existence of God can be discovered through the use of reason, not by means of ideas innate within us, but instead on the basis of experience, with miracles being an important proof. But it also appears that his own evaluation of the correct balance between reason and revelation did seem to change over the years, to the great consternation of interpreters of his thought who would prefer to deal with a more monolithic body of philosophy.

There is no question that, in terms of sheer bulk, Locke wrote a good deal about the Bible and religion.[10] He had an interleaved Bible, two interleaved New Testaments, an octavo Greek New Testament, and a separate notebook with entries about the New Testament.[11] He also had an interleaved Old Testament in quarto.[12] The presence of such biblical books in the library of a seventeenth-century scholar is not in itself the slightest bit surprising. More revealing are Locke's manuscript remains.[13] Among them is a parchment box containing notes by Locke on Richard Simon's critical history of the Old Testament.[14] There is quite a bit on Hebrew chronology, with some lists including notes by Locke.[15] Locke read and took notes on the work of the kabbalists Knorr von Rosenroth, and Francis Mercurius van Helmont.[16] He also preserved a table written by Isaac Newton in 1691 showing the fulfilment of the prophecy of the seven seals and trumpets and its interpretation according to the Book of Revelation.[17] Locke, like Newton, tended to occupy himself increasingly with metaphysical matters in the latter part of his life. Newton's religious interests are often explained away as the distracted jottings of a senile old man. Locke's writings span a longer period, and have therefore been dealt with in a somewhat different way, being forced into the Procrustean bed of Enlightenment reason.

Locke himself was abundantly clear about the crucial importance of biblical knowledge. He proclaimed that it was the duty of the Christian to study the Bible, 'receiving with stedfast belief, and ready obedience, all those things which the spirit of truth hath therein revealed.'[18] Indeed, he expected that a man's willingness to accept the Bible would be taken into account on Judgment Day.[19] Towards this end, Locke produced a paraphrase with notes of the epistles of Paul to the Galatians, 1 and 2 Corinthians, Romans, and Ephesians, which was published posthumously.[20]

The paraphrase was once a very common and accepted method of biblical interpretation, popular in the early modern period, but with long roots almost from the time of the Bible's redaction. Indeed, the Aramaic Targum used by biblical scholars today is less a translation than a paraphrase, the earliest versions of which go back to the second century AD. So too did Erasmus produce Latin paraphrases of every book in the New Testament except Revelation. The fashion reached Britain with *Plaine Discoverie of the Whole Revelation of Saint John* by John Napier (1550–1617), published in Edinburgh in 1593. In the seventeenth century, numerous paraphrases appeared, produced by men such as William Day, Obadiah Walker, Samuel Cradock, Daniel Whitby, and Samuel Clarke. Locke's devoted work on a paraphrase of the Pauline epistles was therefore not as eccentric as it may seem to modern students of his philosophy. The paraphrase was a popular tool and exceedingly useful to anyone trying to fathom the often initially opaque words of Scripture.

Locke used the opportunity of writing a preface to his paraphrase to attack what he viewed as one of the chief reasons for the misunderstanding of the Bible. This, he thought, was the habit of the age of dividing the Scriptures

> into Chapters and Verses, as we have done, whereby they are so chop'd and minc'd, and as they are now Printed, stand so broken and divided, that not only the Common People take the Verses usually for distinct Aphorisms, but even Men of more advanc'd Knowledge in reading them, lose very much of the strength and force of the Coherence, and the Light that depends on it.

Locke complained that 'we pick out a Text here and there, to make it serve our turn; whereas if we take it altogether, and consider what went before, and what followed after, we should find it meant no such thing.'[21]

While never a Hebrew or a Greek scholar, Locke was well aware that any understanding of Scripture would be only as good as the text used. Towards this end, he made himself familiar with the New Testament editions produced by Erasmus, Robertus Stephanus, and Beza. He may also have had access to the work in progress by John Mill (1645–1707) at Oxford, but since Mill was an opponent of Locke's and proposed that the philosopher's works be banned from tutorials with students, it may be that Locke was denied what would have been a very helpful source.[22] Locke corresponded with Newton in 1690 about the famous Trinity proof text in 1 John v. 7 and about another passage in 1 Timothy iii. 16. Newton declined to publish his views, and they did not appear in print until the middle of the next century, but they show that Locke, like Newton, was troubled by these references.[23] One interesting quirk about Locke's perception of scriptural style was the way in which he dealt with variant readings. John Mill, for example, adopted the standard eighteenth-century view that when variant readings exist, it is the more difficult one which is the original, reasoning that copyists would smooth out the difficulties. Locke, however, considered the easier reading original, arguing that Paul's arguments were coherent in themselves, and that difficulties were more likely to have been the inventions of the copyists.[24]

Locke's attitude to variant readings is indicative of some of his most cherished axioms about biblical interpretation. He insisted that the biblical authors wrote truth, completely expressed, and presented in an orderly fashion, so much so that the same words were always applied to the same ideas. The Bible was constructed on the basis of dependent reasonings, that is, every proposition that we find there must either be a conclusion drawn from a previous statement or a premiss which reached fruition in a later conclusion. This was Locke's *principle of coherence*, which explained why he was so against biblical verse-chopping. Locke also championed an atomistic understanding of biblical ideas. Each complex concept, he thought, was made up of simpler ones. The task of the reader is to break down the complex ideas and put them back together again – his *principle of resolution* – using the principle of coherence. Should this fail, the biblical interpreter should study similar ideas using the same words by means of the *principle of comparison*, and then reconstruct the argument sensibly thanks to the principle of coherence. The point of Locke's methodology was to allow the reader to understand Scripture as God intended. The Bible was a cluster of truths related to one another and built up of simple ideas portrayed in a consistent way. It was revelation that could be expounded through the use of human reason.[25]

'The holy scripture is to me, and always will be, the constant guide of my assent;' Locke proclaimed, 'and I shall always hearken to it, as containing infallible truth'.[26] This was as uncompromising a declaration in support of divine revelation as one might wish to have, especially from a philosopher whose lasting reputation has made him seem so much more sceptical. Locke's assurance in biblical truth was built on an even more surprising foundation: miracles. According to Locke, a miracle is 'a sensible operation, which being above the comprehension of the spectator, and in his opinion contrary to the established course of nature, is taken by him to be divine.'[27] On balance, thought Locke,

> The evidence of our Savior's mission from Heaven is so great, in the multitude of miracles He did before all sorts of people, that what He delivered cannot but be received as the oracles of God, and unquestionable truth. For the miracles He did were so ordered by Divine Providence and wisdom that they never were, nor could they be, denied by any of the enemies or opposers of Christianity.[28]

Locke's discussion of miracles is interesting, but not at all subtle, especially because he never satisfactorily addresses the question of why we should believe in miracles in the first place. He distinguishes between two types: those performed by the recipients of revelation to convince others, and those performed by God Himself in order to convince the recipients. But Locke's faith in the divine nature of the biblical text is such that he accepts the very validity of miracles on this basis alone, and then turns around and validates the events described in the text through the citation of miracles. The circularity of the argument does not seem to have troubled Locke. One can only wonder at the possible applications here of the hermeneutic principle that weak arguments by great philosophers are often indications of their rejection of the championed view, forced to be hidden because of the threat of persecution.

A good deal of discussion by Locke specialists over the years has revolved around the question of the comparative standing of revelation and reason in Locke's later thought. In his *Paraphrase*, published posthumously, Locke seems to be arguing that ultimately reason must defer to divine revelation, stressing the limits of human ability. Even in earlier works, we find hints of this trend. In *The Reasonableness of Christianity*, published anonymously by Locke in 1695, he takes great pains to stress the essential simplicity of Christianity, which almost places it beyond the necessity to think deeply about it. Locke recognized 'that reason, speaking never so clearly to the wise and virtuous, had never authority enough to prevail on the multitude, and to persuade the societies of men that there was but one God that alone was to be owned and worshipped.' God gave man 'reason, and with it a law, that could not be otherwise than what reason should dictate'. At the same time, God recognized the limitations of leisure and ability in most people: reason may be a tool for religious knowledge,

> But considering the frailty of man, apt to run into corruption and misery, He promised a deliverer whom in His good time He sent, and then declared to all mankind that whoever would believe Him to be the Savior promised, and take Him, now raised from the dead and constituted the Lord and Judge of all men, to be their King and Ruler, should be saved. This is a plain, intelligible proposition, and the all-merciful God seems herein to have consulted the poor of this world, and the bulk of mankind. These are articles that the labouring and illiterate man may comprehend. This is a religion suited to vulgar capacities, and the state of mankind in this world, destined to labour and travail.[29]

Locke clearly had little patience for 'the controversies at this time so warmly managed', and placed great emphasis on the fundamental articles of religion, chief among them – perhaps the only one – being that Jesus Christ is the

Messiah. The essential Christianity, he believed, could be obtained through reason, but might equally be based on biblical revelation alone.

Locke's argument, then, seems to be that although reason alone might be sufficient proof of God and His majesty for thinking and leisured persons, the Incarnation was necessary in order to provide for the spiritual needs of the intellectually deprived bulk of mankind. Or as Locke put it himself, 'Revelation is natural Reason enlarged by a new set of Discoveries communicated by God immediately, which Reason vouches the Truth of, by the Testimony and Proofs it gives, that they come from God'.[30] Reason need not be suspended in scriptural interpretation: it would confirm what revelation teaches us.

III

But was all of revelation contained in the Bible as defined by the Jews and published by the King's authority? For while Locke was paraphrasing Scripture, another battle was raging about the thorny question of extra-biblical holy books, and the light they might shed on the divine text. The first of these were the Sibylline Oracles. We know a good deal more about them than was possible in the seventeenth century. The Sibylline literature derives from the myth of a prophetess who delivers her predictions spontaneously, unlike other oracles who first need to be consulted. The image of a single individual woman living for a thousand years evolved into a group of such figures, residing in different countries. One of the Sibyls, Sambethe or Sabbe, was said to be the Babylonian wife of Noah's son. Aristophanes mentions a Sibylline literature in Greece in the fifth century BC. These prophetic verses were installed on the Capitol in Rome, guarded over by a college of officials, who permitted them to be studied but not consulted except by express order of the state. Five years after the buildings on the Capitol were destroyed by fire in 81 BC, a commission was ordered to obtain copies of genuine Sibylline verses in Italy and abroad. Augustus had these oracles copied in 17 BC, and five years later had those outside the canon destroyed.

Two different collections of the *Oracula Sibyllina* have survived, designated as Books I–VIII and XI–XIV respectively, although this numbering does not refer to any order in the text. The first group of oracles was compiled by Christians at the beginning of the sixth century, but it includes much older material, the earliest of which is certainly of Jewish origin, with Greek and even Babylonian materials. The first published edition of the Sybilline Oracles was that of Betuleius, who edited the first eight books in 1545 from a manuscript then at Augsburg. The eighth book was not complete in this version, and further editions followed in 1555 and 1599, this third version produced by Johannes Koch (Opsopoeus).

The question of the standing of the Sibylline Oracles, however, was more than a mere classical conundrum. Their eternal presence in Michelangelo's Sistine Chapel immediately suggests this. For the Sibyls were seen in the post-Christian era as pagans who foretold the coming of Christ, his miracles, his death and his resurrection. Indeed, this came to be seen as their primary historical function, and Christian apologists who cited their poetry claimed that they were silent after the birth of Christ. Having completed their task, they were pensioned off. The Church Fathers may have had some lingering doubts about their authority, but they agreed with Augustine that the Sibyls could be used to confound the heathen. Justin Martyr, Tertullian, and St Clement of Alexandria all quote from the Sibyls, and Origen defended their authenticity. Even St Jerome attributed to them divine inspiration. In sum, then, the Sibylline Oracles joined with Josephus in providing the necessary bridge between the Old and New Testaments, between classical and Eastern civilizations and the Christian world. In many respects, one could hardly do without them.[31]

In the seventeenth century, there were basically three revisionist positions that one could take on the Sibylline Oracles as an alternative to those which accepted them as completely authoritative, or at the very least somewhat inspired and useful in polemics against the pagans. Firstly, there was the view of Johannes Marckius, doctor in theology at Gröningen, according to which the oracles were the work of the early Christians. Secondly, there was the far more radical approach of Antony van Dale, Dutch physician, who argued that not only were the Sibylline Oracles complete forgeries, but that they did not cease with the coming of Christ. The third view was that of Isaac Vossius, that the Sibylline Oracles were of Jewish origin. As we have seen, in a sense, all three of these alternative theories were partially correct. We know that in 160 BC an Alexandrian Jew began to rewrite parts of the oracles using Jewish elements, and that the early Christians started retouching the texts as early as the first century AD, without denying the reality of the Sibyls' inspiration. In any case, it is clear that Vossius tried to anchor the Sibylline Oracles in the accepted progression of divine history from Jews to Christians, and save them as an acceptable source of religious data.[32]

Isaac Vossius (1618–89) became an integral part of the English scene, spending the last two decades of his life from 1670 at Windsor. He was very much the son of his father G.J. Vossius (1577–1649), classical scholar, philologist, and theologian. Vossius had spent time as the long-suffering librarian of Queen Christina of Sweden (in whose employ perished Descartes). Isaac Vossius at least had his revenge by selling his father's library twice: to Queen Christina for 20,000 guilders in 1649, and to the general public in 1656 in a public auction. After Christina abdicated in June 1654, Vossius returned to the Netherlands, and became acquainted with Charles de Saint-Évremond

(1610?–1703), the flamboyant sceptic, soldier, poet, and man of society who would be buried in Westminster Abbey. Vossius joined him in London in 1670, and was showered with honours by Oxford and given a prebend in the royal chapel of Windsor. Charles II found him both learned and amusing, famously remarking that Isaac Vossius would believe anything, if only it were not in the Bible.[33]

Isaac Vossius's theory about the Jewish origin of the Sibylline Oracles was revealed to the world in a book published at Oxford in 1679. The reaction was predictably intense, from both sides of the spectrum. One of the best defences of the independent authenticity of the oracles came only after Vossius's death, from Sir John Floyer (1649–1734), the Lichfield physician who was the first to measure the pulse rate. Dr Samuel Johnson remembered 'the celebrated Sir John Floyer' as the man who sent him to be touched by Queen Anne.[34] Floyer declared his opposition to Vossius, and explained why. 'I here present to you in these Oracles', Floyer announced,

> the old *Antediluvian Religion*, and all the Moral Precepts communicated to *Japhet*'s Family, which also contain many Prophesies concerning the Changes which would happen in the Kingdom of *Japhet*'s Posterity; so that we do not wholly derive all our Religion and Learning from the *Jews*, who convers'd formerly very rarely with the *Gentiles*, among whom they were but little known before their Captivity. When the *Chaldeans*, *Aegyptians* and *Greeks* had corrupted the *Noachic* Traditions of Religion, by applying their Sacrifices and Prayers to the Sun, Moon, and Heroes, which were appointed for God's Service, it pleas'd God to inspire the *Sibyls*, that they might restore the true ancient Worship to God alone, and correct all the errors from the old moral Precepts by these *Oracles*: the *Jewish* Men-Prophets, near the same thing, reform'd the Corruptions which Idolatry had introduc'd among them; but Woman-Prophetesses were sent to the *Gentiles*, because they used Women in their Heathen Oracles; and they could be least suspected by them for setting up any new Sect in Philosophy, or Religion.

In other words, the Sibylline Oracles provided the Christian with a means of bypassing the Jewish monopoly on the divine message, and moving one step closer to the very original communication God had with man in the halcyon days of the Garden of Eden when Adam named the animals and had perfect and complete knowledge. Claiming that mankind was originally monotheistic and had only afterwards degenerated into idolatry was an early modern commonplace, championed by Isaac Newton and many others. But what Floyer and his supporters attempted to do was to remove the Jews entirely from the chain of command, to discount their traditions and their learning, even at the expense of downgrading the authority of the Bible itself, and to construct an alternative channel of divine knowledge. Floyer noted that the Christian Fathers supported the Sibylline Oracles, and pointed out that since 'we believe the same Fathers Testimony concerning the Canon of Scriptures, we cannot disbelieve 'em, when they unanimously say, that these Oracles had a divine Inspiration'. This was certainly true, but it was a far cry from Augustine, who found the Oracles useful in confirming Scripture and in debates with pagans, to Floyer, who gave them an independent standing apart from the biblical text itself.[35]

William Whiston, the 'honest Newtonian', was very kind about Sir John Floyer in his own vindication of the Sibylline Oracles, and was not entirely negative about Isaac Vossius either. Like Floyer, Whiston concluded that

It appears therefore, that tho' God gave positive Laws, or an Institution of religious Worship, only to the *Jews*, and intrusted them only with those *Divine Oracles* that related to the same, yet that he did not wholly confine Divine Inspiration to that Nation; but supported the Law and Religion of Nature, and the right Worship of himself, as the One true God, among the Heathen also, all along by these Oracles even till the Light of the Christian Revelation was spread over the World.

Whiston followed his remarks with the Greek and English texts of the Sibylline Oracles, taken out of Floyer's earlier book.[36]

But Isaac Vossius's major opponent was Bernard Le Bovier, sieur de Fontenelle (1657–1757), whose *Histoire des oracles* created such a sensation in 1687. Fontenelle openly admitted that his own book was merely a literary reworking of the research of Antony van Dale, but his outright rejection of the Sibylline Oracles seems also to have been designed to cast doubt on all established religion. An English translation by the proto-feminist Aphra Behn appeared in 1688, while Vossius was still alive, and must have caused him considerable anguish. Fontenelle summarized his objectives on the first page of his work: 'My design is not to give you directly an History of *Oracles*', he wrote, 'I only intend to argue against that common Opinion which attributes 'em to *Daemons*, and will have 'em to cease at the coming of *Jesus Christ*'. From Fontenelle's point of view, it was really irrelevant who began this pious fraud, for the Sibylline Oracles were nothing more than the product of a wish to deceive.[37]

But all of this criticism was as nothing compared with the choice words of Dr Edward Pococke, Regius professor of Hebrew and Laudian professor of Arabic, one of the most celebrated Orientalists of all time. Despite having enjoyed the patronage of G.J. Vossius, Pococke thought nothing of attacking his son, for his work on the Sibylline Oracles threatened to undercut far too much to be tolerated. 'I look not abroad among the new Books', wrote Pococke to his friend Dr Narcissus Marsh (1638–1713), provost of the College of Dublin and later Ussher's successor in the archbishopric of Armagh,

I have not so much as seen *Vossius's* Tract of his Sibyls, and such others as
are with it; but I am told, that he speaks therein Things that are deroga-
tory to Rabbinical Learning (but that matters not much, as for other
Things) and particularly (which is *magis dolendum*) to bring Disrespect and
Contempt on the *Hebrew* Bible; and all authoritative, without good Proof
or Reason: And I hear, that by some at Coffee-Meetings, it is cried up. It
may be suspected, that the Intention is to bring it into Doubt, whether we
have any such Thing, as a true Bible at all, which we may confide in, as
God's Word. It is, I see, by some wished, that the Verity of the Original
Text might be vindicated from such sceptical Arguments, by some of Learning and Vigour, such as yourself. However, I doubt not, but that, by God's
Providence, as the *Hebrew* Text hath hitherto stood firm, so it will stand on
its own Bottom to wear out all Assaults against it, and be, what it always
was, received as the undoubted Word of God, when all the Arguments and
Objections against it are vanish'd into Smoke.[38]

From where Pococke stood, Isaac Vossius looked like a dangerous sceptic
because he cast doubt on the Masoretic monopoly of the Hebrew Bible and
dared to suggest that other classical texts such as the Sibylline Oracles might
enhance the meaning of Scripture.

Dr Marsh in Dublin agreed with Pococke completely, and if anything was
even more emphatic. 'I am very much grieved', he replied to his English
colleague, 'at what you say concerning some Mens Design to invalidate the
Authority of the *Hebrew* Text, and thereby of all the Old Testament'.[39] Vossius
now became in Marsh's mind the leader of a sceptical conspiracy which by
suggesting alternative routes to divine knowledge secretly took aim at the
very heart of Protestantism itself. Marsh hoped Pococke would take up the
challenge, and denounce the son of his old patron in public. A fortnight later,
Marsh wrote again to Pococke, pressing him to consider entering the fray:

I find, Dr. *Vossius's* last, as well as former Books, have not done much Good
(I wish they have not done the contrary) here: We have not many, that can
judge of the Original; but I hope to breed up good Store that Way, since
we have an *Hebrew* Professor's Place lately settled on the College, to which
Lecture I make all the Bachelors of Arts attend, and be examined thrice
every Week, and they are likewise to be publickly examined in *Hebrew*,
before they can take their Degree of Master in Arts, which I sometimes
do myself. I say, I think, we have not many in the whole Kingdom, that
can judge of the Original *Hebrew*.

This was the chief reason, Marsh claimed, that Isaac Vossius was able to get
away with such gross theological improprieties. Marsh prayed 'that God will
raise up some Man to vindicate (I may say) his own Cause: But I must add,

that all Mens Eyes are fixt upon you; and I dare say, none will have the Confidence to think of putting Pen to Paper on such a Design, whilst you live.'[40]

The panic expressed by Narcissus Marsh and others like him is quite understandable in view of the substantial academic investment that they had made in understanding the Hebrew verity. Indeed, Marsh achieved immortality largely through this work, by means of the establishment of Marsh's Library in Dublin, the first free public library in Ireland. The collection is brimming over with Hebrew, Aramaic, Syriac, Arabic, and Turkish books and manuscripts, as well as a vast amount of additional material in other Oriental languages. Marsh managed to purchase the entire library of Edward Stillingfleet, the Latitudinarian bishop of Worcester who died in 1699, and placed it among his own collection. Although Marsh had a crisis of confidence in Irish Oriental learning and its future which prompted him to dispatch nearly a thousand Hebrew and Syriac codices to his friend Pococke at the Bodleian, Marsh's Library remained the centre of Hebrew learning in Ireland. In fact, it was there that James Joyce warned Stephen Daedalus that beauty was not to be found 'in the stagnant bay of Marsh's library where you read the fading prophecies of Joachim Abbas'.[41] Champions of the Sybilline Oracles would not find it easy to get readers' tickets to Marsh's Library.

But Edward Pococke disappointed Marsh, and would not attack Isaac Vossius directly. Leonard Twells, Pococke's eighteenth-century biographer, pondered the reason for this reticence, and came to the conclusion that Pococke was reluctant to align himself with either of the two sides, whose partisans often took rather extreme positions:

> Some may think our Author went too far, in supposing, that the *Hebrew* Text was always, and in every Particular, read as it is at present; but if he err'd in this, he certainly err'd on the right Side, it being safer to suppose the Original *Hebrew* utterly uncorrupt, than to call its Purity in Question so oft as *Capellus* and *Vossius* did.[42]

Twells's 'all-or-nothing-at-all' explanation, however, is rather implausible. For Edward Pococke was also one of the first English Hebraists to recognize the potential importance of the Samaritan Pentateuch, and to encourage the acquisition of a copy of this important document. It was the Italian traveller Pietro della Valle who first obtained copies of the Samaritan Pentateuch. In 1616, Pietro visited Palestine and Damascus, and in the latter city purchased two manuscripts from a Samaritan. One of these he gave to the French ambassador in Constantinople; the second he kept for himself, and thereby provided the first Samaritan Pentateuch to arrive in Europe.[43] Scholars soon discovered that the Pentateuch used by the Samaritans, a Jewish sect established in about the fourth century BC and still surviving today, is not an independent version, but a particular form of the Hebrew text written in a different script. Although the Samaritan Pentateuch differs from the Masoretic text in as many as 6,000 places, most of these are unimportant, and the others are pleonastic, apart from a number of alterations designed to further the interests of the sect itself.[44]

The introduction of the Samaritan Pentateuch into the European biblical arena was bound to create a good deal of disturbance. As we have seen, scholars had long disputed over the relative value of the Masoretic text and the Septuagint, but this was a new problem. The fact that the Samaritan Pentateuch agreed with the Septuagint in about one-third of the variant readings led it to be aligned with the Greek text in seventeenth-century biblical discussion. Roman Catholic scholars defended the use of the Septuagint, as well as Jerome's Latin Vulgate (*c.* AD 400): they recognized the authority of the Church as the final religious arbiter, and were not tied to the biblical word alone. Catholic biblical authorities such as Johannes Morinus (1591–1659), J.H. Hottinger, and of course Richard Simon (1638–1712) therefore promoted the usefulness of the Samaritan Pentateuch in supplying alternative readings. Protestants, on the other hand, were generally unable to cast any doubt whatsoever on the Masoretic text of the Old Testament, without risking the breakdown of *sola fide* along with *sola scriptura* and, despite the inclusion of a Samaritan text in Brian Walton's Polyglot Bible, tended to reject the Samaritan Pentateuch outright: it was not until Benjamin Kennicott (1718–83) wrote in its defence in eighteenth-century Oxford that Protestants gradually came to see that its use was not necessarily an act of gross atheism.[45]

From our point of view, what is interesting is how involved Pococke was in the discovery and exploitation of this text which was a rival to the Masoretic Hebrew Bible, and a source that might prove even more revisionist than the Greek Septuagint chronology or the Sibylline Oracles. Pococke and his circle even went one step further by actually making contact with the Samaritans living in contemporary Nablus. J.J. Scaliger in 1589 had been the first Westerner to persuade the Samaritans to answer direct written queries. He sent them letters from Cairo and Nablus, and received a reply in Hebrew the following year.[46] But now the man on the spot was Pococke's successor as minister to the English factory at Aleppo, Robert Huntington (1637–1701). In 1672, the Samaritans sent Huntington at Jerusalem a Pentateuch for the Jews of England, with a covering letter to them written from Nablus by Merchib-Ben-Jacob. Huntington was also encouraged in his work by Job Ludolf (1624–1704) the German Orientalist, who himself reached the Samaritans in the 1680s through the agency of a local Jew from Hebron named Jacob Levy. Pococke was very involved in all this exciting activity, and corresponded with Huntington, Ludolf, and others in an attempt to see what revelation the Samaritan traditions and texts could offer.[47]

On the face of it, one would have thought that a man like Edward Pococke, who was so opposed to Isaac Vossius's use of the Septuagint and the Sibylline Oracles as alternative non-Masoretic routes to divine wisdom, would also shrink from using the Samaritan Pentateuch, whose textual message was often at variance with that of the Masorites. But not so. Even Robert Huntington himself, the searcher of the Samaritans, opposed Isaac Vossius and argued that he had gone too far. In a letter from Aleppo dated 24 May 1681, Huntington wrote to Pococke with reference to reports of Vossius's work that had been sent halfway across the world to Syria. 'I have not seen *Vossius de Sibyllis*,' Huntington confessed to his mentor,

> but to decry the *Hebrew* Text has long been his Design and Practice. And it is a great while since *Hulsius* and *Horn* have taken Notice of it; but I am no Judge of the Controversy. Whilst Men speak and fight too not for Truth, but Victory, we may well expect heterodox Opinions and seditious Actions.[48]

In other words, Huntington saw no contradiction between championing the Samaritan Pentateuch and the Hebrew Masoretic text at one and the same time, but denied Vossius's right to cast his net even further and include the Septuagint chronology and the Sibylline Oracles.

By the same token, in a reverse application of the identical principle, one would have expected Richard Simon to have offered Isaac Vossius some measure of support. But Simon no less than Pococke thought that Vossius was appalling, and wrote his 'animadversions upon a small treatise of Dr I.V. concerning the Oracles of the Sibylls'.[49] As far as Simon was concerned, the entire Hebrew Bible was too insecure a foundation on which to build massive chronologies, and generally he saw Vossius as far too credulous to make a first-rate biblical critic.

But Isaac Vossius was indeed an important forerunner of the kind of biblical critic who would become commonplace only after the work of Benjamin Kennicott at Oxford in the mid-eighteenth century. Kennicott was also a champion of the Samaritan Pentateuch, like Pococke, and his famous defence of this ancient text provoked a mass of hostile reaction. But by the time he wrote, a good deal was already known about the Samaritans' religion and customs, and sixteen Samaritan manuscripts existed in England, including seven copies of the Pentateuch deposited at Oxford, Cambridge, and the British Museum. By Kennicott's day, the Jews of India and even the Chinese Jews were being canvassed for manuscripts that might throw light on the original Hebrew verity which had been clouded by time.[50] This sort of scriptural exploration had been pioneered by the Jesuits who first reached China in the late sixteenth century, but such a multi-textual approach was new among Protestants: Isaac Vossius stood at the genesis of this tradition.

It is not surprising, then, to find that Vossius was more strongly opposed in the 1680s than Kennicott would be in the 1750s, when biblical criticism was becoming a fact of life in Germany, and after Richard Bentley in England had already applied the same tools to an analysis of the less controversial Greek New Testament. Nevertheless, even in Vossius's day, other scholars had cast doubt on the Masoretic text. Archbishop Ussher himself admitted privately that the Hebrew Bible must have suffered the same fate as any other ancient manuscript, and was very actively involved in bringing copies of the Samaritan Pentateuch to England.[51] But he simultaneously argued that the Septuagint was in many respects a forgery.[52] Newton had doubts about the literal purity of the Old Testament, yet had a naïve belief in the truth of biblical data.[53] But Ussher and Newton sought extra-Masoretic evidence in order to demonstrate the truth of the Hebrew Old Testament; Vossius sought to open alternative Jewish supernatural routes to divine wisdom and, like Giordano Bruno and the Egyptian Hermeticists, found that there were limits to critical experimentation. Isaac Vossius's contribution in the history of Protestant biblical criticism was to draw the borders while standing on the outside: Benjamin Kennicott would 'build a fence around the biblical law', as the Talmud puts it, while standing well within.

IV

Locke's attitude to the Bible went some way towards the streamlining of religion, and towards eliminating what he saw as unnecessarily controversial issues which would have no effect on the salvation of an individual believer. Inspired in part by his writings, other men, collectively known as the Deists, tried to eliminate the supernatural elements which they thought further obscured the issue. Perhaps the most learned among them was John Toland (1670/1–1722), the impecunious Irishman whose name almost more than any other is associated with Deism. Like Vossius, Toland is also important for having championed another extra-biblical text as a source of divine knowledge.

If Locke is somewhat difficult to characterize, the Deists are even more so. Many people thought that Deism was a completely new phenomenon on the religious horizon. Jonathan Edwards (1703–58) defined Deists as 'professed infidels':

> They ben't like the heretics, Arians and Socinians, and others, that own the Scriptures to be the word of God, and hold the Christian religion to be the true religion, but only deny these and these fundamental doctrines of the Christian religion; they deny the whole Christian religion . . . And they deny the whole Scripture; they deny that any of it is the word of God.[54]

At the end of the nineteenth century, Leslie Stephen tried to smooth out the discontinuities of the Deists by arguing that they themselves underwent an evolution, from the early 'constructive' Deists who tried to substitute natural religion and morality for Christian doctrine, to the 'critical' Deists who were only interested in demonstrating the tenets of the Christian story to be naïve or even ridiculous.[55] Perhaps Paul Hazard was closer to the mark when he observed that 'If Deism rejected the God of Israel, Abraham, and Jacob, it at least believed that there was a God. If it denied Revealed Religion, at least it would not admit that the Heavens were empty.'[56]

Historians often look back to Lord Edward Herbert of Cherbury (1583–1648) as the first recognizable Deist, albeit *avant la lettre*. Herbert was ambassador to Paris for James I, a friend of Bacon and Casaubon, and the older brother of George Herbert the poet. Herbert's work *De veritate* (1624) was the first to develop a religious philosophy which did not require a special revelation, but was based on reason alone. That being so, his religion was extraordinarily minimalist, and consisted of only five key points:

1. There is Supreme God.
2. This Sovereign Deity ought to be Worshipped.
3. Virtue with Piety . . . the most important part of religious practice.
4. vices and crimes . . . must be expiated by repentance.
5. There is Reward or Punishment after this life.

Herbert's insistence that these five points comprised all of the absolutely necessary elements of religion, and that they could be demonstrated by reason alone, without the need for revelation, prefigure many of the arguments of the Deists. So Herbert was also an important influence on Locke, as should now be clear.[57]

The belief that there was a natural religion which underlay all religions of revelation could not but radically alter the conception of Scripture. One of the most important, and earliest, of the Deists who confronted the problem directly was Charles Blount (1654–93), who began his attack in a deceptively roundabout fashion by publishing a translation with commentary of the two first books by Philostratus on Apollonius of Tyana.[58] Here was a neo-Pythagorean sage with supernatural powers, such as clairvoyance, knowledge of the languages of birds and animals, and so forth, which he enhanced during his wanderings in Persia, India, and Egypt, stopping in Rome during Nero's reign, and dying as a very old man at the end of the first century AD. The interesting point was that a cult of Apollonius flourished in Asia and Syria as a pagan answer to Christianity, promoted in Rome by the Syrian dynasty there, especially by the empress Julia Domna. By publishing a translation of Apollonius's life, Blount was subtly making the point that it might be very difficult to determine who was the genuine Messiah, Jesus or Apollonius, since both were held to be miracle-workers. Bayle would take the same line, describing Apollonius as one of the most remarkable people who ever lived, a description usually reserved for Jesus himself. There was an enormous literature on Apollonius at the end of the seventeenth century and the beginning of the next, and shortly before the French Revolution, Blount's edition appeared in both Paris and Berlin in French.[59]

In Blount's more mature work, such as *Oracles of Reason*, his last book, we get a more direct assault on the biblical narrative, but in such a way as paradoxically to sow the seeds of more constructive biblical criticism. This he did by drawing on the work of his contemporary, John Spencer (1630–93), who reversed the direction of influence by arguing that the origin of Old Testament religious institutions and ceremonies was to be found in Egyptian practices then current. The advantage of this theory was that Spencer could thereby explain some of the more absurd and abhorrent practices to be found in the Bible: the Israelites had spent so much time in Egypt as the prisoners of idolatry that God had to wean them away to true religion. This He did by circumscribing the Israelites with petty ceremonial laws which taught them the discipline required by true religion. At the same time, He retained many harmless Egyptian customs to help ease the transition.[60]

The notion of divine education would be of immense importance in later centuries as a means of explaining the inconvenient elements of biblical narrative, as it was applied not only by Lessing, but by numerous others who were offended by the lack of reason in many divine proclamations. Spencer drew heavily on Maimonides, the darling of seventeenth- and eighteenth-century biblical commentators, who stressed the notion of 'accommodation', the adaptation by God of divine ideas to human capacities. Spencer was able to see beyond the search for the origins of divine institutions and to try to reconstruct the mentality behind their establishment in the first place.[61]

John Toland was even more controversial than Spencer. He converted to Protestantism at the age of sixteen, took his MA at the University of Edinburgh, and studied at Leiden for two years under Frederick Spanheim the younger, where he also met Le Clerc. Toland returned to England in January 1694 and stayed in Oxford for almost two years, working on his first controversial book, the most important deistical tract that had yet appeared. This was *Christianity not Mysterious*, published in 1696, at first anonymously, but almost immediately thereafter in a second enlarged edition bearing his name. Toland began by noting that although people welcome improvements in arts and sciences, they are loath to contemplate such changes in the realm of religion. Toland posited a new hermeneutical key: reason, which should be applied unflinchingly to the Bible and to religion in general in all situations. The essential doctrines of Christianity were simple and well within the sphere of human reason. On these sound foundations, however, the agents of 'priestcraft' had erected superfluous 'mysteries', unintelligible and incomprehensible beliefs. Some of these were adapted from pagan concepts by ignorant and credulous Church Fathers. Others were more cynically introduced in order to support particular church doctrine at a later stage. The point, however, was that the unmysterious New Testament must be distilled from ecclesiastical doctrine which constantly exploits the Bible in order to justify religious ceremonies (especially in the case of the Roman Catholics) or questionable theological doctrines (especially in the case of the Protestants).[62]

As we have already seen, so Locke too stressed the paramount importance of reason in religious discussion, but he reserved a place for revelation in supplying certain human deficiencies. Toland saw himself as a disciple of Locke (causing Locke a good deal of nervous worry) and went one step further, arguing that not only could reason be used in understanding religion, but that nothing contrary to reason should be allowed at all. Indeed, the claim has been made that Locke's book on the reasonableness of Christianity may have been an answer to Toland, an attempt to delineate the distinctions between the two men.[63]

Toland in his mature works continued this sceptical trend, basing himself on reason but not denying the validity of Scripture when properly used. In his *Letters to Serena* (Sophie Charlotte, queen of Prussia whom Toland had visited in 1701), Toland followed Spencer in arguing that the Israelites had obtained many of their key doctrines from the Egyptians, especially the immortality of the soul, heaven and hell.[64] Some of this close reading of the biblical text was continued in Toland's fascinating work on *Nazarenus: or Jewish, Gentile, and Mahometan Christianity* which he published in 1718 with a corrected second edition appearing in the same year.[65] To understand the crucial importance of this book, we shall need to stray rather far afield.

V

'BARNABAS, Gospel of. A writing in Italian, apparently forged not earlier than the 15th cent. by a native of Italy who had renounced Christianity for Islam.' In this laconic fashion, the *Oxford Dictionary of the Christian Church* describes what must be the most implausible forgery of all time.[66] Purporting to be an authentic eyewitness account of the life of Christ composed in first-century Palestine, the Gospel of Barnabas is in fact written in Italian on sixteenth-century watermarked paper and includes phrases which are strikingly similar to lines from Dante. George Sale (1697?–1736), in his 1734 translation of the Koran, described the provenance of this curious 75,000-word manuscript, 255 leaves of 6 × 5 inches bound in leather-covered boards and divided into 222 chapters. According to Sale, there was once a monk named Fra Marino who had read in Irenaeus something about a Gospel of Barnabas, so he went round to his friend Pope Sixtus V (1585–90), who denied all knowledge of such a document. The pope, being old and frail, dozed off during their meeting, so Fra Marino poked around looking for something to read. The first thing he laid his hands upon was the Gospel of Barnabas. Fra Marino slipped the codex up his sleeve and left the room.

The contents of the mysterious manuscript fully justified the pope's reluctance to reveal it. According to the Gospel of Barnabas, it was not Jesus who was crucified on the cross, but Judas, who was magically transformed into the Saviour's likeness and crucified against his will. Even more surprisingly, the Lord announces to mankind that they should watch for 'He it is whom the nations look for, to whom the secrets of God are so manifest that, when he cometh into the world, blessed shall they be that shall listen to his words'. This wonderful figure, however, is not Jesus, but 'Muhammad, the Messenger of God.' Fra Marino was so taken by this prophecy that he immediately converted to Islam.

Who would believe such a tale? For one thing, New Testament apocrypha were a shekel a cubit even in the Middle Ages. There was the *Gospel According to the Hebrews* and *The Gospel According to the Egyptians*, and gospels in the names of Peter, Marcion, Thomas, Philip, and the Twelve Apostles in a sort of joint-authorship. Apart from these works, which were largely written to legitimize Gnostic and other heretical interpretations, there were the texts that were created to fill in the gap between Jesus's infancy and the beginning of his ministry thirty years later. There was the *Childhood Gospel of Thomas*, the *History of Joseph the Carpenter*, the *Departure of Mary*, and more.[67] Not one of these is written in Italian.

John Toland thought the Gospel of Barnabas genuine, or at least he claimed that this was his view. Toland's interest in the case began with his *Life of Milton* (1698). An unfortunate passage in that book seemed to express doubt about the veracity of the New Testament, and Toland leaped to his own defence in a further book, *Amyntor, or a Defence of Milton's Life* (1699), in which he provided a list of New Testament apocrypha and promised that his doubts went as far as these non-canonical works alone. According to Toland's own account, however, in 1709 he was shown 'a Mahometan Gospel, never before publicly made known among Christians, tho they have much talkt about the Mahometan's acknowledging the Gospel.' Furthermore, Toland recounts, the 'learned gentleman, who has been so kind as to communicate it to me (*viz.* Mr. CRAMER, Counsellor to the King of *Prussia*, but residing at *Amsterdam*) had it out of the library of a person of great name and authority in the said city'. 'Cramer' is certainly Johan Jacob Cramer (1673–1702), a Swiss Orientalist and diplomat, who may have obtained the document from the library of Gregorio Leti, which had been sold eight years earlier. Cramer gave the manuscript to Prince Eugene of Savoy in 1713, and it remains in the Austrian National Library as Codex 2662. A translation and commentary were produced by Lonsdale and Laura Ragg and published by the Clarendon Press in 1907.[68]

Toland was entranced by this new gospel, which promulgated a radically different version of the life of Christ, denied that Jesus was crucified and then resurrected, and proclaimed Muhammad as the Saviour of mankind. The result of his study and further research was *Nazarenus* (1718), in which Toland argued that this Gospel of Barnabas was in fact the holy book of the Ebionites, the Jewish Christian sect of the first centuries of the new faith, who lived on the wrong side of the Jordan. The Ebionites, poor and extremely ascetic, believed in the continued validity of the Mosaic law. They were also 'docetic', that is, they denied it was Christ who suffered on the cross. The man crucified may have been Judas Iscariot, or even Simon of Cyrene, but it was not Jesus.

As a work of New Testament scholarship alone, Toland's book is fascinating. It deals unflinchingly with the shifting sands of early Christian groups, not only the Ebionites, but also the Nazarenes, those Jewish Christians of Syria who obeyed Jewish law and used the Aramaic *Gospel According to the Hebrews*. Toland would probably have liked to know about the Elkesaites, neighbours of the Ebionites, who revered their 'Book of Elkesai ['sacred power']' given to them by an angel 96 miles high. Like the Ebionites, they rejected the upstart Paul, his epistles, and his entire marketing programme outside the confines of the Jewish world. According to tradition, Muhammad lived for a time in an Elkesaite community, which definitely thickens the plot.

Nazarenus is a book often cited but little read. It is usually described as promoting Gentile–Jewish syncretic Christianity and as attacking all professed religions, but this is an unjust description, for that was not all he wrote. For one thing, although the discussion of the Gospel of Barnabas is the centrepiece of the book, it only comprises Letter I. The second letter deals with another text entirely, the Codex Armarchanus, stolen from the King's Library in France in 1707 by the renegade priest Jean Aymon and brought to the Netherlands.[69] The manuscript (now in the British Library) is an important source for tenth-century Irish Church history. For Toland, it was useful because it demonstrated that the primitive Irish Church rejected an entire litany of bad things including transubstantiation, images, saints, confession, celibacy, monks, fasting, and much more. Put together, Toland delivers the promise on his title page, that *Nazarenus* will suggest a new version of 'the Original Plan of Christianity occasionally explain'd in the history of the Nazarens, wherby diverse Controversies about this divine (but highly perverted) institution may be happily terminated.'

Professor Justin Champion, who edited the modern edition of the text, makes great weight of a 70-page autograph draft of *Nazarenus* written in

French and dedicated to Eugene of Savoy, also to be found in the Austrian National Library (Codex 10325). Champion looks carefully at the entire question of literary forgeries, bringing in Anthony Grafton's argument that humanism was first and foremost a process of discriminating between true/false, authentic/forged, godly/spurious.[70] Champion rightly argues that Toland played with this convention in *Nazarenus*, using genuine scholarship to attack Christianity itself by undermining faith in the exclusivity of its most important texts, or as Champion rather obscurely puts it, acting as 'a ludic avatar of the critical ambitions of Erasmian scholarship'. In other words, Toland's preferred strategy for attacking Christianity in this particular book was to be 'relentlessly textual', avoiding other issues such as inspiration, inerrancy, or the divinity of the authors.[71]

Champion is very good at placing Toland in the context of what has been written about that obfuscating man. Robert Sullivan argued that Toland was at the very borders of Christian belief, but remained within them.[72] David Berman and Margaret Jacob presented Toland as more thoroughgoingly anti-religious, his gestures towards Christianity merely a convenient cover in an era of religious persecution.[73] It is one thing to argue that there was a secret private Toland and a public Toland, but it is quite another for those who study him to disagree so totally about the clandestine qualities of the inner man. Champion, for his part, sees Toland as more of a 'public writer', whose work was deliberately ambiguous and could be read in different ways by different audiences, unlike the Bible, which was supposed to have only one divine meaning.[74]

So did Toland believe that the Gospel of Barnabas was genuine or did he see it for the fake it was? According to Champion, 'It seems likely that Toland did not believe in the textual truth of Christian revelation'. Why then advocate the veracity of a book that was so palpably false? Champion argues that Toland promoted the authenticity of the false gospel in order 'to engage with a cultural discourse that held at its heart notions of sacred authenticity and originality', and thereby attack the ecclesiastical institutions that authorized (and were authorized by) Scripture. By doing this, Champion claims, Toland could undermine Christian notions of canonicity, parody patristic writers, promote primitive Christianity, and put the Muslim example on the table. The implication of the Gospel of Barnabas was that it was possible to be a good Christian even if you were faithful to Jewish ceremonial practices (like the Ebionites) and thought that Muhammad was also a messiah. Toland showed that there were different schools of thought in primitive Christianity, and salvation was not dependent on subscribing to any particular one. The New Testament could then be seen as a record of religious practice containing words of advice rather than doctrinal propositions. It was only the priests who turned this tolerant system into one based on strict injunctions. Toland, in other words, claimed to have identified the original plan of Christianity, which was not prescriptive at all. In our own times, therefore, there was no reason why Jews, Christians and Muslims could not live together in harmony, promoting alternative but equally valid descriptions of religion.[75]

Some of the sources for Toland's radical views must have been obvious even at the beginning of the eighteenth century. Spinoza's *Tractatus Theologico-Politicus* (1670) was one clear influence. So was 'An Account of the Rise and Progress of Mahometanism' (*c.* 1671) by Henry Stubbe (1632–76), which showed connections between Ebionites, Nazarene Christianity, and Islam.[76] There was also the *Critical History of the Text of the New Testament* by Richard Simon, which appeared in English in 1689 and 1692. The seventh and eighth chapters of Simon's work discussed the Ebionites and Nazarenes at great length, dwelling on the Gospel According to the Hebrews.[77]

Toland's work was recognized for what it was, an attempt to blur the congruity between Church and Scripture and to suggest that there were alternative readings to the text that formed the basis of organized religion. The Gospel of Barnabas had a new lease of life, thanks to Toland. His *Nazarenus* put this manuscript on the map, and prompted Sale's mention of the text in his Koran translation of 1734. When John W. Youngson went out to the East as a Victorian Church of Scotland missionary, he found so many Muslim scholars citing the Gospel of Barnabas without ever having seen it, that he himself searched for the text until he found it in Vienna and persuaded fellow missionary Canon Ragg and his learned wife to produce the edition for the Clarendon Press published in 1907. His plan of discrediting the text through examination rather backfired, however. Since that time, the Gospel of Barnabas has gone through countless reprintings in the Muslim community, and reverberates in cyberspace in pro and con websites, opposition coming not only from Christians who object to deviant views of the Life of Christ and/or to Islam in general, but from within the Islamic world itself.

One of the reasons for Islamic opposition is the usefulness of the Gospel of Barnabas to the Ahmadiyyah movement, an Islamic sect founded at the end of the nineteenth century by Hazrat Mirza Ghulam Ahmad (*c.* 1830–1908), who eventually claimed to be a messiah himself, appointed by Allah. Ghulam Ahmad pinpointed a tomb, said to be that of a Kashmiri prophet named 'Yus Asaph', as the actual tomb of Jesus, who had secretly left Palestine after the crucifixion incident and travelled through Afghanistan to his final resting place in Kashmir.[78] Thanks to Toland, this claim received further justification in the docetic Gospel of Barnabas.

Scholars have also needed to take into account the discovery of an incomplete Spanish manuscript of the Gospel of Barnabas in 1976 at the University of Sydney, Australia. George Sale saw it at the beginning of the eighteenth century in the collection of a Hampshire rector, and from him it seems to have passed through the hands of Thomas Monkhouse of Queen's College, Oxford and John Nickolls (*c.* 1745), ending up in Dublin before going down under. A good case has been made for a Morisco (crypto-Muslim) origin for the Gospel of Barnabas, which would fit in well with Toland's interest in the Jews and their welfare, and indeed might help explain the usefulness of such a forgery.[79]

Both in 1588 and 1595, manuscripts were found in Granada which seemed to throw light on early Christianity, and which were submitted for approval to Pope Sixtus V in Rome. In the first instance, under the ruins of a minaret a lead box was discovered which contained a bone of St Stephen, a painting, and a prophecy by St John concerning Granada, helpfully written in Latin, Arabic, and Castilian. In 1595 a number of further manuscripts turned up, including the 'Truth of the Gospel' by the Virgin Mary herself, who had it from Gabriel. The manuscript was now in Spain thanks to St James, who hid it there to prevent alterations to the text. James prophesied that the book would be discovered by a holy priest aided by the Muslims (God's most recently chosen people) led by a great conqueror (the Sultan?) who would call a church council on Cyprus (home of Barnabas). It is more than possible that the Gospel of Barnabas was an attempt by local Moriscos to create yet another forged holy text which might indicate ways in which Christians and Muslims could find common ground. We know that the Spanish *Gospel* was in existence at least in 1634, when it was first mentioned by a Morisco scholar. According to recent work by Dr Luis F. Bernabé Pons, by the time the forged Gospel was finished, it was already useless, since the Moriscos were expelled from Spain between 1609 and 1614. The manuscript in Rome is merely the Italian translation of the Spanish original, he argues, that had been sent to Pope Sixtus V in the hope of authentication. If it could be proven that Jesus himself proclaimed Muhammad the Messiah, then the course of history might be diverted to a more tolerant future.[80]

It is fascinating to think that John Toland in eighteenth-century England was in essence taking up the very torch laid down by converted Muslims in Granada over a century before, and with the same purpose. Toland may not have believed in the veracity of the Gospel of Barnabas, but neither did the original forgers, whoever they were. But both they and Toland were united in the hope that Christianity could be made to tolerate people who saw God in a different light. Indeed, some distinguished scholars such as Shlomo Pines have argued for the existence of a genuine substratum to the forgery which throws light on the early Jewish-Christians.[81]

Apart from anything else, this is a wonderful story. Novels have been written on the theme, from Irving Wallace's *The Word* (1972) about a forged Gospel of James, to Nicolas Saudray's *Le Maître des fontaines* (1976) concerning a lost gospel of the Nazarenes, to James Redfield's *The Celestine Prophecy* (1994) about an ancient manuscript discovered in the rain forests of Peru containing nine key insights into life. So too did *The Holy Blood and the Holy Grail* boys, Michael Baigent and Richard Leigh, hint darkly about the secrets of the Nazarenes being hidden from mankind by the sinister Roman Catholic Church. Toland's *Nazarenus* belongs in that number, but is far and away the most scholarly of the lot, and deserves to be more carefully read.

Toland defended various parts of his general argument in later works. In his study of *Origines Judaicae*, Toland stood up to French bishop Pierre Daniel Huet (1630–1721), and used Strabo (63BC?–?AD24) the Greek geographer to demonstrate that the earliest Jews were not superstitious. When Moses established the Jewish religion it was based on the Ten Commandments and therefore very close to the law of nature. The senseless ceremonial laws and sacrifice rituals which God gave to the Israelites were part of divine punishment for their idolatry.[82] Toland's admiration for the Jews also provoked him into making concrete proposals for their naturalization in England and admission on an equal standing with gentiles.[83] So too in *Hodegus* did Toland confront the problem of miracles, explaining them in purely naturalistic terms. The pillar of fire which went before the Israelites in the desert was simply a beacon described in literary terms. Old Testament miracles therefore did not contradict his thesis that the original religion of the Israelites was uncorrupted by superstition and was as close to natural religion as one might possibly hope for.[84]

Sometimes Toland's biblical scholarship was almost an accidental by-product of other polemics. As we have seen, Toland produced a life of John Milton in 1698 which was also printed as a preface to Milton's prose works in three volumes. In the course of his discussion of the authenticity of *Eikon Basilike*, attributed to Charles I, Toland remarked that we now can understand the inclusion of 'so many supposititious pieces under the name of Christ and his apostles'. Immediately he was attacked by Offspring Blackall (1654–1716), who thought Toland was refering to the canonical Gospels rather than to the apocryphal writings, and thereby provoked him into a more comprehensive defence as well as to ask whether the canon of the New Testament might have unjustly excluded other authentic writings, such as the Gospel of Barnabas.[85] Unlike Blount, therefore, Toland did genuinely attempt to strengthen the authority of the Bible, and he hardly deserves his reputation as a cryptoatheist. His argument was that there was nothing in the Scripture which was irredeemably contrary to reason, and that with a bit of scholarship and common sense it should be possible to unmask the original divine meaning.

VI

His patron the earl of Shaftesbury (1671–1713) was more sceptical, presenting his case with care in the collection of his own works which he had the foresight to edit himself. Like Blount, Shaftesbury uses Spencer, and like Toland, he was sceptical about the value of miracles in proving biblical truths. Shaftesbury threw his weight behind the notion of natural religion, emphasizing the reality of natural law which made it reasonable for people to act morally. The place of the Bible in such a scheme was therefore severely diminished, for it was no longer necessary to have scriptural examples before one's eyes, which in any case were more likely than not to promote immorality and other offences.[86]

Locke had been responsible for Shaftesbury's education; Anthony Collins (1676–1729) came to know Locke much later in life, but like Toland saw himself as the great man's disciple and spiritual descendant, who took the criterion of reason one crucial step forward. Collins began by conceding that the Bible was not a philosophical treatise, but was composed according to the principles of accommodation. Nevertheless, although we need not understand everything in Scripture as a perfectly literal reflection of what actually occurred, there was nothing in religion which was contrary to, or above, reason.[87] But it was his provocative *Discourse of Free Thinking* (1713) which really set the cat among the pigeons. Collins was not specifically trying to dethrone the Bible, but was making the point that the spectacular lack of agreement by religious authorities should alone convince us that each individual believer should approach the text armed with reason rather than prejudice. This is what he meant by 'free-thinking'.[88]

These more general views about religion and the Bible were considerably fleshed out in the context of Collins's epic dispute with William Whiston, in the days when Whiston was still a spokesman for orthodoxy. Whiston gave the Boyle Lectures in 1707 on the accomplishment of Scripture prophecies, which were published in book form the following year. Whiston argued that prophecies in the Old Testament could have only a single meaning: either they referred to later events in the Old Testament itself, or they predicted something that would occur at the time of Jesus. The notion of typology was unacceptable to him: a prophecy could not refer simultaneously to two different events.[89] Whiston amplified these views in a later work on the text of the Old Testament, arguing that both the Masoretic Hebrew text and the surviving text of the Septuagint had been perverted by the Jews by the beginning of the second century after Christ. It was for this reason that Whiston was one of the few Protestants of his time who supported the Samaritan Pentateuch as an uncorrupted version of Scripture. Whiston also explained by this means why the quotations of the Old Testament in the New were different from those in the versions currently used, as was the case with citations in Philo and Josephus. Distilling a copy of the original version of the Bible as known to Jesus and his earliest followers, he argued, would go a long way towards deciphering the meaning of prophecy.[90]

Anthony Collins replied to Whiston, accepting his basic arguments and turning them against both the Bible and Christianity itself. Like Whiston, Collins accepted that there could be only one meaning for each prophecy in the Old Testament: referring to something that would occur either later in the same text, or in the New Testament, but not both together. Like Whiston, Collins rejected typology as a logically flawed concept, noting in any case that this sort of allegory was common in the time of Christ, but was unknown to the Jews of the Old Testament. Collins set his sights on several Old Testament proof texts, showing that they did not refer to later events in the New. The reference in Isaiah vii. 14, for example, was to the prophet's own son, not to Christ. Collins was also sceptical about the claim that the Jews had managed to forge the text of the Old Testament without anyone noticing it, and was doubtful that, even if so, Whiston could after this passage of time restore the Bible to its original splendour. Collins made great use of the work of the Dutch Arminians, of Hugh Grotius (1583–1645), and especially of Willem Surenhuys (Surenhusius) (1666–1729), who defended and explained the inaccurate quotations of the Old Testament in the New.[91]

The line of attack which Collins had chosen was to prove very fruitful for those who would minimize biblical authority and would relocate the rela tionship between the two Testaments. Collins snapped the connection between the two sacred books, rejecting typology, the glue that held them together. In doing so, he also raised the entire issue of literary licence in the Bible, noting that allegory as well as prophecy comprised the biblical text, and that we need to be attuned to the symbolic qualities of scriptural language.

Collins had many supporters and more detractors. Among the more interesting of his followers was Thomas Bullock, chaplain to the bishop of Norwich, who argued that Christianity was not based on the Old Testament at all, but was a completely new religion introduced by Jesus. The references to the Old Testament in the New were merely part of the campaign of the early Christians to recruit Jews and to present familiar aspects of their tradition in the hope of winning them over to the faith.[92]

The views which Collins championed, drawing on previous work from Locke to Toland, were easily recognized as potentially destabilizing and revolutionary. The reaction could sometimes be no less problematic. Thomas Woolston (1670–1733) of Sidney Sussex College, Cambridge, had made his name as an extreme champion of allegory and typology, preaching on the Old Testament in his college chapel and publishing his discourses in 1705 at the University Press. Like Toland, Woolston aimed at reducing all scriptural miracles to rational explanations. But Woolston was a devoted student of Origen, and applied an extreme allegorist interpretation to nearly every event described in the Old Testament. Jesus among the Romans was prefigured by

Moses with the Pharaoh; Moses led the children of Israel out of Egypt as
Christ redeemed the world. With correct knowledge and a good deal of study,
every detail of the Old Testament might be linked to a corresponding part
of the life of Christ and the history of the early Church.[93] Indeed, Woolston's
devotion to allegory and typology was so extreme that he began to question
the actual historical validity of both the virgin birth and the Resurrection.
Christ rising from the dead, he said, was the allegorical parallel of Christians
emancipating themselves from Jewish ceremonial law. This was too much for
ecclesiastical authority to bear and he was indicted in 1725 for blasphemy,
although in the end the charges were dropped.[94]

Undeterred by this brush with the law, Woolston produced a six-part
discourse on the miracles in the New Testament, like Toland giving rational
explanations for what was said to have occurred, but in Woolston's case
not in order to be critical about the Bible, but in order to provide himself
with further scriptural fodder for his typology machine. By the time the
fourth discourse was published, the authorities had enough, and revived
the prosecution against him, trying him at the Guildhall in March 1729.
Woolston was found guilty and sentenced to a year's imprisonment and a
fine of £100 but, failing to find the money, remained incarcerated until his
death.[95]

As Woolston well knew, the danger lurking behind Collins's interpretation
was that the fragile connection between the two Testaments would completely
break down, leaving the entire history from Creation to Chronicles behind
as the life of Christ proceeded in a stately fashion towards Resurrection. This
was the dream of Thomas Morgan (d. 1743), whose hostility to Israelite religion and Judaism spilled over, or perhaps derived from, his negative attitude
to the Old Testament. Morgan emphasized the concept of 'moral philosophy',
which he defined as 'the Knowledge of God, Providence, and Human
Nature'. The existence of God was posited by the intrinsic order to be found
in the universe, which Morgan, like Newton, believed required the periodic
intervention of God to keep running properly. All that we need to know in
the realm of religion and morality can be derived through the use of reason,
but God in His wisdom has supplemented reason with revelation as a further
demonstration of the designated path.

Like other deistical writers before him, Morgan had a difficult time in
accepting the Old Testament as part of any divine plan for revealing truth.
The moral character of the patriarchs and the kings, and the numerous tedious
ceremonies and pointless sacrifices were hard to reconcile with the wishes of
the Christian God. Morgan followed Blount in blaming the Egyptians for
having introduced superstition among the Jews, causing them to lose the
knowledge they had about God and religion. Sacrifices, which had originally

been merely feasts, were transformed into rituals according to the Egyptian rite. Joseph, meanwhile, introduced clergy and priestcraft as a negative and restraining factor. Like Spencer, Morgan emphasized the concept of accommodation, arguing that a strict ceremonial law was the only method Moses could adopt for keeping the Israelites under control as they had been degraded and rendered superstitious by long years under Egyptian influence. In this way, Morgan could explain at a stroke the degeneration of the Israelites from the recipients of God's message in the time of Abraham, and also demonstrate that the Old Testament was in fact the history of a Middle Eastern people with no direct relevance to the European Christian. Morgan rejected typology as did Collins, and refused to apply to Israelite ceremonies the allegorical interpretation which a man like Woolston used to shore up the narrow strait between the Old Testament and the New.[96]

Morgan is often represented as a somewhat disreputable figure among the Deists, despite his self-proclaimed medical credentials. Jacob Ilive's (1705–63) image was the same but more so, and rests largely on the oration he gave at Joiners' Hall on 24 September 1733 in which he preceded Morgan in expressing extreme distaste about the Old Testament, but combining this view with certain fantastic elements. Ilive claimed that God created this world as a place of residence for Satan, and that it is in fact the hell against which we have been so often warned. The notion of a separate hell apart from earth is one of the many deceitful fancies of the lying clergy. The fallen angels, meanwhile, were embodied in men, who might still be reconciled to God through repentance. Those who miss their chance will be condemned to live in darkness when the entire earth returns to its original chaos by means of a non-material fire. The similarities between Ilive's views and those of the Gnostics was lost on no one, but they are instructive as to what inferences might be drawn from a rejection of the Old Testament and Israelite history.[97]

Perhaps the most impressive deistic reinterpretation based on a rejection of the Old Testament as part of the Christian story came from Matthew Tindal (1657–1733) in his *Christianity as Old as the Creation*, published in 1730. Tindal was a notorious high-liver at All Souls, who changed his religion several times at the most advantageous moments, although he always denied that he did so from any venal motives. Nevertheless, his book is rather ingenious, and in many ways merits its reputation as a high point of the deistical writings. Tindal's argument, presented in the form of a dialogue, is that Christianity is not a new religion at all, but a 'Republication of the Religion of Nature', based on reason and the law of nature itself. This religion corresponds to true morality, which is the nature of God. Revelation, once again, functions to confirm what mankind can discover for itself, but often fails to, though not for lack of inherent faculties. Organized religion, with its rituals and ceremonies, is merely superstition, although public worship may be beneficial if the maximum amount of flexibility is allowed as to actual practice.

The Bible was the subject of Tindal's thirteenth chapter, and he found it hard to reconcile the Scriptures with his own definition of religion. The Old Testament was unworthy of rational man, with its anthropomorphic God and its immoral biblical heroes. The New Testament was also problematic, especially as Jesus and the Apostles clearly thought that the end of the world was rather more nigh than it actually was, and thereby undercut any claim for infallible prophesying. In the end, Tindal had to adopt the rather vague rule of thumb calling 'to admit all for divine Scripture, that tends to the Honour of God, and the Good of Man; and nothing which does not.' That is to say, anything in the Bible which is congruent with the law of nature ought to be accepted, but nothing else on mere scriptural authority. Jesus was often hard to understand, as his words 'were accommodated to the then Way of speaking', but we need to avoid sectarian interpretations of the Bible, which is a text open to all. Tindal's emphasis on the moral and ethical teachings of Scripture inevitably led to the denigration of the purely historical sections which would therefore have little to teach rational Christians. Indeed, ethical Christianity would hardly need Jesus or the Bible at all.[98]

VII

At least in a general way, the Deists were primarily interested in questioning and even dismantling the Newtonian synthesis which had prevailed in so many aspects of seventeenth-century thought and religion. As yet, the Deists concentrated on particular aspects of the picture: Collins turned his critical eye to prophecy, while Woolston attacked the conventional view of miracles. Quite obviously, the notion of constant divine intervention was wearing very thin. What was required was to look at the entire framework and attack conventional perceptions at the weakest point. This was the achievement of David Hume (1711–76), who rightly recognized that the consensus among thinkers regarding science and religion was based on the reality of miracles and the fulfilment of prophecy. Much work had already been done by the Deists in undermining these claims, and many of their arguments remained unchallenged.

Hume presented his case in most convincing fashion in *An Enquiry Concerning Human Understanding* (1748). Section X, 'Of Miracles', is a clear exposition of one of the key problems in biblical studies, and for Christianity in general. J.H. Randall, in his survey of the history of philosophy, described Hume's work thus:

one of the classic philosophical instances of an irrefutable argument permanently accepted as valid, he proved so conclusively that intelligent men have rarely questioned it since, that a miracle, in the sense of a supernatural event given as a sign of the divinity of its worker, cannot possibly be established.[99]

Hume admitted that there were certainly events which might be justly described as 'marvellous', such as the attitude of the Indian prince when frost was first described to him. But such men might reasonably deduce that although they had never seen water in any state but fluid, 'they never saw water in Muscovy during the winter; and therefore they cannot reasonably be positive what would there be the consequence.' A far different case is that of the 'really miraculous'. As Hume defined it, 'A miracle is a violation of the laws of nature', or alternatively, 'a transgression of a law of nature by a particular volition of the Deity, or by the interposition of some invisible agent.' Hume argued that even if it could be shown that the events recorded did actually take place, any supernatural claims for their origin would be impossible to demonstrate because no witness sufficiently infallible could be produced.

From these premises it was a short jump for Hume to assert 'that a miracle can never be proved, so as to be the foundation of a system of religion.' Such a claim would be entirely against human reason, and so it should be, Hume writes, since 'Our most holy religion is founded on *faith*, not on reason; and it is a sure method of exposing it to put it to such a trial as it is, by no means, fitted to endure'. This was the tactic of 'those dangerous friends or disguised enemies to the *Christian Religion*, who have undertaken to defend it by the principles of human reason.' This was presumably a disingenuous swipe at Locke, who abandoned the championing of reason when confronted with the insurmountable problem of religious truth.

But the chief proving ground had to be the Bible, and Hume chose the Pentateuch for a close reading according to the principles of those defenders of reason that he pretended to despise:

Here then we are first to consider a book, presented to us by a barbarous and ignorant people, written in an age when they were still more barbarous, and in all probability long after the facts which it relates, corroborated by no concurring testimony, and resembling those fabulous accounts, which every nation gives of its origin.

Anyone working solely from the standpoint of reason, looking at the Bible as if it had a human rather than a divine author, would find it impossible to accept what is written there at face value. 'I desire anyone to lay his hand upon his heart,' dared Hume,

and after a serious consideration declare, whether he thinks that the falsehood of such a book, supported by such a testimony, would be more extraordinary and miraculous than all the miracles it relates.

Hume continued by making the point that everything he said about
miracles applied equally to prophecy, which is in essence a form of miracle,
since it reflects a process ordinarily beyond the capacities of mankind.

When Hume reflected on the wider implications of his own analysis, there
was only one inference which could be drawn:

> upon the whole, we may conclude, that the *Christian Religion* not only was
> at first attended with miracles, but even at this day cannot be believed by
> any reasonable person without one. Mere reason is insufficient to convince
> us of its veracity: and whoever is moved by *faith* to assent to it, is con-
> scious of a continued miracle in his own person, which subverts all the
> principles of his understanding, and gives him a determination to believe
> what is most contrary to custom and experience.

Hume's style here is more than somewhat sarcastic, but he was quite correct
in arguing that the strategy of basing or even limiting religious belief to what
could be anchored in reason was dangerous in the extreme. 'The religious
philosophers,' he affected to complain,

> not satisfied with the tradition of your forefathers, and doctrine of your
> priests (in which I willingly acquiesce), indulge a rash curiosity, in trying
> how far they can establish religion upon the principles of reason; and they
> thereby excite, instead of satisfying, the doubts, which naturally arise from
> a diligent and scrutinous inquiry.

Hume topped up his demonstration of the incompatibility of the Bible, faith,
and reason by attacking in Section XI the cosmological proof for the existence of God – the 'watch in the heath' argument later made famous by
William Paley. Hume's point was that no matter how wonderful and beneficial the effect – such as order in the universe – we have no justification for
making inferences about the cause. Even assuming the existence of a Creator,
we can say nothing at all about His character or motivations. The world as
we know it may be a sort of cosmic sick joke.

Taken as a whole, Hume's critique of conventional religious assumptions
was devastating. The Deists' debate had already passed, and while many of
their more wild claims, such as the Egyptian origin of Israelite religion, were
no longer given a serious hearing, the questions they raised had not been put
to rest. Hume's work, written in a far more moderate manner and far less
sensationalist, was able to reap the rewards of pioneers such as Blount, Toland,
and Morgan. From our point of view, Hume dealt a serious blow to those

who championed the Bible as a source of inerrant historical truth. At a stroke, many of the advances in biblical interpretation that had taken place in the last century became frighteningly irrelevant. If the Bible was really such an unreliable book written by a such a barbarous and ignorant people, then it was hardly worth applying to it the new-found techniques of textual criticism developed in France and England. When Hume examined the Bible not as the undisputed word of God but as 'the production of a mere human writer and historian', the contradictions and absurdities found therein rendered the entire enterprise of questionable use.

Hume's focus on miracles in general and biblical miracles in particular also helped set the goalposts for future discussion. Hume was essentially interested in 'violation miracles', the transgression of a law of nature in order to make a religious or metaphysical point. Focusing on Scripture, he was much less concerned with 'coincidence miracles' whose religious significance is largely in the eye of the beholder, such as the philosopher's hypothetical train that miraculously stops inches before hitting a child playing on the tracks. Hume well knew that apart from such impressive miracles as turning water into wine, Christianity simply could not do without the Resurrection. As Paul himself admitted, 'if Christ be not risen, then is our preaching vain, and your faith is also vain'.[100] Doubting Thomas wanted to see for himself,[101] but in Hume's view, even his testimony must be relegated to the sphere of inadmissible hearsay evidence.

VIII

By the middle of the eighteenth century, David Hume seemed, at least to fellow philosophers, to have destroyed the key concepts of providence, prophecy, and especially miracles, all of which could no longer be used by reasonable men to justify their Christian faith. The Bible was degraded to a temporal literary product of a primitive tribe living in uncivilized times. After the minimalization of the biblical text promoted by the Latitudinarians, Locke, the Deists, and Hume, the Bible came to be seen in far more general terms, with basic truths that were rather simple to comprehend. The Scriptures were descholarized, even streamlined. The rejection of the notion that study of the Bible was necessarily complicated and out of the reach of ordinary people, however, was fundamentally different from the prevailing concepts of biblical interpretation during the English Civil War a century before. During Cromwell's time, it was an act of faith that everything written in Scripture was crystal clear and it was criminally obscurantist to erect scholarly barriers between the godly readers and their divine text. The point that Hume, Locke and their predecessors were making was that the *core* of biblical teaching was

transparent, and any further study for religious or moral purposes was unnecessary, or at worst mere antiquarianism. This is one reason that biblical paraphrases became more popular during the middle of the eighteenth century,
a popular response to the streamlining of Scripture. We stand at the very end
of the period when the deficiencies of the biblical text could be noted but
still not affect religious business as usual.

CHAPTER 5

The Occult Bible: Aestheticization and the Persistence of the Supernatural

The bishopric of St David's in Wales was always famously poor. When the Welshman Henry Tudor changed his name to Henry VII, one of his first acts was to try to improve the state of the Welsh episcopate, but he and his successors were always defeated by the poverty of the see. There were forty bishops of St David's between the beginning of the sixteenth century and the end of the nineteenth, but only half of them stayed put; the rest got themselves translated to more lucrative and less isolated postings.[1] But St David's was a good place to be a trainee bishop, and quite a number of well-known figures got their start there, including the infamous Archbishop William Laud, scourge of the Puritans, who was executed in 1645.[2]

Among this illustrious group of eastward-looking bishops of St David's was Robert Lowth (1710–87), a New College man who held the professorship of poetry at Oxford for nearly ten years from 1741, before he began his steady rise in the episcopate. Lowth was given the Welsh see in 1766, but hardly had time to unpack before he returned in glory the same year as bishop of Oxford. He soon showed himself to be one of the most able clerics of his day, and a translation to London in 1777 was followed six years later by the offer of the archbishopric of Canterbury, which he actually turned down.[3]

How does a professor of poetry get offered the job of primate of the Anglican Church? In the case of Robert Lowth, it was by making the astonishing claim that, above else, the Bible was Literature, and that its poetry conformed to all the canons of verse which we have a right to expect from great art. Indeed, according to Lowth, Hebrew poetry is ontologically the most ancient and the best of all

> than which the human mind can conceive nothing more elevated, more beautiful or more elegant; in which the most ineffable sublimity of the subject is fully equalled by the energy of the language and the dignity of the style. And it is worthy observation that as some of these writings exceed

in antiquity the fabulous ages of Greece, in sublimity they are superior to the most finished productions of that polished people.[4]

By choosing the word 'sublimity', Lowth was also signalling his appreciation of the prime and nearly universal aesthetic categories of his day, the 'sublime' and the 'beautiful'. As Kant (1724–1804) expressed it in his celebrated discussion of the concept, the sublime 'is a magnitude which is like itself alone', unimaginable power beyond compare, inspiring respect and fear. The merely beautiful, on the other hand, has an identifiable form capable of representation, and thus it generates love.[5] Edmund Burke (1729–97) wrote about the sublime in his youth (1757), and made this idea the basis of his conception of monarchy when reflecting on the Revolution in France forty years later.[6] The 'sublime' was the most overused intellectual buzz word of the eighteenth century, and Robert Lowth wants us to know that he is *au fait* with the very latest literary jargon.[7] From our point of view, Lowth and his defence of the Bible as Literature are crucially important for understanding the way in which the radical Hebraic millenarianism of Cromwell's day was aestheticized and transformed into a benign contemplative pastime suitable for a scholarly bishop in rural eighteenth-century Wales.

I

Lowth was very keen on biblical poetry: indeed, he saw it everywhere in the sacred text, arguing against tradition that even 'the writings of the Prophets [are] in general poetical', especially Isaiah, who was 'the first of all poets for sublimity and eloquence'.[8] Earlier biblical commentators had seen the prophets as masterful orators; but poets – this was something new.

It also carried within it a contradiction which needed to be resolved, for 'sublimity' and 'poetry' do not necessarily go together. The sublime, as Lowth defines it, is 'that force of composition, whatever it be, which strikes and over-powers the mind, which excites the passions and which expresses ideas at once with perspicuity and elevation, not solicitous whether the language be plain or ornamented, refined or familiar'. According to Lowth, the sublime is the essence of poetry: 'in a word, reason speaks literally, the passions poetically.'[9]

In many ways, this is a very odd claim to make. The emphasis on the passions is certainly very Romantic and eighteenth-century, and in this we should hardly be surprised. On the other hand, Lowth and his contemporaries had very definite ideas on what poetry was and how it should be written, and this did not include stream of consciousness. Lowth would have hated *Finnegans Wake*.

First of all, for Lowth, poetry is metrical. The Hebrew Bible obviously is not. This is a problem which Lowth resolves with resounding circularity:

> But since it appears essential to every species of poetry that it be confined to numbers and consist of some kind of verse (for indeed, wanting this, it would not only want its most agreeable attributes but would scarcely deserve the name of poetry), in treating of the poetry of the Hebrews it appears absolutely necessary to demonstrate that those parts at least of the Hebrew writings which we term poetic are in metrical form.

In other words, since poetry is metrical and the Bible is poetry, it must therefore be metrical: the facts must conform to the theory. Anyway, Lowth explains, 'scarcely any real knowledge of the Hebrew versification is now to be obtained'.[10]

But even more important than the identification of metre in true poetry, there was what Lowth calls 'parallelism'. As Lowth defined it, 'parallelism' is a rhetorical device

> chiefly observable in those passages which frequently occur in the Hebrew poetry in which they treat one subject in many different ways, and dwell upon the same sentiment; when they express the same thing in different words, or different things in a similar form of words; when equals refer to equals, and opposites to opposites: and since this artifice of composition seldom fails to produce even in prose an agreeable and measured cadence, we can scarcely doubt that it must have imparted to their poetry, were we masters of the versification, an exquisite degree of beauty and grace.[11]

Lowth goes on to delineate three distinct varieties of parallelism: (1) the *synonymous*, in which 'the same sentiment is repeated in different but equivalent terms'; (2) the *antithetic*, in which 'a thing is illustrated by its contrary being opposed to it'; and (3) the *synthetic or constructive*, 'in which the sentences answer to each other not by the iteration of the same image or sentiment, or the opposition of their contraries, but merely by the form of construction'.[12] Parallelism, this 'artifice of composition', works in the Bible because it is perfectly suited to Hebrew, 'so that what in any other language would appear as superfluous and tiresome repetition, in this cannot be omitted without injury to the poetry.'[13]

In other words, somewhere between metre and parallelism, the untamed passions of the sublime − mortal man confronted with omnipotent God − are directed into the controllable channels of biblical poetry. How unlike the home life of the inferior classical poets:

> For what is meant by that singular frenzy of poets which the Greeks, ascribing to divine inspiration, distinguished by the appellation of

'enthusiasm', but a style and expression directly prompted by nature itself and exhibiting the true and express image of a mind violently agitated? when, as it were, the secret avenues, the interior recesses of the soul are thrown open, when the inmost conceptions are displayed, rushing together in one turbid stream, without order or connection.[14]

Just as God created order out of chaos when He inspired biblical verse, He was displeased with extravagant poetry which 'was without form, and [therefore] void'.

So the Bible was Literature, and its Hebrew text was not only poetry, but that of the highest quality, since the divine hand played a major role in the editing, and ensured that the *sublime* fear and awe which we experience when contemplating the Godhead might be subtly transformed into the containably *beautiful*. Constraining the unruly passions was obviously a good thing for an eighteenth-century English bishop, especially one who spent even a few months in Wales, but applying conventional literary categories to the Bible might have other effects as well.

If Robert Lowth could be brought back to life and restored to his old job teaching poetry at Oxford, after a lunch or two with the luminaries of the English Faculty he would probably start using the word 'transparency'. By this he would mean that there is a reality behind the text, which in its 'transparency' enables us to see it clearly. Moses was a real and living person, whose existence is unaffected by whether or not the events of his life are ever told, or how many trees fall in the forest to make books about him. Jesus walked, and his existence outside of the Bible is testified paradoxically by the very fact that his story is told in four separate versions in the Gospels, demonstrating a complete dissociation of form and content.

This is not exactly literature in the way in which we might understand the term. Frank Kermode, writing about the Bible as a literary creation, begins by quoting Henry James, who confessed in the preface to *The Portrait of a Lady* that he always invents the characters first and then builds the story around them. According to Kermode, the opposite is true in the Bible, where the story is the driver, as the narrative moves 'from fable to written story, from story to character, from character to more story'.[15] Just as there is no point in asking, 'How many children had Lady Macbeth?' since she is merely a fictional character in a play, we should understand that a figure like Judas was invented somewhere between Mark and Matthew in order to flesh out the betrayal of Jesus and to produce a more satisfying literary creation.[16]

Robert Lowth would never endorse such a view of biblical literature, in which it is argued that instead of being a transparent window, the objects under scrutiny have been embedded in the glass itself, and thus have no independent reality. By publicizing the notion of the Bible as Literature, Lowth cut the ribbon on a new waterway which would open up into an ocean of modern criticism that stretches from California to Calcutta and back again. But it would be wrong to think that this waterway swept all before it, gathering strength in nineteenth-century German Higher Criticism and culminating in the writings of D.F. Strauss, Ernest Renan, Erich Auerbach, Northrop Frye, Frank Kermode, Edmund Leach, Robert Alter, and their respective Jewish and Christian clones and critics. For as important as this Higher Criticism/Bible as Literature stream is for the development of the European mind, it never completely washed away the parallel line on which travelled those scholars who continued to see the Bible as a source of secret and esoteric wisdom. These men and women did not see the Bible as Literature in the sense of an artefact which itself creates the reality we perceive in the narratives of Moses and Jesus. Yet nor was the Bible merely a transparent medium, unimportant in itself, for better viewing of the living reality which lay on the other side. The biblical critics of this third group championed what one might call 'the occult Bible', in that they endowed the Scriptures themselves with supernatural qualities which might be accessed by mankind today living in the contemporary mundane world. In their view, there *was* a reality behind the text, a *content* which could be separated from *form*. At the same time, they learned from Lowth, and others before and after, that form was also important, for within the sacred words and structures of the Bible lay other less accessible and more esoteric secrets. In their devotion to winkling out the mysteries of the biblical texts they pioneered numerous techniques of literary criticism, and were quick to adopt the conclusions of religious professors of poetry like Robert Lowth, whose research only confirmed what they already knew: that the writings of Shakespeare and Milton were children's nursery rhymes when compared with the Hebrew poetry and prose of the First Author Himself.

Certainly, it is possible to exaggerate the originality of Robert Lowth in promoting the notion of the Bible as Literature. Even people in ancient times recognized that the Bible was a pretty good read. Lowth himself paid tribute to Rabbi 'Azarias', the celebrated Azariah de'Rossi, the sixteenth-century Jewish expert on chronology, whose book *Me'or Einayim* was an important work of biblical exegesis in which the concept of parallelism is clearly stated.[17]

A perhaps less obvious precursor is our old friend Joseph Mede (1586–1668), the Cambridge don whose discovery of *The Key of the Revelation* (London, 1643) eventually established the book of the Apocalypse as a literary artefact. Mede had been struck by a remark made to St John the Divine (Rev. xvii) by 'one of the seven angels which had the seven vials' regarding the identity of 'the great whore that sitteth upon many waters'. The 'woman which thou sawest', revealed the angel, 'is that great city, which reigneth over the kings of the earth', that is to say, Rome. According to Mede, the seventeenth chapter of the Book of Revelation is therefore the 'key' which opens up the book from the inside, in that it simultaneously shows us the interpretative method which we need to use (allegory) and warns us that there is only one possible interpretation for each allegorical figure (in the paradigmatic case, Rome).

Mede used this information to deconstruct the entire text of the book, showing that instead of recounting future events sequentially, the Book of Revelation in fact represents a more limited number of events in architecturally constructed 'synchronisms' which are repeated a number of times using different allegorical figures. Perhaps this is how time itself will be organized in the future, after the coming of the Messiah, when the souls in heaven will be permitted to take part in a variety of episodes, each time playing a different character.[18]

Reading the Book of Revelation as Joseph Mede wants us to is not an easy task. Moses wished 'that all the Lord's people were prophets' (Num. xi. 29), but Mede would have none of that. He established a sort of school for the canonical interpretation of the Bible, especially its millenarian bits, and drove home the idea that verse-mining and quoting out of context was unacceptable. Every passage in the Bible needed to be seen against the background of the structure of the complete text, which was planned with such exactitude that it could be conceived of spatially as a sort of temple of words. In other words, Joseph Mede was arguing that the Bible was Literature, and that the only people fully qualified to interpret the text were scholars of this literature. Mede may not have accurately predicted the coming of the Messiah, but he did prophesy the coming of the English Professor, who makes claims about textual knowledge and brooks no challenge to his interpretative hegemony, which in any case is reserved for an elite group of scholars. Mede's temple of words becomes Derrida's 'prison house of language'.

Biblical critics like Joseph Mede and Robert Lowth, then, despite their devotion to Scripture, prophecy, and the millennium, became part of a process of damping down the religious excitement of Cromwellian England, when anyone could open a bible and calculate the Second Coming from Daniel, Revelation, and a virtually unlimited number of disconnected proof texts. This is not to deny that there were still many wild-eyed millenarian radicals in eighteenth-century England, and they could still command a following, like Richard Brothers (1757–1824) and Joanna Southcott (1750–1814). Joseph Priestley (1733–1804) and even David Levi (1740–99) were names to be reckoned with by anyone who took seriously the Second Coming of Christ. But the process by which the Bible became more than just a text, but actual Literature, would create a rather new and more scholarly school of millenarian interpretation, whose theories were even more unlikely than those of the popular prophets of the English Civil War.

Many histories of the Bible tend to emphasize those thinkers in the past whose beliefs seem comfortably like our own, or may be seen as helping move us in that direction. Such theological 'Whig History' passes over some of the schools of thought which were central in their own time. Both the Hutchinsonians and the Swedenborgians, for example, have been excised from the history of the English Bible because they seem to stand for a world view that was supposed to have disappeared with Spinoza and Newton. In some ways they are an historical inconvenience. From our point of view, they are important because their highly literary way of looking at the biblical text had the effect of helping to aestheticize Scripture, and thereby reduce the revolutionary potential of unrestricted individual millenarian interpretation.

II

Nowhere is this tendency towards 'Whig History' more apparent than in the almost complete neglect suffered by the Hutchinsonians, who ruled the roost in eighteenth-century Oxford, and long afterwards in Scotland.[19] In a sense, they were Hebraic alchemists, trapped somewhere between superstition and science. Their theology was based on the notion that only the consonants in the Hebrew Bible were divinely ordained, and that the vowels were a Jewish invention designed to pervert the original meaning of Scripture. As the Old Testament text itself is and remains a consonantal skeleton, their claim had immediate appeal to many Christians who began to test the waters of Hebrew scholarship. This approach was not in itself new, but the innovative nature of Hutchinsonian interpretation was demonstrated in their belief that the consonants themselves could be constituted into words by the use of any vowels which happened to fit, so as to give the text a variety of meanings. This, in English, would be to argue that *bad*, *bode*, *bid*, *bed*, and *bud* were all possible meanings whenever the consonants *bd* appeared in a word. As the Hebrew language is largely built on three-letter consonantal roots, such an axiom opened up the possibility of a much-expanded spectrum of possible interpretations for nearly all words. Such complicated word play was well within the infinite capabilities of the Almighty, and part of the multi-layered message of the Bible. The Old Testament became a sort of code-book containing all of the secrets of the universe, which now became available to the creative Hebraist.[20]

In many ways, the Hutchinsonians were merely a variety of the Christian kabbalist school which sought gentile messages within the Jewish Holy Writ. For centuries, Christian Hebraists had postulated, for example, that the first three letters of the Hebrew Bible, *beth*, *resh* and *aleph* were in reality abbreviations for *ben, ruach*, and *av,* 'son, spirit, and father'. Others noted that the addition of the Hebrew letter *shin* to the unpronounceable Tetragrammaton, the Name of God, created an approximation of the name of Jesus: the unsayable becomes articulate; the spirit made flesh. It was even argued that when written vertically the Tetragrammaton appears to be the stick figure of a man. The Hutchinsonians were very much in this spirit, and they regarded Newton as one of their chief bogeymen in that he sought in nature laws which should rightly be derived from re-reading the divine message to be found in the Old Testament itself.[21]

The founder of this school of thought was John Hutchinson (1674–1737), a Yorkshireman who was employed as a land steward in the household of the duke of Somerset. It was in this capacity that he met John Woodward (1665–1728), the duke's physician, who was slowly working on an attempt to reconcile the Old Testament with the geological evidence which even then was beginning to undermine the chronological narrative in the Bible. Hutchinson applied to the duke of Somerset for permission to leave his service and devote himself, like Woodward, to a study of science and religion, but when his noble employer heard of the project, he resolved to sponsor it himself. Hutchinson was provided with a sinecure, a house, and even the right to present to one of the duke's Sussex livings, which would enable him to employ a research assistant, Julius Bate (1711–71), who with Robert Spearman (1703–61) would edit and publish the founder's works after his death. Their efforts were essential, as Hutchinson's prose style was very nearly impenetrable.[22]

Hutchinson's Hebraic learning was more than a mere tool towards biblical understanding. In the eyes of his followers it was nothing less than a means of deconstructing the secrets of the universe by the use of a method far more effective than any trickery employed by the Newtonians. Hutchinson himself gave numerous examples of how his theory might be implemented. He pointed out, for example, that the word in Hebrew for the firmament described in Genesis is *rakia,* a derivative of the root *rka,* which 'signifies an opening, or dividing asunder, a drawing, or stretching out, according as where it is found, and what it is understood of – to expand, extend, distend, stretch'. On this basis, Hutchinson was able to conclude that the firmament at Creation consisted originally of air and water, and like 'a Plate of ductile Metal hammer'd, of Wings expanded, or such Things, is extending one Edge one Way, and the other the other Way'. Another example illustrates Hutchinson's principle that all words derived from the single root were not only related but virtually interchangeable. The two Hebrew consonants *shin* and *mem,* making the sounds 'sh' and 'm', together can be read either as 'a name' or 'a place', or in the plural, 'heavens'. As Hutchinson explained, in his inimitable prose, we can therefore see 'the Thing, to be the same as Place . . . Place and

Things are the same; and tho [*shin/mem*] be a General Name for Place, and Heaven be the Matter or Place which includes all'.[23]

But of course his most famous etymological demonstration was the emphasis on the common root of the words 'glory' and 'heavy', so that gravity could be seen as the product of the glory of God. 'Glory does not appear to be a Root, or have a separate Idea', Hutchinson surmised, 'but to imply that the Root of Weight is applied to beneficial Purpose, or to valuable Actions, or Things, so Glory'.[24] By equating gravity with God's glory, Hutchinson was able to argue that it was the divine will which caused objects to fall rather than any universal and impersonal laws. The creative application of unpointed (and therefore unvocalized) Hebrew allowed Hutchinson and his followers to disregard Newton and to reject his principles, especially those which postulated gravitation as a non-mechanistic, and therefore almost occult force. The problem was that Newton's knowledge of Hebrew was inadequate to understand the Old Testament in its original and therefore divine form. 'One would think', Hutchinson's editors argued, 'that such an one, born in a Christian country, who had access to examine books dictated by the Supreme Author of this system, would first have qualified himself to read and understand them, before he had dared to reject revelation, to set up a scheme in direct opposition thereto, stolen from the worst and blindest of the heathens'. Newton's experiments were misconceived from the start, and it was ludicrous to claim that 'some children's gewgaws, a three corner'd piece of glass, a hole in a window, the pendulum of a clock   may, it seems, become the foundation of mighty discoveries'. These, Hutchinson argued, 'shew no more than a few very singular properties of the *names'* of God, the key word being, of course, interchangeable with 'the heavens'.[25]

III

Certainly, from the philological point of view, Hutchinson's Hebraism belongs on the dust heap of wrong-headed ideas. His scholarship was demolished and ridiculed virtually in his own time by Benjamin Kennicott, fellow of Exeter College, Oxford, and Radcliffe librarian. This is why Leslie Stephen, who wrote John Hutchinson's entry in the *Dictionary of National Biography*, dismissed as a 'little eddy of thought' this 'school which, at the middle of the century, represented the influence upon theology of the great University of Oxford'. Stephen believed that we see here 'the crotchets of weak minds', but as he himself admits, the influence of the Hutchinsonians was enormous in the eighteenth century and demands explanation, if only to gain an understanding of the less than universal acceptance of Newtonianism in religious circles.[26] For it was especially in Oxford that Hutchinsonianism was adopted with a fervour, as a sort of High Church theological science. 'Was not I talking of religious sects?' wrote Horace Walpole (1717–97) to a friend in the country during September 1753,

> Methodism is quite decayed in Oxford, its cradle. In its stead, there pre-
> vails a delightful fantastic system, called the sect of the Hutchinsonians, of
> whom one seldom hears anything in town. After much inquiry, all I can
> discover is, that their religion consists in driving Hebrew to its fountain-
> head, till they find some word or other in every text of the Old Testament,
> which may seem figurative of something in the New. As their doctrine is
> novel, and requires much study, or at least much invention, one should
> think that they could not have settled half the canon of what they are to
> believe – and yet they go on zealously, trying to make and succeeding in
> making converts.[27]

Walpole was quite right about the growing strength of the movement. When Edward Gibbon (1737–94) came up to Magdalen College in 1752, hoping to become an Orientalist, he was dissuaded from the subject by his tutor. He noted that the only serious fellow student he found was George Horne, 'a young fellow (a future Bishop), who was deeply immersed in the follies of the Hutchinsonian system'.[28] Bishop Horne would indeed become the central figure in the movement at Oxford during the height of the school in the second half of the eighteenth century.

That Hutchinsonianism survived to be lampooned by Walpole was due not only to the publication of the master's works in 1742 by his disciples Robert Spearman and Julius Bate, but also to its adoption by a number of prominent intellectuals. First among these was Alexander Stopford Catcott (1692–1749), whose sermon on 16 August 1735 at the mayor's chapel before the corpora-tion of Bristol and Lord Chief Justice Hardwicke on the 'Supreme and Infe-riour Elahim' provoked the first serious debate about Hutchinsonianism and the scientific evidence contained in the Old Testament, effectively chal-lenging the Newtonian synthesis. His son Alexander Catcott (1725–1779) promoted Hutchinsonianism at Oxford in the middle of the century, and later at Bristol as vicar of Temple Church.[29] But the creed became genuinely respectable with its adoption by Duncan Forbes (1685–1747), the celebrated Scottish president of the Court of Session, who in 1732 made a public con-fession of his new-found faith.[30]

Even those who preferred Newton to Hutchinson in science, and Kenni-cott to Hutchinson in biblical scholarship, had to admit that some gold might be found among all of the dross. As the poet Alexander Pope (1688–1744) pointed out in 1736, 'Hutchinson is a very odd man and a very bad writer, but he has struck out very great lights and made very considerable discov-eries by the way, as I have heard from people who know ten times more of these matters than I do'. This was also the view held by Lord Bolingbroke: 'Does Lord Bolingbroke understand Hebrew?' Pope was asked. 'No, but he understands that sort of learning and what is writ about it'.[31] As Walpole noticed, in order to adopt the Hutchinsonian *torah*, it was necessary to learn a very great deal of Hebrew, and this in itself commanded respect.

Once Forbes and the Catcotts adopted Hutchinsonianism, his theories were given the respectability which allowed them to find a strong foothold in mid-eighteenth-century Oxford and to spread simultaneously to Scotland. One of the most distinguished Hutchinsonians in Gibbon's time was his fellow student George Horne (1730–92), president of Magdalen College from 1768, and bishop of Norwich two years before his death. Horne's tutor at University College, George Watson (1723?–73) was also a believer, as was William Jones of Nayland (1726–1800), the celebrated churchman who became Horne's chaplain at Norwich. Walter Hodges (1695–1757), the provost of Oriel College, was another follower of Hutchinson. William Stevens (1732–1807), editor of the works of Jones of Nayland, carried the principles of Hutchinsonianism into the nineteenth century, especially among the members of 'Nobody's Friends', the club founded by members of his group in 1800. Stevens, Jones of Nayland, and their associates have often been seen as the link between the Nonjurors of the seventeenth century, and the Tractarians and leaders of the Oxford Movement in the nineteenth.[32]

So too in Scotland were the Hutchinsonians influential. According to one clergyman who had been ordained about 1820, at that time there was hardly a single non-Hutchinsonian minister in the diocese of Aberdeen.[33] Chief among these was certainly the Reverend John Skinner (1721–1807), the incumbent of Longside, Aberdeenshire for sixty-five years. Skinner was imprisoned in 1753 for having conducted church services during the late Jacobite uprising, and while in jail had time to contemplate the controversy over the notorious Jew Bill of that year which would have given some Jews limited civil rights. Skinner applied himself to Hebrew, in part to provide better and more scholarly arguments against emancipation, and was soon led to adopt the Hutchinsonian interpretation of Scripture.[34] Skinner's son of the same name (1744–1816) became bishop of Aberdeen, and passed the see on to his own son (1769–1841).[35] From this nest came, among others, Alexander Nicol (d. 1828), appointed Regius professor of Hebrew at Oxford in 1822, who with his brother 'read Hebrew without the points'.[36] Another Scottish Hutchinsonian was the Reverend James Andrew (1774?–1833), who in 1823 published his 'Hebrew Dictionary and Grammar without points'.[37]

Hutchinsonianism was also transplanted to America, where it became the ruling method of scriptural interpretation at King's College, New York, which after the Revolution would be renamed Columbia University. The conquest of King's was due to the conversion of its first president, Samuel Johnson

(1696–1772), a leader in the revolt against Congregationalism at Yale in the 1720s, and later the most noteworthy disciple of George Berkeley in America. Johnson was much interested in science, and was drawn at first to Newton, but rejected him when he came across Duncan Forbes's *Letter to a Bishop*, and turned instead to the twelve volumes of Hutchinson's works. Johnson hoped that he would be succeeded at King's by George Horne, and wrote to Archbishop Thomas Secker in 1760 towards that end, but he was rejected out of hand on the grounds of his Hutchinsonianism and his opposition to Newton. Perhaps Johnson took comfort in the fact that although Secker's man Miles Cooper got the post, he was 'not unskilled in Hebrew'. After Samuel Johnson's retirement from King's College he devoted himself entirely to Hebrew and produced his own Hebrew–English grammar on Hutchinsonian principles.[38]

By the beginning of the nineteenth century, the interpretative side of Hutchinsonianism was wearing very thin, and Kennicott's monumental collation of existing Hebrew manuscripts of the Old Testament had demonstrated beyond all doubt that variations did exist, and were inevitable once one began to think of the Old Testament as an ancient book like any other. Yet Hutchinsonianism continued to find adherents and even admirers. William Kirby (1759–1850), for example, discussed Hutchinsonianism in his Bridgewater Treatise, admitting that although they have 'perhaps gone too far in an opposite direction' from Newton and other modern scientists, yet Hutchinsonians recognized that 'in order rightly to understand the voice of God in nature, we ought to enter her temple with the Bible in our hands'.[39] Samuel Taylor Coleridge (1772–1834) too turned to the Hutchinsonians for an interpretation of the meaning of the word 'firmament', concluding that

> We are far from being Hutchinsonians, nor have we found much to respect in the twelve volumes of Hutchinson's works, either as biblical comment or natural philosophy: though we give him credit for orthodoxy and good intentions. But his interpretation of the first nine verses of Genesis xi. seems not only rational in itself, and consistent with after accounts of the sacred historian, but proved to be the literal sense of the Hebrew text. His explanation of the cherubim is pleasing and plausible: we dare not say more. Those who would wish to learn the more important points of the Hutchinsonian doctrine in the most favorable form, and in the shortest possible space, we can refer to Duncan Forbes's Letter to a Bishop. If our own judgement did now withhold our assent, we should never be *ashamed* of a conviction held, professed, and advocated by so good, and wise a man, as Duncan Forbes.[40]

Indeed, Coleridge's copy of Forbes's book is annotated, and bears the marks of careful reading.[41] In sum, Coleridge saw 'the Cabbala of the Hutchinsonian School as the dotage of a few weak-minded individuals', but adopted some of their interpretations and appreciated their emphasis on the Old Testament and on the Hebrew text.[42]

IV

The Hutchinsonians became extinct and with them their distinctive and original theology, despite the fact that in their time they dominated whole areas of the English theological establishment. The Swedenborgians suffered a reverse fate, since their longevity in the form of a rather eccentric but by no means unsuccessful religious sect has had the effect of trivializing their interpretation of the Bible and of the metaphysical meaning of Christianity. In the long run, Swedenborg would be a decisive influence on later millenarians and mystics as diverse as the Mormons, Mary Baker Eddy (1821–1910), Madame Blavatsky (1831–91), and the Reverend Sun Myung Moon (b. 1920).[43] A contemporary of prophets like Richard Brothers and Joanna Southcott, Emanuel Swedenborg (1688–1772) was a scientist and philosopher of the first rank, whose religious views were unremarkable until he was in his middle fifties. Swedenborg is important for us in another way as well, for he provides a link and a channel into the world of the 'radical Enlightenment', where his followers mixed with Freemasons and neo-Rosicrucians in an attempt to find the keys that would unlock the occult secrets of the universe. Professor Margaret Jacob argued that in order to understand the origins of 'our politics and of democratic discourse' we should look back to the lodges of the eighteenth-century Freemasons: 'Rather than imagining the Enlightenment as represented by the politics of Voltaire, or Gibbon, or even Rousseau, or worse as being incapable of politics, we might just as fruitfully look to the lodges for a nascent political modernity.'[44] While Professor Jacob's thesis has not met with universal acceptance, her notion of a 'radical Enlightenment', centring around exclusivist societies such as the Freemasons, deserves a great deal of further investigation. Professor J.M. Roberts, in his pioneering study of secret societies, points out that in the *ancien régime* there was little scope for private activity outside the family. All this began to change in the early eighteenth century with the appearance of coffee houses, clubs, and salons . . . and exclusivist societies such as the Freemasons. England played a large part in this fashion, not only because a movement like Freemasonry was kept firmly under upper-class control, but also because England itself was fashionable in the first third of the eighteenth century. 'La preponderance anglaise', Professor Roberts reminds us, was felt in a variety of spheres, in politics, the army, and the economy, and also in the intellectual world. Newton and Locke had barely left the stage, advanced religious toleration was apparent, social mobility was a possibility, and parliamentary rule a comparative reality.

England had a particularly attractive culture and society during those years, which in part accounts for the success of Freemasonry abroad, especially in France.[45]

So too can 'Anglomania' – a contemporary word – be used to account for the Swedish connection. Swedenborg made at least eleven visits to England, living at Cheapside but avoiding public notoriety, not so much because of his opinions, but because of poor English made even more opaque by a speech impediment. By the time Swedenborg died in London in 1772 and was buried in the Swedish Church, he had delineated an impressive philosophy more suited to an intellectual school than a radical religious sect. Swedenborgianism was also out of step for another reason, in that Swedenborg and his followers opposed the Newtonian synthesis because they themselves were materialists in their philosophy (albeit of a unique kind) and thought that Newton was attributing occult properties to matter which should be seen as inert.

Emanuel Swedenborg was born in Stockholm in 1688, the son of a man distinguished in Swedish theology. His father changed his name from Swedberg when ennobled in 1719, in recognition of a career that would include the posts of court chaplain, professor of theology at Uppsala, and bishop of Skara. His son Emanuel studied at Uppsala until 1709, and then spent five years abroad, in England, France, and the Netherlands, where his primary aim was to learn of the latest advances in mathematics and natural science. Swedenborg seems already to have come under the strong influence of Eric Benzelius (1675–1743), his brother-in-law. Benzelius was mystically inclined, visiting Leibniz at Hanover in 1697, moving on to Francis Mercurius van Helmont (1614?–99) to sort out the Pythagorean kabbalah, and travelling to London to meet the members of the Philadelphian Society. Returning to Sweden in 1700, Benzelius turned more seriously to the study of Hebrew, using the services of a converted Jew named Johan Kemper. The two men worked on a kabbalistic interpretation of the New Testament and on annotations to Philo, talking of founding a pansophic college in Sweden. The young Swedenborg lived in Benzelius's house from 1703 and was surrounded by this combination of arcane scholarship and mystical lore.[46]

Swedenborg came to England in 1710, despite the tense political relations between the two countries in the run-up to the Jacobite rebellion, the 'Fifteen. There he came under the wing of the Swedish ambassador and may have been involved in revolutionary Jacobite and Freemason circles. He had opportunity to meet, and may have met, such luminaries as William Penn (1644–1718) and Lord Bolingbroke (1678–1751). Swedenborg seems to have visited Dr Jean Esdras Edzardi, whose family had converted many Jews in Hamburg by devising a convincing mixture of kabbalah and the New Testament. It has sometimes been claimed that Swedenborg himself joined a Freemasonic lodge, but as its politics would have been Jacobite, all records were destroyed after the failure of the rebellion in 1715.

With perfect hindsight, Emanuel Swedenborg's activities during those years do look like an ideal preparation for the occult views that he would hold in later life. But here too it is possible to exaggerate. When in Hanover shortly thereafter, he attempted to pay a call on Leibniz but found him away in Vienna. In this, Swedenborg was following in the footsteps of his mentor Benzelius, but any discussion they might have had would have touched on more than esoteric matters, we can be sure. Swedenborg's relations with Rabbi Haim Samuel Jacob Falk (1708–82), the so-called 'Baal Shem of London', a mystical magician whose exploits made him a well-known figure in late eighteenth-century London, are also more than mystifying. Falk in his commonplace book makes a reference to a certain 'Emanuel, a servant of the king of France', which may refer to Swedenborg with his Jacobite leanings.[47]

In any case, it was at Wellclose Square, near Falk's house, that Swedenborg had his first vision of Christ, on 7 April 1744. His life could never be the same again, although it was not until a year later that his mission was divinely confirmed. Swedenborg spent the remaining twenty-seven years of his life dedicated to purely religious questions, publishing about thirty books, all in Latin, mostly anonymously. That in itself points to the nature of Swedenborgianism as an esoteric philosophy more than a mass movement, and his theology should be seen in a more serious context than has often been the case. We need first, therefore, to examine his mature philosophy, especially in light of the fact that he claimed to have received his ideas from personal visits to the spiritual world rather than from mere reflection.

Swedenborg's goal was no less than to discover the substance that held the universe together. This task was complicated by his insistence that the world had more than a simple natural or physical aspect. He tinkered with the idea of magnetism, which would later become the preferred medium of Franz Anton Mesmer (1734–1815), but finally settled on the notion that the common bond was some sort of electrical vibration or very fine indestructible substance.[48] This latter object, he believed, was the soul of man, which not only is immortal but has actual dimensions. The spiritual and natural worlds, therefore, were merely different manifestations of the same substance. (Here Swedenborg is revealing himself as a student of Descartes's body/soul/mind debate, and indeed his thought is thoroughgoingly Cartesian.) Influenced by his near-interlocutor Leibniz, Swedenborg elaborated that all life derived from a single source, but it was organized on different levels or *series*: natural/physical, rational/living/intelligent/moral, and spiritual. Every particular object in the universe had its own place or *degree* in each of these three series. These parallels were called *correspondences*. Swedenborg was also influenced by the Platonic idea that none of the series could survive without a constant *influx* or spiritual input from God, the spiritual sun. Each degree or item in each series enjoyed a particular influx, which passed through the spiritual series, down through the rational, and finally the natural series. As a result, each item or degree on the spiritual plane had its exact counterpart in another item on the rational and natural planes, united by the fact that they were each touched by the same influx. These axioms had Platonic consequences, so that man's love and wisdom found perfect expression in the essence of God on a higher plane. Swedenborg was also therefore anti-trinitarian: Christ is God in human form, and at the crucifixion God retained some human aspects which He maintains on His highest plane, making Him a sort of divine human.[49]

Swedenborg saw himself as commissioned to announce the seventh and last revelation to a New Church, the very same body described in the Book of Revelation as the New Jerusalem. This organization commenced in 1757 when Jesus returned to earth, not as an inferior fleshly messiah, but this time interiorly and spiritually, by opening the eyes of men to the true meaning of the Bible. Swedenborg's Bible was somewhat shorter than usual, as he excluded 37 of its 66 books on the grounds that they were bereft of spiritual meaning. Nevertheless, he had great respect for the surviving scriptures, and his colossal *Arcana coelestia* was in effect an extended and unfinished commentary on Genesis and Exodus. But it is his last work, *The True Christian Religion* (1771), that is the clearest epitome of his thinking on this subject, as on most others.

Here Swedenborg approaches the difficulties in extracting holy truth from the Bible:

> The natural man, however, cannot thus be persuaded to believe that the Word is divine truth itself, in which are divine wisdom and divine life; for he judges it by its style which reveals no such things. Yet the style of the Word is a truly divine style, with which no other however lofty and excellent can be compared. The style of the Word is such that it is holy in every sentence, in every word, and sometimes in every letter; and therefore the Word unites man to the Lord and opens heaven.

The kabbalistic tincture of this sentiment hardly needs to be spelled out. Indeed, Swedenborg's theory of correspondences, when specifically applied to Scripture, takes on more than a superficial kabbalistic tone:

> That everything in nature and in the human body corresponds to spiritual things is shown in *Heaven and Hell*. But what correspondence is, has been hitherto unknown, although it was perfectly understood in the most ancient times; for to the men of that time the science of correspondence was the science of sciences, and was so universal that all their manuscripts

and books were written by correspondences. The book of Job, a book of the ancient church, is full of correspondences. The hieroglyphics of the Egyptians and the myths of antiquity were the same. All the ancient churches were representative of spiritual things; the ceremonial laws of their worship were pure correspondences; so was everything in the Israelitish church. The burnt-offerings, sacrifices, meat-offerings and drink-offerings were correspondences in every detail; so was the tabernacle with everything in it; and also the feasts of unleavened bread, of tabernacles, and of first fruits; also the priesthood of Aaron and the Levites and their holy garments . . . Moreover, all the laws and judgments relating to their worship and life were correspondences. Now, because divine things manifest themselves in the world by correspondences, the Word was written by pure correspondences; and for the same reason, the Lord, because He spoke from the divinity, spoke from correspondences. For everything from the divinity flows into such natural things as correspond thereto; and these outward things then conceal in their depth the divine things called celestial and spiritual.

Here, in this long extract, we see some of the key elements of Swedenborg's mystical biblical interpretation. Like the kabbalists, he thought that there was another parallel meaning to the scriptural word. Like the Deists and many others before them including Maimonides, Swedenborg championed the notion of 'accommodation', arguing that God had adapted His message to the ability of His hearers to comprehend what He was saying, but reserving a deeper meaning for those with greater spiritual insight. Like Mede and Hutchinson, Swedenborg advocated a prolonged close reading of the biblical text by the use of techniques which had been vouchsafed to him alone, in order to undermine the surface reading and penetrate to the divine truths lurking below.[50]

Interestingly, Swedenborg also showed some similarity to the deistical biblical critics in his fascination with the contribution made by other ancient peoples to our understanding of God's Word. According to Swedenborg, he had 'been informed' by the spirit world that 'the men of the most ancient church, which existed before the flood, were of so heavenly a genius that they conversed with the angels of heaven; and that they had the power to do so by correspondences.' So whenever they saw something on earth, they were able to determine its corresponding form on the spiritual plane. Swedenborg also claimed that 'Enoch and his associates (Gen. v. 21–4), made a glossary of correspondences from the speech of the angels, and transmitted this knowledge to posterity.' This fact was to have an enormous impact. 'As a result,' Swedenborg explains, 'the science of correspondences flourished in many kingdoms of Asia, particularly in Canaan, Egypt, Assyria, Chaldea, Syria,

Arabia, Tyre, Sidon, and Nineveh, and was thence communicated to Greece, where it became mythical, as may be seen from the oldest Greek literature.' We can see, therefore, Swedenborg explains, that

> Religion has existed from the most ancient times, and the inhabitants of the earth everywhere have a knowledge of God and some knowledge of life after death; but this is not from themselves or their own intelligence, but from the ancient Word, and afterwards from the Israelitish Word. From these two Words religion spread to India and its islands, through Egypt and Ethiopia to the kingdoms of Africa, from the maritime parts of Asia to Greece, and thence to Italy. But, as the Word could only be written symbolically, that is, by mundane things corresponding to and therefore signifying heavenly things, the religion of the Gentiles became idolatrous, and in Greece mythical; and the divine properties and attributes were looked upon as so many gods, dominated by a supreme deity called Jove, possibly from Jehovah. And they had a knowledge of paradise, the flood, the sacred fire, and the four ages, from the golden age to that of iron. (Dan. ii. 31–5)

In orthodox fashion, if somewhat eccentrically, Swedenborg thereby postulates the Hebrews as the source of eternal wisdom, a little lower than the angels.[51]

Swedenborg also sought to account for the evident degeneration of the Hebrews from purveyors of a divine monopoly to the superstitious Jews with whom we are familiar today. In his view, in 'the course of time the representative rites of the church, which were correspondences, began to be turned into idolatry and also into magic.' It was not by accident, but by 'the divine providence of the Lord' that the Israelites lost the 'science of correspondences', which was eventually 'amongst the Israelitish and Jewish nation totally obliterated.' Since their worship consisted entirely of correspondences, this was a crucial loss, and what had originally been a symbolic and pure worship gradually became superstitious. Not only the Jews, but other ancient peoples began to confuse the symbol with the thought expressed and, for example, worshipped images of calves and oxen, forgetting that originally these were powerless objects which merely signified 'the affections and powers of the natural man'. Fortunately, the 'knowledge of correspondences remained among many eastern nations, even till the coming of the Lord'. This is why the wise men came from the East, bearing symbolic gifts. Indeed, the 'ancient Word, which existed in Asia before the Israelitish Word, is still preserved among the people of Great Tartary', a fact which was personally confirmed to Swedenborg by 'spirits and angels who came from that country'. 'But the science of correspondences was completely unknown to the Israelitish and Jewish nation, although all the details of their worship, and all the statutes and judgments given them by Moses, and everything contained in the Word, were pure correspondences.' Apart from divine intention, the reason for this is that Jews 'were at heart idolaters' and were more interested in the ceremonies than in their spiritual meaning. This is also why they were unable to recognize the messianic role of Jesus, since they were prepared for a messiah who would give them an earthly kingdom and 'who should exalt them above all the nations in the world, and not one who should take care of their eternal salvation.'[52]

According to Swedenborg, the 'science of correspondences, which is the key to the spiritual sense of the Word, is to-day revealed, because the divine truths of the church are now being brought to light.' This was a fact which he had been taught during his sojourns in the spiritual world, and indeed his description of the role of the Bible there was truly fantastic. In that higher place, he recalled,

> The Word is kept in the shrines of the angelic temples and shines like a great star, sometimes like the sun with a halo of beautiful rainbows; this occurs when the shrine is first opened. All the truths of the Word shine, as I learnt on seeing that, when any verse is written on paper and thrown into the air, the very paper shines in the form in which it has been cut; so that spirits can by the Word produce various shining forms, even those of birds and fishes. But what is still more wonderful, if any person rubs his face, hands, or clothes against the open Word, so as to touch the writing, his face, hands, and clothes shine as if he were standing in the brilliance of a star. This I have often seen with wonder; and it showed me why the face of Moses shone when he brought down the tables of the covenant from Mount Sinai.

On the other hand, sometimes an opposite process also occurs in the spiritual world, for

> if any person obsessed by falsities looks at the Word lying in its sacred place, darkness shrouds his eyes, and the Word appears to him black and sometimes as if covered with soot; while, if he touches the Word, a loud explosion follows, and he is hurled into a corner of the room, where he lies for a time as if dead. If any one obsessed by falsity writes a passage from the Word on a piece of paper and throws it in the air, a similar explosion follows, and the paper is torn to pieces and vanishes; the same thing happens if the paper is thrown into the nearest corner. This I have often seen.

While somewhat kabbalistic in flavour, then, Swedenborg's attitude to the biblical text was, if possible, even more mystical, based on what he believed himself to have witnessed in the spiritual world.[53]

Swedenborg's view of the Hebrew language itself is original and unique. 'There was once sent down to me from heaven', he revealed, a piece of paper covered with Hebrew characters; the letters were curved as among the ancients, not straight as they are to-day, and had little extensions at the top. The angels with me said that each letter had a complete meaning which was largely expressed by the curves and their extensions . . . They told me that writing in the third heaven consists of letters variously curved and inflected, each of which has a special meaning; that the vowels I and E are replaced by Y and EU, and that A, O, and U have a specially rich sound; that they do not pronounce consonants roughly, but smoothly, and for this reason some Hebrew letters had dots in them to indicate a soft pronunciation. They added that hard sounds are used in the spiritual heaven because the truth of that heaven admits of hardness, whereas the good of the Lord's celestial kingdom, or third heaven, does not.

Like the kabbalists, Swedenborg also thought that the very words and letters of the Bible had mystical powers which awaited deciphering by the illuminati.[54]

Certainly, it is very difficult to argue with a man who claimed to 'have been permitted by the Lord to be in the spiritual and natural worlds at one and the same time; thus I have conversed with angels as with men, and have become acquainted with the state of those who after death pass into that hitherto unknown world.' Heaven, he revealed, was constituted as a *homo maximus*, a giant man, with the parts of his body consisting of angels. Swedenborg testified that he had 'conversed with all my relatives and friends, also with departed kings, dukes and men of learning, and this continually for twenty-seven years.'[55] Sometimes entrance was gained by the technique of taking one breath every thirty minutes.

Apart from spirits and angels, some other sources for Swedenborg's interesting biblical theology suggest themselves. Chief among these is Jacob Boehme (1575–1624), the German mystic who became notorious for stressing the dualism of God which required evil as a complement to His divine goodness. Boehme's most famous disciple in Swedenborg's time was William Law (1686–1761), whose influence on the Wesleys, and whose connection with the Philadelphian Society of Jane Lead (1623–1704) and Francis Lee (1661–1719) is well documented.[56] Swedenborg denied having read Boehme, but there were some very obvious similarities with Law's theology. Among these was the notion that God emitted an 'eternal nature', which was His very body and being, and which was in effect the spiritual world. This higher reality had its counterpart in a lower celestial realm made up of the opposing principles to be found in God's nature – fire/light, good/evil, and so on. This was the angelic world. Below this was an even lower existence, the material world, created by the rebellion of the angels, in which the dualities were no longer in balance. Nevertheless, connections and analogies between the three different levels existed and remained in operation. Man himself, originally an angel, was now a denizen of the material world, and was in effect a spirit trapped in a physical body. Jesus, by taking human form, injected a divine element into mankind, providing the hope of his restoration to the spiritual existence. Law, unlike Boehme, was optimistic that this reunion would eventually occur, hell would be destroyed, and all mankind would be saved. Swedenborg's ideas were so similar that he appealed to many old Behmenists, such as Thomas Hartley (1709–84), who had a great influence on Samuel Taylor Coleridge.[57]

Swedenborgianism thus began as a philosophy and only gradually mutated into a sect, largely through having been picked up by the rector of a Manchester parish named John Clowes (1734–1831), a former member of Wesley's 'Holy Club' who had begun with the writings of William Law and chanced upon Swedenborg's Latin works in 1773. Clowes remained within the bosom of the Anglican Church, even refusing a bishopric in 1804, and introducing only as much of Swedenborg's views into his sermons as he thought the market would bear. The new gospel spread throughout Lancashire, at the same time that the Methodists were making important inroads in this area. Both groups began within the Established Church, and only later, and very reluctantly, declared their independence. Furthermore, the Methodists, like the followers of Swedenborg, placed great emphasis on non-rational religious revelation: convulsions rather than visions, but nevertheless part of the same mixture of folk traditions and respectable religion.

John Wesley (1703–91), the founder of Methodism, was himself in two minds about this strange alliance. He wrote about Swedenborg in his journal that

> Any one of his visions puts his real character out of doubt. He is one of the most ingenious, lively, entertaining madmen that ever set pen to paper. But his waking dreams are so wild, so far remote both from Scripture and common sense, that one might as easily swallow the stories of 'Tom Thumb' or 'Jack the Giant-killer'.

Later on, after reading 'that strange book', Swedenborg's *Theologia coelestis*, Wesley added that

> It surely contains many excellent things. Yet I cannot but think the fever he had twenty years ago, when he supposes he was 'introduced into the society of angels', really introduced him into the society of lunatics; but still there is something noble, even in his ravings.[58]

Similarly, there was a certain amount of migration between the two groups at the popular level, especially as the Methodist chapel became too much of a symbol of respectability for many Lancashire workers to stomach. Swedenborgianism also appealed to groups outside the Methodist sphere of influence, such as those in the Huguenot community, attracted no doubt by Swedenborg's connection with Freemasonry and other European occultists, such as the French Prophets.

Like the Methodists, the Swedenborgians found themselves drawn almost inevitably into institutionalization, although one group opposed to separation gathered around Jacob Duché (1738–98), chaplain of the Asylum for Female Orphans in Lambeth. The first step was the foundation in about 1783 of the Theosophical Society, which read and discussed Swedenborg's works. The great man's manuscripts had been shipped back to Sweden after his death, where they could not be published, but were now beginning to appear in greater numbers, thanks to Clowes's determination and effort. The very word 'theosophical' was redolent of Freemasonry, and promised a combination of biblical study and fashionable neoplatonism. One of their prominent members, General Charles Rainsford (1728–1809), was heavily involved with kabbalah, Freemasonry, alchemy, and astrology. Continental Freemasonic circles were informed, aware, and excited by the existence of Swedenborgian reading groups in England, and these contacts were extended during the 1780s. Rainsford was an important link, and he promoted the Swedenborgian visitation at the Congrès du Philalethes, organized by the French speculative Freemasonic lodge of the Amis Réunis in 1784–5, and again in 1787. Swedenborgian representatives attended the meeting in 1784, which had primarily been called to unite Freemasons on the Continent and to agree on some common elements of doctrine. As a result, some of the leading lights there came to England to see the new philosophy for themselves, including the Marquis de Thomé, Count Tadeusz Grabianka, and even the notorious 'Count' Cagliostro (1743–95), the champion of 'Reformed Egyptian Freemasonry', who would end his life a prisoner in a tiny Inquisition cell.[59]

This occult tinge was given a somewhat more Christian and less 'pagan' motif in 1785 when on the advice of the Marquis de Thomé, they renamed themselves the Society for Promoting the Heavenly Doctrines of the New Church designed by the New Jerusalem in the Revelation of St John. The new name preserved at least one element of Swedenborgianism's attraction, which was its almost Romantic emphasis on the spiritual, as opposed to the arid rationalism of the Enlightenment and its influence on the Established Church. Far from being a theological system opposed to empirical science, Swedenborgianism might be seen as a truly pioneering creed, extending the principle of experimentation to the spiritual realm. Almost everyone believed that there were spiritual forces at work in our material world; the Swedenborgians were the first to do something about it and, unlike the Methodists, were not so quick to ascribe these powers to the Devil.[60]

By 1788 it was clear that the followers of Swedenborg would have to open their own chapel and the society was renamed the New Church. Ordinations and baptisms soon began, and the group settled into the traditional pattern of English Dissent, without giving up the occult impulses which created it in the first place. Swedenborg's voluminous writings assumed the character of a third testament, and the man himself was increasingly venerated. The New Church underwent a crisis when Swedenborg's *Conjugal Love* was translated into English and published in 1794, for in this book he declared that a man could take a 'concubine' to slake his lust, or even to leave his lawful wife if he found a more fitting spiritual partner at a later stage. Swedenborgians were also accused, by the abbé Barruel (1741–1820) and others, of being with the Deists one of the illuminist sects that were indirectly responsible for the French Revolution and the political disturbances of the age. The post-millennial theology of the Swedenborgians, it was said, in claiming that Christ had already returned, also called on believers to be alert for manifestations of his renewed glory, which most obviously could include revolutionary political change. The Unitarians were also post-millennialist, and the Swedenborgians seem to have lost many followers to that less demanding sect. By the turn of the century, the Swedenborgians were insisting that the Second Coming was spiritual rather than political, and did not involve a restructuring of national governments, but by then their period of dramatic expansion had ended.

The Swedenborgians became more respectable and even more intellectual, especially under the leadership of Samuel Noble (1779–1853) who was chiefly interested in publishing accurate translations of the founder's writings. This more philosophical inclination, which probably would have been blessed by Swedenborg himself, ensured that they would never become a truly popular sect. Not only were the holy books in Latin, but it was a very long time before more simplified versions of Swedenborg's writings appeared. In any case, Swedenborg's theology was contemplative more than congregational or social, and was unsuited for the sort of passionate community that the Methodists engendered. Even if northern congregations attracted greater number of artisans and people who were locally active, in the south Swedenborgianism would retain a decidedly intellectual tinge. This was not to everyone's taste, as the poet William Blake (1757–1827) would discover.

Blake had been a follower of Swedenborg, but by 1790 he already had severe doubts. 'Thus Swedenborg boasts that what he writes is new; tho' it is only the Contents or Index of already publish'd books', Blake complained,

A man carried a monkey about for a shew, & because he was a little wiser than the monkey, grew vain, and conciev'd himself as much wiser than seven men. It is so with Swedenborg: he shews the folly of churches, &

exposes hypocrites, till he imagines that all are religious, & himself the single one on earth that ever broke a net.

Now hear a plain fact: Swedenborg has not written one new truth. Now hear another: he has written all the old falshoods.

Blake was cross partly because in his view Swedenborg's theology was not completely original: 'Thus Swedenborg's writings are a recapitulation of all superficial opinions, and an analysis of the more sublime – but no further.' Indeed, he wrote, 'Any man of mechanical talents may, from the writings of Paracelsus or Jacob Behmen, produce ten thousand volumes of equal value with Swedenborg's, and from those of Dante or Shakespear an infinite number.'[61] The fact was that, despite Swedenborg's frequent conversations with angels and other spiritual beings, his writing was in the last analysis an amplification and exposition of the divine truths already vouchsafed to mankind in the Bible, or at least those chapters that were left after he wielded his pruning hook on the text. But Swedenborgianism was enormously influential on an entire group of writers and poets, not only Blake, but also Balzac, Baudelaire, Emerson, Yeats and Strindberg. Indeed, one almost hears Swedenborg talking of a 'chain of signifiers' when he writes about the world of correspondences, and for that alone we should be wary of putting him too firmly '*sous rature*'.

V

The interpretative systems of men like Mede, Lowth, Hutchinson, and Swedenborg were so complex and intricate that they either commanded belief or compelled their detractors to invest a good deal of time and energy in preparing a refutation. We tend to think of millenarianism and messianism as doctrines which by their very nature are intrinsically radical and destructive of the existing religious and social order. In point of fact, when the apocalyptic belief systems themselves become exceedingly complex, the intellectual property of an elite group of highly trained religious philosophers, then the net effect may be conservative in nature. Terry Eagleton makes this point about much of eighteenth-century literature, when he notes the Romantic

> stress upon the sovereignty and autonomy of the imagination, its splendid remoteness from the merely prosaic matters of feeding one's children or struggling for political justice. If the 'transcendental' nature of the imagination offered a challenge to an anaemic rationalism, it could also offer the writer a comforting alternative to history itself.[62]

The Bible, as Literature, requiring canonical interpretation of an artful text, could be quarantined in a protected zone separate from the cares and needs of everyday life. This process of damping down may also have been the result of the concrete pictorial representation of the Apocalypse by William Blake and others, which inevitably transformed the unthinkable sublime into the merely beautiful.[63] The aestheticization of millenarianism which occurred in eighteenth-century England alongside the more exciting messianism of people like Richard Brothers or Joanna Southcott kept eschatology safe.[64]

This is still the case. The Canadian critic Northrop Frye, himself a clergyman, wants us to believe that the goal of all literature is to create a 'self-contained literary universe' in which 'we have moved into the still center of the order of words'. When Frye turned his attention to the most divine work of literature, he called his book on the Bible, *The Great Code*.[65] With the help of professors we can enter that 'still center', decipher the great code, and live in Canada. Having read and internalized the writings of Robert Lowth and German Higher Criticism, they produced that utopian hybrid of a messiah who comes on time.

CHAPTER 6

Divine Copyright and the Apotheosis of the Author in Eighteenth-Century England

'The highest praise of genius is original invention', wrote Samuel Johnson of Milton, and this quotation has been cited more times than his biography of the poet has been read.[1] A good deal has been written during the past decade about the emergence of a new conception of the author during the second half of the eighteenth century, most of it emphasizing the novelty of the authorial stance which Johnson praised so highly.[2] The claim has been made that between the Renaissance and about 1750, the writer was valued primarily as a master craftsman who plied his trade and exhibited his skill. The author was expected to make good and pleasing use of raw materials available to anyone. This indeed was his greatness, to fashion something aesthetically beautiful out of the ideas and images around him. The Renaissance author declined to emphasize his originality: many published their works anonymously precisely to avoid notoriety. Even if an author did publish his work under his own name, it was not recognized as the product of his individual labour, according to the Lockian definition that one's labour defines one's individual worth and freedom.[3] The Renaissance author's published work was owned by his bookseller, who derived all the profits from sales of books and who gave the writer a flat fee for a craftsman's job well done. It was therefore impossible to earn one's living as a writer. The Renaissance author was forced to rely on patrons, who in turn supported the writer materially, but did not value him more than any other servant or craftsman.

This Renaissance paradigm, according to current theory, began to break down in the seventeenth century. A key figure here is Ben Jonson, who constructed himself and his writing by publishing his work in standard and permanent folio form.[4] At the same time, Jonson played an important role in the designation of Shakespeare as the authorial model, despite the fact that little is known about the Bard's life, most of his plots were unoriginal, and he never published his own work.[5]

The great struggle over the birth of the modern author, however, was in the commercial arena, with the epic battle over the issue of copyright.[6] This is the implication of Michel Foucault's diktat that 'Texts, books, and discourses really began to have authors (other than mythical, "sacralized" and "sacraliz ing" figures) to the extent that authors became subject to punishment, that is, to the extent that discourses could be transgressive.'[7] The protagonists were the London booksellers versus the provincial publishers. In order to protect their right to keep making money from the works of the authors they published, the strategy of the London booksellers was to contend that a writer's labour produced a commodity of permanent worth much like land itself, the ultimate form of property. Provincial booksellers made most of their money on reprints, so they hoped to convince Parliament and the courts that literary property was more like a patent on a new invention. It might temporarily allow the inventor to reap a certain financial benefit, but ultimately good ideas belonged freely to mankind. In their argumentation, the London booksellers were driven to proclaim the notion of the modern author, an individual producing a unique work from the intellectual labour of his own private thoughts. At the end of the day, the famous Copyright Statute of Queen Anne (1710) allowed for only a fourteen-year exclusive right of publication, followed by a second term of the same length if the author was still among the living. Despite a number of important court cases, the notion of permanent copyright was decisively defeated.

According to the current interpretation of this chain of events, it was two generations later that the concept of the authorial 'genius' began to be accepted.[8] Samuel Johnson is given the credit for being the first major writer to liberate himself from the comfortable shackles of the patronage system when he preferred to publish his dictionary without the embrace of Lord Chesterfield's patronage.[9] Alexander Pope may have been the first English poet to make a living at writing.[10] Beginning in Germany, an idea evolved that the author was a writer whose work was designed to convey a unique experience whose very distinctiveness would provide the reader with pleasure.[11] No longer was the aim of literature to demonstrate virtuosity, to awaken in the reader an appreciation for craftsmanship with known materials and forms. From the middle of the eighteenth century, the author was an economically self-sufficient genius whose greatness lay in producing something substantially different and original, to create admiration in the reader who recognized a greater intellectual Other. William Wordsworth (1770–1850) saw genius in this way, and Edward Young's essay of 1759, so influential in Germany, provided the philosophical underpinning for the concept of authorial genius.[12]

This dichotomy – the Renaissance writer pirouetting before wealthy and aristocratic patrons, versus the Enlightenment author as creative literary capitalist – may be too stark, even if satisfying a basic need for binary opposition and order among chaos. For one thing, the world looks very different if we begin with the modern author and look backwards, as opposed to beginning with the Renaissance and looking forward to the Enlightenment and after. Men like Machiavelli were no strangers to self-serving glory and fame; even while grovelling for Medici patronage, he succeeded in presenting himself and his work as a most distinct Other.[13]

That being said, and those reservations being expressed, there is no doubt that the eighteenth-century author was a more independent figure than his or her counterpart of two hundred years before. Protected by the Copyright Act, relying on a hugely expanded literary market-place, a writer could more easily strut the intellectual stage proclaiming genius. This was true not only for those authors most directly affected by public support, the playwrights, but also those whose works appealed to a smaller and more distinctly learned clientele. For whatever we decide about the emergence of the modern author, the same sort of strictures applied to those who published scholarly works.

Richard Bentley (1662–1740) and Benjamin Kennicott provide us with examples of the classic case of the scholarly author who attempted to cross the boundary between the university and the outside world, to appeal to a more general public. Bentley was a fellow of Trinity College, Cambridge and the greatest New Testament scholar of his age. Kennicott was at Exeter College, Oxford and was the foremost eighteenth-century gentile expert on the Old Testament. Both proposed to provide new and corrected editions of their chosen Testaments, and both tried to be self-financing by floating them on a sea of subscriptions. But there the difference ends. Bentley's work met with general encouragement, despite his abusive personality. Kennicott, writing thirty years later, was greeted by a flurry of opposition from those Hebraic alchemists, the Hutchinsonians, and others whose attitude to the biblical text would make a modern American Fundamentalist blush. Comparing the work of Bentley and Kennicott may not only provide us with the key to understanding the evolution of modern biblical criticism, but also throw light on the contemporary debate over the birth of the modern author.

I

The name of John Mill has certainly been eclipsed by that of Richard Bentley, his successor. It was Mill, however, who first laid the groundwork in England for the revision of the original Greek text of the New Testament and, even more significantly, helped create the atmosphere that made such an attempt possible. His biography itself is uneventful. He went up to Queen's College, Oxford, became a fellow, and in 1680 was appointed chaplain to King Charles II. Mill obviously suffered from few confessional problems, since he was willing to serve in the same capacity both Charles's Roman Catholic brother James II, and his Protestant successor William III after the Glorious Revolution. He married once, but his wife lived less than a year and he was loath to repeat the experiment. Mill became principal of St Edmund Hall in 1685, a post which he retained until his death in June 1707.[14]

John Mill worked on his revised edition of the New Testament for thirty years. Indeed, it was his life's work in more than a conventional way: a fortnight after it was published, Mill died. According to the prolegomena to his great work, he started on his texts after he gave up the post of senior bursar of Queen's College in July 1678, urged on by his Orientalist friend Edward Bernard (1638–96), the Savilian professor. The real inspiration for Mill's work, however, seems to have been Dr John Fell (1625–86), the dean of Christ Church, and later bishop of Oxford. Fell's was the first edition of the Greek New Testament published at Oxford in 1675, a rather poor and badly printed octavo volume which included maybe a dozen manuscripts in the Bodleian, and even these with incomplete references.[15] Any serious study of the New Testament manuscripts would have to take into consideration more than a hundred different exemplars, and it was a task that Fell might have turned to, had he not been called to the bishopric of Oxford the year after his own volume appeared. Bernard suggested John Mill as a likely successor, and Fell agreed. It was a work much desired, and even Queen Anne was moved to tell Mill to hurry it up in August 1705.[16]

The task that Mill faced was daunting. There was, of course, Erasmus's Greek and Latin New Testament published at Basle in 1516. He also had the Complutensian Polyglot which was printed two years before Erasmus, but published only in 1522. These two points of heritage were fabulously unequal. The Spanish Polyglot appeared in only 600 copies and was already quite rare, while Erasmus set out to make a best-seller. Erasmus was also more creative: when his Greek text of the Book of Revelation ran out, he simply made up the Greek on the basis of the Latin Vulgate. Several other key editions of the New Testament followed.[17]

Simon de Colines produced a revision of the third edition of the Erasmus text in 1534, making a few changes, and omitting 1 John v. 7, the Trinity proof text which Erasmus eventually restored under great pressure. De Colines's son-in-law Robert Estienne, the great printer, published his own New Testaments, the third edition of which, appearing in 1550, used a traditional text, but noted in the margin variants from the Complutensian Polyglot and fifteen manuscripts. This was the copy of the New Testament that was printed in the Polyglot (1654–7) of Brian Walton, thus making it the standard Greek text of the New Testament used in England.

The final important source which Mill had before him came from Calvin's successor Theodore Beza, who gave his Codex Bezae ('Codex D') to

Cambridge in 1581. This manuscript included everything from the Gospels to Acts, and helped form the basis of Beza's own published text. Beza also used ten additional manuscripts, the Syriac version, and the Arabic version in Latin, but did not allow these peripheral exemplars to affect the main substance of the text. He therefore found himself differing from Estienne in 176 places. Beza's text was reprinted throughout the sixteenth century, and formed another part of the heritage of the New Testament revision.

Brian Walton's Polyglot (1654–7) included the New Testament as volume 5, including not only the Greek text, but also Latin, Syriac, Arabic, and Ethiopic versions, with the Gospels in Persian. Walton added complex tables and essays, and this volume was published separately after his death, in 1673 and again in 1777. The sixth and final volume of Walton's Polyglot was a huge collection of critical material, with variant readings from the more esoteric versions, as well as two groups of variants from the different Greek manuscripts. Walton had marginal notes from Estienne's third edition, and suggestions from fourteen other manuscripts, including the Codex Bezae. Walton claimed that he had used variants 'gathered out of above forty old Greek MSS.'[18] These included Estienne's fifteen MSS, the Codex Alexandrinus which had been given to Charles I by the Greek patriarch in 1627 (and about which more later), and fourteen new manuscripts acquired by Irish Archbishop James Ussher, nearly all of which were to be found at Oxford and Cambridge. All of this does not add up to forty plus, but perhaps Walton was including those used in the Complutensian Polyglot. Still, it was Walton who called the Codex Alexandrinus 'Codex A', and thereby started the convention of designating the different uncial manuscript versions of the New Testament in this fashion.

The last New Testament Mill had to consider was that produced at Amsterdam in 1658 at the Elzevir Press by Etienne de Courcelles (Curcellaeus) of Geneva (1586–1659). Curcellaeus worked in France for a time, and in 1643 went to Amsterdam to take Simon Episcopius's distinguished chair. He wrestled with the question of 1 John v. 7 like others before him. Curcellaeus put the phrase in square brackets and noted that it is not to be found either in many older Greek and Latin manuscripts or in Syriac, Arabic, or Ethiopic; nor is it cited by many of the Fathers, nor is it to be found in some of the printed versions of the New Testament that had appeared before his own.

John Mill prepared for his task not only by eye-piercing work among the manuscripts and by close attention to the work of his predecessors from Erasmus to Curcellaeus, but also by keeping up to date with the latest biblical criticism from France. His prolegomena makes it clear that he knew of Richard Simon's critical history of the text of the New Testament, published in 1689. Mill testified that it was his reading of Simon that sent him back to patristic quotations of the New Testament and encouraged him to look for less obvious sources of textual transmission.

The *Novum Testamentum Millii* was published on 9 June 1707.[19] The prolegomena alone was a prodigious feat: 200,000 words of Latin and Greek, covering 168 pages in double columns of 78 lines each. It was divided into three parts. The first 38 pages discussed the canon of the New Testament, followed by 115 pages regarding the transmission of text, including an analysis of the various manuscripts and printed versions. The last 15 pages delineated the special features of his own edition. In total, Mill in his prolegomena described 32 printed editions of the Greek New Testament, and mentioned three others; eight works of variant readings; two editions of Matthew in Hebrew;[20] 87 MSS and three catenae (series of patristic comments on Scripture). Much of the work was done by Mill himself. He collated 33 MSS and more than 13 of the early printed editions of the Greek New Testament. Critics might argue that Mill knew no Oriental language apart from Hebrew, and that when he compared the Arabic with the Syriac versions he was in fact using the Latin texts of both. One might even quarrel about the amount of Hebrew that Mill had. Johann Jacob Wetstein, his later competitor in the same field, would argue that there were 10,000 errors in Mill.[21] But it was still a prodigious feat.

The text of the Greek New Testament was essentially copied from Estienne's edition of 1550, 809 pages in all, with only about thirty changes. At the bottom of the page, Mill included parallels from other places in the Bible and, more importantly, similar patterns which he discerned in patristic and classical sources. His notes could be extensive: pages 740–9 were devoted exclusively to the *comma Johanneum* (1 John v. 7), the controversial proof text for the Trinity.

Once completed, Mill's edition of the New Testament was rapidly made available to the public. The imprimatur of the vice-chancellor of Oxford and the dedication are dated 25 March 1707, and it was actually published on 9 June, sporting an engraving which eternalized the presentation of the work to Queen Anne. According to advertisements in the *London Gazette*, it cost 36 shillings, but could be had in better quality at a higher price. It was sometimes bound in two or three volumes, but we do not know how many copies were printed.

Gerard of Maastricht, in the prologue to his own Greek New Testament published in 1711, said that Mill had found 30,000 variants, and that figure has been imprinted in the critical mind ever since.[22] This achievement alone should have procured Mill unqualified praise, but in a sense he spoiled the unadulterated effect himself by following Brian Walton's lead in prefacing his book with a highly political Latin epistle to the queen in which he denounced both Roman Catholics and the French in general. He also gratuitously minimized the contribution of William III, who was said to have needed the thoroughly English Marlborough to complete the routing of the French. This no doubt did not endear him to the Dutch, who used Ludolph Küster

(1670–1716), himself a serious scholar, to revitalize Mill's edition within a very short time. Küster had been made professor at Berlin at the age of thirty, but was allowed to travel freely. He was in England from 1700 to 1705, and thus was aware of Mill's work, and indeed would later become a close friend and associate of Richard Bentley. Küster returned to Berlin, but soon was to be found living in Utrecht, where he set about revising Mill and reorganizing the work in a more useful way. His first edition was published at Rotterdam in 1710, and in its third version, published at Amsterdam in 1746, essentially pirated Mill's work to the extent that Küster's version became the European standard edition.[23] Charles Butler (1750–1832), the Catholic critic, in his classic survey of sacred literature, noted that Mill's 'work formed a new aera in Biblical criticism.' Indeed, 'While sacred criticism lasts, his learning, indefatigable industry, and modest candour, will be spoken of with the highest praise.'[24]

Mill was also noticed by Jean Le Clerc (1657–1736), the great Protestant biblical critic and associate of Locke. Le Clerc wrote two articles (before 1708, and 18 September 1708) in the *Bibliothèque Choisie* (Amsterdam), as did Jacques Lenfant (1661–1728), the celebrated pastor of the French Protestants at Berlin (5 June 1708 and 31 December 1708). Both men had visited England, and indeed, Queen Anne was said to have wanted to make Lenfant her chaplain after Mill's death. So these two leading biblical critics had their ears very close to English soil, and their words carry some weight. Le Clerc's views were probably the more important, and he was favourable, although he did not accept all of Mill's proposals, and was disappointed that the paper was too thin and the printing not up to the Eurostandard. He also thought that it was useless to start with Estienne's text as the baseline, and thereby pile up insignificant variants.

Another important torchbearer of Mill's was the Protestant biblical critic Christopher Matthew Pfaff (1686–1760), who had a chair at Tübingen, and then at Giessen University. He also came to England, and spent the winter of 1708–9 at Oxford. He was primarily interested in Mill's methodology, in the 'critical canons' he used to divide the wheat from the chaff in the Greek New Testament. Mill did not distinguish these canons in so many words, but his predecessor Bishop Fell had already done so in his New Testament published at Oxford in 1675, citing thirty-seven criteria by means of which he could do his work. Pfaff tried to put all of this methodology into order, and in some ways helped to systematize Mill's major advances, in his *Dissertatio* published at Amsterdam in 1709.[25]

Other, more minor, attempts were made to improve on Mill's work before Bentley took up the chase. Joseph Hallet (1691?–1744), a Unitarian minister, published in 1728 an index of the Greek manuscripts and various versions used by both Mill and Küster.[26] Further attempts to correct Mill's text were made by William Bowyer the younger (1699–1777) in 1763[27] and Edward

Harwood (1729–94) in 1776.[28] Dr Edward Wells (1667–1727) produced a Greek and English New Testament between 1708 and 1719, the first attempt since Beza to print a corrected text. His English was that of the Authorized Version adjusted to fit the Greek, so in a sense it is the first genuine Revised Version of the English Scriptures.[29] The final work worthy of mention is that of Daniel Mace, a Presbyterian minister at Newbury (d. 1753), who in 1729 published (anonymously) a Greek New Testament with the translation in parallel columns, very useful for someone actually working with the text. He had a straightforward approach to Scripture, and steadfastly opposed all those who would 'substitute Popish absurdity for British sense'.[30]

II

In most discussions of eighteenth-century biblical scholarship, John Mill is seen as merely the precursor of Richard Bentley, the cantankerous classicist and excoriated Master of Trinity College, Cambridge. Apart from his combative nature, Bentley is most widely remembered for his epic role in the 'Battle of the Books' over whether the 'Ancients' or the 'Moderns' were to be credited with having made the greater contribution to Western civilization. Swift's caustic portrayal of the dispute gave Bentley eternal life in the history of English literature, but has partially obscured his efforts in New Testament scholarship. Although Bentley never produced the edition which he hoped would make all others superfluous, his pioneering research helped put the subject on a new footing.

The outlines of Bentley's life are quickly told, in part because he was the subject of one of the classic biographies written in English, that by J.H. Monk, published in 1833.[31] Bentley was born in Yorkshire, and went up to St John's College, Cambridge at the age of fourteen. From 1683 to 1689 he lived in the house of Dr Edward Stillingfleet, then dean of St Paul's, as tutor to his son. Stillingfleet was a leading theologian and philosopher, and his collection of books, now mostly in Marsh's Library in Dublin, was one of the best in his day. When Stillingfleet became bishop of Worcester in 1689, Bentley took orders the following year and became his chaplain. In any case, during those years Bentley was in Oxford when his pupil went up to Wadham, and it was then that he met John Mill. Bentley had great success in Oxford, and acquired a substantial reputation. When Robert Boyle died in 1691 and left money to finance lectures which would rout infidels and atheists, it was Bentley who was invited to give the first one the following year, and another in 1694. At that time, he was made keeper of the royal libraries, and elected to the Royal Society, followed by an appointment in 1695 as chaplain in ordinary to King William III. Bentley actually lived in St James's Palace as royal librarian, and this gave him the opportunity to consort with Newton, Locke, Wren, and Evelyn. From 1700, and for the next thirty-eight years, he was master of Trinity College, Cambridge, a post which embroiled him in endless quarrels with the fellows. He was Regius professor of Divinity from 1717, and vice-chancellor of Cambridge University.

This barebones sketch of Bentley's life hardly does justice to the activities of one of the most learned and colourful figures of early eighteenth-century English intellectual life, but it is just that richness that debars further elaboration here, for it would only diminish the story itself. Nevertheless, even a brief survey of Bentley's life would have to include the famous Phalaris dispute, in which Bentley tangled with Sir William Temple (1628–99), diplomat and statesman, on the question of whether the epistles of Phalaris were genuine. Temple had had the misfortune to hold up this work along with Aesop's *Fables* as examples of the superiority of ancient prose works to those of the moderns in his 'Essay upon Ancient and Modern Learning'.[32] Bentley knew that Phalaris was a late Greek forgery, and that Aesop's *Fables* contained much later material, but he never sought the controversy. His own involvement began when his bookseller Thomas Bennett was commissioned to produce a special edition of the classical work for Christ Church, Oxford, which intended to give the book as a Christmas present to all its members. Bentley told the bookseller that although the proposed edition would probably sell many copies, the text itself was a fake. The only result was that when the book was published under the name of Charles Boyle (1676–1731), later the earl of Orrery, the supposed editor took the opportunity to offer Bentley gratuitous insults for his ignorance.

Meanwhile, William Wotton (1666–1727), a Cambridge-educated clergyman, seized the moment to publish his *Reflections upon Ancient and Modern Learning* (1694), attacking Temple and his expressed views.[33] Bentley came aboard in the second edition of the *Reflections* (1697) which included his dissertation upon the epistles of Phalaris and the *Fables* of Aesop: this revealed that the Christ Church volume was in fact the work of incompetent dons hoping to attract patronage by giving the dubious credit to an aristocratic undergraduate.[34] An enormous 'Battle of the Books' was soon launched, involving all of the above-named protagonists, as well as Francis Atterbury (1662–1732), Temple protégé Jonathan Swift (1667–1745), and many others.[35] In this scholarly squabble, as in many others of a like nature, it was Bentley who was right.

Bentley recalled years later that his Hebrew studies began when

He wrote, before he was twenty-four years of age, a sort of *Hexapla*; a thick volume in quarto, in the first column of which he inserted every word of the Hebrew Bible alphabetically; and in five other columns, all the various interpretations of those words in the Chaldee, Syriac, Vulgate, Latin, Septuagint, and Aquila, Symmachus, and Theodotian, that occur in the whole Bible. This he made for his own use, to know the Hebrew, not from the late rabbins, but from the ancient versions; when, bating Arabic, Persic, and Ethiopic, he read over the whole Polyglot.[36]

A letter from William Wotton dated 14 May 1689 from St John's College, Cambridge, reveals that Bentley had already expressed an interest in the palaeography of the Codex Bezae and the Codex Claromontanus, two early manuscript versions of the New Testament.[37] John Mill himself wrote to Bentley about the same subject on 31 March 1691.[38] Ludolph Küster was already writing to Bentley in September 1708 concerning possible dedications for 'the Niew Edition of Dr. Mils Testament, which y have undertaken'.[39]

Biblical studies were not his primary concern, however, but they were not neglected. His early attitude to the text of the Bible may be reflected in a story too wonderful to be excluded as apocryphal. According to William Whiston,

> When Dr. *Bentley* was courting his Lady, who was a most excellent Christian Woman, he had like to have lost her by starting to her an Objection against the Book of *Daniel*, as if its Author, in describing *Nebuchadnezzar's* Image of Gold, *Daniel* vi. to be 60 Cubits high, and but 6 Cubits Broad, knew no better, than that Mens Height were 10 Times their Breadth, whereas it is well known to be not more than 6 Times. Which made the good Lady weep.

All was forgiven, however, and Bentley married Mrs Joanna Bernard on 4 January 1701.[40]

Bentley's interest in the New Testament as a classical text should probably be traced back to the paraphrase of that sacred book produced by Daniel Whitby (1638–1726).[41] Whitby followed up this work with a large folio study of John Mill's version of the New Testament, in which he made the following pronouncement:

> Although I acknowledge that Divine Providence has not so watched over Holy Scripture that no errors may have crept into it, yet it is agreeable to Reason to suppose that He who has established the Scriptures as the sole Rule of the Church for all time has had regard for this rule in such a way that it should never be inadequate or unsuitable for securing this end. For neither can infinite wisdom ever fail in its intention, nor can highest goodness, not to say justice, demand that the Christians should under gravest penalty order their life according to a standard which is insufficient for the purpose owing to corruptions that have become mixed with it

The problem with Mill's work, Whitby suggested, was that it seemed to provide ammunition to those who would attack Christianity. 'I GRIEVE', he wrote, 'therefore and am vexed that I have found so much in Mill's Prolegomena which seems quite plainly to render the standard of faith insecure, or at best to give others too good a handle for doubting'. To rectify this problem, Whitby provided his own five critical principles for biblical scholarship, the upshot of which was that not only was the text of the New Testament secure, since none of the variants found to date could cause any major changes in Christian theology or faith, but Mill's entire enterprise should be disregarded in favour of the received text as it stood.[42]

Whitby's work had exactly the opposite effect to that he had hoped. Anthony Collins (1676–1729) pounced on the revealed difficulties in the biblical text in his notorious (if anonymous) *Discourse of Free-Thinking*, which appeared in 1713. 'Free-Thinking', as he defined it, is 'The Use of the Understanding, in endeavouring to find out the Meaning of any Proposition whatsoever, in considering the nature of the Evidence for or against it, and in judging of it according to the seeming Force or Weakness of the Evidence'. Applying this dictum to the conduct of the clergy, he praised them for 'Their owning and labouring to prove the Text of the Scripture precarious', specifically referring the reader to Mill's famous 30,000 variants and to the scruples of Daniel Whitby.[43]

As might be expected, Collins's arguments were not allowed to stand without reply. They were officially condemned by Dr Benjamin Ibbot (1680–1725), the chaplain to the archbishop of Canterbury, in his Boyle Lectures for that year, in which he particularly addressed the issue of the text of Scripture.[44] Many others had their say as well, including William Whiston[45] and Jonathan Swift.[46] Among this distinguished group was Richard Bentley, who sheltered behind a Latin pseudonym while delivering his deadly salvo. His reply to Collins is so delightfully wicked that the following long extract gives an exemplary introduction to the man and his style:

> The Doctor's Labours, says he, make the whole Text precarious; and expose both the Reformation to the *Papists*, and Religion it self to the *Atheists*. God forbid! we'l still hope better things. For surely those *Various Readings* existed before in the several Exemplars; Dr. *Mill* did not make and coin them, he only exhibited them to our View. If Religion therefore was true before, though such Various Readings were in being: it will be as true and consequently as safe still, though every body sees them. Depend on't; no Truth, no matter of Fact fairly laid open, can ever subvert True Religion.
>
> The 30,000 Various Lections are allow'd then and confess'd: and if more Copies yet are collated, the Sum will still mount higher. And what's the Inference from this? . . . If there had been but One Manuscript of the *Greek*

Testament, at the restoration of Learning about Two Centuries ago; then we had had no *Various Readings* at all. And would the text be in a better condition then, than now we have 30,000? So far from That; that in the best single Copy extant we should have had Hundreds of Faults, and some Omissions irreparable. Besides that the Suspicions of Fraud and Foul Play would have been increas'd immensely.

It is good therefore, you'l allow, to have more Anchors than One; and another *MS.* to join with the first would give more Authority, as well as Security. Now chuse that Second where you will, there shall be a Thousand Variations from the First; and yet Half or More of the Faults shall still remain in them both.

A Third therefore, and so a Fourth, and still on, are desirable; that by a joint and mutual help All the Faults may be mended: some Copy preserving the True Reading in one place, and some in another. And yet the more Copies you call to assistance, the more do the Various Readings multiply upon you: every Copy having its peculiar slips, though in a principal Passage or two it do singular service. And this is fact, not only in the New Testament, but in all Antient Books whatever.

'Tis a good Providence and a great Blessing, That so many Manuscripts of the New Testament are still amongst us; some procur'd from *Egypt*, others from *Asia*, others found in the *Western* Churches. For the very Distances of Places, as well as Numbers of the Books, demonstrate; that there could be no Collusion, no altering nor interpolating One Copy by another, nor All by any of them.

This passage could hardly be bettered to stand as Bentley's credo for critical work yet to come.[47]

But the real declaration of serious intent only came eight years later, in Bentley's revealing letter to William Wake (1657–1737), newly elevated to the archbishopric of Canterbury in 1716. It is indeed, as Bentley warned his correspondent, 'a long letter about those unfashionable topics, Religion and Learning.' Bentley was concerned about 'what an alarm has been made of late years with the vast heap of Various Lections found in MSS. of the Greek Testament.' The variations provided ammunition for the Catholics against the *sola scriptura* Protestants, and for the atheists against them both. This was clearly seen in the dispute over Anthony Collins's book on *Free-Thinking*, although Bentley flattered himself that he had gone some way towards neutralizing its poison. 'But since that time', he wrote,

I have fallen into a course of studies that led me to peruse many of the oldest MSS. of the Greek Testament and of the Latin too of St. Jerom, of which there are several in England, a full thousand years old. The result of which has been, that I find I am able (what some thought impossible) to give an edition of the Greek Testament exactly as it was in the best exemplars at the time of the Council of Nic[a]e[a, AD 325]; so that there shall not be twenty words, nor even particles, difference; and this shall carry its own demonstration in every verse, which I affirm cannot be so done of any other ancient book, Greek or Latin; so that that book, which, by the present management, is thought the most uncertain, shall have a testimony of certainty above all other books whatever, and an end be put at once to all Various Lections now or hereafter.

Even if Bentley's sights were set impossibly high, it was a lofty goal, worthy of the ascent.

Bentley's letter, despite its historic importance, is a piece of personal correspondence, and in it he gives some idea of how he came to decide on his great project. It began 'by degrees' when out of curiosity he checked the text of a couple of Paul's epistles with the fifth-century Codex Alexandrinus (later tagged as 'A'), which had been given to Charles I by the Patriarch of Constantinople in 1627, and was still an exciting new source.[48] His copy of Mill's celebrated edition being at hand, he recalls,

I was surprised to find several transpositions of words, that Mill and the other collators took no notice of; but I soon found their way was to mark nothing but changes of words; the collocation and order they entirely neglected; and yet at sight I discovered what a new force and beauty this new order (I found in the MS.) added to the sentence. This encouraged me to collate the whole book over to a letter, with my own hands.

This is Bentley the editor in a nutshell: revising the text, and improving it so as to bring it into line with the high literary and intellectual standard which he represented.

Bentley reported to Wake the importance of the manuscript in Paris now known as 'C', the fifth-century vellum on which is written about 60 per cent of the New Testament, but over which in the twelfth century were penned Greek translations from the works of Ephraem of Syria, a fourth-century Church Father. Nevertheless, Bentley assures us, 'even now, by a good eye and a skilful person, the old writing may be read under the new.' Collating this Codex Ephraemi Rescriptus with the Greek New Testament as printed, Bentley detected over 200 variants, which turned out to agree almost entirely with 'our noble Alexandrian'. Bentley reckoned that if the oldest Greek manuscripts were properly collated, Mill's 30,000 variants could be reduced to even less than 200.

Unlike his mentor John Mill, Richard Bentley actually had a plan, a method, general principles which guided his work. In order to get as close as possible to the Greek text current at the Council of Nicaea in AD 325,

Bentley not only needed to find the oldest Greek manuscript possible, but also to demonstrate that this text was generally received at the time when it was written. He argued that this could be achieved by comparing that Greek manuscript with the oldest received *Latin* text that could be found. Such a received Latin text must represent a received Greek text, and where such a Latin version is essentially the same as the oldest Greek manuscripts that we have, then we can surmise that this Greek text is not merely very old, but was also the text accepted by the Church when the Latin version was made. Bentley affirmed that we could not simply use Pope Clement VIII's 1592 edition of the Sixtine Vulgate as a standard, since it is very different from the Alexandrian manuscript of the New Testament. But if we use Latin manuscripts a thousand years old, Bentley reports, then 'the success is, that the old Greek copies and the old Latin so exactly agree (when an able hand discerns the rasures and the old lections lying under them), that the pleasure and satisfaction it gives me is beyond expression.' Further evidence might be had by looking at quotations from the New Testament in the Greek Fathers from before Nicaea, such as Origen, who died many years before the council sat. Where Origen agrees, say, with the Vulgate, we can be reasonably sure that we have here a quotation from the New Testament as it existed at Nicaea. In other words, Bentley's method involved not only an appeal from recent documents to antiquity, the first five centuries of Christianity, but also an appeal to agreement between the Greek and Latin texts.

Bentley had something to say to Archbishop Wake about the 'hard fate' of the printed New Testament. 'After the Complutenses and Erasmus, who had but very ordinary MSS., it has become the property of booksellers', he complained.[49] Meanwhile, the so-called received text of Robert Stephens, 'set out and regulated by himself alone, is now become the standard. That text stands, as if an apostle was his compositor.' Indeed, Bentley pointed out, 'No heathen author has had such ill fortune'. The numerous errors in the first printing of classical authors were corrected by later scholars. 'But if they had kept to the first published text, and set the Various Lections only in the margin, those classic authors would be as clogged with variations as Dr. Mill's Testament is.' The revised Vulgates of Popes Sixtus V and Clement VIII represent hardly any advance, since 'though I have not yet discovered any thing done *dolo malo*, they were quite unequal to the affair. They were mere Theologi, had no experience in MSS., nor made use of good Greek copies'. They could hardly be blamed, wrote Bentley imperiously, 'for it is not every body knows the age of a manuscript.' Bentley's letter finally draws to a close:

> I am already tedious, and the post is a going. So that, to conclude, in a word, I find that by taking two thousand errors out of the Pope's Vulgate, and as many out of the Protestant Pope Stephens's, I can set out an edition

of each in columns, without using any book under nine hundred years old, that shall so exactly agree word for word, and, what at first amazed me, order for order, that no two tallies nor two indentures can agree better.

Bentley promised to 'alter not a letter of my own head without the authority of these old witnesses', which in light of his reputation today for promiscuous editing seems almost comical. The result would be not only a more faithful text, but a more aesthetically beautiful New Testament. 'My Lord,' Bentley warned, 'if a casual fire should take either his Majesty's library or the king's of France; all the world could not do this.'[50] A reply from the archbishop was soon forthcoming, encouraging Bentley in general and suggesting 'printing the Latin in a column against the Greek'.[51]

Bentley spent the next thirteen years engrossed in producing a revised version of the Greek New Testament text that would return to the standard set at the Council of Nicaea in AD 325. The man who took credit for inspiring Bentley in his great task was Johann Jacob Wetstein of Basle, who himself would later become a celebrated editor of the New Testament. Wetstein turned up in Trinity College at the beginning of 1716 and met him there and later at the King's Library in London where Bentley was librarian. Wetstein told Bentley that he had recently managed to collate the Codex Ephraemi Rescriptus in Paris and, on hearing this exciting news, Bentley urged his visitor to publish his findings. Wetstein, in turn, joined his voice to those of others who suggested that Bentley himself might like to take on this noble task.[52] Bentley's letter to Wake in April 1716 was the first announcement of the new project, and the fact that Archbishop Wake himself had done a bit of collating for Mill's New Testament while living in Paris during the reign of Charles II went some way towards ensuring ecclesiastical support.[53]

Bentley's correspondence during the following year is filled with ample testimony of his dedication to producing a better copy of the New Testament. Wetstein was his first ally, writing him informative letters from Paris in French regarding the progress of his research.[54] Others sent him manuscripts and encouraged him in his endeavours, such as Thomas Rud (1668–1733) of Durham, who also begged Bentley to 'write a Dissertation in answer to the vulgar objection against various readings, that they render the Text precarious.' Rud thought that Bentley could print such a dissertation as part of the prolegomena to the improved New Testament.[55] Bentley was aware of the grave misgivings which many Protestants had about tinkering with the foundations of *sola scriptura*. 'Nothing will satisfy them but I must be put by the Professor's chair', he complained sardonically to Samuel Clarke, Newton's mouthpiece, 'and the Church is in great danger from my New Testament.'[56]

One of the key issues in Bentley's New Testament would obviously be the controversial proof text of the Trinity, I John v. 7, which Erasmus had bravely omitted from his first edition and then was persuaded to restore, on the basis of a manuscript in Ireland. Bentley first expressed the way he intended to tackle this thorny problem in a letter of reply to an anonymous correspondent on the first day of 1717. Rumour had reached this unknown enthusaist 'from common fame' that Bentley intended to leave out that troublesome yet essential verse from his proposed edition. Bentley replied with a sort of potted intellectual autobiography:

> About a year ago, reflecting upon some passages of St. Hierom, that he had adjusted and castigated the then Latin Vulgate to the best Greek exemplars, and had kept the very order of the words of the original, I form'd a thought, *a priori*, that if St. Jerom's true Latin exemplar could now be come at, it would be found to agree exactly with the Greek text of the same age; and so the old copies of each language (if so agreeing) would give mutual proof, and even demonstration, to each other. Whereupon, rejecting the printed editions of each, and the several manuscripts of seven centuries and under, I made use of none but these of a thousand years ago, or above, (of which sort I have 20 now in my study, that one with another make 20,000 years). I had the pleasure to find, as I presaged, that they agreed exactly like two tallies, or two indentures; and I am able from thence to lead men out of the labyrinth of 60,000 various lections, (for St. Jerom's Latin has as many varieties as the Greek), and to give the text, as it stood in the best copies in the time of the Council of Nic[a]e[a], without the error of 50 words.

After this introduction to his basic beliefs and methods, Bentley was in a position to answer the question posed: 'And what will be the event about the said verse of John,' he admitted, 'I myself know not yet; having not used all the old copies that I have information of.' But the main point which Bentley wished to emphasize was that 'the fate of that verse will be a mere *question of fact.*' Indeed, he affirmed, 'if the fourth century knew that text, let it come in, in God's name'; otherwise he would leave it out.[57]

The Trinity proof text was among the scholarly subjects uppermost in Bentley's mind throughout the first half of 1717, when the rest of his thoughts were devoted to securing the Regius professorship of Divinity at Cambridge, said to be by far the richest in Europe.[58] Like Bentley's other forays into university politics, this was a tricky business, and his actions were characteristically high-handed and very possibly illegal. For our purposes, what is interesting is that Bentley chose the controversial topic of the Trinity proof text as his theme for his *praelectio*, or probationary lecture, delivered on 1 May 1717 before a large audience, the day before the election to the chair, which he duly won.[59] The text of his lecture is now lost, but what he said can be reconstructed from contemporary reports. William Whiston heard from someone who had been present that Bentley 'entirely gave up that text, and publicly proved it to be spurious'.[60] J.H. Monk, Bentley's celebrated biographer, cites evidence from 'Atwood the Esquire Beadle' who was actually present, and wrote in his manuscript journal 'that he read away the text (1 St. John, v. 7) to the utmost of his power.'[61] Conyers Middleton (1683–1750) was probably there, but in any case was writing in Cambridge and for those who certainly had been there. Four years after the fact he stated that 'He has already, we know, determined against the genuineness of the famous passage of St. John, 1 Epistle v. 7. For what reason has he condemned it as spurious? Why because some manuscripts and some Fathers have omitted it.'[62] Richard Porson (1759–1808), Regius professor of Greek at Cambridge, while of another generation, had seen the text of the talk and recalled that 'Bentley read a public lecture, which is still extant, to prove the verse spurious.'[63]

If Bentley's opponents – of whom there were many – had any reason to doubt his intention to rock the boat when necessary, his lecture on the eve of his elevation to the Regius professorship of Divinity must have made them ill at ease. From 1717, Bentley was busily occupied with his New Testament project, in the run-up to the public flotation of his *Proposals* three years later. His first chief collaborator was J.J. Wetstein, the Swiss visitor who had lit the spark of New Testament scholarship in Bentley's breast at the beginning of the previous year. Wetstein was devoted to the task of collating Greek manuscripts of the New Testament and would have continued to serve Bentley for many years. But classical scholarship was only his hobby; he was at that time a chaplain in the Dutch army and would soon have to return to his post with the expiration of his leave of absence. Bentley might have continued to employ Wetstein, but he remained partially deaf to the Swiss scholar's plaintive hints, even when they came from his military quarters at Bois-le-Duc. Wetstein gave up on Bentley as an employer, and resolved to return to Basle and serve as his father's clerical assistant. 'I wish you a good journey home,' wrote Bentley without a trace of irony, 'and hope you will continue, even there, to assist me in my designed edition of the New Testament, which proceeds beyond my expectation. Whatever you send me of collations from the oldest Greek or Latin MSS. shall be thankfully acknowledged as well as honourably rewarded'.[64] Wetstein, for his part, lamented that he required some compensation for all of this work, 'besides weak eyes, and a disqualification for other pursuits.'[65]

Wetstein was replaced with a native Englishman named John Walker (1692?–1741), who had become a fellow of Trinity College in 1716. Bentley had had his eye on this young man while Walker was still an undergraduate whose Greek and Latin manuscript work was very promising. Walker was dispatched to Paris in 1719 where he stayed for nearly a year, at Bentley's expense. It was not cheap, as this was the height of the South Sea Bubble. 'The Rent of my Lodgings is raised upon me this morning', Walker reported at the end of December, 'and the price of everything is raised a third part since I cam hither, by that infinite Number of Strangers that continue yet to flock hither every day.'[66] This situation improved little, for among his reports concerning manuscript collations Walker took care to ask what Bentley's immediate plans were. 'I beg you would let me know,' he wrote the following February, 'whether you have occasion for me longer than one Year out of England, and whether in any other place besides Paris. Paris has been so dear all this winter that there is no living in it but for those People who have dealt in the Actions of Misisippi; I pay near half more for every thing, than I did when I came first here'.[67] He was worried that he might be duplicating some of Wetstein's work, and asked Bentley for details of the manuscripts already collated.[68] Walker also travelled quite a bit, careful not to 'miss any opportunity of examining the Libraries wherever we passed'. He returned to England in August 1720.[69]

The difficulties of the sort of scholarship undertaken by such patient men as Wetstein and Walker are not to be underestimated. Walker was fortunate in having won the affection of the Benedictine monks of St-Maur, to whom Bentley had promised some help with an edition of Origen. Not only did the monks allow Walker free run of their manuscripts, but they took him in and gave him a room and (more importantly) a fire at their monastery of St-Germain-des-Prés. A number of monks even helped Walker with the work of collation itself.[70] Bentley's grand-half-nephew Thomas, himself a classical scholar and interested in the various renditions of Plutarch, had a more difficult time. He was working in the Vatican Library, 'in what they call the Palatine Library, and another large room that has nothing but the MSS. left by Christina of Sweden; of which they have not yet made a Catalogue!' There were many important books and manuscripts there,

> But what can a body do with such great Books, where they only allow the use of them for 3 hours in a morning, and that but 5 times a week, or but 3 or 4 times? for all holidays, &c., are vacancies; all Christmas, and, they tell me, May, June, July entirely; besides that, you are obliged to sit in the same room with 8 or ten others, some working and some chattering. At that rate it would take one 4 or 5 years to go through all Plutarch's Works.[71]

Walker's return to England was Bentley's signal to bring before the public his proposal to print a corrected version of the New Testament. It was clear to him that such a work would have to be published by subscription, as it was by no means certain that he could recoup his investment by sales alone.[72] Details of the New Testament according to Richard Bentley were furnished to the public in the form of two printed sheets setting out his goals and aspirations.[73]

The main point of the project was stated clearly and succinctly at the outset:

> The author of this edition, observing that the printed copies of the New Testament, both of the original Greek and ancient vulgar Latin, were taken from manuscripts of no great authority, such as the first editors could then procure; and that now by God's Providence there are MSS. in Europe, (accessible, though with great charge) above a thousand years old in both languages; believes he may do good service to common Christianity, if he publishes a new edition of the Greek and Latin, not according to the recent and interpolated copies, but as represented in the most ancient and venerable MSS. in Greek and Roman capital letters.

Bentley recalled that his interest was sparked by Jerome's claim to have compared 'the whole Latin Vulgate to the best Greek exemplars, that is, to those of the famous Origen'. Bentley 'took thence the hint' and discovered for himself that the Vulgate did indeed agree in both words and order of words with the oldest Greek MSS. Now, he affirmed, he

> believes that he has retrieved (except in very few places) the true exemplar of Origen, which was the standard to the most learned of the Fathers, at the time of the Council of Nic[a]e[a] and two centuries after. And he is sure, that the Greek and Latin MSS., by their mutual assistance, do so settle the original text to the smallest nicety, as cannot be performed now in any Classic author whatever: and that out of a labyrinth of thirty thousand various readings, that crowd the pages of our present best editions, all put upon equal credit to the offence of many good persons; this clue so leads and extricates us, that there will scarce be two hundred out of so many thousands that can deserve the least consideration.

This work of collation is supplemented by use of the versions in Syriac, Coptic, Gothic, and Ethiopic, and of all the Greek and Latin Fathers of the first five Christian centuries. Bentley also promised to include notations of various readings which fell within this time period, so 'that the reader has under one view what the first ages of the Church knew of the text; and what has crept into any copies since, is of no value or authority.'

Bentley admitted in his *Proposals* that he was playing with religious fire: 'The author is very sensible,' he wrote, 'that in the Sacred Writings there's no place for conjectures or emendations. Diligence and fidelity, with some judgment and experience, are the characters here requisite.' Bentley did not trifle with the fundamental concept of *sola scriptura*: 'He declares, therefore, that he does not alter one letter in the text without the authorities subjoined in the notes'. In all places where the biblical text is amended and corrected, Bentley promised to provide as well the 'received text' of Stephanus, and the Sixtine Vulgate of Popes Sixtus V and Clement VIII. Any unsupported suggestions would be relegated to the prolegomena where he would attempt to make his case openly and judiciously.

In brief, Bentley proudly affirmed, that in this his revised edition of the New Testament, 'he is of no sect or party; his design is to serve the whole Christian name. He draws no consequences in his notes; makes no oblique glances upon any disputed points, old or new.' Bentley wanted to set his New Testament as the new benchmark, in his words, 'a Charter, a Magna Charta, to the whole Christian Church; to last when all the ancient MSS. here quoted may be lost and extinguished.'

Not forgetting matters of the mundane world, Bentley closed his *Proposals* by promising to print his epic New Testament 'with the best letter, paper, and ink that Europe affords', which was the chief reason that he was publishing the edition by subscription in the first place. It would appear in two folio volumes. The purchase price for the small paper edition he set at three guineas, one guinea to be paid on subscribing. The 'great paper' edition cost two guineas more. The actual printing of the book would commence only when sufficient funds were collected, and the number of copies printed would be exactly equal to the number of copies subscribed. Lastly, Bentley announced that his full partner in all profits and losses would be 'the learned Mr. John Walker, of Trinity College in Cambridge; who with great accurateness has collated many MSS. at Paris for the present edition.'

Bentley made the somewhat rash decision of including with his modest *Proposals* a 'specimen' of the sort of biblical criticism that he was putting on public offer. This consisted of the twenty-second chapter of the Book of Revelation, the last one in that biblical book and, indeed, the concluding section of the New Testament itself. It may be that Bentley wanted to imply, at least subliminally, that the entire editorial work was done, and all that was required was public funding for the Bentley New Testament to roll off the presses in the original Greek. In any case, Bentley already had done all of the work on the Book of Revelation that could be done, since the MSS abroad which had not yet been fully collated lacked the Apocalypse.

While the New Testament project had been stewing in Bentley's mind for a number of years, the actual production of these *Proposals* seems to have been conducted with unprofitable speed. Later on, when responding to his critics, he would say in his defence that the 'Proposals being drawn up in haste, in one evening by candle-light, and printed the next day from that first and sole draught, (which haste likewise hindered him from revising that sheet, and so left several false accents and points in the specimen itself,) he consulted not St. Hierom, but cited the passage by memory'. In the event, the quotation was misremembered, and it was easy for his many enemies to allege that he was deliberately manipulating the evidence in order to fit his theories about the relationship between the Greek and Latin versions of the New Testament.

What had gone wrong? Unquestionably, his characteristic over-confidence was a crucial factor. As Monk put it so well,

> The truth is, that it never occurred to him as probable that his present adversaries, keen and inveterate as they were, would think of attacking him in the department of criticism; and a paper of proposals, which he regarded only in the light of an advertisement, did not seem to demand that care and circumspection which he reserved for the publication itself.[74]

Be that as it may, Bentley had laid himself open to severe criticism, just at the moment when his enemies were looking for any weapon at hand to deprive him of the Regius professorship of Divinity.

The first into the field was his old adversary Conyers Middleton, 'the most malignant of a malignant crew', whose anonymous *Remarks* by 'a Member of the University of Cambridge' were as vicious as they were unfair.[75] While it may have been true that the *Proposals* included a slipshod specimen, it was going too far to lambast Bentley for having treated the first editors of the Greek New Testament with 'barbarity and injustice', and to describe the great classical scholar as having 'neither talents nor materials proper for the work he had undertaken'. Middleton accused Bentley of having been ungrateful to his predecessor Mill, and launched a full-blast attack on publication by subscription, despite himself having used the same method in the past. But 1720 was the year of the disastrous collapse of the South Sea scheme, and bad investments were on everybody's mind. As Middleton put it, 'most people are agreed in opinion, that he has borrowed his scheme from Change-Alley, and in this age of bubbles, took the hint to set up one of his own.' At the end of the day, Middleton predicted, there was not 'the least question that *Bentley's Bubble* will be as famous and profitable as the best of them.'[76]

Bentley would have done well to ignore Middleton's outrageous attacks and to have concentrated instead on his revised New Testament and its marketing. But this was not the measure of the man, who could not resist the temptation of a literary quarrel. Unfortunately, Bentley in his fury entirely missed his mark, and directed his venom not at the anonymous true author of the *Remarks*, but at another of his sworn enemies from his own college, Dr John Colbatch (1664–1748). Colbatch had begun academic life as a Bentley protégé, tutoring and doing the Grand Tour with the son of the duke of Somerset, chancellor of Cambridge University. Colbatch was the recipient of various lucrative church posts, apart from the professorship of casuistical divinity. It may have been his refusal of Bentley's offer to rule Trinity College as vice-master that set them at odds, but they were never again to be friends.[77]

Bentley never mentions Colbatch by name in his little book, nor does he reveal himself without guile, but the references to both author and victim were so legion that no one was fooled, nor were they meant to be. Colbatch, for his part, was not amused at being called 'cabbage-head', 'insect', 'maggot', 'vermin', 'gnawing rat', 'snarling dog', 'ignorant thief', and 'mountebank', and at having his clergyman brother described as a lunatic who wore 'a beard to his girdle, sufficient for a Greek Patriarch'.[78]

Bentley was now clearly in the wrong, and Colbatch sought to make the most of this. He published a declaration denying any connection with the initial attack on Bentley's *Proposals*.[79] He also applied to the aged vice-chancellor of Cambridge, who declined to act, as did the members of Trinity College. But the Heads of Colleges publicly censured Bentley for this latest example of rude behaviour, and Colbatch felt he finally had Bentley on the run.[80] Colbatch then began a prosecution in the vice-chancellor's court against the university printer and bookseller Crownfield, in the hope that he would finger the author who had brought this legal action to their door. The new vice-chancellor Dr Crosse tried to persuade Colbatch that Crownfield had immediately stopped selling the pamphlet after it had been declared a libel and that therefore there was no cause for prosecution. They tried to bribe Colbatch with the honour of presenting the university's thanks to the earl of Nottingham on the occasion of his having written a reply to William Whiston's recent attack on the Trinity. But Colbatch demurred, arguing sulkily that 'it was not fit that one who had such a slur upon him, should appear before persons of honour'.[81]

Colbatch's friends persuaded him to be silent, on the grounds that it would not do to seek redress both at law and in the public press. Colbatch's cudgels were taken up by the man who had started all of the problems in the first place, Conyers Middleton. This latest work, four times as long as his first, is infinitely more dignified. More importantly, Middleton signed his name to the piece and indirectly apologized to Colbatch for the trouble that had been caused. Indeed, the entire work is a model of civility in which Middleton dissects Bentley with elegance and wit. Bentley's weakest point was clearly that his much-vaunted specimen was defective, which did not augur well for the promised publication itself. Middleton used this careless blunder to great sarcastic advantage. But even apart from this embarrassing oversight, Middleton had a point when he criticized Bentley for consistently harping on the claim that the Vulgate in Latin always follows the order of the words in the Greek manuscripts. On this basis, Bentley had argued that we need to revise the Greek text to fit the word order in the Vulgate, on the assumption that St Jerome was telling the truth when he said that he had used the oldest and the best Greek manuscripts available at the time of writing. Middleton objected that this was an interesting working hypothesis, but it was a theory only, and even the celebrated Richard Bentley was obliged to demonstrate its effectiveness.[82] Middleton's piece was not the only one which appeared in the aftermath of Bentley's *Proposals*, but it was by far the most effective.[83]

The impact of all this criticism is difficult to gauge. Bentley told Bishop Francis Atterbury that he had never bothered to look at Middleton's piece, indeed, 'he scorned to read the rascal's book; but if his Lordship would send him any part which he thought the strongest, he would undertake to answer it before night.'[84] Such a cavalier attitude to published criticism does not fit what we know of Bentley's character. Subscription money continued to pour in despite the pamphlet wars, and may have amounted to as much as 2,000 guineas. As his critic Bishop Richard Smalbroke (1672–1749) told him, 'it is generally believed you have already received so large a Sum of Money, either in the Way of Bounty or Subscription, as will very amply support the Expenses of the propos'd Examination.'[85] According to the antiquary Thomas Hearne (1678–1735),

> A young Gentleman lately told me that, dining with [Charles Paulet] the Duke [of Bolton], within this twelve Month, among a great many others that din'd there, there happen'd to be D^r. Bently, and that the D^r. going out of the room after Dinner, the Duke propos'd to the Company a Subscription to the D^{rs} Ed. of the New Testament in Greek, and, all of them coming into it, collected for the D^r. about 100 Guineas, wch he deliver'd to the D^r. upon the Drs Return into the Room.[86]

Bentley did face a disappointment in the Board of Treasury's refusal to regard his New Testament as a national treasure in the making and to allow him to import the paper for it duty free. J.J. Wetstein, Bentley's first research assistant, believed that the master of Trinity was so infuriated by this rejection that he abandoned the entire project in revenge.[87] Colbatch also suggests this, writing to Middleton after his recent salvo against Bentley:

> I heartily congratulate you upon the universal and highly deserved applause that your last piece meets with every where; by which, according to all that I can speak with or hear from, you have laid Bentley flat on his back. Mr. Eachard writes me by last post from London, that he is every where teased and mortified about it; and that the loss of his paper project puts him beyond all patience.[88]

But despite the enduring life of this anecdote, it seems to be untrue and, at least in Wetstein's case, the result of a misunderstanding. In any case, despite the paper problem, Bentley was immediately on the move again once his project had been floated, borrowing manuscripts and planning a summer of study at the Bodleian.[89]

Over the next decade, Bentley continued to work intermittently on his New Testament, without neglecting other important projects, such as his new edition of Homer, and his relentless terrorism against the fellows of Trinity College, Cambridge. The major task which needed to be tackled was the collation of the ancient New Testament manuscript at the Vatican. One of Bentley's co-workers there was a German baron named Philippe de Stosch who lived in Rome, where he did a bit of spying for the British government.[90] The baron enjoyed the services of an Italian named Mico in this endeavour.[91]

But most of the work was done in those years by his grand-nephew Thomas Bentley (1693?–1742), grandson of Richard Bentley's half-brother. Following in the footsteps of his famous great-uncle, Thomas went up to Trinity College, Cambridge after completing his education at St Paul's School in London, took his BA in 1711 and his MA four years later. By 1718 he was a fellow of the college at which his great-uncle was master, and was publishing several small classical studies. But Thomas Bentley refused to take religious orders, so by the rules of the college he lost his fellowship after seven years as a Master of Arts, continuing in the capacity of college librarian, being also awarded the degree of doctor of laws. Thomas Bentley had literary ambitions, and in 1725 he made a Grand Tour of continental libraries, pausing at Paris, Rome, Naples, and Florence. While there, he worked diligently on behalf of his great-uncle, being one of the few people who always managed to stay in the great man's favour.[92]

We have already come across Thomas Bentley's amusing report to his great-uncle about the tiresome working conditions at the Vatican Library.[93] The open and friendly style of the younger man's letter remained constant, and seems to give some indication of the personality behind the text. By August 1726, Thomas Bentley had already done Naples and was now back in Rome. 'There can be no doubt of the sincerity of my thanks for the present you have made me,' he wrote, 'unexpected and in time of need.' The implication, perhaps, is that Richard Bentley was not supporting the labours of his grand-nephew any more than he paid for the research expenses of J.J. Wetstein years before. 'I have seen most of the Testaments in the Vatican', reported Thomas Bentley. 'The finest and oldest is of all the Bible, which I suppose is that Mico collated. Had you a collation of all the New Testament from him?' In any case, Thomas Bentley continued with the work of collation, not waiting for a reply from Cambridge. 'I am always wanting money, or in fear of wanting; and yet I live soberly and *sagement*.'[94] Had his health been more robust, Thomas Bentley might have stayed a while longer on the Continent. Although he seems not to have been as helpful as John Walker, his letters are certainly more interesting and lively, and would have given greater pleasure to the historian.

Sadly, Bentley devoted little time during the following years to the New Testament project which was designed to put the Christian world on a more secure footing. This is somewhat puzzling, as they were years of comparative peace in Bentley's stormy academic life. He had been deprived of his degrees by the Cambridge University court in 1718 for failing to appear in a minor suit brought against him by his old adversary Conyers Middleton. At the end of March 1724, however, the university was compelled to restore them, and no new controversies of that nature erupted until 1728, when another old enemy, Dr Colbatch, began a ten-year war which only ended with Bentley's final victory in 1738 against those who would have deprived him of the mastership of Trinity College. As his Victorian biographer R.C. Jebb put it, the controversy lasted a year longer than the Peloponnesian War.[95]

Bentley's last attempt to discharge the obligation to his subscribing public came during a summer break from his busy campaigning schedule against his adversaries at Cambridge University. In the summer of 1729 he wrote to Dr Patrick Delany (1685?–1768), friend of Jonathan Swift and chancellor of Christ Church Cathedral, Dublin. Bentley was concerned about the famous Greek manuscript in Dublin, the Codex Montfortianus, which contained the disputed Trinity proof text from John, and wrote to its owners to obtain more information about it. Delany replied with a facsimile of the crucial passage, and concluded his covering letter with the encouraging message that

> This is all the information I can give upon this controversy; which I am sorry to see revived in an age wherein the early editions of the New Testament ought, in my humble opinion, to have more weight than perhaps all the manuscripts now extant put together. No man who knows the character of the early editors, can doubt the credit of those manuscripts they published from.[96]

At the same time, Baron de Stosch, his man in Rome, posted to Bentley a large number of notes regarding the manuscript in the Vatican. The implication in the letter is that Bentley required this information urgently.[97]

But that was that. Despite these professions of haste, and notwithstanding the fact that Bentley's working copy was well advanced both in text and notes, nothing happened. All he needed were the collations from the Vatican manuscript to reward his subscribers and the entire scholarly world with the fruits of his divine labour. Yet no book text was ever delivered to the press after this last spurt of energy in the summer of 1729. Bentley's great biographer Monk, musing on this academic mystery, agreed that

> After this time I discover no trace of his being occupied upon his projected edition: the contest which he waged with his prosecutors allowed him but little intermission for several years; and in those short intervals

other literary objects were pressed upon him, and when at length greater leisure arrived, it found him disabled by age for the exertion requisite to complete the work.[98]

Bentley's projected New Testament died in July 1729, although the unstoppable John Walker seems to have been making collations for his patron as late as 1732.[99]

One project which diverted Bentley's energies was his famously misguided effort to restore *Paradise Lost* to its Miltonic glory. Bentley was hard at work by 1730, and had it finished by 1732. Both contemporaries and modern critics are in strenuous agreement that in this effort Bentley failed on a grand scale.[100] Bentley himself implied in the preface that the notes for his new edition came straight off the top of his head and were 'put to the Press as soon as made'. Yet Bentley's Milton gives us a clue to his grand design and his philological philosophy as pursued in his projected New Testament as well. Thomas de Quincey (1785–1859) saw this in his Victorian review of Monk's biography of Bentley. If we consider all of Bentley's work, de Quincey observed,

> The same quality of sagacity, or the power of *investigating* backward (in the original sense of that metaphor), through the corruptions of two thousand years, the primary form of the reading which lay buried beneath them, – a faculty which in Bentley was in such excess that it led him to regard every MS. as a sort of figurative Palimpsest in which the early text had been overlaid by successive layers of alien matter, – was the fruitful source both of the faults and the merits of his wonderful editions.[101]

Bentley's method of deconstructive reconstruction failed spectacularly when applied to Milton, but it used the same tools that had been employed to such great effect with regard to the New Testament.

The final scene to the story of Bentley's New Testament provides a tragi-comic flourish. The collections of the King's Library and the Cottonian manuscripts were moved about quite a lot during the eighteenth century, from Cotton House, to Essex House (near Temple Bar), and latterly to Abingdon House, Little Dean's Yard, next to (and now part of) Westminster School, which had been bought for the specific purpose of giving the library a home. Sadly, fire broke out at Abingdon House on the night of 23 October 1731, and destroyed many manuscripts in the collection.[102] Bentley happened to be nearby, and risked his life in order to save the Alexandrian manuscript from oblivion. An eyewitness described Bentley emerging from the flames in his dressing gown, clutching the codex to his breast.[103] In the event, over 200 volumes were destroyed or badly damaged. After the fire, the two collections were moved to the Old Dormitory at Westminster and, finally, in 1752, to Montagu House – the British Museum.[104] Given Bentley's prophetic remarks in 1716 about the possibility of a fire destroying the Codex Alexandrinus, we might almost credit the man with some of the supernatural powers that his admirers thought he possessed.

What Bentley never accomplished in life, he may have hoped to achieve after his death in 1742. He made his nephew Richard the sole executor of his will, and left to him his entire library and all of his papers and manuscripts. Richard Bentley the deceased may have hoped that his namesake would cut the Gordian knot and publish the New Testament as it stood. But the younger Richard was of a different stamp. He became rector of Nailston in Leicestershire three years later, in 1745, and stayed there until 1786, when he himself went to join his uncle in a Better Place. Young Richard refused to recognize any literary responsibility and sold part of the books immediately, keeping what remained at the parsonage. The subscribers to the New Testament received their money back, and Bentley's manuscript for the corrected Holy Book was given to Trinity College, along with Bentley's revised Homer and other classical notes.[105] The younger Richard Bentley remained a fellow of Trinity College until his death, taking a DD in 1750. A good number of Bentley's classical books, with marginal notes, and the great man's literary correspondence, had been given to Dr Bentley's son-in-law Richard Cumberland (1732–1811), the celebrated dramatist. Cumberland gave the papers to Trinity, and sold the books to James Lackington (1746–1815), the bookseller, who in turn made a gift of them to the British Museum.[106] In the end, by this crooked path, scholarship was served after all.

III

Bentley's great project came to nothing, but it was an important precedent, and it was only a matter of time before someone would attempt the same global revision of the Old Testament. The man who took up the challenge was Benjamin Kennicott, fellow of Exeter College, Oxford from 1747, Radcliffe librarian from 1767, a pupil of Thomas Hunt (1696–1774), the Regius professor of Hebrew. Kennicott's life work was the collation of the existing manuscripts of the Hebrew Bible in an attempt to eliminate errors which had been introduced over the centuries, while still acknowledging the divine inspiration of Scripture itself. The problem, Kennicott argued, was that 'what was thus inspir'd by God, was committed to the Care of Men; and we must acknowledge, that *we have had this Treasure in Earthen Vessels*'. Kennicott was well aware of the opposition that his work would meet. 'If this were not a known case', he complained, 'it would seem strange – that Men, pretending to an Acquaintance with Languages, should allow Mistakes to have been introduced in transcribing the New Testament, and not allow the same as to the Old', especially when we consider the fact that some parts of this book were written as much as 1,500 years before the Gospels. Indeed, Kennicott argued,

> To suppose such an absolute Freedom from Error in the Transcribers of these Books, the most ancient in the whole World – what is it else, but to suppose *a constant Miracle wrought in favour of every such Transcriber*, and the Divine Assistance communicated in the Formation of every Letter? – And this Infallibility continued down to these times; as there seems no particular Aera assignable for its Termination: at least, it seems to have been as necessary, 'till the Invention of Printing, as it could have been before.

Such a claim, Kennicott maintained, was not consistent with a rational and unprejudiced examination of the problem.[107]

Kennicott described the shock he received when he went over to the Bodleian Library in about 1751 to put to the test his theory of the imperfect Old Testament text. Kennicott sought out the manuscript copies of the Old Testament there, 'without expecting any great matters from them; having frequently been assur'd by considerable Writers – that the Jews (the *later* Jews, at least) had transcrib'd their sacred Books so carefully, and with a superstitious Exactness number'd every Sentence and Word and Letter, that no material Differences could be found in any of the MS copies now extant'. Instead, Kennicott found ample evidence of the vagaries of textual transmission, for although the manuscripts, 'in general, were writ with great Care ... yet, the very best and most accurate of them wore the Marks of human Imperfection'. Kennicott thereupon resolved to collect and collate the various readings, in order to reproduce as closely as possible the original Hebrew text, 'to separate *the pure Gold* from the Dross and Defilement, which it has contracted by Time and Accidents'.[108]

It seems to have been Bishop Thomas Secker (1693–1768) of Oxford who suggested to Kennicott in March 1758 that he collate the surviving Old Testament manuscripts on a grand scale and thereby provide the scholarly world with the same sort of benefit that Bentley had very nearly supplied for the New Testament.[109] Kennicott's proposals for this great endeavour were issued at Oxford on 21 January 1760 and, like Bentley, he intended to produce his work on a platform of public subscriptions.[110] A second appeal was issued on 18 December 1760, with a list of subscribers appended.[111] Kennicott did not lack backers, and subscriptions eventually totalled £9,119 7s. 6d.[112] European enthusiasm was also forthcoming. The king of Denmark offered him the run of six very ancient manuscripts; the duc de Nivernois in France pledged his support; the king of Sardinia sent him four quarto volumes of variant readings; and the stadtholder of Holland gave him an annual donation of 30 guineas.[113]

Like Bentley, Kennicott had his man scouring the Continent for manuscripts: Paul Jacob Bruns of Lübeck (1743–1814) collated Old Testaments for him at Rome and elsewhere.[114] Kennicott also had help with Hebrew at home from his wife Ann Chamberlayne, who according to her friend the novelist Fanny Burney (1752–1840), 'has rendered herself famous also, by having studied that language, after marriage, in order to assist her husband in his edition of the Bible; she learnt it so well as to enable herself to aid him very essentially in copying, examining, and revising.' Ann Kennicott was friends with the wife of David Garrick (1717–79) the actor, and Hannah More (1745–1833), the religious author.[115] Bishop Shute Barrington (1734–1826) left her an annuity of £100, and Bishop Beilby Porteus (1731–1808) of London, Lowth's successor, left his 'dear and pleasant friend Mrs. Kennicott' £500 of 3 per cent stock.[116] Ann Kennicott herself founded two scholarships at Oxford which took effect upon her death at Windsor on 25 February 1830, nearly half a century after the passing of her husband.[117]

Kennicott, unlike Bentley, wanted his subscribers to see immediate value for money, and to know where their generous support was going. For this reason, he produced every year between 1760 and 1769 a pamphlet 'On the Collation of the Hebrew Manuscripts of the Old Testament', a sort of shareholders' annual report.[118] The result of Kennicott's great labour was his monumental *Vetus Testamentum Hebraicum, cum variis lectionibus*, the first volume of which was published at Oxford in 1776, the second following there four years later.[119] This second volume of 1780 also included a 'Dissertatio Generalis' regarding the manuscripts of the Old Testament.[120] When completed, the entire work was presented by Kennicott himself to King George III.[121] The manuscript collations were given to the Bodleian Library on 17 December 1760.[122]

Even Kennicott's supporters probably shared the views of Dr Johnson, that 'although the text should not be much mended thereby, yet it was no small advantage to know, that we had as good a text as the most consummate industry and diligence could procure'.[123] But nowhere was the absolute rejection of Kennicott and all he stood for more apparent than among the Hutchinsonians, that determined group of Christian kabbalists, champions of the 'occult Bible' that we met in the previous chapter. Even though Newton was their chief target of abuse, Kennicott came in for his fair share of opposition, not only because he canonized with scholarship the hated vowel points, but because he tampered with the accepted consonantal skeleton of the Hebrew Bible itself. The version which the Hutchinsonians had subjected to their intense scrutiny was shown to be nothing more than the Hebrew Bible printed at Venice in 1524–5 from a late medieval manuscript. Kennicott sought to get behind this late text, by using not only Syriac and early Latin versions, but also the Septuagint and even the Samaritan Pentateuch, written in

Hebrew and containing variant readings and alterations.[124] Kennicott's search even brought him to try to make contact with the Jews of China, in the hope that they would have preserved pre-Talmudic manuscripts.[125] Kennicott's parallel texts effectively undermined the biblical literalism of the Hutchinsonians and all those who were determined to adopt an occult approach to the Old Testament. His grammatical knowledge, used with great effectiveness against the Hutchinsonians in Oxford itself, supported this major blow against the school.

Ironically, in many respects the method used by John Hutchinson was very similar to that of Kennicott, and, indeed, of Hebrew scholars in England and Europe since the Renaissance. Hutchinson's editors described how their mentor would apply his principles when at work:

> In order to take a nearer view of the *Mosaic* philosophy, the original text must be consulted, simply as it stands, divested of those points or pricks for vowels which the modern *Jews* contrived: for this purpose our author chuses generally to follow the *Latin interlineary* version, as the most literal, and fittest to show the order of the *Hebrew* words; then, to investigate the true idea each word is intended to convey, he collates the different senses given it in the *Lexicons*. The authorities he makes most use of are, the *Roman* edition of *Marius de Calsio's concordance* of the *Hebrew* with other Eastern languages, *Castelli's lexicon heptaglotton, Schindler's pentaglot,* and *Buxtorff's* large *rabinical dictionary*.[126]

This is the way all Christian Hebrew scholars would go about trying to understand the text of Scripture, although they would of course have the added advantage of the vowels.

Kennicott came out directly against the Hutchinsonians as early as 1756, in a short anonymous pamphlet directed against three recent sermons. Two aspects of the problem troubled Kennicott more than all others: the pseudo-scientific learned conceit of the Hutchinsonians, and the fact that they were invited to deliver sermons on formal occasions under the official auspices of Oxford University. It seemed ridiculous, even to as great an innovator as Kennicott, to argue that the entire Hebrew language 'had been lamentably misunderstood, and the genuine meaning of both the Old and New Testaments dangerously conceal'd; till there arose, in the 18th century, this great champion of truth and revelation, this original in the discovery of roots physical and theological'. As Kennicott saw it, the entire Hutchinsonian doctrine was clear proof that 'A little learning is a dangerous thing':

> For if a little learning and a great deal of conceit should prompt a man abusively to censure his superiors for not patronizing, and his equals for not encouraging, his own crude notions; should prompt him insolently to

prescribe to the world wrong systems of science and (what may emphatically be call'd) vain philosophy; the consequence must be, that men truly learned will express their contempt at this manifestation of vanity and impertinence in the dictator.

Kennicott claimed that of late the 'behaviour of the *Hutchinsonian* Divines, in this University and in other parts of the kingdom, is now become matter of general complaint'. Nevertheless, he did acknowledge the success of the Hutchinsonians in managing to 'insinuate themselves into the good opinion of young Gentlemen', chiefly by claiming that all other divines were either mistaken in their theology or positively wicked.[127]

The Hutchinsonians declined to reply in print to Kennicott's rather general attack on their abilities and their motives. They waited until he had published his second dissertation on the state of the printed Hebrew text of the Old Testament, and then unleashed Thomas Rutherforth (1712–71), professor of divinity in Cambridge, to make their objections known. Kennicott's major claim in this, his second introductory work, was that the Samaritan Pentateuch provided an important and under-used source for understanding the original text of Scripture which had been corrupted over the centuries. Kennicott, once again, was striking at the heart of Hutchinsonian Hebraic Fundamentalism. Rutherforth gleefully reported instances in which Kennicott himself seems to have been a less than accurate copyist, but noted that

> Though I should have been sorry to have had the *Hebrew text* entrusted with you to be new-modelled, as you might think proper, in a critical edition of it; yet as I was desirous, that the *Hebrew* MSS might be collated, I was glad to find, that you would undertake to collate them; because I knew of no one, so well qualified for this kind of work as yourself, who would be willing to set down to it.

Rutherforth therefore was willing to have Kennicott continue in his work:

> though I agreed with you, that there are errors in the printed Hebrew copies, yet in one point I could not help differing from you. As far as I was able to judge, no emendation could be so fully established by any or by all the means of emending, which you had proposed, as to warrant you in giving it a place in the *text*, if you should ever publish an edition of the Hebrew bible.

Kennicott, meanwhile, advertised a reply to Rutherforth's work before it had even appeared.[128] His pamphlet covered familiar ground,[129] as did Rutherforth's reply in turn.[130]

So too did Kennicott meet with more sober opposition abroad. Kennicott's Jewish sometime assistant Joseph Adolphe Dumay was perhaps the author of the anonymous and hostile letters printed at Paris in 1771 with a false Rome imprint.[131] These were immediately translated into English by the Hutchinsonian William Stephens (1732–1807) and published at London in 1772.[132] Kennicott soon issued a reply, claiming that the libel against him was the handiwork of six Capuchins in the convent of St Honoré at Paris.[133] But Stephens soon reproduced the original letter, this time with an answer to Kennicott's self-defence.[134] Kennicott's champion on this occasion was George Sheldon, the vicar of Edwardston in Suffolk.[135] But the dispute had travelled widely, even to Rome, where a further attack on Kennicott was actually published in 1772. Ever faithful, Paul Jacob Bruns responded (albeit ten years later, but at least in the same city), with a Latin translation of Kennicott's defence and some material of his own.[136]

Yet the controversy over Kennicott's work continued, merging into the birth of scientific biblical criticism of the Old Testament in Germany. O.G. Tychsen was unhappy with his work,[137] and the great Johann David Michaelis (1717–91) was also somewhat critical of Kennicott's efforts.[138] Michaelis's criticism was worth replying to from a scholarly point of view, and Kennicott did so in a long Latin letter which was printed at Oxford in 1777, and actually included by Michaelis in the twelfth part of the *Bibliotheca orientalis* with his own further reply.[139] Kennicott waited until the second volume of his Old Testament appeared before launching a pre-emptive defence against Michaelis in 1782.[140] Michaelis, however, was a worthy academic adversary, and even if his disagreements with Kennicott caused the Hutchinsonians premature glee, in the long run the German biblical critics would cause more damage to the fragile shell of literal biblical understanding than could have been foreseen at the end of the eighteenth century.

IV

Richard Bentley and Benjamin Kennicott, each in his own way, helped build the foundations which would revolutionize the study of the Bible in the Protestant world. The very different public reactions to their respective projects tell us a good deal both about the development of modern biblical criticism, and about the concept of the author in eighteenth-century England and after. It was exactly during the years which separated Bentley and Kennicott that the modern notion of the author as an original and creative individual arose. Although much has been written in recent years about the changing authorial role during this period with regard to poetry and prose, it has not been appreciated that the apotheosis of the author was also important in the development of eighteenth-century biblical criticism.

Bentley lived in the years of the great debate over the issue of copyright, and the struggle between authors and publishers to claim ownership of the fruits of literary labour. Kennicott worked in the period after this battle was already won and the concept of the author was already recognized. But this was not the only distinction. Their tasks were very different, and this fact helps explain why the public was so accepting of Bentley and so critical of Kennicott.

Bentley was in search of the text of a work written by human authors (albeit under divine guidance), the New Testament as ratified by the fourth-century Council of Nicaea. He was not trying to obtain the original words of Jesus Christ and his Apostles, but to reconstruct the text as 'copyrighted' by the Church at a critical point in its history. This particular text became the standard, regardless of any variation from the original author's intentions, much as Ben Jonson's folio edition of Shakespeare's works set the earliest determination of textual memory. Bentley was thus not a biblical critic in the full modern sense of the word. Indeed, he had much more in common with the Roman Catholic view that the Vulgate of St Jerome was the standard text of Scripture, whose authority obviated the necessity of searching further back in textual prehistory. Once Bentley had succeeded in determining the 'copyrighted' text of the New Testament, it could be used not only for strictly religious purposes, but also as a commodity which could be marketed to the faithful and for missionary endeavours.

Kennicott's aims were far more ambitious, which helps explain the great ire he aroused among the Hutchinsonians and many other of his critics. By the late eighteenth century, the concept of the autonomous author had long been established. The principle of copyright had survived a number of challenges in the courts, and the supreme role of the author in creating a new and original work was recognized beyond dispute. Kennicott bypassed the 'copyrighted' Jewish version of the Old Testament, the Hebrew Bible as published at Venice in 1524–5. He was in search of the *original* text as first committed to writing on Mount Sinai through the agency of Moses himself, recording the very Hebrew words of God whose power was so awesome that through their pronunciation God had created the universe.

Kennicott was also an innovator in that he challenged the Jewish monopoly on the Old Testament and on the Hebrew language itself. Renaissance scholars of Hebrew such as Reuchlin and many others came to the Jews to learn, and to apply what they had learned to the eternal truths of Christianity. Kennicott in effect was cutting the Jews out of the inheritance of Scripture by claiming to have discovered a method of textual criticism which would reveal God's message in its pristine Sinaitic glory. Even Bentley, for all his celebrated arrogance, did not claim to teach Greek to the Nicaean Fathers.

Bentley was trying to reconstruct the '*copyrighted*' text of *human* authors; Kennicott wanted to restore the *original* text of a *divine* author. This made all the difference, and the fear that his quest would undermine the entire structure of religious faith transformed Kennicott into the object of concerted attack, of which the Hutchinsonians were the most prominent manifestation.

The fictional Miss Dorothea Brooke thought that 'Perhaps even Hebrew might be necessary – at least the alphabet and a few roots – in order to arrive at the core of things, and judge soundly on the social duties of the Christian.'[141] George Eliot was poking gentle fun here at such old-fashioned sentiments, but they did not die in the nineteenth century. In this sense at least, the Hutchinsonians did stand for the future, and their success and survival remind us that the path to modern biblical criticism leads as much to Fundamentalism as it does to the academic study of Scripture.

CHAPTER 7

Ten Little Israelites: Counting Out the Bible in Victorian England

Every Oxford academic longs to have a book on the open shelves of the Bodleian Library. The implication is that one's *opus* is consulted so often, by so many different people, that consigning it to the bowels of the bookstack would be to insult generations of librarians by assigning them a task of sisyphean pointlessness. The third book on the English side of the Upper Reading Room's open shelves is *Mimesis: The Representation of Reality in Western Literature*, by Erich Auerbach (1892–1957). As is well known, Auerbach wrote the book while in exile in Istanbul, having been forced out of the University of Marburg, and published it in German in 1946. The appearance of an English translation in 1953 at Princeton University Press made him famous.[1]

Auerbach's brief was to study '"the interpretation of reality" [*Wirklichkeit*] through literary representation [*Darstellung*] or "imitation"'.[2] One of the difficulties in Auerbach's work is that he shrinks from defining his terms, preferring to tell by showing. He gives a sort of methodological summary in the Epilogue, however, reminding the reader of where he has already been. *Mimesis*, Auerbach says, examines 'three closely related ideas, which give the original problem form'.[3] The first of these is the role played by the ancient doctrine of the three styles: elevated (suitable for tragedy), low (good for comedy), and something in the middle (useful for works dealing with social reality). This doctrine finally broke down in early nineteenth-century France with writers like Stendhal and Balzac, whose works depicted random individuals from everyday life, where the tragic situation was dependent on current mundane circumstances.[4] A later development of this process would be known as modern realism.

Auerbach's second organizational concept derived from his insight that this great notion of three appropriate styles was in fact an idea that had not been continuously recognized and applied since classical times, but indeed, like much else, had been somewhat artificially revived in the sixteenth and seventeenth centuries by advocates of the rigorous imitation of classical literature. Before that time, throughout the Middle Ages and the Renaissance period, 'a serious realism had existed', which paid no attention at all to the ancient doctrines of levels of style. Indeed, the first and greatest break with that doctrine can be found in the story of Christ, which combines everyday reality with the highest and most sublime tragedy.

For his third idea, Auerbach grasped that these two breaks with the doctrine of stylistic levels – that in the story of Christ and that in the works of Stendhal and Balzac – had occurred under completely different conditions, leading to distinctive notions of realism. Throughout the Middle Ages and the Renaissance, realism was 'figural', that is, an occurrence on earth might signify not only itself, but also another event more distant in linear time, which it predicts, and which the second occurrence confirms in turn. These two events are no less real for being linked; together they signify a unity within the divine plan, which is reflected in everything that happens in this mundane world. Certainly there were many events which remained significant only in the here and now and were outside of any organizing principle. But many other occurrences were linked both horizontally to each other, and vertically to God. Modern realism, in contrast, was something else entirely, a flat horizontal universe for immediate apprehension and consumed by time.

Erich Auerbach went about describing these important shifts in literature, philosophy, and religion by jumping into his first text, the *Odyssey*, letting himself be carried down the ages until he rested by serene shores on the other side of Virginia Woolf. He would shrink, he said, from a more systematic method, which would lead to 'hopeless discussions', especially and 'above all concerning the definition of the concept realism'.[5] Instead, Auerbach insisted on 'citing for every epoch a number of texts and using these as test cases for my ideas'.[6] Some of these gobbets of literature were rather obscure, for 'the great majority of the texts were chosen at random.'[7] Nevertheless, at the end of his work, Auerbach could declare that 'I am convinced that these basic motifs in the history of the representation of reality – provided I have seen them correctly – must be demonstrable in any random realistic text.'[8]

Auerbach's *Mimesis* is a grand narrative of a most interesting sort, consisting of 537 pages of text, with no footnotes. It may be, as Auerbach himself claimed in the Epilogue, that it was only his exile in Istanbul, far away from European libraries and easy access to sources, that gave him the courage to write a book about a theme in literature that spans 2,500 years. His study of realism put a subject on the table in a new and interesting way, and it has been seminal in contemporary discussions of nineteenth-century literature. Among these literary works we must place the Bible.

It is striking that Auerbach himself used the Bible as a paradigmatic text, in the very first chapter of *Mimesis*. His book begins with a comparison of the tale of Odysseus's nurse in Homer with the story of the sacrifice of Isaac in the Old Testament. Auerbach notes that when the old nurse discovers the scar that identifies Odysseus, the story is told using all the detail that can be brought to hand. No loose ends are left hanging; everything is foregrounded. In the Bible, on the other hand, there is much that is not told, and we as readers are meant to understand that further detail lies hidden in the background. It is from the Bible that we derive our modern realistic tradition, and as a literary creation it serves as a model, the *Urtext* which represents realism in Western (!) literature.

According to Auerbach, the great realistic revolution of modern times took place in early nineteenth-century France. After reading Stendhal and Balzac, it would be quite impossible for a cultivated Frenchman ever to feel quite the same satisfaction with Racine. But how would he henceforth read the Holy Scriptures? What would a 'realistic' Bible look like for a nineteenth-century Frenchman? Or more relevantly here, for a Victorian Englishman?

As we have seen, the English Bible in the eighteenth century underwent a process of aestheticization, by which means the Scriptures came to be seen not merely as another form of literature, but as the paradigm of how mankind should deploy words. No longer could the biblical text be understood as merely transparent, allowing us to see the truth which lay behind it. By the end of the eighteenth century, most scholars would have to concede that the biblical text was itself important, and Christians were generally in dire need of authoritative guidance from clergymen and professors in order to tease out divine truth. Robert Lowth and the other pioneers of biblical criticism saw poetry as the highest expression of literature, and this was the dominant view throughout the eighteenth century before the novel had come of age. Only through poetry could the sublime be expressed in words. Indeed, a very extreme Kantian position on the sublime might even argue that since the real world of 'things-in-themselves' is unknown and unknowable, poetry is more real than direct sense data.

At the same time, however, the ways in which the 'real world' could be represented began to change, in a direction that would have profound effects on biblical criticism. Among the key milestones and influences on this directional change was the publication of *Robinson Crusoe* in 1719. Daniel Defoe's realistic fiction promulgated a new model for a story told as a kind of detailed reportage. Defoe, in the role of anonymous editor of a genuine narrative, asserted in the preface to the first edition that the book was 'a just History of Fact; neither is there any Appearance of Fiction in it'. When attacked for having passed off fiction as truth, 'Robinson Crusoe' himself protested that 'the Story, though Allegorical, is also Historical' in that it contained much genuine information: 'all those Parts of the Story are real Facts in my History, whatever borrow'd Lights they may be represented by'.[9] In Defoe's day, a 'history' was simply a relation of incidents, which might be either true or imaginary. Only later on in the eighteenth century was a clear distinction made between a 'novel' and a 'history'.[10] Inevitably, there was a mutual influence between the way literature was understood and the methods of biblical interpretation. In the long run, nineteenth-century readers of the Bible came to expect of Scripture what they would find in contemporary novels: an artful literary expression depicting events and situations that might be recognizable as part of life.

But what was 'life'? Did 'life' have any signification, or was it a meaningless succession of random events? Auerbach is certainly right to say that something changed in the nineteenth century, but he never hazards a guess as to the cause of the shift. He takes the role of circus ringmaster, pointing to the most exciting performances and proclaiming their virtues to the crowd. What happened in fact was the collapse of the providential universe, and this in turn was primarily due to the excessive tinkering of scholars, not in France, but in Germany and England, with what had hitherto been regarded as the most ultimate, perfect – and realistic – book: the Bible.

By 'providential universe', we should understand the world view according to which not only is God a living presence in our lives, but our lives themselves are unfolding according to divine plan and intention.[11] This view of events in the mundane world is not automatically at odds with the concept of free will. Even though there is a divine blueprint, many of us will fail to heed its instructions, and will no doubt suffer the consequences of this misdirection. Nevertheless, God is there (rather than here), as the transcendent watchmaker who put the entire operation into motion. This is the view of the universe one gets in the two classic statements of the providential world view, Joseph Butler's *The Analogy of Religion* (1736) and William Paley's *Natural Theology* (1802).[12] But the providential universe was hardly the invention of English theologians. The notion of 'poetic justice' is as old as the hills, or at least the Greeks. As H.D.F. Kitto put it succinctly in regard to classical drama, the 'divine background holds up to us, so to speak, the system of co-ordinates against which we are to read the significance of what the human actors do and suffer.'[13] An audience watching a play in ancient Greece or reading a story in eighteenth-century England would recognize as true to life, 'real', a plot that unfolded according to the axioms of God's divine plan. The author of a book takes on a number of divine attributes, including creation and omniscience, and literary characters, like ordinary mortals, ignore the transcendental blueprint at their peril. The task was to find the hints and patterns in everyday life that help us draw a facsimile of the divine plan. As readers and humans we are engaged in a very similar project – reading a text – either a written book or the Book of Life. Just as life unfolds according to God's plan and everything in life turns out 'for the best', or at least has some (often hidden) significance, so too in novels before the middle of the nineteenth century do things come out all right, reach some kind of satisfactory closure by the time we reach the final page.

Back to Robinson Crusoe again: his problem was that he completely failed to see the signs all around him. He used his free will in the wrong directions. He set to sea without asking his father's permission and found not freedom but slavery at the hands of a Turkish pirate, followed by servitude to nature herself. Only at the end does he understand that obedience to God's will is the single way forward.[14]

But something happens in the middle of the nineteenth century that makes the ending of a book like *Great Expectations* seem just a little too pat. The chance meeting between Pip and Estella in the grounds of Satis House, both 'happening' to visit there for the first time since the events of 300 pages earlier, came to be seen as an unbelievable artistic device, not 'real'. At the beginning of the century, there was nothing wrong at all with a healthy overdose of coincidence, for what looks to us mere mortals like coincidence is in reality a clue left behind by God's providence.

For the later Victorians, such literary neatness simply wouldn't wash. God was still there, but now He was more here than there, immanent rather than transcendent, a friend or a father Who cares and stays near to help, a divine ruler active in human affairs on a continuous basis. He is here for us if we search for Him through the darkness. By Thomas Hardy's day (and he died in 1928), sometimes things didn't turn out quite completely all right, as Jude the Obscure discovered. Henry James described the dramatic process very well in 1908: 'Really, universally, relations stop nowhere, and the exquisite problem of the artist is eternally to draw, by a geometry of his own, the circle within which they shall happily *appear* to do so.'[15] The universe had become rather meaningless and has stayed like that ever since.

The descent of God from transcendently On High to immanently Among Us fits in well with the burgeoning Romantic movement throughout Europe, itself a product of Pietism, Methodism, and the general religious revival in eighteenth-century Germany, Britain, and America. Discussions about reality and man's place in the natural world were being stimulated by the popularity of Immanuel Kant and his publicists, especially F.W.J. von Schelling (1775–1854), who himself was reinterpreted (some might say plagiarized) by Samuel Taylor Coleridge.[16] But the concept of what is real, possible, believable, was heavily dependent on religion, and in England, Protestantism remained strongly biblical. At mid-century, the Victorian Bible suffered a number of shocks from which it would never really recover and, like other traditional forms of literature, was heavily influenced by the rise of the novel.

We have already seen how new concepts of authorship and notions of the Bible as literature changed the way the Scriptures in English were understood by their readers. Demanding that the Bible be like *Robinson Crusoe*, 'a just History of Fact', put an unbearable strain on Holy Writ. For the greatest danger to the traditional understanding of *sola scriptura* lay just with those people who had no doubts that the precise factual Word of God was contained therein. It is curious how much the Victorian period parallels the revolutionary implications of textual criticism during the European Renaissance four hundred years before. Then it was the innocuous science of *philology* which began in pious examination of the Bible and ended in revealing worrying anomalies. So too in the seventeenth century did biblical *chronology* follow the same path from piety to destabilization. In the nineteenth century it was the meddling with *quantification* which shook the biblical faith of many people and had a greater effect than a hundred reprints of the writings of the Deists. The German biblical scholars began by taking the Bible as God's last words, and His numbers as divine. Their calculations of the length and breadth of the Exodus parade of Israelites, the exact number of the children of the Children of Israel, and numerous other quantifiable biblical conundrums, drilled holes into the pillar of *sola scriptura* that their further research did nothing to repair. The German conquest of the Bible was unstoppable, and swept over England like a clergyman's nightmare.

I

German biblical criticism came to England with Lessing. Gotthold Ephraim Lessing (1729–81) was born in Saxony, the son of a Lutheran minister, and went up to the University of Leipzig at the age of seventeen. Curiously, Lessing abandoned theology to go on the stage, but by the time he met his exact contemporary Moses Mendelssohn (1729–86), his philosophical interests had been reawakened. Lessing returned to Leipzig in 1755, moving three years later to Berlin, two years after that to Breslau, and returning to Berlin in 1765 in the hope of becoming royal librarian. A year later he was back in the theatre at Hamburg, but in 1769 he was given the dream appointment of librarian of the duke of Brunswick's collection at Wolfenbüttel.[17]

Lessing's earliest writings on theology may give some indication as to the direction his interests would take.[18] His first published work was a 'Vindication of Hieronymus Cardanus' (1754), in which he rejected the accusations of atheism that were laid against Girolamo Cardano (1501–76) for his favourable evaluation of non-Christian religions in his work *De subtilitate* (1550). Lessing's point was that Cardano's failure to include the strongest argument in defence of Islam, namely, that Muslims believe in one God and life after death without the theological need for supernatural miracles or resurrection, proves that in spite of it all he was a devout Christian.[19]

But Lessing soon showed himself to be far from that. Lessing had plans to publish a series entitled *Zur Geschichte und Literatur. Aus den Schätzen der herzoglichen Bibliothek zu Wolfenbüttel* ('Contributions to Literature and History from the Ducal Library at Wolfenbüttel'), and in February 1772 his noble employer gave him leave to print anything he liked, as long as he refrained from attacking religion. While it is true that the actual word 'religion' did not appear in the title of his series, it was inconceivable that Lessing would have been silent in this important area. He began by putting out an unpublished note by his hero Leibniz, defending the notion of the torments of hell, although he denied it in private.[20] Lessing carried on Leibniz's arguments, but it was clear that something meatier would be more appropriate for the new publication.

At that time, Lessing was especially concerned with the work of the so-called 'neologists', who (like the Deists in England) were attempting to provide a rational foundation for Christianity by explaining away all supernatural elements, even at the expense of draining out everything that made religion a faith. In a letter to his brother Karl at the beginning of 1774, Lessing complained that the neologists, 'under the pretext of making us rational Christians, they are making us very irrational philosophers.'[21] Lessing believed that by softening the irrational edges of Christianity, the neologists were hoodwinking more people than the austere supernatural orthodox Protestants ever did, since their arguments were so superficially plausible. 'I only prefer the old orthodox theology (at bottom, tolerant),' he wrote to Karl, 'to the new (at bottom, intolerant) because the former is in manifest conflict with human reason, while the latter might easily take one in. I make agreement with my obvious enemies in order to be able to be the better on my guard against my secret adversaries.'

While in Hamburg, Lessing became acquainted with the family of Hermann Samuel Reimarus (1694–1768), who taught Oriental languages at the Gymnasium Johanneum there. His son J.A.H. Reimarus was both Lessing's friend and physician. Through him and his sister Elise, Lessing learned that Reimarus had left a huge unpublished manuscript entitled 'Apologie oder Schutzschrift für die vernünftigen Verehrer Gottes' ('Apology or Defence for Rational Worshippers of God'). It was clear that the text could not be published as it stood: it was simply too radical (and too long and diffuse) to appear in print unedited.[22] Now at Wolfenbüttel, Lessing decided to publish anonymous fragments of it in his 'Contributions to Literature and History', which was globally spared the attentions of a censor.[23] Thanks to his plot, Reimarus's authorship was not known for sure until 1814, when Dr Reimarus donated his father's manuscripts to libraries in Hamburg and Göttingen.[24]

Lessing published the first fragment in 1774, calling it 'On the Toleration of the Deists', and claiming it was the work of an anonymous writer: 'I have been quite unable to discover how and when it came into our Library', Lessing lied, even suggesting that the author might be the notorious and safely dead German Deist J. Lorenz Schmidt (1702–49), who had conveniently passed away in Wolfenbüttel.[25] This first text was rather innocuous, suggesting that any rational person who follows the ethical and moral teachings of Jesus may call himself a Christian.

Three years later, in 1777, having tested the waters, Lessing dropped his theological bomb, in the form of five separate fragments, which together comprised a brutal attack on Christianity itself. From our point of view, it is the third fragment which is most relevant, being devoted to 'The Passage of the Israelites Through the Red Sea'. Assuming the Old Testament to be the Word of God and completely accurate down to the smallest details, Reimarus focused on the references in Exodus xxxviii. 26 and Numbers i. 46 to 603,550 warriors aged 'twenty years and upward' having left Egypt. In Exodus the context is a tax for the tabernacle; in Numbers the figure is given in connection with the census of the Israelites. Reimarus estimated that this would have entailed a general population of about three million Israelites, who would have required 300,000 oxen and cows and 600,000 sheep and goats. Now, if the Israelites moved in a column ten deep, the length of this parade would have been 180 miles, and it would have taken them a minimum of nine days to cross the Red Sea! Over a century later, Albert Schweitzer (1875–1965) was still impressed. In his view,

The monograph on the passing of the Israelites through the Red Sea is one of the ablest, wittiest, and most acute which has ever been written. It exposes all the impossibilities of the narrative in the Priestly Codex, and all the inconsistencies which arise from the combination of various sources; although Reimarus has not the slightest inkling that the separation of these sources would afford the real solution of the problem.[26]

The fourth fragment dealt with the fact that the Old Testament omits any discussion of a life after death, which might indicate that it was not 'written to reveal a religion'. The fifth fragment analysed the contradictions between the different evangelists concerning the Resurrection, casting doubt on the whole business.

Lessing published these documents with some conclusions and comments, taking the opportunity to launch the first fifty-three paragraphs of his own *Die Erziehung des Menschengeschlechts* ('The Education of the Human Race'), properly published only in 1780, as if it were the work of someone else.[27] Lessing's argument was that there is progress in human history, and we ourselves are in a better position to separate history from myth than many of those who lived at the time when the biblical events took place. The positive religions represented stages in the advance of humanity from infancy to maturity. Christianity demonstrates a more developed stage of religion as the primitive Israelite tribesmen progressed to being followers of a more complex ethical faith. Indeed, this was the reason that there was no doctrine of immortality in the Old Testament: it took a very long time until mankind had evolved to the point where it could be understood and accepted. The evangelists themselves were ordinary men, lacking divine inspiration, and errors and omissions were only to be expected. Like Toland and many others, Lessing was advocating that we read the Bible like any other book.[28]

Many of these issues were followed up in Lessing's epic controversy with Johann Melchior Goeze (1717–86), the pastor of the Lutheran Church of St Catharine at Hamburg. Lessing's wife had just died (10 January 1778) shortly after giving birth to a child which did not itself long survive. He was in a fighting mood. In 1778 he published a longer and stronger fragment, 'On the Intentions of Jesus and His Disciples', in which Reimarus argued that despite the later development of the Christian religion, the Jesus of history was a simple Jewish peasant without dreams of a world religion, and would not have understood either the concept of Atonement or that of Resurrection.[29] These were bold pronouncements. Indeed, Albert Schweitzer believed that this last of the Reimarus fragments represented 'perhaps the most splendid achievement in the whole course of the historical investigation of the life of Jesus, for he was the first to grasp the fact that the world of thought in which Jesus moved was essentially eschatological.'[30]

This last fragment was really quite enough for the duke of Brunswick, who told Lessing that it was time that the censor examined his writings before publication. Lessing drew on his theatrical background and produced an answer in dramatic form, his famous *Nathan der Weise* (1779). It was a plea for religious toleration in which Nathan the Jew, Saladin the Muslim, and the Knight Templar could all live in harmony, emphasizing the positive elements of their respective religions. Lessing had been a Freemason at least since 1771 when he was initiated into a lodge in Hamburg, and similar concepts are prominent in his five Masonic dialogues, *Ernst und Falk* (1778–80).[31]

Apart from the fact that Lessing provoked a good deal of controversy about important issues by publishing Reimarus's fragments, he is crucial for the history of the English Bible in that he utilized the arguments of the Deists to promote a new understanding of the text. Assuming that Reimarus's arithmetic was accurate, and that the story of the Exodus was impossible to accept exactly as written, what then? Did it matter if the Old Testament had no doctrine of a future life?[32] Lessing's argument was that it really is not important if the Old Testament is incomplete or even wrong, since it reflects a much earlier and more credulous stage in the education of mankind. The concept of the development of religion is usually associated with Cardinal J.H. Newman (1801–90), but not only did it appear much earlier, in Lessing, but through the translation of *Education* in 1858 Lessing's views were made available in England, and provided the inspiration for Frederick Temple's article on that subject in the notorious *Essays and Reviews* (1860), about which more below.

II

The real breakthrough came with the work of W.M.L. de Wette (1780–1849), especially his introductions to the Old Testament, which began appearing in 1806. De Wette's idea, not to put too fine a point on it, was that

> From the nature of things and the fate of all ancient books, we must suppose that the Old Testament, in spite of the holy zeal of the Jews to maintain its purity, – which may be called the influence of the Holy Ghost, – would become disfigured by the faults of the transcribers, unless a continual miracle took place.[33]

Such a continual miracle being unlikely, de Wette put forward a view of the Old Testament notable for being the first which is substantially different from that appearing in the Bible itself. 'The design of criticism', he proclaimed, 'is *to determine what was originally written by the author*, consequently to ascertain facts.'[34]

This task was crucial when dealing with the all-important question of miracles. 'Now,' reasoned de Wette,

> since it is at least doubtful, to a cultivated mind, that *such miracles actually took place*, the question naturally rises, Did they *appear* so to the eye-witnesses, and to such as were actively engaged in the events recorded in this history? or did the writer understand them as natural events, but yet portray them in a poetico-miraculous light?

De Wette looked carefully at those miracles in the Old Testament that appear more than once, such as burnt offerings. His analysis revealed that

> The miraculous in the historical books diminishes just in proportion as they approach historical times, and that it entirely ceases in that period from which we have contemporary accounts. In the earliest times, men have intercourse with God; later, angels appear; still later, the prophets perform the miraculous; but in the times after the exile, from which we have contemporary history, the miraculous ceases altogether.[35]

What does this mean? These questions are dealt with at length in a chapter provocatively entitled 'Origin and Progress of the Mosaic Mythology'. 'The conclusion that these accounts of miraculous events are entirely forged would be too rash', de Wette wrote. Some forgery there may have been in the books of Daniel and Second Maccabees, 'but it can scarcely be so in the books of Moses.' De Wette came to this view, not because of pious obligation, but rather due to his understanding that 'Here a genuine historical legend lies at the foundation, which was connected with certain monuments, supported by popular songs, and preserved in the mouth of the people.' Furthermore, we know that the 'analogy of other nations plainly shows us that popular traditions are not reduced to writing until a late period.' We find etymological myths, which explain place names, for example, as in 'the same manner, the legends of the Arabs are connected with names and proverbs.' There are also 'idealo-poetic' elements by which 'means the tradition was transformed, gradually into the miraculous and the ideal.' A good example, de Wette thought, was the parting of the Red Sea. In Exodus xiv. 22 we get the 'historical statement': 'And the children of Israel went into the midst of the sea upon the dry *ground*: and the waters *were* a wall unto them on their right hand, and on their left.' Fair enough, but a bit later on, in Exodus xv. 8 we are subjected to 'lyric exaggeration': 'And with the blast of thy nostrils the waters were gathered together, the floods stood upright as an heap, *and* the depths were congealed in the heart of the sea.' Behold the birth of a miracle in popular tradition.[36]

De Wette made no allowance for the fact that he was dealing with Holy Writ and divine history, but treated the biblical text as he would have done any ancient document. 'In reducing these legends to writing,' he explained,

> the authors of these books scarcely design to write a history. They were the less inclined to it as this design had exerted so small an influence in preserving the legend. They exercised the rights of the religious imagination natural to their countrymen, and the more freely, as this had formerly been so active in developing and embellishing the same legends, and as the substance of them was so indefinite and fluctuating.

Apart from this, de Wette posits, the 'author of Deuteronomy had read the earlier Mosaic books.'[37] Simple as that: no beating around the bush about Mosaic authorship: the Pentateuch was an edited volume.

It was also an epic. 'If an historical narrative, written without critical investigation of the facts, but treated so as to suit religious and poetical ideas, is an epic composition, then the Pentateuch may be called the theocratic epic poem of the Israelites, without denying that there is an historical basis at the bottom.'[38] Not that there is anything wrong with an epic: every culture should have at least one, and the Old Testament betrays its epic quality in two ways. Firstly, it is shown in 'the poetic form of the narrative', demonstrated by what de Wette calls '*Anschaulichkeit und Gemütlichkeit*' (intuitiveness and spiritedness), and by the 'rhythmic elevation of the style'. Secondly, it is apparent in the subject matter, especially the appearance of miracles and the 'supernatural intercourse of man with God', de Wette notes, 'for the epic loves the miraculous'. Indeed, there was a kind of epic slippery slope: it began with popular legend, which created the original extraordinary event, was passed down to the epic poets, 'who needed miracles to answer the end they proposed' and even 'sometimes developed the miraculous legend still further, and sometimes invented new miracles.' Even more typically, 'they also availed themselves of the right, so frequently used by the poets and prophets, of constructing symbolical poems.' What starts out as 'natural and simple' in the Elohistic part of the Pentateuch becomes miraculous with the Jehovist and is further embellished by the time the story is retold in Chronicles. 'The story of the manna in Ex. xvi.,' de Wette reveals, 'is obviously designed to impress men with the holiness of the Sabbath.'[39]

A story designed, a book written, an author implied – and in this case, more than a single author, and certainly not Moses. 'After coming to these results,' de Wette wrote, 'we find no ground and no evidence to show that the books of the Pentateuch were composed by Moses. The only reason such a claim is made at all, he explains, is that 'the Jews were of this opinion'. Anyone with a knowledge of the development of Syriac and Aramaic can see that the Hebrew language would also be expected to change between the time of Moses and the period of the composition of the final books of the Old Testament, yet the style is far too uniform:

> – still, even then, it would be absurd to suppose that one man could have created beforehand the epico-historical, the rhetorical and poetic style, in all their extent and compass, and have perfected these three departments of Hebrew literature, both in form and substance, so far that all subsequent writers found nothing left for them to follow in his steps.[40]

Such an eventuality was even more unlikely than miracles.

W.M.L. de Wette was a pioneer, but like many others who expressed revolutionary ideas that would eventually become part of mainstream thought, he spoiled his chances for greater influence in his own lifetime by hitching his wagon to a permanently unfashionable philosophy. When de Wette had been a student at the University of Jena he attended lectures by Jakob Friedrich Fries (1773–1843) and eventually the two became close friends. Fries was a follower of Kant, and tried to improve on the great man's philosophy, explicating areas which had hitherto been unclear. In Fries's case it was the issue of how we can sense eternal ideas which are unknown, and his answer was that we have a capacity for what he called *Ahndung* (inkling), by means of which we come to express these ideas in symbolic artistic form. Among these artistic forms are myths, which are not bits of bungled history or primitive science, but one of the ways in which the human spirit expresses its intuition of divine ideas. Fries's attitude to myth comes through very clearly in de Wette's writings.[41]

Fries was also notoriously anti-Semitic, the author of a book succinctly titled 'On the Danger Posed by the Jews to German Well-Being and Character' (1816). Fries refused to see Judaism as a religion at all, condemning it as a state within a state, founded on principles of barbarous morals and a love of money, and one which should not be tolerated in any decent society. So too did de Wette describe Judaism as a religion of *Unglück* (misfortune) in his work entitled 'Characteristic Features of Hebrew Religion' (1807). But de Wette was more interested in ancient Jews than in their more modern representatives.

De Wette's work was daring in its time, and there were echoes in other parts of Germany from scholars thinking along the same lines. Among these were Wilhelm Gesenius (1786–1842), whose fame would rest on his Hebrew lexicon (1810–12) and grammar (1813). Gesenius was well aware that the lack of linguistic development in the Hebrew language between Genesis and Chronicles could only mean that there was a later recension of the biblical text.[42] Another scholar working towards similar conclusions was Johann Friedrich Leopold George (1811–73). He was very shocked by his reading of David Friedrich Strauss's (1808–74) *Life of Jesus* (1835), lost his faith, and became a Hegelian philosophy professor. George went further than de Wette by taking the biblical books entirely apart. Whereas de Wette was puzzled by the fact that the rituals in Leviticus and Numbers seemed more developed than in Deuteronomy, George argued simply that the Bible was even more of a jumble than we thought, reflected in the fact that the last book in the Pentateuch was not the last to be written. In this he came close to postulating the existence of P, a third author along with E and J, a thesis which would later be championed by Julius Wellhausen, George's colleague at the University of Greifswald.[43]

By the time that Strauss published his notorious *Life of Jesus* in 1835, then, there was already quite a momentum in play. The last interesting figure in the post-de-Wette group of German professors was Wilhelm Vatke (1806–82), who published his *Biblical Theology* in the same year as Strauss; this inevitably led to his name being coupled with that controversial figure, even apart from the significant fact that the two men actually worked together for forty-three years (1831–74). Vatke was a student of Gesenius, Schleiermacher, and Hegel, and his own work was extremely Hegelian, with a constant emphasis on development. Interestingly in that regard, Vatke paid special attention to sun metaphors in religion, arguing that worship of earth's star was a higher form of devotion. Like Friedrich Max Müller at the end of the century, Vatke saw the sun everywhere around him. He argued that it was a Phoenician Temple architect who introduced mythological solar symbols into the sanctuary and thereby elevated the Israelite cult of Yahweh to a higher plane. Even the story of Samson properly understood was really about how the sun god triumphed over the worship of Baal.[44] As regards that other touchstone, Josiah's law book, Vatke had doubts regarding the entire tale. How likely, he asked, was it that idolatrous servants would have kept such a document in the Temple itself? Probably the only written materials found there were a few chapters from Exodus.

Vatke also brought a greater historical sense to the development of Judaism. He argued that after the fall of Jerusalem, people either continued to worship local Canaanite gods or adopted those of their Babylonian overlords. Contact with the religions of Babylon and Persia introduced an entire pantheon of new concepts, such as Satan and Resurrection, and by the second century before Christ, a new *Jewish* theological system had developed. Unlike many of his colleagues, however, Vatke argued that this change from Israelite ideology and nature worship to Jewish theology was a step forward, indeed the high point in the history of Judaism.[45]

These new ideas did not meet with immediate success in Germany, to say the least, despite the general picture that we usually have of the rampant rise of Higher Criticism there. Vatke's career suffered a terminal blow with the death of his teacher Schleiermacher in 1834. As bad luck would have it, the man who succeeded to de Wette's chair at Berlin in 1828 was the arch-conservative Ernst Wilhelm Hengstenberg (1802–69), and he was now top dog in Vatke's academic universe. Vatke was systematically kept out of a chair and, having married money, turned into a gentleman scholar at Berlin, keeping the post warm but producing nothing further.

Hengstenberg, indeed, was one of the leaders of the group which tried to halt the tide of the new biblical criticism, and to avoid asking the questions that could not be answered. He had trained originally as an Arabist and had lots to say about such learned subjects as the Samaritan Pentateuch. But he also believed that reason must give way before faith, a research method which led him to argue that Moses had written the entire Pentateuch, that Chronicles gives an accurate account of Levitical rituals, and that a certain prophet named Isaiah wrote all sixty-six chapters in the book called by his name.

With the benefit of hindsight, Hengstenberg's work does indeed seem like the last gasp of a decaying faith in the absolute authenticity of the biblical text as it has come down to us. He knows this, and informs his readers right at the beginning that

> Such a work as the Pentateuch can be maintained as genuine, only as long as it is expounded as a sacred book. An inability to penetrate its depths – the exposition of it as a profane author – the diluting of its meaning, contain (in the germ) the denial of its genuineness; and if this is not immediately

developed, it is a mere inconsequence, which the course of events will set aside; for every tendency will, sooner or later, arrive at maturity.

It was a slow, step-by-step process of demolition. Hengstenberg even blamed poor Michaelis, who 'by clearing the foundations of the genuineness of the Biblical writings, has injured them more than those who have more directly attacked them. He destroyed the kernel, and then vainly declaimed against those who attempted to injure the shell.'[46]

Hengstenberg's remarks, originally published in Berlin in 1831, were enormously prescient. As we shall see, it proved to be much easier to deal with outright opponents of religion than with the well-meaning pious biblical scholars who genuinely sought to clear up the paradoxes in Scripture, unable to imagine that no amount of learning could make infallible what was after all an ancient document subject to the same vagaries as any other. Furthermore, Hengstenberg and his crowd not only objected to what was said, but also to *how* it was expressed. He had only pity for D.F. Strauss (who reminded him of the seventeenth-century English biblical critic John Spencer in more than one way):

> Both possess acuteness, but with such almost incredible deficiency in profundity of thought as oftentimes to cast a doubt on their acuteness. In both there is the same icy coldness – the same religious feebleness – the same attitude for stifling devotional sentiment, so that the emotions of piety never once appear, even as a transient influence, to interrupt the train of their speculations.[47]

What was the point of devoting so much time and energy to writing a life of Jesus, if it was not itself done out of a spirit of devotion?

Hengstenberg objected to the element of sensationalism in the work of the new critics. De Wette's claims, for example, he thought to be 'so ridiculously arbitrary' that if his subject had been other, either literary or historical, then he would have been wholly ignored. 'And even if he had succeeded in exciting some notice in his day,' Hengstenberg continued, 'a work like that of Vatke, had he chosen to exercise his acuteness on Herodotus, for example, instead of the Pentateuch, would have fallen still-born from the press. It would have been considered as transgressing the proper limits of philosophical enquiry.'[48]

The rot had set in as early as Johann Gottfried Eichhorn (1752–1827), the famous Protestant theologian, who 'labours to explain away every thing supernatural, every thing that presupposes the presence of a living, personal God.'

> The shining of Moses' face, he thinks, could only have been deemed miraculous as long as the nature of electricity was not known. Had Eichhorn, instead of Moses, been in a storm on Mount Sinai, on his descent he would

have shone equally so, down to his toes, if he had previously thrown off his clothes.

The fundamental mistake which biblical critics of Eichhorn's stamp made, in brief, was that 'the dread of the supernatural led to a denial of the genuineness of the Pentateuch.'[49]

Hengstenberg's theological agenda was abundantly clear: there was nothing wrong with preconceived ideas as long as they were right, as was manifestly the case with traditional views of the Old Testament. A much more subtle and superficially progressive form of theology came from Heinrich Ewald (1803–75), who was born in Göttingen, studied in Göttingen, and taught in Göttingen. When Hanover was annexed to Prussia in 1866 he was the only professor who refused to take the loyalty oath, which was in effect a resignation from his university post. He was by all accounts an extraordinary figure, both for his numerous political stands which often put his academic career at risk, and for his diligence as a scholar.[50] Ewald spent a good deal of time in England, and in 1862 paid his last visit, staying with Friedrich Max Müller at Oxford. Müller recalled him as 'the only man I remember who, after copying Hebrew MSS. for twelve hours at the Bodleian with nothing but a sandwich to sustain him, complained of the short time allowed there for work.'[51]

The problem which Ewald posed for the more progressive biblical critics in mid-nineteenth-century Germany was that he too looked rather progressive, at least in his choice of method and his refusal to adopt stonewalling tactics. He had studied with Eichhorn, and despite Hengstenberg's hysteria, Ewald remembered his teacher's belief in the Mosaic authorship of the Pentateuch, and he agreed with him. But Ewald was not afraid to make use of the latest historiographical trends in order to elucidate what he knew to be the truth. In Ewald's day, the last word was Barthold Georg Niebuhr (1776–1831) and his *Römische Geschichte*, published at Berlin in 1811–12. The study of mythology was becoming increasingly fashionable and it was Niebuhr's belief that classical legends and other non-historical literature could provide a solid base on which one could build a reliable account of actual events. All that was required was a healthy dose of imagination.[52]

This was a quality with which Ewald was manifoldly blessed. His master work reflected the belief that only daring hypothesis can enable us to convert garbled mythological traces into something substantial. Ewald's *History of Israel* was published at Göttingen between 1843 and 1859, and an English translation appeared between 1867 and 1886. Ewald argued that the Old Testament was originally composed of three 'Great Books' – 'Origins' (the Pentateuch and Joshua), 'Kings', and a 'Great Book of Universal History to Greek Times'. Ewald's work was monumental and, like Niebuhr, his intuition went very far indeed beyond his evidence. But at least he had shown that the new criticism need not be completely revolutionary, as long as we took a good deal on faith.

A deep belief in Christ and his divine mission also lay behind what might be seen as the culmination of the more conservative trend that began with Hengstenberg and those who were unwilling to sell the Old Testament for a mess of revisionist biblical interpretation – *Heilsgeschichte* (salvation history). At the simplest level, this term referred to the idea that the history we find recorded in the Bible is no ordinary chronicle of events but is itself a highly didactic drama in which God uses the dual techniques of prophecy and fulfilment in order to convey a message to mankind. The scholar whose name is usually associated with this school of thought is Johannes Christian Konrad von Hofmann (1810–77), a pupil of Ranke's in Berlin, who taught at Erlangen for over thirty years until his death. Hofmann had nothing against the application of Ranke's methodological techniques to history *per se*. They were simply inappropriate for the study of the Bible, in which the text operated according to radically different internal principles. As with any written product of a single author, it was the deconstruction of the self-conscious artifice which was important and which compelled study. People who lived with faith in Christ had no need for philological or archaeological acrobatics. Biblical scholarship can help us understand the prophecies better in their own linguistic and historical setting, but is worthless if we miss the main point that history is an organic process directed by God Himself.[53]

III

It would seem to be very comprehensive to present the state of German Higher Criticism at mid-century as consisting of two schools of thought: a progressive party represented by de Wette, as opposed to the forces of reaction led by Hengstenberg and the lions of *Heilsgeschichte*. To some extent, this is how the situation appeared to Victorian observers. Oddly enough, however, if we look at *Essays and Reviews* (1860), that watershed document that announced the emancipation of English biblical studies, we find that only one contemporary German scholar rates an entire chapter all to himself: Christian Carl Josias von Bunsen (1791–1860). Unlike most of the other scholars in the field, he was not a professional theologian but a career Prussian diplomat. His work brought him to England, first in 1838–9, and then for a much longer period as Prussian minister in London (1842–54). Bunsen was very well liked in England, in no small part because he was married to Frances, an extremely capable Englishwoman.[54] He became friends with Thomas Arnold (1795–1842), and with the translators of Niebuhr's history of

Rome, Connop Thirlwall (1797–1875) and Julius Hare (1795–1855).[55] The influence of Niebuhr was important. Bunsen had worked for the great classicist in Rome when Niebuhr was appointed Prussian minister to the Vatican in 1816. Bunsen himself succeeded Niebuhr in that post in 1824, and remained there until he was recalled in 1838. Throughout his time in Rome, Bunsen held a *salon* for German and English intellectuals, which won him many friends. He spent the years 1839–41 as minister to Switzerland, and was translated to the plum posting in England in 1842.[56] Bunsen described his first meeting with Niebuhr in 1815, at the age of twenty-four:

> My visits to Niebuhr, Schleiermacher, and Solger demand the first notice, but I can now only speak of those to Niebuhr. It would be hard to describe my astonishment at his command over the entire domain of knowledge. All that can be known seems to be within his grasp, and everything known to him to be at hand, as if held by a thread. He met me at once with the advice to carry out my project of an Oriental journey of linguistic research for the Prussian Government.[57]

Although diplomatic work took up much of Bunsen's time in later life, he remained keenly interested in the Middle East of his day, and was involved in the founding of the Anglo-German Protestant bishopric at Jerusalem in 1841.

By the time Bunsen met Niebuhr, he already had a general idea of what his scholarly work would be, but the meeting crystallized a plan of action. In a letter to his sister from Rome at the end of 1817, Bunsen looked back on the progression of his thoughts. His basic principle always had been, he explained, to study the 'consciousness of God in the minds of man, and that which in and through that consciousness, He has accomplished, especially in language and religion'. By Christmas 1812, Bunsen had the idea of making a comprehensive study of 'heathen antiquity', beginning with the East, followed by Greece and Rome, and concluding with his own Teutonic nations. A couple of years later, he recalled,

> I arrived at this conclusion, that as God had caused the conception of Himself to be developed in the mind of man in a two-fold manner, – the one through revelation to the Jewish people through their patriarchs, the other through reason in the heathen; – so also must the enquiry and representation of this development be twofold; – and as God had kept these two ways for a length of time independent and separate, so should we, in the course of the examination, separate knowledge from man, and his development from the doctrine of revelation and faith, firmly trusting that God in the end would bring about the union of both.[58]

The result of Bunsen's ruminations was a five-volume study of *Egypt's Place in Universal History*, the first three volumes appearing at Hamburg in 1845, completed by the last two at Gotha in 1856–7. The English translation, published by Longmans, kept pace with the German originals.[59]

Like thinkers all over Europe, Bunsen had been entranced by the decipherment of hieroglyphics in 1822 by Jean François Champollion (1790–1832), which opened a window into a culture which many thought to be the first developed civilization in the history of mankind. Bunsen's particular slant was philological, and he cited Friedrich Schlegel (1772–1829) as his inspiration for believing 'the great truth, that a method has been found of restoring the genealogy of mankind, through the medium of language; not by means of forced, isolated etymologies, but by taking a large and comprehensive view of the organic and indestructible fabric of individual tongues, according to the family to which they belong.'[60] Bunsen thanked his fortune in having become acquainted in 1836 with Richard Lepsius (1810–84), who helped him in his Egyptian studies and had his own radical ideas about biblical chronology.[61] But he never forgot the influence of Niebuhr, for 'he is in our estimation the highest model of an historical critic; an honour which would seem to depend, not on the negation, but on the recognition and restoration, of true historic principles.'[62] What was true for the study of ancient Egyptians was also true for the Bible:

> Historical faith and historical science have the same object in view, but they start from opposite points. In the contemplation of human history, Faith begins, as the Sacred Books do, with the Divine origin of things, and, starting from the great facts of creation and the unity of the human race, considers the events handed down principally in their connection with that Divine origin. The stronger and the more pure this faith is, the more free and independent will be the position it occupies in regard to the question, really unimportant, if viewed from that position, concerning the external shell of the divine kernel. The question is, whether the external history, related in the Sacred Books, be externally complete, and capable of chronological arrangement. Science on the other hand ascends from the clear historical periods to the dark ages. Her task is to sail up the stream of universal history, and she fulfils it in the hope of being able to hold out the hand to Faith who sits at the source, and, on her part, sees Science patiently and joyfully plodding up her thorny path. For Faith alone appreciates the full importance of that path, because Faith alone perceives the goal. To her it is immaterial whether Science discover truth in a spirit of scepticism or of belief – and truth has been really found by both courses, but never by dishonesty or sloth.[63]

Bunsen argued that we need not slavishly accept every historical detail in the Old Testament as gospel truth. Take the thorny question of the 603,550 Israelite fighting men aged twenty and upwards who left Egypt at the Exodus.

Simple mathematics could not produce such a figure from the fifty-six couples who came to Egypt to start with at the time of Joseph, even after the passage of the 430 years that Israel sojourned there.[64]

Putting all preconceptions aside, Baron Bunsen searched for 'those threads of the research which lie beneath the unsightly and time-worn surface, and which yet may prove the thread of Ariadne.'[65] After five volumes, Bunsen's conclusions were startling indeed. He argued that there was an historical connection between the ancient histories of the Greeks, the Israelites, the Egyptians, and Asia. Indeed, he argued,

> The religion of Egypt is merely the mummy of the original religion of Central Asia. The mythology of the Egyptians is the deposit of the oldest mythological belief of mankind, which took a new colouring westward in Upper Mesopotamia, and was petrified in the valley of the Nile by the influence of an African sky, and by the overpowering force of solar symbolism.[66]

That is to say, Bunsen wrote, that 'Primeval Asia, on the whole, is the starting-point of an intellectual movement, by the action of which we are ourselves consciously and unconsciously affected.' Bunsen also rejected claims that had been made for the importance of Egypt in the development of the Mosaic religion. According to Baron Bunsen, 'Moses adopted no part of the Egyptian customs or symbols: what was common to them both came from primitive Asia.' Indeed, the 'popular sentiment reflected in Abraham, in Moses, and in the primitive religion from the creation to the flood, and the expression of it, is rooted in the mythological life of the East in the earliest times.'[67]

Baron Bunsen was well aware that in deciding the paternity claims of ancient Egypt, and positing the peoples of central Asia as the religious and cultural ancestors of the biblical patriarchs, he was being radical and highly idiosyncratic. 'It is a very mistaken course pursued by Spencer, and latterly by Hengstenberg,' he warned, 'which led them to look for an Egyptian origin in the religious institutions and symbols of the Jews. Every argument adduced in support of it is a fallacy.' Bunsen's reference, of course, was to John Spencer, master of Corpus Christi College, Cambridge, whose great work, *De Legibus Hebraeorum ritualibus et earum rationibus* appeared there in 1685. Spencer had argued that Moses was an Egyptianized Hebrew, who used the principles of the Egyptian mysteries in devising Israelite ritual law. According to Spencer, Moses also learned in Egypt the underlying concept of the hieroglyphic ethos, that is, the importance of concealing a deeper philosophy within a code accessible to adepts alone. As Spencer himself noted:

> God gave the Jews a religion that was carnal only in its frontispiece, but divine and wonderful in its interior in order to accommodate his

institutions to the taste and usage of the time lest his Law and cult should seem deficient in anything transmitted in the name of wisdom.

Just as Egypt kept its secrets hidden under the veil of hieroglyphs, so too did Moses conceal his philosophy under the cover of ritual law. Similar ideas were expressed by Ralph Cudworth, William Warburton (1698–1779), and Bunsen's own countryman Karl Leonhard Reinhold (1757–1825), among many others.[68]

But this was not Baron Bunsen's view. His studies revealed that mankind began in China about twenty thousand years before Christ, in a sort of earthly paradise. Some unrecorded natural catastrophe led to a removal, and the original human race began to subdivide some time between 15,000 and 12,000 BC. The biblical flood took place only afterwards, between 11,000 and 10,000 BC. As the human race broke up, so did its language, splitting into a 'Semitic-Hamitic' group and another one Bunsen called 'Turanian-Aryan'.[69] Egypt came along, therefore, at a rather advanced stage of human existence, and was *not* the source of all wisdom. Egypt was, however, the bridge between the original human race and later ages, passing along a sense of God.

Baron Bunsen's Bible was therefore read in a rather innovative way, but it was still read as a fundamentally authoritative religious work. Indeed, a number of years later, Bunsen published a three-volume study entitled *God in History or the Progress of Man's Faith in the Moral Order of the World*. Here he discussed the religions and languages of mankind, and affirmed his expectation of the Coming of the Messiah exactly as depicted in Scripture, who would bring with him salvation, peace, and divine judgment.[70] At the same time, Bunsen was not afraid to disregard biblical chronology, especially the strait-jackets of Exodus xii. 40 (which posited 430 years for Jacob's family in Egypt) and 1 Kings vi. 1 (setting 480 years between Exodus and the building of the Temple). Bunsen placed Jacob's family in Egypt before the Hyksos period, and targeted the Exodus at 1320 BC.[71] Much of this work in the field of comparative biblical chronology was continued by his son Ernest de Bunsen (1819–1903), one of the Baron's brood of five sons and five daughters.[72] The elder Bunsen was also a great popularizer, publishing a nine-volume 'Bible for the People' (1858–70) which summarized recent biblical scholarship for the attentive Protestant reader.

Baron Bunsen's personal flair and his accomplished English wife made him a popular figure who during his lifetime remained untarnished by accusations of heterodoxy. Nevertheless, some of the issues and methodology which Bunsen raised were potentially explosive, and at least some critics could put the problem in a wider context. The *Westminster Review* pointed out that

Bunsen has parodied and misapplied in historical investigations the maxim which Lyell employed successfully in accounting for geological phenomena. Lyell inferred similar effects from like causes; and whatever the scale of the phenomena, he had unlimited time at his disposal, during which to suppose the action of necessary forces. But Bunsen would infer dissimilar consequents from like antecedents; and as a Biblical reconciler, the time he requires is denied him, for the records stubbornly refuse to grant it.

Geology, philology, theology: something would have to give: 'It is impossible for any researches in philology to throw light upon such an intimate problem as that', and in any case, Bunsen's scientific philological research was rendered fruitless so long as he believed (as he did) in supernatural linguistic intervention at the Tower of Babel. 'Now if such an event be supposed to have taken place,' objected the *Westminster Review*, 'it must arrest at once all scientific investigation.'[73]

IV

Baron Bunsen died in 1860 and, as we shall see, that year was the most important watershed in English biblical studies. Indeed, it is almost impossible to avoid the cardinal historiographical sin of Whiggish hindsight when looking at the efforts of English biblical critics to internalize the new advancements in hermeneutics which were reported from Germany. Yet much work had been done in nineteenth-century England before 1860, and we should give these pioneers their due before returning to Bunsen's era.

Alexander Geddes (1737–1802) is much more of an eighteenth-century figure, but his work was important and frequently cited thereafter. Geddes was a French-trained Scottish Roman Catholic who was not above maintaining friendships with Anglicans and Unitarians as well. He knew about the work in Germany of Eichhorn and others, and himself came to reject the supernatural elements in the biblical narrative. His plan for publishing a new translation of the Bible was supported by Lowth, but ultimately opposition proved overwhelming and the project was dropped.[74] Another early nineteenth-century figure was Adam Clarke (1762?–1832), an Irish Methodist who recounted that he began biblical studies at the age of twenty-one when he found a half-sovereign while gardening and used the money to buy a Hebrew grammar.[75] His great commentary on the Bible, published between 1810 and 1825, was altogether traditional, but he did incorporate both science and philology when appropriate, arguing, for example, that the Hebrew word *nachash* which appears in the account of the Fall refers not to 'serpent' but to 'ape', as in the Arabic word *hanasa*. Clarke also puzzled over the size of Noah's ark. But more prophetically for the history of biblical arithmetic, he was troubled by the figure of 603,550 fighting men who were said to have been part of the Israelite Exodus. Clarke suggested that this would produce a total Israelite population of about 3,263,000. Their survival in the desert could only be attributed to divine miracle. Later commentators would find those numbers even harder to swallow than manna.[76]

Another early commentator was Thomas Hartwell Horne (1780–1862), who was actually born in Chancery Lane and hardly stirred from that narrow street. He studied at Christ's Hospital, and was tutored there at the age of ten by his fellow classmate Samuel Taylor Coleridge. By confession he was a Methodist, but by profession a poorly paid barrister's clerk. He turned to other work, compiled the index to the Harleian Manuscripts in the British Museum and later began a classified catalogue of all the printed books there, until much later a decision was made simply to list the books alphabetically by author. Somehow despite all of this he found time to produce a three-volume introduction to biblical criticism, which appeared in 1818 and went through many editions both in Britain and the United States, becoming a classic text. Although Horne does acknowledge Eichhorn's existence, his work is little affected by it. Yet even Horne could not but admit that he saw evidence in the Book of Joshua of an 'accidental derangement of the order of the chapters in this book, occasioned probably by the antient mode of rolling up manuscripts'. Horne noted other problems as well, but neglected to draw any rationalist conclusions.[77]

Since the relevant portion of Jewish history largely took place in biblical times as far as Christians were concerned, the authors of general histories of the Jews had to take a stand about scriptural interpretation as well. In 1818, the American Hannah Adams (1755–1831) published a history of the Jews from about the time of Christ until her own day, with a good deal of information gleaned about the Lost Ten Tribes, the Samaritans, and other related subjects. 'The preservation of the Jews as a distinct people,' she wrote, 'is an event unparalleled in the annals of history.' But the impact of more modern biblical criticism was not felt at all in her book.[78]

A rather different work was produced by Henry Hart Milman (1791–1868): *The History of the Jews* consisted of three little anonymous volumes published between 1829 and 1830 in John Murray's 'Family Library' series. Milman was ex-Eton and Brasenose College, Oxford, and began life hoping to make a career as a man of letters. Having failed to interest the public in a succession of poetic and dramatic works, he turned to scholarship. In 1827 he was selected to deliver the Bampton Lectures, and produced an unexceptional series on the Apostles. His history of the Jews made a much greater noise, treating them as just another Oriental tribe. Abraham, Milman wrote, was 'an independent Sheik or Emir'. Miracles and supernatural intervention in the Bible were as real or believable as any other tales from the mysterious East. Official reaction was swift and clear: the book was withdrawn, and Murray's 'Family Library' was shut down entirely just to be sure. Milman's history of the Jews was not republished until 1863, once the great mid-century theological crisis was in full swing. Other editions would follow.

'The Jews,' Milman wrote, 'without reference to their religious belief, are among the most remarkable people in the annals of mankind.' Their own annals, the Bible, however, must be read with understanding. Take, again, the thorny arithmetical problem of the 603,550 Israelite fighting men of Exodus. This, he noted, 'according to the usual calculations, would give the total sum of the people at 2,500,000 or 3,000,000.' It was an unacceptably large number. Milman cited Niebuhr, who claimed that the crossing of the Red Sea took place near Suez, where the water is only two miles across:

> Not to urge the literal meaning of the waters being a wall on the right hand and on the left, as if they had stood up sheer and abrupt, and then fallen back again, – the Israelites passed through the sea, with deep water on both sides; and any ford between two bodies of water must have been passable only for a few people at one precise point of time.

Biblical numbers, in general, just did not compute. 'I protest against hazarding the veracity of that which is historically true in the Mosaic records', he wrote, 'on what is vulgarly called the Bible chronology, a system, or rather many conflicting systems (no two of the ancient copies or versions agree), which rest on precarious and irreconcilable arguments.'[79]

Samuel Smiles, who wrote John Murray's biography, recalled that 'Milman was preached against, from Sunday to Sunday, from the University and other pulpits, in the most unmeasured language, as one of the most dangerous and pernicious of writers.'[80] Milman, for his part, insisted that the 'often-repeated charge of following the Germans is rank nonsense. Except in one passage, where I have given different opinions, and theirs among the rest, there is *not one explanation of a miracle* borrowed from a German divine. I have used them only for other purposes.'[81] By the end of March 1830, Milman confessed to his publisher that 'I am weary to death of the Jews, I almost wish they were with the Egyptians at the bottom of the Red Sea.'[82]

Milman's career, however, was relatively unaffected by his unorthodox views. In 1835, Sir Robert Peel defied opposition and made Milman canon of Westminster and also gave him the plum rectorship of St Margaret's Westminster. When Milman's history of Christianity under the Empire appeared in 1840, however, as Lord Melbourne said, it was ignored as if the clergy had taken a universal oath never to mention it to anyone.[83] In 1849, Milman became dean of St Paul's, which was an ideal position for him, and which kept him fully occupied with plans and improvements.

Samuel Davidson (1806–98) found it rather more difficult to be a biblical maverick. He began life as a Presbyterian in Ulster, and in 1835 was appointed professor of biblical criticism at Belfast College. Becoming estranged from that denomination, he migrated in 1843 to the new Lancashire Independent College as professor of biblical literature and ecclesiastical history. The following year he visited Germany, and began to realize that his entire subject was undergoing profound change. In 1854, Longman publishing house approached him with an offer to help produce a new edition of Horne's introduction to the Scriptures. Davidson agreed to take on the Old Testament, and suggested the self-educated ex-ironmonger Samuel Prideaux Tregelles (1813–75) to do the New (1857–72). Davidson's work appeared as the second volume of the tenth edition of Horne's classic text, published in October 1856.

The reaction of his colleagues in Manchester was overwhelmingly negative. It was bad enough that Davidson denied the Mosaic authorship of the Old Testament, but there was even the claim that he was not only wrong but dishonest, having plagiarized his heresy from German so-called authorities. An official sub-committee was set up, and Davidson published a pamphlet defending himself. This not satisfying the committee, Davidson resigned. He had many supporters, however, and eventually a donation of £3,000 was presented to him, which enabled him to continue his work as a private scholar in Cheshire. He moved to London in 1862 after being elected a Scripture examiner at the University of London, continuing his writing and contributing to the *Westminster Review* and other periodicals.[84]

Something of his frustration comes out in his thoroughly revised introduction to the Old Testament, which he published in 1862 in the wake of the mid-century biblical ferment. 'Should any think that his handling of the subject has been occasionally free,' he explained,

> they are reminded that there is a time to utter the conclusions of the higher criticism; that superstition should not enslave the mind for ever; and that the Bible is far from being yet understood by the majority of readers in all its parts and bearings. It is, indeed, a perilous thing at the present day to publish anything connected with the Scriptures that does not square with the narrow notions of noisy religionists. Scientific theologians have fallen on evil days and evil tongues. Persecution assails them if they do not repeat the only ideas and phrases which they are *supposed* to accord with the honour of Scripture. They are maligned from pulpit and press for the glory of God. But the Almighty Father of mankind has given His servants talents to be used conscientiously as well as diligently in His service; and if in the exercise of these talents some arrive at results different from those of others, it is cowardly to suppress them should their dissemination tend to enlighten the mind or purify the heart.[85]

That Davidson had begun his career by keeping an open mind can be seen even in his *Sacred Hermeneutics*, written while he was still living in Belfast, before going to Manchester, where he would be dismissed from his chair for heterodoxy. The seventh chapter of Davidson's book is a study of German systems of biblical interpretation, in which the different schools are nicely categorized and explained.[86]

A more mischievous attitude to the Bible in this period before the hermeneutical tidal wave hit England was exemplified in the work of Francis William Newman (1805–97), brother of the more famous cardinal. 'Much as we love each other,' wrote his brother John Henry, 'neither would like to be mistaken for the other'.[87] When Francis Newman went up to Oxford in 1821, he lodged with his brother at Seale's Coffee House on the corner of Holywell and Broad Street, but they soon parted company. Francis Newman had a spectacular undergraduate career (unlike his late-blooming brother), achieving a stupendous double first in classics and mathematics. He was elected a fellow of Balliol, but resigned in 1830, unable to subscribe to the Thirty-Nine Articles. By that time he had become acquainted with the millenarian John Nelson Darby (1800–82) in Dublin and, as if in balance, was attracted to a more rationalist approach to religion. In September 1830 he went on an ill-conceived but highly romantic mission to Syria, having numerous and dangerous adventures before travelling down the Euphrates by raft to Baghdad. Returning to England, he became a Baptist, taught classics at Manchester College, Oxford, and in 1846 was appointed to the chair of Latin in University College, London.[88] There he became a popular and eccentric figure, translating 'Rebilius Cruso' and 'Hiawatha' into Latin for use in his classes, championing such causes as women's suffrage and vegetarianism, and opposing vivisection and vaccination.[89] According to one who knew him, his 'slender form and acute physiognomy were often made more striking by peculiarities of dress.'[90] One of his first acts after taking up his new post in London was to publish a biblical history from Samuel to the Babylonian exile, harping on inaccuracies in the Bible and emphasizing the late editing of the text itself. In its way it was rather radical for the times, and set against the background of Francis Newman's colourful personality, captive university audience, and filial relationship to a man whom many Victorians loved to hate, his views on the Bible had wider currency than otherwise they might have done.[91]

V

It is important to appreciate how much Germany was a closed book before Bunsen, and how haphazard were the bits of information that came wafting in, sometimes from unexpected sources. Thomas Beddoes (1760–1808) the innovative physician was one of these. He had resigned his readership in chemistry at Oxford in 1792 as a roundabout act of sympathy with the French Revolution, and six years later established a 'Pneumatic Institute' for the cure of disease by inhalation. His assistant Humphry Davy made his first great discoveries there, and published his first work in a collection edited by Beddoes. But however misguided was Beddoes's science, he was an avid reader of German periodicals, and told his friend Coleridge what was in them, fostering the great poet's lifelong interest in the latest word in biblical interpretation.[92] A similar sort of conduit was Henry Crabb Robinson (1775–1867), lawyer, reporter, and foreign editor of *The Times*. Robinson had studied at the University of Jena in his youth, and was acquainted with Goethe, Schiller, and Madame de Staël. He was very *au fait* with German biblical criticism, and in England was friends not only with Coleridge but with the entire set: Lamb, Wordsworth, Southey, and many others.[93]

Sometimes German biblical criticism could be a stick with which to beat others even more radical. John Pye Smith (1774–1851), for example, used the Germans against the Unitarians. But he himself denied that the world was of recent origin, or that all organic life began in the same place, although he did believe that only eight people survived the Flood, and we are their descendants.[94] Some very negative and often rather distorted views of German biblical criticism came to England via those who hoped to immunize the English from its effects. Hugh James Rose (1795–1838) spent a year in 1824–5 in Germany for health reasons, and there discovered the horrors of German rationalist theology. When he returned to England as select preacher at Cambridge he delivered four sermons, which he then published, warning his countrymen of imminent danger and ultimately blaming the philosophy of Kant. 'I believe I am correct in saying,' Rose clarified, 'that Schleiermacher is almost the only divine in Germany, who is likewise a great scholar.' But Rose was at pains to note that one of the reasons for the straying of the Germans was that they lacked what England had: articles and formularies of faith and an episcopal form of government. Many readers felt that Rose was underestimating the threat which the country now faced from German rationalism.[95]

Edward Bouverie Pusey (1800–82) thereupon published his first book in order to make it clear that there was no reason to feel safely theologically complacent in England. In this year, 1828, Pusey was on the eve of being appointed Regius professor of Hebrew at Oxford by the duke of Wellington, the beginning of a great ecclesiastical career in defence of High Anglicanism. Pusey's point was that articles and formularies can also produce a 'dead orthodoxism', a formally correct belief without any true spiritual feeling behind it. This seemed to him to be the direction that the Church of England was taking, and we could do worse than to look at the fervent aspects of German Pietism. The only result of Pusey's book, and its sequel, was paradoxically to win for himself a temporary reputation as a Pietistic rationalist, and in the end Pusey gave instructions in his will that these misunderstood works should never be reprinted.[96]

As yet, much of the information coming from Germany was unsystematic and garbled. Perhaps the first book which properly presented the German new historicism to English readers was Peter von Bohlen's introduction to Genesis. Von Bohlen (1796–1840) was born into a poor family, and when his father died he was sent to a military orphanage. Turning out too short for the army, he became a domestic servant to a French general, and then was farmed out to a German mercantile house with an English partner. Here he learned English, and after being given a copy of Sir William Jones's works by the English consul in Hamburg, von Bohlen moved on to Hebrew, Arabic, and Persian and became the assistant librarian there. Local supporters paid the way of this talented young man to the University of Halle, where he studied Hebrew with Gesenius and Arabic with Freytag, and later on, Sanscrit with Schlegel. Eventually he became professor at Königsberg. Von Bohlen had spent some time in London, Wiltshire, and the Isle of Wight as a private tutor to the aristocratic Lansdowne family in the 1830s, which helped make him more widely known in England.

Von Bohlen's commentary on Genesis had been published in German in 1835, but although his work had been printed in Boston in 1843, only in 1855 did he make his appearance in England. It was not a moment too soon, since conservative Germans had already come out in English translation, many from the press of T. & T. Clark in Edinburgh. Hengstenberg, Tholuck, and Hävernick (1832–47). Von Bohlen did not believe that Moses wrote the Book of Genesis, and he doubted many of the details given in the Pentateuch. The figure of 603,550 fighting men given in Exodus was impossible to justify, producing a total Israelite population of about 2.5 million, the support of which would have required more than manna. Von Bohlen thus also put his finger on one of the key disproof texts which would worry later commentators. He argued that the laws of Leviticus became known only in the reign of Josiah, and were enforced only on the return from Babylon, when the Pentateuch received its final form. As von Bohlen himself began his book, 'Among all the civilized nations of antiquity, the dawn of genuine history (whether more or less authentic) is preceded by a series of myths and legends, whose patriotic object it uniformly is, to trace the origin and to exalt the early glories of the people.'[97]

VI

Back, then, to Baron Bunsen, who died in 1860, and might have been surprised both at the ensuing controversy over his opinions and the fact that his work was only the first shot in the mid-Victorian battle of the biblical books.[98] Indeed, Bunsen's researches formed a significant part of the watershed Victorian challenge to biblical authority, the publication of a collection of pieces in 1860 entitled *Essays and Reviews*.[99] Lecky, looking back on the nineteenth century from the vantage point of its very end, mused that

> No change in English life during the latter half of the nineteenth century is more conspicuous than the great enlargement of the range of permissible opinions on religious subjects. Opinions and arguments which not many years ago were confined to small circles and would have drawn down grave social penalties, have become the commonplaces of the drawing-room and of the boudoir. The first very marked change in this respect followed, I think, the publication in 1860 of the 'Essays and Reviews,' and the effect of this book in making the religious opinions which it discussed familiar to the great body of educated men was probably by far the most important of its consequences.[100]

What was so shocking for readers was not only the content of the ideas expressed, but the fact that six of the seven co-authors were clergymen. One of them (Rowland Williams) was even vice-principal of a theological college.

Assuming our archetypal Victorian would have ploughed through the whole book, what would he (or she) have found? The first chapter was unoriginally entitled 'The Education of the World' and was written by Frederick Temple (1821–1902). Struggling out of an impoverished childhood, Temple made a name for himself as a scholar and later fellow at Balliol College. In 1857, he was appointed headmaster of Rugby School: Matthew Arnold had been his friend and contemporary at Oxford, along with Benjamin Jowett and A.P. Stanley. Despite having contributed to the notorious *Essays and Reviews*, Temple went on to greater accomplishments, including the posts of bishop of Exeter (1869), London (1885), and finally (1896) the archbishopric of Canterbury.[101]

Temple's essay was not very distinguished, being a *rechauffé* sermon delivered originally at Rugby School Chapel. Temple gave Jowett the finished version after spending only ten hours in revising the text. He took his title from Lessing's 'The Education of the Human Race', which had already appeared in English, arguing what was by now an old chestnut that humankind underwent collectively the same process of growth and maturation passed through by an individual adult. But Temple's message with regard to the Bible was forthrightly clear:

> If geology proves to us that we must not interpret the first chapters of Genesis literally; if historical investigations shall show us that inspiration, however it may protect the doctrine, yet was not empowered to protect

the narrative of the inspired writers from occasional inaccuracy; if careful criticism shall prove that there have been occasionally interpolations and forgeries in that Book, as in many others; the results should still be welcome.

The simple reason for this optimism, Temple explains, is that the

substance of the teaching which we derive from the Bible will not really be affected by anything of this sort. While its hold upon the minds of believers, and its power to stir the depths of the spirit of man, however much weakened at first, must be immeasurably strengthened, in the end, by clearing away any blunders which may have been fastened on it by human interpretation.

What we need to realize, Temple explains, is that the 'immediate work of our day is the study of the Bible.'[102]

The second piece in the volume was a 'review' rather than an 'essay', dedicated to 'Bunsen's Biblical Researches', and written by Rowland Williams (1817–70). Ex-Eton and King's College, Cambridge, Williams was appointed in 1850 vice-principal and professor of Hebrew at the theological college of St David's, Lampeter. Four years later he preached a series of lectures at Cambridge, the second of which, on the subject of 'rational godliness', gave him a reputation for free-thinking. This was compounded by the interruption of the series by the death of his father, sparking the rumour that the sermons were halted by university authority. Williams's argument was that we need to accept the fact that there is a human element in the biblical text, and that revelation is progressive and available to people completely outside the Judaeo-Christian tradition. Williams published these sermons and others in 1855,[103] and expanded the ideas in a work entitled *Christianity and Hinduism*, published the following year.[104] It was this book which brought him to Bunsen's attention, and the two men met at Heidelberg in 1857.[105]

Rowland Williams was thus very receptive to the idea of a new volume of essays and reviews on important and controversial theological matters, and promised to bring in other Cambridge authors to the project.[106] Initially, Williams was unsure whether to write about Bunsen or Renan, but chose the baron as a way of helping to introduce German Higher Criticism to a wider English audience. Ironically, Williams made Bunsen much more controversial in death than he was in his lifetime.

The third essay, on the evidences of Christianity, was produced by Baden Powell (1796–1860), the Savilian professor of geometry at Oxford (and father of the founder of the Boy Scout movement much later). Powell was already well known as a champion of science against religion, and had published a number of works on the subject. One of these was concerned with *The Order of Nature* (1859), which he argued was completely uniform, thereby contradicting the possibility of miracles. Christianity, in Powell's view, was primarily about morality and ethics. Powell's essay in the controversial volume of 1860, 'On the Study of the Evidences of Christianity', was essentially a summary of this book.[107]

Henry Bristow Wilson (1803–88) wrote an essay on 'The National Church', which in some ways is the least interesting of the lot. Many agreed with his plea for greater comprehension in Anglican communion and his argument that dogmatic statements in theology must necessarily be provisional. Wilson was a don at St John's College, Oxford, until he was presented to an East Anglian vicarage in 1850. He was also a communicator of ideas to a wider public. Wilson edited the religion and philosophy section of the *Westminster Review* (replacing Mark Pattison, also an Essayist), and edited the *Oxford Essays* (1855–8), an annual review in which the authors took sole responsibility for their work. This was the model which would be used in *Essays and Reviews*. Among Wilson's authors were three of the 'seven against Christ'.[108]

Charles Wycliffe Goodwin (1817–78), the fifth member of the group, was an expert in Egyptology, and wrote an essay 'On the Mosaic Cosmogony'. According to those who knew him, his interest in Egypt was sparked at the age of nine by reading an article on 'Hieroglyphics' in the December 1826 number of the *Edinburgh Review*. Resigning his Cambridge fellowship rather than take clerical orders, Goodwin was called to the bar, eventually serving as a judge in the Supreme Court for China and Japan and dying in Shanghai.[109] But Egypt was his chief delight, along with related subjects, which led to Baden Powell's request to contribute to *Essays and Reviews*, the only non-clergyman (just) so to do. Goodwin surveyed the recent books which tried to reconcile Genesis with geology, works by William Buckland (1784–1856), Thomas Chalmers (1780–1847), Hugh Miller (1802–56), and John Henry Pratt (d. 1871). His conclusion was that although the Bible does contain much revelation, this does not include 'physical truths, for the discovery of which he [man] has faculties specially provided by his Creator.'[110]

The last two essays were written by the most distinguished of the contributors, Mark Pattison and Benjamin Jowett. Mark Pattison (1813–84) became rector of Lincoln College, Oxford, the year following his appearance in *Essays and Reviews*. His contribution on 'Tendencies of Religious Thought in England, 1688–1750' was so wholly unobjectionable that nothing could be said against him apart from the company he kept.[111]

The fame of Benjamin Jowett (1817–93), however, eclipsed all others, and it was his essay 'On the Interpretation of Scripture' which concluded the volume. Jowett's success at Oxford began from the moment he set foot in Balliol. He was even elected a fellow of the college while still an undergraduate (1838). Jowett survived the storm over Newman's famous 'Tract XC' on the Articles of Religion, noting later that 'But for the providence of God, I might have become a Roman Catholic'. In the summer of 1855, Jowett was appointed Regius professor of Greek. By that time, his unorthodox theological views were well known, and his Oxford enemies took revenge by freezing his salary at £40 per annum, the level set by Henry VIII when he established the chair three centuries before. The other Regius professors were paid at a more competitive rate, and despite numerous appeals to Convocation, only in 1865 was Jowett's salary increased to £500. Apart from this annoying act of revenge, neither Jowett's career nor his reputation as a classicist were damaged by *Essays and Reviews*. He was elected to the mastership of Balliol in September 1870, and devoted himself fully to the welfare of the college and Oxford University until his death twenty-three years later. Earlier in 1870 he had contemplated producing yet another volume of *Essays* in concert with Henry Wilson, in which he himself would write on the religions of the world, but the elevation to the mastership of Balliol effectively killed the project.[112]

Essays and Reviews was published on 21 March 1860, and went through thirteen editions over the next nine years, along with authorized and pirated editions produced abroad. The first edition of 1,000 copies was published by Parker and Sons, the well-established liberal London house which also printed books for Cambridge University Press and the Society for Promoting Christian Knowledge. The thirteen editions together ran to 24,250 copies: even *On the Origin of Species* (1859) only sold 17,000 copies in seventeen years.[113] By contemporary standards, *Essays and Reviews* was undoubtedly a best-seller.

Although reviews of the book began to appear within a fortnight of publication, it was the article in October by Frederic Harrison (1831–1923) in the *Westminster Review*, the great secular Utilitarian quarterly, that first propelled it to public attention and notoriety. Harrison would become one of the most prominent English believers in Positivism as a religious faith. By 1860 he had already lost interest in his fellowship at Wadham College, Oxford, and for the past two years had been trying to make a go of the law, while primarily occupying himself with intellectual matters.

Harrison was really the first to grasp the importance of *Essays and Reviews*: 'A book has appeared which may serve to mark an epoch in the history of opinion', he wrote. Harrison understood that in theory this was a composite volume from the pens of seven different thinkers working independently, yet he saw it as 'a manifesto from a body of kindred or associated thinkers; if it be not rather an outline of the principles of a new school of English theology.' The principles of this virtual manifesto were three in number: (1) the concept of human development or moral and intellectual evolution; (2) the validity of German textual Higher Criticism for elucidating biblical texts; and

(3) the role of science in replacing a belief in inerrant Scriptures. Looked at in its entirety, Harrison wrote, *Essays and Reviews* promulgated views which were 'incompatible with the religious belief of the mass of the Christian public, and the broad principles on which the Protestantism of Englishmen rests'.[114]

Frederic Harrison's review was a red flag that could not be ignored, and certainly not by Samuel Wilberforce (1805–73), who had been bishop of Oxford since 1845. In that year, John Henry Newman was received into the Roman Catholic Church and E.B. Pusey replaced him as the High Church gadfly, barely recognizing Wilberforce's spiritual authority. Wilberforce was constantly involved in controversy during his twenty-five years at Oxford, and most recently had written in the *Quarterly Review* (July 1860) against Darwin's *On the Origin of Species*. A few days before that publication he had famously debated with T.H. Huxley (1825–95) in Oxford itself, at a meeting of the British Association. Wilberforce could not ignore *Essays and Reviews*, especially once Harrison the Positivist had singled it out as ripe for attack.

Wilberforce hated everything about *Essays and Reviews*, especially its 'scarcely veiled Atheism' and its 'German rationalism'. He denounced Jowett's plea to 'Interpret the Scripture like any other book'. If one were to accept the views of the Essayists, then the Bible 'becomes a medley of legend, poetry, and oral tradition, compiled, remodelled, and interpolated by a priestly order centuries after the times of the supposed authors'. The Essayists were merely parroting the 'rational views of Paine and Voltaire'; their 'whole apparatus is drawn bodily from the German Rationalists' and ultimately we see that to 'our own Deists in the last century belongs the real shame of originating this attack upon the faith'. The approach of the Essayists was quite *passé*, Wilberforce revealed, since E.W. Hengstenberg, himself a German, had 'already abundantly repelled objections and fallacies of German rationalism'. Finally, Wilberforce noted, the fact that the Essayists publish their views while enjoying 'the status and emolument of Church of England clergymen is simply moral dishonesty'.

Wilberforce predicted, perhaps with a good deal of nervous bravado, that *Essays and Reviews* would find few supporters:

> We cannot believe that they will exert any wide-spread influence in the Church of our land, or amongst our people. The English mind is too calm, too sound, too essentially honest to be widely or deeply affected by such speculations as these – and more especially from such mouths. The flattering appeal which they make to unassisted human reason, and the gratification which they afford to the natural pride of the human heart, may win for them a certain following, but the great body of Church-of-England men will stand aloof from them.[115]

Wilberforce's article appeared anonymously, but it was pretty clear who had written it. The *Quarterly Review* had to print the January number five times to meet the demand.[116]

On 16 February 1861, *The Times* published on page ten a letter dated four days earlier from the archbishop of Canterbury, John Bird Sumner (1780–1862), ostensibly to William Robert Fremantle (1807–95), one of Wilberforce's rather obscure Oxford clergymen. The letter condemned *Essays and Reviews*, and to it were appended the names of twenty-five bishops, including that of Wilberforce, who had actually drafted this so-called 'Episcopal Manifesto'.[117] By now, the controversy over *Essays and Reviews* was reaching crisis proportions. Arthur Penrhyn Stanley (1815–81), the dean of Westminster and leading Broad Church theologian, tried to find a *via media* between the parties. His article in the liberal *Edinburgh Review*, however, failed to achieve this.[118] The next part of the struggle would leave the pages of intellectual journals and enter the courts.

Rowland Williams and Henry Bristow Wilson were the most vulnerable to the formal charge of heresy, and they were the first to feel the wrath of ecclesiastical law. In 1861 charges of heresy were brought against them in the Court of Arches, the civil law church court of the ecclesiastical province of Canterbury. Proceedings could be started by a letter from a bishop asking that the Dean of Arches, a life appointment, hear the case (alone and without a jury), and give a judgment. Appeals against his verdict were heard before the Judicial Committee of the Privy Council. In 1861 the Dean of Arches was Dr Stephen Lushington (1782–1873), sometime head of Doctors' Commons (the association of ecclesiastical lawyers).[119] On 1 June 1861 Walter Kerr Hamilton (1808–69), bishop of Salisbury, sent to Lushington his 'Letters of Request', a large manuscript written on vellum, and Williams was charged. Thomas Turton (1780–1864), bishop of Ely, did the honours for H.B. Wilson on 16 December 1861.[120]

Williams's hearing began on 19 December 1861 and went on for five days; another session the same length took place 7–16 January 1862. Sir Robert Joseph Phillimore (1810–85), prosecuting Williams, warned that unless the Essayists were stopped, 'The Hebrew Scriptures will take their place upon the bookshelf of the learned, beside the Arabian and Sanscrit poets'. Wilson's case went on for four days between 22 February and 3 March 1862. Dr Lushington gave his preliminary 'interlocutory' decision on 25 June 1862, admitting some articles of indictment and rejecting others.[121] Lushington's final verdict was handed down on 15 December 1862. Williams was condemned for his views on biblical inspiration, the doctrine of propitiation, and justification by faith. Wilson was found guilty in regard to his views on biblical inspiration as well, 'covenanted and uncovenanted mercies', and for rejecting the idea of the everlasting punishment of the wicked.

Their punishments were not insignificant. Williams and Wilson were required to bear the costs of the entire trial, which were considerable, and were suspended from office for one year. The case against Jowett was conducted in Oxford University's Chancellor's Court; it lasted exactly one week (13–20 February 1863) and ended when the articles themselves were not admitted. Williams and Wilson were not so lucky, so the two men immediately appealed to the Judicial Committee of the Privy Council, appearing in person when the meetings began on 19 June 1863.

The hearing was concluded on 26 June, and on 8 February 1864 the decision of the Court of Arches was reversed by Lord Westbury, the Lord Chancellor. Court costs from the original trial were to be borne by each party, not by the defendants alone. According to contemporary wit, Westbury had 'dismissed Hell with costs, and took away from orthodox members of the Church of England their last hope of everlasting damnation.'[122]

The defeat of Wilberforce and his supporters at the Privy Council was a major blow to those who saw themselves as upholding Civilization against the barbarian onslaught. The most galling thing about the judgment was that for appeals involving offences against ecclesiastical law, both the archbishops of Canterbury and York were full members of the Judicial Committee, along with the bishop of London. Those distinguished clergymen sat as actual judges, not merely experts. Truly they had let the side down. Charles Thomas Longley (1794–1868), archbishop of Canterbury, had already denounced *Essays and Reviews*. William Thomson (1819–90), archbishop of York, had edited *Aids to Faith* (1861), a rebuttal volume to *Essays*, and was rewarded by being appointed, in rapid succession, bishop of Gloucester and Bristol, and in 1862, York. Archibald Campbell Tait (1811–82), bishop of London (and later Canterbury) was in close personal contact with Wilson, Temple, and Jowett, but he put his name as well to the Episcopal Manifesto published in *The Times*, condemning *Essays and Reviews*.[123] At the end of the day, however, the mild dissenting protests of the three bishops simply weren't enough.

Wilberforce, for his part, took his protest to the streets, or at least to the quads.[124] On 9 February 1864, the day after Lord Westbury acquitted Williams and Wilson, Pusey wrote to fellow Tractarian John Keble (1792–1866) and to Henry Phillpotts (1778–1869), bishop of Exeter, concerned about the effects the decision would have on doctrinal matters. He also wrote to Wilberforce and to Gladstone about the same issues. Wilberforce responded on 21 February 1864, enclosing a draft document written by W.R. Fremantle of Episcopal Manifesto fame. This was the original text, later reworked by Pusey, of the 'Declaration on the Inspiration of the Word of God, and the Eternity of Future Punishment, by Clergymen of the United Church of England and Ireland', better known as the 'Oxford Declaration of the Clergy'. On 25 February 1864 a general meeting was held in the Holywell Music Room, at which time the document was approved and signatures were collected. It was thereupon printed and sent to each of the 24,800 Anglican clergymen in Britain and Ireland: eventually 10,906 signed.[125]

Wilberforce simply would not give in. His next step was to pursue a campaign for a 'synodical condemnation' in the Convocation of Canterbury, which met only three days after the judgment of the Privy Council was given. After much discussion, making full use of Wilberforce's formidable debating skills, *Essays and Reviews* was the subject indeed of a 'synodical condemnation', affirmed on 24 June 1864. Westbury, the Lord Chancellor, argued in the House of Lords on 15 July that the very concept of a 'synodical judgment' was meaningless. Making oblique reference to Wilberforce's nickname of 'Soapy Sam', Westbury announced: 'I am happy to tell your lordships that what is called a synodical judgment is simply a series of well-lubricated terms – a sentence so oily and so saponaceous that no one could grasp it.' Wilberforce concluded the Lords debate by affirming that 'We are set in trust in this land for this – that we may be the depository of the truth which God has revealed, as held by this reformed Church of England.' Westbury replied briefly and, as *The Times* reported it, 'The subject then dropped' (16 July 1864, p. 8).

The trial of the Essayists was not the last prosecution for heresy in England. Charles Voysey (1828–1912), the man who published the Wolfenbüttel fragments in English, argued after the decision of the Privy Council that the Church of England was shown to be flexible on the key issues of biblical inspiration, Original Sin, the Atonement, and eternal punishment. He was tried in 1869 in the Chancery Court of the archbishop of York and was found guilty the following year; the decision was confirmed by the Privy Council in February 1871, with Tait in attendance.[126] Later on, Charles Gore and his liberal Roman Catholic contributors to *Lux Mundi* in 1889 were assailed by elderly opponents of *Essays and Reviews*, but nothing came of it.[127]

The fact of the matter is that the Church of England had been forced to deploy ecclesiastical machinery in order to try to silence arguments rather than to engage with them. Contemporaries saw this quite clearly. *Punch* summed up the problem on 16 March 1861, in an issue full of satires and references to the controversy over that diabolical book:

> Denounce Essayists and Reviewers,
>   Hang, quarter, gag or shoot them –
> Excellent plans – provided that
>   You first of all refute them.
>
> By all means let the Hangman burn
>   Their awful book to ashes,
> But don't expect to settle thus
>   Their heterodox hashes.

Some heresies are so ingrained,
　　E'en burning won't remove them,
A shorter and an easier way
　　You'll find it − to disprove them.

Be this, right reverends, your revenge,
　　For souls the best of cure[s] −
Essay Essayists to upset,
　　And to review Reviewers.[128]

VII

Even as the controversy over *Essays and Reviews* was raging in the pages of intellectual England's literary reviews and the chambers of the ecclesiastical courts, it was clear that something positive would have to be built on the ruins of what had been so thoroughly destroyed. As more rigorous criteria separated 'history' from 'fiction', new authoritative figures needed to be found who could help navigate the Holy Scriptures to a safe place of scriptural rest. Cast in the role of Victorian hermeneutic hero, oddly enough, was our old friend the seventeenth-century Dutch Jew Baruch Spinoza (1632–77), reinvented by the most exact arbiter of contemporary taste and culture, Matthew Arnold.

It would not be much of a gamble to suggest that most English-speakers even today first read Spinoza's *Tractatus Theologico-Politicus* in the sturdy Victorian translation of R.H.M. Elwes, published by G. Bell & Son at London in 1883. Few bother to read the translator's introduction to that volume, which began with a German quotation from Heine about Spinoza's glory, launching Elwes into his first sentence, a reminder to the reader that 'A very few years ago the writings of Spinoza were almost unknown in this country.' Indeed, the only authoritative studies of Spinoza published before 1880, he insisted, 'to which the English reader could be referred were the brilliant essays of Mr. Froude and Mr. Matthew Arnold'. In recent years, he noted, there was a 'stir of tardy recognition' among Victorian intellectuals for Spinoza, who 'shrank with almost womanly sensitiveness from anything like notoriety'. Elwes suggested that the 'first recognition of his true character came probably from Germany through Coleridge'.

> It may strike those who are strangers to Spinoza as curious, that, notwith-standing the severely abstract nature of his method, so many poets and imaginative writers should be found among his adherents. Lessing, Goethe, Heine, Auerbach, Coleridge, Shelley, George Eliot; most of these not only admired him, but studied him deeply. On closer approach the apparent anomaly vanishes. There is about Spinoza a power and a charm, which

appeals strongly to the poetic sense. He seems to dwell among heights, which most men see only in far off, momentary glimpses. The world of men is spread out before him, the workings of the human heart lie bared to his gaze, but he does not fall to weeping, or to laughter, or to reviling: his thoughts are ever with the eternal, and something of the beauty and calm of eternal things has passed into his teaching. If we may, as he himself was wont to do, interpret spiritually a Bible legend, we may say of him that, like Moses returning from Sinai, he bears in his presence the witness that he has held communion with the Most High.[129]

Elwes insisted that his translations 'may claim to be the first version of Spinoza's works offered to the English reader'. He must have known that this was not quite true, especially not for the *Tractatus Theologico-Politicus* [*TTP*]. An English edition had appeared as early as 1689 (reprinted in 1737), and another by W. Maccall was produced in 1854, although he was right in noting that 'the book has become so rare as to be practically inaccessible.'[130] George Eliot (1819–80) worked on a translation of *TTP* in 1849, although it was never published.[131] But the translation that really set the cat among the pigeons was the work of Robert Willis (1799–1878), and published by Trübner & Co. at London in 1862.[132] Matthew Arnold was furious when he had a look at it, and retorted with a salvo of essays that (Mormon-style) retroactively baptized Spinoza as a liberal Victorian biblical critic.

Matthew Arnold (1822–88) started life with the considerable advantages which would make him Victorian England's foremost critic and an acclaimed poet. His father Thomas Arnold had been appointed headmaster of Rugby School in 1828, and by the time of his early death fourteen years later had managed to revolutionize the English public school system. Matthew Arnold was a pupil at Rugby, and then went up to Balliol, where he got a second despite having won the Newdigate Prize with his poem 'Cromwell' in 1843, the year before he took his degree. In 1847 he took a post with Lord Lansdowne who served in the cabinet, and who gave him a proper job as a schools inspector in 1851, in order to finance his marriage to Frances Lucy Wightman in June of that year. Arnold stuck to this work until two years before his death, even after he had permanently made his mark on English letters, travelling throughout England and Europe inspecting schools and reporting on the general state of education.

Arnold's poetry is no longer in vogue. In his day, however, he had a significant following, which helped him get elected in 1857 to the chair of poetry at Oxford, aided by the fact that the man who held the chair before him, the celebrated John Keble, was his godfather. Arnold held the chair for ten years, and it provided the academic backdrop to his popular writing and his endless perambulations around Britain.

Like his father, Arnold was very concerned about religion. Although most of his specifically religious work was produced from about 1870,[133] it was in 1862 that he began his vendetta against the South African bishop of Natal, John William Colenso (1814–83), textually bludgeoning the silly man almost to death. His chosen weapon was Spinoza, and because of this Arnold popularized Spinoza's religious philosophy in a number of important and influential publications, so that it can truly be said that he reincarnated him for the English-speaking world. Why this quintessential Victorian moralist and liberal should crave the company of a self-effacing Dutch Jew who died two centuries earlier is the question before us.

John William Colenso, the Cambridge-trained bishop of the new province of Natal, was a Cornishman devoted to his work, which chiefly was converting the Zulus to Christianity. Towards this end, a few years after his arrival there in 1854, he produced a Zulu grammar and began translating the Bible into that language. He was assisted in this task by a certain William Ngidi, who posed common-sense questions about the biblical narrative that Colenso was hard pressed to answer. Colenso's background was mathematics, and he had published an impressive number of school textbooks in algebra and geometry, based on his experience teaching at Harrow after taking his degree and becoming a fellow of St John's, Cambridge.[134]

Colenso began with the numerical facts presented in the Pentateuch and they just didn't add up. The Bible tells us that 'about six hundred thousand on foot *that were* men, beside children' made the sojourn in the desert, confirmed by the figure of 603,550 warriors aged 'twenty years old and upward' cited in Exodus and Numbers. Using figures based on the London birth- and death-rate statistics given in *The Times* for a week in September 1862 (1,852 births/1,147 deaths), Colenso posited that there must have been 2–2.5 million Israelites. That's a lot of Hebrews. Colenso deployed his considerable skills in arithmetic and, like Reimarus and others before him, simply couldn't crunch the numbers. It would have been impossible for the 'threescore and ten' individuals in Jacob's family who went down to Egypt (Gen. xlvi. 27) to have increased even to two million in four to five generations. He estimated that the Israelites would have had about two million sheep and oxen. At five sheep per acre (based on figures from nineteenth-century New Zealand and Australia), that would mean that about 25 square miles of grazing area would have been required for the sheep alone: 'larger than Hertfordshire', Colenso notes sagely.

Worse was yet to come. Numbers iii. 43 reports that there were 22,273 first-born males among the Israelites. Looking again at the benchmark of 603,550 males aged twenty and over, then each family would have to have had about forty-two boys, each married woman would have had to give birth to an average of fifteen sons and fifteen daughters, and only 10 per cent of the men could have a wife or daughter at all. Colenso calculated that if the Israelites made their exodus 'in a wide body, fifty men abreast, as some suppose to have been the practice in the Hebrew armies, then, allowing for an interval of a yard between each rank, the able-bodied warriors alone would have filled up the road for about *seven miles*, and the whole multitude would have formed a dense column more than *twenty-two miles long*'. Crossing the Red Sea apparently took much longer than we had ever imagined.

Witnessing must have been difficult, if we are to believe that Aaron followed the commandment of the Lord to gather 'all the congregation together unto the door of the tabernacle' (Lev. viii. 3). Using the principles he taught in his arithmetic textbook, Colenso argued that if we allow 'two feet in width for each full-grown man, nine men could have stood in front' of the door, and if we take into account that there were over 600,000 men altogether, if they stood 'side by side, as closely as possible, in front, not merely of the *door*, but of the whole *end* of the Tabernacle, in which the door was, they would have reached, allowing 18 inches between each rank of nine men, for a distance of more than 100,000 feet, – in fact, nearly *twenty miles!*'

There were also various numerical problems about sacrifices: 'for the two millions of people, each Priest must have had to sprinkle the blood of 50,000 lambs in about two hours, that is, at the rate of about *four hundred lambs every minute for two hours together*'. Aaron and his two sons (Num. iii. 10) were already exhausted every day from the effort of sacrificing and consuming the sin-offerings after childbirth (Lev. xii. 6–7). At about 250 births per day, figuring five minutes per sacrifice, that would be 42 hours per day 'without a moment's rest or intermission', not including the time it took each priest to eat eighty turtle-doves, assuming that they could be found and caught in the desert. Apart from all that, since Deuteronomy xxiii. 12–14 recorded that toilet needs were prohibited within the camp, this meant a journey of about six miles each way for people living in the centre of the settlement, by which time they probably would have had to start out all over again.[135]

Not all of Colenso's work was destructive; he also had a lot to say about the text of the Old Testament, claiming that Samuel was the author of the E document, and Solomon that of J, but for people of a literalist bent, Colenso's book was a severe blow to their faith. It was undoubtedly an impressive achievement: over 3,500 pages in seven parts. As Paul Hazard wrote about the dry-as-dust scholars who naïvely totted up the life-spans of the patriarchs and were shocked that biblical chronology did not work, 'when these learned gentlemen finish their task . . . they will have sown more seeds of unrest in quiet minds, and done more to undermine faith in history, than all your open scoffers and anti-religious fanatics ever succeeded in doing.'[136] The subtext of Colenso's work was that if we are no longer required to believe the biblical numbers, then perhaps parts of the biblical narrative were not exactly true either. Colenso freed his readers to look for the biblical message in the spirit rather than the letter of the law, or even in the writings of other religions and cultures, an important message for the missionaries he represented.

The reaction to Colenso was quite fierce, both for and against. He was already in trouble for having published in 1861 a new translation and commentary of the Book of Romans 'explained from a missionary point of view', which adopted Frederick Denison Maurice's (1805–72) more liberal concept of the 'penal substitution theory' that Christ died for our sins.[137] In many respects, Colenso was arguing the case for which Wilson was condemned in the Court of Arches, and the entire book seemed to smack of Jowett's radical views on the epistles of St Paul. Robert Gray (1809–72), the Tractarian bishop of Cape Town and Colenso's metropolitan, argued that 'there *are* difficulties in Holy Scripture – difficulties which have probably been permitted to be there to try the humility and faith of God's people, to invite them reverently to examine and inquire'.[138] William Connor Magee (1821–91), later archbishop of York, agreed that the inconsistencies in the Bible were present 'by God's special providence' to teach people that mathematical certainty and faith were two separate matters.[139] Even the 'intelligent Zulu' William Ngidi had second thoughts after being visited by Bishop Gray.[140]

The first part of Colenso on the Pentateuch was printed in South Africa between April and May 1862, and was published in England on 29 October 1862, just as the tenth edition of *Essays and Reviews* appeared, and by Longman, the same publisher. Colenso's book sold 8,000 copies in the first three weeks, and the two books were inextricably linked.[141] As the poet Robert Browning (1812–89) wrote:

> The candid incline to surmise of late
> That the Christian faith proves false, I find;
> For our Essays-and-Reviews' debate
> Begins to tell on the public mind,
> And Colenso's words have weight:[142]

Colenso himself declared in the preface to his book that he had begun serious research on the subject in January 1861 after reading *Essays and Reviews* and the responses it provoked, especially *Aids to Faith*. Colenso argued that Lushington's 'interlocutory judgment' allowed him under the Articles of Religion to modify his subscription to the Anglican Formularies which required him to 'unfeignedly believe all the Canonical Scriptures of the Old and New Testament'. He had immersed himself in Hengstenberg, de Wette and his student Friedrich Bleek, and others, and completed his first draft in February or March 1861, under the shadow of the case in the Court of Arches. By May of the same year, Colenso had come to the official attention of the Convocation of Canterbury, as Wilberforce once again led the attack, particularly against the renegade bishop's view of the Atonement. The same bishops, led by Hamilton of Salisbury and Sumner of Winchester, who had been exercised over *Essays*, were upset about Colenso. When they tried to depose Colenso, he came to England and lived with his family in hired rooms at Kensington for nearly three years until Westbury delivered his judgment in favour of Colenso at the Judicial Committee of the Privy Council on 20 March 1865.[143]

Many rallied to his support. Stanley and Jowett exchanged some letters in which they championed Colenso, although they wished that his tone was not so argumentative. 'An excellent man, and an able book;' Stanley informed Jowett,

> but it is so written as to vex me a good deal. I have urged upon him, if possible, to write it more like a defence, and less like an attack. Every additional work composed about the Elohistic and Jehovistic elements, &c. &c., as if to destroy the Bible – when it really should be as if to bring out a series of interesting and instructive facts in and about the Bible – is so much done to drive us further and further from the haven where we would be. No man ought ever to write himself down as a heretic.[144]

Mark Pattison, writing in the *Westminster Review*, acclaimed Colenso for reading the Bible as one would any text, asking 'Who the persons are that are speaking to us in those books? On what evidence is their authority grounded that they should be believed, whether they speak concerning God, or the world, or of history?'[145] There were favourable and mixed reviews, often comparing Colenso with *Essays and Reviews*.[146] Swinburne, Dickens, Thackeray, and George Eliot supported Colenso. Anthony Trollope helped pay for legal costs, Tennyson spoke on Colenso's behalf, and Garibaldi wrote to Colenso affirming that they were fellow fighters for the emancipation of mankind. Sir Charles Lyell the evolutionary geologist became a close friend and got him elected to the Athenaeum, the London club to which many intellectuals and literary men belonged.[147] Matthew Arnold, however, was dead against Colenso, and not just because he himself was a member of the Athenaeum and did much of his writing there (or in the North Library of the British Museum, since neither place used gas lamps, which made his eyes run). Bishop Colenso was a moving target that Arnold could not afford to miss.[148]

VIII

'The tone of my Colenso article is a little sharper than I could wish,' Arnold confessed to his mother, 'but the man is really such a goose that it is difficult not to say sharp things of him.'[149] Arnold's essay was published as 'The

Bishop and the Philosopher' in the January 1863 number of *Macmillan's Magazine*, and formed the basis of later articles about Colenso and Spinoza that he would include in his collected works. His argument was very simple: 'Religious books come within the jurisdiction of literary criticism so far as they affect general culture.' The mission of such books was to ensure that 'the raw are humanised or the cultivated are advanced to a yet higher culture', what Arnold liked to call 'edification'. According to this principle, he felt compelled in the name of literary criticism 'to try the book of the Bishop of Natal, which all England is now reading.' Arnold was unconvinced that most people were able to accept new ideas in general, not to mention destructive biblical criticism: 'Old moral ideas leaven and humanise the multitude: new intellectual ideas filter slowly down to them from the thinking few; and only when they reach them in this manner do they adjust themselves to their practice without convulsing it.' Colenso's book failed to satisfy either 'the multitude' or 'the thinking few'. Certainly the first and larger group would not know what to make of Colenso's demolition of the sacred text:

> He finds the simple everyday Englishman going into church, he buries him and the sacred fabric under an avalanche of rule-of-three sums; and when the poor man crawls from under the ruins, bruised, bleeding, and bewildered, and begs for a little spiritual consolation, the Bishop 'refers him' to his own Commentary on the Romans, two chapters of Exodus, a fragment of Cicero, a revelation to the Sikh Gooroos, and an invocation of Ram.

As for 'the thinking few', they might demand of Colenso, '*What then?*' If the Bible is not an inspired document, then what place is it to have in religion and society? 'What is the new Christianity to be like? How are Governments to deal with national Churches founded to maintain a very different conception of Christianity?' These are the questions that Hegel in Germany and Renan in France were now attempting to answer, Arnold reported.

But even those great scholars may be reinventing the wheel: 'I will make what I mean yet clearer by a contrast', Arnold explained,

> At this very moment is announced the first English translation of a foreign work which treats of the same matter as the Bishop of Natal's work, treats of it in an unorthodox way. I mean a work signed by a great name – to most English readers the name of a great heretic, and nothing more – the *Tractatus Theologico-Politicus* of Spinoza.

Arnold delineated what he liked about Spinoza, and why he thought that the Dutch Jew made such an admirable contrast to the benighted South African bishop. First of all, Spinoza wrote in Latin, 'the language of the instructed few – the language in which Coleridge desired that all novel speculations about religion should be written', and Spinoza himself expressly declared that he was writing for that elevated group of people alone. More importantly, Spinoza gives an answer to the question '*What then?*', which naturally follows the demolition of conventional religion, something that Colenso was incapable of doing. True it was that despite Spinoza's caveats, here was Arnold exulting in the fact that *TTP* was coming out in an English translation: but times had changed since Spinoza wrote, and 'the English branch of the race of Japhet' was ready to take strong intellectual drink without falling down drunk with despair:

> The author of the *Tractatus Theologico-Politicus* is not more unorthodox than the author of the *Pentateuch Critically Examined*, and he is far more edifying. If the English clergy must err, let them learn from this outcast of Israel to err nobly! Along with the weak trifling of the Bishop of Natal, let it be lawful to cast into the huge cauldron, out of which the new world is to be born, the strong thought of Spinoza![150]

Alas, Arnold's hope that Spinoza would write good Victorian prose was almost immediately dashed, reminding us that even a hundred years ago it was still possible to review a book before having actually read it. Writing about Willis's translation in the *London Review* a few days later, he made his anger known to all:

> We part from this book with sincere resentment. This publication is discreditable to all concerned in it; advantage has been excited about Biblical criticism, to try and palm off upon the British public an article which is, in the translator's own language, most 'mendacious.' And we have been compelled to perform a task which is revolting to us, and which is not the task we had thought to perform. We had thought to speak of a great thinker and his philosophy; and, instead of that, we find ourselves with these hangman's hands.

Arnold gave numerous examples of schoolboy mistakes in Latin translation, carved up the editor and his work, and advised his acolytes to read *TTP* in another language: 'If he knows neither Latin, French, nor German, he must wait for a proper English translation. The present English translation let no man buy.'[151]

Matthew Arnold spent all of 1863 almost obsessed with Spinoza, and determined to promote him as the unsung father of modern Higher Criticism of the Bible, whose claims to paternity had been obstructed by the rambunctious Germans. Arnold admitted that 'it was a German (Goethe) who first interested me in Spinoza, so he naturally connects himself in my mind with Germany and German thought.'[152] Years later, however, he would thank T.H. Huxley for a letter,

> First, because it put the saddle on the right horse, and made me indebted to Spinoza and not to the Germans. It makes me rather angry to be affiliated to the German Biblical critics: I have had to read masses of them, and they would have drowned me if it had not been for the corks I had brought from the study of Spinoza. To him I owe more than I can say.[153]

Indeed, Arnold had been preparing to launch Spinoza on the British public ever since reading Colenso's curious first volume. 'I suspect it is Colenso's book which has reanimated the orthodox party against Jowett and the Essayists', he wrote to his mother on 19 November 1862,

> I think, *àpropos* of Colenso, of doing what will be rather an interesting thing. I am going to write an article called 'The Bishop & the Philosopher' contrasting Colenso and Co.'s jejune and technical manner of dealing with Biblical controversy with that of Spinoza in his famous treatise on the Interpretation of Scripture: with a view of showing how, the heresy on both sides being equal, Spinoza broaches his in that edifying and pious spirit by which alone the treatment of such matters can be made fruitful, while Colenso and the English Essayists, from their narrowness and want of power more than from any other cause do not. I know Spinoza's works very well, and shall be glad of an opportunity of thus dealing with them; – the article will be in Fraser or Macmillan I don't know which.[154]

To his French friend Charles Augustin de Sainte-Beuve (1804–69), Arnold revealed that 'Je vien d'écrire sur le grand hérétique, Spinoza, à propos d'un petit hérétique l'évêque Colenso, dont un livre absurde sur la Pentateuque a jeté tout notre monde religieux dans l'émoi!'[155]

When Arnold first became interested in Spinoza is not entirely clear. His earliest explicit reference to our hero comes in a letter to his friend Arthur Hugh Clough (1819–61) on 23 October 1850, noting that 'Locke is a man who has cleared his mind of vain repetitions, though without the positive and vivifying atmosphere of Spinoza about him. This last, smile as you will, I have been studying lately with profit.'[156] Yet Arnold certainly knew of Spinoza's work several years earlier, since he was one of the authors that his younger brother Thomas Arnold (1823–1900), later professor of English at University College Dublin, took with him to New Zealand in November 1847, along with books by Hegel, Rousseau, and Emerson.[157] Arnold was already boning up on Spinoza a number of years before Colenso stupefied the academic world. He read Spinoza's *Ethics*, in George Eliot's unpublished manuscript translation, at the beginning of January 1851.[158] *TTP* appears in Arnold's *Note-Books* for 1856, and was on his reading list in September 1858. He was very careful about noting his reading plans and had booked in the *TTP* for summer 1860; he took it with him to the country in September 1862, so that

Spinoza was ripe in his mind when the bishop of Natal became a household name.[159]

Arnold knew, however, that Colenso was an unworthy foil for the great Jewish philosopher, and was in himself rather an embarrassment both to English letters and religious life. In despair, Arnold would cry that

> It is really the strongest possible proof of the low ebb at which, in England, the critical spirit is, that while the critical hit in the religious literature of Germany is Dr Strauss's book, in that of France M. Renan's book, the book of Bishop Colenso is the critical hit in the religious literature of England.[160]

Even *The Times* had a go at this easy target once Arnold had given his imprimatur for the ridiculing of Colenso, recounting sarcastically how the bishop began translating the Bible with the help of

> an intelligent Zulu, a sort of coloured Spinoza, as it would seem. This *enfant terrible* . . . began to ask impertinent questions, which Dr. Colenso found a difficulty in answering. . . . Instead of Dr. Colenso converting the Zulu, the Zulu converted Dr. Colenso.[161]

Yet although there was a good deal that was comical about Colenso, Arnold knew that by contrasting the bishop of Natal with Spinoza, he himself was 'edifying' the nation and working towards a view of the Bible which could be both critical and constructive. Arnold soon had another opportunity of clarifying his position the following month, February 1863, when he reviewed the first part of his friend Arthur Penrhyn Stanley's *Lectures on the History of the Jewish Church*, which had just appeared. Stanley was Regius professor of ecclesiastical history at Oxford, the pupil and biographer of Thomas Arnold, a close family friend, and had written one of the books that Colenso had attacked.[162] Arnold's review was more than a puff, however, and he used the article in *Macmillan's Magazine* to continue blasting the bishop and trumpeting Spinoza as the answer to a Victorian clergyman's prayers. Stanley was added as a sort of warm-up to Spinoza, since the professor had also written a book on religious matters that 'fulfils the indispensable duty of edifying at the same time that it informs.' Colenso had cut the ground from naïve but pious Englishmen:

> Puzzled by the Bishop's sums, terrified at the conclusion he draws from them, they, in their bewilderment, seek for safety in attacking the sums themselves, instead of putting them on one side as irrelevant, and rejecting the conclusion deduced from them as untrue. 'Here is a Bishop,' many of Stanley's brethren are now crying in all parts of England – 'here is a Bishop who has learnt among the Zulus that only a certain number of people can stand in a doorway at once, and that no man can eat eighty-eight pigeons

a day, and who tells us, as a consequence, that the Pentateuch is all fiction, which, however, the author may very likely have composed without meaning to do wrong, and as a work of poetry, like Homer's.'

The reader, Arnold writes, turns to Stanley expecting him to prove 'that any number of persons can stand in the same doorway at once, and that one man can eat eighty-eight pigeons a day with ease', but instead finds that the professor brushes aside such tedious scriptural arithmetic, and rejects Colenso's entire approach. 'Even if the Bishop's sums are right,' says Stanley in Arnold's vernacular paraphrase,

> they do not prove that the Bible narrative is to be classified with the Iliad and the Legends of Rome. Even if you prove them wrong, your success does not bring you a step nearer to that which you go to the Bible to seek. Carry your achievements of this kind to the Statistical Society, to the Geographical Society, to the Ethnological Society. They have no vital interest for the religious reader of the Bible. The heart of the Bible is not there.

This was also the message of that 'born thinker' Spinoza, writing in his 'austere isolation'.[163]

The time had come for Arnold to put his thoughts about Spinoza in order, and to lay down the law for Victorian aesthetes like himself. This he did in his classic essay, 'Spinoza and the Bible' which was built upon his earlier controversy with Colenso, but when he republished the piece in his celebrated book, *Essays in Criticism*, he deleted all references to the bishop of Natal as unworthy of his great theme.[164] Arnold's mission was not to praise Spinoza but to unbury him. In a letter to his mother on 7 January 1863, when the controversy with Colenso was at its height, Arnold wrote that, with regard to Spinoza,

> You say very justly that one's aim in speaking about such a man must be rather to modify opinion about him than to give it a decisive turn in his favour: indeed the latter I have no wish to do, so far as his doctrines are concerned – for, so far as I can understand them, they are not mine. But what the English public cannot understand is that a man is a just and fruitful object of contemplation much more by virtue of what spirit he is of than by virtue of what system of doctrine he elaborates.[165]

Spinoza went too far even for Arnold, but in his character and his approach he fulfilled the dual criteria of being both edifying and instructive, so he is worthy of both our study and our praise.

Arnold's essay on Spinoza is one of his best, a masterpiece of Victorian literary criticism. He begins by quoting the edict of excommunication, and proclaims that in expelling Spinoza from their midst, the Jews of Amsterdam 'remained children of Israel, and he became a child of modern Europe.' Despite the *herem*, and notwithstanding 'Voltaire's disparagement and Bayle's detraction', indeed

> in spite of the repellent form which he has given to his principal work, in spite of the exterior semblance of a rigid dogmatism alien to the most essential tendencies of modern philosophy, in spite, finally, of the immense weight of disfavour cast upon him by the long repeated charge of atheism, Spinoza's name has silently risen in importance, the man and his work have attracted a steadily increasing notice, and bid fair to become soon what they deserve to become, – in the history of modern philosophy the central point of interest.

High praise indeed from the chief apostle of culture in his time.

The problem with writing about Matthew Arnold is that any paraphrase of his style does him a terrible injustice, since his prose is far more skilful than ours. He is especially good when putting words into other people's mouths: we have already seen the lines he gave Stanley in an imaginary debate with Colenso's followers. Here too he gives Spinoza a set speech, affirming that

> I will show these people, that, taking the Bible for granted, taking it to be all which it asserts itself to be, taking it to have all the authority which it claims, it is not what they imagine it to be, it does not say what they imagine it to say. I will show them what it really does say, and I will show them that they will do well to accept this real teaching of the Bible, instead of the phantom with which they have so long been cheated. I will show their governments that they will do well to remodel the national churches, to make of them institutions informed with the spirit of the true Bible, instead of institutions informed with the spirit of this false phantom.

Spinoza therefore returned to the Bible, Arnold recounts, 'to read it over and over with a perfectly unprejudiced mind, and to accept nothing as its teaching which it did not clearly teach.'

The result of Spinoza's research, Arnold explains, was that the divine authority of the Bible consists in 'a revelation given by God to the prophets', received by these good men 'through the means of words and images'. These prophets were chosen for their task, not because of the 'perfection of their mind', but because 'the prophets excelled other men by the power and vividness of their representing and imagining faculty'. The words and images which they conjured up were not absolute reflections of reality, and this is why the prophets differed, Micah imagining God sitting on a throne, Daniel imagining him as an old man with a white robe and hair, Ezekiel as a fire, and so on. But these discrepancies were of no importance, since God's purpose was to convey a clear message: 'The sum and substance of this revelation was simply: *Believe in God, and lead a good life.*' This is the duty of everyone, not one nation in particular, and 'this law is universal, written in the heart, and one for all mankind.' As was true in the time of the prophets, so too does it follow today that philosophy or science and theology can never conflict, since they occupy separate realms of thought and inhabit totally different conceptual universes: 'Theology demands perfect obedience, philosophy perfect knowledge: the obedience demanded by theology and the knowledge demanded by philosophy are alike saving.' In sum, Arnold wrote, Spinoza is telling us that 'These are the fundamentals of faith, and they are so clear and simple that none of the inaccuracies provable in the Bible narrative the least affect them, and they have indubitably come to us uncorrupted.' It is this message that makes Spinoza's work 'most interesting and stimulating to the general culture of Europe.' By now, Arnold no longer needed Colenso as the straw man; Victorian England was ready for Spinoza unwired.

It is not at all surprising that Matthew Arnold connects Spinoza's name with that of D.F. Strauss, whose *Leben Jesu* (1835) was translated in 1846 into English by George Eliot and became the touchstone of Victorian Higher Criticism, although Arnold thought him rather too destructive. What is strange is how close he came to the much later views of another Strauss, Leo, in trying to work out the contradictions in the writings of Spinoza himself. Arnold noted here and there 'the silence or ambiguity of their author upon a point of cardinal importance', and tried to work out how that could be so in a man of exceptional genius, as Spinoza was. This was especially felt in regard to the key question of miracles. Why should Spinoza have rejected a whole host of supernatural biblical events, such as the parting of the Red Sea, the resurrection of the Shunammite's son, and the rainbow after the Flood, assigning to each a perfectly reasonable natural explanation, only to turn around and assert that it was a real divine voice which was heard on Mount Sinai? Arnold's critical sense led him to conclude that

> No intelligent man can read the *Tractatus Theologico-Politicus* without being profoundly instructed by it: but neither can he read it without feeling that, as a speculative work, it is, to use a French military expression, *in the air*; that, in a certain sense, it is in want of a base and in want of supports; that this base and these supports are, at any rate, not to be found in the work itself, and, if they exist, must be sought for in other works of the author.

In other words, Spinoza's views on miracles, for example, can only be elucidated within the context of everything he wrote about miracles. Not quite Leo Strauss, but as Arnold said of Spinoza and might have said about himself, a 'philosopher's real power over mankind resides not in his metaphysical formulas, but in the spirit and tendencies which have led him to adopt those formulas.'

The crucial fact for Arnold was the intense relevance of Spinoza for his own time. A man like Colenso should never have achieved the notoriety that he did, since Spinoza had already demolished his arguments two centuries before. Spinoza for Arnold was the 'lonely precursor of German philosophy', and 'he still shines when the light of his successors is fading away; they had celebrity, Spinoza has fame.' Arnold was no sycophantic philosophical groupie, however; he was attracted to Spinoza the man and the thinker, but what drew him to this seventeenth-century Jew was his timelessness:

> What a remarkable philosopher really does for human thought, is to throw into circulation a certain number of new and striking ideas and expressions, and to stimulate with them the thought and imagination of his century or of after-times.

In this, Spinoza was completely successful, for Arnold was able to bring him to bear on some of key issues which troubled the Victorians, especially the relation between science and religion, and the conflict between the intellect and the imagination or feeling. Arnold returned to Spinoza and many of these themes in his later writings, especially in *Literature and Dogma* (1873), but 'Spinoza and the Bible' retains much more of the passion of his struggle with Colenso for positing how cultured Englishmen should read their Bibles.

IX

From what has been said before, it should come as a surprise that despite Matthew Arnold's unflagging devotion to Spinoza, a good case could be made for seeing the man as a rabid racist and an anti-Semite. This rather dubious distinction is largely based on the fourth chapter of his celebrated book, *Culture and Anarchy* (1869), entitled 'Hebraism and Hellenism'. Taking his cue from Heine, who had originally posited this binary opposition,[166] Arnold set up an almost simplistic division between two forces, or ways of living. The first he characterized by the name of 'Hebraism', to which he applied words and phrases such as doing, energy, practice, conduct, obedience, strictness of conscience, and practising one's duty. The opposite of 'Hebraism' was said to be 'Hellenism', sketched out with the aid of terms and concepts such as thinking, knowing, intelligence, ideas, seeing things as they really are, spontaneity of conscience, knowing one's duty, and of course, Arnold's catch phrase, 'sweetness and light'. The aim of both of these 'forces', as he called them, was identical, despite their polar distinctions, namely, 'man's perfection or salvation'. Christianity, Arnold argued, was in essence a form of Hebraism, in that it set doing above knowing: 'Self-conquest, self-devotion, the following not our own individual will, but the will of God, *obedience*, is the fundamental idea of this form'.

Looked at in the largest possible scale, Hebraism and Hellenism were the two forces which determined European history and culture. Each alone was only part of the story: 'the evolution of these forces, separately and in themselves, is not the whole evolution of humanity, – their single history is not the whole history of man; whereas their admirers are always apt to make it stand for the whole history.' Indeed, 'Hebraism and Hellenism are, neither of them, the *law* of human development, as their admirers are prone to make them; they are, each of them, *contributions* to human development'. We can see these two forces struggling throughout history:

> As the great movement of Christianity was a triumph of Hebraism and man's moral impulses, so the great movement which goes by the name of the Renascence was an uprising and re-instatement of man's intellectual impulses and of Hellenism. We in England, the devoted children of Protestantism, chiefly know the Renascence by its subordinate and secondary side of the Reformation. The Reformation has been often called a Hebraising revival, a return to the ardour and sincereness of primitive Christianity.

Nevertheless, the Renaissance was also a return to classical values, so one could say that in the sixteenth century, 'Hellenism re-entered the world, and again stood in the presence of Hebraism, – a Hebraism renewed and purged', that is, Protestantism.

So far so good, and anyone who read only this far in this fourth chapter of *Culture and Anarchy* might have thought that the Jews were on the winning team. Yet it is just at this moment that Arnold disabuses us of this optimism, with a healthy dose of nineteenth-century racism:

> Science has now made visible to everybody the great and pregnant elements of difference which lie in race, and in how signal a manner they make the genius and history of an Indo-European people vary from those of a Semitic people. Hellenism is of Indo-European growth, Hebraism is of Semitic growth; and we English, a nation of Indo-European stock, seem to belong naturally to the movement of Hellenism.

It was Puritanism that perverted the destiny of 'our race', in that it was 'a reaction of Hebraism against Hellenism' and it won the day. In almost Leibnizian fashion, however, Arnold admitted that although it was sad that the advancement of the Renaissance and its values was checked in England, 'if Hellenism was defeated, this shows that Hellenism was imperfect, and that its ascendancy at that moment would not have been for the world's good.' The history of (European) mankind was a development from paganism to Hebraism to Christianity to Hellenism, and 'Puritanism was no longer the central current of the world's progress, it was a side stream crossing the central current and checking it.' The illegitimate victory of Semitic Hebraism over an Indo-European people who should have been the standard-bearers of Hellenism implied a 'contravention of the natural order' which always must produce 'a certain confusion and false movement, of which we are now beginning to feel, in almost every direction, the inconvenience.' Arnold called upon Englishmen everywhere to begin 'going back upon the actual instincts and forces which rule our life', that is, to reject 'a main element in our nature', a tendency towards Hebraism over Hellenism, expressed by 'our preference of doing to thinking'.[167]

Arnold's contrasting of the Hebraic and Hellenistic geniuses in *Culture and Anarchy* was not an aberration of mind or a passing fancy. Indeed, he wrote to his mother in June 1869 that 'the chapters on Hellenism and Hebraism are in the main, I am convinced, so true that they will form a kind of centre for English thought and speculation on the matters treated in them.'[168] He was even more expansive in his lectures, *On the Study of Celtic Literature* (1867), when he tried to show that the English race drew on a unique formula of different bloods deriving from the German, Norman, and Celtic races, each blood having its own particular character whose qualities remained preserved in the mixture. Our enlightened sensitivities can surely not condemn him outright, or link him inevitably with grand racial theorists such as Joseph Arthur de Gobineau (1816–82). Many other thinkers, Jews included, were swept away by the notion that each race or people was characterized by immutable qualities, good or bad. The distinction between Hebraism and Hellenism was, as we have seen, one which Arnold lifted from Heinrich Heine. Moses Hess (1812–75) preferred the contrast between Rome and Jerusalem. Disraeli wrote about the difference between Saxon hard work and Norman good manners. Even George Eliot's *Daniel Deronda* (1876) revolves around the premises that a Jew brought up as an English aristocrat of Spanish blood, would in later life begin to show behavioural patterns typical of his people, such as the unexplained compulsion to seek out fellow Jews and a spooky tendency towards prophecy. One of Arnold's recent biographers argues that we shouldn't take all this too seriously: his racist musings were not very logical and even have a quality of self-mockery about them: 'We might be reading a psychoanalytic transcript by a relaxed Matthew, dreamily telling us what he sees when we say to him words such as "Germans", "Celt", or "Englishman."'[169]

It is also true that Matthew Arnold had a number of close Jewish friends. As a young man of twenty-five, he became an ardent fan of 'Rachel' (1822–58), a famous deep-voiced German-Jewish actress at the Théatre Français, spent six weeks following her from performance to performance, and after her early death wrote three sonnets (1863) in memory of this woman

'Sprung from the blood of Israel's scatter'd race'.[170] He also had a relationship with Louisa, Lady de Rothschild (née Montefiore) which would have been scandalous had not both their characters been quite above reproach.[171] Meeting some of her German cousins in London in 1863, Arnold exclaimed, 'What women these Jewesses are! with a *force* which seems to triple that of the women of our Western and Northern races'.[172] Arnold was a great admirer of Emanuel Deutsch (1829–73), who worked at the British Museum from 1855, taught George Eliot Hebrew, and served as the model for 'Mordecai' in *Daniel Deronda*. Deutsch was almost invited to contribute an article to *Essays and Reviews*, but instead wrote a celebrated essay on the Talmud for the *Quarterly Review* meant for the general English reader, and Arnold liked his work: 'I met Mr Deutsch the other day, and had a very long talk with him about Hebraism & Hellenism', he wrote to Lady de Rothschild,

> I was greatly interested in seeing him, and any diffidence I felt in talking about my crude speculations to such a savant was set at rest by his telling me that he was distinctly conscious, while writing his article on the Talmud, that if it had not been for what I had done, he could not have written the article in the Quarterly, and the British public could not have read it.

The reference, apparently, is to a few quotations from 'The Ethics of the Fathers' in 'The Bishop and the Philosopher': once Arnold had quoted from the Talmud, he sincerely believed, it was a signal to the cultivated few to admit an interest in the subject.[173] Indeed, his Edwardian biographer suggested that 'Arnold's remote ancestors had belonged to the Ancient Race, and had emigrated from Germany to Lowestoft, where they dwelt for several generations.'[174] Even Hilaire Belloc (1870–1953) accepted this particular 'history' as 'fact'.[175]

X

We have already seen how Matthew Arnold was at pains to make Spinoza his intellectual mentor, while minimizing the influence of the Germans on his thinking. But he well knew that it was in Germany that the notion of a coherent and absolute biblical text began to come apart, at least from the later eighteenth century when Johann Gottfried Eichhorn declared that 'My greatest labour I have had to devote to a hitherto unworked field, to the investigation of the inner nature of the various scriptures of the Old Testament, with the help of the Higher Criticism (not a new term to any humanist).'[176] This new approach to the Bible fitted in well with contemporary German ideas about each society undergoing its own *Fortgang* (progress) as it fulfils its historical potential, cultures yielding to one another as *Entwicklung* (development) takes place, just as *Bildung* was a corresponding process on the indi-vidual level. Arnold learned about these weighty matters at the source, by reading Johann Gottfried von Herder, especially his *Ideen zur Philosophie der Geschichte der Menschheit* (1784–91), which Arnold owned in the Leipzig, 1828 edition, although he presumably also cribbed from the English translation which appeared in 1800. Arnold's copy of Herder is now in the Yale library, and one can see that he read and marked carefully the first seven books, the part about the general philosophy of history before Herder launches into his exhaustive narrative of the progress of mankind from China and the Orient up until sixteenth-century Europe, emphasizing all the way the axiom of *Entwicklung* from lower forms, cultural evolution.

The problem with change is that things never stay the same, and while this is probably for the best in history, it is a concept that can wreak havoc in theology. The Oxford of young Matthew Arnold's day was still the university of Cardinal Newman, who had injected the notion of development into Roman Catholic theology, arguing that we can no longer sweep under the edicule the fact that the nineteenth-century Church is not the same as that of Saint Peter. It need not be, Newman argued, and we have no reason to fear the notion of change or development, as was the universal practice in Rome. It was not religious truth that was changing, he explained, but our apprehension and understanding of those eternal verities that grew, as a small child learns about the unchanging world around him as he grows to maturity.

Arnold admired Spinoza but refused to go down the road with him in the darkness (or light) of godlessness. Arnold rejected what he called 'Strauss's passion for demolition'.[177] He was a religious man, but could not ignore con-temporary philosophical trends, especially ones which were in vogue and known to his many readers. In Arnold's very first foray against Colenso, he berated the bishop for having tried to tear down the naïve faith of the mul-titude without following up the destruction with a simple '*What then?* What follows from all this? What change is it, if true, to produce in the relations of mankind to the Christian religion?' This is what Arnold got from Spinoza, who at a stroke denied the importance of Colenso's arithmetic and the more sophisticated work of the Germans, who dissected the Bible and laid bare the wheels and pulleys that made up the biggest conjuring trick in the history of mankind. There was no point in looking for the original text of the Bible, because there was none: 'to know accurately the history of our documents is impossible, and even if it were possible, we should yet not know accurately what Jesus said and did; *for his reporters were incapable of rendering it, he was so much above them.*'[178] By positing that the only essential message in the Scrip-ture was moral and uncomplicated – '*Believe in God, and lead a good life*' – Spinoza provided for Arnold the kind of weighty and dignified ancient (or at least antique) authority that allowed him to have his Eucharist and eat it too.

For no Victorian could do without development, without progress. Arnold and his friends wrote a good deal about Homer, as a code-word for the Bible, half with a sublime fear that the biblical narratives would dissolve in the same fog that had made Troy and the wanderings of Odysseus more fairy-tale than true history.[179] The best illustration of the Victorian intellectual vertigo was written in about 1888 by Robert Browning, five years after Elwes's *TTP*, in a poem actually entitled 'Development'. 'My Father was a scholar and knew Greek', he began, and told the story of how, as a boy of five, when learning that his father was reading about the siege of Troy, he asked what the story was about and was treated to a re-creation of the tale with chairs, tables, and the family cat. Later on his father gives him Alexander Pope's translation of the *Iliad*, and encourages him to learn Greek so as to tackle the original text, which was enchanting until he came across the work of Friedrich August Wolf (1759–1824), who argued that Homer's works were simply a compilation of oral tradition:[180]

> And, after Wolf, a dozen of his like
> Proved there was never any Troy at all,
> Neither Besiegers nor Besieged, – nay, worse, –
> No actual Homer, no authentic text,
> No warrant for the fiction I, as fact,
> Had treasured in my heart and soul so long –
> . . . though Wolf – ah, Wolf!
> Why must he needs come doubting, spoil a dream?
>
> But then 'No dream's worth waking' – Browning says:
> And here's the reason why I tell thus much.
> I, now mature man, you anticipate,
> May blame my Father justifiably
> For letting me dream out my nonage thus,
> And only by such slow and sure degrees
> Permitting me to sift the grain from chaff,
> Get truth and falsehood known and named as such.
> Why did he ever let me dream at all,
> Not bid me taste the story in its strength?
> Suppose my childhood was scarce qualified
> To rightly understand mythology,
> Silence at least was in his power to keep . . .

Sitting over a copy of Aristotle's *Nicomachean Ethics* a few lines later, however, Browning admits that

The 'Ethics': 'tis a treatise I find hard
To read aright now that my hair is grey,
And I can manage the original.
At five years old — how ill had fared its leaves!
Now, growing double o'er the Stagirite,
At least I soil no page with bread and milk,
Nor crumple, dogsear and deface — boys' way.[181]

Unlike Wolf, Spinoza allowed Arnold to 'sift the grain from chaff, Get truth and falsehood known and named as such', without losing the essence of the divine prophecy that was essential for mankind's salvation — '*Believe in God, and lead a good life*'. This is why our friend R.H.M. Elwes, writing five years before Arnold's passing, could affirm that we may say of Spinoza that 'like Moses returning from Sinai, he bears in his presence the witness that he has held communion with the Most High.'[182]

CHAPTER 8

Unsuitable Paternity: Darwin, Anthropology, and the Evolutionist Bible

The notion of the implacable incompatibility of science and revelation is a modern one, barely more than a century old. It is only to modern perceptions that Isaac Newton the millenarian looks odd at the head of the Royal Society.[1] At the beginning of the nineteenth century, it might still be argued that nature was a museum demonstration of God's plan and, if properly viewed, might reveal new insights otherwise unobtainable, perhaps even from Scripture. The argument from design was, and remains, a most powerful demonstration of God's existence and His works. William Paley's (1743–1805) famous metaphor – of the natural world being as obviously the product of some intelligence as a watch found in 'crossing a heath' – implies that further scientific investigation is more likely to confirm rather than to weaken religious belief. This would all change with the controversy over Darwin.[2]

I

The scientific threat to theology, however, began not with Darwin and biology but with geology, which seemed at first to be a handmaiden of Scripture. Even in the seventeenth century, John Ray (1627–1705) recognized that fossils must be the remains of living things, and that their very existence was difficult to reconcile with the account of Creation revealed in Genesis.[3] But in those days, the proper response was not to jettison Genesis, but to revise the geology, just as Newton disputed the length of the Great Pyramid rather than abandon the belief that a secret of the universe was concealed in its measurements. This drive to reconcile geology with Scripture found its fullest expression in *Telluris theoria sacra* by Thomas Burnet (1635?–1715) published in Latin in 1681 and in an English translation three years later. Burnet argued that at Creation the earth was perfectly smooth and stood upright, although since the poles were slightly higher than the equator, all the rivers flowed towards the tropics. The Garden of Eden was exactly in the middle of the southern hemisphere, enjoying perpetual spring, since without a tilted axis there were no seasons, and in such a Californian climate the patriarchs could easily reach their recorded ages. The Flood, however, put an end to this. The earth tilted to its present angle of about 20 degrees, and the water under the crust cracked and spilled over the land, aided but not caused by a significant quantity of rainfall. Burnet determined the amount of water needed to cover the earth, and concluded that rainfall would simply not be enough. The end result was that the surface of the earth became irregular and broken, an imperfect shape suitable for post-lapsarian man. At the End of Days, he predicted, the earth would suffer a great inferno, in which the blazes of Britain would be particularly prominent as her subterranean coal caught fire. When the dust literally settled, it would return the earth's shape to its original perfectly spherical form. Jesus would begin his millennial reign, followed by the war of Gog and Magog, and the elevation of the saints to heaven, after which time the earth would become a star.[4]

Certainly, Burnet was not the first to conceive of the state of the earth after the Fall as being substantially inferior to what had prevailed in the age of Edenic purity. As Burnet shrewdly pointed out,

> When this idea of the earth is present to my thoughts, I can no more believe that this was the form wherein it was first produced, than if I had seen the Temple of Jerusalem in its ruins, when defaced and sacked by the Babylonians, I could have persuaded myself that it had never been in any other posture, and that Solomon had given orders for building it so.[5]

Descartes earlier had argued that the earth had originally been a sun which had cooled and contracted into a nucleus contained by a rocky shell, over which was an expanse of water covered by a smooth outer crust. Like Burnet, Descartes explained that the collapse of the crust and the escape of the water underneath created the topography of the world as we know it today.[6] Joseph Glanvill (1636–80) said that the earth at the End of Days would become a comet.[7] So too did Robert Hooke (1635–1703) discuss a shift in the earth's centre of gravity, arguing that ''Tis not impossible but that some of these great alterations may have alter'd also the magnetical Directions of the Earth; so that what is now under the Pole or Aequator, or any other Degree of Latitude may have formerly been under another'.[8] These ideas were already in the air, and Burnet's views did not seem absurd to Newton, who told him that 'Of our present sea, rocks, mountains &c I think you have given the most plausible account.'[9]

Thomas Burnet's theory, however, was not mere biblical literalism. Indeed, Burnet wrote to Newton in January 1681 claiming that there was a good deal of accommodation in Moses's version of history. The Fall was a long and slow process of decay, and the Garden of Eden was a myth. Burnet's geology sparked a hugh controversy, which continued into the beginning of the next century.[10] Among the most prominent of Burnet's critics was William Whiston, who published a defence of the traditional scheme in 1696, objecting to the view that biblical history is 'a meer Popular, Parabolick, or Mythological relation; in which the plain Letter is no more to be accounted for or believ'd, than the fabulous representations of *Aesop*, or at best than the mystical Parables of our Saviour.' Whiston readily admits that the literal Mosaic narrative cannot be seen as a 'Nice and Philosophical account of the Origin of All Things', but nevertheless sees the story of the Creation of the world in six days as being 'an Historical and True Representation of the formation of our single Earth out of a confused Chaos, and of the successive and visible changes thereof each day, till it became the habitation of Mankind.' By using a combination of the Bible and Newtonian physics, it should be possible to understand exactly what occurred. His most famous application of this research principle described the influence of comets in the divine work. Genesis tells us that the chaos was 'without form and void', a clear reference to the atmosphere of a comet, from which the earth was initially formed, and a hint that the End of Days would occur by the collision of a comet with the earth. Edmond Halley (1656–1742), also an old Newtonian, had already applied a strikingly similar explanation to the Flood, which he saw as being caused by the gravitational pull of a comet's close approach, and read papers to the Royal Society in December 1694 in which he argued his case with great effect.[11] When Halley's paper was finally published forty years later, this tardiness was explained by his fear at the time that he would suffer persecution from the religious authorities, and that in any case no one would believe him.[12]

Genesis and geology, then, were two valid and useful sources of information, but as the Bible was infallible and the evidence from the ground was open to a wide variety of interpretations and explanations, it was the earth that had to move. The apparent inconsistencies between science and Scripture were addressed directly by the Bridgewater Treatises. Francis Henry Egerton, the eighth earl of Bridgewater (1756–1829) was a fellow of the Royal Society and All Souls, and the non-resident rector of two parishes in Shropshire. He lived in Paris with a huge collection of boots, a garden teeming with rabbits, and a house full of cats and dogs, some of which were dressed in yellow coats and fed at table by his servants and his illegitimate daughters. While verging on the eccentric, the earl of Bridgewater also had charitable instincts, and indeed it was his collection that became the Egerton MSS at the British Library. He also left £8,000 to the president of the Royal Society for sponsoring a series of works 'on the power, wisdom and goodness of God, as manifested in the Creation'. These were the Bridgewater Treatises.[13]

Two of these addressed the question most directly. William Whewell
(1794–1866), a fellow of Trinity College, Cambridge, and later to become
master of his college and professor of moral philosophy, wrote on astronomy
and physics.[14] An even more important work was produced by William
Buckland, whose career would include the posts of dean of Westminster,
canon of Christ Church, and incumbent of the chair of geology at Oxford.
Buckland was accused of knowing all the ologies except theology, but his
treatise defended the claim that each day of Creation was of unspecified
length: either that, or the chronology in Genesis was not complete. Buckland
also argued that the entire story of the Flood needed to be re-examined in
light of recently discovered geological evidence.[15]

But the major problem was still chronology, a science which had changed
very little since Newton's day. As William Buckland put it succinctly, minds
'which have been long accustomed to date the origin of the universe, as well
as that of the human race, from an era of about six thousand years ago, receive
reluctantly any information, which if true, demands some new modification
of their present ideas of cosmogony'.[16] There were certainly solutions which
might accommodate all of the evidence. Philip Gosse (1810–88) argued that
God created rocks with fossils already inside in order to try the faith of the
godless geologists.[17] But even he could not ignore the more sophisticated
challenge of Sir Charles Lyell (1797–1875), the Scottish geologist who was for
a time professor of his subject at King's College, London during the first years
of that institution's foundation. Lyell promoted the concept of development
in geology, emphasizing gradualism and what would be called 'unifor-
mitarianism'. This was the thesis that the present holds the key to the past,
that there are no significant changes in either rate or intensity of development, so that we need merely to observe what happens in our own time and
extrapolate backwards. Lyell published his *Principles of Geology* in 1830–3 in
which these views were advanced.[18]

Lyell was unhappy about the use that Darwin would make of his geology,
applying to the natural world the concepts that Lyell used with regard to the
inorganic. Lyell never was anything but a practising Anglican, and argued
hopefully that the reason advanced vertebrates were not found from the
earliest period is not that they didn't exist, but that they simply had not
yet been discovered. Birds, he pointed out, decay easily and leave few if any
traces. He also saw his own work as a confirmation of religion as evidenced
by the long-standing cosmological argument:

In our attempts to account for the origin of species, we find ourselves still
sooner brought face to face with the working of a law of development of
so high an order as to stand nearly in the same relation as the Deity himself
to man's finite understanding, a law capable of adding new and powerful

causes, such as the moral and intellectual faculties of the human race, to a system of nature which had gone on for millions of years without the intervention of any analogous cause. If we confound 'Variation' or 'Natural Selection' with such creational laws, we deify secondary causes or immeasurably exaggerate their influence.

Man might therefore stand in awe at the system of nature which God had created. At the same time, however, Lyell substantially contributed to wiping out Archbishop Ussher's seventeenth-century chronological framework, which allowed mankind less than 6,000 years for gradual development, surely impossible at the current rate of change.[19] Even so, although the chronological outline was considerably expanded, there always remained the possibility that Adam and Eve existed, albeit at a much earlier date than had hitherto been expected from biblical evidence. Adam and Eve were necessary not only for biblical literalists, but for theologians, for without the Fall a new theory of Christ's Atonement would have to be hammered out. The geologists had done their work; it remained for the biologists to eliminate our first parents.

Lyell had championed the principle of gradual development in the world of rocks, but even before Darwin, the application of this idea to living creatures was tentatively put forward by Robert Chambers (1802–71), the Scottish journalist and publisher who would achieve a kind of immortality with his famous *Encyclopaedia*. As Chambers accurately put it, his *Vestiges of the Natural History of Creation* 'is the first attempt to connect the natural sciences into a history of creation.' Chambers not only published his book anonymously in October 1844, but exhibited a paranoid fear of discovery to the extent that he went so far as to collect and deliver proofs via messenger. 'For reasons which need not be specified,' he wrote, 'the author's name is retained in its original obscurity, and, in all probability, will never be generally known.' Indeed, the mysterious author of the book was not known for forty years, during which time various names were suggested, including Thackeray, Prince Albert, Byron's daughter, and Darwin himself. It was a huge best-seller: nearly 24,000 copies in eleven British editions, with the first four editions appearing within the first six months.[20]

Chambers's simple idea was that all of nature was subject to natural laws, both in its inorganic and organic manifestations:

> Let us seek in the history of the earth's formation for a new suggestion on this point. We have seen powerful evidence, that the construction of this globe and its associates, and inferentially that of all the other globes of space, was the result, not of any immediate or personal exertion on the part of the Deity, but of natural laws which are expressions of his will. What is to hinder our supposing that the organic creation is also a result of natural laws, which are in like manner an expression of his will?

Chambers provided further proof of the extension of geological principles into the realm of living creatures:

> More than this, the fact of the cosmical arrangements being an effect of natural law, is a powerful argument for the organic arrangements being so likewise, for how can we suppose that the august Being who brought all these countless worlds into form by the simple establishment of a natural principle flowing from his mind, was to interfere personally and specially on every occasion when a new shell-fish or reptile was to be ushered into existence on *one* of these worlds? Surely this idea is too ridiculous to be for a moment entertained.

Chambers's belief in multiple worlds in no way diminishes the logical sense of his argument.[21]

Chambers was above all else anxious to stress that his discovery of a common law for the inorganic and organic realms actually served religion rather than worked against it:

> Those who would object to the hypothesis of a creation by the intervention of law, do not perhaps consider how powerful an argument in favour of the existence of God is lost by rejecting this doctrine. When all is seen to be the result of law, the idea of an Almighty Author becomes irresistible, for the creation of a law for an endless series of phenomena – an act of intelligence above all else that we can conceive – could have no other imaginable source, and tells, moreover, as powerfully for a sustaining as for an originating power.

The key concept, Chambers thought, was development, that is, development or evolution towards a better position, a higher form. This was also true with regard to human races, Chambers suggested, with the white race (of course) being at the top of the pyramid:

> Thus the whole is complete on one principle. The masses of space are formed by law; law makes them in due time theatres of existence for plants and animals; sensation, disposition, intellect are all in like manner developed and sustained in action by law. It is most interesting to observe into how small a field the whole of the mysteries of nature thus ultimately resolve themselves. The inorganic has one final comprehensive law, GRAVITATION. The organic, the other great department of mundane things, rests in like manner on one law, and that is, – DEVELOPMENT. Nor may even these be after all in twain, but only branches of one still more comprehensive law, the expression of that unity which man's wit can scarcely separate from Deity itself.

Evolution, development, was the end result of the law which God had ordained and set in motion at Creation. God set the ball rolling, and fixed the course, so that the outcome was never in doubt, although it may have taken some time. In other words, evolution was now seen as part of the argument from design.[22]

The idea of evolution was not entirely new, and did not necessarily imply a complete rejection of the biblical narrative and its theological implications. From classical and Renaissance beginnings, J.-B. de Lamarck (1744–1829) proposed that changes in the environment cause modifications in the structure of animals and plants, characteristics which are transmitted to offspring. Darwin's grandfather Erasmus Darwin (1731–1802) had a similar idea. But their views were not widely known, and Chambers was the one who appeared as a maverick.

Charles Darwin's (1809–82) book *On the Origin of Species by Means of Natural Selection* (1859) was therefore not completely unexpected. Already by 1842 he had a plan of combining the idea of development and evolution with a theory of natural selection such as appeared in Thomas R. Malthus's (1766–1834) *Essay on the Principle of Population* (1798). Much had been done in the field of chronology, and a good deal of new raw material was available, even the observations of pigeon-fanciers regarding cross-breeding. While Darwin's views might be seen as part of God's plan, and indeed there were times, he confessed, when he himself saw it that way, generally speaking he was not a religious man and unlike Lyell did not object to atheistical implications being drawn from his work. The notion of the survival of the fittest was problematic enough; Darwin's claim in *The Descent of Man* (1871) that the human race derived from an anthropoid animal made his name a byword for atheism.

It was during the period between *Origin* and *Descent* that the concept of an implacable contradiction between theology and science crystallized. We often think of the famous debate between Bishop 'Soapy Sam' Wilberforce, then of Oxford, later of Winchester, and Thomas Henry Huxley, Darwin's self-appointed bulldog, biologist, and later president of the Royal Society. According to Wilberforce's biographer and popular opinion, Huxley proclaimed at that debate in Oxford that he 'would rather be descended from an ape than a bishop', but Huxley's version is somewhat softer.[23] Another important signpost was the Oxford Declaration of 1864, denouncing all those who denied that the entire Bible was the Word of God. It was signed at first by over 700 people, and in the end nearly 11,000 clergymen added their name to the list. Sedgwick and Gosse signed, but many others did not, objecting to the very concept of what was in effect a fortieth Article of Religion. *The Times* published a leading article on the subject in May 1864, and certainly by then it was clear to most people that science was a problem.[24]

Darwin, indeed, was comparatively tame next to a scientist like John Tyndall (1820–93), the Ulster physicist and authority on crystals and glaciers who after the Oxford Declaration began attacking the claims of theology to pronounce on the state of the physical world. The British Association had been founded in 1831 for scientists, and when Tyndall was asked to be its president and to address its meeting at Belfast, he delivered a speech which would become famous and even more well known in book form as *Fragments of Science for Unscientific People*. Here he adopted a completely rational and materialist position, deriving even consciousness from matter itself. Since Joseph Butler (1692–1752) published *The Analogy of Religion* (1736), Tyndall noted,

> It is hardly necessary to inform you that . . . the domain of the naturalist has been immensely extended – the whole science of geology, with its astounding revelations regarding the life of the ancient earth, having been created. The rigidity of old conceptions has been relaxed, the public mind being rendered gradually tolerant of the idea that not for six thousand, nor for sixty thousand, nor for six thousand thousand thousand, but for aeons embracing untold millions of years, this earth has been the theatre of life and death. The riddle of the rocks has been read by the geologist and palaeontologist, from subcambrian depths to the deposits thickening over the sea-bottoms of to-day. And upon the leaves of that stone book are, as you know, stamped the characters, plainer and surer than those formed by the ink of history, which carry the mind back into abysses of past time compared with which the periods which satisfied Bishop Butler cease to have a visual angle.

He also urged his fellow scientists not to let theology 'intrude on the region of objective *knowledge*, over which it holds no command'; religion should be allowed to serve its proper function, as it was 'capable of being guided to noble issues in the region of *emotion*, which is its proper and elevated sphere.'[25]

Historians rallied round the scientists against the obscurantist die-hard theologians. W.E.H. Lecky (1838–1903) in Ireland and J.W. Draper (1811–82) in America published histories of the rise of rationalism and the gradual and inevitable defeat of religious blindness.[26] Andrew Dickson White (1832–1918), the president of Cornell University, gave a Phi Beta Kappa oration at Brown University which had an effect similar to Tyndall's at about the same time. He repeated his lecture at other universities, printed it in the *Popular Science Monthly*, and published it in expanded form as *The Warfare of Science* in 1876 with a preface by the atheistic Ulsterman himself. Further editions appeared, eventually adding the words *with Theology* to the title so as to leave no one in doubt where the enemy might be found.[27]

II

Evolution, or at least development, were the concepts, then, which occupied the hearts and minds of churchmen, scientists, and intellectuals alike. These principles found their way into almost every aspect of the human sciences. Even such a staunch anti-modernist as the venerable John Henry Newman could not but be affected, although there is no doubt that his musings on the subject long predated Darwin. As early as 1833, Newman published his study on the Arians of the fourth century, and broached what he regarded as the Church's 'economical method'. Newman argued that 'the exterior world, physical and historical, was but the manifestation to our senses of realities greater than itself. Nature was a parable: Scripture was an allegory: pagan literature, philosophy, and mythology, properly understood, were but a preparation for the Gospel.' Everything we thought we knew about Christianity was the product of imperfect understanding. Even the most basic principles of the Christian faith were but an economical shadow of the thing itself. This 'economical method' of the Church was a means of 'accommodation to the feelings and prejudices of the hearer, in leading him to the reception of a novel or unacceptable doctrine'. This imprecision in doctrinal matters, coupled with the perceived development of human understanding, led Newman to condemn the fourth-century Arians, heretics who relied on the 'mere private study of Holy Scripture' to create 'a systematic doctrine from the scattered notices of the truth which Scripture contains'. The Bible could not be used alone to teach the faith: the Church was the source of Christian dogma, and merely used 'Scripture in vindication of its own teaching'.[28]

Newman returned specifically to the problem of development in 1842, and the following year gave a sermon on 'The Theory of Developments in Religious Doctrine'. His text was 'But Mary kept all these things, and pondered them in her heart'. Newman argued that Mary should be 'our pattern of Faith, both in the reception and in the study of Divine Truth. She does not think it enough to accept, she dwells upon it; not enough to possess, she uses it; not enough to assent, she develops it'. When such a breakthough occurs, 'the great idea takes hold of a thousand minds by its living force and grows in them, and at length is born through them, perhaps in a long course of years, and even successive generations; so that the doctrine may rather be said to use the minds of Christians, than to be used by them.'[29]

Newman worked up these ideas into *An Essay on the Development of Christian Doctrine* (1845), which one of his most recent biographers has proclaimed as 'the book that is the theological counterpart of the *Origin of Species*, which it pre-dates by over a decade.'[30] Newman describes his work as 'an hypothesis to account for a difficulty', namely, that Christian doctrine has undergone so many changes and variations that it is apparently impossible to speak of a

continuity of doctrine since the time of the Apostles. The Protestants, he
notes, tend to give up on the idea of historical Christianity altogether and to
rely on the Bible alone. Anglicans seek a middle ground, and cleave to the
broadest and most widely accepted tenets of the faith. Newman sought to
confront the problem directly, and made much of the distinction between an
'idea' and its 'aspects'. A 'living' idea, he claimed, is one which will eventually grow into a 'body of thought'. Newman defined the process 'called the
development of an idea' as 'the germination, growth, and perfection of some
living, that is, influential truth, or apparent truth, in the minds of men during
a sufficient period.' The development of an idea 'is not like a mathematical
theorem worked out on paper, in which each successive advance is a pure
evolution from a foregoing, but it is carried on through individuals and bodies
of men; it employs their minds as instruments, and depends upon them while
it uses them.' Newman proposed no fewer than seven 'tests' which allow us
to distinguish between genuine developments as opposed to corruptions, and
devotes most of his book to providing 'illustrations' of these tools.[31]

What is extremely interesting is that even if he could not have been influenced by Darwin, the same cannot be said about biology. Looking for a way
of explaining the development of doctrine, Newman turns to an extended
natural metaphor, and develops it in characteristic purple prose:

> It is indeed sometimes said that the stream is clearest near the spring. What-
> ever use may fairly be made of this image, it does not apply to the history
> of a philosophy or sect, which, on the contrary, is more equable, and purer,
> and stronger, when its bed has become deep, and broad, and full. It neces-
> sarily rises out of an existing state of things, and, for a time, savours of the
> soil. Its vital element needs disengaging from what is foreign and tempo-
> rary, and is employed in efforts after freedom, more vigorous and hopeful
> as its years increase. Its beginnings are no measure of its capabilities, nor of
> its scope. At first, no one knows what it is, or what it is worth. It remains
> perhaps for a time quiescent: it tries, as it were, its limbs, and proves the
> ground under it, and feels its way. From time to time, it makes essays which
> fail, and are in consequence abandoned. It seems in suspense which way
> to go; it wavers, and at length strikes out in one definite direction. In time
> it enters upon strange territory; points of controversy alter their bearing;
> parties rise and fall about it; dangers and hopes appear in new relations,
> and old principles reappear under new forms; it changes with them in order
> to remain the same. In a higher world it is otherwise; but here below to
> live is to change, and to be perfect is to have changed often.[32]

It may still be a matter of debate whether his *Essay* was influenced by
evolutionary ideas, if only because the first edition was published in 1845,
and the second heavily revised version appeared in 1878. Newman's point,

after all, was that it was mankind who developed, gradually apprehending widening aspects of the Christian truth which is itself static and
unchanging.[33]

Newman's case aside, it is undeniable that the notions of development and
evolution were in the air. For one of the most interesting and perhaps unexpected results of the general acceptance of the evolutionary theory was the
emergence of Victorian anthropology and comparative religion. If there were
really men before Adam, then it was the scientist's duty to try to learn about
these primitive people. As their longevity was substantially shorter than that
of the biblical patriarchs, there was no alternative but to try to look at the
lifestyle and habits of contemporary primitive peoples and to distil from these
observations some conclusions about human life thousands of years ago. It
was no accident that this approach was applied only in the Victorian period,
since it required both the crystallization of empire and the development of
efficient seagoing transportation. Of course, the relevance of Aborigines to
Genesis was predicated on the notion that all mankind shared certain basic
common physical and mental characteristics, and to some extent on the idea
that all societies passed through roughly the same stages. It also appeared to
Victorian anthropologists demonstrably true that change on this scale was
generally for the better, and that societies could be ranked chronologically on
the basis of their complexity. Christianity's Fall of Mankind had been transformed by Darwin and his followers to the Rise of Man.[34]

This change in direction in itself had worrying implications, since it implied
that we too might have been cannibals or idol-worshippers in the distant past.
Some churchmen and their scholarly allies sought to prove that, on the contrary, societies often developed downwards, and regressed towards barbarism.
The most cogent representative of this view was archbishop of Dublin
Richard Whately (1787–1863), whose lecture in 1854 'On the Origin of
Civilisation' made the case most clearly for inevitable degeneration and the
supernatural beginnings of culture.[35] 'It is easier to sink than to rise,' he
postulated, but nevertheless it has been a tradition since ancient times 'that
the savage state was the original one, and that mankind, or some portion of
mankind, gradually raised themselves from it by the unaided exercise of their
own faculties.' This axiom, Whately pointed out, is never actually proven,
merely stated. The truth of the matter regarding savages is quite the reverse,
that 'there is no one instance recorded of any of them rising into a civilised
condition, or, indeed, rising at all, without instruction and assistance from
people already civilised.' The natives themselves recognize this, and those that
have pulled themselves out of a brute, savage condition 'always have some tradition of some foreigner, or some Being from heaven, as having first taught
them the arts of life.' Wherever one looks across the globe, 'they all agree in
one thing, in representing civilisation as having been introduced (whenever

it *has* been introduced) not from *within*, but from *without.*' One did not need
to believe in Adam and Eve to accept this fact:

> According to the present course of things, the first introducer of civilisa-
> tion among savages, is, and must be, Man in a more improved state, in the
> *beginning*, therefore, of the human race, this, since there was no *man* to effect
> it, must have been the work of *another Being*. There must have been, in
> short, something of a REVELATION made, to the first, or to some sub-
> sequent generation, of our species.

This is what logic tells us, without having recourse to religion.[36]

At the same time, we can now see that there was no conflict at all with
the Bible, for

> this miracle (for such it clearly is, being out of the present course of nature)
> is attested *independently* of Scripture, and consequently in *confirmation* of the
> Scripture-accounts, by the fact that civilised Man exists at the present day.
> Each one of us Europeans, whether Christian, Deist, or Atheist, is actually
> a portion of a standing *monument* of a former communication to mankind
> from some superhuman Being. That Man could not have *made* himself, is
> often appealed to as a proof of the agency of a divine *Creator*; and that
> mankind could not, in the first instance, have *civilised* themselves, is a proof
> of the same kind, and of precisely equal strength, of the agency of a divine
> *Instructor*.

Whately's analysis, he thought, produced conclusions which 'agree precisely
with what is recorded in the oldest book extant', the Book of Genesis. Man
is shown there 'as originally existing in a condition which, though far from
being highly civilised, was very far removed from that of savages.' There is
already a certain amount of division of labour, and humans knew about
agriculture and the domestication of animals:

> But I have been careful, as you must have observed, to avoid appealing, in
> the outset, to the Bible as an authority, because I have thought it impor-
> tant to show, independently of that authority, and from a monument actu-
> ally before our eyes, – the existence of civilised Man – that there is no
> escaping such conclusions as agree with the Bible narrative.

Not missing a chance to take aim at the book that had rocked the biblical world, Whately continued:

> There are at the present day, philosophers, so-called, some of whom make
> boastful pretensions to science, and undertake to trace the Vestiges of
> Creation; and some who assume that no miracle can ever have taken place,
> and that the idea of what they call a 'book-revelation' is an absurdity; and

these you cannot meet by an appeal to our Scriptures. But if you call upon them to show how the existing state of things can have come about *without* a miracle and without a revelation, you will find them (as I can assert from experience) greatly at a loss.

Even though there were many anthropologically inclined thinkers who had difficulty conceiving of self-propelled cultural evolution, Whately thought it 'remarkable' that none of 'these eminent men seem to have thought of the inference, though they were within one step of it, that the first beginnings of civilisation must have come from a *superhuman* instructor.' The conclusion was obvious, and Whately expressed it with characteristic clarity:

> It appears, then, that all the attempts made to assail our position have served only to furnish fresh and fresh proofs [*sic*] that it is perfectly impregnable. That some communication to Man from a Superior Being – in other words, some kind of Revelation – must at some time or other have taken place, is established, independently of all historical documents, in the Bible or elsewhere, by a standing monument which is before our eyes, the exis-tence of civilised man at this day.

In its essentials, the story of the Garden of Eden still stood, based upon the bedrock of divine revelation and human logical deduction.[37]

Diffusionism, rather than independent evolution, might then account for improvement in man's status in some areas since the Fall. This idea was given a great boost by the discovery of Assyrian and Babylonian cuneiform texts and their decipherment in the 1870s. The existence of Flood narratives among the Babylonians, and other apparent biblical parallels, led even non-believers to posit either the Babylonians or, later on, the Egyptians or even the North Arabians, as the source of much of the world's culture. Diffusionism was not completely overwhelmed by the evolutionist mode. Those travellers who reported a regression in the tribes with which they came into repeated contact seemed to lend even anthropological support to this view, as well as the almost universal myth of an earlier Golden Age.[38]

Travellers' reports and myths; ethnography and mythology: these were the two methodological tools which would be so important to Victorian anthro-pologists searching for the origins of religion. The results of their delibera-tions would have crucial effects on the status of the Bible in Britain.

Let us look first at ethnography, or that part of it which has a direct bearing on our interests here: comparative religion. This field as it came to be con-ceived in the nineteenth century was in a sense a more intellectualized version of anthropology conducted among non-Christian peoples of more complex societies. The practitioners of this revitalized discipline of comparative reli-gion looked for knowledge of the Godhead in all higher religions throughout the world, but especially in India. Not only was India quite simply more accessible both in terms of transport and politically, but it was almost part of the European experience because the Indo-European language group was becoming recognized as the ancestor of Europeans' own speech.[39]

Frederick Denison Maurice, professor and Christian Socialist, was among the best known of the men who tried to find the common ground between the great religions of the world.[40] Their banner was the 'comparative method', a term coined by Auguste Comte (1798–1857), which had already had great success in so many fields. Philology, anatomy, and zoology had all profited from its use, and it was only natural that it should be applied at some stage to the history of religions. The comparative method authorized the collection of a limitless amount of ethnographic information from a wide variety of cultures. If a psychic unity existed among mankind, as its practitioners believed, then there was nothing wrong with using ethnographic data from any part of the world. Just as Darwin posited a slow but progressive evolution of the human body, so too could the human mind be seen to develop from the primitive psyche to its modern form.

F.D. Maurice, indeed, had a number of even more disturbing things to say to those Victorians whose faith rested on the biblical text. He wondered firstly about the paternalistic attitude which Christians often took towards other religions. Before we set forth as missionaries to the so-called heathen, he suggested, we need to ask ourselves some hard questions:

> Was the gift worth bestowing? Were we really carrying truth into the distant parts of the earth when we were carrying our own faith into them? Might not the whole notion be a dream of our vanity? Might not particular soils be adapted to particular religions? and might not the effort to transplant one into another involve the necessity of mischievous forcing, and terminate in inevitable disappointment? Might not a better day be at hand, in which all religions alike should be found to have done their work of partial good, of greater evil, and when something much more comprehensive and satisfactory should supersede them? Were not thick shadows overhanging Christendom itself, which must be scattered before it could be the source of light to the world?

Maurice delivered these statements before a public audience, as one of his Boyle Lectures, and implied that the great scientist would have agreed with him.[41]

Maurice's more controversial argument was related to the nature of revelation itself, and, by implication, to the status of the Bible in his more tolerant world:

> Faith it is now admitted has been the most potent instrument of good to the world; has given to it nearly all which it can call precious. But then it

is asked, is there not ground for supposing that all the different religious systems, and not one only, may be man's constitution? Are not they manifestly adapted to peculiar times and localities and races? Is it not probable that the theology of all alike is something merely accidental, an imperfect theory about our relations to the universe, which will in due time give place to some other? Have we not reason to suppose that Christianity, instead of being, as we have been taught, a revelation, has its roots in the heart and intellects of man, as much as any other system?

Long before Durkheim, then, Maurice was claiming that society created religion, and not the other way around. With this statement he undercut not only the Christian concept of human origins, but the authoritative status of the Bible.[42]

F.D. Maurice had opened his Boyle Lectures by praising the work of 'a young German, now in London, whose knowledge of Sanskrit is profound', and who had it in mind to translate and publish all the Vedas.[43] This was Friedrich Max Müller (1823–1900), a German scholar from a distinguished intellectual family, brought to England by Baron Bunsen (the controversial biblical critic and Prussian minister to London), and whose work would put flesh on the ideological framework of comparative religion. Max Müller was engaged by the East India Company in 1847 to translate the Rig Veda, which he did from Oxford, living at first near the Press. He soon became an Oxford fixture, elected to a fellowship at All Souls; inviting Jenny Lind to sing at a party there; having Alexander Graham Bell up to his house at 7 Norham Gardens to demonstrate the telephone, the microphone, and the phonograph; and entertaining the kings of Sweden and Siam together for tea.[44] He was the favourite for the Boden chair of Sanskrit in 1860, and had the vocal support of E.B. Pusey, the Regius professor of Hebrew, and many others.[45] But his German origins and his friendship with the 'heretical' Bunsen worked against him, and it went to [Sir] Monier [Monier-]Williams (1819–99), himself a fine scholar, who would later found the Indian Institute at Oxford. Max Müller took his defeat very badly, but eventually began 'to feel that I shall do more, as I am now, than if I were in the easy-chair of Sanskrit.'[46]

Max Müller was correct in the assessment of his own prospects. In the first place, Oxford was so keen not to lose him that later they created a chair of philology especially for him, Max Müller's name being mentioned in the statute of foundation. As his wife recalled, it was this new chair 'that led him on from the Science of Language to the Sciences of Thought and Religion.'[47] When Max Müller proposed to leave his chair in 1875 and to return to Germany, all forces were mobilized to persuade him to stay, including appointing a deputy to lecture in the great man's stead.[48] More importantly, Max Müller at that time conceived the idea of publishing what would become his eternal monument in fifty volumes, *The Sacred Books of the East*. 'Apart from the interest which the Sacred Books of all religions possess in the eyes of the theologian,' he proclaimed in the prospectus for the project,

> and, more particularly, of the missionary, to whom an accurate knowledge of them is as indispensable as a knowledge of the enemy's country to a general, these works have of late assumed a new importance, as viewed in the character of ancient historical documents.[49]

It was to this need that Max Müller applied himself in his most glorious project.

The first volume of *The Sacred Books of the East translated by Various Oriental Scholars and edited by F. Max Müller* was published by the Clarendon Press in 1879. The warning to the reader was published on the very first page. 'Readers who have been led to believe', he proclaimed, that these 'are books full of primeval wisdom and religious enthusiasm, or at least of sound and simple moral teaching, will be disappointed on consulting these volumes.' They are different and varied texts from another time and another place, and the labour to understand them is prodigious. But the effort is worth making:

> To watch in the Sacred Books of the East the dawn of the religious consciousness of man, must always remain one of the most inspiring and hallowing sights in the whole history of the world; and he whose heart cannot quiver with the first quivering rays of human thought and human faith, as revealed in those ancient documents, is, in his own way, as unfit for these studies as, from another side, the man who shrinks from copying and collating ancient MSS., or toiling through volumes of tedious commentary.

Max Müller swore to tell the whole truth about these documents, even if it meant leaving untranslated 'frequent allusions to the sexual aspects of nature' found therein. 'Scholars also who have devoted their life either to the editing of the original texts or to the careful interpretation of some of the sacred books, are more inclined, after they have disinterred from a heap of rubbish some solitary fragments of pure gold, to exhibit these treasures only than to display all the refuse from which they had to extract them.'[50] This was an academic vice which Max Müller promised to avoid, but which did little to prevent him from getting involved in a public dispute with Bishop Reginald S. Copleston of Colombo (Bp. 1875–1902) and others in the Letters column of *The Times* and elsewhere regarding the charge that he was constructing a sanitized picture of Eastern religions and proclivities.[51]

From the strictly religious point of view, the work of Max Müller helped promote Indian wisdom as not at all inferior to Christian truth, and led his readers to ponder whether God indeed did not reveal Himself to different peoples in different ways at different times. But Max Müller was perhaps even more well known for his interesting theory of mythology, which brings us to the second aspect of Victorian anthropological methodology. Max Müller called his theory 'solarism', arguing that most of the gods and heroes of the Indo-European peoples began life as metaphors for the observed power of the sun. The ancient Aryans proclaimed their deep feelings towards this absolute power in stories we call 'myths' because they were unable to express themselves in straightforward philosophical discourse. The reason for this failure was linguistic: the primitive Aryan spoke a language which was deficient in abstract nouns but plentiful in active verbs, itself a symptom of the fact that primitive man tended to attribute life to inanimate objects. In time, and with concurrent linguistic development, the original meaning of these figurative and metaphorical homilies was no longer remembered or understood, although the stories themselves were preserved, as myths. In Max Müller's famous phrase, myths were therefore a 'disease of language', an artefact created by a linguistic deficiency. It was his emphasis on the primacy of language that prevented Max Müller from accepting Darwin with open arms. His wife recalled that when the two finally met in 1874 after a long correspondence, the 'conversation turning on apes as the progenitors of man, Max Müller asserted that if speech were left out of consideration, there was a fatal flaw in the line of facts. "You are a dangerous man," said Darwin, laughingly.'[52] Despite its ingenuity, Max Müller's interpretation remained a distinctly minority view, although the so-called 'Nature Mythology School' did include among its adherents such distinguished British scholars as George W. Fox the classicist and Robert Brown (1844–1912) the Semitic scholar.[53]

III

Max Müller's ruminations concerning the origin of myths derive from a much longer tradition of discussion about mythology and the origin of religion itself, which was extremely active during the Enlightenment, and which fed into nineteenth-century anthropological discussions with no sense of chronological incongruity. We need to look quickly at these thinkers' views in order to see the subject through their eyes. Montesquieu (1689–1755) argued that religion was a social utility. Edward Gibbon claimed that religion was an historical phenomenon which might be of some use to the state. The *philosophes* of the early Enlightenment tended to follow Lucretius and see religion as the product of fear, especially the fear of death. Baron d'Holbach (1723–89), the French materialist philosopher, invented the term 'anthropomorphism' to describe the transformation of human emotions into divine beings. As d'Holbach saw it, religion based on fear was destructive of human happiness, and the fear of God's wrath led to religious persecution. Fear created the gods, and organized religion came into being when a class of priests claimed knowledge, and therefore power, towards propitiating them. Eventually, a huge parasitic institution developed, preying on society at large. D'Holbach was uncompromising in his detestation of religion. Even the beneficial effects of religious belief, he argued, such as the maintenance of state and society, were at origin based on fear of death, or divine retribution in the afterlife.[54]

Enlightenment thinkers also pondered the essence of primitive mentality and in large measure set the terms for the Victorian anthropologists. It was axiomatic that primitive people had no capacity for abstract ideas, a view which held implacable sway until Lévi-Strauss. John Locke argued that the origin of idol worship (including the veneration of saints) derived from the tendency of common people to see everything in concrete terms. David Hume thought that most of mankind could not maintain themselves at the abstract level of monotheism and therefore had a tendency to backslide to a polytheistic system where each god would have control over a specific element of nature. Charles François Dupuis (1742–1809), who played a key role in the first part of the French Revolution, gave a more specific explanation in the same vein, arguing that religion was a degenerate form of scientific knowledge. The common people were unable to remain at the high level of abstraction achieved by the ancient philosophers, especially the Egyptians, and regressed to worshipping the symbols of the ideas they could no longer understand.[55]

But of course it was Giambattista Vico who changed European perceptions of primitive man, although despite being revived by Jules Michelet (1798–1874) in the nineteenth century, his direct influence on the Victorian anthropologists is uncertain. Vico's *New Science*, revised in a third edition in the year of his death, presented a new and interesting view of how primitive people think, especially with regard to religion, which Vico considered as the first of the three *principi* which are the basis of human society, the other two being marriage and burial. Like others of his time, Vico thought that the origin of religion was fear, specifically the fear of thunder, the source of which early man called Jove. This first name was the product not of reasoning but of *fantasia*, an act of imagination. The figure of Jove, found in every nation, was a *universale fantastico*, an imaginative universal.

Vico proclaimed that 'the first peoples were poets', and that this fact was the 'master key' of his new science. By this he meant that the language of primitive man was more concrete and limited in vocabulary, and therefore more prone to metaphoric and poetic expression. Poetry was older than prose. The heroes of mythology were 'poetic characters', that is, they were metaphors, expressing popular abstract ideas in concrete form. Myths were not simply stories, but were 'histories of customs', specific illustrations of the 'poetic logic' of primitive man. Vico insisted that the primitive mind is the same even in different cultures, which would explain the similarities in mythical themes. He also claimed that all nations have a common nature because they begin with the experience of thunder/Jove, and all go through the same course (*corso*) of development in three ages. In each of these phases, gods, heroes, and humans are respectively the focus of attention, the last phase being a decline, after which the *corso* comes to an end and the civilization falls, only to be re-established by a *ricorso* which repeats the entire experience all over again. Vico believed that the universal nature of his explanation provided the evidence of the working of providence in history.

By positing that all nations have a common pattern of genesis and development, Vico had no need to apply the diffusionist argument at all, since he did not have to argue that all of civilization emanated from a single source. Most importantly, it was Vico who virtually created the notion of a primitive mentality, challenging the Renaissance assumption that human nature was the same everywhere and at all times. His insistence that the primitive mind was characterized by a 'poetic mode of thought' and was in any case quite different from our own way of thinking makes him a clear forerunner of Victorian anthropological views.[56]

Most of these views of religion from the period of the early Enlightenment were characteristically negative about the beneficial effects of divine worship. They saw religion at best as an attempt by primitive people to understand their world, and at worst as a concerted fraud which exploited confusion and fear. Vico was somewhat more positive, but the *philosophe* who really gave dignity to primitive man was Jean Jacques Rousseau (1712–78). The key text was *Émile, ou traité de l'éducation*, which appeared in 1762, and the central religious passage was the confession of the vicar of Savoy. Religion was presented as the product of the love of God rather than the fear of Him. What was needed was a religion of the heart, unfettered by institutional forms. This sort of pure worship was preserved among the uneducated peasants, Rousseau argued, and even primitive man was closer to the divine than his civilized counterparts. Mythology should therefore be seen as a code to be broken, a testimony to the time when humanity was nearest to God. Rousseau's religion of the heart was taken over by the German Romantics, especially Johann Gottfried von Herder (1744–1803). He saw the birth of a people's religion as the most creative moment in the development of a *Volk*, the driving force of a national identity.

Victorian anthropology, then, had to deal with many theoretical ghosts when approaching questions of religion and mythology. While it is true that new data were converging at a fast rate, everywhere from Australia to Babylonia and onwards to Africa and peasant Europe, these problems could hardly be dealt with in isolation, and the *philosophes* of the Enlightenment were often the silent partners of nineteenth-century anthropological discussion.

IV

Ethnography and mythology were the methods used by Victorian anthropologists in trying to understand the origin and nature of religion, and they drew on both the negative Enlightenment understanding and the more positive Romantic view of religion. The 'solarism' of Max Müller was more than a little reminiscent of Vico's understanding of the primitive mind, although it is not clear that a chain of influence can be demonstrated. Max Müller, however, was the target of severe attack, especially by Andrew Lang (1844–1912), the Scottish polymath. Lang objected that the same myths which Max Müller had observed in the Indo-European peoples also appeared among groups outside the Aryan sphere of influence, primitive people who may or may not have had a requisite number of abstract nouns in their quiver. In any case, Lang objected, the solarists never seem to be able to agree on what exactly the underlying fact of the various myths actually was:

> Again, the most illustrious etymologists differ absolutely about the true sense of the names. Kuhn sees fire everywhere, and fire-myths; Mr. Müller sees dawn and dawn-myths; Schwartz sees storm and storm-myths, and so on. As the orthodox teachers are thus at variance, so that there is no safety in orthodoxy, we may attempt to use our heterodox method.

Instead, Lang suggested that we should see the myths of primitive people as growing out of a certain set of material, social, and psychological conditions. As these were often held in common by primitive peoples living at the same level of existence, it is no wonder that similar stories evolved.[57]

Yet despite the very effective attacks by Lang and others, men like Max Müller and the Victorian ethnologists and scholars of other religions and cultures had stated a very important principle regarding the Bible and other received religious texts and truths. Max Müller insisted, admittedly in a private letter to his wife, 'that the Old Testament is a genuine old book, full of all the contradictions and impossibilities which we have a right to expect in old books, but which we seldom see in books written on purpose.'[58] More expansively, in a letter to the duke of Argyll, he explained that

> I look upon the account of Creation as given in Genesis as simply historical, as showing the highest expression that could be given by the Jews at that early time to their conception of the beginning of the world. We have learnt, certainly since Kant, that the knowledge of beginnings is denied to

us, that all we can do is to grope back a little way, and then to trust. I think I have a right to accept a special beginning of man, because I cannot account for what he is, if I look upon him as the product of anything else known to me.[59]

Max Müller had created for himself a limbo world between the older scepticism towards the inerrancy of Scripture, and the more modern anthropology which would actively seek to find a replacement for Adam and Eve.

But the full flowering of evolutionary anthropology did not come until the work of [Sir] Edward Burnett Tylor (1832–1917). His celebrated book on *Primitive Culture* (1871) is often regarded as the founding document of modern British anthropology, a sentiment strengthened by the fact that Tylor became the first professor of anthropology at Oxford (1896–1909). Tylor also accepted the view that there was a fundamental unity to mankind, making the similarities between cultures far greater than the differences: 'surveyed in a broad view, the character and habit of mankind at once display that similarity and consistency of phenomena which led the Italian proverb-maker to declare that "all the world is one country," "tutto il mondo è paese"'. This axiom in turn led Tylor to argue that there was an organic law of development and progress in human institutions uniform throughout the world, following the evolutionary pattern of the simple to the more complex.[60]

Tylor found it difficult to understand how anyone could think otherwise. Nevertheless, he admitted,

> The idea of the original condition of man being one of more or less high culture, must have a certain prominence given to it on account of its considerable hold on public opinion. As to definite evidence, however, it does not seem to have any ethnological basis whatever. Indeed, I scarcely think that a stronger counter-persuasion could be used on an intelligent student inclined to the ordinary degeneration theory than to induce him to examine critically and impartially the arguments of the advocates of his own side.

Tylor was well aware, however, that this entire issue spread far beyond the bounds of mere anthropological speculation, and knew 'that the grounds on which this theory has been held have generally been rather theological than ethnological.' Even so, Tylor pointed out, biblical criticism had moved on during the past century, especially with regard to the question of Adam and Eve and the Garden of Eden, and 'it must be remembered that a large proportion of modern theologians are far from accepting such a dogma.' The whole idea of attempting 'to ground scientific opinion upon a basis of revelation' was in Tylor's view 'objectionable'. Indeed, he thought it 'inexcusable if students who have seen in Astronomy and Geology the unhappy results of attempting to base science on religion, should countenance a similar attempt in Ethnology.'[61]

Tylor reserved special attention to Archbishop Richard Whately of Dublin, who had been a key champion of the 'degeneration theory'. Whately had asserted that the creation of mankind at a stage above the barbarous was due to divine revelation. Yet, as Tylor makes clear, even if we accept the principle that the origin of civilization is divine, we need not assume that this first civilization was at a high level: 'Its advocates are free to choose their starting-point of culture above, at, or below the savage condition, as may on the evidence seem to them most reasonable.' Tylor traces the degenerist position back to a misreading of the *Römische Geschichte* (1811–32) by Barthold Georg Niebuhr, in which it is stated that 'no single example can be brought forward of an actually savage people having independently become civilized'. Whately understood this remark to mean that civilization must have begun at a high level through divine intervention and that savages are degenerated civilized man. Tylor argued that there are also no examples of a civilized people falling independently into a savage state, and that even if there were, it would not negate the opposite phenomenon. Furthermore, degeneration probably is a greater factor in lower cultures than in higher ones – the Iroquois, for example, made better cabins in the century before Tylor. Such degeneration as does exist, he reasoned, is 'by no means indeed the primary cause of the existence of barbarism and savagery in the world, but a secondary action largely and deeply affecting the general development of civilization.' Looking at the process in its widest sense, Tylor argued, it 'may perhaps give no unfair idea to compare degeneration of culture, both in its kind of operation and in its immense extent, to denudation in the geological history of the earth'.[62]

In brief, Tylor completely rejected one of the most fundamental myths of European civilization, that of an Edenic Golden Age. Not only was such a past logically unlikely, but it went against the very grain of human behaviour. As Tylor put it in characteristically purplish prose,

> We may fancy ourselves looking on Civilization, as in personal figure she traverses the world; we see her lingering or resting by the way, and often deviating into paths that bring her toiling back to where she had passed by long ago; but, direct or devious, her path lies forward, and if now and then she tries a few backward steps, her walk soon falls into a helpless stumbling. It is not according to her nature, her feet were not made to plant uncertain steps behind her, for both in her forward view and in her onward gait she is of truly human type.[63]

Human history, in sum, was the story of progress rather than degeneration.

Almost more interesting than Tylor's general theory was the way in which he proved it. What he did was to collect data regarding primitive peoples, viewing them as living fossils, preserving isolated bits from the common development of mankind. Since mankind was a unity, and since the development of human nature was the same everywhere, Tylor was able to string together information and examples from widely distant parts of the globe. The theoretical basis of his method was his 'doctrine of survivals'. By 'survivals', Tylor meant the 'processes, customs, opinions, and so forth, which have been carried on by force of habit into a new state of society different from that in which they had their original home, and they thus remain as proofs and examples of an older condition of culture out of which a newer has been evolved.' They survived in the first place because of social or religious conservatism, and although they were no longer functional, they could tell us something about mankind in its earlier stages of development. An example in speech would be the 'k' in the word 'knight', which once had a speech function but now remained as a mere silent but observable trace. Furthermore, Tylor writes, 'it is quite a usual thing in the world for a game to outlive the serious practice of which it is an imitation. The bow and arrow is a conspicuous instance.'[64]

In his general book on *Anthropology* (1881), Tylor expanded his views on myth and religion, arguing that both forms came from a common source: the primitive habit of animating nature. The 'savage philosopher', as Tylor called him, knows that the 'anima', the soul, exists, because the dead appear to him in visions and dreams. It was a natural step to extend the privilege of possessing an 'anima' to non-human objects such as animals, plants, and stones. Tylor invented the term 'animism' to describe this cultural phenomenon, and called for the study of myths to see what we could learn about mankind's earliest history.[65]

Tylor's emphasis on primitive survivals had a crucial effect in the history of Victorian anthropology, not the least because he helped turn armchair ethnographers into encyclopaedists of culture. One of the most striking turns of mind before Tylor is how often Victorians made far-reaching pronouncements on subjects as complex and challenging as the origins of culture and religion. Johann Wilhelm Mannhardt (1831–80), the German folklorist, called on his colleagues to stop theorizing and do more fieldwork among contemporary European peasants. They retained beliefs, he insisted, that preserve traces of Aryan ideas crystallized over four millennia earlier. Mannhardt promoted his 'law of similarity', positing that when customs are similar, albeit in different societies, we may assume that the motives in performing the customs are also similar. Contemporary ethnographic reports, therefore, provided the anthropologist with a window through which to view early man.

The Victorian anthropologists were in agreement that their theories might be applied to all cultures at all times. It was inevitable that at some point the culture under discussion would be ancient Israel. Folklore, the more benign face of anthropology, was the first to come forward. The term 'folklore' seems to have been coined in 1846 by William John Thoms (1803–85) the British antiquary and clerk to the House of Lords, although the first field collection of local myths and legends may have been Thomas Croker's (1798–1854) study of southern Ireland over twenty years before.[66] But of course it was the brothers Grimm, Jacob (1785–1863) and Wilhelm (1786–1859), whose collection of *Kinder- und Hausmärchen* (1812–19) inaugurated the field of folklore in Germany, and in turn influenced their colleague at Göttingen, Heinrich Ewald (1803–75), the great scholar of the Old Testament. Ewald was very impressed with the Grimms' assertion that myths were the basic form of folk tradition, and that they were originally stories about gods. The Grimms also posited that the saga was an expression of popular beliefs and fears, containing supernatural elements which drew on the world of myth. In his history of ancient Israel, Ewald made use of the notion that human memory preserves through saga and myth certain ancient events and forms them into larger units. More recent memories tended to displace older ones, and important figures were more likely to become magnets for narratives which originally had no connection with them. While the monotheism of the Old Testament meant that the mythical element was suppressed, Ewald nonetheless suggested that the Bible itself may have been influenced by the very same folklore processes which had been observed at work in the European peasantry of his own time.[67] With Heinrich Ewald, biblical anthropology was born, and Darwin came to Deuteronomy.[68]

V

With the benefit of hindsight, all of this looks like the prehistory of *The Golden Bough*. Certainly James Frazer's eccentric masterpiece is part of the same tradition, one in which the Bible would be of critical importance. This was due in large measure to the contribution of Frazer's friend and mentor, William Robertson Smith (1846–94). Born in Aberdeenshire, Smith was the son of a schoolmaster ordained late into the conservative Free Church of Scotland. He studied at Aberdeen University, and then New College, Edinburgh, where he served as research assistant to the physics professor along with fellow student Robert Louis Stevenson. Smith continued his work with Andrew Bruce Davidson (1831–1902), and then did a stint in Germany, absorbing the latest trends in biblical scholarship and theology. His reward came with the professorship of Hebrew and Old Testament at the Free Church College in Aberdeen. Other appointments included positions on the editorial committees of the splendid ninth edition of the *Encyclopaedia Britannica* and the Revised Version of the Bible.[69]

It was when working for the *Britannica* that Smith first got into trouble, and in a way that would not only change his life but result in Frazer's inspiration and increased use of anthropology in biblical scholarship. The *Encyclopaedia Britannica* appeared volume by volume in alphabetical order, and Smith was commissioned to write some of the early articles, including 'Angel' and, fatefully, 'Bible'. Certainly today these articles seem not only uncontroversial but, more importantly, unprovocative. But to the Free Church of Scotland, they came as something of a bombshell. Most galling, perhaps, was Smith's adoption of an evolutionary stance with regard to the Holy Book itself:

> A just insight into the work of the prophetic party in Israel was long rendered difficult by traditional prejudices. On the one hand the predictive element in prophecy received undue prominence, and withdrew attention from the influence of the prophets on the religious life of their own time; while, on the other hand, it was assumed, in accordance with Jewish notions, that all the ordinances, and almost, if not quite, all the doctrines of the Jewish church in the post-canonical period, existed from the earliest days of the theocracy. The prophets, therefore, were conceived partly as inspired preachers of old truths, partly as predicting future events, but not as leaders of a great development, in which the religious ordinances as well as the religious beliefs of the Old Covenant advanced from a relatively crude and imperfect to a relatively mature and adequate form.[70]

The result of such tentative German-style criticism was a slow-motion scandal. Charges were brought against Smith in 1878, the case was heard two years later, and in 1881 he was removed from his chair. Smith's scholarly standing was sufficient for him to obtain the appointment in 1883 as Lord Almoner Reader in Arabic at Cambridge, including a fellowship at Trinity College. In 1885 he was made a fellow of Christ's College, which remained his home until his death nine years later.

Freed from the Free Church, Smith was now able to produce his most innovative and interesting work. In 1881, he published a book on the Old Testament in which he argued that revelation itself was gradual and progressive. God accommodated Himself to the social and psychological situation of each generation. Making his point most provocatively, Smith proclaimed that

> It is our duty as Protestants to interpret Scripture historically. The Bible itself has a history. It was not written at one time, or by a single pen. It comprises a number of books and pieces given to the Church by many instrumentalities and at various times. It is our business to separate them one by one, and to comprehend each piece in the sense which it had for

tho first writer, and its relation to the needs of God's people at the time when it was written. In proportion as we succeed in this task, the mind of the Revealer in each of His many communications with mankind will become clear to us.

Spinoza had finally come to Scotland. Kennicott had as well, for Smith was clear that we should apply the normal methods of textual criticism to the Scriptures, just as we would to any ancient text, for 'the transmission of the Bible is not due to a continued miracle, but to a watchful Providence ruling the ordinary means by which ancient books have all been handed down.' Any analysis of a particular book of the Old Testament, then, must begin with the historical background in order to elucidate the life and times of the writer and his milieu.[71]

Once at Cambridge, Smith continued his work with a study of ancient kinship and marriage, preoccupied, like others, with the idea that originally kinship had been determined by the female line.[72] The appearance of the work of Julius Wellhausen (1844–1918) in English in 1885 was a great milestone in biblical criticism, and it was William Robertson Smith who wrote the introduction. Amplifying the so-called controversial views of his original encyclopaedia article, Smith proclaimed that Wellhausen provided the key to understanding the Old Testament as a whole, for his argument was that it was untrue that Israel had the entire biblical law from the time of Moses. The law was an institution that grew slowly, and was transformed by the prophets into something very different to what the Children of Israel understood in the desert.[73] As Smith would later describe this process,

> The religious constitution of Israel, then, as laid down by Moses and con-solidated in the institution of the kingship, was not the entirely unique thing that it is frequently supposed to be. Indeed, if Moses had brought in a whole system of new and utterly revolutionary ideas he could not have carried the people with him to any practical effect.[74]

Far from being the first step on the slippery slope towards atheism, Smith argued, Wellhausen in effect demonstrated the hand of providence inexorably leading the Jews to the Christian Gospel.

But it was *Lectures on the Religion of the Semites* (1889) which assured Smith lasting fame and authority. For our purposes, the significance of this book is that in it Smith was applying the most advanced principles of Victorian anthropology to the ancient society of the Bible. Despite the great fascination his contemporaries had with India and Australia, what interested Smith was the sociology of the people who provided the foundation of Christianity. Some of the main concepts of his book are already familiar to us. First and foremost was the axiomatic belief in the evolutionary progress of society.

We hardly need to invoke Darwin and his geological predecessors here since Smith himself uses such an analogy:

> The record of the religious thought of mankind, as it is embodied in religious institutions, resembles the geological record of the history of the earth's crust; the new and the old are preserved side by side, or rather layer upon layer.[75]

This evolutionary process could be discovered to the researcher, Smith wrote, by the use of the comparative method, on the assumption that there was a psychic unity to man, and that all societies were subject to similar principles of development:

> This account of the position of religion in the social system holds good, I believe, for all parts and races of the ancient world in the earlier stages of their history. The causes of so remarkable a uniformity lie hidden in the mists of prehistoric time, but must plainly have been of a general kind, operating on all parts of mankind without distinction of race and local environment; for in every region of the world, as soon as we find a nation or tribe emerging from prehistoric darkness into the light of authentic history, we find also that its religion conforms to the general type which has just been indicated. As time rolls on and society advances, modifications take place. In religion as in other matters the transition from the antique to the modern type of life is not sudden and unprepared, but is gradually led up to by a continuous disintegration of the old structure of society, accompanied by the growth of new ideas and institutions.[76]

The job of the anthropological biblical critic, Smith thought, was to try to isolate by means of the comparative method the most basic components of society.

In these beliefs, Smith was not alone, but they were not universally accepted. Some scholars thought that blind use of the comparative method simply went against common sense. Archibald Henry Sayce (1845–1933) the Oxford Assyriologist, for example, proclaimed:

> I must enter a protest against the assumption that what holds good of Kaffirs or Australians held good also of the primitive Semite. The students of language have at last learnt that what is applicable to one family of speech is not necessarily applicable to another, and it would be well if the anthropologist would learn the same lesson.[77]

So too did the great Orientalist Theodor Nöldeke (1836–1930) object to the use of outlandish ethnographic data and their application to ancient Arabia: 'We must not idealize these Arabs,' he warned, 'but Robertson Smith is too inclined to regard them as utter barbarians and too readily applies to them analogies from North American Indians and aboriginal Australians.'[78] Never-theless, despite these nay-sayers, the use of disparate information had a certain attractive logic to it, and was generally accepted.

What, then, was the basic component of biblical society, according to Robertson Smith? In a word, it was sacrifice. More than half of his *Lectures on the Religion of the Semites* is about sacrifice, emphasizing the social and ritualistic aspects of the rite over questions of belief and theology. Indeed, Smith insisted that religion was primarily a social activity, which meant that the conscious intentions of the believer were relatively unimportant. Sacrifice lay at the heart of Semitic religion: it was an act of communion between a social group and a supernatural being with whom that group hoped to reaf-firm its union. In its most primitive form, sacrifice was the religious feast at which the group killed and ate the totemic animal from which they thought themselves descended. The most important relationship was not that of the individual to his or her god, but that of 'all the members of a community to a power that has the good of the community at heart, and protects its law and moral order'. There was a 'solidarity of the gods and their worshippers as part of one organic society'. As society developed, so did religious and political institutions, and new gods appeared on the scene as well: 'a society and kinship of many gods began to be formed, on the model of the alliance or fusion of their respective worshippers'. The underlying meaning of this sociological evolution was that church organization and political organization were two aspects of the same thing.[79]

Certainly, by this point, both contemporary and modern readers may detect the influence of the work of Numa Denis Fustel de Coulanges (1830–89), whose study of *La Cité antique* (1864) would also mould the thought of his pupil Émile Durkheim (1858–1917). Fustel de Coulanges was convinced that the root of society was to be found in religion: 'The religious idea was, among the ancients, the inspiring breath and organizer of society', he wrote. 'Social laws were the work of the gods; but those gods, so powerful and beneficent, were nothing else than the beliefs of men'. Fustel, unlike Robertson Smith, thought that earliest society was based on the patriarchal family, but that family was formed not by nature but by religion. This in essence was due to the fact that among primitive peoples, ancestor worship and the survival of the soul after death were strong beliefs. As a result, groups of people would coalesce around the worship of a common ancestor. In time, he mused, these groups would become tribes, and eventually these tribes would evolve into cities. Fustel used evidence from both Greek and Roman times, but also wove together information from Africa and North America, in true nineteenth-century anthropological fashion.[80]

In many ways, Robertson Smith went even further. He argued that with the domestication of animals, the wild totemic animal was replaced with the worship of livestock. Agriculture became sedentary rather than nomadic; the joyful, totemic, communion sacrifice became replaced with a solemn sacrifice of tribute and expiation; the cohesive democratic social group evolved into a class society dominated by a priestly cult. At the same time, the original family or kin unit became part of a larger social structure centring around a town or a cult site. These important changes were part of the result of increased numbers and higher density of population. People allowed the priests to sacrifice for them instead of doing it themselves. What had been communion now became a gift or a tribute. The gods themselves became alienated from men, less like family and more like kings. Robertson Smith was not entirely against these developments, since as he was a believing and committed Christian, comparisons with the Eucharist were never far behind; but it is striking that he was able to apply contemporary anthropological views to such a thorny issue in his own religious tradition.[81]

Robertson Smith consistently placed the emphasis on what people do rather than what they claim to believe. This principle, applied to ancient Semitic and biblical society, led him to his famous postulation that ritual precedes myth. Social action comes before belief; the actual rite predates the religious explanation. Robertson Smith's argument was that 'antique religions had for the most part no creed; they consisted entirely of institutions and practices'. The first expression of religious ideas came in ritual acts rather than words. Therefore, when looking at Semitic religion we should concentrate on their totemic and sacrificial ritual, and see how it related to social conformity, paying less attention to traditional theological questions and the entire issue of religious creeds. Instead, he insisted, we should realize that the true relation is the other way around: myths offer an explanation of what the community is already doing in its rituals, and the myths are not binding in a Christian doctrinal sense on the worshippers themselves.

This postulate could be demonstrated quite simply by noting that any tribesman, Semitic or otherwise, would not be bothered by varying interpretations of the same rite, but would be very disturbed if the ritual itself was altered in form or mode of execution. Belief was not compulsory: 'What was obligatory or meritorious was the exact performance of certain sacred acts prescribed by religious tradition.' Indeed, man is first and foremost an actor: he does something to make the gods help him. He sings, dances, or acts out what he wants the gods to do. The mythic explanation of the ritual arises when for some reason the ritual falls into disuse, due to religious reform, or simple forgetting or misunderstanding with time. The words, which had been a mere handmaiden of sacred action, now take on an independent life of their own. The libretto becomes the entire opera. Indeed, Robertson Smith explained,

> So far as myths consist of explanations of ritual, their value is altogether
> secondary, and it may be affirmed with confidence that in almost every
> case the myth was derived from the ritual, and not the ritual from the
> myth; for the ritual was fixed and the myth was variable, the ritual was
> obligatory and faith in the myth was at the discretion of the worshipper.

The proper way to understand a myth is to examine the ritual it attempts to
explain or, if the ritual no longer survives, to use the myth to reconstruct the
ritual, especially as myths are often attempts to rationalize rituals which are
still practised but no longer understood.

In brief, then, Robertson Smith was arguing that religious institutions are
older than religious beliefs. The effect of this postulate was of immense importance, not only for anthropology, but also for the study of religion. Robertson Smith directed scholarly attention to behaviour rather than belief. He
wanted to know how rituals yielded results for the social group as a whole,
pushing aside the question of what the participants in the rituals actually
thought they were doing. The 'real' purpose of the rituals might be different
from what the believers themselves thought. The road to Durkheim's 'manifest' and 'latent' functions of religion was thus already well established.

The third aspect of Robertson Smith's thought which is of interest to us
here is his theory of totemism. This is a subject which has become a chestnut in anthropological studies, but in his day it was new and exciting. In
essence, totemism refers to the symbolization of individuals or social groups
using particular images, often plants or animals, and the resulting relationship
of identity and power with those images. According to Robertson Smith,
totemism is a phase of religious belief through which all societies pass, including ancient Israel. He was strongly influenced here by the work of his friend
John Ferguson McLennan (1827–81), who had argued that the very earliest
forms of society consisted of social units of common blood but divided
into different groups, each of which identified itself with a totem animal.[82]
Interestingly, Robertson Smith was convinced that early humans were
totemic in religious practice and never polytheistic, much less monotheistic
as had often been claimed. In general, he thought that primitive peoples were
social rather than individualistic in religious inclination. The development of
a religious life associated with the individual was a characteristic of a higher
form of spiritual consciousness.

In another work, Robertson Smith argued that the prophets of Israel helped
the nation evolve from an understanding of God as a local *baal*, to the point
where they saw Him as a personal and individual God, the basis of morality,
and so on:

> But while the religion of Jehovah had thus acquired a fixed national char-
> acter, it would be a great mistake to suppose that it already presented itself

to the mass of the people, as it did to the later Jews, as something altogether dissimilar in principle and in details from the religions of the surrounding nations. The Jews after the exile not only had a separate religion, but a religion which made them a separate nation, distinct from the Gentiles in all their habits of life and thought. In old Israel it was not so. The possession of a national God, to whom the nation owed homage, and in whose name kings reigned and judges administered justice, was not in itself a thing peculiar to Israel. A national religion and sacred laws are part of the constitution of every ancient state, and among the nations most nearly akin to the Hebrews these ideas took a shape which, so far as mere externals were concerned, bore a close family likeness to the religion of Jehovah.

Indeed, he writes, 'but for the continued word of revelation in the mouths of the prophets, Israel's religion might very well have permanently remained on this level, and so have perished with the fall of the Hebrew state.'[83] The prophets of Israel were ahead of the society in which they lived, but not too far ahead.

The fourth and last useful element of Robertson Smith's book is his general view on the relationship between religion and society, some of which has already been discussed. As he saw it, what was crucial was the social basis of belief and values:

A man did not choose his religion or frame it for himself; it came to him as part of the general scheme of social obligations and ordinances laid upon him, as a matter of course, by his position in the family and in the nation ... Religion did not exist for the saving of souls but for the preservation and welfare of society, and in all that was necessary to this end every man had to take his part, or break with the domestic and political community to which he belonged.[84]

The worship of supernatural beings is the central process in the formation of belief. Group worship and social action reinforced social bonds by emphasizing those which held that group together. Such worship also releases tensions and contributes to the unity of the group. This unity, in turn, is the central foundation of religion. Looking at it another way, the belief in God, the idea of God Himself, grows out of a political system.[85]

Robertson Smith occupies a rather interesting place both in the historiography of Victorian anthropology, and in the development of modern biblical criticism. Despite his unwavering Christian faith, he was uncompromising about the application of new anthropological and historical techniques to the biblical text and narrative. 'The records of our religion are historical documents,' he asserted, 'and they claim the same treatment which has been so fruitfully applied to the other sources of ancient history. They claim it all the more because the supreme religious significance of this history gives it an interest to which no other part of ancient history can pretend.' The message of God is preserved in the Bible, but like other ancient texts it has become misunderstood and encrusted with debris:

> It is far easier for the English reader to gain a just view of the present state of inquiry in Greek or Roman history and literature than to learn what modern scholarship has done for the history and literature of the Hebrews. And yet it is manifestly absurd to think that the very best use of the Bible can be made by those who read it for the nourishment of their religious life, so long as the history of the revelation which it contains is imperfectly understood.

Robertson Smith himself had suffered from British obscurantism in biblical criticism, and delivered an uncomprising denunciation of such tendencies of thought:

> The timidity which shrinks from this frankness, lest the untrained student may make a wrong use of the knowledge put into his hands, is wholly out of place in Protestant Churches, and in modern society, which refuses to admit the legitimacy of esoteric teaching.[86]

It remained for Robertson Smith's atheistic protégé to take the next step.

VI

James George Frazer (1854–1941), like Robertson Smith, came from a Free Church of Scotland background. Frazer was an undergraduate at Trinity College, Cambridge, and once he entered he never left, although his fellowship had to be renewed three times until it was confirmed for life at the age of forty-five. It was his great friend James Ward (1843–1925), the professor of moral philosophy and logic who suggested to Frazer that he might enjoy E.B. Tylor's *Primitive Culture*. It was a book that changed his life. Frazer was thus already interested in anthropology when he met Robertson Smith at some point during the two years that he spent at Trinity before moving on to Christ's College.[87] In the preface to the first edition of *Lectures on the Religion of the Semites*, Smith thanks his new friend quite lavishly:

> In analysing the origin of ritual institutions, I have often had occasion to consult analogies in the usages of early peoples beyond the Semitic field. In this part of the work I have had invaluable assistance from my friend, Mr. J.G. Frazer, who has given me free access to his unpublished

collections on the superstitions and religious observances of primitive nations in all parts of the globe. I have sometimes referred to him by name, in the course of the book, but these references convey but an imperfect idea of my obligations to his learning and intimate familiarity with primitive habits of thought.

In the second edition, Robertson Smith thanked Frazer for correcting the proofs.[88]

Robertson Smith influenced Frazer's life work in yet another practical way. As we have seen, Smith was one of the chief editors of the celebrated ninth edition of the *Encyclopaedia Britannica*, which was being published in alphabetical order during those years. Smith met Frazer by the time they had reached the letter 'T', a fateful letter in the anthropologist's dictionary. Brushing aside Frazer's objections that he really didn't know anything about the subject, Smith assigned him the articles on 'Taboo' and 'Totemism'. The first article would be the embyronic draft of *The Golden Bough*; the second for his two works on totemism, the second of which would inspire Freud to make his own contribution to the field.[89] Of the two articles, the one on taboo is the more enlightening, since it gives a sense of how Frazer would use ethnographic information from a wide variety of sources, mixing in Old Testament examples with classical data and reports from the Australian outback. Frazer expresses himself in the type of prose that made him widely read:

> The original character of the taboo must be looked for not in its civil but in its religious element. It was not the creation of a legislator but the gradual outgrowth of animistic beliefs, to which the ambition and avarice of chiefs and priests afterwards gave an artificial extension. But in serving the cause of avarice and ambition it subserved the progress of civilization, by fostering conceptions of the rights of property and the sanctity of the marriage tie, – conceptions which in time grew strong enough to stand by themselves and to fling away the crutch of superstition which in earlier days had been their sole support. For we shall scarcely err in believing that even in advanced societies the moral sentiments, in so far as they are merely sentiments and are not based on an induction from experience, derive much of their force from an original system of taboo. Thus on the taboo were grafted the golden fruits of law and morality, while the parent stem dwindled slowly into the sour crabs and empty husks of popular superstition on which the swine of modern society are still content to feed.

We can also see the influence of his anthropological forebears, and his stress on the evolutionary use of what is in essense a superstitious practice.

But it was Frazer's *The Golden Bough* that had the greatest impact on so many aspects of European intellectual life. Robertson Smith died in 1894, and by then Frazer had rejected his mentor's emphasis on religion as a social institution in which the group was the prime unit. Frazer had come to see religion as more of a philosophical system devised by individuals and based on supernatural sanctions. This system would endure until it was replaced by a better one, science. Robertson Smith had been content to draw his material only from the world of the Semites; Frazer cast his net much wider, but everything he said was meant to apply to the biblical peoples as well. It was most likely a book by Ernest Renan (1823 92) about Nemi that pointed Frazer towards the motif of the dying god, but he refrained from acknowledging this debt because Robertson Smith thought the Frenchman was a fake, and might have therefore refused the dedication of *The Golden Bough*.[90]

The theme of *The Golden Bough* is not directly relevant to biblical studies, but its echo would be heard everywhere. In brief, Frazer's argument was that the priest-king at Nemi, who ruled until he was killed by a usurper, was in effect the incarnation of the tree-spirit, that is, a man who claimed to be a god and could control nature. This king must always be at the height of his powers, since the implication otherwise was that natural forces were winding down. Frazer brought examples from around the world to show that survivals of these practices still exist in the experience of primitive peoples and contemporary peasants. He linked Nemi with the myth of Balder, including the plucking of the mistletoe by Loki and the death of Balder by burning. This in turn led him to look at mistletoe worship and midsummer bonfires. Frazer concluded that Balder's life was lodged in the mistletoe and this is why he could be killed only by that plant. He interpreted Virgil's golden bough in the sixth book of the *Aeneid* as being the mistletoe as well (which Virgil does not say), which led him to the conclusion that the priest at Nemi was the king of the wood, and personified the oak tree on which the golden bough grew. According to the story, the king could be killed only by a runaway slave who would break off the golden bough as a preliminary part of fighting the priest-king. The book itself in its many editions is a long and very often rambling discussion of the ramifications of this story, through much of which Nemi, Balder, and the Golden Bough are completely lost from sight. But Frazer's methodology and his remarks on religion and science would become a permanent part of Western consciousness.

This pattern was especially clear in the second edition of *The Golden Bough*, published in 1900. The original subtitle of the book, 'A Study in Comparative Religion', was changed to read, 'A Study in Magic and Religion'. Frazer had by now come to see mankind as going through definite stages: 'an Age of Religion has thus everywhere, as I venture to surmise, been preceded by an Age of Magic'. Primitive man first tries to compel nature, and when that fails, he begs. This, in turn, is followed by a more efficient kind of compulsion, called science. The discussion of magic is extremely interesting, and according to his recent biographer is 'Frazer's single most important contribution to the anthropology of religion.'[91]

The Old Testament was merely another source of ethnographic data, and Frazer was not above making great leaps of logic on the basis of little hard exegetic evidence. His discussion of the Book of Esther and the Jewish holiday of Purim, for example, is stunning in its wrong-headedness. According to Frazer, the story is not that of Jews escaping mass murder in Persia, but yet another Middle Eastern holiday of misrule, of Babylonian origin, based on agricultural magic, and in its original form involving human sacrifice. Purim began as the rite which ratified the gods' approval for a king's rule for another year, a ritual which originally had involved ritual murder, but which at some point made use of a mock king instead. This explanation also solved the meaning of the Passion narrative. Frazer claimed that at Purim the Jews would stage a passion play starring two prisoners who would play Haman (the mock king who is killed) and Mordecai (the true king who is enthroned). Jesus, playing the part of Haman, was killed; Barabbas, appearing as Mordecai, was spared: even his name has the ring of a role title. Frazer thought his theory solved the question of whether the pattern of the dying/reviving god, common to the Middle East, also existed in Palestine. Most people thought not. Frazer, on the other hand, argued that Jesus was included among the adherents of this motif, and was given the undesirable role of Haman in the first place because his revolutionary preaching had angered the wrong people.[92]

Frazer's reinterpretation of Purim and the Book of Esther quite naturally did not go down well with either Christians or Jews. He knew that himself, and warned his good friend the rabbinical scholar Solomon Schechter (1850–1915) that the second edition of his book would get him into trouble everywhere. Reviews this time were far more negative, not only from Jews like Chief Rabbi Moses Gaster (1856–1939), but also from Andrew Lang, the scourge of the solarists. Indeed, Lang's review was so severe that when Frazer read it he had to quit writing and take a long holiday to recover from the blow.

The third edition of *The Golden Bough* (1911–15) repaired much of the damage and incorporated the development of his recent thinking, which was not nearly so anti-religious. The first thing to go was his interpretation of Purim, especially the claim that Jesus was crucified while playing Haman in a *Purimspiel*. Frazer's main point in this flight of fancy was to show that the Palestinian Jews already had the motif of the dying and resurrected god, so it was easy for them to accept the story of Jesus when it crystallized. Frazer also made it clear that he did not think that Jesus was a mythical figure, and he even compares him with Muhammad. Jesus fitted in well with Frazer's notion of the great role that individuals had in history, in helping mankind make the inevitable progression from magic to religion and finally to science. 'Quite apart from the positive evidence of history and tradition,' he ruled, 'the origin of a great religious and moral reform is inexplicable without the personal existence of a great reformer.' But since Frazer never threw anything out, he printed the Purim idea in an appendix, with some new information that he had since acquired.[93] Still, at least he accepted now that religion, as misguided as it was, might have beneficial effects, a theme he had first advanced in his encyclopaedia article on totemism back in 1888. Some of these ideas were further developed in his book, *Psyche's Task* (1909), in which he actually argued that the four most important pillars of modern life owe their origins to 'superstition': respect for (monarchical) government; respect for private property; respect for marriage and sexual morality; and respect for human life.[94]

As Frazer himself admitted, the story of Balder the Beautiful, and all of the waffling about the golden bough was 'little more than a stalking-horse to carry two heavy pack-loads of facts'. Nevertheless, Frazer had an enormous influence on all historians of religion and biblical scholars. His distinction between religion and magic; his notion of the magician being closer to the scientist than to the priest; his use of anthropological data from a wide variety of sources – all this shows Frazer to have been himself a 'stalking-horse' for later historical works, especially the studies of religion, magic, and the occult which were published in the 1970s.[95] His understanding of the Old Testament as just another text on the evolutionary ladder was in itself a product of the penetration of Darwinian ideas which had begun many years before. In many obvious ways, the next step in the story needs to be the work of Emile Durkheim, but this is beyond our brief. Durkheim's belief was that if one sees religion in functional terms, it was indispensable. But as a means for explaining the world, it is dead. Durkheim hoped to find the rational organizations that would replace the latent functions which had previously been performed by religion. Religion was dead, but sociology would provide its successor. The emergence of Fundamentalism under Durkheim's nose would prove him wrong.

Conclusion: The End of a World and the Beginning of Fundamentalism

Marcus Kalisch (1825–85) was one of the few Jews who was what one might call a 'player' in the general discussion of how the English Bible was read. He was born in Pomerania, educated in Berlin, and took his doctorate at Halle, before coming to England and serving as secretary to the chief rabbi and tutor to the sons of the Rothschild family. 'Almost marvellous is the progress which the Biblical sciences have made since the beginning of this century'; he mused, 'it amounts to a total regeneration, and comprises nearly all branches of sacred literature.' Yet there was another side to these developments as well, for

> modern criticism also has its defects; like every new principle, it has been pursued with one-sided rigour; the desire of consistency has led to extremes. The treasures of old, especially the Jewish commentators, were neglected; the positive basis was deserted; every traditional conception was rejected as prejudice and an illusion. The sacred records were dismembered, transposed, falsified; the most aerial conjectures were framed; and the palm was awarded to those, who excelled the rest in boldness and fanciful theories. Instead of penetrating into the notions of the Bible, these critics forced upon it ideas which were nothing but the emanations of their individual preconceptions; and instead of commenting with calm examination, violence and destruction were their constant weapons. Can it cause astonishment, that under such hands the spirit of the holy books vanished, and that the most venerable documents were degraded to an aggregate of contradictions, enigmas, and singularities?[1]

Kalisch wrote those words in 1855, before the controversy over *Essays and Reviews*, and prior to the forced discussion of the issues which Bishop Colenso put on the table. But his words were very prescient, for it is that combination of admiration for the work that had been accomplished in biblical studies, with a feeling that perhaps too much had been sacrificed, that characterized many Bible readers in the last four decades or so of the nineteenth century. Three landmarks stand out during this period, so much so that it is difficult to avoid writing ends-oriented Whig history when thinking about them: the work of Wellhausen (1878+), the production of the Revised Version of the English Bible (1881–5), and the beginnings of Fundamentalism in the United States (1910).

Julius Wellhausen in some ways was much more of a symbol of the new biblical scholarship than a pioneer in his own right. Certainly his history of Israel, first published in 1878 and then in other editions, became an important set text, and transformed him into the Darwin of Deuteronomy. But many of his ideas had been circulating for at least twenty years in Germany, where it was becoming accepted even among deeply religious scriptural scholars that the Pentateuch was not written by Moses. Wellhausen's work was also conducted against the backdrop of the discovery of new manuscripts, some of them forgeries,[2] but including the ancient codex (later called 'Aleph') which Konstantin von Tischendorf (1815–74) found in the monastery of Santa Katarina in the Sinai Desert.[3] Many if not most professors of biblical studies in Germany already recognized that Genesis to Numbers and parts of Deuteronomy had been put together by an author called J, who himself rewrote materials collected from what came to be known as the *Grundschrift* ('book of origins'). This earlier text was the work of a certain E (distingushed from J in that he called God 'Elohim' while J used the Tetragrammaton JHVH), or even two writers, an earlier and a later E. This *Grundschrift* had the basic biblical narrative from the beginning of Genesis, including much of Exodus, Leviticus, and parts of Numbers. Deuteronomy came much later, written in about the seventh century BC, followed by the editorial work which turned the Pentateuch and Joshua into a more or less coherent text, P, the priestly document. There was not much that was completely new about the so-called 'documentary hypothesis', but Wellhausen stated the case in a most convincing way and had a great influence in Britain, especially after his book appeared in an English translation in 1885. Soon it was a commonplace that the Bible was made up of four different documents, labelled J E D P in order of composition.[4]

At the same time that the Bible was being taken apart in Germany, it was being put together in a new way in Britain. The demand for a new and more accurate translation of the Bible into English had been in the air even before the King James Version was complete. Something was done about it at the end of the nineteenth century.

In the generation after Brian Walton's Cromwellian struggle for a new text, one of the most prominent of those who demanded a change was Charles Le Cène (1647?–1703), the Huguenot exile in London who worked throughout his life on a new French translation of the Bible, which was finally

published in 1741 after his death.[5] Le Cène called for a new translation at the
turn of the century, in a book published in English in 1701. The people, he
wrote, 'are always in danger of being deceiv'd, as long as the Translations continue as they now are.' Le Cène believed that a translation should not be too
literal, as a result of which 'it is almost impossible to understand them.' Indeed,
he thought, 'the Generality of Christian Translators have likewise fallen into
the same fault, even with respect to the New Testament, which they have
often made to speak *Hebrew* and *Greek* in their own Language.' Le Cène also
confronted directly the fact that there were significant variations among the
surviving ancient biblical manuscripts: this seemed to point to a dilution
of the truth, which was perhaps now impossible to find. He looked to the
original biblical commentators for guidance:

> The *Jews* are so far from imagining that there has no alteration happened
> in the letters of the Sacred Text, That the *Talmudists* acknowledge XII dif-
> ferent Readings, and the Author of *Sopherim* almost 200. *Elias Levita* has
> counted 148. *Buxtorf* has remarkt 1,014, without reckoning those of *Daniel*,
> which are often repeated in *Ezekiel*. Father *Morinus* has observed 1,200 in
> the great Bible at *Venice*; and the *Mazorets*, besides the fore-mention'd, have
> remarked more than 200 differences betwixt the *MSS.* of the Eastern and
> Western *Jews*, tho' they have not put them on the Margin of their Bibles,
> as they have done their other scrupulous Observations. And there are at
> this Day more than 200 Places wherein the Bibles of the Eastern and
> Western *Jews* do differ; yet they don't accuse one another of corrupting
> the Text: And the Bibles of the *Spanish Jews* are more correct than those
> of the *German Jews*, and yet the former don't reproach the latter on this
> Account: because they suppose it has happen'd by the fault of Transcribers,
> rather than by any Malice or Design in them.[6]

Proposals to print a new translation of the Bible, or parts of it, preferably
by subscription, continued throughout the eighteenth century. John Russell,
who described himself as a fellow of Merton and chaplain to the bishop of
Peterborough, thought it best to reprint the Lollard Bible.[7] Others called for
reprints of the Septuagint, or the Ethiopic, Coptic, and Armenian versions, or
even Walton's Polyglot as a way of looking again at the text before us.[8]
Matthew Pilkington (1705–65), prebendary of Lichfield, called for the use of
Hebrew manuscripts to give us 'a more correct and intelligible Translation of
the Bible.'[9] There was also a proposal for printing the Bible and the Book
of Common Prayer in Manx, since there were 20,000 people on the Isle of
Man, 'the far greater Number of which are entirely ignorant of the *English*
Language'.[10]

Tinkering with the text was a possibility, but this was not always appreciated. Benjamin Blayney (1728–1801), vice-principal of Hertford College, was

employed by the Clarendon Press to produce a corrected Authorized Version. This did appear at Oxford in 1769, but as luck would have it, most of the copies were destroyed in a fire at Paternoster Row in the Bible Warehouse.[11] Blayney was helped in his work by William Newcome (1729–1800), the one-armed fellow of Hertford College and later Irish bishop and finally archbishop of Armagh. Newcome had an even more radical view of the need for change than his friend. The King James Version was well and good, Newcome thought,

> But since that period the biblical apparatus has been much enriched by the publication of polyglots; of the Samaritan pentateuch; of ancient and modern versions; of lexicons, concordances, critical dissertations and sermons; books of eastern travels; disquisitions on the geography, customs, and natural history of the East; accurate tables of chronology, coins, weights, and measures. Many Hebrew and Samaritan MSS. many early printed editions of the Hebrew scriptures, have been collated by Kennicott and De Rossi; the eastern languages, which have so close an affinity with the Hebrew, have been industriously cultivated at home and abroad; the Masoretic punctuation is now ranked among useful assistances, but is no longer implicitly followed; and the Hebrew text itself is generally allowed to be corrupt in many places, and therefore capable of emendation by the same methods which are used in restoring the integrity of all other ancient books.

Newcome included in his work a handy list of the different editions of the Bible and in which private hands they were deposited.[12]

Charles Butler, the first Roman Catholic barrister since the Glorious Revolution and a celebrated legal writer, also had something to say about new versions of the Bible, in his famous survey of the subject. He detailed many editions of the Scriptures, in many different languages, but was somewhat wary about the endless fiddling with the minutiae of the text. 'The merit of Doctor Kennicott's labours is generally acknowledged;' he wrote,

> his opinions on the state of the Hebrew text are generally received, and the high pretensions of the Masorah are generally rejected. Still, however, the ancient opinions have some advocates. They do not go so far as to assert, that, a collation of Hebrew manuscripts, is perfectly useless, but they think it may be prized higher than it deserves: that, when manuscripts of an earlier date than the Masorah are sought for, it should not be forgot, that, the Masorites had those manuscripts, when they settled the text; and what hopes, can there be, they ask, that at the close of the eighteenth century, after the Hebrew has long ceased to be a spoken language, a christian, so much of whose time is employed in other pursuits and distracted

by other cares, can make a better use of those manuscripts than was actually made of them by the Masoritic literati, whose whole time, whose every thought, from their earliest years to their latest age, was devoted to that one object.

The Masorites, he was arguing, represented the limit of legal memory.[13]

So far there was a good deal of talk, but little biblical action. It was the lot of John Bellamy (1755–1842) actually to produce a new Bible. Bellamy was a born controversialist. As early as 1792, he revealed that he had

> no other Motive but that of recommending to others, those just and solid *Truths* contained in *the Holy Word*, and which I am not ashamed to acknowledge, I had not the least conception of (though connected many years with a respectable Religious Community) nor should I ever have understood the Scriptures, if I had not met with the writings of that Servant of the Lord, Emanuel Swedenborg.[14]

Bellamy's Hebraic researches resulted in his unintentionally amusing reply to the claim by Adam Clarke that 'the agent employed in the fall of man' was in fact 'the ouran-outang monkey, and not the serpent'.[15] He also wrote a comparative history of religions, in reply to the famous Jewish auto-didact David Levi, who made the life of Joseph Priestley so miserable.[16]

But it was John Bellamy's plan to produce a new translation of the Bible that aroused even greater controversy, especially after his proposals were revealed to the public. Among his strongest opponents was Thomas Burgess (1756–1837), the Hebraist bishop of St David's and, later, Salisbury. Burgess was a powerful reformer of Welsh religious life, and a prolific writer of more than a hundred works. Burgess rejected Bellamy's plan for what he called 'a splendid, expensive, and voluminous translation of the Bible', and summarized his objections to the new translation succinctly in a short list:

1. It cannot answer the *end proposed*;
2. the plan is very *defective*;
3. and, at the same time, *too expensive* for a work of general utility.

Looking at Bellamy's idea, Burgess could only lament that anyone would want to attempt once again 'that important and necessary duty, which appears to have been performed with a most punctilious and rigid accuracy by KING JAMES's TRANSLATORS.'[17]

Undaunted, John Bellamy pressed ahead, and published his Pentateuch in 1818, at 16 shillings, 24 shillings on large paper, dedicated to the prince regent and blessed with the subscriptions of a host of royalty, bishops, and lesser clergymen. 'It may be necessary to inform the Public,' Bellamy pointed out, 'that no translation has been made from the original Hebrew since the 128th year of

Christ.' The book before the reader was the product of twenty years' labour, representing thirty years of biblical study. Bellamy prefaced his work with a discussion of previous translations, not forgetting the obligatory jibes against his old Jewish enemy David Levi. 'I have in the following pages shewn the *absolute integrity of the Hebrew text*, that it is as perfect as the autograph of Moses', he wrote. 'Many things in the following pages will appear new; yet they will be found perfectly consistent with the meaning of the sacred writer.'[18]

Some of Bellamy's biblical phrases must have appeared new and strange to a reader born and bred on the King James Version. This was clear on the first page:

> In the beginning GOD created, the substance of the heaven, and the substance of the earth.
>
> 2. Now the earth was without form, even a waste; also darkness was upon the face of the deep: but the spirit of GOD moved, upon the face of the waters.
>
> 3. Then GOD said, BE LIGHT: and LIGHT WAS.
>
> 4. And GOD saw, that the light, was good: thus GOD divided, the light, from the darkness.
>
> 5. And GOD called the light day; and the darkness, he called night: so the evening and the morning, were the first day.

The word 'substance' twice in the first line of Holy Writ was somewhat jarring, and Bellamy took pains to explain how it got there. It was a translation of the Hebrew word *eth*, which everyone except Bellamy then and now believes to be a curious grammatical feature of Hebrew, a meaningless sound which simply points to the direct object following. Bellamy argued that *eth* is not merely a grammatical feature, but 'signifies the very SUBSTANCE of the thing spoken of'.[19]

Bellamy's newfangled Pentateuch was not an unqualified success. It was panned in the influential *Quarterly Review*.[20] Thomas Burgess, for example, had had few expectations for it, but he was unprepared for the sheer scale of foolishness in the final publication. In his view,

> The great defect of Mr. Bellamy's work (exclusive of his very imperfect knowledge of the Hebrew language, and incorrect use of the English,) is an *extreme irreverence for the Scriptures*, shewn in the species of commentary which he has adopted, and the disputatious, contemptuous, unscriptural sport with which it is conducted, in its ill-placed redundance of undigested verbal speculation and its licentious departure from received interpretations of Scripture, and established doctrines.

At the same time, Burgess admitted that 'Mr. Bellamy's undertaking has, however, found an advocate in Sir James Bland Burges'.[21] Oddly enough, this was true. Sir James Bland Burges (1752–1824) was a colourful political and diplomatic personality who turned to literature at the age of forty-three after retiring from government. Three years before his death he inherited the estate of his old friend John Lamb, and took that surname as his own, confusing historians ever since. In any case, Burges was convinced indeed by Bellamy's work, and called on both Church and State to 'direct an immediate revision of our Received Version, or, what might perhaps be more recommendable, a New Translation of the Original Text.'[22]

With all the confidence of a politician, Burges had backed his man, and found himself thereby the object of much derision. Henry John Todd (1763–1845), career clergyman and editor of Milton, lamented 'both the mis-application of the advocate's learning, and the occasion which he has given for opposition to the plea of good intention'. Indeed, he thought, 'the Reasons of Sir James Burges, in favour of a new Translation of the Holy Scriptures, may impose upon the judgement of such, as are swayed by a name rather than an argument. They are therefore more particularly to be guarded against.'[23] Bellamy and Burges were also attacked by John William Whittaker (1790?–1854), clergyman, Arabist, and astronomer, with the help of the Syndics of Cambridge University Press 'who have with great lib-erality defrayed all the expenses of this publication'. Whittaker was scath-ing and nasty over 331 pages, criticizing not only the quality of Bellamy's Bible, but also the conditions under which it had appeared, and the system of subscription wherein the great and the good are easily persuaded to give their support to a worthy project of which they know very little. As for Bellamy, despite his claims of thirty years' study of Hebrew, it was clear that he did not understand the language: 'I shall therefore give no reasons why [eth] does not mean "substance"'. Appendix (A) helpfully contained 'A List of the Chief Violations of Grammar Committed by Mr. Bellamy'.[24] Buoyed by his success, Whittaker followed up his first attack on Bellamy and Burges with another the following year, also paid for in full by the grateful Syndics.[25] Burges, now called Lamb, had his final say, but it was a hopeless case to make.[26]

Bellamy's Bible certainly provoked a good deal of controversy, and soon generated its own historiography. Richard Laurence (1760–1838), Regius professor of Hebrew at Oxford, and soon to become an Irish archbishop, decided to provide an historical overview of those who had tried and failed to find an alternative to the Authorized Version. 'In the preceding chapter,' notes Laurence,

I have given a short account of the writers upon the subject under con-sideration, who flourished in the last century. And here perhaps I might terminate the enquiry. But at the commencement of the present century one of so peculiar a character has appeared in the catalogue of biblical translators, that it would be as improper to overlook, as it is mortifying to notice him. I allude to *Mr. J. Bellamy*, who supported by a liberal subscription has recently undertaken to give a new translation of the Bible from the Hebrew alone.

It was the issue of public subscription, and of such distinguished people, that galled him the most:

Foreigners it is to be hoped will not form their estimate of the present state of Hebrew erudition among us from so illiterate a production, notwithstanding the respectable subscription which has been obtained to encourage it. For in this country, it should be recollected, the plausible projector, and importunate promoter, of every undertaking, apparently useful, and certainly laborious, solicit not public patronage in vain; and seldom is incapacity presumed, until it be detected.

There was simply no reason at this time to attempt a new translation of the Bible into English:

When imperfections therefore are imputed to our established translation, these imperfections must be understood to consist, not in *theological,* but simply in *philological,* inaccuracies. And it is only upon a scale of this kind, that we are to estimate the importance attached to them. The *absolute necessity* then of the proposed measure being wholly out of the question, and the *great expediency* of it resting upon such a basis, have not our rulers always acted with wisdom and discretion in resisting the headstrong torrent of literary opinion, and in not suffering themselves to be borne down by its impetuosity?

Will there ever be time when it will be possible to consider a new translation of the Bible?

When biblical critics *are agreed* upon the formation of an improved text, it will then I apprehend be time enough to take the public adoption of that text into consideration.[27]

Bellamy, for his part, continued in his project, and in 1832 petitioned the House of Commons for support, to no avail. By 1841 he had translated and published everything from Genesis to Song of Songs, but died in November of the following year. After his death, his manuscripts were championed by Peter Stuart of Liverpool, who published Bellamy's Daniel in 1863, and the minor prophets in 1867.[28] By the time Bellamy died, the revised word from Germany was already spreading across the Channel. Further attempts to prevent a revised version were put forward, most notably by Solomon Caesar

Malan (1812–94), the Oriental linguist, and Alexander M'Caul (1799–1863), the Hebraist and missionary to the Jews.[29]

But the need for change was now too obvious to be ignored. The Convocation of Canterbury appointed a committee in February 1870, which recommended that they 'should nominate a body of its own members to undertake the work of revision, who shall be at liberty to invite the co-operation of any eminent for scholarship, to whatever nation or religious body they may belong.' They were ordered to 'introduce as few alterations as possible into the text of the AV, consistently with faithfulness' and 'to limit, as far as possible, the expression of such alterations to the language of the Authorized and earlier English versions'. In any case, any and all changes had to be approved by a two-thirds majority. Proposed changes which were supported by only a simple majority would be relegated to the margins. The plan of the translators was to try to remain consistent to the Hebrew and Greek, using the same word throughout the English text. They also printed the Psalms and other poetical parts of the Bible as verse. The volumes appeared in due course: the New Testament first, in 1881; followed by the Old Testament in 1885; and the Apocrypha ten years later. From 1899, it was permissible to use the Revised Version in Anglican services. The Americans involved in the project produced their own American Standard Version (1901), including some of the emendations which had been rejected by the parent body. It was this text that was the basis of the Revised Standard Version (1946–57) which has in large measure finally succeeded in overtaking the efforts of King James's scholars.[30]

Yet just as the American Standard Version was being produced, an implicit acknowledgement of the acceptability and importance of the latest biblical scholarship, a new movement was growing up in the United States which rejected it root and branch. It would eventually become known as Fundamentalism, a term more often used than understood, like Feudalism, or Fascism. It is therefore often applied to phenomena in a variety of different contexts, creating such misnamed hybrids as Islamic and Jewish 'Fundamentalism'.

The name itself derives from a series of a dozen pamphlets known as *The Fundamentals*, three million copies of which were published between 1910 and 1915. This project was the brainchild of Lyman and Milton Stewart, California oilmen who had heard a preacher in Los Angeles storming against the infidel professors of theology at the University of Chicago Divinity School. The Stewarts convinced the preacher, A.C. Dixon, to supervise putting their case forward to the general public in a series of small works championing a millenarian interpretation of Scripture and underwritten by the brothers to the amount of $300,000. A committee of 'Fundamentalists' was formed, most of whom were already involved with the Moody Bible

Institute in Chicago. One of these men, Louis Meyer, was a converted Jew who ran a ministry for the Jews there and who became the second editor of the series.[31]

The pamphlets dealt with the key issues of the inerrancy, inviolability, and authenticity of the Bible, but with much else as well. The authors of *The Fundamentals* attacked German biblical criticism, contending that the ancient Hebrew records must be authentic, since God had chosen the Jews as the people to hear and convey His message. They stressed that recent archaeo-logical findings, or some of them at least, tended to confirm the accuracy of biblical history. As one of the authors, William G. Moorhead, put it: 'Ancient Judaism has one supreme voice for the chosen people, and its voice was prophetic . . . If any man deny the inspiration of the Old Testament, sooner or later he will deny that of the New.'[32]

As is readily seen, Fundamentalism was not a new idea, but rather an emphasis on Martin Luther's original precepts of *sola fide* and *sola scriptura*, the basis tenets of Protestantism which stressed faith (rather than performed sacra-ments) and the Bible as the very bedrock of Christianity. Fundamentalism, or Evangelicalism as it has come to be called, includes churches of many sects, but primarily Baptists, who restrict full membership to those who are able to choose. In the 1920s, they became famous for their opposition to Darwin's doctrine of evolution. A number of American states had passed laws against the teaching of evolution, and this statute was challenged in the courts in 1925 by the American Civil Liberties Union, in the person of John T. Scopes, a science teacher in Dayton, Tennessee who had agreed to serve as the defen-dant in a landmark case. The resulting trial, and the sparring between Clarence Darrow for the defence and William Jennings Bryan as assistant prosecuting attorney, entered into the realm of legend and literature, obscuring the incon-venient fact that Scopes was actually convicted and fined $100, although this ruling was eventually reversed on technical grounds by the Tennessee Supreme Court.[33]

Fundamentalism enjoyed a great revival after the Second World War along with other religious beliefs, represented by figures such as the great Billy Graham (b. 1918), who dressed like a business executive and used the mass media and huge rallies to convince people to dedicate their lives to Christ. Graham's preaching emphasized individual sins rather than biblical theology or Darwinian evolution, implying that dedicating oneself to his message was almost an economic and social investment, leading to measurable rewards on earth. His success was phenomenal, as he prayed with presidents and consolidated his position as the American Protestant pope. Post-war Fundamentalists replaced one foreign atheistic enemy with another, as Darwinianism was pushed aside by Communism as the godless theology of America's enemies. Men like Jerry Falwell (b. 1933), Pat Robertson (b. 1930), and Hal Lindsey (b. 1929) promoted Fundamentalist views of biblical prophecy and messianism to a genuinely mass audience of many millions.

It would be difficult to measure the strength of Fundamentalism in the world today, but at least in the United States, the religious culture is ripe for acceptance. America is a very religious country, a place where 95 per cent of the population believes in God, 65 per cent believe in the Devil, 72 per cent in angels, 71 per cent in life after death, and 80 per cent in miracles. According to the National Survey of Religious Identification (NSRI) more than 20 per cent of the American population – 50 million Americans – can be called 'Evangelical Protestants'.[34]

While the term itself refers to a wide variety of groups, most would probably subscribe to the 'Five Points of Fundamentalism': (1) the inerrant inspiration of the Bible, preserved without error in the original manuscripts; (2) the virgin birth; (3) the Atonement; (4) the Resurrection; and (5) the miracle-working power of Jesus Christ. The Niagara Bible Conference, held in 1878, added a number of key doctrines, including (1) the Trinity; (2) the total depravity of man; (3) the necessity of a new birth for salvation; and (4) the premillennial Second Coming of Christ, that is, the notion that Jesus will come before the thousand-year reign of the saints.

The Fundamentalists also have their own biblical text, the Scofield Reference Bible, still published by Oxford University Press. Cyrus I. Scofield (1843–1921) had been a soldier from Tennessee in the Confederate army, a man with a somewhat scandalous past involving drunkenness and marital difficulties. This did not stop him from becoming a lawyer in Kansas and a political figure there, but this glory did not last long, and he was soon accused of stealing political funds. He was jailed in St Louis for forgery in 1879, and it was while he was in prison that Scofield experienced a remarkable religious conversion. He was released and began to practise law in St Louis, where he met and became a devoted disciple of James H. Brookes (1830–97), the Fundamentalist leader of the Niagara Bible Conference and editor of the first major American Fundamentalist periodical, *The Truth for Christ*. Scofield took on a ministry at the Dallas First Congregational Church, and started a publication called *The Believer*. He also became a key figure in the activities of the Moody Bible Institute in Chicago, and a participant in the various Bible and prophecy conferences.[35]

Scofield began working on his extraordinary edition of the Bible in about 1901. His purpose was to guide readers to the prophetic themes contained within the Bible and to give them the proper messianic interpretation. Using the King James Version as his text, Scofield employed section headings, lucid footnote explanations, and cross-references to other biblical texts, so that reading the Testaments becomes an adventure in code-breaking. The Scofield Reference Bible was first published in 1909, and has been in print ever since,

being perhaps the single most influential publication in the history of messianic theology. For the more naïve reader, there was little to distinguish the
Word of God from that of Scofield, and his footnotes easily acquired almost
canonical status. Most importantly, Scofield adopted the Dispensationalist millenarian scheme in its entirety, proclaiming the stages of mankind's spiritual
development which would ultimately lead to the Rapture of the faithful to
heaven, the seven years of tribulation, and the Second Coming of Christ.
Scofield himself, having produced the monument which still bears his name,
became leader of the Dallas Seminary, the institution where Hal Lindsey and
many other Fundamentalist millenarians were trained.[36]

Hal Lindsey's prophetic text, *The Late Great Planet Earth* was first published
in 1970 and has since sold over 20 million copies.[37] It has even been translated into Hebrew, a sort of mirror image of the linguistic journey followed
by the Bible itself. Lindsey accepts every jot and tittle in the two Testaments
as God's last words, and sees them as forming a divine code-book with a
precise description of mankind's future. Even Calvin never envisioned such
detail, which Lindsey presents in the form of maps illustrating the period
before the End of Days. In his straightforward approach to Scripture, and his
belief that a full interpretation of the text is available to everyone, Lindsey
recalls the very basic principle of *sola scriptura* which seemed so revolutionary in the early sixteenth century.

American Fundamentalism is often portrayed as an eccentric and primitive
throwback to more intolerant times when God was in His heaven and Adam
and Eve lost Paradise. Even their intense interest in the Signs of the Times,
especially in the Land of Israel, seems Cromwellian in direction and intensity. There is no doubt that most Fundamentalists would reject the idea that
the biblical tinkering of the past two hundred years has brought mankind any
closer to understanding the Bible. They might even argue that what appears
to us as demonstrable evidence of multiple authorship was implanted by God
to try our souls, just as Philip Gosse insisted that the world was divinely
created with the fossils already on site. From the viewpoint of our story, the
birth of the Fundamentalist movement brings us right back to the beginning,
when scriptural authority was axiomatic and the Bible was self-evidently
God's Last Words to mankind. Far from being a deviant group of religious
extremists, Fundamentalists are actually those whose theological position is
closest to the message of the Protestant revolution, while *we* are the ones who
have gone into the sunset of the 'horizon of expectations'.

Notes

Abbreviations

BL   British Library
Bodl. Lib.   Bodleian Library
Brit. Jnl. Hist. Sci.   British Journal of the History of Science
Bull. John Rylands Lib.   Bulletin of the John Rylands Library
Cal. S.P. Dom.   Calendar of State Papers, Domestic
Cal. S.P. Span.   Calendar of State Papers, Spanish
Cal. S.P. Ven   Calendar of State Papers, Venetian
DNB   Dictionary of National Biography
Hist. Cat.   Historical Catalogue of Printed Editions of the English Bible 1525–1961, ed. A.S. Herbert, et al. (London and New York, 1968)
Jnl. Hist. Ideas   Journal of the History of Ideas
Jnl. Theol. Stud.   Journal of Theological Studies
OED   Oxford English Dictionary
PRO   Public Record Office
SP   State Papers
Stud. Church Hist.   Studies in Church History

Preface: The Biblical Reader and the Shifting Horizon of Expectations

1   Stanley E. Fish, 'Interpreting the Variorum', Critical Inquiry, 2 (1975–6), 476.
2   Hans Robert Jauss, Towards an Aesthetic of Reception (Brighton, 1982), ch. 1: 'Literary History as a Challenge to Literary Theory'. The title of the original lecture in April 1967 was 'What Is and For What Purpose Does One Study Literary History?', a paraphrase of the title of Friedrich Schiller's inaugural lecture at the University of Jena (1789), substituting the word 'literary' for 'universal'. See also Wolfgang Iser, Theorie ästhetischer Wirkung (Munich, 1976), trans. as The Act of Reading: A Theory of Aesthetic Response (Baltimore, 1978).
3   Fish, 'Variorum', pp. 465–85, esp. pp. 473–4, 481, 483–4.
4   Stanley E. Fish, 'Literature in the Reader: Affective Stylistics', New Literary History, 2 (1970–1), 123–62, esp. pp. 126–7, 140. On p. 145, Fish explains that 'the reader is the informed reader'.
5   Karl Popper, 'Natural Laws and Theoretical Systems', in Theorie und Realität (Tübingen, 1964), pp. 87–102, esp. pp. 91, 102: quoted in Jauss, 'Literary', pp. 40–1.

6 J.C. Dannhauer, *Hermeneutica sacra* (Strasburg, 1654); R. Burthogge, *Organum Vetus & Novum* (London, 1678), p. 70: 'Ratiocination Speculative, is either Euretick or Hermeneutick, Inventive or Interpretative'. Cf. *OED*, s.v. 'hermeneutic'.

7 Martin Heidegger, *Sein und Zeit* (1927), trans. as *Being and Time* (Oxford, 1962), pp. 191–2.

8 Hans-Georg Gadamer, *Wahrheit und Methode* (Tübingen, 1960), trans. as *Truth and Method* (London, 1975).

9 Ibid., p. 258.

10 Ibid., p. 263.

CHAPTER I *The Prehistoric English Bible*

1 M.M. Knappen, *Tudor Puritanism: A Chapter in the History of Idealism* (Chicago, 1939), ch. 1.

2 Jacob Burckhardt, *The Civilization of the Renaissance in Italy: An Essay* (Phaidon edn, London, 1960), pp. 162–3, from 2nd German edn (1868), trans. S.G.C. Middlemore.

3 Quoted from a manuscript source in Moshe Idel, 'The Magical and Neoplatonic Interpretations of the Kabbalah in the Renaissance', in *Jewish Thought in the Sixteenth Century*, ed. B. Cooperman (Cambridge, 1987), pp. 186–242, esp. pp. 186–7. See also idem, 'Hermeticism and Judaism', in *Hermeticism and the Renaissance*, ed. I. Merkel and A. Debus (Washington, 1988), pp. 59–76.

4 Burckhardt, *Renaissance*, p. 170.

5 See generally, A.W. Pollard, *Records of the English Bible* (London, 1911); C. Anderson, *Annals of the English Bible* (London, 1845–55); D. Wilson, *The People and the Book: The Revolutionary Impact of the English Bible, 1380–1611* (London, 1976); and I. Green, *Print and Protestantism in Early Modern England* (Oxford, 2000).

6 Martin Luther, *An Appeal to the Ruling Class of German Nationality as to the Amelioration of the State of Christendom* (1520), in *Martin Luther*, ed. J. Dillenberger (New York, 1961), pp. 412, 414.

7 See generally, Thomas Frognall Dibdin, *An Introduction to the Knowledge of Rare and Valuable Editions of the Greek and Latin Classics* (4th edn, London, 1827), i. 1–43 (polyglot Bibles); 44–81 (Hebrew Bibles); 82–168 (Greek Bibles and Testaments); B. Hall, 'Biblical Scholarship: Editions and Commentaries', in *The Cambridge History of the Bible*, iii, ed. S.L. Greenslade (Cambridge, 1963), 38–93.

8 He was created cardinal in 1507, and in an expedition to Africa two years later, captured Oran. He was regent of Castile for Charles V (1516–17), and died within hours of being sacked by the emperor. For his life, see first his authorized biography commissioned by the University of Alcalá, and the basis for all later works: Alvaro Gomez de Castro, *De rebus gestis a Francisco Ximenio, Cisnerio, Archiepiscopo Toletano* (Alcalá, 1560). See also Eugenio de Robles, *Compendio de la vida . . . del Cardenal F. Ximenez de Cisneros* (Toledo, 1604); Valentin Esprit Fléchier [bishop of Nîmes], *Histoire du Cardinal Ximenes* (Amsterdam, 1693); B[asil Richard] Barrett, *The Life of Cardinal Ximenes* (London, 1813); Michel Baudier, *Histoire de la vie et de l'administration du Cardinal Ximénès* (Paris, 1851); Karl Joseph von Hefele [bishop of Rottenburg], *The Life of Cardinal Ximenez* (London, 1860), based on the German original pub. Tübingen, 1844, largely a defence of the Spanish Inquisition; J.P.R. Lyell, *Cardinal Ximenes* (London, 1917).

9 Others included Corpus Christi College at Oxford, the Collège de France, and the University of Wittenberg, which was endowed by Frederick of Saxony with chairs in each of the three languages.

10 William H. Prescott, *History of the Reign of Ferdinand and Isabella* (London, 1838), iii. 509–10, relying on Gomez, *Ximenio*, fo. 218 and Robles, *Ximenez*, ch. xviii.

11 According to J. Le Long, *Bibliotheca sacra* (Leipzig, 1709), i. 13–20.

12 Another reason to pinpoint 1522 as the date of circulation is that Erasmus's third edition of his Greek New Testament (1522) shows no clear influence of the Complutensian Polyglot, while his fourth edition does.

13 He also made Henry VIII 'Defender of the Faith' (11 Oct. 1521). Leo X died of malaria and was replaced by Hadrian VI (1522–3), the Dutchman who was the last non-Italian pope until John Paul II.

14 Gomez, *Ximenio*, fo. 38

15 A photograph of a typical page is printed as plate 12, *Cambridge History*, iii.

16 Uncial MSS are the oldest of the New Testament, written in large letters on vellum: from the Latin word *uncia*, an inch, large, applied to letters.

17 Hall, 'Biblical Scholarship', p. 51.

18 Ibid.

19 Christian D. Ginsburg, *Introduction to the Massoretico-Critical Edition of the Hebrew Bible* (London, 1897), pp. 906–25. The most bitter controversy over the Complutensian Polyglot was between Wetstein (against) and Goeze (for): Michaelis sided with Goeze and the Complutensian: see Michaelis, below.

20 J.D. Michaelis, *Introduction to the New Testament* (Cambridge, 1793, 1801), ii (1). 440–1: trans. of his *Einleitung in die göttlichen Schriften des Neuer Bundes* (4th edn, Göttingen, 1788).

21 Charles Butler, *Horae biblicae* (London, 1797), i. 78–9.

22 Prescott, *Ferdinand and Isabella*, iii. 401 and n.

23 Modesto Lafuente y Zamalloa, *Historia general de España* (Madrid, 1850–67), x. 453n.

24 Ginsburg, *Introduction*, p. 918: Ginsburg had no doubt that Prescott accepted the story 'as an authentic fact'.

25 (Milan, 1481) with Magnificat/Benedictus; and a psalter published by Aldus Manutius before 1498: he also produced six chapters from the Gospel of John in 1504.

26 Erasmus to Willibald Pirckheimer, 2 Nov. 1517, from Louvain: *Erasmi epistolae*, ed. P.S. and H.M. Allen (Oxford, 1906–58), iii. 116–19, esp. p. 117 = no. 694.

27 *Erasmus's Annotations on the New Testament . . . Facsimile of the Final Latin Text with All Earlier Variants*, ed. A. Reeve (London and Leiden, 1986–90). See also E. Rummel, *Erasmus' Annotations on the New Testament* (Toronto, 1986); A. Rabil, Jr., *Erasmus and the New Testament: The Mind of a Christian Humanist* (San Antonio, 1972).

28 See generally, R.H. Bainton, *Erasmus of Christendom* (London, 1969); J. McConica, *Erasmus* (Oxford, 1991).

29 Erasmus to John Colet [*c.* Dec.] 1504, from Paris: *The Collected Works of Erasmus*, ed. B.M. Corrigan, *et al.* (Toronto, 1974–), ii. 87 (letter 181).

30 Erasmus to Reuchlin [Basle, August 1514]: *Collected Works*, iii. 7–8 (letter no. 300).

31 In fact, the verse actually does not appear even in the version of the Vulgate prior to AD 800: B. Metzger, *The Text of the New Testament* (Oxford, 1964), p. 102. It appears in the Authorized Version (1611) but was omitted from the Revised Version of 1881.

32 Quoted in Bainton, *Erasmus*, p. 169.

33 Ibid.

34 Ibid., p. 175: from the preface to the Paraphrase of Matthew. Cf. J.C. Olin, *Christian Humanism and the Reformation* (New York, 1987).

35 Cajetan in the preface to his commentary on the Psalms (1530). Andreas Osiander

(Nuremberg, 1522; Cologne, 1527) and Pellican (1539) also rewrote the Vulgate with reference to the original Greek and Hebrew texts. Paolo Sarpi agreed with Cajetan on this point, and wrote about it in his history of the Council of Trent.

36 The second edition appeared in Paris, 1532; the third of Paris, 1538–40 cited many new manuscripts whose variant readings were identified by code letters. In 1545, Estienne produced at Paris two octavo volumes which printed the Vulgate and the Zurich Latin Bible in parallel columns.

37 Estienne published three folio volumes at Geneva in 1557, the first two being the 1546 Old Testament Vulgate with a new Latin Apocalypse based on the Greek text of the Complutensian Polyglot; the third being Beza's first Latin version of the New Testament, i.e. not the Vulgate at all.

38 A second edition appeared in 1539, a quarto with Erasmus's Latin New Testament and the Apocalypse from the Complutensian Polyglot. The two folio volumes were also reprinted in 1546. For much more on Münster and his work, see below, pp. 20–1.

39 Among Leo Jud's collaborators was Beza's tutor Cholinus (who provided a new translation of the Apocalypse) and Rodolph Gualther [Rudolph Walter, 1519–86] (who revised Erasmus's Latin New Testament). This edition included the innovation of enclosing with square brackets words added to the text to make the meaning clear.

40 See generally, J.H. Bentley, *Humanists and Holy Writ: New Testament Scholarship in the Renaissance* (Princeton, 1983).

41 F.A. Yates, *The Occult Philosophy in the Elizabethan Age* (London, 1979), p. 1. See also J.S. Mebane, *Renaissance Magic and the Return of the Golden Age* (London, 1989).

42 On Pico generally, with reference to the kabbalah, see e.g. Ernst Cassirer, 'Giovanni Pico della Mirandola: A Study in the History of Renaissance Ideas', *Jnl. Hist. Ideas*, 3 (1942), 123–44, 319–46.

43 On kabbalah generally, see Gershom Scholem, *Major Trends in Jewish Mysticism* (Jerusalem, 1941); idem, *kabbalah* (Jerusalem, 1974). On Christian kabbalah, see J.L. Blau, *The Christian Interpretation of the Cabala in the Renaissance* (New York, 1944); F. Secret, *Les Kabbalistes chrétiens de la renaissance* (Paris, 1964); W.J. Bousma, 'Postel and the Significance of Renaissance Cabalism', *Journal of the Warburg and Courtauld Institutes*, 17 (1954), 318–32; Yates, *Occult Philosophy in the Elizabethan Age*. See now the major new reinterpretation in M. Idel, *Kabbalah: New Perspectives* (New Haven and London, 1988).

44 Burckhardt, *Renaissance*, p. 120.

45 Johannes Reuchlin, *De rudimentis Hebraicis* (Pforzheim, 1506); idem, *De verbo mirifico* (Basle, 1494); idem, *De arte Cabalistica* (Haguenau, 1517). For an interesting discussion of the Egyptian tradition, see Martin Bernal, *Black Athena* (London, 1987).

46 Idel, 'Magical', p. 212.

47 C. Wirszubski, *A Christian Kabbalist Reads the Law* [Hebrew] (Jerusalem, 1977); Flavius Mithridates, *Sermo de passione domini*, ed. C. Wirszubski (Jerusalem, 1963); S. Simonsohn, 'Some Well-Known Jewish Converts during the Renaissance', *Revue des Etudes Juives*, 148 (1989), 17–52.

48 Idel, 'Magical', p. 187.

49 Moshe Idel, 'Kabbalah and Ancient Theology in R. Isaac and Judah Abrabanel' [Hebrew], in *The Philosophy of Love of Leone Ebreo*, ed. M. Dorman and Z. Levy (Haifa, 1985), pp. 73–112. Cf. idem, 'Kabbalah, Platonism and Prisca Theologia: The Case of R. Menasseh ben Israel', in *Menasseh ben Israel and His World*, ed. Y. Kaplan, M. Mechoulan, and R.H. Popkin (Leiden, 1989), pp. 207–19.

50 David B. Ruderman, *Kabbalah, Magic, and Science: The Cultural Universe of a Sixteenth-Century Jewish Physician* (Cambridge, Mass., 1988).

51 See also H.H. Ben-Sasson, 'The Reformation in Contemporary Jewish Opinion', *Proceedings of the Israel Academy of Sciences and Humanities*, 4 (1970), 239–326.

52 D.S. Katz, 'The Language of Adam in Seventeenth-Century England', in *History and Imagination: Essays in Honour of H.R. Trevor-Roper*, eds Hugh Lloyd-Jones, Valerie Pearl, and Blair Worden (London, 1981), pp. 132–45.

53 [Conrad Pellicanus], *De modo legen. et intelli. hebraevm* (Strasburg, 1504), printed by J. Grüninger. The work was originally leaves F ix–xxviii of Gregorius Reisch, *Margarita philosophica* (Basle, 1535), a famous compendium of useful knowledge. A facsimile is reprinted in pamphlet form by E. Nestle (Tübingen, 1877).

54 Reuchlin, *De rudimentis Hebraicis*.

55 See esp. the Hebrew grammars by the Roman Catholic scholars Nicolaus Clenardus of Louvain, *Tabula in grammaticen Hebraeam* (Paris, 1540), with further editions; and Sanctes Pagninus of Lucca, *Thesaurus linguae sanctae* (Lyons, 1529), also with further editions. The latter's Hebrew grammar of 1546 was printed by Robert Estienne and thereby became the best presented Hebrew grammar of its time.

56 Sebastian Münster, *Epitome Hebraicae grammaticae* (Basle, 1520), printed back-to-front; idem, *Institutiones grammmaticae in Hebraeam linguam* (Basle, 1524), including a polyglot text of the Book of Jonah.

57 From the prefaces, respectively, of Münster's *Opus grammaticum consummatum* (Basle, 1542), with further editions; and his *Absolutissima* (1525) [see n. 64], as quoted in J. Friedman, *The Most Ancient Testimony: Sixteenth-Century Christian-Hebraica in the Age of Renaissance Nostalgia* (Athens, Ohio, 1983), pp. 44–8.

58 Generally, see G.E. Weil, *Elie Levita humaniste et massorète 1469–1549* (Paris, 1963).

59 In his *Linguarum duodecim characteribus differentium alphabetum* (Paris, 1538), fo. 3: 'Elias Germanus, quo usus sum Venetiis'. Postel's pupil Guy Le Fèvre de la Boderie praises Levita in the preface to his *Dictionarium Syro-Chaldaicum* (Antwerp, 1573), originally part of the Antwerp Polyglot Bible (1572).

60 The pupil was Georges de Selve, who later became the French ambassador to Venice.

61 Paul Fagius also supplied a Latin foreword to Levita's Aramaic dictionary, *Lexicon Chaldaicvm* (Isny, 1541).

62 See the edition of Prague, 1660.

63 These books were: (1) *Sefer ha-Harkavah* (Rome, 1518); (2) *Sefer ha-Bachur* (Rome, 1518), later called *Dikduk Eliyyah ha-Levi* (Isny, 1542), and further editions; (3) *Luach beDikduk haPealim ve-ha-Binyanim* (unpublished).

64 Sebastian Münster, *Grammatica Hebraica absolutissima* (Basle, 1525).

65 Sebastian Münster, *Composita verborum & nominum Hebraicorum* (Basle, 1525), with further edns; idem, *Dictionarium Hebraicum* (Basle, 1525): the Bodleian's copy [8°.T.21.Th.BS] is 'E libris Edw. Pocockii'.

66 Sebastian Münster, *Opus grammaticum consummatum* (Basle, 1542), with further edns.

67 Sebastian Münster, *Hebraica Biblia* (Basle, 1534), with annotations and commentary.

68 Sebastian Münster, *Chaldaica grammatica* (Basle, 1527). Levita had published an Aramaic dictionary at Isny in 1514.

69 Sebastian Münster, *Kalendariù Hebraicum* (Basle, 1527).

70 Sebastian Münster, *Ioel et Malachias* (n.p., 1530). David Kimchi (1160–1235), also known as 'Radak' from the initials of his name, was one of the members of the medieval Jewish family of grammarians and biblical scholars in Narbonne, Provence.

71 Sebastian Münster, *Praecepta Mosaica* (Basle, 1533).

72 Sebastian Münster, *Tredecim articuli fidei Iudaeorum* (n.p., 1529).

73 Sebastian Münster, *Evangelium secundum Matthaeum in lingua Hebraica cum versione Latina* (Basle, 1537), ded. to Henry VIII (sigs a2ʳ–a4ʳ). The Bodleian's copy of the Basle, 1557 edn [8°.Z.202.Th] has the signature on the title page of 'Joannes Dee 1562', and a few underlinings and notes. The dedication to Henry VIII is sigs aa2ʳ–8ʳ in the 1557 edition. Münster's translation derived from an imperfect MS copy of Matthew's gospel in Hebrew made in 1385 for polemical purposes by Shem Tob b. Shaprut, a Jew of Tudela in Castile. The book is 154 pages. Actually, it is not quite true that Münster was the first to translate Matthew: Jacob ben Reuben, *Milkhamot ha-Shem* (*c.* 1170) has some of Matthew in Hebrew, and Raymond Martini (*c.* 1220–*c.* 1284) has some quotations in Hebrew from the New Testament.

74 In the concluding section of his *De orbis terrae concordia* [(Basle, 1544)].

75 Generally, see Ginsburg, *Introduction*, ch. 13, where each publication is meticulously described.

76 It was printed without vowels with David Kimchi's commentary.

77 Bomberg's first Hebrew work was a Pentateuch (Venice, Dec. 1516).

78 Bomberg obtained a privilege to print Hebrew books for Jews in 1516.

79 Other Jews who worked for Bomberg included Elijah Levita, David Pizzighettone, Kalonymus ben David, and Abraham de Balmes. Bomberg had Felix Pratensis's Latin translation of Psalms (Venice, 1515) printed at his own expense at another publishing house.

80 The next edition of a rabbinical Bible was that published by the Adelkind brothers at Venice in 1548.

81 The story goes that Plantin's daughter Magdelaine read the proofs aloud in five languages: she did certainly know Latin and Greek: Plantin to Cayas, 4 Nov. 1570: *Correspondance de Christophe Plantin*, ed. Max Rooses (Antwerp, 1883–1920), ii. 175–6.

82 The Hebrew punches were manufactured by Plantin and Guillaume Le Bé (1525–98), a French typecutter trained by Robert Estienne.

83 Francesco Giorgio, *L'Harmonie du monde* (Paris, 1578): from the first Latin edition published at Venice in 1525, *De harmonia mvndi* (n.p., n.d.). Generally on Giorgi and the La Boderie brothers, see Yates, *Occult Philosophy in the Elizabethan Age*, pp. 29–35, 65–7. Giorgi worked actively for Henry VIII's divorce: see D.S. Katz, *The Jews in the History of England, 1485–1850* (Oxford, 1994), pp. 24–6, 29–33. See also F.A. Yates, *The French Academies of the Sixteenth Century* (London, 1947), pp. 43–4; B. Rekers, *Benito Arias Montano* (London, 1972), pp. 45ff.; H. de la Ferrière-Percy, *Les La Boderie* (Paris, 1857). A third brother, Antoine, served as ambassador to England (1606–11) and his memoirs were published in five volumes in 1750. He is quoted extensively in D.H. Willson, *King James VI & I* (London, 1956).

84 *L'Heptaple de J. Picus, comte de la Mirande, translaté par N. Le F. de la B.*, printed with the translation of Giorgi's work, pp. 829–78. See also C. Wirszubski, 'Francesco Giorgio's Commentary on Giovanni Pico's Kabbalistic Theses', *Journal of the Warburg and Courtauld Institutes*, 37 (1974), 145–56, now Jewish National and University Library, MS Yah. Var. 24.

85 Gui Le Fèvre de la Boderie, *L'Encyclie des sécrets de l'eternité* (Antwerp, [1570]). He also translated a book against Islam, Juan Andrés, *Confusion de la secte de Muhamed* (Paris, 1574).

86 Idem, *La Galliade, ou de la révolution des arts et sciences* (Paris, 1578).

87 W.J. Bouwsma, *The Career and Thought of Guillaume Postel* (Cambridge, Mass., 1957). Frances Yates notes that the French translation of Giorgi is dedicated to

'Monsieur Després,' one of the few people certainly known to have been a member of the 'Family of Love'.

88 Génébrard's pupil was the French diplomat and kabbalist Blaise de Vigenère.

89 In G. Génébrard, *Chronologia Hebraeorum maior, quae Seder olam rabba inscribitur* (Paris, 1578), pp. 75ff. For the influence of Eldad ha-Dani, see D.S. Katz, *Philo-Semitism and the Readmission of the Jews to England, 1603–1655* (Oxford, 1982), pp. 145–6.

90 Plantin also printed Hebrew Bibles for export to the Jews of North Africa (1567), and may have produced a Hebrew prayer book that appeared anonymously at Antwerp in about 1577.

91 Arias Montanus also published in 1575 a Latin translation of the travels of Benjamin of Tudela, the late twelfth-century Jewish explorer. Cf. the translation by Constantine l'Emperour, published at Antwerp in 1633. See generally for his later career, Rekers, *Benito Arias Montano*; A.F.G. Bell, *Benito Arias Montano* (Oxford, 1922).

92 On Tremellius, see C. Roth, 'Jews in Oxford after 1290', *Oxoniensia*, 15 (1950), 64–8; *DNB*. Junius's son Franciscus Junius (1589–1677), the philologist and antiquary, was for thirty years tutor and librarian to Thomas Howard, earl of Arundel. The elder Junius also had a daughter, who married G.J. Vossius.

93 Exceptions are S. Brock, 'An Introduction to Syriac Studies', in *Horizons in Semitic Studies: Articles for the Student*, ed. J.H. Eaton (Birmingham, 1980), pp. 1–33; and W. Strothmann, *Die Anfänge der syrischen Studien in Europa* (Göttingen, 1971).

94 Theseus Ambrosius, *Introductio in Chaldaicam linguam, Syriacam, atque Armenicam, & decem alias linguas* (Pavia, 1539). The correspondence between Ambrosius and Postel is fos. 192b–200b.

95 Ibid., fos. 140–1.

96 On Tyndale generally, see J.F. Mozley, *William Tyndale* (London, 1937); R. Demaus, *William Tyndale* (London, 1871); D. Daniell, *William Tyndale* (London, 1994) and *The Bible in English* (New Haven and London, 2003).

97 *Tyndale's Old Testament*, ed. D. Daniell (New Haven and London, 1992), 'W.T. To the Reader', p. 5. Cf. John Strype, *Ecclesiastical Memorials* (Oxford, 1822), i/2, pp. 364, 367; Mozley, *Tyndale*, pp. 44–50.

98 C. Haigh, *English Reformations: Religion, Politics and Society under the Tudors* (Oxford, 1993), p. 59.

99 Petition of Humphrey Monmouth, draper, of London, to Wolsey and the Council, 19 May 1528: *Letters & Papers of Henry VIII*, iv (2), no. 4282. Cf. John Foxe, *Acts and Monuments*, ed. S.R. Cattley and G. Townshend (London, 1837–41), iv. 618.

100 *Tyndale's Old Testament*, ed. Daniell, p. 5.

101 Petition of Humphrey Monmouth, draper, of London, to Wolsey and the Council, 19 May 1528.

102 According to A.G. Dickens, *The English Reformation* (London, 1964), p. 74, Roy was 'born of Jewish stock in Calais'.

103 The unhappy customer was Johann Dobneck (Cochlaeus), dean of the church of the Blessed Virgin at Frankfurt, who was having printed an edition of the works of Rupert, a former abbot of Deutz [*DNB*]. He told the story in his book, *De actis et scriptis Martini Lutheri* (1549 edn), p. 132ff. The only surviving copy is the fragment in the Grenville Collection of the British Library, which is missing the title page: 31 folios in all, ending suddenly in the middle of Matthew xxii. Quentell's name does not appear in the text that we have, but he was almost certainly the printer: *Hist. Cat.*, p. 1.

104 Edward Lee to Henry VIII, December 1525, from Bordeaux: *Original Letters Illustrative of English History*, ed. Sir Henry Ellis (London, 1824–46), series 1, I.

180–4; M. Dowling, *Humanism in the Age of Henry VIII* (London, 1986), p. 42; Mozley, *Tyndale*, pp. 57–74.

105 Dowling, *Humanism*, p. 43.

106 S. Brigden, *London and the Reformation* (Oxford, 1989), p. 159, with MS citations; W.A. Clebsch, *England's Earliest Protestants* (New Haven, 1964), pp. 139–42; *Original Letters*, ed. Ellis (3rd ser.), ii. 86 [*DNB*], Haigh, *Reformations*, p. 60. Cf. *Letters & Papers of Henry VIII*, iv (2), p. 1158n., referring to Tunstall's order, printed in Foxe, *Acts and Monuments* and cited by Strype, *Memorials*, i. 165.

107 Mandate of the archbishop of Canterbury to John Voysey, bishop of Exeter, 3 Nov. 1526: *Letters & Papers of Henry VIII*, iv (2), no. 2607. Also on the list was Tyndale's *The Obedience of a Christian Man* and *The Parable of the Wicked Mammon*.

108 Brigden, *London*, pp. 183–4; Augustino Scarpinello to Francesco Sforza, duke of Milan, 16 Dec. 1530: *Cal. S.P. Ven.*, *1527–33*, p. 271; Haigh, *Reformations*, pp. 64–5.

109 John Strype, *Ecclesiastical Memorials* (London, 1721), i. 79 & App. xvii and xxii; *Hist. Cat.*, p. 2.

110 *Cal. S.P. Ven.*, iii. 642; *Cal. S.P. Span.*, iv/1.509 (pp. 820–1); *Two London Chronicles from the Collections of John Stow*, ed. C.L. Kingsford (Camden Soc., Miscellany, xii, 1910), p. 5; Brigden, *London*, pp. 183–4.

111 Petition of Humphrey Monmouth, draper, of London, to Wolsey and the Council, 19 May 1528. Cf. Strype, *Memorials* (1822 edn), i/2, pp. 364–7.

112 John Strype, *Ecclesiastical Memorials* (Oxford, 1820–40), I (2), pp. 54–5: cf. pp. 63–5; Haigh, *Reformations*, p. 60.

113 Foxe, *Acts and Monuments*, iv. 670–1: John Fox, *An Universal History of Christian Martyrdom* (London, 1824), pp. 253–4.

114 The book had been at the Bristol Baptist College since 1784: *Guardian Weekly*, 8 May 1994.

115 *Hist. Cat.*, pp. 1–2.

116 It seems to have been printed by Martin de Keyser for Govaert van der Haghen: *Hist. Cat.*, pp. 7–8 [no. 15]. This is therefore often called the 'G.H.' edition.

117 Ibid., p. 3; *The Library*, Sept. 1947/8, p. 85. There are copies in both the British Library and the Bodleian.

118 *DNB*, s.v. 'Joye, George (d. 1553)'. The author of the entry, however, doubts that Joye was the translator, noting that 'the verbal differences are too thorough to render this theory probable.' A.S. Herbert, in his *Historical Catalogue*, p. 3, catagorically lists the book [no. 3] as Joye's. Joye also produced eight preliminary leaves of a translation of Isaiah [no. 5] (1531: Martin de Keyser at Antwerp) [Bodleian]; another Psalter [no. 9] (1534: Martin Emperour [de Keyser]); ?Proverbs [no. 10] (1534?: Thomas Godfray, London); Jeremiah [no. 11] (1534: widow of Christopher of Endhoven alias C. Van Ruremund, Antwerp) [BL, C.25.d.7.(2)]; a version of Tyndale's NT 'diligently ouersene and corrected' [no. 12] (1534, 16°, same printer, Antwerp) [BL, only copy, G.12180]; a carefully revised edition of Tyndale's 1525 NT and including a second preface in which Tyndale defends his own translation against Joye's corrections [no. 13] (1534, 8°, Martin Emperour [de Keyser], Antwerp) [BL C.23.a.5]; a further reprint of his 1534 16° modification of Tyndale's NT, now also in 16° [no. 17] (1535: Catharyn Widowe [of . . .]) [BL, only copy, C.36.bb.3].

119 *Hist. Cat.*, p. 3; *The Library*, Sept. 1947/8, pp. 85 ff. There are copies in both the British Library and the Bodleian.

120 See now the edition edited by David Daniell.

121 Only one copy exists, in the British Library, discovered in 1861.

122 Foxe, *Acts and Monuments*, v. 363–5 (cf. iv. 635).

123   A.G. Dickens, *Thomas Cromwell and the English Reformation* (London, 1959), pp. 122–3.

124   *Hist. Cat.*, p. 7 [no. 13].

125   See M. Dowling, 'Anne Boleyn and Reform', *Journal of Ecclesiastical History*, 35 (1984), 30–46; E.W. Ives, *Anne Boleyn* (London, 1986), chs 13–14.

126   [Vaughan to Henry VIII], [18 Apr.] 1531: *Letters & Papers of Henry VIII*, v, no. 201. The book in question was *An Answere unto Sir Thomas Mores Dialogue Made by Willyam Tindale* ([London, 1530]): also ed. H. Walter (Parker Soc., Cambridge, 1850). See also *The Confutation of Tyndale's Answer* in Thomas More, *Complete Works* (New Haven and London, 1963–), p. viii. See generally, J.A. Guy, *The Public Career of Sir Thomas More* (Brighton, 1980).

127   This is Dickens's explanation, in *Cromwell*, p. 111.

128   The emphasis and gaps appear in the original: [Cromwell] to Vaughan, [May 1531]: *Letters & Papers of Henry VIII*, v, no. 248, from BL, Cotton MSS, Galba Bx, fos. 338–41: repr. *Thomas Cromwell on Church and Commonwealth*, ed. A.J. Slavin (New York, 1969), pp. 149–53. Cf. *Letters & Papers of Henry VIII*, v, no. 21.

129   Vaughan to Henry VIII, 20 May 1531: *Letters & Papers of Henry VIII*, v, no. 246; Vaughan to [Cromwell], 20 May 1531: ibid., no. 247; Vaughan to Cromwell, 19 June 1531: ibid., no. 303. Cromwell's letter, ibid., no. 248 seems to me to be out of order: it should come before no. 246 and no. 247. Cf. Thos. Jermyn to Cromwell, 19 [June] 1531: *Letters & Papers of Henry VIII*, no. 304: 'Has sent to Master Tyndall, this Monday, the 19th inst., and his servant has delivered to him the King's letter, so that he cannot deny its receipt.'

130   *Letters & Papers of Henry VIII*, v, pp. 121 (no. 265); 165 (no. 354); [Sir T. Elyot] to the duke of Norfolk, 14 Mar. 1532: ibid., no. 869.

131   Vaughan to Cromwell, [14 Nov.] 1531: ibid., no. 532; same to same, 14 Nov. 1531: ibid., no. 533. Sir Thomas Elyot to Cromwell, 18 Nov. 1554: ibid., no. 1554. Cf. a rather crawling letter, same to [same], 9 Dec. 1531: ibid., no. 574.

132   F.D. Logan, 'The Origins of the So-Called Regius Professorships: An Aspect of the Renaissance in Oxford and Cambridge', *Stud. Church Hist.*, 14 (1977), 277; G.L. Jones, *The Discovery of Hebrew in Tudor England: A Third Language* (Manchester, 1983), pp. 190–201. For lists of incumbents, see *The Historical Register of the University of Oxford* (Oxford, 1900), pp. 50–1; and *The Historical Register of the University of Cambridge*, ed. J.R. Tanner (Cambridge, 1917), pp. 76–7. See generally, I. Baroway, 'Toward Understanding Tudor–Jacobean Hebrew Studies', *Jewish Social Studies*, 18 (1956), 3–24.

133   Vaughan to Cromwell, 13 Apr. 1536: *Letters & Papers of Henry VIII*, x, no. 663.

134   Mozley, *Tyndale*, ch. 13.

135   See generally, J.F. Mozley, *Coverdale and his Bibles* (London, 1953).

136   *Hist. Cat.*, pp. 9–11 [no. 18]: copies in both the British Library and the Bodleian. Coverdale's sources were the Vulgate, Tyndale's translations, the German version of Zwingli, and Leo Juda (Zurich, 1524–9), Pagnini's Latin (1528) and Luther's German version (finished 1532). Coverdale's version of 1537 [no. 32] was the first folio Bible printed in England, produced by James Nycolson at Southwark. The same year also saw the production of a quarto version of the same [no. 33], the first Bible of that size printed in England as well.

137   *Documents Illustrative of English Church History*, ed. H. Gee and W.J. Hardy (London, 1896), pp. 269–74.

138   Haigh, *Reformations*, pp. 129–35.

139   *Hist. Cat.*, pp. 18–19 [no. 34]: a copy is in the British Library. Cf. Haigh, *Reformations*, p. 135.

140   *Documents*, ed. Gree and Hardy pp. 275–81; Haigh, *Reformations*, p. 135. The second

edition of April 1540, a folio with Cranmer's prologue, became the standard text, 'Cranmer's Bible': *Hist. Cat.*, pp. 29–30 [no. 53].

141 Haigh, *Reformations*, pp. 156–9. For Gardiner's opposition to Cranmer on this issue, see G. Redworth, *In Defence of the Church Catholic* (Oxford, 1990), pp. 160–4. For some examples of local leaders (the mayor of Sandwich and the vicar of Faversham) trying to outlaw Bible reading, see *Letters & Papers of Henry VIII*, xviii (2), p. 546, pp. 299, 308, 358.

142 P.O. Kristeller, *Renaissance Thought* (New York, 1955), ch. 5.

143 See, e.g., Jones, *Discovery of Hebrew*, pp. 115–22; D.M. Karpman, 'William Tyndale's Response to the Hebraic Tradition', *Studies in the Renaissance*, 14 (1967), 110–30; G. Hammond, 'William Tyndale's Pentateuch: Its Relation to Luther's German Bible and the Hebrew Original', *Renaissance Quarterly*, 33 (1980), 351–85; idem, *The Making of the English Bible* (London, 1982); *William Tyndale's Five Books of Moses Called the Pentateuch*, ed. J.I. Mombert (London, 1884) [new edn ed. F.F. Bruce (Arundel, 1971)]; Clebsch, *Protestants*, p. 138.

144 *Tyndale's Old Testament*, ed. Daniell, pp. 5–6.

145 Note that Erasmus and Tyndale died at almost the same time, Erasmus in July 1536 and Tyndale in October of the same year.

146 The metaphor is A.G. Dickens's: *English Reformation*, p. 37.

147 NB that there were 14 editions of the English Bible produced in the 1560s; 25 in the 1570s; 26 in the 1580s; and 31 in the 1590s, mostly drawing on Tyndale: Haigh, *Reformations*, p. 276, from the *Short-Title Catalogue*.

148 The story of the King James Bible has been told so often that I do not need to tell it again here. Some recent books include B. Bobrick, *Wide as the Waters* (New York, 2001), A.E. Mcgrath, *In the Beginning* (New York, 2001), and A. Nicolson, *God's Secretaries* (New York, 2003).

149 A.W. Pollard, *Records of the English Bible* (Oxford, 1911), pp. 58–60.

150 Although the word 'Jehovah' first appears in the thirteenth century.

151 Tyndale, *Obedience*, preface: quoted in *Tyndale's Old Testament*, ed. Daniell, p. xv.

CHAPTER 2 *In Pursuit of a Useful Bible: Scriptural Politics and the English Civil War*

1 Thomas Hobbes, *Leviathan* (London, 1651); ed. M.J. Oakeshott (Oxford, 1946), pp. 207–8.

2 Thomas Hobbes, *Behemoth*, ed. F. Tönnies (London, 1889), pp. 21–2.

3 Francis Bacon, *The New Organon*, ed. L. Jardine and M. Silverthorne (Cambridge, 2000).

4 John Foxe, *The Acts and Monuments*, ed. Josiah Pratt (London, 1853–70), iii. 719.

5 *DNB.*; S.A. Stussy, 'Michael Sparke, Puritan and Printer' (Univ. Tennessee PhD thesis, 1983); H.R. Plomer, 'Michael Sparke, Puritan Bookseller', *The Bibliographer*, I (1902), 409–19. Sparke was also the editor of the ever-popular *Crums of Comfort* (44 edns between 1628 and 1755), a collection of prayers for times of personal crisis.

6 [Michael Sparke], *Scintilla, or a Light Broken into darke Warehouses* (London, 1641), p. 3. Cf. repr. in *A Transcript of the Registers of the Company of Stationers of London; 1554–1640 AD*, ed. E. Arber (London, 1875–94), iv. 35–8 [1st numbering]; and *Hist. Cat.*, pp. 182–7.

7 T. Watt, *Cheap Print and Popular Piety, 1550–1640* (Cambridge, 1991), chs 5–6.

8 J. Vowell [Hooker], *The Description of the City of Excester* (Devon and Cornwall Record Soc., 1919), ii. 75; C. Haigh, *English Reformations* (Oxford, 1993), p. 194.

9   *Hist. Cat.*, pp. 61–2.
10 *Correspondence of Matthew Parker* (Cambridge, Parker Soc., 1853), pp. 261–2.
11 *Reports of Cases in the Courts of Star Chamber and High Commission*, ed. S.R.
    Gardiner (Camden Soc., 145, 1886), p. 274 [19 Apr. 1632].
12 *Hist. Cat.*, p. 134 (no. 311).
13 Ibid. (no. 313).
14 Now in the University of Heidelberg library: *Hist. Cat.*, p. 134 (no. 313).
15 Ibid., p. 136 (no. 318).
16 Ibid., pp. 136–7 (no. 319).
17 Ibid., pp. 138–9 (no. 322).
18 Ibid., p. 139 (no. 323).
19 Ibid., p. 146 (no. 355).
20 Ibid., pp. 105–6 (no. 208): 'Printed by Iohn Legate, Printer to the Vniuersitie of
    Cambridge. Anno Do. 1591. May 29.'; ibid., p. 158 (no. 424). Cf. *300 Years of
    Printing the Authorized Version of the Holy Bible at Cambridge, 1629–1929* (Cambridge,
    1929).
21 *Hist. Cat.*, p. 162 (no. 444).
22 Peter Heylyn, *Cyprianus Anglicus* (London, 1668), p. 228.
23 *Hist. Cat.*, p. 162.
24 William Kilburne, *Dangerous Errors* (Finsbury, 1659): repr. in intro. to W.J. Loftie, *A
    Century of Bibles* (London, 1872), pp. 31–49; *Hist. Cat.*, p. 162.
25 *DNB*.
26 *Hist. Cat.*, pp. 167–8 (no. 475).
27 Ibid., p. 157 (no. 420).
28 The New Testament alone is ibid., pp. 169–70 (no. 481). An extract from the
    complete Bible, but issued separately, is ibid., p. 168 (no. 476).
29 *Vitae passionis et mortis Jesu Christi . . . exposita per P. Joannem Bourghesium
    Malbodiensem e Societate Jesu* (Antwerp, 1622), esp. plate 76 between pp. 388–9.
30 From 'a person in England to two confidents in Scotland', 11 July 1638: in
    *Memorials and Letters Relating to the History of Britain in the Reign of Charles the
    First*, ed. [Sir] Dav. Dalrymple [Lord Hailes] (Glasgow, 1766), ii. 42.
31 [Michael Sparke], *A Second Beacon fired by Scintilla . . . Wherein is Remembred the
    Former Actings of the Papists in their Secret Plots: And Now Discovering their Wicked
    Designes to Set Up, Advance, and Cunningly to Usher in Popery; By Introducing Pictures
    to the Holy Bible* (London, 1652), p. 6.
32 William Prynne, *Canterburies Doome* (London, 1646), pp. 109–10; cf. pp. 471, 491,
    497, 515. See also *The History of the Troubles and Tryal of . . . William Laud* (London,
    1695), pp. 335–6.
33 Kilburne, *Dangerous Errors*, p. 6. The Bible itself is *Hist. Cat.*, p. 176 (no. 520).
34 *Hist. Cat.*, p. 274 (no. 1142).
35 Kilburne, *Dangerous Errors*, pp. 12–13; *Hist. Cat.*, pp. 177–8 (no. 528), which
    describes two nearly identical editions, supposedly printed in 12° by Robert
    Barker at London, one of which seems to be the counterfeit Bible described by
    Kilburne, although both may have been actually printed in Holland.
36 *Hist. Cat.*, p. 178 (nos 529–32). Cf. the list of errors in Lea Wilson, *Bibles,
    Testaments, Psalms and other Books of the Holy Scriptures in English, in the Collection of
    Lea Wilson* (London, 1845). See also the list of English Bibles printed abroad in
    Hist. Cat., p. 187.
37 *Hist. Cat.*, p. 191 (no. 577). The private collector was named as George Livermore,
    whose reproduction of the Souldiers Pocket Bible, printed in 1861, was distributed
    in 50,000 copies and five editions to the Union troops. Another facsimile edition
    appeared ed. F. Fry (London, 1862), and a further copy in 1894. Another edition

was published in 1895 at London with a preface by Field Marshal Viscount Wolseley. The edition used in the Spanish-American War was published by the American Tract Society. Apart from Livermore's copy of the 1643 original edition, another copy is to be found in the Thomason Collection at the British Library, bearing the date 3 August. Another (slightly different) edition appeared in 1693 for the use of the English army in Flanders, but with the passages quoted in the by now ubiquitous King James Version: *Hist. Cat.*, p. 229 (no. 830) which notes that a facsimile edition was published at London in 1862.

38 *Cal. S.P. Dom., 1652–3*, p. 395 (Council of State proceedings, 9 June 1653).

39 *Hist. Cat.*, p. 195 (no. 601). According to Christopher Anderson, *The Annals of the English Bible* (London, 1845), ii. 559, a quarto edition of this Bible was published at Amsterdam in 1644.

40 *Hist. Cat.*, p. 200 (no. 634).

41 Ibid., p. 213 (no. 719 & 720).

42 Ibid., p. 217 (nos. 744–6).

43 William Maitland, *History of London* (London, 1739), p. 667; Anderson, *Annals*, ii. 559–60; *Hist. Cat.*, p. 217.

44 *Commons Journal, 1651–1659*, p. 245 (11 Jan. 1652–3), p. 264 (4 Mar. 1652–3); PRO, SP.18/26, fos. 260–264ᵛ (*Cal. S.P. Dom., 1652–3*, pp. 73–4).

45 *Hist. Cat.*, p. 192 (no. 579). It is a folio reprint of the 1640 edition (pp. 180–1, no. 545).

46 Niccolò Machiavelli, *The Prince and the Discourses* (New York, 1950): *The Prince*, ch. xxv.

47 See now A. Walsham, *Providence in Early Modern England* (Oxford, 1999).

48 Thomas Gataker, *Of the Natvre and Vse of Lots; A Treatise Historicall and Theologicall* (London, 1619); idem, *A Ivst Defence of Certaine Passages in a Former Treatise concerning the Nature and Vse of Lots, Against such Exceptions and Oppositions as haue beene made thereunto by Mᵣ I.B.* (London, 1623).

49 *Tyndale's Old Testament*, ed. David Daniell (New Haven and London, 1992), p. 63.

50 B. Hilton, *The Age of Atonement: The Influence of Evangelism on Social and Economic Thought, 1785–1865* (Oxford, 1989).

51 J. Bossy, *Christianity in the West, 1400–1700* (Oxford, 1985), p. 38.

52 Stephen Marshall, *Meroz Cursed* (London, 1641). Cf. reply disagreeing with verse-mining by Edward Symmons, *Scripture Vindicated* (Oxford, 1644).

53 The almanacs for 1656–9 and 1662 are now missing. Jessey's Scripture-Kalendar was revived later by 'J.S.' in 1668. Wing wrongly ascribes the edition of 1645 to Henry Jessop on the basis of Thomason's extension of the printed initials: see B.S. Capp, *Astrology and the Popular Press* (London, 1979), pp. 365, 377.

54 [Henry Jessey], *1654. The Scripture-Kalendar* (London, 1654), title page, last page; idem, *1661. The Scripture-Kalendar* (London, 1661), sig. Bʳ⁻ᵛ and *passim*; Capp, *Astrology*, pp. 171–2.

55 B. Ball, *A Great Expectation* (Leiden, 1975), p. 125n. I have not been able to verify this reference.

56 H[enry] J[essey], *The Lords Loud Call to England* (London, 1660), title page, p. 4. Wood noted on his copy (Bodl. Lib., Wood 643[3]) that 'This pamphlet came out in Yᵉ middle of Aug: 1660'. Jessey's full name is cited on sig. A2ʳ, and dated 13 Aug. 1660.

57 All anonymous, without notion of publisher or place: *Mirabilis Annus, Or The Year of Prodigies and Wonders* (1st imp., 1661); *Mirabilis Annus Secundus: Or The Second Year of Prodigies* (1662); *Mirabilis Annus Secundus Or, The Second Part of the Second Years Prodigies* (1662).

58   Ibid., title page.

59   The computation of prodigies was made by Ball, *A Great Expectation*, pp. 111–15.
     On these works, see also K. Thomas, *Religion and the Decline of Magic* (Penguin
     edn, Harmondsworth, 1973), p. 111; and C.E. Whiting, *Studies in English Puritanism*
     (London, 1931), pp. 547–51.

60   *Mirabilis Annus*, sig. A4ᵛ (preface).

61   *Mirabilis Annus Secundus* [first part], sig. A3ᵛ (preface).

62   E[dward] W[histon], *The Life and Death of Mr. Henry Jessey* (n.p., 1671), p. 108.

63   *Mirabilis Annus Secundus* [first part], preface.

64   W. Lamont, *Richard Baxter and the Millennium: Protestant Imperialism and the English
     Revolution* (London, 1979), p. 31.

65   Richard Baxter, *The Life of Faith* (London, 1670), p. 142: written in 1660. Cf.
     Reliquiae Baxterianae, ed. Matthew Sylvester (London, 1696), ii. 432–3; Lamont,
     Baxter, p. 31.

66   See esp. C. Webster, *The Great Instauration* (London, 1975), for more on this entire
     milieu and its effect on the development of modern science.

67   Bodl. Lib., Wood 643(4).

68   Philip Henry, *Diaries and Letters*, ed. M.H. Lee (London, 1882), p. 101: entry for 12
     Dec. 1661; cf. p. 105.

69   Anthony Wood's notes on the title page of Bodl. Lib., Wood 643(4). The first
     impression has 64 pp.; in the second the text is spread out to 88 pp.

70   Colonel Francis Basset of Taunton to Nathaniel Crabb, 25 Dec. 1660: PRO SP.
     29/24, fo. 84ʳ⁻ᵛ.

71   Examination of Jessey, 8 Dec. 1661: PRO, SP. 29/45, fos. 48ʳ–49ʳ. See also
     information concerning Jessey, 11 Sept. 1661: SP. 29/41, fo. 106ʳ⁻ᵛ; arrest warrant of
     Jessey, 27 Nov. 1661: SP. 44/5, p. 59; Jessey to William Howard, 10 Dec. 1661: SP.
     29/45, fos. 56ʳ, 57ʳ; examination of Francis Smith, 19 Dec. 1661: ibid., fo. 136ʳ;
     Jessey to Charles II and Council, ? Dec. 1662: SP. 29/65, fo. 168ʳ; examination of
     Wickham, 3 Nov. 1662: SP. 29/62, fo. 42ʳ; *Mirabilis Annus Secundus*, sig. A4ʳ⁻ᵛ. For
     the background to the government hysteria, see W.C. Abbott, 'English Conspiracy
     and Dissent, 1660–1674', *American History Review*, 14 (1908–9), 513–15; B.S. Capp,
     The Fifth Monarchy Men (London, 1972), p. 209.

72   W[histon], *Life and Death*, pp. 84, 94; White Kennett, *A Register and Chronicle*, i
     (London, 1728), p. 833.

73   Peter Crabb to Bennet, 22 Sept. 1663: PRO, SP. 29/80, fos. 192ʳ–193ᵛ. The *Cal.S.P.
     Dom.*, *1663–4*, pp. 277–8, has Jessey travelling to Holland, but it is clear from the
     original letter that the reference is to Knollys.

74   Cromwell to Walton, 5 July 1644, in Oliver Cromwell, *Writings and Speeches*, ed.
     W.C. Abbott (Cambridge, Mass., 1937–47), i. 287–8.

75   Cromwell to 'a worthy member of the House of Commons' [11 July? 1645] ibid.,
     i. 364–6.

76   Cromwell to Fairfax (commander of Parliamentary army), 28 June 1648: ibid., i.
     618–19, esp. p. 619.

77   Cromwell to Lenthall, 20 Aug. 1648: ibid., i. 634–8, esp. p. 638.

78   Cromwell to Oliver St John (solicitor-general), 1 Sept. [1648]: ibid., i. 644–5, esp.
     p. 644.

79   Cromwell to Philip, Lord Wharton, 2 Sept. 1648: ibid., i. 646.

80   Cromwell to Colonel Robert Hammond, 25 Nov. 1648: ibid., i. 696–9.

81   Cromwell to Dorothy Cromwell, 13 Aug. 1649: ibid., ii. 103–4.

82   Cromwell to Lenthall, [25] Nov. 1649: ibid., 171–4, esp. p. 173.

83   John Hodgson, *Memoirs*, ed. Sir Walter Scott (Edinburgh, 1806), pp. 147–8: 'And,
     the sun appearing upon the sea, I heard Nol say, "Now let God arise, and his

enemies shall be scattered [Psalm lxviii.v.1];" and he, following us as we slowly marched, I heard him say, "I profess they run!" and then was the Scots army all in disorder and running, both right wing, and left, and main battle.'

84 Cromwell to Lenthall, 4 Sept. 1650: in *Writings and Speeches*, ed. Abbott, ii. 321–5, esp. 324–5.

85 Cromwell to John Cotton, 1651: ibid.

86 See, for example, the important works by N. Cohn, *The Pursuit of the Millennium: Revolutionary Millenarians and Mystical Anarchists of the Middle Ages* (London, 1957, rev. edn, London, 1970); E. Hobsbawm, *Primitive Rebels* (Manchester, 1959); E. Hobsbawm and G. Rudé, *Captain Swing* (London, 1969); E.P. Thompson, *The Making of the English Working Class* (London, 1963); G. Leff, *Heresy in the Later Middle Ages* (Manchester, 1967); D. Weinstein, *Savonarola and Florence* (Princeton, 1970); H. Kaminsky, *A History of the Hussite Revolution* (Berkeley, 1967); W. Lamont, *Godly Rule* (London, 1969); J.F.C. Harrison, *Robert Owen and the Owenites in Britain and America* (London, 1969); R.E. Lerner, *The Heresy of the Free Spirit in the Later Middle Ages* (Berkeley, 1972).

87 Esp. Capp, *Fifth Monarchy*.

88 Generally, see M.E. Reeves, *The Influence of Prophecy in the Later Middle Ages* (Oxford, 1969); idem, *Joachim of Fiore and the Prophetic Future* (London, 1976); idem, and B. Hirsch-Reich, *The Figurae of Joachim of Fiore* (Oxford, 1972), B. McGinn, *The Calabrian Abbot* (New York, 1985); idem, *Visions of the End: Apocalyptic Traditions in the Middle Ages* (New York, 1979).

89 That is, the study of 112 ministers who published at least three books between 1640 and 1653: Capp, *Fifth Monarchy*, p. 38.

90 For more on Venner and his risings, see Capp, *Fifth Monarchy*; C. Hill, *The World Turned Upside Down* (London, 1972).

91 William Medley, *A Standard Set Up* (London, 1657), pp. 12–22.

92 [Anon.], *A Character of England* (London, 1659), repr. *Harleian Miscellany*, ed. T. Park (London, 1808–13), x. 192.

93 M.M. Knappen, *Tudor Puritanism* (2nd edn, Chicago, 1970), p. 442.

94 H. Gee and W.J. Hardy, *Documents Illustrative of English Church History* (London, 1896), p. 477; E.C.S. Gibson, *The Thirty-Nine Articles* (London, 1898).

95 John Rogers, *To . . . Cromwell. A Few Proposals relating to Civil Government* (London, 1653), broadsheet; Edmund Ludlow, *Memoirs*, ed. C.H. Firth (Oxford, 1894), i. 358–9; Anthony Morgan to Henry Cromwell, 3 Mar. 1657, in *Cromwell, Writings and Speeches*, ed. Abbott, iv. 418–19; *Clarke Papers*, ed. C.H. Firth (Camden Soc., 2nd ser., 49, 54, 61, 62, 1891–1901), iii. 4, iv. 21; *Thurloe State Papers*, ed. T. Birch (London, 1742), i. 240; *Cal. S.P. Dom.*, *1652–3*, pp. 339–40; Capp, *Fifth Monarchy*, pp. 63, 117–18; *Staffordshire and the Great Rebellion*, ed. D.A. Johnson and D.G. Vaisey (Staffordshire, 1964), p. 72.

96 L.D. [Samuel Highland], *An Exact Relation* (London, 1654), repr. in *Somers Tracts*, ed. W. Scott (2nd edn, London, 1809–15), vi. 266–84, esp. p. 278; A. Woolrych, *Commonwealth to Protectorate* (Oxford, 1982), p. 271.

97 Woolrych, *Commonwealth*, p. 272.

98 [John Cotton], *An Abstract or the Lawes of New England* (London, 1641). The 1655 edition included a preface by William Aspinwall the Fifth Monarchist. Others who advocated adopting the Mosaic law included John Brayne, *The New Earth* (London, 1653), and John Spittlehouse, *The First Addresses* (London, 1653).

99 Woolrych, *Commonwealth*, p. 272.

100 Exod. xx. 8–11.

101 M.M. Knappen, *Tudor Puritanism* (2nd edn, Chicago, 1970), pp. 443–4; S. Bacchiocchi, *From Sabbath to Sunday* (Rome, 1977), pp. 16–55.

102   E.g. 12 Rich. II, c.6; 27 Hen. VI, c.5: see J. Wigley, *The Rise and Fall of the Victorian Sunday* (Manchester, 1980), pp. 204–8 for a list of statutes.
103   Knappen, *Puritanism*, pp. 444–5.
104   Quoted in C. Hill, *Society and Puritanism* (2nd edn, New York, 1967), p. 210.
105   R. Cox, *The Whole Doctrine of Calvin about the Sabbath* (Edinburgh, 1860), p. 91.
106   William Tyndale, *An Answer to Sir Thomas More's Dialogue*, ed. H. Walter (Cambridge, Parker Soc., 1850), pp. 97–8.
107   Knappen, *Puritanism*, pp. 445–6; Hill, *Society*, pp. 149–50: see e.g. 5 & 6 Edw. VI, c.3 (repealed under Mary but re-enacted in 1604) which authorized harvest labour on Sunday 'or at any times in the year when necessity shall require to labour, ride, fish or work any kind of work, at their free wills and pleasure'.
108   Dr Williams's Library, MS Morrice B II, fo. 9ᵛ: quoted in P. Collinson, 'The Beginning of English Sabbatarianism', *Stud. Church Hist.*, 1 (1964), 208.
109   Thomas Shepard, *Theses sabbaticae* (London, 1649), preface, sig. B; W.U. Solberg, *Redeem the Time* (Cambridge, Mass., 1977), pp. 1–2. A similar viewpoint can be found in William Gouge, *Gods Three Arrows* (London, 1631), p. 5; and from John Dod, preaching in Coggeshall: *Cal. S.P. Dom.*, *1636–7*, p. 514. Cf. W. Hunt, *The Puritan Moment* (Cambridge, Mass., 1983), pp. 259, 274.
110   J.E. Neale, *Elizabeth I and her Parliaments* (London, 1953–7), ii. 58–60, 394–5.
111   J. Tait, 'The Declaration of Sports for Lancashire (1617)', *English Historical Review*, 32 (1917), 561–8. Tait located a copy of this hitherto lost document in *Manchester Sessions*, i, ed. E. Axon (Record Society of Lancashire & Cheshire, 42, 1901), pp. xxiv–xxvii.
112   *The Constitutional Documents of the Puritan Revolution*, ed. S.R. Gardiner (3rd edn, Oxford, 1906), pp. 99–103: Declaration of Sports reissued 18 Oct. 1633. For the background to this action, see S.R. Gardiner, *History of England . . . 1603–1642* (2nd edn, London, 1883–4), iii. 248–52; vii. 318–23; *Victoria County History of Somerset*, ii (1911), 43–6; T.G. Barnes, 'County Politics and a Puritan Cause Célèbre: Somerset Churchales, 1633', *Transactions of the Royal Historical Society*, 5th ser., 9 (1959), 103–22; R.C. Richardson, 'Puritanism and the Ecclesiastical Authorities', in *Politics, Religion and the English Civil War*, ed. B. Manning (London, 1973), pp. 15–16.
113   Gardiner, *History*, vii. 322; C. Russell, *Parliaments and English Politics 1621–1629* (Oxford, 1979), pp. 96–7, 157, 183, 234, 276; idem, 'The Parliamentary Career of John Pym, 1621–9', in *The Elizabethan Commonwealth*, ed. P. Clark *et al.* (Leicester, 1979), p. 152; *Commons Debates 1621*, ed. W. Notestein *et al.* (New Haven, 1935), ii. 96; iii. 299; iv. 377–8.
114   G.M. Trevelyan, *History of England* (3rd edn, London, 1945), p. 453. The two most thoughtful pieces of work are Hill, *Society*, ch. 5: 'The Uses of Sabbatarianism'; and Collinson, 'Beginning'. See also R.L. Greaves, 'The Origins of English Sabbatarian Thought', *Sixteenth Century Journal*, 12 (1981), 19–34; K.L. Sprunger, 'English and Dutch Sabbatarianism and the Development of Puritan Social Theology (1600–1660)', *Church History*, 51 (1982), 24–38; K.L. Parker, *The English Sabbath* (Cambridge, 1988); and idem, 'Thomas Rogers and the English Sabbath: The Case for a Reappraisal', *Church History*, 53 (1984), 332–47. See also D.S. Katz, *Sabbath and Sectarianism in Seventeenth-Century England* (Leiden, 1987). An older work, still useful, is M. Levy, *Der Sabbath in England* (Leipzig, 1933). For the Sabbath in later times, see Wigley, *Victorian Sunday*; and D. Eshet, 'Life, Liberty and Leisure: Sunday Observance in England and the Cultural Ideological of Modern Leisure' (UCLA PhD thesis, 1999). The primary sources are meticulously catalogued in R. Cox, *The Literature of the Sabbath Question* (Edinburgh, 1865). See also M. Weber, *The Protestant Ethic and the Spirit of Capitalism*, trans. T. Parsons (New York, 1958), p. 167.

115 Gardiner, *History*, iii. 247.

116 Knappen, *Puritanism*, pp. 447–9.

117 M. James, *Social Problems and Policy during the Puritan Revolution* (London, 1930), pp. 9, 14–15, 21.

118 Hill, *Society*, ch. 5, *passim*.

119 Ibid., esp. pp. 146, 159, 167, 172, 209, 213, 216.

120 *Constitutional Documents of the Reign of James I*, ed. J.R. Tanner (Cambridge, 1930), p. 49.

121 Gardiner, *History*, vii. 318–19.

122 Tait, 'Declaration', p. 565. Dr Hill claims that it is especially in 'the fierce discussions as to whether God intended Saturday or Sunday to be observed as the day of rest' that an element of 'mere irrational Bibliolatry' enters into the Sabbath question: *Society*, p. 146.

123 Mark ii. 27.

124 Bacchiocchi, *Sabbath*, p. 17.

125 See D.S. Katz, *Philo-Semitism and the Readmission of the Jews to England, 1603–1655* (Oxford, 1982), ch. 1.

126 P. Heylyn, *The History of the Sabbath* (London, 1636), pp. 259–60. On Brabourne, see Katz, *Philo-Semitism*, pp. 34–8.

127 Samuel Fisher, *The Rustick's Alarm to the Rabbies* (London, 1660), esp. i. 52–4, ii. 39, 78–9, 103–4, 109, 118–19, 157, 176; iii. 3, 22.

128 Ibid., i. 52.

129 Caton to Fell, 15 Mar. 1657–8, from Leiden: Friends' House Library, London, MS Caton III, p. 507.

130 These pamphlets were eventually published as: [Margaret Fell], *For Manasseth Ben Israel. The Call of the Jewes out of Babylon* (London, 1656); idem, *A Loving Salutation to the . . . Jewes* (London, 1656). Her later works to the Jews are: *A Call to the Universal Seed of God* (London, 1664); *A Call unto the Seed of Israel* (London, 1668); and *The Daughter of Sion Awakened* (London, 1677). See generally, I. Ross, *Margaret Fell: Mother of Quakerism* (London, 1949). Fell's correspondence regarding the translation is: Fell to Fisher, Mar. 1656: Friends' House Library, London, MS Spence III, p. 37; Fell to Stubbs, [?1656], ibid., pp. 38–40.

131 Ames to Fell, 17 Apr. 1657, from Utrecht: Friends' House Library, London, MS Swarthmore 4/28r (transcr. i. 71–4).

132 That this translator was Spinoza was asserted by H.G. Crosfield, *Margaret Fox of Swarthmoor* (London, 1913), p. 50n; W.I. Hull, *The Rise of Quakerism in Amsterdam 1655–1665* (Philadelphia, PA, 1938), p. 205; Ross, *Fell*, p. 94; D. Carrington, 'Quakers and Jews', *Jewish Chronicle Special Supplement: Tercentenary of the Settlement of the Jews in the Brit. Isles 1656–1956* (27 Jan. 1956), p. 46; H.J. Cadbury, 'Spinoza and a Quaker Document of 1657', *Medieval and Renaissance Studies* (1943), 130–3; idem, ed., *The Swarthmore Documents in America* (London, 1940), p. 7; L. Feuer, *Spinoza and the Rise of Liberalism* (Boston, 1958), p. 49; L. Roth, 'Hebraists and Non-Hebraists of the Seventeenth Century', *Journal of Semitic Studies*, 6 (1961), 211; J. van den Berg, 'Quaker and Chiliast: The Contrary Thoughts of William Ames and Petrus Serrarius', in *Reformation, Conformity and Dissent: Essays in Honour of Geoffrey Nuttall*, ed. R. Buick Knox (London, 1977), pp. 182–3.

133 A copy of Fell's *Loving Salutation* in Hebrew is in the Friends' House Library, London, Tracts vol. 133, 38. The translation is followed by a letter in Hebrew by Samuel Fisher, 'to all the House of Jacob at all corners of the earth', Tract 38a. This pamphlet has now been published in a modern edition by R.H. Popkin and M.S. Singer as *Spinoza's Earliest Publication?* (Assen/Maastricht, 1987), with an introduction and commentary.

134   Martin Luther, 'How Christians Should Regard Moses', in *Works*, ed. J. Pelikan
       and H.T. Lehman (St Louis and Philadelphia, 1955–67), xxxv. 171, from the
       sermon of 27 Aug. 1525.

CHAPTER 3   *Cracking the Foundations: Biblical Criticism and*
the Newtonian Synthesis

1   Nicholas Gibbens, *Qvestions and Dispvtations Concerning the Holy Scriptvre* (London,
     1602), pp. 316–18.
2   Ibid., p. 120.
3   [Henry Walker], *Five Lookes over the Professors of the English Bible* (London, 1642),
     title page, sig. A^v, A^{v}3. The title page has a nice engraving of Arminians,
     Protestants, Brownists, and Anabaptists all pulling the Bible in different directions.
4   Arthur Jackson, *A Help for the Understanding of the Holy Scripture* (n.p., 1643), i. sig.
     A6^r, p. 224.
5   J[ohn] Downame, *Annotations Upon all the Books of the Old and New Testament*
     (London, 1645), sig. B2^r. A second and greatly enlarged edition was published at
     London in 1651.
6   Theodore Haak, *The Dutch Annotations Upon the Whole Bible* (London, 1657).
7   Arthur Jackson, *Annotations Upon . . . the Old Testament* (London, 1658), p. $\star$3^v.
8   William Nisbet, *A Scripture Chronology* (London, 1655), sig. +4^v–+5^r.
9   Thomas Allen, *A Chain of Scripture Chronology; from the Creation of the World to the
     Death of Jesus Christ* (London, 1659), esp. sig. a^r; pp. 32, 42–3, 48–9, 50–1, 74–5.
10   The literature on Hobbes and religion, and on Hobbes and Bible, is so huge that
     no note could begin to do justice to the subject.
11   Thomas Hobbes, *Leviathan*, ed. M. Oakeshott (Oxford, 1960), pp. 242–3 (ch. 32).
12   Ibid., p. 77 (ch. 12).
13   Ibid., p. 396 (ch. 43).
14   Ibid., p. 50 (ch. 8).
15   Ibid., pp. 255–6 (ch. 34).
16   Ibid., pp. 225–65 (ch. 34), 291–304 (ch. 38).
17   Ibid., pp. 404–5 (ch. 44).
18   Ibid., p. 419 (ch. 45).
19   Ibid., pp. 291–2 (ch. 38).
20   Ibid., p. 285 (ch. 37).
21   Ibid., pp. 284–5 (ch. 36).
22   Ibid., pp. 254–5 (ch. 33).
23   Ibid., pp. 398–9 (ch. 44).
24   Ibid., p. 246 (ch. 32).
25   Ibid., p. 248 (ch. 33).
26   Ibid., p. 254 (ch. 33).
27   Ibid., pp. 254–5 (ch. 33).
28   Ibid., p. 342 (ch. 42).
29   Ibid., p. 339 (ch. 42).
30   On Walton generally, see (apart from *DNB* art. by D.S.M[argoliouth]), A. Wood,
     Fasti Oxonienses, ed. P. Bliss (London, 1815–20), ii. 81–5; idem, *Athenae Oxonienses*,
     ed. P. Bliss (London, 1813–20), iii. 535, 812, 840; iv. 107, 238, 280, 302, 429. Most
     comprehensively, see Henry John Todd, *Memoirs of the Life and Writings of the Right
     Rev. Brian Walton* (London, 1821).
31   Brian Walton, *An Abstract of a Treatise Concerning the Payment of Tythes and Oblations
     in London* ([London], 1641).

32　An early indication of his unpopularity occurred on 5 May 1636, when he
appeared before the High Commission: *Cal. S.P. Dom., 1635–6*, p. 502. Cf. *The
Articles and Charge Proved in Parliament against Doctor Walton, Minister of St.
Martins Organs . . . Wherein his Subtile Tricks, and Popish Innovations are Discovered* (London,
1641); *Commons Journal.*, ii. 396 (25 Jan. 1641–2). Walton later compounded for his
estate, which had been confiscated: *Calendar of the Committee for Compounding*,
p. 1544.

33　Walton's first wife died in May 1640, and he later married Fuller's daughter Jane,
by whom he had a son.

34　PRO, SP. 18/26, fos. 260ʳ–264ᵛ [*Cal. S.P. Dom., 1652–3*, pp. 73–4]: the actual
document is fos. 262ʳ–263ʳ. The quotation about possible Ainsworth MSS. is
written on a bit of paper attached by a paper clip to fo. 261ᵛ, and is itself
designated fo. 261. It may have fallen off since this was written.

35　*Commons Journal*, 1651–9, pp. 245 (11 Jan. 1652–3), 264 (4 Mar. 1652–3).

36　[Brian Walton], *A Brief Description of an Edition of the Bible* ([London, 1652]):
broadsheet. Those who had missed the boat paid more: in a letter to J. Buxtorf
the younger at Basle, Walton quotes the price at £50.

37　*Biblia sacra polyglotta* (London, 1655–7), six folio volumes.

38　The supervising group consisted of David Stokes (1591?–1669), Abraham
Wheelock (1593–1653), Herbert Thorndike (1598–1672), Edward Pococke (about
whom see below), John Greaves (1602–52), John Vicars (1604–60) and Thomas
Smith (1615–1702). When Wheelock died in 1653, Thomas Hyde (1636–1703) took
his place. John Lightfoot (about whom see below) was invited to participate but
declined. Much of the work was done by Edmund Castell (about whom see
below), whose *Lexicon Heptaglotton* (London, 1669) was in some sense a
supplement to the Polyglot: Castell would complain that he was inadequately
compensated for his work with Walton. See Thorndike's account of the project:
Cal. S.P. Dom., 1655–6, pp. 285–6; *1656–7*, p. 322.

39　*Cal. S.P. Dom., 1651–2*, p. 328.

40　*Cal. S.P. Dom., 1653–4*, pp. 58–9 (29 July 1653).

41　See T.F. Dibdin, *An Introduction to the Knowledge of Rare and Valuable Editions of the
Greek and Latin Classics* (4th edn, London, 1827), i. 20–31.

42　*Briani Waltoni in biblia polyglotta prolegomena* (Leipzig, 1777); and (Cambridge, 1827),
ed. Francis Wrangham. See also *Briani Waltoni . . . Biblicus apparatus chronologico-
topographico-philologicus*, ed. J.H. Heidegger (Zurich, 1673)

43　Brian Walton, *The Considerator Considered* (London, 1659): also repr. in Todd,
Walton, ii. 1–307, followed by the editor's notes.

44　Brian Walton, *Introductio ad lectionem linguarum orientalum* (London, 1655), with the
preface repr. in the Netherlands as *Dissertatio in qua de linguis orientalibus*
(Deventer, 1658).

45　*Cal. S.P. Dom., 1660–1*, p. 235.

46　*Cal. S.P. Dom., 1661*, pp. 49, 69.

47　*Bibliotheca Waltoniana* (London, 1683), an auction catalogue for the sale of 30 Apr.
1683.

48　Castell to Hearne, cited in Dibdin, *Introduction*, p. 32n.

49　Michaelis published the Syriac part of the lexicon at Göttingen in two quarto
volumes in 1788. The Hebrew section was also published separately at Göttingen
in 1790–2.

50　Receipt of the vice-chancellor: J. Nichols, *Illustrations of the Literary History of the
Eighteenth Century* (London, 1817–58), iv. 28; Castell's will, 24 Oct. 1685: BL, Baker
MS 24, pp. 268–71. For more on Castell, see Wood, *Athenae*, ed. Bliss, iii. 883;
Wood, *Fasti*, ed. Bliss, ii. 48.

51 See generally, John Lightfoot, *The Whole Works*, ed. John Rogers Pitman (London, 1822–5); and *Works*, ed. G. Bright and J. Strype (London, 1684). Lightfoot wrote an important book on *The Temple* (London, 1650), which was a key subject for Newton and many others of an apocalyptic bent: see below, p. 108.

52 In a house on High Street opposite Queen's Lane, near the place that Jacob the Jew would in 1650 open the first coffee house in England. This was prophetic in view of Pococke's Arabic–English edition of a MS on *The Nature of the Drink Kauhi, or Coffe, and the Berry of Which it is Made Described by an Arabian Phisitian* (Oxford, 1659).

53 Pococke's collection of 420 Oriental MSS was bought by Oxford University in 1693 for £800 and is in the Bodleian: see Richard Davis, *Catalogi variorum librorum* (London, 1692), a bookseller's auction catalogue for 11 Apr. 1692. The Bodleian acquired more of Pococke's printed books in a bequest of 1821–2: W.D. Macray, *Annals of the Bodleian Library* (2nd edn, Oxford, 1890), p. 161, with a MS notation in the Duke Humfrey's copy correcting the purchase price of the MSS from £600 to £800, citing the vice-chancellor's accounts.

54 See generally Leonard Twells, *The Lives of Dr. Edward Pocock* (London, 1816); and Edward Pococke, *The Theological Works* (London, 1740), including a biography by Twells; P.M. Holt, 'The Study of Arabic Historians in Seventeenth Century England: The Background and the Work of Edward Pococke', *Bulletin of the School of Oriental and African Studies*, 19 (1957), 444–55; M. Feingold, 'Oriental Studies', in *The History of the University of Oxford, Volume IV: Seventeenth-Century Oxford*, ed. N. Tyacke (Oxford, 1997), pp. 449–503.

55 Edward Pococke, *Specimen historiae Arabvm, sive Gregorii AbulFarajii Malatiensis* (Oxford, 1650). It was reprinted in 1806 at Oxford in a sumptuous boxed edition ed. Joseph White (1745–1814), with an appendix by Antoine Isaac Silvestre de Sacy (1758–1838), the French Orientalist. It also includes a lovely engraving of the 'Arbor Pocockiana' fig tree.

56 Edward Pococke, *Porta Mosis* (Oxford, 1655).

57 John Locke to [Humfry Smith], 23 July 1703: *The Correspondence of John Locke*, ed. E.S. de Beer (Oxford, 1976–89), viii. 37–42 (no. 3321): the letter is long and full of interesting anecdotes about Pococke.

58 William Paley, *Natural Theology* (London, 1802), p. 1.

59 Generally here, see F. Oakley, 'Christian Theology and the Newtonian Science: The Rise of the Concept of the Laws of Nature', *Church History*, 30 (1961), 433–57; D. Kubrin, 'Newton and the Cyclical Cosmos: Providence and the Mechanical Philosophy', *Jnl. Hist. Ideas*, 28 (1967), 325–46; M. Todd, 'Providence, Chance, and the New Science in Early Stuart Cambridge', *Historical Journal*, 29 (1986), 697–711; J.E. McGuire, 'Force, Active Principles, and Newton's Invisible Realm', *Ambix*, 15 (1968), 154–208.

60 R.G. Collingwood, *The Idea of Nature* (London, 1946).

61 Clarke to Leibniz, 26 Nov. 1715: *The Leibniz–Clarke Correspondence*, ed. H.G. Alexander (Manchester, 1956), p. 14.

62 In 'Remarks upon the Observations Made upon a Chronological Index of Sir Isaac Newton, Translated into French by the Observator, and Publish'd at Paris', *Philosophical Transactions*, 33 (1724–5), 315–21, printing Newton's letter of 27 May 1725.

63 Vico published Conti's letters in the 1730 edition of *The New Science*.

64 F.E. Manuel, *Isaac Newton Historian* (Cambridge, 1963), p. 35 blames William Whiston for the book's publication. According to his view, Whiston was still angry with his former patron and wanted to see the book in print so he could publicly

refute it. According to Robert Westfall, *Never at Rest* (Cambridge, 1980), however, Newton's heirs were anxious to capitalize on his reputation, and sold the manuscript to a bookseller at once. Conduitt was married to Newton's niece Catherine Barton in 1717, and became very involved with Newton during the last years of his life.

65   Westfall, *Never at Rest*, p. 815.

66   Gen. v. 3,6. For the outline of biblical chronology, I am indebted to the concise remarks in *The Oxford Companion to the Bible*, ed. B.M. Metzger and M.D. Coogan (New York, 1993), s.v. 'Chronology'.

67   Ussher to Selden, 2 Nov. 1627: James Ussher, *The Whole Works*, ed. C.R. Elrington (Dublin, 1847–64), xv. 383–4. On chronology generally, see A.T. Grafton, 'Joseph Scaliger and Historical Chronology: The Rise and Fall of a Discipline', *History & Theory*, 14 (1975), 156–85; idem, 'Scaliger's Chronology', *Journal of the Warburg and Courtauld Institutes*, xlviii (1985), 100–43; J. Barr, 'Why the World Was Created in 4004 BC: Archbishop Ussher and Biblical Chronology', *Bull. John Rylands Lib.*, 67 (1984–5), 575–608; idem, 'Luther and Biblical Chronology', *Bull. John Rylands Lib.*, 72 (1990), 51–67; H. Trevor-Roper, 'James Ussher, Archbishop of Armagh', in *Catholics, Anglicans and Puritans* (London, 1987), ch. 3; Manuel, *Isaac Newton*.

68   Edward Gibbon, *Memoirs of My Life* (Penguin edn, Harmondsworth, 1984), pp. 72–3.

69   Trevor-Roper, 'Ussher', p. 159.

70   P. Hazard, *The European Mind, 1680–1715* (Penguin edn, Harmondsworth, 1973), p. 60 [French edn, 1935].

71   Isaac Newton, *The Chronology of Ancient Kingdoms Amended, To which is Prefix'd, A Short Chronicle* (London, 1728), p. 43: dedicated to the queen by John Conduitt.

72   Ibid., pp. 79–95.

73   Ibid., pp. 51–7. Generally, see A.B. Ferguson, *Utter Antiquity: Perceptions of Prehistory in Renaissance England* (Durham, NC, 1993), esp. ch. 1.

74   Theophilus Gale, *The Court of the Gentiles* (London, 1669–70)

75   The manuscript is far more disorganized than some recent commentary would suggest. Most of it is Jewish National and University Library, Jerusalem, MS Yahuda 16.2. Some of it is in Latin, some in English, some in Newton's hand, and some in the hand of his amanuensis (but no relation) Humphrey Newton. Further details regarding the MS can be found in Westfall, *Never at Rest*, pp. 351–2n. See also, idem, 'Isaac Newton's *Theologiae Gentilis Origines Philosophicae*', in *The Secular Mind*, ed. W. Wager (New York, 1982), pp. 15–34.

76   Newton, *Chronology*, pp. 332–46 and following three plates.

77   Isaac Newton, 'A Dissertation upon the *Sacred Cubit* of the *Jews* and the *Cubits* of the several Nations; in which, from the Dimensions of the greatest *Egyptian* Pyramid, as taken by Mr. *John Greaves*, the antient Cubit of *Memphis* is determined', in John Greaves, *Miscellaneous Works*, ed. Thomas Birch (London, 1737), ii. 405–33. John Greaves was professor of astronomy at Oxford. Between 1638 and 1640 he travelled in the Middle East and climbed the Great Pyramid twice. His work was summarized in his *Pyramidographia: or A Description of the Pyramids in Aegypt* (London, 1646), including a very accurate cross-section of the Great Pyramid. For the ultimate pyramid book, see P. Lemesurier, *The Great Pyramid Decoded* (London, 1977).

78   Jewish National and University Library, Jerusalem, MS Yahuda 17.3, fos. 8–11: repr. Westfall, *Never at Rest*, p. 354.

79   Newton to Locke, 14 Nov. 1690: Locke, *Correspondence*, ed. de Beer, iv. 164–5 (no. 1338).

80   Le Clerc to Locke, 1/11 Apr. 1691: ibid., pp. 247–9 (no. 1381). See also M.I.
      Klauber, 'Between Protestant Orthodoxy and Rationalism: Fundamental Articles in
      the Early Career of Jean LeClerk', *Jnl. Hist. Ideas*, 54 (1993), 611–36
81   See Isaac Newton, *Correspondence*, ed. H.W. Turnbull, *et al.* (Cambridge, 1959–77),
      iii (no. 384) for proof that Newton did not know that the letters had been sent
      on.
82   Newton to Locke, 26 Jan. 1691–2: Locke, *Correspondence*, ed. de Beer, iv. 376 (no.
      1457).
83   Newton to Locke, 16 Feb. 1691–2: ibid., p. 387 (no. 1465).
84   Peter King, *The Life of John Locke* (2nd edn, London, 1830), i. 423–34: 'Remarks on
      Sir Isaac Newton's Three Letters'.
85   *Two Letters of Sir Isaac Newton to Mr. Le Clerc, Late Divinity Professor of the
      Remonstrants in Holland. The Former Containing a Dissertation upon the Reading of the
      Greek Text, I John, v.7. The Latter Upon That of I Timothy, iii.16. Published from
      Authentick MSS in the Library of the Remonstrants in Holland* (London, 1754).
86   'An Historical Account of Two Notable Corruptions of Scripture. In a Letter to a
      Friend. Now First Published Entire from a MS. in the Author's Hand-writing in
      the Possession of the Rev. Dr. Ekens, Dean of Carlisle', in Isaac Newton, *Opera*,
      ed. Samuel Horsley (London, 1779–85), v. 493–550.
87   Bodl. Lib., MS New College 361/4, fos. 2–41: repr. Newton, *Correspondence*, iii.
      83–129 (no. 358): Newton to a friend, 14 Nov. 1690. It is in fact two letters, the
      first dealing with the passage from John and the second from Timothy, written
      carefully in Newton's hand. Ibid., iii. 129–44 (no. 359): Newton to a friend
      [?John Locke], [?Nov. 1690], is headed by Newton, 'The Third Letter', and is a
      sequel to the previous text. It exists in two manuscripts: Bodl. Lib., MS New
      College 361/4, fos. 49ᵛ–68; and fos. 70–83. The first MS is badly mutilated
      and has been pasted on to larger sheets, with missing words added in Newton's
      later handwriting. The second MS was begun by Newton and completed by his
      nephew John Conduitt from folio 80, who notes on it that it is a 'Copy from an
      old MS pasted on Paper with various Readings The Third Letter'. It is the first
      manuscript that is printed ibid., iii. 129–44, as the second is merely a copy by
      Newton and Conduitt from the first.
88   The manuscript is now in Trinity College, Dublin.
89   This and following quotations from King's College, Cambridge, MS 5: repr. S.
      Mandelbrote, '"A duty of the greatest moment": Isaac Newton and the Writing of
      Biblical Criticism', *Brit. Jnl. Hist. Sci.*, 26 (1993), 296.
90   M. Foucault, *Discipline and Punish: The Birth of the Prison* (New York, 1979), pp.
      136–41 [French edn, 1975].

CHAPTER 4   *Streamlined Scriptures: The Demystification of the Bible*

1   E. Cassirer, *The Philosophy of the Enlightenment* (Princeton, 1951), p. 134: first pub.
     1932.
2   Voltaire to Frederick William, prince of Prussia (= nephew of Frederick the Great
     and succeeded him on throne of Prussia in 1786), 28 Nov. 1770: *Voltaire in His
     Letters*, ed. S.G. Tallentyre (New York, 1919), p. 233. Voltaire used this line on other
     occasions as well.
3   René Descartes, *Meditations on First Philosophy in Which the Existence of God and the
     Distinction of the Soul from the Body are Demonstrated*, trans. D.A. Cress (3rd edn,
     Indianapolis, 1993), p. 43 (Meditation V): first pub. 1641.
4   For the best recent account of the subject, see M.I.J. Griffin, *Latitudinarianism in*

the Seventeenth-Century Church of England (Leiden, 1992), based on his 1962 Yale Ph.D. thesis, updated and edited by R.H. Popkin.

5 See R.H. Popkin, *The History of Scepticism from Erasmus to Spinoza* (3rd edn, Berkeley, 1979); B. Dooley, *The Social History of Skepticism: Experience and Doubt in Early Modern Culture* (Baltimore, 1999); L.I. Bredvold, *The Intellectual Milieu of John Dryden* (Ann Arbor, 1934).

6 John Sergeant, *Sure-Footing in Christianity* (London, 1665). Among the Latitudinarians who wrote against Sergeant were John Tillotson, *Rule of Faith* (London, 1666), repr. in *Works* (Edinburgh, 1772), iii. 249–516; and Edward Stillingfleet, *Discourse . . . Faith* (London, 1688).

7 Tillotson, *Works*, i. 549–50; ii. 448 [sermons 73, 168].

8 Ibid., pp. 182–3; ix. 333 [sermons 30, 229].

9 William Chillingworth, *The Religion of Protestants a Safe Way to Salvation* (London, 1638), pp. 54, 57. On the legal implications, see T. Waldman, 'The Origins of the Legal Doctrine of Reasonable Doubt', *Jnl. Hist. Ideas*, 20 (1959), 299–316.

10 See the very useful book by J.S. and J.W. Yolton, *John Locke: A Reference Guide* (Boston, 1985), esp. pp. xxi–xxvi ('Writings by John Locke').

11 These are, respectively, Bodl. Lib., Locke MS 16.25 (LL no. 309); Locke 9.40 (LL no. 2862) and Locke 9.103–7 (LL no. 2864); LL no. 2862; Locke fo. 30.

12 LL. no. 307.

13 See generally, *A Summary Catalogue of the Lovelace Collection of the Papers of John Locke in the Bodleian Library*, ed. P. Long (Oxford, 1959).

14 Bodl. Lib., MS Locke c. 32, fos. 1^r–23^r: sparsely filled 5 × 7-inch pages.

15 Bodl. Lib., MS Locke c. 27, fos. 56^r 66^r: two lists of Hebrew chronology written by S. Brownover, 1680; fos. 90^r–91^v: two lists of Hebrew chronology, the second of which is written by Peter King, 1685; fos. 258^t–261^v: lists of Hebrew chronology with notes by Locke.

16 Bodl. Lib., MS Locke c. 27, fos. 75^r–77^v: 'Dubia circa Philosophiam Orientalem', extracts with notes by Locke from Christian Knorr von Rosenroth, *Adumbratio kabbalae Christianae* (Frankfurt, 1684); fos 248^{r-v}: notes on resurrection headed 'F.M.V.H.', certainly Francis Mercurius Van Helmont's, *Seder Olam* (London, 1694).

17 Bodl. Lib., MS Locke c. 27, fo. 88.

18 John Locke, *A Vindication of the Reasonableness of Christianity* (London, 1695), in *The Works of John Locke*, (London, 1823), vi. 176.

19 *The Correspondence of John Locke*, ed. E.S. De Beer (Oxford, 1976–89), vi. 629–30.

20 John Locke, *A Paraphrase and Notes on the Epistles of St Paul to the Galatians, 1 and 2 Corinthians, Romans, Ephesians*, ed. A.W. Wainwright (Oxford, 1987).

21 Ibid., pp. 105–7. Locke here is quoting John Selden (1584–1654), historian and Orientalist.

22 Mill's New Testament was published only in 1707, after Locke's death. For Mill on Locke, see Locke, *Correspondence*, viii. 269.

23 Newton to Locke, 14 Nov. 1690: ibid., iv. 164–5. For more on this MS, see above, pp. 108–11. See also, M. Cranston, *John Locke* (London, 1957), pp. 338–9, 354–5; F. Manuel, *A Portrait of Isaac Newton* (Cambridge, Mass., 1979), pp. 184–5, 371–2.

24 Mill's method was first stated by Johannes Albrecht Bengel: see B.M. Metzger, *The Text of the New Testament* (2nd edn, Oxford, 1968), p. 112, A. Fox, *John Mill and Richard Bentley* (Oxford, 1954), pp. 147–8.

25 See esp. P.A. Schouls, *The Imposition of Method: A Study of Descartes and Locke* (Oxford, 1980), pp. 216–51.

26 John Locke, *A Letter to Edward Ld. Bishop of Worcester*, in *Works*, iii. 96.

27 John Locke, 'A Discourse of Miracles', first published in the *Posthumous Works of Mr. John Locke* (London, 1706): *Works*, viii. 256–65: esp. p. 256.

28   [John Locke], *The Reasonableness of Christianity, as Delivered in the Scriptures*
     (London, 1695): *Works*, vi.

29   Ibid.

30   John Locke, *An Essay concerning Human Understanding* (London, 1690), ed. P.H.
     Nidditch (Oxford, 1975), 4.19.4.

31   For the original Greek text, see *Sibyllinische Weissagungen: Urtext und Übersetzung*,
     ed. A. Kurfess (Berlin, 1951); *Oracula Sibyllina*, ed. A. Rzach (Prague, 1891).
     Generally, see H.W. Parke, *Sibyls and Sibylline Prophecy in Classical Antiquity*
     (London, 1988); H.N. Bate, *The Sibylline Oracles Books III–V* (London, 1918); M.S.
     Terry, *The Sibylline Oracles* (London, 1890); Y. Am[ir], 'Sibyl and Sibylline Oracles',
     Encyclopaedia Judaica, xiv. 1489–91. Cf. S.A. Hirsch, *A Book of Essays* (London,
     1905), pp. 219–59.

32   Isaac Vossius, *De Sibyllinis aliisque quae Christi natalem praecessere Oraculis* (Oxford,
     1679) [repr. Leiden, 1680], dedicated to Thomas Browne.

33   'Le Roi *Charles II* connoissoit bien son caractere; car l'entendant un jour debiter
     des chose incroyables de ce Pays [China], il se tourna vers quelques Seigneurs qui
     étoient avec lui & leur dit: *ce sçavant Theologien est un étrange homme, il croit tout hors
     la Bible*': Jean-Pierre Nicéron, *Mémoires pour servir à l'histoire des hommes illustres
     dans la république des lettres* (Paris, 1727–45), xiii. 133.

34   James Boswell, *Life of Johnson* (Oxford, 1983), p. 32.

35   John Floyer, *The Sibylline Oracles* (London, 1713), sigs A2ʳ–A3ʳ.

36   William Whiston, *A Vindication of the Sibylline Oracles* (London, 1715), pp. 36, 78,
     83; the book is dedicated to Richard Bentley. For more on Whiston, see J.E.
     Force, *William Whiston: Honest Newtonian* (Cambridge, 1984).

37   Fontenelle, *The History of Oracles and the Cheats of the Pagan Priests* (London, 1688).

38   Edward Pocock, *The Theological Works*, ed. Leonard Twells (London, 1740), i. 74.

39   Marsh to Pococke, 17 Apr. 1680: ibid., p. 75.

40   Marsh to Pococke, 29 Apr. 1680: ibid.

41   James Joyce, *Ulysses* (New York, 1961), p. 39. Joyce himself visited Marsh's Library
     only twice, on 22 and 23 October 1902, to read the prophetic books of Joachim
     Abbas, the *Vaticinia* (Venice, 1589): L. Hyman, *The Jews of Ireland* (Shannon, 1972),
     p. 349.

42   Pocock, *Works*, ed. Twells, i. 78.

43   Pietro della Valle, *Viaggi* (Bologna, 1672), i. 406–8, 424: selections repr. in
     R. Röhricht, *Bibliotheca geographica Palaestinae* (Jerusalem, 1963), p. 947.

44   Generally, see J.D. Purvis, *The Samaritan Pentateuch and the Origins of the Samaritan
     Sect* (Cambridge, Mass., 1968); O. Eissfeldt, *The Old Testament: An Introduction*
     (Oxford, 1965), pp. 694–5, 782.

45   Purvis, *Samaritan Pentateuch*, pp. 74–5; *The Bible in its Ancient and English Versions*,
     ed. H. Wheeler Robinson (Oxford, 1940), chs 2 and 4.

46   N. Shor, 'Reports of Samaritans in the Writings of Western Christian Travellers
     from the 14ᵗʰ until the end of the 18ᵗʰ Centuries' (Hebrew), *Cathedra*, 13 (1979),
     185n; H. Adams, *The History of the Jews* (London, 1818), pp. 499–500. The answer
     in Hebrew which Scaliger received in 1590 is translated into Latin in Silvestre de
     Sacy, *Mémoire sur l'état actuel des Samaritains* (Paris, 1812), pp. 16–23.

47   Shor, 'Reports', p. 186; Adams, *History*, pp. 500–2. Ludolf's answers from the
     Samaritans are reprinted in J. Morinus, *Antiquitates ecclesiae orientalis* (London,
     1682). Their last letter was dated 1689, and reached him in 1691. Huntington sent
     the material he received from the Samaritans to Thomas Marshal of Oxford, who
     kept up the correspondence until his death in 1685: Adams, *History*, pp. 500–3,
     from material in l'Abbé Gregoire, *Histoire des sectes réligieuses* (Paris, 1810).

48   Pocock, *Works*, ed. Twells, i. 75. But cf. the report in the *Journal de Trévoux*, 17

(1706), 1818–19: 'Cependant ayant fait de nouvelles recherches, j'ay enfin découvert que ce refus de communier étoit chimerique. On ne le lui proposa pas seulement. Il étoit trop éloigné de la situation d'esprit qu'il faut pour faire une action aussi sainte & aussi religieuse que celle-là.'

49 Richard Simon, *Critical Enquiries into the Various Editions of the Bible* (London, 1684); idem, *Opuscula Critica adversus Isaacum Vossium* (Edinburgh, 1685).

50 See D.S. Katz, 'The Chinese Jews and the Problem of Biblical Authority in Eighteenth- and Nineteenth-Century England', *English Historical Review*, 105 (1990), 893–919. Vossius's obsession with China was famous: see Nicéron, *Mémoires*, xiii. 132–3, 141.

51 Ussher to Selden, 2 Nov. 1627: James Ussher, *The Whole Works*, ed. C.R. Elrington (Dublin, 1847–64), xv. 380–7; Ussher to Louis Cappel (Cappellus) the Huguenot Hebraist, n.d. (before 1652), ibid., vii. 589–609; H. Trevor-Roper, 'James Ussher, Archbishop of Armagh', in *Catholics, Anglicans and Puritans* (London, 1987), p. 158.

52 Ussher, *Works*, 1. 269–70.

53 Newton admitted that the Masoretic text had already been corrupted by scribes before codification, and therefore preferred the Septuagint because it was older and therefore closer to the truth: F.E. Manuel, *Isaac Newton, Historian* (Cambridge, Mass., 1963), pp. 61, 148.

54 Jonathan Edwards, *Works*, ed. J.E. Smith, *et al.* (New Haven, 1957–), ix. 432. See also G.R. McDermott, *Jonathan Edwards Confronts the Gods: Christian Theology, Enlightenment Religion, and Non-Christian Faiths* (New York, 2000).

55 Leslie Stephen, *History of English Thought in the Eighteenth Century* (London, 1876), chs iii & iv. There is also much about the Deists in H.W. Frei, *The Eclipse of Biblical Narrative* (New Haven, 1974).

56 P. Hazard, *The European Mind 1680–1715* (Harmondsworth, 1973), p. 293: first pub. 1935.

57 Edward, Lord Herbert of Cherbury, *De veritate*, trans. M.H. Carré (Bristol, 1937), esp. pp. 291, 293, 296, 298, 300. For a good deal on the Deists, see H.G. Reventlow, *The Authority of the Bible and the Rise of the Modern World* (London, 1984), trans. of German orig., 1980.

58 Charles Blount, *The Two First Books, of Philostratus, Concerning the Life of Apollonius Tyaneus* (London, 1680). Cf. [idem], *Miracles, No Violations of the Laws of Nature* (London, 1683).

59 So too in the fourth century did Hierocles compare Apollonius's miracles with those of Jesus. Cf. *Philostratus*, ed. F.C. Conybeare (Loeb edn, 2 vols, 1912), with life and letters, which are attributed to Apollonius on very doubtful grounds. Philostratus also wrote *Life of the Sophists*. Cf. John Bradley, *An Impartial View of the Truth of Christianity: with the History of the Life and Miracles of Apollonius Tyanaeus* (London, 1699). A gospel according to Apollonius was published in this century. Cf. Maria Dzielska, *Apollonius of Tyana in Legend and History* (Rome, 1986).

60 John Spencer, *De legibus Hebraeorum ritualibus et earum rationibus* (Cambridge, 1685).

61 See the interesting article by A. Funkenstein, 'Maimonides: Political Theory and Realistic Messianism', *Miscellanea Mediaevalia*, 11 (1977), 81–103.

62 [John Toland], *Christianity not Mysterious* (London, 1696).

63 By M. Jacob, *The Newtonians and the English Revolution, 1689–1720* (Ithaca, NY, 1976), p. 214.

64 John Toland, *Letters to Serena* (London, 1704). Baron d'Holbach published a French translation of this work under the title *Lettres philosophiques* at Amsterdam ['London'], in 1768.

65 John Toland, *Nazarenus: or, Jewish, Gentile, and Mahometan Christianity* (London,

1718) incl. (App., pp. 1–8) 'Two Problems, Historical, Political, and Theological, concerning the Jewish Nation and Religion'. The Appendix also has more on the Gospel of Barnabas, pp. 9–13. See now the edition, ed. Justin Chamption (Oxford: Voltaire Foundation, 1999).

66   Generally, see D. Sox, *The Gospel of Barnabas* (London, 1984); J. Slomp, 'The "Gospel of Barnabas" in Recent Research', *Islamochristiana*, 23 [internet version]; J. Bowman, 'The Gospel of Barnabas and the Samaritans', *Abr-Nahrain*, 30 (1992), 20–33; idem, 'The Debt of Islam to Monophysite Syrian Christianity', *Nederlands Theologisch Tijdschrift*, 19 (1964–5), 177–201; W.E.A. Axon, 'On the Mohammedan Gospel of Barnabas', *Jnl. Theol. Stud.*, 3 (1901–2), 441–5.

67   See E.J. Goodspeed, *Strange New Gospels* (Chicago, 1931); *The Apocryphal Jesus: Legends of the Early Church*, ed. J.K. Elliott (Oxford, 1996).

68   *The Gospel of Barnabas*, ed. L. and L. Ragg (Oxford, 1907), also produced in numerous pirated editions published in the tens of thousands, such as my copy (9th edn, Karachi: Azimi Printers, 1982). See also L. Ragg, 'The Mohammedan "Gospel of Barnabas"', *Jnl. Theol. Stud.*, 6 (1904–5), 424–33.

69   Toland acted as the fence in the theft: see A. Goldgar, *Impolite Learning* (New Haven, 1994), pp. 179–81.

70   A. Grafton, *Forgers and Critics: Creativity and Duplicity in Western Scholarship* (Princeton, 1990).

71   John Toland, *Nazarenus*, ed. J. Champion (Oxford, 1999), pp. 6, 13.

72   R. Sullivan, *John Toland and the Deist Controversy: A Study in Adaptations* (Cambridge, Mass., 1982).

73   D. Berman, *A History of Atheism* (London, 1980); M. Jacob, *The Radical Enlightenment* (London, 1981).

74   Toland, *Nazarenus*, ed. Champion, pp. 14–15.

75   Ibid., pp. 65–6.

76   [Henry Stubbe], 'An Account of the Rise and Progress of Mahometanism with the Life of Mahomet and a Vindication of him and his Religion from the Calumnies of the Christians': BL, MS Harl. 1876 (complete), 6189 (complete); MSS Sloane 1709, 1786 (fragments): first printed, ed. Hafiz Mahmud Khan Shairani (London, 1911), and repr. (Lahore, 1954). See P.M. Holt, *A Seventeenth-Century Defender of Islam: Henry Stubbe (1632–76) and His Book* (London, 1972); J.R. Jacob, *Henry Stubbe, Radical Protestantism and the Early Enlightenment* (Cambridge, 1983); N. Matar, *Islam in Britain, 1558–1685* (Cambridge, 1998); idem, *Turks, Moors, and Englishmen in the Age of Discovery* (New York, 1999).

77   Richard Simon, *A Critical History of the Text of the New Testament* (London, 1689–92). Cf. Simon's *A Critical History of the Old Testament* (London, 1682).

78   There is a good deal of literature about this claim. See Nicholas Notovitch, *La Vie inconnue de Jésus-Christ* (Paris, 1894), trans. as *The Unknown Life of Jesus Christ* (London, 1895), written by a Russian war correspondent who visited India and Tibet in 1887 and claimed that at the lamasery of Himis he learned of a text called the 'Life of Saint Issa, Best of the Sons of Men'. F. Max Müller, about whom much more below (see pp. 282–4), noted that the text does not appear in any record of Tibetan literature and his inquiries at the lamasery convinced him that the entire story was fraudulent: F. Max-Müller, 'The Alleged Sojourn of Christ in India', *The Nineteenth Century*, 36 (1894), 515–22; and J. Archibald Douglas (and F. Max-Müller), 'The Chief Lama of Himis on the Alleged "Unknown Life of Christ"', *The Nineteenth Century*, 39 (1896), 667–78. See also A. Faber-Kaiser, *Jesus Died in Kashmir* (London, 1977); and J. Bock, *The Jesus Mystery* (Los Angeles, 1980). See also *The Crucifixion of Jesus, by an Eye-Witness*, a book used by the Ahmadi Muslims, who believe that Jesus ended up in Kashmir

with the Lost Ten Tribes, described by Goodspeed, *Gospels*, pp. 31–41, and
generally, W.C. Smith, 'Ahmadiyya', *Encyclopaedia of Islam* (2nd edn, Leiden, 1960), i.
301–3. Cf. Al-Haj Khwaja Nazir Ahmad, *Jesus in Heaven on Earth* (Lahore, 1952),
written by a former senior advocate of the Pakistani Supreme Court; and M.A.
Rahim, *Mohammad (Peace Be Upon Him) in Prophecy & in Fact* (Tripoli, 1975).

79 J.E. Fletcher, 'Spanish Gospel of Barabas', *Novum Testamentum*, 18 (1976).

80 Luis F. Bernabé Pons, *El Evangelio de San Bernabé: Un Evangelio Islámico Español*
(Alicante, 1995), based on the author's doctoral thesis (1992) at the university
there.

81 Shlomo Pines, *The Jewish Christians According to a New Source* (Jerusalem, 1966),
based on a lecture (14 June 1966) arguing for a connection between the Gospel
of Barnabas and the Ebionites. Pines was attacked by S. Stern, 'Quotations from
Apocryphal Gospels in 'Abd Al-Jabbar', *Jnl. Theol. Stud.*, 18 (1967), and 19 (1968).
See also *Time Magazine*, 15 July 1966. Cf. R. Blackhirst, *Sedition in Judaea: the
Symbolism of Mizpah in the Gospel of Barnabas* (Bendigo, Australia, 1996), who
largely agrees with Pines; Blackhirst maintains a 'Gospel of Barnabas Home
Page'.

82 John Toland, *Ade sidaemon . . . Annexae sunt ejusdem Origines Judaicae* (The Hague,
1709).

83 [John Toland], *Reasons for Naturalizing the Jews in Great Britain and Ireland, On the
Same Foot with All Other Nations* (London, 1714). It must have been published
between 18 Oct. 1714 and 1 Dec. 1714, because a reply appeared at that time:
[Anon.], *Confutation of the Reasons for Naturalizing the Jews* (London, 1715). Cf.
The Monthly Catalogue, 1, no. 8 (1714), p. 53. The two copies are at the Jewish
Theological Seminary, New York City; and Trinity College Dublin. A reprint can
be found in *Pamphlets Relating to Jews in England in the 17th and 18th Centuries*, ed.
P. Radin (San Francisco, Cal. St. Library, Sutro Branch, 1939), occ. paper, Eng. ser.
no. 3. Generally, see G. Carabelli, *Tolandiana* (Florence, 1975), pp. 188–9. S. Ettinger,
'Jews and Judaism as seen by the English Deists of the 18th Century' [Hebrew],
Zion, 29 (1964), 182–207, argues that, apart from Toland, the Deists' conception of
Jews and Judaism was so negative that we ought to see them as the link between
ancient and classical anti-Judaism and modern anti-Semitism. See also M. Wiener,
'John Toland and Judaism', *Hebrew Union College Annual*, 16 (1941), 215–42 and I.E.
Barzilay, 'John Toland's Borrowings from Simone Luzzatto', *Jewish Social Studies*, 31
(1969), 75–81, who argues that many of the ideas in Toland's work appeared in
Luzzatto's Italian book published in 1638. See also F.E. Manuel, *The Broken Staff:
Judaism through Christian Eyes* (Cambridge, Mass., 1992); and his earlier study, 'Israel
and the Enlightenment', *Daedalus* (1982), 33–52, repr. in his *The Changing of the
Gods* (London, 1983), pp. 105–34.

84 John Toland, *Tetradymus. Containing I. Hodegus* (London, 1720). Note that the third
part of this work, called 'Mangoneutes', is a direct defence of *Nazarenus*.

85 J[ohn] T[oland], *The Life of John Milton* in *A Complete Collection of the Historical,
Political and Miscellaneous Works of John Milton* (London, 1698); J[ohn] T[oland],
Amyntor; or a Defence of Milton's Life (London, 1699); O. Blackall, *Mr. Blackall's
Reasons for Not Replying to a Book Lately Published Entituled Amyntor* (London,
1699). Others who replied included Samuel Clarke, S. Nye, and John Richardson.

86 Anthony Ashley Cooper, 3rd earl of Shaftesbury, *Characteristicks of Men, Manners,
Opinions, Times* (London, 1711), with many further editions.

87 [Anthony Collins], *An Essay Concerning the Use of Reason in Propositions* (London,
1707). A second edition appeared in 1709.

88 [Anthony Collins], *A Discourse of Free-Thinking* (London, 1713). Another edition,
published at 'London' [The Hague] also appeared the same year.

89   William Whiston, *The Accomplishment of Scripture Prophecies* (Cambridge, 1708): the Boyle Lectures.

90   William Whiston, *An Essay towards Restoring the True Text of the Old Testament* (London, 1722). A copy in the British Library [873. l. 10] includes MS notes and corrections by the author.

91   [Anthony Collins], *A Discourse of the Grounds and Reasons of the Christian Religion* (London, 1724). Other editions followed; Baron d'Holbach (1723–89) published a French translation in 1768. Collins replied again (anonymously) in *The Scheme of Literal Prophecy Considered* (London, 1727). See generally, J. O'Higgins, *Anthony Collins: The Man & His Works* (The Hague, 1970).

92   Thomas Bullock, *The Reasoning of Christ and his Apostles* (London, 1725), seven sermons preached at Hackney, Nov.–Dec. 1724.

93   Thomas Woolston, *The Old Apology for the Truth of the Christian Religion against the Jews and Gentiles Revived* (Cambridge, 1705).

94   Thomas Woolston, *The Moderator between an Infidel and an Apostate* (London, 1725). Woolston published two supplements to this work the same year, and a second edition of the entire work in 1729–32.

95   Thomas Woolston, *A Discourse on the Miracles of our Saviour* (London, 1727). Six discourses in all were published between 1727 and 1729: *DNB*.

96   [Thomas Morgan], *The Moral Philosopher. in a Dialogue between Philalethes a Christian Deist, and Theophanes a Christian Jew* (London, 1737–40).

97   Jacob Ilive, *The Oration Spoke at Joyners-hall* (London, 1733). The text for his discourse was John xiv. 2. A second edition appeared at London in 1736. Ilive also wrote *The Book of Jasher . . . translated into English . . . by Alcuin of Britain* (London, 1751), with another edition published (Bristol, 1829).

98   [Matthew Tindal], *Christianity as Old as the Creation: or, the Gospel a Republication of the Religion of Nature* (London, 1730), esp. title page, pp. 232–352. See also the work of the self-taught Deist Thomas Chubb (1679–1747), *The True Gospel of Jesus Christ Asserted* (London, 1738).

99   J.H. Randall, Jr., *The Career of Philosophy* (New York, 1962–5), i. 698. For a diametrically opposed view, see J. Earman, *Hume's Abject Failure: The Argument against Miracles* (New York, 2000). See also D. Johnson, *Hume, Holism, and Miracles* (Ithaca, NY, 1999); S. Buckle, *Hume's Enlightenment Tract: The Unity and Purpose of an Enquiry Concerning Human Understanding* (Oxford, 2001); *Religion and Hume's Legacy*, ed. D.Z. Phillips and T. Tessin (London, 1999); T. Penelhum, *Themes in Hume: The Self, the Will, Religion* (Oxford, 2000).

100   1 Cor. xv. 14.

101   John xx. 25.

CHAPTER 5   *The Occult Bible: Aestheticization and the Persistence of the Supernatural*

1   *A Dictionary of English Church History*, ed. S.L. Ollard and G. Crosse (London, 1912), pp. 535–9.

2   Others included Samuel Horsley (Bp. 1788–93), Thomas Burgess (Bp. 1803–25), and Connop Thirlwall (Bp. 1840–75).

3   *Memoirs of the Life and Writings of . . . Robert Lowth* (London, 1787).

4   Robert Lowth, *De sacra poesi Hebraeorum* (Oxford, 1753); trans. as *Lectures on the Sacred Poetry of the Hebrews* (London, 1787) as thirty-four lectures in two volumes; and again in London (1847) with notes by J.D. Michaelis, the great German

biblical critic. The first English edition of 1787 is used here. This reference, i. 37. Note the outline of Lowth's work, produced in the form of letters to a lady: H.E. Holder, *The Substance of Lowth's Praelections, before the University of Oxford: Digested into Letters, Addressed to Mrs. Ford. Intended as a Supplement to a Hebrew Grammar, Published in the Same Form* (London, 1792).

5 Immanuel Kant, *Observations on the Feeling of the Beautiful and Sublime*, trans. J.T. Goldthwait (Berkeley, 1960): first pub. 1764, and published in English in 1799.

6 Edmund Burke, *A Philosophical Enquiry into the Origin of Our Ideas of the Sublime and Beautiful* (London, 1757), with a second edition (London, 1759) including an additional preface and a new 'Introduction on Taste'; NB the 'World's Classics' edition (Oxford, 1990). His *Reflections on the Revolution in France* was published in 1790. See also S. Blakemore, *Burke and the Fall of Language: The French Revolution as Linguistic Event* (Hanover, NH, 1988).

7 The sublime has once again become a key ingredient of the very latest literary jargon, as any search among the titles of new books will easily reveal.

8 Lowth, *Lectures*, Lecture 18; and esp. i. 166; ii. 4, 84–7. Recognition of Lowth's emphasis on the prophets as poets is made by modern critics such as J.L. Kugel, *The Idea of Biblical Poetry* (New Haven, 1981), p. 172; M. Roston, *Prophet and Poet: The Bible and the Growth of Romanticism* (London, 1965); D. Norton, *A History of the Bible as Literature* (Cambridge, 1993), ii. 59–73; and S. Prickett, 'Romantics and Victorians: from Typology to Symbolism', in *Reading the Text: Biblical Criticism and Literary Theory*, ed. S. Prickett (Oxford, 1991), pp. 182–224.

9 Lowth, *Lectures*, i. 307–9.

10 Ibid., i. 52, 56.

11 Ibid., i. 68–9.

12 Ibid., ii. 35–49.

13 Ibid., i. 101.

14 Ibid., i. 79.

15 F. Kermode, *The Genesis of Secrecy* (Cambridge, Mass., 1979), ch. 4, esp. p. 98.

16 The reference is to L.C. Knights, 'How Many Children Had Lady Macbeth?' in *Explorations* (London, 1945), pp. 1–39. Cf. Edmund Leach, 'Why Did Moses Have a Sister?' in E. Leach and D.A. Aycock, *Structuralist Interpretations of Biblical Myth* (Cambridge, 1983).

17 Lowth, *Lectures*, ii. xxxiii–xli, 54–6.

18 For a good summary of Mede's views, see R.G. Clouse, 'The Rebirth of Millenarianism', in *Puritans, the Millennium and the Future of Israel*, ed. P. Toon (Cambridge, 1970), pp. 56–61.

19 Most of the secondary work on the Hutchinsonians is concerned with their scientific (and especially geological) views: see H. Metzger, *Attraction universelle et religion naturelle* (Paris, 1938), pp. 8, 197; A.J. Kuhn, 'Glory or Gravity: Hutchinson vs. Newton', *Jnl. Hist. Ideas*, 22 (1961), 303–22; M. Neve and R. Porter, 'Alexander Catcott: Glory and Geology', *Brit. Jnl. Hist. Sci.*, 10 (1977), 37–60; G.N. Cantor, 'Revelation and the Cyclical Cosmos of John Hutchinson', in *Images of the Earth* ed. L.J. Jordanova and R. Porter (Chalfont St Giles, 1979), pp. 3–22; C.B. Wilde, 'Hutchinsonianism, Natural Philosophy and Religious Controversy in Eighteenth Century Britain', *Brit. Jnl. Hist. Sci.*, 18 (1980), 1–24; M.C. Jacob, *The Radical Enlightenment* (London, 1981), p. 96; C.B. Wilde, 'Matter and Spirit as Natural Symbols in Eighteenth-Century British Natural Philosophy', *Brit. Jnl. Hist. Sci.*, 15 (1982), 99–131. See also D.S. Katz, 'The Hutchinsonians and Hebraic Fundamentalism in Eighteenth-Century England', in *Sceptics, Millenarians and Jews* [Festschrift for R.H. Popkin], ed. D.S. Katz and J.I. Israel (Leiden, 1990), pp. 237–55; and D.S. Katz, '"Moses's Principia": Hutchinsonianism and Newton's

Critics', in *The Books of Nature and Scripture* ed. J.E. Force and R.H. Popkin (Dordrecht, 1994), pp. 201–11.

20 See generally, [Robert Spearman], *An Abstract from the Works of John Hutchinson* (2nd edn, London, 1755); and John Hutchinson, *The Philosophical and Theological Works*, ed. Robert Spearman and Julius Bate (London, 1749).

21 See D.S. Katz, 'The Phenomenon of Philo-Semitism', *Stud. Church Hist.*, 29 (1992), 327–61, esp. pp. 327–33.

22 Robert Spearman, *A Supplement to the Works of John Hutchinson* (London, 1765), pp. i–v.

23 John Hutchinson, *Moses's Principia. Part II*, in *Works*, ed. Spearman and Bate, ii. 79, 264–5; first pub. 1727.

24 John Hutchinson, *Glory or Gravity*, in *Works*, vi. 7: first pub. 1733–4.

25 [Spearman], *Abstract*, pp. 148–9.

26 L. Stephen, *History of English Thought in the Eighteenth Century* (3rd edn, London, 1902), i. 389–92.

27 Horace Walpole, *Correspondence*, ed. W.S. Lewis, *et al.* (New Haven, 1937–83), xxxv. 156.

28 Edward Gibbon, *Memoirs of My Life* (Penguin edn, Harmondsworth, 1984), p. 80. Magdalen had been a centre of Hebrew studies at Oxford since the Civil War: see D.S. Katz, 'The Abendana Brothers and the Christian Hebraists of Seventeenth-Century England', *Journal of Ecclesiastical History*, 40 (1989), 28–52.

29 Alexander Stopford Catcott, *The Supreme and Inferiour Elahim* (London, 1736). Many of the polemical works written in protest over Catcott's views are bound together as Bodl. Lib., G. Pamph. 250.

30 [Duncan Forbes], *A Letter to a Bishop* (London, 1732), esp. pp. 3, 8, 33.

31 Joseph Spence, *Observations, Anecdotes, and Characters of Books and Men*, ed. J.M. Osborn (Oxford, 1966), pp. 114, 214, 294.

32 See generally, William Jones, *Memoirs of the Life, Studies, and Writings of the Right Reverend George Horne* (London, 1795); George Horne, *Works*, ed. William Jones (2nd edn, London, 1818); William Jones, *Theological, Philosophical and Miscellaneous Works* (London, 1801). Cf. Kuhn, 'Glory'.

33 W. Walker, *The Life and Times of the Rev. John Skinner* (2nd edn, London, 1883), p. 165.

34 John Skinner, *Theological Works* (Aberdeen, 1809), I. xii, xiii, cvi–cxiii, cxxxii–cxliii, cliii–clxxv, cxcv; II. 1–8.

35 W. Walker, *The Life and Times of John Skinner, Bishop of Aberdeen* (Aberdeen, 1887); idem, *Revd John Skinner*, p. 156.

36 Ibid., pp. 159–60. Alexander Nicol held the post for only six years before he died in 1828. He was succeeded as Regius professor by E.B. Pusey, who held the chair for fifty-four years.

37 James Andrew, *Hebrew Dictionary and Grammar* (n.p., 1823).

38 Samuel Johnson, 'Memoirs', in *Samuel Johnson* ed. H. and C. Schneider (New York, 1929), i. 3, 6, 30–1, 45–6; idem, *An English and Hebrew Grammar* (London, 1767). Generally, see T.B. Chandler, *The Life of Samuel Johnson* (New York, 1805), esp. pp. 2, 4–5, 76–85, 116–23, 201–4; E.E. Beardsley, *Life and Correspondence of Samuel Johnson* (New York, 1874); T. Hornberger, 'Samuel Johnson of Yale and King's College: A Note on the Relation of Science and Religion in Provincial America', *New England Quarterly*, 8 (1935), 378–97; I.S. Meyer, 'Doctor Samuel Johnson's Grammar and Hebrew Psalter', in *Essays on Jewish Life and Thought* [Baron Festschrift], ed. J.L. Blau, *et al.* (New York, 1959), pp. 359–74.

39 William Kirby, *On the Power Wisdom and Goodness of God* [7th Bridgewater Treatise] (London, 1835), I. xvii, xlix–l, lxxi (disagreeing with the Hutchinsonians

on the meaning of the word 'cherub'), lxxxiv–v (but agreeing with their understanding of 'firmament' as expansion).

40 S.T. Coleridge, *The Friend*, ed. B.E. Rooke, in *Collected Works* (London, 1971–), iv. III. 502–3 (first pub. 1818). Cf. [Forbes], *Letter*, p. 31.

41 S.T. Coleridge, *Marginalia, I*, ed. G. Whalley, in *Works*, xii. 417.

42 S.T. Coleridge, *The Notebooks*, ed. K. Coburn (London, 1957–), iii. 4401 (March 1818).

43 See J.L. Brooke, *The Refiner's Fire: The Making of Mormon Cosmology* (Cambridge, 1994), esp. pp. 16, 94–5, 166, 199, 205, 257; P. Washington, *Madame Blavatsky's Baboon* (London, 1993), pp. 13–19; E. Barker, *The Making of a Moonie* (Oxford, 1984), esp. p. 44, regarding Moonie leader 'Miss Kim', who had visions of Swedenborg while still a teenager in Korea.

44 M.C. Jacob, *Living the Enlightenment: Freemasonry and Politics in Eighteenth-Century Europe* (New York, 1991), p. 224.

45 J.M. Roberts, *The Mythology of the Secret Societies* (London, 1972), pp. 17–31. Unlike Jacob, who stresses the role of loyal Whig Freemasons, Roberts notes that French Freemasonry was popularized by Jacobite exiles from Scotland and Ireland, who wanted to bring down the entire *ancien régime*: pp. 28–9.

46 See generally the important new work by M.K. Schuchard, *Restoring the Temple of Vision: Cabalistic Freemasonry and Stuart Culture* (Leiden, 2002); and her 'Swedenborg, Jacobitism, and Freemasonry', in *Swedenborg and his Influence*, ed. E.J. Brock, *et al.* (Bryn Athyn, Pa. and London, 1988), pp. 359–79. Benzelius's son-in-law Andreas Norrelius edited Kemper's MSS later on. For Benzelius's correspondence with Leibniz and others, see *Letters to Erik Benzelius the Younger from Learned Foreigners*, ed. A. Erikson (Göteborg, 1980); *Erik Benzelius' Letters to his Learned Friends*, ed. A. Erikson and E.N. Nylander (Göteborg, 1983). Kemper seems to have been a secret follower of Shabtai Zvi: H.-J. Schoeps, *Barocke Juden* (Berne, 1965), pp. 60–82.

47 For more on Falk, see D.S. Katz, *The Jews in the History of England, 1485–1850* (Oxford, 1994), pp. 300–3; and Michal Oron, *Samuel Falk: The Baal Shem of London* [Hebrew] (Jerusalem, 2002).

48 See R. Darnton, *Mesmerism and the End of the Enlightenment in France* (Cambridge, Mass., 1968); A. Winter, *Mesmerized: Powers of Mind in Victorian Britain* (Chicago, 1998).

49 See generally, P.J. Lineham, 'The English Swedenborgians 1770–1840: A Study in the Social Dimensions of Religious Sectarianism' (Ph.D. thesis, Univ. of Sussex, 1978), p. 11. Cf. idem, 'The Origins of the New Jerusalem Church in the 1780s', *Bull. John Rylands Lib.*, 70 (1988), 109–22.

50 Emanuel Swedenborg, *The True Christian Religion* (Everyman edn, London, 1933), pp. 270, 280 (nos 191, 201). See also the very useful book *A Compendium of the Theological Writings of Emanuel Swedenborg*, ed. S.M. Warren (London, 1896).

51 Swedenborg, *True Christian Religion*, pp. 280–1, 332 (nos 202, 275).

52 Ibid., pp. 282–4, 335 (nos 204–5, 279). Swedenborg also notes that scriptural truths might be found in China: cf. D.S. Katz, 'The Chinese Jews and the Problem of Biblical Authority in Eighteenth- and Nineteenth-Century England', *English Historical Review*, 105 (1990), 893–919.

53 Ibid., pp. 285–6 (no. 209).

54 Ibid., pp. 334–5 (no. 278).

55 Ibid., p. 340 (no. 281). See also M. Idel, 'The World of Angels in Human Form', in *Studies in Jewish Mysticism, Philosophy, and Ethical Literature [Isaiah Tishby Festschrift]*, ed. J. Dan and J. Hacker (Jerusalem, 1986), pp. 1–66, esp. pp. 64–6,

where Idel argues that Swedenborg's idea of a *homo maximus* was closer to kabbalistic ideas than to the Cosmic Man of Jaina.

56 See C.D.A. Leighton, 'William Law, Behmenism, and Counter Enlightenment', *Harvard Theological Review*, 91 (1998), 301–20; A.K. Walker, *William Law: His Life and Thought* (London, 1973).

57 See esp. Edward Taylor, *Jacob Behmen's Theosophick Philosophy Unfolded* (London, 1691); D. Hirst, *Hidden Riches: Traditional Symbolism from the Renaissance to Blake* (London, 1964), esp. chs 3 and 7; and A. Koyré, *La Philosophie de Jacob Boehme* (Paris, 1929).

58 John Wesley, *Journal*, ed. N. Curnock (London, 1910–17), v. 354–5 [28 Feb. 1770], 440 [8 Dec. 1771]. Wesley's fullest discussion of Swedenborg's works is dated from Wakefield, 9 May 1782, and published in the *Arminian Magazine*, 6 (London, 1783), 437–41, 495–8, 550–2, 607–14, 669–80. Cf. W.R. Ward, 'Swedenborgianism: Heresy, Schism or Religious Protest?', *Stud. Church Hist.*, 9 (1972), 303–9.

59 See esp. Lineham, 'Origins', pp. 112–13. On Cagliostro, see W.R.H. Trowbridge, *Cagliostro: Splendour and Misery of a Master of Magic* (London, 1910); M. Harrison, *Count Cagliostro* (London, 1942); F. Funck-Brentano, *Cagliostro and Company* (London, 1910); and H.R. Evans, *Cagliostro and his Egyptian Rite of Freemasonry* (New York, 1930). Rainsford's papers are bursting with information about Freemasonry, alchemy and magnetism: BL, Add. MSS 23644–80.

60 Lineham, 'English Swedenborgians', ch. 3; Ward, 'Swedenborgianism'. The standard history of the sect is R. Hindmarsh, *Rise and Progress of the New Jerusalem Church in England, America and other Parts*, ed. E. Madeley (London, 1861).

61 William Blake, 'The Marriage of Heaven and Hell' (*c.* 1790–3), in *Complete Writings*, ed. G. Keynes (London, 1957), pp. 148–60, esp. pp. 157–8. The title itself, of course, is a reference to Swedenborg's book, *Heaven and Hell*.

62 T. Eagleton, *Literary Theory* (Oxford, 1983), p. 20, and generally his *The Ideology of the Aesthetic* (Oxford, 1990). See also C. Gallagher, *The Industrial Reformation of English Fiction, 1822–1867* (Chicago, 1985); and H. Pitkin, *The Concept of Representation* (Berkeley, 1967).

63 R. Paulson, *Representations of Revolution (1789–1820)* (New Haven, 1983); S. Goldsmith, *Unbuilding Jerusalem: Apocalypse and Romantic Representation* (Ithaca, NY, 1993). See also the older standard works on Blake: N. Frye, *Fearful Symmetry: A Study of William Blake* (Princeton, 1947); and H. Bloom, *Blake's Apocalypse: A Study in Poetic Argument* (Garden City, NY, 1959).

64 For some recent objections to the aestheticization of millenarianism, see M.H. Abrams, *Natural Supernaturalism* (New York, 1971); J. Derrida, 'Of an Apocalyptic Tone Recently Adopted in Philosophy', *Oxford Literary Review*, 6 (1984); and J. Baudrillard, 'The Anorexic Ruins', in *Looking Back on the End of the World*, ed. D. Kamper and C. Wulf (New York, 1989).

65 N. Frye, *The Great Code: The Bible and Literature* (New York, 1982).

CHAPTER 6 *Divine Copyright and the Apotheosis of the Author in Eighteenth-Century England*

1 Samuel Johnson, *Lives of the Poets* (London, 1779–81), partly repr. as *Milton*, ed. C.H. Firth (Oxford, 1888), p. 82.

2 The most useful general works include R. Chartier, 'Figures of the Author', in *Of Authors and Origins*, ed. B. Sherman and A. Strowel (Oxford, 1994), pp. 7–22, repr. in his *The Order of Books: Readers, Authors, and Libraries in Europe between the Fourteenth and Eighteenth Centuries* (Cambridge, 1994), pp. 25–59; N.Z. Davis,

'Beyond the Market: Books as Gifts in Sixteenth-Century France', *Transactions of the Royal Historical Society*, 5th ser., 33 (1983), 69–88.

3 On Locke, see R. Brin, 'The Profits of Ideas: *Privilèges en librairie* in Eighteenth-Century France', *Eighteenth-Century Studies*, 4 (1971), 131–68; C. Fox, *Locke and the Scriblerians: Identity and Consciousness in Early Eighteenth-Century Britain* (Berkeley, 1988); J. Tully, *A Discourse on Property: John Locke and his Adversaries* (Cambridge, 1980); J. Dunn, *The Political Thought of John Locke* (Cambridge, 1969).

4 J. Loewenstein, 'The Script in the Marketplace', *Representations*, 12 (1985), 101–14; R. Helgerson, *Self-Crowned Laureates: Spenser, Jonson, Milton, and the Literary System* (Berkeley, 1983).

5 M. De Grazia, *Shakespeare Verbatim: The Reproduction of Authenticity and the 1790 Apparatus* (Oxford, 1991); W.W. Greg, *The Shakespeare First Folio: Its Bibliographical and Textual History* (Oxford, 1955); F.E. Halliday, *The Cult of Shakespeare* (New York, 1960).

6 M. Rose, *Authors and Owners: The Invention of Copyright* (Cambridge, Mass., 1993); H. Ransom, *The First Copyright Statute: An Essay on an Act for the Encouragement of Learning, 1710* (Austin, 1956); E. Eisenstein, *The Printing Press as an Agent of Change* (Cambridge, 1980); E. Armstrong, *Before Copyright: The French Book-Privilege System, 1498–1526* (Cambridge, 1990).

7 Michel Foucault, 'What is an Author?', in *Textual Strategies*, ed. J.V. Harari (Ithaca, NY, 1979), from the French version of 1969; repr. in *The Foucault Reader*, ed. P. Rabinow (Penguin edn, Harmondsworth, 1991), pp. 101–20, esp. pp. 101, 108. Another authoritative text is Roland Barthes's 'The Death of the Author', in *The Rustle of Language* (New York, 1986).

8 See generally M. Woodmansee, 'The Genius and the Copyright: Economic and Legal Conditions of the Emergence of the "Author"', *Eighteenth-Century Studies*, 17 (1984), 425–48; idem, 'The Interests in Disinterestedness: Karl Philip Moritz and the Emergence of the Theory of Aesthetic Autonomy in Eighteenth-Century Germany', *Modern Language Quarterly*, 45 (1984), 22–47; T. Murray, *Theatrical Legitimation: Allegories of Genius in Seventeenth-Century England and France* (New York, 1987).

9 A. Kernan, *Printing Technology, Letters and Samuel Johnson* (Princeton, 1987).

10 D. Foxon, *Pope and the Early Eighteenth-Century Book Trade* (Oxford, 1991).

11 For France, see C. Hesse, 'Enlightenment Epistemology and the Laws of Authorship in Revolutionary France, 1777–1793', *Representations*, 30 (1990), 109–37; and idem, *Publishing and Cultural Poetics in Revolutionary Paris, 1789–1810* (Berkeley, 1991). See also Armstrong, *Before Copyright*.

12 Edward Young, 'Conjectures on Original Composition' (1759), repr. in *English Critical Essays*, ed. E.D. Jones (London, 1922), pp. 270–311. Cf. Woodmansee, 'Genius', p. 430 and generally, for the German distinction between the commonality of ideas versus the originality and uniqueness of the form in which they are expressed.

13 D. Quint, *Origin and Originality in Renaissance Literature* (New Haven and London, 1983).

14 Generally, see A. Fox, *John Mill and Richard Bentley: A Study of the Textual Criticism of the New Testament, 1675–1729* (Oxford, 1954).

15 [John Fell], *Novi Testamenti* (Oxford, 1675).

16 'I hear ye Queen has lately urg'd D^r. Mill (sending an order for that End) to hasten wth his Testament': Thomas Hearne, *Remarks and Collections*, ed. C.E. Doble, et al. (Oxford, 1885–1921), i. 29: 14 Aug. 1705.

17 See Chapter 1, above, and generally J.H. Bentley, *Humanists and Holy Writ: New Testament Scholarship in the Renaissance* (Princeton, 1983). For an annotated list of

Greek New Testaments, see Thomas Frognall Dibdin, *An Introduction to the Knowledge of Rare and Valuable Editions of the Greek and Latin Classics* (4ᵗʰ edn, London, 1827), i. 106–68.

18 Brian Walton, *The Considerator Considered* (London, 1659), cited in Fox, *Mill and Bentley*, p. 48.

19 John Mill, *Novum Testamentum* (Oxford, 1707).

20 Mill, like many others, believed that the Gospel of Matthew was originally written in Hebrew: ibid., p. viiiA.

21 J[ohann Jacob] Wetstein, *Prolegomena ad Novi Testamenti Graeci* (Amsterdam, 1730), pp. 154–5.

22 Gerard of Maastricht's Greek New Testament was published at Amsterdam, 1711–35.

23 Küster also worked in Utrecht on Aristophanes. It was Bentley who convinced him to edit Suidas's lexicon for the University Press at Cambridge; it was published in three folio volumes in 1705.

24 Charles Butler, *Horae Biblicae* (4ᵗʰ edn, London, 1807), i. 159.

25 Christopher Matthew Pfaff, *Dissertatio critica* (Amsterdam, 1709).

26 Joseph Hallet, *Index librorum MSS. Graecorum, et versionum antiquarum* (London, 1728).

27 William Bowyer, *Critical Conjectures and Observations on the New Testament* (4ᵗʰ edn, London, 1812), ed. John Nichols (1745–1826).

28 E[dward] Harwood, *A New Introduction to the Study and Knowledge of the New Testament* (London, 1767–71).

29 Wells, a product of Westminster School and Oxford, edited Xenophon in five volumes at Oxford and wrote many works on various subjects, including both Old and New Testament geographies. His Greek New Testament was printed with many different title pages, which makes it even more confusing: see, for example, *A Paraphrase with Annotations on the New Testament* (London, n.d.). After finishing the New Testament, he went on to the Old. See also his *A Specimen of an Essay for to Find Out and Ascertain the True or Original Reading of the Hebrew Text, in All Places where it Now Differs, Either from the Septuagint Version, or from the Samaritan Pentateuch* (Oxford, 1720).

30 [Daniel Mace], *The New Testament in Greek and English* (London, 1729).

31 James Henry Monk, *The Life of Richard Bentley, D.D.* (2nd edn, London, 1833). Another celebrated biography is that by R.C. Jebb, *Bentley* (London, 1882). See also R.J. White, *Dr Bentley: A Study in Academic Scarlet* (London, 1965), rather spoiled by a purple prose style rarely seen in serious books. Older works include Thomas de Quincey, 'Richard Bentley', in *Works* (London, 1890), iv. 118–236, an extended review of Monk; Hartley Coleridge, *Biographia Borealis* (1833) repr. in his *Worthies of Yorkshire and Lancashire* (London, 1836); Lytton Strachey, *Portraits in Miniature* (London, 1923); Virginia Woolf, *The Common Reader* (London, 1925). The standard edition is *The Works of Richard Bentley*, ed. Alexander Dyce (London, 1836). See also M.L.W. Laistner, 'Richard Bentley: 1742–1942', *Studies in Philology*, 39 (1942), 510–23, repr. in his *The Intellectual Heritage of the Early Middle Ages* (New York, 1983), pp. 239–54.

32 William Temple, *Miscellanea. The Second Part* (London, 1690), pp. 1–72 (1ˢᵗ ser.), esp. pp. 58–9.

33 William Wotton, *Reflections upon Ancient and Modern Learning* (London, 1694).

34 Richard Bentley, *A Dissertation upon the Epistles of Phalaris . . . And the Fables of Aesop* (London, 1697).

35 Swift's famous piece on 'The Battle of the Books', although written at this time, was not published until 1704, in the volume that contained *A Tale of a Tub*. For

more on the controversy, see J.M. Levine, 'Ancients and Moderns Reconsidered', *Eighteenth-Century Studies*, 15 (1981–2), 72–89; idem, 'The Battle of the Books and the Shield of Achilles', *Eighteenth-Century Life*, 9 (1984), 33–61; idem, 'Ancients, Moderns and History', in *Humanism and History: Origins of Modern English Historiography*, ed. J.M. Levine (Ithaca, NY, 1987), 155–77; R. Black, 'Ancients and Moderns in the Renaissance: Rhetoric and History in Accolti's *Dialogue on the Preeminence of Men of his Own Time*', *Jnl. Hist. Ideas*, 43 (1982), 3–32; J.E. Lewis, 'Swift's Aesop/Bentley's Aesop: The Modern Body and the Figures of Antiquity', *The Eighteenth Century*, 32 (1991), 99–118; J.F. Tinkler, 'The Splitting of Humanism: Bentley, Swift, and the English Battle of the Books', *Jnl. Hist. Ideas*, 49 (1988), 453–72; H.R. Jolliffe, 'Bentley Versus Horace', *Philological Quarterly*, 16 (1937), 278–86.

36 Monk, *Bentley*, i. 14. The volume is now in the British Library: Fox, *Mill and Bentley*, p. 117.

37 William Wotton to Bentley, 14 May 1689: *The Correspondence of Richard Bentley, D.D.*, ed. C[hristopher] W[ordsworth] (London, 1842–3), i. 1.

38 John Mill to Bentley, 31 Mar. 1691: ibid., pp. 33–5.

39 Ludolph Küster to Bentley, from Amsterdam, 15 Sept. 1708: ibid., pp. 364–5.

40 William Whiston, *Memoirs* (London, 1749), pp. 107–8.

41 Daniel Whitby, *A Paraphrase and Commentary on the New Testament* (London, 1703).

42 Daniel Whitby, *Examen variantum lectionum Johannis Millii* (London, 1710), p. iii, trans. in Fox, *Mill and Bentley*, p. 106.

43 [Anthony Collins], *A Discourse of Free-Thinking, Occasion'd by the Rise and Growth of a Sect call'd Free-Thinkers* (London, 1713), esp. pp. 5, 46, 87, 88.

44 Benjamin Ibbot, *A Course of Sermons* (London, 1727), esp. pp. 117–37 (1st ser.).

45 William Whiston, *Reflexions on an Anonymous Pamphlet, Entituled, A Discourse of Free Thinking* (London, 1713). Collins and Whiston would have a public dispute in 1724 regarding the literal interpretation of prophecy.

46 [Jonathan Swift], *Mr. C——ns's Discourse of Free-Thinking, Put into Plain English, by Way of Abstract, for the Use of the Poor* (London, 1713).

47 Phileleutherus Lipsiensis [Richard Bentley], *Remarks Upon a Late Discourse of Free-Thinking* (London, 1713), pp. 63–5, with eight editions to 1743.

48 It was for many years in Bentley's possession, as keeper of the King's Library, and was rescued by him from a fire in 1731: see below, p. 203. See also H. Trevor-Roper, 'The Church of England and the Greek Church in the Time of Charles I', in *From Counter-Reformation to Glorious Revolution* (London, 1992), pp. 83–111.

49 But see Bentley himself, *Works*, iii. 353 [from Bentley, *Correspondence*, p. 793].

50 Bentley to William Wake, archbishop of Canterbury, 15 Apr. 1716, from Trinity College, Cambridge: Bentley, *Correspondence*, pp. 502–7, with notes on pp. 791–4, including the fact that the original of this historic letter is now in the library of Christ Church, Oxford. A transcript of most of the letter is now Lambeth Palace, MS Wake 1133, p. 139. Bentley himself makes reference to the letter in his 'Proposals', in his *Works*, iii. 477. Bentley's prophecy was almost fulfilled on 23 Oct. 1731, when nearly 200 books were destroyed or damaged in a fire: see below, p. 203.

51 Bentley to Wake, n.d. [Apr. 1716], from Trinity College, Cambridge: Bentley, *Correspondence*, pp. 507–8.

52 Monk, *Bentley*, i. 397. Monk points out that the same suggestion had been made publicly three years before by his friend Dr Hare.

53 Bentley to Wake, n.d. [April 1716]: *Correspondence*, pp. 507–8: 'I was told, a month ago, that your Grace (when you was at Paris) had made a whole transcript of the

Clermont copy, Greek and Latin, which I hope is true.' The reference is to the Codex Claromontanus, a sixth-century manuscript.

54   J.J. Wetstein to Bentley, 19 July 1716; 29 July 1716: *Correspondence*, pp. 508–10, 510–11.

55   Thomas Rud to Bentley, 22 July 1716: ibid., pp. 512–17.

56   Bentley to Samuel Clarke, 18 Nov. 1716: ibid., pp. 526–9.

57   Bentley to ?, 1 Jan. 1716–17, from Trinity College, Cambridge: ibid., pp. 529–30.

58   According to De Quincey, 'Bentley', p. 147.

59   See Monk, *Bentley*, ii. 8–20.

60   William Whiston, *Historical Memoirs of the Life of Dr. Samuel Clarke* (London, 1730), p. 77; Monk, *Bentley*, ii. 18. Whiston's account is directly contradicted by Daniel Waterland, *Letters to John Loveday*, in *Works*, ed. Van Mildert (2nd edn, Oxford, 1843), vi [1st edn *Works*, x. 410]: Monk, *Bentley*, ii. 18n.

61   Monk, *Bentley*, ii. 18.

62   Conyers Middleton, *Works*, ii. 373; Monk, *Bentley*, ii. 19.

63   Richard Porson, *Letters to Mr Archdeacon Travis, in Answer to his Defence of the Three Heavenly Witnesses, 1 John V.7* (London, 1790), pref., p. viii. Cf. C.O. Brink, *English Classical Scholarship: Historical Reflections on Bentley, Porson, and Housman* (Cambridge and New York, 1986); Monk, *Bentley*, ii. 19.

64   Bentley to Wetstein, 14 Apr. [1717]: *Correspondence*, pp. 532–3; Monk, *Bentley*, i. 120–1.

65   Monk, *Bentley*, i. 121.

66   Walker to Bentley, 29 Dec. 1719, from Paris: *Correspondence*, pp. 563–5.

67   Same to same, 20 Feb. 1720: ibid., pp. 566–8.

68   Same to same, 22 Mar. 1720: ibid., pp. 571–3.

69   Same to same, 30 June 1720: ibid., pp. 605–6.

70   Monk, *Bentley*, ii. 123–5.

71   Thomas Bentley to Richard Bentley, 25 March [1726]: *Correspondence*, pp. 652–7.

72   Monk, *Bentley*, ii. 126–7.

73   Richard Bentley, *Novum Testamentum Versionis Vulgatae . . . Proposals for Printing* [n.p., 1720]. Two editions were printed in the latter part of 1720. The original draft is in Trinity College, Cambridge.

74   Monk, *Bentley*, ii. 130.

75   Cf. *DNB*. It was Conyers Middleton who launched the petty dispute with Bentley in 1718 over the payment of a four-guinea fee which led to the university stripping Bentley of his degrees and a court case between the two which lurched forward intermittently until 1726. The epithet belongs to De Quincey, 'Bentley', p. 124n.

76   [Conyers Middleton], *Remarks, Paragraph by Paragraph, upon the Proposals Lately Publish'd by Richard Bentley* (London, 1721), pp. 18, 39; Monk, *Bentley*, ii. 130–2.

77   *DNB*. De Quincey adds his own personal epithet of 'malicious old toad': 'Bentley', p. 121.

78   [R]J[chard] [B]E[ntley], *Dr. Bentley's Proposals for Printing a New Edition of the Greek Testament* (London, 1721). It is dated from Trinity College, Cambridge, 31 Dec. 1720.

79   John Colbatch, 'Declaration of John Colbatch, D.D. Cambridge, Jan. 20. 1721 disclaiming any connection with *Remarks, Paragraph by Paragraph*', cited in *Richard Bentley, D.D. A Bibliography*, ed. A.T. Bartholomew and J.W. Clark (Cambridge, 1908), p. 22, citing Dyce, iii. 481–2; Monk, *Bentley*, ii. 138–9.

80   'Declaration of the Vice-Chancellor and Heads, Feb. 27. 1720/21, at the insistence of John Colbatch, D.D. pronouncing Bentley's *Proposals* to be "a most virulent and scandalous Libel"': one leaf in Trinity College, Cambridge: Univ. Lib. Cam. MS Baker 27; *Bibliography*, ed. Bartholomew and Clark, p. 23.

81 Monk, *Bentley*, ii.

82 Conyers Middleton, *Some Farther Remarks, Paragraph by Paragraph* (London, 1721).

83 See also [Zachary Pierce (1690–1774), bishop of Rochester] 'Phileleutherus Londinensis', in *Epistolae duae* (London, 1721); 'Philalethes', *A Letter to the Reverend Master of Trinity-College in Cambridge* (London, 1721); *Bibliography*, ed. Bartholomew and Clark, pp. 22–4.

84 Middleton to Colbatch, 9 June 1721: quoted in Monk, *Bentley*, ii. 147.

85 [Richard Smalbroke], *An Enquiry into the Authority of the Primitive Complutensian Edition of the New Testament* (London, 1722), p. 51: repr. in *Somers Tracts*, ed. Walter Scott (2nd edn, London, 1815), xiii. 458–72; and Monk, *Bentley*, ii. 147, who gives the figure of 2,000 guineas.

86 Hearne, *Remarks and Collections*, vii. 322: 30 Jan. 1721–2.

87 Wetstein, *Prolegomena*, p. 156; Monk, *Bentley*, ii. 148n.

88 Quoted in Monk, *Bentley*, ii. 148n.

89 The borrowed MS was an ancient copy of the Gospels owned by the earl of Oxford: J. Nichols, *Illustrations of the Literary History of the Eighteenth Century* (London, 1817–58), i. 88, quoting from the diary of Humphrey Wanley, the keeper of the Harleian Library; Monk, *Bentley*, ii. 148–9.

90 See Philippe de Stosch to Bentley, 9 July 1729 n.s., from Rome: *Correspondence*, pp. 706–7.

91 Monk, *Bentley*, ii. 239.

92 Ibid., ii. 239–42; *DNB*.

93 See above, p. 195.

94 Thomas Bentley to Richard Bentley, 2 Aug. 1726, from Rome: *Correspondence*, pp. 668–73.

95 *DNB*.

96 Monk, *Bentley*, ii. 286–8.

97 Philippe de Stosch to Bentley, 9 July 1729 n.s., from Rome: *Correspondence*, pp. 706–7.

98 Monk, *Bentley*, ii. 289. De Quincey echoes this judgement, perhaps a bit too closely, in 'Bentley', p. 190.

99 Jebb, *Bentley*, p. 163, citing a marginal note in a copy of the quarto Geneva New Testament (1620): Christ Church, Oxford, MS Wake.

100 See esp. J.W. Mackail, 'Bentley's Milton', *Proceedings of the British Academy*, 11 (1925), 55–73; R.E. Bourdette, Jr., 'To *Milton* Lending Sense: Richard Bentley and *Paradise Lost*', *Milton Quarterly*, 14 (1980), 37–49; M.M. Cohen and R.E. Bourdette, Jr., 'Richard Bentley's Edition of *Paradise Lost* (1732): A Bibliography', *Milton Quarterly*, 14 (1980), 49–54; J.K. Hale, 'Notes on Richard Bentley's Edition of *Paradise Lost*', *Milton Quarterly*, 18 (1984), 46–50; J.M. Levine, 'Bentley's Milton: Philology and Criticism in Eighteenth-Century England', *Jnl. Hist. Ideas*, 1 (1989), 549–68. Levine's attempt to see Bentley's work as literary criticism rather than philology is particularly interesting. See also E. Zimmerman, 'Fragments of History and *The Man of Feeling*: From Richard Bentley to Walter Scott', *Eighteenth-Century Studies*, 23 (1990), 283–300.

101 De Quincey, 'Bentley', p. 229.

102 Monk, *Bentley*, ii. 308.

103 Dr R. Freind to Lady Sundon, John Nichols, *Literary Anecdotes of the Eighteenth Century* (London, 1812), ix. 592.

104 Monk, *Bentley*, ii. 308.

105 *The Western Manuscripts of the Library of Trinity College Cambridge*, ed. M.R. James (Cambridge, 1900).

106 Monk, *Bentley*, ii. 415–16.

107   Benjamin Kennicott, *The State of the Printed Hebrew Text of the Old Testament Considered* (Oxford, 1753), i. 7–9. Most of Kennicott's works are helpfully bound together as Bodl. Lib., BS 8° F 122–4. The English letters to Kennicott (with three by him) are now Bodl. Lib. MS Kennicott *c.* 12. The foreign letters are now Bodl. Lib. MS Kennicott *c.* 13, esp. the many letters (*c.* June 1770–74) in *English* from P.J. Bruns, his assistant on the Continent.

108   Kennicott, *State of the Printed Hebrew Text*, ii. 261–2, 556. Cf. idem, *The State of the Printed Hebrew Text of the Old Testament Considered. Dissertation the Second.* (Oxford, 1759), pp. vi–vii, from dedication to Thomas Hunt.

109   *DNB.* Secker became archbishop of Canterbury in 1758.

110   Benjamin Kennicott, *Proposals for Collating the Hebrew Manuscripts* (Oxford, 1760).

111   Benjamin Kennicott, *On the Collation of the Hebrew Manuscripts of the Old Testament* (Oxford, 1760).

112   *DNB.*

113   Ibid.

114   P.J. Bruns's letters to Kennicott are now Bodl.Lib., MS Kennicott *c.* 13, fos. 106–245. Bruns tells Kennicott that he intends to practise his English by writing in that language, so almost all of the correspondence is in English. The letters begin *c.* June 1770, and are very thick until about 1774, with a few dating as late as 1780–1.

115   Fanny Burney, *Diary and Letters of Madame d'Arblay* (London, 1842–6), iii. 237: entry for 28 Nov. 1786. Kennicott married Ann, the sister of Edward Chamberlayne (later Secretary of the Treasury), on 3 Jan. 1771. Another sister married W.H. Roberts, provost of Eton. Many letters between Ann Kennicott and Hannah More are printed in William Roberts, *Memoirs of the Life of Mrs. Hannah More* (London, 1836).

116   *DNB.*

117   Ibid.

118   Benjamin Kennicott, *The State of the Collation of the Hebrew Manuscripts of the Old Testament* (Oxford, 1761), and subsequently to 1769 [?]. The entire series was reprinted as *The Ten Annual Accounts of the Collation of Hebrew MSS. of the Old Testament; Begun in 1760, and Compleated in 1769* (Oxford, 1770). The reports from 1761–8 were translated into Latin and published by N. Barkey as part of the *Bibliotheca Hagana*.

119   Benjamin Kennicott, *Vetus Testamentum Hebraicum, cum variis lectionibus* (Oxford, 1776 and 1780).

120   Kennicott's 'Dissertatio Generalis' was published separately at Oxford in 1780. It was also reprinted by his assistant P.J. Bruns at Brunswick in 1783.

121   *DNB.*

122   Ibid. Much of the material was originally in the Radcliffe Library, but it was transferred to the Bodleian on 10 May 1872, and is now in the New Bodleian.

123   James Boswell, *Life of Johnson*, ed. R.W. Chapman (Oxford, 1980), p. 444: this remark was made in 1770.

124   For Kennicott and the Samaritan Pentateuch, see D.S. Katz, 'Isaac Vossius and the English Biblical Critics, 1670–1689', in *Scepticism and Irreligion in the Seventeenth and Eighteenth Centuries*, ed. R.H. Popkin and A.J. Vanderjagt (Leiden: E.J. Brill, 1993), pp. 142–84.

125   D.S. Katz, 'The Chinese Jews and the Problem of Biblical Authority in Eighteenth- and Nineteenth-Century England', *English Historical Review*, 105 (1990), 893–919.

126   [Robert Spearman], *An Abstract from the Works of John Hutchinson* (2nd edn, London, 1755), p. 42.

127 [Benjamin Kennicott], *A Word to the Hutchinsonians* (London, 1756), pp. 4–5, 6–7, 19.

128 Thomas Rutherforth, *A Letter to the Reverend Mr. Kennicott* (Cambridge, 1761), pp. 1, 3, 5–6, 57–63, 69, 171–3.

129 Benjamin Kennicott, *An Answer to a Letter* (London, 1762), pp. 5–7, 31.

130 Thomas Rutherforth, *A Second Letter* (Cambridge, 1762), pp. 1–3. Cf. Richard Parry, *Remarks upon a Letter* (London, 1763).

131 [J.A. Dumay?], *Lettres de M. l'Abbé de ***, ex Professeur en Hébreu en l'Université de *** au S' K.* (Rome [Paris], 1771).

132 [J.A. Dumay?], *Letters of M' the Abbot of **** (Paris [London], 1772). The claim that Dumay was the author of the letters was made in the Hutchinsonian biography by William Jones, *Memoirs of the Life, Studies, and Writings of the Right Reverend George Horne* (London, 1795), pp. x–xi, 84–109.

133 [Benjamin Kennicott], *A Letter to a Friend Occasioned by a French Pamphlet* (London, 1772).

134 [J.A. Dumay? and William Stephens], *A New . . . Translation of Letters from M. l'Abbé **** (London, 1773).

135 George Sheldon, *Remarks upon the Critical Parts of a Pamphlet Lately Published* (n.p., 1775).

136 *De libello contra B.K. . . . ejusque collationem MSS. Hebraicorum* (Rome, 1772).

137 O.G. Tychsen, *M.O.G. Tychsen . . . befrevetes Tentamen . . . nebst einer Beurtheilung einiger in . . . Kennicott's Pränumerations-Avertissement vorkommenden paradoxen Sätze* (n.p., 1774).

138 Johann David Michaelis, *Neue orientalische und exegetische Bibliothek* (Göttingen, 1786–93), iv. 205–9.

139 Benjamin Kennicott, *Epistola ad celeberrimum professorem Joannem Davidem Michaelis; de Censurâ Primi Tomi Bibliorum Hebraicorum* (Oxford, 1777); repr. (Leipzig, 1777).

140 Benjamin Kennicott, *Contra Ephemeridum Goettingensium criminationes* (Oxford and London, 1782).

141 George Eliot, *Middlemarch* (Penguin edn, Harmondsworth, 1985), p. 88: first pub. 1871–2.

CHAPTER 7 *Ten Little Israelites: Counting Out the Bible in Victorian England*

1 Erich Auerbach, *Mimesis: Dargestellte Wirklichkeit in der abendländischen Literatur* (Berne, 1946), published in English as: *Mimesis: The Representation of Reality in Western Literature* (Princeton, 1953). For the English edition Auerbach added a chapter on Don Quixote (ch. xiv). Reference is to the English-language edition.

2 Ibid., p. 554.

3 Ibid., p. 555.

4 Auerbach was taken to task for what might be seen as an unnecessarily narrow approach to realism – tragic depth and historical concreteness – especially by René Wellek, 'Auerbach's Special Realism', *Kenyon Review*, 16 (1954), 299–307.

5 Auerbach, *Mimesis*, p. 548.

6 This is what Auerbach called 'historicism', defining the nature of a thing from its own history, an idea he assimilated from Vico, whom he had translated into German before his Turkish exile.

7 Auerbach, *Mimesis*, p. 556. In a sense, Auerbach was using the early modern biblical technique of verse-mining, still essential to Fundamentalists today. For a

connection between Auerbach's methodology, Clifford Geertz's anthropology, and New Historicism, see S. Greenblatt, 'The Touch of the Real', *Representations*, 59 (1997), 14–29, repr. in C. Gallagher and S. Greenblatt, *Practicing New Historicism* (Chicago, 2000), ch. 1.

8   Ibid., p. 548. The notion that an individual constructs a complete world view (*Weltanschauung*) during the course of a life (*Lebenslauf*) is usually associated with Wilhelm Dilthey and the so-called Baden School of neo-Kantians. Auerbach, of course, was well aware of this tradition, and in the Epilogue to *Mimesis*, with its sudden autobiographical ending full of pathos, he almost hints that it is his own life, his own *Weltanschauung* which has organized this disparate group of often obscure texts into a coherent history of the representation of realism in Western literature. See M. Holquist, 'The Last European: Erich Auerbach as Precursor in the History of Cultural Criticism', *Modern Language Quarterly*, 54 (1993), 371–91. Auerbach himself referred to *Mimesis* as 'a book that a particular man in a particular place wrote in the early 1940s': 'Epilegomena zu *Mimesis*', *Romanische Forschungen*, 65 (1953), 18: quoted in C. Landauer, 'Auerbach's Performance and the American Academy, or How New Haven Stole the Idea of *Mimesis*', in *Literary History and the Challenge of Philology: The Legacy of Erich Auerbach*, ed. S. Lerer (Stanford, 1996), pp. 179–94, 286–90; M.B. Helfer, *The Retreat of Representation: The Concept of Darstellung in German Critical Discourse* (Albany, 1996).

9   [Daniel Defoe], *Serious Reflections during the Life and Surprising Adventures of Robinson Crusoe* (London, 1720), sigs A2ʳ, A3ʳ (Preface).

10   *OED*, s.v. 'history'. See generally R. Mayer, *History and the Early English Novel: Matters of Fact from Bacon to Defoe* (Cambridge, 1997); and M. Phillips, 'Macaulay, Scott, and the Literary Challenge to Historiography', *Jnl. Hist. Ideas*, 50 (1989), 117–33.

11   For much of what follows, I am indebted to T. Vargish, *The Providential Aesthetic in Victorian Fiction* (Charlottesville, 1985), introduction. See also S. Prickett, 'Poetics and Narrative: Biblical Criticism and the Nineteenth-Century Novel', in *The Bible and European Literature: History and Hermeneutics*, ed. Eric Osborn and Lawrence McIntosh (Melbourne, 1987), pp. 81–97.

12   The books by both Joseph Butler (1692–1752) and William Paley (1743–1805) were published in London.

13   H.D.F. Kitto, *Form and Meaning in Drama* (London, 1956), pp. 243–4.

14   See R.M. Baine, *Daniel Defoe and the Supernatural* (Athens, Georgia 1968).

15   Henry James, *Roderick Hudson* (New York, 1908), pref., p. x. There is quite a lot of critical literature about endings: see F. Kermode, *The Sense of an Ending* (New York, 1966); M. Torgovnick, *Closure in the Novel* (Princeton, 1981), esp. intro.; B.H. Smith, *Poetic Closure* (Chicago, 1968); D. Richter, *Fable's End* (Chicago, 1968); R. Adams, *Strains of Discord: Studies in Literary Openness* (Ithaca, NY, 1968). See also, E. Said, *Beginnings: Intention and Method* (Baltimore, 1975).

16   See generally A. Bowie, *Schelling and Modern European Philosophy* (London, 1993); D. Hedley, *Coleridge, Philosophy and Religion* (Cambridge, 2000).

17   On Lessing generally, see E. Cassirer, *The Philosophy of the Enlightenment* (Princeton, 1951); and T.W. Rolleston, *Life of Gotthold Ephraim Lessing* (Port Washington, 1972 [1889]).

18   See generally, *Lessing's Theological Writings*, ed. H. Chadwick (London, 1956).

19   See A. Grafton, *Cardano's Cosmos: The Worlds and Works of a Renaissance Astrologer* (Cambridge, Mass., 1999).

20   The piece was an attack on Ernst Soner (1572–1612), professor of medicine at Altorf and a closet Socinian. Leibniz thought that the Socinian denial of hell was even more incorrect.

21 G.E. Lessing to Karl Lessing, 2 Feb. 1774: G.E. Lessing, *Gesammelte Werke*, ed.
P. Rilla (Berlin, 1954–8), ix. 596–7: quoted in H.E. Allison, *Lessing and the Enlightenment* (Ann Arbor, 1966), p. 84.

22 Only in 1972 did a complete critical edition finally appear in print, edited by
Gerhard Alexander and published in Frankfurt by Insel Verlag in two volumes.
An English translation by Charles Voysey (1828–1912) of the second half of the
seventh fragment appeared as *Fragments from Reimarus* (London and Edinburgh,
1879); for more on Voysey, see below, p. 247. Modern editions of Reimarus's other
works include: *Die vornehmsten Wahrheiten der natürlichen Religion* (Göttingen, 1985);
Vernunftlehre (Munich, 1979); *Allgemeine Betrachtungen über die Triebe der Thiere,
hauptsächlich über ihre Kunsttriebe* (Göttingen, 1982); *Kleinegelehrte Schriften*
(Göttingen, 1994).

23 The fragments published by Lessing can be found in his *Gesammelte Werke*, ed.
Rilla, vii (frags. 1–6), viii (frag. 7).

24 The final version, written in Reimarus's hand, is in the Hamburg Universitäts-
und Staatsbibliothek. The MS in the Göttingen Universitäts- und Staatsbibliothek
is a copy made by secretaries working for his son. There is a third MS in the
Hamburg Staatsarchiv. Lessing's copy, surrendered to the duke of Brunswick in
1778, alas, is lost. Oddly enough, a comparison between the final Reimarus text
and the fragments published by Lessing suggests that he may have had at his
disposal an older and less detailed version. Lessing revealed to his Jewish friend
Moses Mendelssohn the true author of the fragments, and lent him the MS to
take to Berlin: A. Altmann, *Moses Mendelssohn* (London, 1973), p. 254.

25 The choice was a good one: Schmidt had been imprisoned for his religious
views, had translated Spinoza's *Ethics* and published in 1741 a translation of
Matthew Tindal, *Christianity as Old as the Creation* (1730).

26 Albert Schweitzer, *The Quest of the Historical Jesus: A Critical Study of its Progress
from Reimarus to Wrede* (London, 1910), p. 15.

27 Lessing wrote to his brother (25 Feb. 1780) that he would never admit to being
the author: A.M. Wagner, 'Who is the Author of Lessing's "Education of
Mankind"?', *Modern Language Review*, 38 (1943), 318–27. The work first appeared in
English in the *Monthly Repository of Theology and General Literature*, i (1806), 412–20,
467–73: the pages in the Bodleian copy remain uncut to this day. An American
translation appeared in F.H. Hedge, *Prose Writers of German* (Philadelphia, 1848) and
in England in a new translation by F.W. Robertson in 1858.

28 John Toland, *Christianity Not Mysterious* (London, 1696), p. 49: 'Nor is there any
different Rule to be follow'd in the Interpretation of *Scripture* from what is
common to all other Books.'

29 The sixth and seventh fragments have been published in English as *Reimarus:
Fragments*, ed. C.H. Talbert (London, 1971), in large part a reprint of Voysey's
edition of 1879: See Talbert, pp. 44–57 for a trans. of D.F. Strauss, *Hermann Samuel
Reimarus und seine Schutzschrift für die vernünftigen Verehrer Gottes* (Bonn, 1861–2),
sections 38–40. Until the publication of the entire 'Apology' in 1972, Strauss's
synopsis was the only readily available approach to Reimarus's text.

30 Schweitzer, *Quest*, pp. 22–3.

31 H. Schneider, *Quest for Mysteries: The Masonic Background for Literature in Eighteenth-
Century Germany* (Ithaca, NY, 1947).

32 Lessing was replying here to Bishop William Warburton, *The Divine Legation of
Moses Demonstrated* (London, 1738–41), in which it was argued that it was in fact
the lack of a doctrine of immortality that proved the divine origin of the Bible.
Without the concept of posthumous divine judgment, Warburton argued, society
would collapse, therefore the existence of biblical society implies that God must

have provided some alternative. This took the form of constant divine intervention and miracles, so that every Hebrew was rewarded in this life in direct proportion to his obedience to the law.

33   Wilhelm Martin Leberecht de Wette, *A Critical and Historical Introduction to the Canonical Scriptures of the Old Testament* (Boston, 1843), i. 308. The first German edition appeared in 1817; this translation was done from the Berlin, 1840 edn. See generally, J.W. Rogerson, *W.M.L. de Wette: Founder of Modern Biblical Criticism* (Sheffield, 1992); T.A. Howard, *Religion and the Rise of Historicism: W.M.L. de Wette, Jacob Burckhardt, and the Theological Origins of Nineteenth-Century Historical Consciousness* (Cambridge, 2000).

34   de Wette, *Introduction*, i. 377.

35   Ibid., ii. 36–7.

36   Ibid., pp. 38–9, 40.

37   Ibid., p. 42.

38   Ibid., p. 43.

39   Ibid., pp. 43–4.

40   Ibid., pp. 160–1.

41   For more on de Wette and Fries, see R. Otto, *The Philosophy of Religion Based on Kant and Fries* (London, 1931), pp. 151–215.

42   Wilhelm Gesenius, *Geschichte der hebräischen Sprache und Schrift* (Leipzig, 1815).

43   J.F.L. George, *The Older Jewish Festivals* (1835). See conclusion below.

44   For more on Max Müller, see below, pp. 282–4.

45   Wilhelm Vatke, *Die biblische Theologie* (Berlin, 1835), discussed in J. Robertson, *Old Testament Criticism in the Nineteenth Century: England and Germany* (London, 1984), pp. 69–81. See also O. Pfleiderer, *The Development of Theology in Germany since Kant, and its Progress in Great Britain since 1845* (London, 1890).

46   E.W. Hengstenberg, *Dissertations on the Genuineness of the Pentateuch* (Edinburgh, 1847), i. 2, 12, being an English translation of the second and third volumes of his 'Contributions for the Introduction to the Old Testament' (Berlin, 1831–9). This translation was published by the firm of T. & T. Clark of Edinburgh, which made available to the Victorian reader a good deal of conservative German theology. They also published an English translation of his *Christology of the Old Testament, and a Commentary on the Messianic Predictions* (2nd edn, Edinburgh, 1854–8). An earlier edition, abridged in one volume, was published at London by Rivington in 1847.

47   Hengstenberg, *Dissertations*, i. 3.

48   Ibid., p. 20.

49   Ibid., pp. 31, 43.

50   T.W. Davies, *Heinrich Ewald: Orientalist and Theologian 1803–1903. A Centenary Appreciation* (London, 1903), pp. 4–29.

51   F. Max Müller, *My Autobiography: A Fragment* (London, 1901), p. 287.

52   One of Ewald's colleagues at Göttingen was Karl Otfried Müller (1797–1840), who did for Greece what Niebuhr did for Rome, in his *Introduction to a Scientific System of Mythology* (London, 1844), first published in German at Göttingen in 1825: see J.H. Blok, 'Proof and Persuasion in *Black Athena*: the Case of K.O. Müller', *Jnl. Hist. Ideas*, 57 (1996), 705–24. Cf. R. Pfeiffer, *History of Classical Scholarship from 1300–1850* (Oxford, 1976), pp. 186–7.

53   J.C.K. von Hofmann, *Prophecy and Fulfilment* (1841–2).

54   See *DNB*, s.v. 'Frances Bunsen (1791–1876).' Cf. Augustus J.C. Hare, *The Life and Letters of Frances Baroness Bunsen* (3rd edn, London, 1882).

55   See generally N.M. Distad, *Guessing at Truth: The Life of Julius Charles Hare (1795–1855)* (Shepherdstown, W. Va., 1979).

56 But even the celebrated Bunsen was recalled in 1854 when his Western leanings got in the way of efforts for a Russian alliance promoted by conservatives at the Prussian court.

57 Frances Bunsen, *A Memoir of Baron Bunsen* (London, 1868), i. 84: B. to Lücke, 21 Nov. 1815, from Berlin.

58 Ibid., i. 137–8: B. to his sister Christina, 28 Dec. 1817, from Rome.

59 Christian C.J. Bunsen, *Egypt's Place in Universal History: An Historical Investigation in Five Books* (London, 1848–67), with a second edition of volume 1 also appearing in 1867: used here below.

60 Ibid., i. x.

61 Richard Lepsius, *Discoveries in Egypt, Ethiopia, and the Peninsula of Sinai* (London, 1852), overlapping material with his *Letters from Egypt, Ethiopia, and the Peninsula of Sinai* (London, 1853), esp. pp. 357–506 (concerning chronology), and NB p. 334 (a meeting with Bishop Alexander of Jerusalem). Cf. his *A Tour from Thebes to the Peninsula of Sinai* (London, 1846), recounting the voyage of 4 Mar. – 14 Apr. 1845.

62 Bunsen, *Egypt's Place*, i. xlii.

63 Ibid., p. 176.

64 Ibid., p. 190. Cf. Exod. xii. 40.

65 Bunsen, *Egypt's Place*, 1. p. 174.

66 Ibid., iv. 27. Regarding 'solar symbolism', note that it was Bunsen who brought F. Max Müller to London: see below, pp. 282–4.

67 Ibid., pp. 27–8. Cf. a very similar argument by Carlo Ginzburg, *Ecstasies: Deciphering the Witches' Sabbath* (London, 1989).

68 John Spencer, *De Legibus Hebraeorum ritualibus et earum rationibus* (Cambridge, 1685), i. 157: trans. in J. Assman, *Moses the Egyptian: The Memory of Egypt in Western Monotheism* (Cambridge, Mass., 1997), p. 79, and generally. For more on Warburton, see B.W. Young, *Religion and Enlightenment in Eighteenth-Century England* (Oxford, 1998); and J. Assmann, 'Pictures versus Letters: William Warburton's Theory of Grammatological Iconoclasm', in *Representation in Religion*, ed. J. Assman (Leiden, 2001), pp. 297–311.

69 See J. Winternitz, 'The "Turanian" Hypothesis and Magyar Nationalism in the Nineteenth Century', in *Culture and Nationalism in Nineteenth-Century Eastern Europe*, ed. R. Sussex and J.C. Eade (Columbus, Ohio, 1985), pp. 143–58.

70 See generally Christian C.J. Bunsen, *Christianity and Mankind, their Beginnings and Prospects* (London, 1854), with great reliance on comparative linguistics in historical and anthropological research. See also his *Signs of the Times: Letters to Ernst Moritz Arndt on the Dangers to Religious Liberty in the Present State of the World* (London, 1856); and *The Constitution of the Church of the Future* (London, 1847).

71 C.C.J. Bunsen, *God in History* (London, 1868–70), from the German edition (Leipzig, 1857–8).

72 Ernest de Bunsen, *The Chronology of the Bible* (London, 1874). His own son Sir Maurice de Bunsen (1852–1932) became a prominent English diplomat, described in the *DNB* as a man whose notable accomplishments included 'the art of living'.

73 *Westminster Review*, 17 (1860), 335–6.

74 Alexander Geddes, *Prospectus of a New Translation of the Holy Bible* (Glasgow, 1786); idem, *Proposals and Specimens* (London, 1788); idem, *Critical Remarks on the Hebrew Scriptures* (London, 1800). See R.C. Fuller, 'Dr Alexander Geddes' (Univ. of Cambridge Ph.D., 1968).

75 J.W. Etheridge, *The Life of the Rev. Adam Clarke* (London, 1859), p. 260; *An Account of the Infancy, Religious and Literary Life of Adam Clarke . . . by a Member of his Family* (London, 1833). The grammar was Cornelius Bayley, *An Easy Entrance into the Sacred Language* (London, 1782).

76 Adam Clarke, *The Holy Bible with a Commentary and Critical Notes* (London, 1810–25).

77 Thomas Hartwell Horne, *An Introduction to the Critical Study and Knowledge of the Holy Scriptures* (London, 1818). A much larger and comprehensive edition is the tenth, published at London in 1856, revised by the author in four volumes.

78 Hannah Adams, *The History of the Jews, from the Destruction of Jerusalem to the Present Time* (London, 1818), esp. pp. 498–516, 551, 556–61. See also idem, *A Memoir of Miss Hannah Adams, Written by Herself. With Additional Notices, by a Friend* (Boston, 1832).

79 [Henry Hart Milman], *The History of the Jews* (London, 1829), esp. i. 1, 8, 89, 93–4, 98. In the third volume, Milman has an interesting discussion about Spinoza (pp. 374–83), and on the general influence of the Jews (pp. 426–55). See also his son's book, Arthur Milman, *Henry Hart Milman* (London, 1900).

80 Samuel Smiles, *A Publisher and his Friends: Memoir and Correspondence of the late John Murray* (London, 1891), ii. 298.

81 Milman to Murray, Feb. 1830: ibid., p. 300.

82 Milman to Murray, 29 Mar. 1830: ibid., p. 301.

83 Quoted in *DNB*, s.v. 'Milman, Henry Hart'.

84 [J. Allanson Picton], *The Autobiography and Diary of Samuel Davidson*, ed. A.J. Davidson [his daughter] (Edinburgh, 1899), published by T. & T. Clark. Davidson's pamphlet was published as *Facts, Statements, and Explanations* (London, 1857). See also [Enoch Mellor and James G. Rogers], *Dr. Davidson: His Heresies, Contradictions, and Plagiarisms. By Two Graduates* (Manchester, 1857); Thomas Nicholas, *Dr. Davidson's Removal from the Professorship of Biblical Literature* (London, 1860).

85 Samuel Davidson, *An Introduction to the Old Testament* (London and Edinburgh, 1862), i. v–vi.

86 Samuel Davidson, *Sacred Hermeneutics Developed and Applied, including a History of Biblical Interpretation from the Earliest of the Fathers to the Reformation* (Edinburgh, 1843). Cf. his *Treatise on Biblical Criticism* (Edinburgh, 1852), also published in 1854 in a single volume.

87 J.H. Newman to Lilly, 1877: John Oldcastle, *Cardinal Newman* (London, 1890), p. 5. Cf. *DNB*, *s.v.*, 'Newman, Francis William'. Francis wrote a rather nasty biography of his saintly brother John as well: *Contributions Chiefly to the Early History of the late Cardinal Newman* (2nd edn, London, 1891).

88 I. Giberne Sieveking, *Memoirs and Letters of Francis W. Newman* (London, 1909), written by the niece of Maria Rosina Giberne, to whom Newman twice unsuccessfully proposed marriage, before and after his adventures in the East; but she preferred his brother's way, and eventually became a nun in France. The Sievekings were also related to the Reimarus family. See Francis Newman's autobiography, *Phases of Faith* (London, 1850). See also, B. Willey, 'Francis W. Newman (1805–1897)', in *More Nineteenth Century Studies* (London, 1956), ch. 1; and generally, I. Ker, *John Henry Newman* (Oxford, 1988).

89 Francis William Newman, *Rebilius Cruso: Robinson Crusoe, in Latin; A Book to Lighten Tedium to a Learner* (London, 1884); idem, *Hiawatha: Rendered into Latin* (London, 1862).

90 *DNB*, s.v. 'Newman, Francis William'.

91 Francis William Newman, *A History of the Hebrew Monarchy from the Administration of Samuel to the Babylonish Captivity* (London, 1847). Cf. idem, *On the Historical Depravation of Christianity* (London, 1873).

92 *DNB*, s.v. 'Beddoes, Thomas'.

93 *DNB*, s.v. 'Robinson, Henry Crabb'.

94 John Pye Smith, *The Scripture Testimony to the Messiah* (London, 1847); idem, *On*

the *Relation between the Holy Scripture and some Parts of Geological Science* (London, 1839). Cf. O. Chadwick, *The Victorian Church: An Ecclesiastical History of England* (London, 1966–70), i. 562–3.

95 Hugh James Rose, *The State of the Protestant Religion in Germany* (Cambridge, 1825), esp. p. 145n: pp. 113–83 consists entirely of endnotes, some of which have their own footnotes. A second edition (London, 1829) includes the work originally published as *An Appendix to 'The State of the Protestant Religion in Germany;' Being a Reply to the German Critiques on that Work* (London and Cambridge, 1828). See also J.W. Burgon, *Lives of Twelve Good Men* (London, 1888), i. 116–283, including (248–52), an exchange of letters between Rose and Pusey in March 1838. Hugh James Rose worked closely (and sometimes shared jobs) with his brother Henry John Rose (1800–73), whose contribution to the attack on the Germans was *The Law of Moses, Viewed in Connexion with the History and Character of the Jews* (Cambridge, 1834), the Hulsean Lectures at Cambridge for 1833: see Burgon, *Lives*, i. 284–95.

96 E.B. Pusey, *An Historical Enquiry into the Probable Causes of the Rationalist Character Lately Predominant in the Theology of Germany* (London, 1828); idem, *An Historical Enquiry . . . Part II. Containing an Explanation of the Views Misconceived by Mr. Rose* (London, 1830). See also Edward H. Dewar, *German Protestantism, and the Right of Private Judgment in the Interpretation of Holy Scripture* (Oxford, 1844): Dewar had been the [Anglo-Catholic] chaplain in Hamburg, and was very much against the recent developments in German theology.

97 Peter von Bohlen, *Introduction to the Book of Genesis*, ed. James Heywood (London, 1855), with the editor's short biography. Heywood also connected Lyell's geological discoveries with the work of Bunsen: ibid., i. xxxi–ii.

98 Although see J.L. Altholz, 'Bunsen's Death: Or, How to Make a Controversy', *Victorian Periodicals Review*, 30 (1997), 189–200.

99 *Essays and Reviews* (London, 1860), 1st edn pub. John W. Parker & Son. Later editions were published by Longman. See now the ultimate edition edited by Victor Shea and William Whitla, *Essays and Reviews: The 1860 Text and its Reading* (Charlottesville, 2000). Generally, see J.L. Altholz, *Anatomy of a Controversy: The Debate over 'Essays and Reviews' 1860–1864* (Aldershot, 1994); M.A. Crowther, *Church Embattled: Religious Controversy in Mid-Victorian England* (Newton Abbot, 1970); Basil Willey, 'Septum contra Christum (*Essays and Reviews*, 1860)', in *More Nineteenth Century Studies* (London, 1956), ch. iv; R.V. Sampson, 'The Limits of Religious Thought: The Theological Controversy', in *1859: Entering an Age of Crisis*, ed. P. Appleman, W.A. Madden, and M. Woolf (Bloomington, 1959), pp. 63–80; C.C.J. Webb, *A Study of Religious Thought in England from 1850* (Oxford, 1933); H.D. McDonald, *Ideas of Revelation: An Historical Study AD. 1700 to AD. 1860* (London, 1959); L.E. Elliott-Binns, *Religion in the Victorian Era* (2nd edn, London, 1964); idem, *English Thought, 1860–1900: The Theological Aspect* (London, 1956); H.G. Wood, *Belief and Unbelief since 1850* (Cambridge, 1955); D. Bowen, *The Idea of the Victorian Church* (Montreal, 1968); *Victorian Faith in Crisis*, ed. R.J. Helmstadter and Bernard Lightman (London, 1990).

100 W.E.H. Lecky, *Democracy and Liberty* (London, 1896), i. 424–5.

101 See generally P. Hinchliff, *Frederick Temple* (Oxford, 1998).

102 *Essays and Reviews*, ed. Shea and Whitla, pp. 163–4.

103 Rowland Williams, *Rational Godliness after the Mind of Christ and the Written Voices of his Church* (Cambridge, 1855).

104 Rowland Williams, *Christianity and Hinduism* (Cambridge, 1856).

105 Bunsen, *Memoir*, ii. 429; Bunsen to Max Müller, 27 Apr. 1857: Friedrich Max Müller, *Chips from a German Workshop* (London, 1867–70), iii. 506. Max Müller,

oddly enough, was one of the innocent bystanders wounded in the attack on the Essayists. He was a favourite for the Sanskrit chair at Oxford, but his origins in Germany, the source of the biblical infection, and his friendship with Baron Bunsen inspired a host of MAs to come up to Oxford and vote in Convocation against his appointment: *The Life and Letters of Benjamin Jowett*, ed. E. Abbott and L. Campbell (London, 1897), i. 291; and see below, pp. 282–4.

106 In the end, it was only C.W. Goodwin, the one layman of the group, whom he managed to recruit.

107 Baden Powell, *The Order of Nature Considered in Reference to the Claims of Revelation* (London, 1859). Cf. his *Revelation and Science* (Oxford, 1833). Generally see Pietro Corsi, *Science and Religion: Baden Powell and the Anglican Debate, 1800–1860* (Cambridge, 1988), esp. pp. 215–24 concerning *Essays and Reviews*.

108 There were also *Cambridge Essays* (1855–8): Goodwin contributed an article to it: 'Hieratic Papyri', *Cambridge Essays* (1858), 226–82, which 'marks an epoch in Egyptology', according to Warren R. Dawson, *Who Was Who in Egyptology* (London, 1951), p. 63.

109 See generally Warren R. Dawson, *Charles Wycliffe Goodwin 1817–1878: A Pioneer in Egyptology* (London, 1934).

110 *Essays and Reviews*, ed. Shea and Whitla, p. 208.

111 See Mark Francis, 'The Origins of *Essays and Reviews*: An Interpretation of Mark Pattison in the 1850s', *Historical Journal*, 17 (1974), 797–811; John Sparrow, *Mark Pattison and the Idea of a University* (Cambridge, 1967).

112 *Life and Letters of Benjamin Jowett*, ed. Abbott and Campbell, i. 290–320; P. Hinchliff, *Benjamin Jowett and the Christian Religion* (Oxford, 1987); G. Faber, *Jowett: A Portrait with Background* (London, 1957); J. Barr, 'Jowett and the "Original Meaning" of Scripture', *Religious Studies*, 18 (1992), 433–7.

113 Longman later took over the publication of the book: *Essays and Reviews*, ed. Shea and Whitla, pp. 25–6.

114 [Frederic Harrison], 'Neo-Christianity', *Westminster Review*, 18 (1860), 293–332, esp. pp. 293, 295.

115 [Samuel Wilberforce], 'Essays and Reviews', *Quarterly Review*, 109 (1861), 248–305.

116 *Essays and Reviews*, ed. Shea and Whitla, p. 36.

117 Printed ibid., pp. 649–50.

118 [A.P. Stanley], 'Essays and Reviews', *Edinburgh Review*, 113 (1861), 461–500.

119 See generally S.M. Waddams, *Law, Politics and the Church of England: The Career of Stephen Lushington 1782–1873* (Cambridge, 1992).

120 Formally, Turton was acting for James Fendell, an Ely diocese rector, who was the official 'promoter' in the case against Wilson.

121 Printed as *Essays and Reviews. Judgment Delivered on the 25th of June 1862* (London, 1862). See also R.B. Kennard, *'Essays & Reviews'* (London, 1863), in which some of the important texts are reprinted; *Essays and Reviews*, ed. Shea and Whitla, p. 707.

122 *Essays and Reviews*, ed. Shea and Whitla, p. 765. Bertrand Russell noted much later that 'Belief in eternal hell fire was an essential item of Christian belief until pretty recent times. In this country, as you know, it ceased to be an essential item because of a decision of the Privy Council, and from that decision the Archbishop of Canterbury and the Archbishop of York dissented; but in this country our religion is settled by Act of Parliament, and therefore the Privy Council was able to override their Graces and hell was no longer necessary to a Christian. Consequently I shall not insist that a Christian must believe in hell':

Why I Am Not a Christian (London, 1927), p. 9; first delivered as a lecture to the South London Branch of the National Secular Society (6 Mar. 1927).

123 *Essays and Reviews*, ed. Shea and Whitla, pp. 732–3.

124 *Essays and Reviews* generated a huge literature of response: at least 140 replies have been identified: see Josef L. Altholz, 'The Mind of Victorian Orthodoxy: Anglican Responses to "Essays and Reviews", 1860–1864', *Church History*, 51 (1982), 186–97; repr. in *Religion in Victorian Britain, vol. iv*, ed. G. Parsons (Manchester, 1988), pp. 28–40. For a Wilberforcian view of this material, see *Quarterly Review*, 112 (1862), 445–99.

125 Printed in *Essays and Reviews*, ed. Shea and Whitla, pp. 660–5.

126 Crowther, *Church Embattled*, pp. 127–37.

127 Cf. *Ffoulkes v. Fletcher* at Oxford (1866): Chadwick, *Victorian Church*, ii. 453.

128 Printed in *Essays and Reviews*, ed. Shea and Whitla, p. 837.

129 Benedict de Spinoza, *A Theologico-Political Treatise and A Political Treatise*, trans. R.H.M. Elwes, p. v: vol. 1 (of two) in *The Chief Works of Benedict de Spinoza* (London, 1883–4), being part of Bohn's Philosophical Library. A second, revised edition of both volumes appeared in 1887 in the same series, and the first volume was reprinted in 1895 by Routledge. A facsimile reprint at New York by Dover in 1951 of Elwes's first edition is the one most used. (Cf. a new translation by Samuel Shirley, Leiden, 1989.) Elwes's footnotes show that he was referring to [James Anthony Froude], 'Spinoza', orig. pub. in the *Westminster Review*, 64 (1855), 1–37 and reprinted in his *Short Studies on Great Subjects* (Everyman edn, London, 1906), i. 224–72, based on an earlier article on Spinoza in the *Oxford and Cambridge Review* (1847); and Matthew Arnold's famous article on 'Spinoza and the Bible': see below. Conspicuously absent is the article by George Eliot's partner [George Henry Lewes (1817–98)], 'Spinoza's Life and Works', *Westminster Review*, 39 (1843), 372–407, and reprinted that same year with a title page including his name. See also his much more personal article in the journal he himself edited: 'Spinoza', *Fortnightly Review*, 4 (1866), 386–7.

130 Spinoza, *TTP*, trans. Elwes, p. xxxiiin. Cf. *A Treatise Partly Theological, and Partly Political* (London, 1689), repr. (London, 1737). See also an earlier translation by Charles Blount of chapter 6 of *TTP*, published in *Miracles, No Violations of the Laws of Nature* (London, 1683).

131 George Eliot began working on *TTP* as early as February 1843, had another turn at it in February 1847, and seriously got down to translating it in April 1849. In that month, she was approached by John Chapman (1821–94), who had published her anonymous translation of D.F. Strauss, *The Life of Jesus, Critically Examined* (London, 1846). He had in hand a translation of the *Ethics* by an American named Samuel Hitchcock, and toyed with the idea of printing it with her *TTP*, but it came to nothing. Her translation, or as much of it as she finished, is now lost; Hitchcock's *Ethics* is still unpublished and exists in six copies in the Library of Congress. Perhaps encouraged by this interest, George Eliot began to translate Spinoza's *Ethics* on 8 Nov. 1854 and completed it by 19 Feb. 1856; it should have been published in Bohn's Philosophical Library, but her partner G.H. Lewes quarrelled with Bohn over fees and the project was dropped. The Bohn Philosophical Library, of course, published Elwes's translations in 1883–4. Curiously, the plan was for George Eliot's *Ethics* to be included with a new translation of the *TTP* to be done by a man named Kelly. So it may be that George Eliot's *TTP* had already gone missing or was never completed. Her MS translation of *Ethics*, with a few pages of Lewes's notes, is now at Yale University, and was edited by Thomas Deegan and published in 1981 by the Institut für Anglistik und

Amerikanistik at the University of Salzburg. See *The George Eliot Letters*, ed. G.S. Haight (London, 1954–78), i. 158, 231, 236, 280–1, 321–2; ii. 186, 189, 211, 233; iv. 30–1, 207, 298; v. 182; vii. 95–6, 366; viii. 156–60 (quarrel with Bohn); G.S. Haight, *George Eliot* (Oxford, 1968), pp. 199–200; J. Bennett, *George Eliot* (Cambridge, 1954), 40–42. See also D. Atkins, *George Eliot and Spinoza* (Salzburg, 1978); R. Ashton, *The German Idea: Four English Writers and the Reception of German Thought, 1800–1860* (Cambridge, 1980).

132 Benedict de Spinoza, *Tractatus Theologico-Politicus* [ed. Robert Willis] (London, 1862). A second edition appeared in 1868. Cf. Willis's *Benedict de Spinoza: His Life, Correspondence, and Ethics* (London, 1870). George Eliot described him as 'a valuable person': George Eliot to Charles Bray, 16 July [1855]: *Letters*, ed. Haight, ii. 209.

133 *St. Paul and Protestantism* (1870); *Literature and Dogma* (1873); *God and the Bible* (1875), *Last Essays on Church and Religion* (1877).

134 Generally, see P. Hinchliff, *John William Colenso: Bishop of Natal* (London, 1964); G.W. Cox, *The Life of John William Colenso* (London, 1888); G. Parsons, 'Rethinking the Missionary Position: Bishop Colenso of Natal', in *Religion in Victorian Britain, Volume V* (Manchester, 1997), pp. 135–75; '*Essays and Reviews* and Bishop Colenso's "Great Scandal"', in *Essays and Reviews*, ed. Shea and Whitla, pp. 847–57; A.L. Rowse, *The Controversial Colensos* (Redruth, 1989), which reveals (p. 34) that Colenso called his horse 'Pentateuch'. Colenso's famous school text was called *Arithmetic Designed for the Use of Schools* (London, 1843), published by Longman in many editions.

135 John William Colenso, *The Pentateuch and Joshua Critically Examined* (London, 1862–79), i. 31–40, 58–63, 84–5, 123–4, 131, 147–57. The arithmetical proofs are mostly in Part I of the work, the textual analysis in the second part.

136 P. Hazard, *The European Mind 1680–1715* (Penguin edn, Harmondsworth, 1973), p. 60 [1st French edn, 1935].

137 John William Colenso, *St. Paul's Epistle to the Romans* (Cambridge, 1861).

138 Gray to ?, 30 May 1857: Charles Gray, *Life of Robert Gray* (London, 1876), i. 423.

139 Quoted in Hinchliff, *Colenso*, p. 109.

140 Gray, *Gray*, ii. 141–2.

141 Colenso's figures, reported in Colenso to Th. Shepstone, 2 Mar. 1863, from 23 Sussex Place, London: Cox, *Colenso*, i. 236; in this letter, Colenso crows about his admission to the Athenaeum.

142 'Gold Hair', lines 141–5, in Robert Browning, *The Poems*, ed. J. Pettigrew (New Haven, 1981), i. 764.

143 Although the cases of the Essayists and Colenso were tightly linked and, indeed, were sometimes debated together (as at Convocation on 8 Feb. 1864), in fact they were very different. Colenso had been deposed as bishop and clergyman by the Synod of South African Bishops, led by Gray. Colenso appealed to the Privy Council not in relation to ecclesiastical law but as a citizen of the British empire who had been wronged. He turned the issue into a dispute over colonial jurisdiction, inspired no doubt by the recent case of *Long v. Archbishop Gray of Capetown*, in which another local clergyman had been summarily removed from office. Lord Kingsdown had interrupted the hearings on the Williams and Wilson cases (24 June 1863) to deliver his judgment in favour of the unfortunate William Long. So the issue with Colenso was not heresy, but jurisdiction, exactly what had happened with Jowett: an invalid court had deprived them of their legal rights: Hinchliff, *Colenso*, pp. 142–66; *Essays and Reviews*, ed. Shea and Whitla, pp. 854–5.

144 Stanley to Jowett, end Aug. 1862: in R.E. Prothero and G. Bradley, *The Life and*

Correspondence of Arthur Penrhyn Stanley (London, 1893), ii. 100; Jowett to Stanley, n.d.: *Life and Letters of Benjamin Jowett*, ed. Abbott and Campbell, i. 301.

145 [Mark Pattison], *Westminster Review*, 79 (Jan. 1863), 57–76, esp. pp. 58–9; cf. pp. 376–96.

146 *Athenaeum* (1 Nov. 1862); *Christian Remembrancer* (1863), 25, 252; *Spectator* (1862), 1251; *Eclectic Review* (Dec. 1862), 509; *Fraser's Magazine* (Dec. 1862); *Edinburgh Review*, 117 (1863), 498–516; *Quarterly Review*, 113 (1863), 422–47.

147 *Essays and Reviews*, ed. Shea and Whitla, p. 850; Hinchliff, *Colenso*, pp. 105, 140, 158. The Garibaldi letter is dated 21 Apr. 1864: Durban, Campbell Library: Colenso fos. M78: quoted ibid., p. 158.

148 Colenso himself returned to Durban and arrived there on 4 November 1865. The churchwardens and the dean of his old cathedral physically blocked his way, and he needed to take out an interdict six days later in order to take possession. Gray, for his part, refused to relent, and excommunicated Colenso on 5 January 1866, and Wilberforce in England backed him up, urging the Province of Canterbury to side with Gray and not with an excommunicated heretic. Over the next three years, Colenso's enemies tried to find a man willing to be anti-bishop, and when one (W.K. Macrorie) was consecrated bishop in Cape Town in January 1869, a schism began which continued past Colenso's death on 20 June 1883, and Macrorie's resignation in June 1891. The archbishop of Canterbury appointed a successor, but A.H. Baynes could not overcome the posthumous Colenso faction, and resigned in 1901. Only in 1911 did the bishop of Natal finally recover the endowments which Colenso had administered, and the Colenso affair finally ended: Hinchliff, *Colenso*, pp. 167–95; *Essays and Reviews*, ed. Shea and Whitla, pp. 855–6.

149 Matthew Arnold to his mother, 9 Dec. 1862: *The Letters of Matthew Arnold*, ed. C.Y. Lang (Charlottesville, 1996–), ii. 170. The edition, in progress, supersedes *Letters of Matthew Arnold 1848–1888*, ed. G.W.E. Russell (London, 1895).

150 Matthew Arnold, 'The Bishop and the Philosopher', *Macmillan's Magazine*, 7 (January 1863), 241–56: repr. Matthew Arnold, *The Complete Prose Works*, ed. R.H. Super (Ann Arbor, 1960–77), iii. 40–55.

151 [Matthew Arnold], 'Tractatus Theologico-Politicus', *London Review*, 5 (27 Dec. 1862), 565–7: repr. *Works*, ed. Super, iii. 56–64. Although this review is nominally dated *before* 'The Bishop and the Philosopher', the latter essay was actually on the street before Christmas and thus predates it. The review was published anonymously, which was a common practice. Grant Duff, MP, sent Arnold 'a most beautiful photograph of Spinoza' after reading the essay: Arnold to Frances Arnold, 31 Jan. 1863: *Letters*, ed. Lang, ii. 184; Arnold to Grant Duff, 31 Jan. 1863, ibid., p. 185.

152 Arnold to Hermann Kindt, 6 Feb. 1864: *Letters*, ed. Lang, ii. 279. George Eliot also connected Goethe with Spinoza: *Letters*, ed. Haight, iv. 207; v. 182.

153 Arnold to Thomas Henry Huxley, 8 Dec. 1875: *Letters*, ed. Lang, iv. 290. Cf. W.H.G. Armytage, 'Matthew Arnold and T.H. Huxley', *Review of English Studies*, n.s., 4 (1953), 350.

154 Arnold to his mother, 19 Nov. 1862: *Letters*, ed. Lang, ii. 163. He wrote in a similar vein to his brother Thomas, 29 Nov. 1862: ibid., p. 167.

155 Arnold to Sainte-Beuve, 28 Jan. 1863: ibid., pp. 183–4.

156 Arnold to Clough, 23 Oct. 1850, from Rugby: ibid., i. 176–7. Cf. *The Letters of Matthew Arnold to Arthur Hugh Clough*, ed. H.F. Lowry (London, 1932), p. 117. Note the jokey reference to Matthew vi. 7.

157 K. Allott, *Victorian Studies*, 3 (1960), 320, citing Thomas Arnold to Clough (Nov. 1847), from Matthew Arnold's lodgings in London a week before sailing to New

Zealand: 'I hope I shall like the Free Church people; how alarmed the dear creatures would be, if they knew what a mass of heresy and schism I had got down in the hold. Rousseau! Spinoza!! Hegel!!! Emerson!! Stanley observed that Spinoza and Hegel had probably never crossed the line before': Bodl. Lib., Clough MSS. Thomas Arnold later affirmed that Strauss's *Life of Jesus* had little effect on him, because everything that was revolutionary in that book had already entered his system by his reading of Spinoza: R.H. Super, *The Time-Spirit of Matthew Arnold* (Ann Arbor, 1970), p. 65.

158 Arnold's diary, in *Letters*, ed. Lang, i. 181–5. This is odd, because Arnold seems not to have met George Eliot until 26 Dec. 1876: G.H. Lewes's diary, cited in *George Eliot Letters*, ed. Haight, ix. 184.

159 Arnold, *Works*, ed. Super, iii. 415.

160 Matthew Arnold, 'The Function of Criticism at the Present Time', repr. in *Essays in Criticism* (1865); Matthew Arnold, *Selected Prose*, ed. P.J. Keating (Penguin edn, Harmondsworth, 1970), p. 150. The references are to David Friedrich Strauss, *Leben Jesu* (1835), translated into English in 1846 by George Eliot; and to Ernest Renan (1823–92), *La Vie de Jésus* (1863).

161 *The Times*, 16 Feb. 1863, p. 8, col. 4: quoted in Arnold, *Works*, ed. Super iii. 416.

162 Arthur Penrhyn Stanley, *Lectures on the History of the Jewish Church*, Part I: Abraham to Samuel (London, 1863). Cf. idem, *The Life and Correspondence of Thomas Arnold, D.D.* (London, 1844). Stanley himself was rather a supporter of Colenso, as we have seen, although he did not agree with all of his methods: 'of course arithmetic is entirely beyond me', he wrote a bit sarcastically. 'But I bow, as always, so here, to the greatest living authority in *his own subject*': Stanley to J.C. Shairp, Oct. 1862: R.E. Prothero and G.G. Bradley, *Life and Correspondence of Arthur Penrhyn Stanley* (London, 1893), ii. 101. Cf. Arnold to his mother, 4 Feb. 1863: *Letters*, ed. Lang, ii. 187.

163 Matthew Arnold, 'Dr. Stanley's Lectures on the Jewish Church', *Macmillan's Magazine*, 7 (Feb. 1863), 327–36: in *Works*, ed. Super, iii. 65–82.

164 'Spinoza and the Bible' began as an article entitled 'A Word More about Spinoza', originally intended for *The Times*, but finally published in *Macmillan's Magazine*, 9 (Dec. 1863), 136–42, for which he received a cheque for seven guineas: Arnold to Alexander Macmillan, 2 Dec. 1863: *Letters*, ed. Lang, ii. 253. He changed the title to 'Spinoza' for the first edition of *Essays in Criticism* (1865), but took heed of critics who noted that without reprinting 'The Bishop and the Philosopher', it made the piece seem too abrupt and incomplete. For the second edition of *Essays in Criticism* (1869), Arnold expanded 'Spinoza' to include whole passages from his review of *TTP* published in Dec. 1862. 'Spinoza and the Bible' repr. in *Works*, ed. Super, iii. 158–82.

165 Matthew Arnold to his mother, 7 Jan. 1863: *Letters*, ed. Lang, ii. 176.

166 In his *Ludwig Börne. Eine Denkschrift* (1840): see Arnold, *Works*, ed. Super, v. 435–6.

167 Matthew Arnold, *Culture and Anarchy* (London, 1869): *Works*, ed. Super, v. A second edition appeared in 1875, and a third in 1882. For more on Hebraism vs. Hellenism, see the special issue of *Poetics Today*, 9, no. 2 (1998), 'Hellenism and Hebraism Reconsidered: The Poetics of Cultural Influence and Exchange'. See also L. Gossman, 'Philhellenism and Antisemitism: Matthew Arnold and his German Models', *Comparative Literature*, 46 (1994), 1–39; B. Cheyette, *Constructions of 'the Jew' in English Literature and Society: Racial Representations, 1875–1945* (Cambridge, 1993), pp. 14–23; G.W. Stocking, Jr., 'Matthew Arnold, E.B. Tylor, and the Uses of Invention', *American Anthropologist*, 65 (1963), 783–99: repr. in his *Race, Culture, and Evolution* (Chicago, 1982), 69–90; and V.P. Pecora, 'Arnoldian Ethnology', *Victorian Studies*, 41 (1998), 355–79.

168 Arnold to his mother, 12/13 June 1869: *Letters*, ed. Lang, iii. 350.

169 Park Honan, *Matthew Arnold: A Life* (London, 1981), p. 333. For more on Arnold's
     anthropological thinking, see: F.E. Faverty, *Matthew Arnold: The Ethnologist*
     (Evanston, IL, 1951); Stocking, 'Matthew Arnold, E.B. Tylor and the Uses of
     Invention'; M. Demarest, 'Arnold and Tylor: The Codification and Appropriation
     of Culture', *Bucknell Review*, 34 (1990), 26–42; J.P. Farrell, 'Matthew Arnold and
     the Middle Ages: The Uses of the Past', *Victorian Studies*, 13 (1970), 319–38; F.M.
     Alaya, 'Arnold and Renan on the Popular Uses of History', *Jnl. Hist. Ideas*, 28
     (1967), 551–74.

170 Honan, *Arnold*, pp. 109–10.

171 Ibid., pp. 316–18; R. apRoberts, *Arnold and God* (Berkeley, 1983), pp. 165–70.
     Other useful secondary works on Arnold's religion are: B. Willey, 'Arnold and
     Religion', in *Matthew Arnold*, ed. K. Allott (London, 1975), pp. 236–58; L. Trilling,
     Matthew Arnold (New York, 1939); S. Prickett, 'Biblical Prophecy and Nineteenth
     Century Historicism: The Joachimite Third Age in Matthew and Mary Augusta
     Arnold', *Journal of Literature and Theology*, 2 (1988), 219–36.

172 Arnold to his mother, 29 Oct. 1863: *Letters*, ed. Lang, ii. 238.

173 Arnold to Lady de Rothschild, 9 Aug. 1868: *Letters*, ed. Lang, iii. 279. See also
     same to same, 4 Nov. 1867, in which Arnold praises Deutsch's essay: ibid., p. 185.
     See Emanuel Deutsch, 'The Talmud', *Quarterly Review*, 123 (Oct. 1867), 417–64.
     For Deutsch and *Essays and Reviews*, see *Essays and Reviews*, ed. Shea and Whitla,
     p. 28. Generally, see Constance Battersea, *Lady de Rothschild: Extracts from her
     Notebooks with a Preface by her Daughter* (London, 1912), i. 458–9; and Lucy Cohen,
     Lady de Rothschild and her Daughters, 1821–1931 (London, 1935).

174 G.W.E. Russell, *Matthew Arnold* (London, 1904), pp. 162–3.

175 Hilaire Belloc, *The Jews* (London, 1922), p. 47, where he reveals that Robert
     Browning was also of Jewish ancestry!

176 '. . . durch Hülfe der höheren Kritik (eines keinem Humanisten neuen Nahmens)
     wenden': Johann Gottfried Eichhorn, *Einleitung in das Alte Testament* (3rd edn,
     Leipzig, 1803), i. vi [1st edn, Leipzig, 1780–83]: quoted in Roberts, *Arnold*, p. 27.

177 Arnold, 'Spinoza': *Works*, ed. Super, iii. 179.

178 Matthew Arnold, *Literature and Dogma* (London, 1873); this quotation *Works*, ed.
     Super, vi. 268.

179 See, esp., Matthew Arnold, *On Translating Homer* (London, 1862): *Works*, ed. Super,
     i. 97–216.

180 Friedrich August Wolf, *Prolegomena in Homerum I* (1795).

181 Robert Browning, 'Development', in *The Poems*, ed. Pettigrew, ii. 918–21.

182 Spinoza, *TTP*, trans. Elwes, p. ix.

CHAPTER 8   *Unsuitable Paternity: Darwin, Anthropology,
and the Evolutionist Bible*

  1 Even R.S. Westfall, *Never at Rest: A Biography of Isaac Newton* (Cambridge, 1980),
     p. 21n felt it necessary to include a long autobiographical footnote justifying his
     discussion of Newton's alchemy.

  2 William Paley, *Natural Theology: or, Evidences of the Existence and Attributes of the
     Deity, Collected from the Appearances of Nature* (London, 1802), pp. 1–4. Generally, see
     especially B.M.G. Reardon, *Religious Thought in the Victorian Age* (London, 1971),
     pp. 285–98; and M.L. Clarke, *Paley* (London, 1974).

  3 N.C. Gillespie, 'Natural History, Natural Theology, and Social Order: John Ray
     and the "Newtonian Ideology"', *Journal of the History of Biology*, 20 (1987), 1–49.

4 [Thomas Burnet], *Telluris theoria sacra* (London, 1681): 2nd edn, 1689; 3rd edn, 1702. It appeared in English, also without the author's name, as *The Theory of the Earth* (London, 1684), with up to seven editions by 1759. Cf. a modern edition (Carbondale, Ill., 1965). On Burnet and the Burnet controversy, see K.B. Collier, *Cosmogonies of Our Fathers: Some Theories of the Seventeenth and Eighteenth Centuries* (New York, 1934); R. Porter, *The Making of Geology: Earth Sciences in Britain 1660–1815* (Cambridge, 1977). See also the entertaining presentation in S.J. Gould, *Time's Arrow, Time's Cycle: Myth and Metaphor in the Discovery of Geological Time* (Cambridge, Mass., 1987), ch. 2.

5 Burnet, *Theory*, p. 121 (modern edn).

6 René Descartes, *Principia philosophiae* (1644); cf. U.B. Marvin, *Continental Drift* (Washington, DC, 1973), p. 29.

7 Joseph Glanvill, *Lux orientalis* (London, 1682), pp. 137–41.

8 Robert Hooke, 'A Discourse of Earthquakes', in *Posthumous Works*, ed. R. Waller (London, 1705), p. 328. Cf. E.T. Drake and P.D. Komar, 'Speculations about the Earth: The Role of Robert Hooke and Others in the 17th Century', *History of Geology*, 2 (1983), 11–16; N.A. Rupke, 'Continental Drift before 1900', *Nature*, 207 (1970), 349–50.

9 Newton to Burnet [Jan. 1680–1]: *The Correspondence of Isaac Newton*, ed. H.W. Turnbull *et al.* (Cambridge, 1959–77), letter 247.

10 For a checklist of replies to Burnet, see M. Macklem, *The Anatomy of the World: Relations between Natural and Moral Law from Donne to Pope* (Minneapolis, 1958), pp. 97–9. Indeed, Burnet's work injected new vigour into the debate between the Ancients and the Moderns: see R.F. Jones, *Ancients and Moderns: A Study of the Rise of the Scientific Movement in Seventeenth-Century England* (2nd edn, St Louis, 1961), pp. 266, 342.

11 William Whiston, *A New Theory of the Earth* (London, 1696), pp. 2–3, and esp. introductory essay on 'The Mosaick History of the Creation', pp. 1–94 (1st numbering). See also J.E. Force, 'Some Eminent Newtonians and Providential Geophysics at the Turn of the Seventeenth Century', *History of Geology*, 2 (1983), 4–10; idem, *William Whiston: Honest Newtonian* (Cambridge, 1985). See generally, N.M. de S. Cameron, *Biblical Higher Criticism and the Defense of Infallibilism in 19th Century Britain* (Lewiston, NY, 1987), App. A: 'Interpreting Genesis in the Light of Science', pp. 290–318. For more on comets, see C. Webster, *From Paracelsus to Newton: Magic and the Making of Modern Science* (Cambridge, 1982), pp. 27–41; S. Schechner Genuth, *Comets, Popular Culture, and the Birth of Modern Cosmology* (Princeton, 1997).

12 Edmond Halley, 'Some Considerations about the Cause of the Universal Deluge, laid before the Royal Society', *Philosophical Transactions*, 33 (1724–5), 118–25.

13 *DNB*, s.v., 'Egerton, Francis Henry'. Apart from the those discussed below, other writers included Adam Sedgwick (1785–1873), the Cambridge geologist, and Peter Mark Roget (1779–1869) of thesaurus fame. Of the eight treatises, exactly half were written by Edinburgh-trained physicians.

14 William Whewell, *Astronomy and General Physics Considered with Reference to Natural Theology* (London, 1833). Cf. idem, *Of the Plurality of Worlds* (London, 1853). See generally, M. Fisch, *William Whewell: Philosopher of Science* (Oxford, 1991); and C.Q. Raub, 'Robert Chambers and William Whewell: A Nineteenth-Century Debate over the Origin of Language', *Jnl. Hist.Ideas*, 49 (1988), 287–300.

15 William Buckland, *Geology and Mineralogy Considered with Reference to Natural Theology* (London, 1836), esp. pp. 18–26. The comment on the ologies comes from the *Record*, 20 Nov. 1845. Generally, see N.A. Rupke, *The Great Chain of History: William Buckland and the English School of Geology (1814–1849)* (Oxford, 1983).

Buckland's most violent opponent was William Cockburn, dean of York, e.g. in his *Letter to Professor Buckland, Concerning the Origin of the World* (London, 1838); idem, *The Bible Defended* (London, 1844).

16 Buckland, *Geology*, pp. 8–9.

17 Edmund Gosse, *Father and Son: A Study of Two Temperaments* (Penguin edn, Harmondsworth, 1983), p. 104: 1st pub. 1907.

18 Charles Lyell, *Principles of Geology, being an Attempt to Explain the Former Changes of the Earth's Surface, by Reference to Causes Now in Operation* (London, 1830–3).

19 Charles Lyell, *The Geological Evidences of the Antiquity of Man with Remarks on Theories of the Origin of Species by Variation* (London, 1863), p. 469. Lyell also cited Friedrich Max Müller's views on the evolution of language as support for his own on the development of species (pp. 454–5). For more on Max Müller, see pp. 282–4 below.

20 See now J.A. Secord, *Victorian Sensation: The Extraordinary Publication, Reception, and Secret Authorship of 'Vestiges of the Natural History of Creation'* (Chicago, 2000).

21 [Robert Chambers], *Vestiges of the Natural History of Creation* (London, 1844), pp. 153–4.

22 Ibid., pp. 157–8, 306, 359–60.

23 What actually happened is still a confused matter, Huxley and posterity have given the victory to science rather than theology. The debate seems to have become famous only after the publication of Darwin's biography (1887) and Huxley's (1900). See also S. Gilley and A. Loades, 'Thomas Henry Huxley: The War between Science and Religion', *Journal of Religion*, 61 (1981), 285–308.

24 See above, pp. 246–7.

25 John Tyndall, *Address Delivered before the British Association Assembled at Belfast* (London, 1874), pp. 35, 61. Cf. idem, *Fragments of Science for Unscientific People* (London, 1871). See the very long entry on Tyndall in the *DNB* (which includes the enigmatic observation that 'He had generally, like Faraday, to bespeak a hat on account of the unusual length of his head').

26 W.E.H. Lecky, *History of the Rise and Influence of the Spirit of Rationalism in Europe* (London, 1865); J.W. Draper, *History of the Intellectual Development of Europe* (London, 1864); idem, *History of the Conflict between Religion and Science* (New York, 1875). See also J.P. von Arx, *Progress and Pessimism: Religion, Politics, and History in Late Nineteenth Century Britain* (Cambridge, Mass., 1985), ch. 3: 'W.E.H. Lecky and the History of Retrogression'.

27 A.D. White, *The Warfare of Science* (London, 1876); idem, *A History of the Warfare of Science with Theology in Christendom* (New York, 1896).

28 J.H. Newman, *The Arians of the Fourth Century* (London, 1833), esp. pp. 56, 79; I. Ker, *John Henry Newman: A Biography* (Oxford, 1988), pp. 49–52.

29 J.H. Newman, *Fifteen Sermons Preached before the University of Oxford* (3rd edn, London, 1872), pp. 313, 316–17 [Sermon XV, 1843]; Ker, *Newman*, pp. 257–66.

30 Ker, *Newman*, p. 300.

31 J.H. Newman, *An Essay on the Development of Christian Doctrine* (London, 1845), pp. 27, 36, 37, 57–93.

32 Ibid., pp. 38–9.

33 See esp. F.L. Cross, 'Newman and the Doctrine of Development', *Church Quarterly Review* (1933), 245–57, who sees the genesis of Newman's idea in a seventeenth-century Jesuit debate. Cf. O. Chadwick, *Newman* (Oxford, 1983); G. Faber, *Oxford Apostles* (London, 1933).

34 See generally, O. Chadwick, *The Victorian Church* (3rd edn, London, 1971–2), ii. 33–9; and J.W. Robertson, *Anthropology and the Old Testament* (Sheffield, 1984): first pub. 1978. For the history of anthropology during this period, see: G.W. Stocking,

Jr., *Victorian Anthropology* (New York, 1987); idem, *After Tylor: British Social Anthropology 1888–1951* (Madison, 1995); H. Kuklick, *The Savage Within: The Social History of British Anthropology, 1885–1945* (Cambridge, 1991).

35 Richard Whately, 'On the Origin of Civilisation', repr. in his *Miscellaneous Lectures and Reviews* (London, 1861), pp. 26–59.

36 Ibid., pp. 28, 32, 35–6, 40–1.

37 Ibid., pp. 41–2, 44, 50.

38 The discoveries at Babylonia prompted the appearance of what was called the 'Pan-Babylonian School' in Germany. Their rivals were the members of the so-called 'Heliocentric School' of Samuel Henry Hooke (1874–1968) and others, who still favoured Egypt as the cultural centre. The North Arabian theory was championed by Hugo Winckler (1863–1913) in Germany, author of *The History of Babylonia and Assyria* (London, 1907), translated from the German edition of the previous year; and in England by Thomas Kelly Cheyne (1841–1915), *Traditions & Beliefs of Ancient Israel* (London, 1907), who ruled that from 'a textual point of view, it seems to me difficult to deny that the Exodus of which the original tradition spoke was from a region in N. Arabia' (p. xviii). A.S. Peake, writing about Cheyne in the *DNB*, posits that his championship of the North Arabian theory 'crossed at last the boundary beyond which sanity ceases.' Indeed, Cheyne's conversion, he thought, 'is one of the most tragic episodes in the history of scholarship.' See also J.A. Montgomery, *Arabia and the Bible* (Philadelphia, 1934), who agrees that 'the fact remains that not from the wisdom of the Egyptian, Babylonian, and Greek civilizations came our Western religions, but out of Arabia' (p. 188).

39 See generally, E.J. Sharpe, *Comparative Religion: A History* (2nd edn, London, 1986).

40 See generally, Lytton Strachey's long article in the *DNB*; A. Vidler, *Witness to the Light: F.D. Maurice's Message for Today* (New York, 1948); idem, *F.D. Maurice and Company* (London, 1966); D. Young, *F.D. Maurice and Unitarianism* (Oxford, 1992). Older works include F. Higham, *Frederick Denison Maurice* (London, 1947); and C. Jenkins, *Frederick Denison Maurice and the New Reformation* (London, 1938).

41 Frederick Denison Maurice, *The Religions of the World and their Relations to Christianity* (London, 1847), pp. 2–3: his Boyle Lectures.

42 Maurice, *Religions*, pp. 8–9. It is for this reason that men like Allan Bloom, *The Closing of the American Mind* (New York, 1987) and Alasdair Macintyre, *Whose Justice? Which Rationality?* (London, 1988), accuse among others the early anthropologists of encouraging the fall of absolute moral standards.

43 Maurice, *Religions*, p. xiii.

44 Georgina Max Müller, *The Life and Letters of the Rt. Hon. Friedrich Max Müller* (London, 1902), i. 1, 28–9, 47, 57–8, 74, 211, 217; ii. 48, 409. See also Max Müller's *Auld Lang Syne* (London, 1898), which includes an amusing portrait of the author in uniform and armed with a sword; and his *My Autobiography: A Fragment* (London, 1901). His collected essays appeared as *Chips from a German Workshop* (London, 1867–70). See also, J.H. Voight, *Max Müller: The Man and his Ideas* (Calcutta, 1967); and N.C. Chaudhuri, *Scholar Extraordinary: The Life of Professor the Rt. Hon. Friedrich Max Müller, P.C.* (London, 1974).

45 Max Müller, *Life and Letters*, i. 241–5.

46 Max Müller to Stanley, 17 Apr. 1861: ibid., i. 246–7. The testimonials for Max Müller are preserved in the Bodleian Library as G.A. Oxon. c. 76 (181–3); and G.A. Oxon. 8° 179 (26, 26*, 26**, 26***, 27).

47 Max Müller, *Life and Letters*, i. 242, 350.

48 Ibid., p. 499; ii. 2–6.

49 Ibid., ii. 9.

50   F. Max Müller, 'Preface to the Sacred Books of the East', in *The Sacred Books of the East*, ed. F. Max Müller (Oxford, 1879–1910), I. ix–xxxviii, esp. pp. ix–xi.

51   The dispute began in 1886, and had a revival in 1895: Max Müller, *Life and Letters*, ii. 194–5. Curiously, Copleston was greatly admired by Andrew Lang when they were up at Oxford together: Andrew Lang, *Adventures among Books* (London, 1905), p. 34.

52   Max Müller, *Life and Letters*, i. 468; and cf. his letter to Darwin on the same subject, 7 Jan. 1875: i. 476 and his 'Address to the Anthropological Section of the British Association at the Meeting Held at Cardiff in August, 1891', *Journal of the Royal Anthropological Institute of Great Britain and Ireland*, 21 (1892), 172–92. Generally, see G. Beer, 'Darwin and the Growth of Language Theory', in *Nature Transfigured: Science and Literature, 1700–1900*, ed. J. Christie and S. Shuttleworth (Manchester, 1989), pp. 152–70; idem, *Darwin's Plots: Evolutionary Narrative in Darwin, George Eliot and Nineteenth-Century Fiction* (London, 1983); R.M. Young, *Darwin's Metaphor: Nature's Place in Victorian Culture* (Cambridge, 1985); and P.J. Bowler, *The Invention of Progress: The Victorian and the Past* (Oxford, 1989). See also J. Winternitz, 'The "Turanian" Hypothesis and Magyar Nationalism in the Nineteenth Century', in *Culture and Nationalism in Nineteenth-Century Eastern Europe*, ed. R. Sussex and J.C. Eade (Columbus, 1985), pp. 143–58.

53   For solarism, see R. Ackerman, *J.G. Frazer: His Life and Work* (Cambridge, 1987), pp. 76–7; R.M. Dorson, 'The Eclipse of Solar Mythology', in *Myth: A Symposium*, ed. T.A. Sebeok (Bloomington, Ind., 1958), pp. 25–63; S. Connor, 'Myth and Meta-myth in Max Müller and Walter Pater', in *The Sun is God: Painting, Literature and Mythology in the Nineteenth Century*, ed. J.B. Bullen (Oxford, 1989), pp. 199–222; G. Schrempp, 'The Re-Education of Friedrich Max Müller: Intellectual Appropriation and Epistemological Antinomy in Mid-Victorian Evolutionary Thought', *Man*, n.s., 18 (1983), 90–110. Cf. Robert Brown, *Language and Theories of its Origin* (London, [1881]); idem, *Researches into the Origin of the Primitive Constellations of the Greeks, Phoenicians and Babylonians* (London, 1899–1900).

54   Generally, see F.E. Manuel, 'A Psychology of Everyday Religion', in *The Changing of the Gods* (Hanover and London, 1983), pp. 52–71.

55   Charles François Dupuis, *Origine de tous les cultes, ou religion universelle* (Paris, 1795). Cf. the extract printed as *Christianity a Form of the Great Solar Myth* (London, n.d.); and the reply to Dupuis by John Prior Estlin, *The Nature and the Causes of Atheism* (Bristol, 1797).

56   The literature on Vico is prodigious. The standard English translation of the major work is *The New Science of Giambattista Vico*, ed. T.G. Bergin and M.H. Fisch (Ithaca, NY, 1961[1], 1968[2]). The most useful general secondary works are L. Pompa, *Vico: A Study of the 'New Science'* (Cambridge, 1975); I. Berlin, *Vico and Herder* (New York, 1976); D.P. Verene, *Vico's Science of Imagination* (Ithaca, NY, 1981); P. Burke, *Vico* (Oxford, 1985), esp. ch. 2.

57   Andrew Lang, *Custom and Myth* (London, 1884), dedicated to E.B. Tylor; idem, *The Making of Religion* (London, 1898).

58   Max Müller to his wife, 29 Nov. 1874, after hearing the 'heretical' Bishop Colenso preach in Balliol Chapel. Colenso visited Oxford first as Max Müller's guest; then as a guest of Benjamin Jowett, the master of Balliol; and was forbidden to preach in the city church at Carfax by the bishop of Oxford: Max Müller, *Life and Letters*, i. 468–9.

59   Max Müller to the duke of Argyll, 4 Feb. 1875: ibid., p. 481.

60   E.B. Tylor, *Primitive Culture: Researches into the Development of Mythology, Philosophy, Religion, Art, and Custom* (London, 1871), p. 5. NB his approving remarks regarding Max Müller on p. 20.

61   Ibid., pp. 31–3.
62   Ibid., pp. 34, 37, 41–3. The Niebuhr reference Tylor gives is Part I, p. 88.
63   Ibid., p. 62.
64   Ibid., pp. 15, 65–6.
65   E.B. Tylor, *Anthropology* (London, 1881), esp. pp. 341–4. Tylor sometimes preferred
     the expression 'rude philosopher' (p. 343). He discussed animism in *Primitive
     Culture* as well, devoting chapter 11 to the subject.
66   'Ambrose Merton' [William John Thoms], *Athenaeum*, 862 (1846), p. 3 [22 Aug.]:
     'What we in England designate as Popular Antiquities, or Popular Literature
     (though . . . it . . . would be most aptly described by a good Saxon compound,
     Folk-Lore, – the Lore of the People)': *OED*, 'folklore'; [Thomas Croker], *Fairy
     Legends and Traditions of the South of Ireland* (London, 1825–8). Generally, see R.M.
     Dorson, *The British Folklorists: A History* (London, 1968); and J.W. Rogerson,
     Anthropology and the Old Testament (Sheffield, 1984): 1st pub. (Oxford, 1978), ch. 4.
67   Heinrich Ewald, *Geschichte des Volkes Israel* (Göttingen, 1843), pub. in English:
     (London, 1867–86). Cf. Rogerson, *Anthropology*, pp. 67–8.
68   The next German Old Testament scholar to take up the same themes was H.
     Gunkel, *Das Märchen im Alten Testament* (Tübingen, 1917); cf. Rogerson,
     Anthropology, pp. 68–9.
69   On Smith generally, see T.O. Beidelman, *W. Robertson Smith and the Sociological
     Study of Religion* (Chicago and London, 1974); J.W. Rogerson, *The Bible and
     Criticism in Victorian Britain: Profiles of F.D. Maurice and William Robertson Smith*
     (Sheffield, 1995); J.S. Black and G. Chrystal, *The Life of William Robertson Smith*
     (London, 1912). See also R.A. Jones, 'Robertson Smith and James Frazer on
     Religion', in *Functionalism Historicized*, ed. G.W. Stocking, Jr. (Madison, 1984),
     pp. 31–58; and M. Wheeler-Barclay, 'Victorian Evangelicalism and the Sociology
     of Religion: The Career of William Robertson Smith', *Jnl. Hist. Ideas*, 54
     (1993), 59–78.
70   W. R[obertson] S[mith], 'Bible', *Encyclopaedia Britannica* (9th edn, Edinburgh, 1875),
     iii. 634.
71   W.R. Smith, *The Old Testament in the Jewish Church: Twelve Lectures on Biblical
     Criticism* (Edinburgh, 1881), pp. 20–1, 26; a second enlarged edition was published
     in 1892. Replies to this book include: W.H. Green, *Professor Robertson Smith on the
     Pentateuch* (London, 1882), esp. p. 69; Robert Watts, *The Newer Criticism and the
     Analogy of the Faith* (Edinburgh, 1881).
72   W.R. Smith, *Kinship and Marriage in Early Arabia* (Cambridge, 1885); a new edition
     appeared at London in 1903.
73   J. Wellhausen, *Prolegomena to the History of Israel* (Edinburgh, 1885).
74   W.R. Smith, *The Prophets of Israel and their Place in History* (Edinburgh, 1882),
     p. 53.
75   W.R. Smith, *Lectures on the Religion of the Semites. First Series. The Fundamental
     Institutions* (new [2nd] edn, London, 1894), p. 24. These were the Burnett Lectures
     for 1888–9, of which the first nine (of eleven) were read in Aberdeen; they were
     first published at Edinburgh in 1889 and a third edition was published at London
     in 1927. Smith's failing health prevented him from preparing for publication the
     second (March 1890) and third (December 1891) series of Burnett Lectures.
76   Smith, *Semites*, pp. 30–1.
77   *The Academy*, 36 (30 Nov. 1889), 357–8.
78   Th. Nöldeke in *Zeitschrift der Deutschen Morgenländischen Gesellschaft*, 40 (1886), 155,
     from a review of *Kinship and Marriage*; trans. in Rogerson, *Anthropology*, pp. 33–4.
79   Smith, *Semites*, esp. pp. 32, 39, 55.
80   [Numa Denis] Fustel de Coulanges, *The Ancient City: A Study on the Religion,*

Laws, and Institutions of Greece and Rome (Boston, 1874), p. 175 and *passim:* originally published as: *La Cité antique* (Paris, 1864). Cf. idem, *Histoire des institutions politiques de l'ancienne France* (Paris, 1888–92). Cf. S. Lukes, *Emile Durkheim: His Life and Work: A Historical and Critical Study* (2nd edn, Harmondsworth, 1985).

81   Note that Robertson Smith was also deviating here from E.B. Tylor, who saw sacrifice as much more of a cheerful gift. The entire subject of sacrifice, of course, would become central to modern anthropology, in the work not only of Durkheim, but also of Sigmund Freud (1856–1939), E.E. Evans-Pritchard (1902 73), and also for Henri Hubert (1872–1927) and Marcel Mauss (1872–1950), who together published *Sacrifice: Its Nature and Function* (London, 1964): French orig., 1899.

82   J.F. McLennan, *Primitive Marriage: An Inquiry into the Origin of the Form of Capture in Marriage Ceremonies* (Edinburgh, 1865), cf. new edn by University of Chicago Press, 1970: this book grew out of his article on 'Law' for the 8th edition of the *Encyclopaedia Britannica*. McLennan also argued that within this group, inheritance was in the female line, despite the custom of female infanticide. This in turn led to polyandry (one wife/several men), and eventually to the dominance of the male line over the female. Interestingly, McLennan worked for G.H. Lewes (George Eliot's companion) for two years after coming down from Cambridge: *DNB*.

83   Smith, *Prophets*, pp. 49–50, 55.

84   Smith, *Semites*, pp. 28–9.

85   Note that the Roman Catholic anthropologist E.E. Evans-Pritchard will oppose this view, held by both Robertson Smith and Durkheim, and will argue that God stands outside of society altogether, and that His role in society is only one aspect of the eternal God. Evans-Pritchard in general will be far more interested in belief than in action: see E. Evans-Pritchard, 'The Meaning of Sacrifice among the Nuer', *Journal of the Royal Anthropological Institute of Great Britain and Ireland*, 84 (1954), 21–33; idem, *Nuer Religion* (Oxford, 1956).

86   Smith, *Prophets*, pp. vii–viii.

87   Generally, see Ackerman, *Frazer.*

88   Smith, *Semites*, pp. ix, xi. A.A. Bevan (1856–1930), professor of Arabic at Cambridge, was also thanked for help with the proofs.

89   The books in question are, of course, J.G. Frazer, *The Golden Bough* (London, 1890[1], 1900[2], 1911–15[3]); idem, *Totemism* (Edinburgh, 1887); idem, *Totemism and Exogamy: A Treatise on Certain Early Forms of Superstition and Society* (London, 1910); Sigmund Freud, *Totem und Tabu* (1913). See also R. Fraser, *The Making of The Golden Bough: The Origins and Growth of an Argument* (London, 1990).

90   Ackerman, *Frazer*, pp. 82–95. Cf. Ernest Renan, *Le Prêtre de Nemi: drame philosophique* (Paris, 1886).

91   Frazer, *Golden Bough* (2nd edn, London, 1900), esp. i. 75; Ackerman, *Frazer*, p. 167.

92   Frazer, *Golden Bough* (2nd edn, London, 1900), iii. 186–98. Cf. his *Folk-lore in the Old Testament* (London, 1918).

93   Frazer, *Golden Bough* (3rd edn, London, 1911–15), ix. 412–23, esp. p. 412n.

94   J.G. Frazer, *Psyche's Task. A Discourse concerning the Influence of Superstition on the Growth of Institutions* (London, 1909).

95   For Frazer's influence, see *Sir James Frazer and the Literary Imagination: Essays in Affinity and Influence*, ed. R. Fraser (London, 1990).

Conclusion: The End of a World and the Beginning of Fundamentalism

1 M.M. Kalisch, *A Historical and Critical Commentary on the Old Testament, with a New Translation* (London, 1855–72), i. iii–iv. But interestingly, Kalisch could refer to 'the acute and incisive demonstrations of Colenso': ibid., iii.vi.

2 The most famous forgery of the late nineteenth century was that of the Shapira Scrolls, offered to the British Museum by Moses Wilhelm Shapira (c. 1830–84), a Russian convert to Anglicanism who had an antiquities shop at Christians' Street in Jerusalem, and who committed suicide in Rotterdam after being denounced as a scoundrel. Sadly, most of the arguments used against their authenticity would equally have led to the rejection of the genuine Dead Sea Scrolls, discovered in 1947. The Shapira Scrolls were auctioned at Sotheby's in 1885, and were bought by Bernard Quaritch the bookseller, who exhibited them at the Anglo-Jewish Historical Exhibition (1887). They have since disappeared, but photographs and much additional information is preserved as BL, Add. MS 41294. See also J.M. Allegro [who worked on the Dead Sea Scrolls], *The Shapira Affair* (Garden City, NY, 1965); N.A. Silberman, *Digging for God and Country: Exploration, Archaeology and the Secret Struggle for the Holy Land, 1799–1917* (New York, 1982), pp. 131–46; O.K. Rabinowicz, 'The Shapira Forgery Mystery', *Jewish Quarterly Review*, 47 (1956–7), 170–83; A.D. Crown, 'The Fate of the Shapira Scroll', *Revue de Qumran*, 27 (1971), 421–3; M. Mansoor, *The Case of Shapira's Dead Sea (Deuteronomy) Scroll of 1883* (New York, 1956).

3 L. Schneller [his son-in-law], *Search on Sinai: The Story of Tischendorf's Life and the Search for a Lost Manuscript* (London, 1939); M. Black and R. Davidson, *Constantin von Tischendorf and the Greek New Testament* (Glasgow, 1981). On 3 Sept. 1862, a Greek named Constantine Simonides (b. c. 1820) published a letter in the *Guardian* claiming that he himself had forged the Codex Sinaiticus in 1840. In 1853, Simonides had sold some biblical MSS to the British Museum, and in 1860 had deciphered others owned by Liverpool antiquary Joseph Meyer which were denounced as forgeries and in 1863 ruled indeed to be fakes: J.K. Elliott, *Codex Sinaiticus and the Simonides Affair* (Thessaloniki, 1982).

4 J. Wellhausen, *Prolegomena zur Geschichte Israels* (Berlin, 1883), first published in 1878 as *The History of Israel*, but renamed for the second edition.

5 Charles Le Cène, *La Sainte Bible, nouvelle version Françoise* (Amsterdam, 1741): very rare, due to its confiscation at Gröningen in 1747, having already been banned by the synod of the Walloon Church, five years before.

6 [Charles Le Cène], *An Essay for a New Translation of the Bible* (2nd edn, London, 1727), pp. 12, 20–1, 34: first pub. (London, 1701), trans. from French.

7 John Russell, *Proposals for Printing by Subscription, the Holy Bible, Containing the Old Testament and the New. Translated into English, With Arguments to Each Book, and Comments upon the Text, by John Wickleffe* (n.p., 1719). Russell hopefully includes a sample of the first verse of Genesis.

8 *Proposals for Printing by Subscription, in the University Press at Oxford, the Two Other Parts of the Septuagint* (n.p., n.d.=1710); *A Discourse Concerning the Usefulness of the Oriental Translations of the Bible . . . Being a Proposal for Printing the Ethiopic, Coptic, and Armenian Versions, as a Supplement to Bishop Walton's Polyglot* (London, 1735); *Plan and Specimen of Biblia-Polyglotta Britannica, or, an Enlarged and Improved Edition of the London Polyglott-Bible* (London, 1810).

9 Matthew Pilkington, *Remarks upon Several Passages of Scripture* (Cambridge, 1759), title page.

10 *A Proposal for Printing the Holy Bible, Common Prayer, and Other Religious Books, In the Manks Language* (broadsheet: 4 May 1764); *List of Benefactions towards*

Printing the Holy Scriptures, &c. in the Manks Language (broadsheet: 12 June 1765).

11 *The Holy Bible*, ed. Benjamin Blayney (Oxford, 1769); *DNB*. Blayney also produced an edition of the Samaritan Pentateuch in ordinary Hebrew characters, with notes, and new translations of Jeremiah, Lamentations, and Zechariah.

12 William Newcome, *An Historical View of the English Biblical Translations: The Expediency of Revising by Authority Our Present Translation: and the Means of Executing such a Revision* (Dublin, 1792), pp. 239–40; 387–427 (list). See also the strangely similar anonymous work, *The Reasons for Revising by Authority Our Present Version of the Bible, Briefly Stated, and Impartially Considered* (Cambridge, 1788).

13 Charles Butler, *Horae biblicae* (n.p., 1797), pp. 66–7.

14 J. Bellamy, *Jesus Christ the Only God* (London, 1792), pp. v–vi.

15 John Bellamy, *The Ophion: or the Theology of the Serpent, and the Unity of God* (London, 1811)

16 John Bellamy, *The History of All Religions* (London, 1812).

17 [Thomas Burgess], *Reasons Why a New Translation of the Bible Should Not Be Published Without a Previous Statement and Examination of All the Material Passages, Which May Be Supposed to be Misinterpreted* (Durham, 1816), pp. 13, 16.

18 John Bellamy, *The Holy Bible, Newly Translated from the Original Hebrew: with Notes Critical and Explanatory* (London, 1818), printed for the translator.

19 Ibid., pp. 1–2, 4n.

20 *Quarterly Review*, 37.

21 [Thomas Burgess], *Reasons Why a New Translation of the Bible Should Not be Published* (2nd edn, London, 1819), pp. iii–iv.

22 James Bland Burges, *Reasons in Favour of a New Translation of the Holy Scriptures* (London, 1819), p. 152.

23 Henry John Todd, *A Vindication of Our Authorized Translation and Translators of the Bible* (London, 1819), pp. vii–viii.

24 John William Whittaker, *An Historical and Critical Enquiry into the Interpretation of the Hebrew Scriptures, with Remarks on Mr. Bellamy's New Translation* (Cambridge, 1819), pp. v–xv, 286, 301–31.

25 John William Whittaker, *Supplement to an Historical and Critical Enquiry into the Interpretation of the Hebrew Scriptures, with Remarks on Mr. Bellamy's New Translation* (Cambridge, 1820).

26 James Bland Lamb, *A Reply to the Reverend Mr. Todd's Vindication* (London, 1820). See also *Selections from the Letters and Correspondence of Sir J.B. Burges*, ed. J. Hutton (London, 1885).

27 Richard Laurence, *Remarks upon the Critical Principles and the Practical Application of those Principles, Adopted by Writers, Who Have at Various Periods Recommended a New Translation of the Bible as Expedient and Necessary* (Oxford, 1820), pp. 29–30, 51–2, 55–6, 62.

28 Biographical 'Prefatory Notice' by Peter Stuart in John Bellamy, *The Book of Daniel* (London, 1863), pp. i–iv.

29 S.C. Malan, *A Vindication of the Authorized Version of the English Bible* (London, 1856); Alexander M'Caul, *Reasons for Holding Fast the Authorized English Version of the Bible* (London, 1857).

30 A revision of the RSV appeared in 1989 as the New Revised Standard Version. Other popular translations include the New English Bible (1961–70), updated in the Revised English Bible (1989); and the Roman Catholic Jerusalem Bible (1966), updated in the New Jerusalem Bible (1985).

31 Generally, see E.R. Sandeen, *The Roots of Fundamentalism: British and American*

Millenarianism 1800–1930 (Chicago, 1970); G.M. Marsden, *Fundamentalism and American Culture: The Shaping of Twentieth-Century Evangelicalism 1870–1925* (New York, 1980); P.S. Boyer, *When Time Shall Be No More: Prophecy Belief in Modern American Culture* (Cambridge, Mass., 1992); D.S. Katz and R.H. Popkin, *Messianic Revolution: Radical Religious Politics to the End of the Second Millennium* (London, 1999).

32   D.A. Rausch, *Zionism within Early American Fundamentalism, 1878–1918* (New York, 1979), p. 286.

33   In 1987, the US Supreme Court ruled that it was unconstitutional to compel public schools to teach Fundamentalist 'creation science', since this was merely disguised religious doctrine rather than proper science. Two years later, however, the California Board of Education, under pressure from religious groups, ruled that evolution itself was only an unproved theory, and should be taught as such.

34   B.A. Kosmin and S.P. Lachman, *One Nation Under God: Religion in Contemporary American Society* (New York, 1993), pp. 9, 197: still the most comprehensive and reliable statistical survey of American religion; 'America and Religion: The Counter-Attack of God', *The Economist* repr. *National Times* (Oct.–Nov. 1995), 29.

35   A.C. Gaebelein, *The History of the Scofield Reference Bible* (New York, 1943), p. 11; Rausch, *Zionism*, pp. 77–8; Boyer, *Time*, p. 97.

36   Oxford University Press claims that they sold perhaps as many as 10 million copies by 1967, when they put out a revised edition: Boyer, *Time*, p. 98.

37   Hal Lindsey (with undefined assistance from Carole C. Carlson), *The Late Great Planet Earth* (Grand Rapids, 1970) and many editions thereafter.

Suggestions for Further Reading

What follows is a rather idiosyncratic list of the secondary sources that I found most inspiring, or at least interesting, in writing this book. At the risk of sounding like a professor, there really is no substitute for looking at the raw materials of history, the books that were written by people who lived in the period about which I have been writing, most of whom would have been surprised to find themselves quoted in the twenty-first century.

Generally

Above all sources I would have to recommend the *Dictionary of National Biography*, both the great nineteenth-century printed monument, and the completely new computerised version. Although I was one of the section editors for the new *DNB*, I have not yet seen the finished product, and I can only hope that my colleagues have retained some of the wit and whimsy of the Victorian tomes.

Two older general sources are: Thomas Frognall Dibdin, *An Introduction to the Knowledge of Rare and Valuable Editions of the Greek and Latin Classics* (4th edn, London, 1827); and *The Bible in its Ancient and English Versions*, ed. H. Wheeler Robinson (Oxford, 1940). Two very useful tools are *A Dictionary of Biblical Interpretation*, ed. R.J. Coggins and J.L. Houlden (London, 1990); and *The Oxford Companion to the Bible*, ed. B.M. Metzger and M.D. Coogan (New York, 1993).

General secondary books which cover a good deal of ground are *The Cambridge History of the Bible*, iii, ed. S.L. Greenslade (Cambridge, 1963); H.G. Reventlow, *The Authority of the Bible and the Rise of the Modern World* (London, 1984), a translation of the original German edition of 1980; and H.W. Frei, *The Eclipse of Biblical Narrative* (New Haven and London, 1974). A new book which has not yet been published at the time of writing but which promises to be very interesting is David Daniell, *The Bible in English* (New Haven and London, 2003).

Preface: The Biblical Reader and the Shifting Horizon of Expectations

The key text from my point of view is Hans Robert Jauss, *Towards an Aesthetic of Reception* (Brighton, 1982), ch. 1: 'Literary History as a Challenge to Literary Theory'.

Chapter 1   The Prehistoric English Bible

An essential bibliographical tool is the *Historical Catalogue of Printed Editions of the English Bible 1525–1961*, ed. A.S. Herbert, *et al.* (London and New York, 1968). Also useful is A.W. Pollard, *Records of the English Bible* (Oxford, 1911).

Important secondary works include: D. Wilson, *The People and the Book: The Revolutionary Impact of the English Bible, 1380–1611* (London, 1976); I. Green, *Print and Protestantism in Early Modern England* (Oxford, 2000); and J.H. Bentley, *Humanists and Holy Writ: New Testament Scholarship in the Renaissance* (Princeton, 1983).

For the father of the English Bible, see David Daniell, *William Tyndale* (New Haven and London, 1994) and Daniell's edition of *Tyndale's Old Testament* (New Haven and London, 1992).

Recent books on the King James Bible include: B. Bobrick, *Wide as the Waters* (New York, 2001); A.E. McGrath, *In the Beginning* (New York, 2001); and A. Nicolson, *God's Secretaries* (New York, 2003).

For the Jewish angle, see D.S. Katz, *The Jews in the History of England, 1485–1850* (Oxford, 1994); G.L. Jones, *The Discovery of Hebrew in Tudor England: A Third Language* (Manchester, 1983); and also D.B. Ruderman, *Kabbalah, Magic, and Science: The Cultural Universe of a Sixteenth-Century Jewish Physician* (Cambridge, Mass., 1988).

Although desperately unfashionable, I would still recommend A.G. Dickens, *The English Reformation* (London, 1964), followed by Dickens's *Thomas Cromwell and the English Reformation* (London, 1959).

Chapter 2   In Pursuit of a Useful Bible

A very interesting book is T. Watt, *Cheap Print and Popular Piety, 1550–1640* (Cambridge, 1991). For more on radical religion and the Bible, see *Puritans, the Millennium and the Future of Israel*, ed. P. Toon (Cambridge, 1970).

Regarding the Sabbath question, there is an obscure book by D.S. Katz, *Sabbath and Sectarianism in Seventeenth-Century England* (Leiden, 1987). See the extraordinary bibliographical survey of books and their contents by R. Cox, *The Literature of the Sabbath Question* (Edinburgh, 1865).

For the Jewish angle again, see D.S. Katz, *Philo-Semitism and the Readmission of the Jews to England, 1603–1655* (Oxford, 1982).

Chapter 3   Cracking the Foundations

Generally, see the very French book (in English) by Paul Hazard, *The European Mind, 1680–1715* (Penguin edn, Harmondsworth, 1973), first published in Paris in 1935, and in English in 1953.

On Newton, there is the huge biography by Robert Westfall, *Never at Rest* (Cambridge, 1980), and the more specific and very detailed book by F.E. Manuel, *Isaac Newton Historian* (Cambridge, 1963).

Chapter 4   Streamlined Scriptures

One should start with R.H. Popkin, *The History of Scepticism from Erasmus to Spinoza* (3rd edn, Berkeley, 1979), and then look at B. Dooley, *The Social History of Skepticism: Experience and Doubt in Early Modern Culture* (Baltimore, 1999). An excellent if largely unread study is M.I.J. Griffin, *Latitudinarianism in the Seventeenth-Century Church of England* (Leiden, 1992). See also P.A. Schouls, *The Imposition of Method: A Study of Descartes and Locke* (Oxford, 1980).

For John Toland and company, see R. Sullivan, *John Toland and the Deist Controversy, A Study in Adaptations* (Cambridge, MA, 1982); and M. Jacob, *The Radical Enlightenment* (London, 1981). We now have the fascinating text by John Toland, *Nazarenus*, ed. J. Champion (Oxford, 1999).

If possible, one should not miss Richard Simon, *A Critical History of the Old Testament* (London, 1682), followed by his *A Critical History of the Text of the New Testament* (London, 1689–92).

For the Jews, see F.E. Manuel, *The Broken Staff: Judaism Through Christian Eyes* (Cambridge, MA, 1992); and Manuel's earlier study, 'Israel and the Enlightenment', in his *The Changing of the Gods* (London, 1983), pp. 105–34.

Chapter 5 The Occult Bible

A general guide is D. Norton, *A History of the Bible as Literature* (Cambridge, 1993); and *Reading the Text: Biblical Criticism and Literary Theory*, ed. S. Prickett (Oxford, 1991). Other interesting studies include R. Paulson, *Representations of Revolution (1789–1820)* (New Haven and London, 1983); and S. Goldsmith, *Unbuilding Jerusalem: Apocalypse and Romantic Representation* (Ithaca, NY, 1993).

An excellent survey, perhaps somewhat difficult to find, is P.J. Lineham, 'The English Swedenborgians 1770–1840: A Study in the Social Dimensions of Religious Sectarianism' (Ph.D. thesis, Univ. of Sussex, 1978).

Chapter 6 Divine Copyright and the Apotheosis of the Author in Eighteenth-Century England

On the whole question of authorial rights, see M. Rose, *Authors and Owners: The Invention of Copyright* (Cambridge, MA, 1993), H. Ransom, *The First Copyright Statute: An Essay on An Act for the Encouragement of Learning, 1710* (Austin, TX, 1956); E. Eisenstein, *The Printing Press as an Agent of Change* (Cambridge, 1980); and E. Armstrong, *Before Copyright: The French Book-Privilege System* (Cambridge, 1990).

Hugh Trevor-Roper believed that the second-best biography of all times was James Henry Monk, *The Life of Richard Bentley, D.D.* (2nd edn, London, 1833). Another celebrated biography is that by R.C. Jebb, *Bentley* (London, 1882). Particularly about the Bible, see also A. Fox, *John Mill and Richard Bentley: A Study of the Textual Criticism of the New Testament, 1675–1729* (Oxford, 1954).

Chapter 7 Ten Little Israelites

By far the best and most comprehensive survey of the literature is J. Robertson, *Old Testament Criticism in the Nineteenth Century: England and Germany* (London, 1984). Other important studies include: T.A. Howard, *Religion and the Rise of Historicism: W.M.L. de Wette, Jacob Burckhardt, and the Theological Origins of Nineteenth Century Historical Consciousness* (Cambridge, 2000); R. Ashton, *The German Idea: Four English Writers and the Reception of German Thought, 1800–1860* (Cambridge, 1980); and O. Chadwick, *The Victorian Church: An Ecclesiastical History of England* (London, 1966–70).

The ultimate edition of a key text, supplemented by a mountain of material, appears as Victor Shea and William Whitla, *Essays and Reviews: the 1860 Text and its Reading* (Charlottesville, 2000).

Chapter 8 Unsuitable Paternity

An older survey, still useful, is K.B. Collier, *Cosmogonies of Our Fathers: Some Theories of the Seventeenth and Eighteenth Centuries* (New York, 1934). I personally love reading the terrible trio: W.E.H. Lecky, *History of the Rise and Influence of the Spirit of Rationalism in Europe* (London, 1865); J.W. Draper, *History of the Conflict between Religion and Science* (New York, 1875); A.D. White, *A History of the Warfare of Science with Theology in Christendom* (New York, 1896).

Regarding the history of anthropology during this period, see: G.W. Stocking, Jr., *Victorian Anthropology* (New York, 1987); and his *After Tylor: British Social Anthropology 1888–1951* (Madison, 1995); H. Kuklick, *The Savage Within: The Social History of British Anthropology, 1885–1945* (Cambridge, 1991); and specifically, J.W. Robertson, *Anthropology and the Old Testament* (Sheffield, 1984): first published in 1978. See also E.J. Sharpe, *Comparative Religion: A History* (2nd edn, London, 1986).

For Darwin and the Bible, see G. Beer, 'Darwin and the Growth of Language Theory', in *Nature Transfigured: Science and Literature, 1700–1900*, ed. J. Christie and S. Shuttleworth (Manchester, 1989), pp. 152–70; and Beer's *Darwin's Plots: Evolutionary Narrative in Darwin, George Eliot and Nineteenth-Century Fiction* (London, 1983).

On the author of *The Golden Bough*, see the biography by R. Ackerman, *J.G. Frazer: His Life and Work* (Cambridge, 1987); and *Sir James Frazer and the Literary Imagination: Essays in Affinity and Influence*, ed. R. Fraser (London, 1990).

A new and comprehensive study is J.A. Secord, *Victorian Sensation: The Extraordinary Publication, Reception, and Secret Authorship of Vestiges of the Natural History of Creation* (Chicago, 2000).

Conclusion: The End of a World and the Beginning of Fundamentalism

Generally, see E.R. Sandeen, *The Roots of Fundamentalism: British and American Millenarianism 1800–1930* (Chicago, 1970); G.M. Marsden, *Fundamentalism and American Culture: The Shaping of Twentieth-Century Evangelicalism 1870–1925* (New York, 1980); P.S. Boyer, *When Time Shall Be No More: Prophecy Belief in Modern American Culture* (Cambridge, MA, 1992); and D.S. Katz and R.H. Popkin, *Messianic Revolution: Radical Religious Politics to the End of the Second Millennium* (London, 1999).

Don't forget to join the twenty million people who have read Hal Lindsey (with undefined assistance from Carole C. Carlson), *The Late Great Planet Earth* (Grand Rapids, MI, 1970) and many editions thereafter.

Index